PUBLIC POLICY IN AMERICA

GOVERNMENT IN ACTION

Second Edition

Dennis J. Palumbo
Arizona State University

HARCOURT BRACE COLLEGE PUBLISHERS
Fort Worth Philadelphia San Diego New York Orlando Austin San Antonio
Toronto Montreal London Sydney Tokyo

Publisher	Ted Buchholz
Acquisitions Editor	David Tatum
Project Editor	Publications Development Company
Senior Production Manager	Ken Dunaway
Cover Design	Jim Taylor

Address for Editorial Correspondence: Harcourt Brace Jovanovich College Publishers, 301 Commerce Street, Suite 3700, Fort Worth, Texas 76102.

Address for Orders: Harcourt Brace & Company, 6277 Sea Harbor Drive, Orlando, Florida 32887. 1-800-782-4479, or 1-800-433-0001 (in Florida).

ISBN: 0-15-500383-6

Library of Congress Catalog Card Number: 94-75332

Printed in the United States of America

2 3 4 5 6 7 8 9 0 1 090 9 8 7 6 5 4 3 2 1

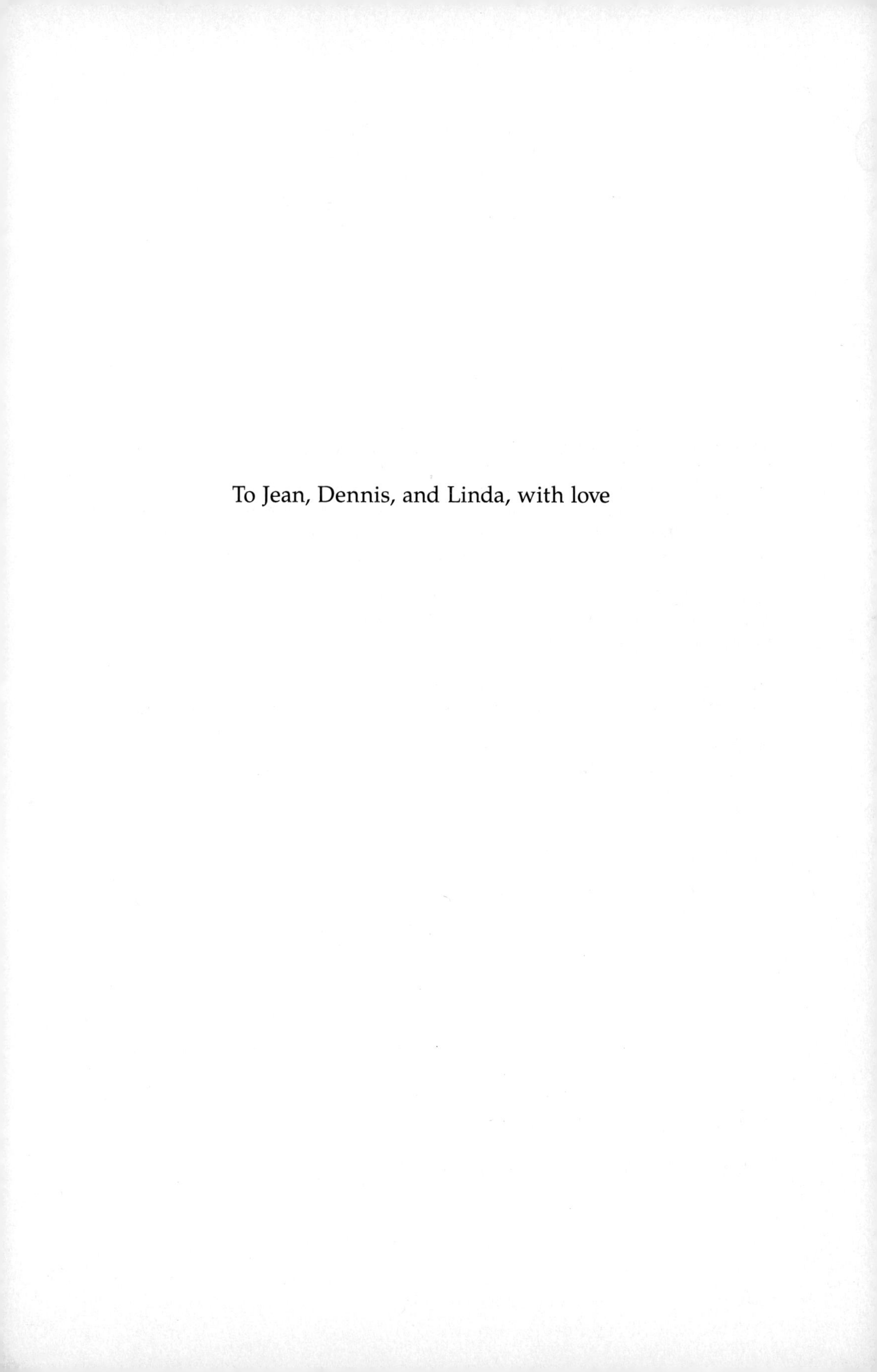

To Jean, Dennis, and Linda, with love

Preface to Second Edition

There is both pleasure and pain involved in doing a second edition of a book. There is pleasure in the fact that the book has received enough interest to justify revising it. It is also nice to see that the policy cycle model is a reasonably good way to view public policy. Many of the analyses that were done using the model proved to be both accurate and have endured over time.

I have tried to improve the model by adding an additional conceptual framework that complements and enhances the policy cycle; this is the constructionist perspective. The first edition stressed the notion of problem definition, because *who* defines the nature of the policy problem and *how* it is defined is a key factor in determining *what* the results of policy making will be. Constructionism, which is introduced in Chapter 1, is the position that "claimsmakers" construct problems and promote a particular definition or perspective about them. Problems, in this view, exist only because claimsmakers construct them and make the public and policymakers aware of their existence. There has been severe criticism of this idea, particularly by critical theorists (which can't be considered here). At the same time, constructionism helps illuminate policymaking. It is, in a way, a cousin of agenda setting, but it adds another dimension that is helpful for understanding public policy. This framework is added in several places in the book but especially in the chapter on crime.

The pain of doing a second edition is primarily in the fact that a tremendous amount of literature has been added during the past few years, not only to the process of policy making, but also to each of the substantive policy areas. Keeping up with it all is quite a job. In addition, I have added material on environmental policy making, connecting it with energy policy.

Finally, I would like to express my appreciation to my editor David Tatum who has shown a great deal of patience waiting for me to meet innumerable deadlines. I would also like to thank the production team at Publications Development Company who did much to make the book production process move swiftly and smoothly. I'm delighted that I was finally able to finish the revisions.

DENNIS J. PALUMBO

Preface to First Edition

I began writing this book in 1981. Although I had a general idea of what I wanted it to be like, many of the details were not fully developed. During the summer of 1981, I saw newspaper headlines proclaiming that the U.S. Senate had decided, by a close vote, when life begins. The issue was abortion, which was generating heated debate at the time. But it seemed odd that the Senate felt it had the power to decide when life begins. I decided then that this would be an appropriate issue with which to begin the book, although I was a little concerned the controversy might fade from view by the time the book was finished.

I didn't need to worry, of course. Abortion is as controversial today as it was in 1981. Many policy issues are like that; there really is no "solution" to them. Like stress for an individual, they are a part of social life itself. But the way we address policy issues reveals a great deal about who we are as a society, and about how our political system functions. How we handle controversial policy issues has a large impact on our social health. We can learn more about ourselves, our politics, our economics, and our social relations by analyzing policy issues than by any other means.

The field of policy studies has grown significantly during the past decade or so. Although there are a number of books that deal with public policy, most of these books either describe the policy-making process or focus almost entirely on issues. This book represents the first attempt to integrate the policy cycle or policy-making process with policy issues. By bringing the two together, I have attempted to make the study of public policy more than a study of current issues.

The book is intended as the principal text in courses in public policy. However, it also can be used as a supplement in American government courses. Instructors in public administration, sociology, economics, and other disciplines concerned with public policy may also find the book useful. I have tried to integrate knowledge from a number of areas as well as to provide a conceptual framework and point of view. I hope that this makes the book more interesting and useful.

Many ideas in this book were developed through interactions with colleagues and friends. The debts I have incurred are largely indirect; some of the people who helped me develop my ideas may not even be aware of their contributions. It therefore gives me great pleasure to acknowledge Mike Musheno, Steven Maynard-Moody, Paula Wright, Elaine Sharp, Yvonna Lincoln, Egon Guba, Stuart Nagel, and Rita Kelly. In addition, I have been fortunate, as editor of the *Policy Studies Review,* to have access to a number of articles that were submitted to the Review for publication. I have cited a number of these articles in the book.

I also would like to acknowledge the marvelous comments and suggestions made by David Rosenbloom, Syracuse University; Janet Weiss, University of Michigan; Larry Elowitz, U.S. Air Command and Staff College; David D. Dabello, Ohio University; and Thomas R. Dye, Florida State University. I have been especially fortunate to have had the excellent editing skill of Nancy Hornick of Harcourt Brace Jovanovich. Her sharp and meticulous editing contributed a lot to the book. I am also grateful to Amy Dunn, the production editor, and to Martha Gilman, the designer of the book. Finally, I am grateful to the fine word-processing skills of Marian Buckly and to Joe Yeh, who helped put together the material for permissions and check the bibliographic entries for accuracy.

Responsibility for any errors that remain in the book belongs entirely to me.

DENNIS J. PALUMBO

Contents

Part I

THE POLICY CYCLE

This book is divided into two parts. The first part describes the various stages of the policy cycle beginning with agenda setting and ending with policy evaluation, and the second part describes how the policy cycle is applied to policy issues in health care, social welfare, crime and justice, education, and energy.

The policy cycle is a useful conceptualization of how policy is made at all levels of government in the United States. There is no claim that this is the only way to study policy making. Nor are all of the various stages that we might depict included in Part I. However, all of the essential stages of the policy cycle—such as agenda setting, policy formulation, implementation, and evaluation—have been included. The strategy in Part I will be to describe the policy cycle in general rather than the specific policy making process of the national, state, and local governments in the United States. Where necessary, the specific differences among these levels of government are discussed.

The emphasis in Part I is on the *process* by which policy is made. There are two major reasons for this emphasis. First, it is possible to get a more complete and general understanding of how policy is made by focusing on the process rather than on the various institutions of government—that is, the U.S. Congress, presidency, and courts. The latter approach gives us a disjointed and cluttered understanding of policy because it overwhelms us with detail. The second reason for emphasizing the policy-making process is that democracy is more aptly conceived of as a process of making decisions rather than as a specific substantive result. For example, a benevolent dictator can produce a social system in which everyone is approximately equal but that system would not be democratic if the people did not participate in bringing about that equality.

Studying the process of policy making has become more popular among political scientists because it gives a more complete overview of policy. Prior to the policy-making orientation, the principal focus in political science was on the *formulation* of public policy, with specific emphasis on the roles of Congress, the president, and the courts in this stage. This focus was broadened when it became apparent that understanding how problems get onto the public agenda is also very important. Knowing how issues get onto the public agenda helps us understand why some issues are never considered by government and the way in which agenda setting influences subsequent developments in policy formulation.

About the time that political scientists were recognizing the importance of agenda setting they were also discovering another important stage in the cycle known as implementation. Both of these stages demonstrated that formulation was indeed only one, and perhaps not even the most important phase of policy making. The final stage, evaluation of public policies, demonstrates how difficult it is to measure the substantive impact of public policy and how little influence knowledge has on the shape and direction of public policy making. By increasing our understanding of the various stages of the policy cycle, we see each substantive area of the public policy—that is, health, education, and welfare—in a fresh, new light.

The reader can follow one of two different strategies in using this book. First, after reading the chapter on agenda setting, he or she can turn to the policy chapters and read the agenda setting sections for each policy. By doing this, the reader can get a complete overview of agenda setting, and each policy area, before turning to the formulation stage. This same strategy can be followed for each stage. Alternatively, the reader can study the chapters in Part I in sequence, and then study how these are applied in Part II in the five policy areas. Either one of these strategies should provide readers with understanding of policy making in America today.

1

The Public Policy Approach to Understanding Politics in America

■ THE NATURE OF PUBLIC POLICY

In midsummer of 1981 the *Los Angeles Times* published the following page one banner headline: "Senate Panel Decides, 3 to 2, When Life Begins." At the top of the story the headline continued: "Says Start Is Time of Conception." This headline might have been written by the newspaper tongue in cheek, because it is somewhat presumptuous for a governmental agency to decide when life actually begins. But the decision behind the headline illustrates the vast impact that government can have on the lives of millions of men, women, and (unborn) children whenever it makes policy.

The Senate panel in this decision was trying to change public policy on abortion which, at that time, was that a woman had a legal right to an abortion in the first three months of pregnancy.* This right had been affirmed in a 1973 U.S. Supreme Court decision in *Roe v. Wade,* which culminated years of political activity on the part of a large number of organized groups.† Critics said that if the Senate panel's decision was approved by Congress, it would make a woman who has an abortion subject to prosecution for murder. Opponents argued further that, if passed, it would be declared unconstitutional by the U.S. Supreme Court, that some kinds of birth control methods could be outlawed by the bill, and that a woman who loses her unborn child because of smoking or drinking could be prosecuted.

The Senate proposal was delayed until a subcommittee considered an alternative way of achieving the same result. These committee proposals finally made their way to the full Congress a year later but were defeated in September 1981 by large votes. This was not the end of the abortion question. The pressure has continued into the 1990s for legislation restricting a woman's ability to get an abortion and Congress still has been unable to say specifically when life begins. In his 1984 presidential election campaign, President Reagan came out against the pro-choice or pro-abortion groups which gave the anti-abortionists or pro-life groups a big boost. The anti-abortionists mounted a nationwide campaign that included a movie that purported to show a fetus attempting to escape the probe of the doctor who was in the process of performing an abortion. The debate escalated in 1986 and violence erupted as anti-abortionists bombed a number of abortion clinics across the country.

In 1991, the right to life's militant tactics got national attention when they blocked two abortion clinics in Wichita, Kansas. Federal Judge Patrick Kelly issued a court order that the clinics be kept open and threatened the protesters with jail. But U.S. Attorney General Richard Thornburgh filed a friend-of-the-court brief saying that the federal courts did not have jurisdiction in the case and that the matter should be left to state jurisdiction. Anti-abortion groups continued to block abortion clinics and violence escalated. In 1993, a doctor was shot as he was on his way to a clinic and other doctors asked the federal government to protect them.

The abortion issue is a volatile one because it draws out the intense involvement of well-organized, opposing interests in our society. While the American Civil Liberties Union worked with a number of women's groups to bring *Roe v. Wade* to the U.S. Supreme Court, the Catholic Church of America reportedly spent millions of dollars to reverse the Supreme Court decision and to restrict the impact of the decision at state and local levels. Further, this issue is emotionally and ideologically charged. It brings out conflicts over women's role in society as well as deep disagreements over what constitutes human life.

* See the last section of this chapter for a complete description of the abortion issue.
† *Roe v. Wade,* 410 U.S. 113 (1973).

As such, abortion serves as a rich example of one of the most controversial problems brought to government for resolution. Because it is so controversial, many people are disturbed by it. But one cannot avoid an issue just because it is controversial. Many other public policy issues are controversial. Nuclear energy, capital punishment, busing, affirmative action, the right to die, and pornography, among others, generate intense feelings and controversy. These, as well as a number of less volatile policy issues will be discussed throughout the book.

Admittedly, the abortion issue is more emotional than most policy issues. Feelings on both sides are so strong that it is difficult to find a "scientific" answer to the question of when life begins or when a fetus becomes a person. But all policy issues are controversial even if they are not as emotional, otherwise they would have not reached the governmental policy agenda. Moreover, policy issues do not have a solution in the same way that a mathematical problem has. There often is not a compromise that is satisfactory to all sides. Most often, solutions are only temporary, subject to revision and change as conditions, groups, and perspectives change. Public policy is a constantly moving target rather than a set of problems that can be solved serially.

Individuals involved in the abortion issue ponder questions about the boundaries and effectiveness of government action. For example, is abortion a legitimate concern of government? If so, whose interest should government protect in deciding to legislate abortion policy? Would *any* government restrictions work, given our society's heavy use of abortions to resolve a host of economic and social problems such as unwanted pregnancies, differential ability of the poor versus rich to afford abortions or teenage pregnancies? And, if a restrictive policy could be enforced, what would its impact be on women in general, and on poor versus rich women in particular?

In attempting to answer these questions, important elements of public policy are revealed. First, public policy is society's attempt to find solutions to problems facing people in their everyday lives. Not *all* problems become a matter of concern for public policy; the abortion issue was not on the federal government agenda for many years. It received national attention only after the sensational Sherri Finkbine case in 1964, described in Chapter 2.

The problem presented in the abortion issue is complicated: What is a woman to do when she is facing an unwanted pregnancy? Those in favor of outlawing abortion are attempting, on moral grounds, to eliminate abortion as a choice for women in almost all circumstances. Those favoring outlawing abortions include the Moral Majority and those who believe in the "right to life" of an unborn fetus. Thus they are generally referred to as "right-to-life" groups. Their solution for avoiding pregnancies is basically a moral one that favors sexual abstinence. Opposing them are those in favor of planned parenthood, population control, and the right of women to make their own decisions about what to do with their bodies. They generally are referred to as "pro-choice" groups. As Kristin Luker writes, "If the status of the embryo has always been ambiguous, as argued here, then to attribute personhood to the embryo is to make the social statement that pregnancy is valuable and that women should subordinate other parts of their lives to that central aspect of their social and biological selves" (1984, 8).

How an issue is portrayed or constructed is crucial to each side: The pro-choice groups do not want to be characterized as being pro-abortion for that would open them up to the charge that they are in favor of abortion for frivolous reasons such as gender selection or as a means of birth control. Similarly, the opposition wants to be called the right-to-life side because it conveys their argument that a fetus is a person from the time of conception.

Because policy is an attempt to find answers to difficult problems, the answer selected invariably will have opposition; there never is *total* agreement that a particular policy is the best way to solve the problem. Declaring by law that life begins at the time of conception might create more problems than it solves and may not be the best way to address this particular issue. Finding the right public policy for any problem is not easy. The War on Poverty of the Johnson administration, for example, is one way to try to approach the problem of poverty. But there are other alternatives, such as the negative income tax, or private charity.

Policy solutions seldom provide final, complete, settled, or finished answers to social problems. "Policies and programs," said newspaper columnist Walter Lippman, "are only instruments for dealing with particular circumstances." There are no final or ultimate solutions to problems such as poverty, illness, old age, defense, crime, lack of energy, unemployment, pollution, inflation, racial discrimination, poor education, inadequate housing, dirty environment, bad neighborhoods, decaying cities, unfair competition, bad labor management relations, the money supply, unsafe working conditions, inadequate streets, bad garbage disposal, insufficient food, low productivity, dangerous buildings, declining cities, and the myriad other problems that society faces every day. Policies aimed at solving or, more often, simply ameliorating the deleterious effects of these social problems will be replaced by new policies as the balance of political power shifts from one time to another, as it becomes apparent that a particular policy is not working, as newer and more ingenious solutions are discovered, or as society's perception of the problem changes.

Consider the abortion issue again. Prior to the 1960s, the right to get an abortion was permitted only on medical grounds. Interest groups supporting legalized abortion and state regulations governing abortion reflected this. Health care professionals supported abortion for "therapeutic" reasons, as in cases where carrying a fetus to term endangered the life or health of the mother, or in cases of rape. Arguments limiting abortion to such cases were accepted by most policymakers. State regulations reflected this and, in most instances, forbade abortion except in such cases.

By the late 1970s, however, the abortion issue had become a life-style issue (Tatalovich 1981). The question became: Does a woman have final determination over her own body and consequently the "right" to elective abortion? The *Roe v. Wade* and *Doe v. Bolton* Supreme Court decisions cleared the way for the life-style controversy by nullifying "all state laws which had banned abortions except for 'therapeutic' need" (Tatalovich 1981, 3).* The Court based its decision on the right to privacy. In so doing, the Court "denied any validity to the ethical belief which was central to the pro-life position" (10). What had been accepted abortion policy on moral and medical grounds prior to 1973 was no longer accepted policy because the definition of the problem had changed.

In making public policy, the government is attempting to ameliorate many of the problems that cannot be addressed through private means alone. Defending the country, for example, cannot be achieved through private actions alone. The same is true of many of the other problems cited earlier. There is, of course, a continuing debate about *which* problems can be handled better through private means rather than by government action, and this decision itself is a policy decision. For example, inadequate or poor education, some believe, can be corrected better through private enterprise than through public agencies (see Chapter 9); but the same is not true of things such as infectious disease. Generally, conservatives like to keep the list of problems that government regulates to a minimum, with defense, maintaining fair competition, and roads among the necessities. Liberals, on the other hand, want to expand the list and have much less faith that private initiative or enterprise can help resolve social problems such as unequal educational opportunity, poverty, unemployment, crime and lawlessness, mass transportation, environmental protection, racism, and many others.

Public policy deals with small issues as well as momentous ones. The abortion issue involves religious beliefs, women's rights, and morality. Not all public policy problems are as momentous as this one. Policy also deals with less visible issues such as a police department's policy toward preventive patrols, a fire department's policy about false alarms, or a probation policy about how to supervise repeat offenders. These seldom become issues of national importance.

An important distinction should be made between *formal* and *informal* policy. An agency may be required to follow a general policy that is mandated for all agencies. Such is the case with affirmative action. All government agencies are supposed to follow the same policy. But the particular way in which affirmative action policy is implemented will vary from place to place, depending on a number of factors. These will be described later in the book. The way in which a policy is implemented is the informal aspect of that policy; this is often more important in determining a policy's ultimate impact than the formal policy. For example, the formal or legally required policy may prohibit agencies from discriminating against minorities when hiring. But a particular agency may find a way to mollify or mitigate the

* *Doe v. Bolton*, 410 U.S. 179 (1973).

effects of this policy. Thus, the informal policy followed by an agency may be at variance with and even more powerful than the formal policy.

Public policy is *prescriptive* in that it provides a set of goals or objectives that an agency, group, or person would like to achieve. For example, we may say that one basic aim of government policy in the United States, at least for the past half century, has been to reduce the amount of poverty that exists in our society. This has been a general goal of government policy, although success in achieving it has been uneven.

Public policy also is *descriptive* in that it refers to actual actions being taken by governmental agencies. For example, the government's poverty policy includes payments to families that have dependent children. Many say that this approach perpetuates rather than reduces poverty (see Chapter 7). There is, of course, always a question about whether what the government is doing (descriptive aspects) will actually achieve the goals it would like to (prescriptive aspects). This is part of the debate that exists for any policy question.

Public policy also is *symbolic* in that it often is adopted more for what it appears to do than what it actually does. For example, many politicians advocate a war on drugs in order to achieve a drug-free society. But it is unlikely that policies adopted to do this actually will eradicate drugs (see Chapter 8).

Public policy seldom takes a uniform and consistent direction. Federal government policy may conflict with that of states and localities, as in the case of abortion policy. Many states have laws that are more restrictive than federal policy and there is a ceaseless struggle over which will dominate. Moreover, what actually is implemented often is at variance with what is *intended* by various policy-making bodies. According to political scientist Alfred Marcus (1982), policy is what we intend to do; implementation is what we actually do.

Finally, policy in any particular area such as health, education, or justice is not singular; there are often a multitude of different policies emanating from governments over the course of time. Some attempt to correct mistakes or problems that were caused by earlier policies. Such is the case with regard to health care policy (see Chapter 7), where a number of bills have been passed in the 1980s in an attempt to contain the costs caused by the 1945 Hill-Burton and the 1965 Medicare and Medicaid Acts.

■ DEFINING PUBLIC POLICY

Public policies are constantly changing as they are shaped and reshaped, modified and changed, and sometimes rejected for new policies. In fact, a policy is like a moving target; it is not something that can be observed, touched, or felt. It must be inferred from the series of intended actions and behaviors of the many government agencies and officials involved in the making of policy over time. Policy is process, or an historical series of intentions, actions, and behaviors of many participants. A law passed by Congress can be observed; a court decision can be read, as can regulations promulgated by government

departments and memoranda written by agency administrators; a political party's platform can be read and a politician's policy statements can be heard. But these things, by themselves, are not policy. Policy, like politics, is complex, invisible, and elusive. It is an analytic category used by researchers who study government activity over time (Heclo 1973), not something that can be captured by pointing out a single event or decision.

Because of this, there may be disagreement about just what meaning any particular decision has for a public policy. For example, in the spring of 1981 the nation's air traffic controllers went on strike. The Reagan administration decided to fight the strike by sticking to the letter of the law which states that it is illegal for federal employees to strike. President Reagan ordered that the striking controllers be fired. Whether or not this response to the air traffic controllers' strike had an effect on the policy of the Federal Mediation and Conciliation Service, depends upon one's interpretation of the event. The FMCS is an independent federal agency that helps resolve public worker disputes on the state and local level. According to Reed Larson, director of the National Right to Work Committee in 1981, the Reagan decision was a "turning point in enforcement of the law where labor disputes were concerned" (*Kansas City Times*, August 23, 1981, 1-G). In previous disputes, striking workers were given amnesty when the strike was settled. But following this dispute, Larson felt that FMCS would no longer be able to provide this kind of out, and in the future would have to fire all illegally striking workers. Thus, the Reagan approach represents a new policy, according to Larson. But according to Paul Bowers, director of the regional FMCS office in St. Louis, the Reagan stance meant "no change in policy at all." Public workers would continue to strike and continue to receive amnesty.

Thus policy—like beauty—is somewhat in the eyes of the beholder and not an objective truth that can be discerned by research. The two views represented by Larson and Bowers depend on how strictly one wants to apply the "law on the books." Larson, who favored lessening the power of unions, chose to interpret the law literally, whereas Mr. Bowers did not. Thus, the law itself is not policy; it depends on how it is interpreted and by whom.

In this case Bowers was wrong; the striking air traffic controllers were not granted amnesty. By the early 1990s, union strength declined and its membership dropped to less than 13 percent of the total workforce, its lowest level since the early 1930s.

In order to define public policy, it helps to distinguish the following terms:

1. *Functions of government* The general activities that are considered to be legitimate purposes of government such as providing for the country's defense, regulating interstate commerce, or maintaining public safety.
2. *Policies* The intentions (contained in politicians' statements, party platforms, campaign promises, and so on) that guide action in pursuing these functions.

3. *Agencies* The governmental units (that is, legislatures, courts, administrative agencies) responsible for formulating and implementing these policies.
4. *Laws* The specific acts passed by legislatures in pursuance of public policy.
5. *Regulations* The rules or orders issued by administrative agencies in pursuance of policy.
6. *Decisions* The particular choices made by government officials in formulating and implementing public policy.
7. *Programs* The specific activities engaged in by agencies in implementing public policy.

These elements of government are all interrelated in complex ways. A discrete decision, for example, would be John F. Kennedy's choice to blockade Cuba as a way of preventing the Soviets from placing missiles in Cuba, or Ronald Reagan's choice that the air traffic controllers' strike in August 1981 was illegal and that every striker should be fired. These decisions can be analyzed using the same methods and models as a policy, but by themselves they are not policies. Instead, each decision is one event in a sequence of events that determine policy over time. The Reagan decision to fire the air traffic controllers might be part of a long-range policy aimed at reducing the power of unions. In fact, the strikers themselves called the decision a "union busting" tactic. But it would not be policy unless a number of subsequent decisions were made that had the effect of reducing the power of unions, such as legislation aimed at further restricting a union's right to strike.

A program also may be viewed as separate from a policy. It may be defined as a specific means adopted for carrying out a policy. To illustrate, assume that the governor of a state is disturbed about the high rate of drunk driving in the state. As part of her campaign for office she vows to improve public safety in the state. Following her reelection, she sends a number of bills to the legislature. She recommends to the legislature that a *law* be passed that includes a mandatory jail sentence, suspension of the driver's license, and a $500 fine for anyone convicted of drunk driving, even if it is the first offense. The governor also issues an *order* to the state police telling them to crack down on drunk drivers. The *law* passed by the legislature and the governor's *decisions* are all part of her *policy* to improve public safety. The state police set up two *programs* as a way of reducing the number of people who drive while drinking alcoholic beverages. One is an educational program aimed at informing people about the hazards of mixing drinking and driving and the other is saturation policing of streets and highways on weekends and weekday evenings.

This example clarifies the distinction among a policy, decision, law, and program. But it should not be assumed that there is a neat, logical movement from a policy statement to a law and then to a program. Instead, there is a complex interaction among them. Policies, decisions, laws, and programs are distinct and interrelated at times, but at other times, they may be independent of each other. A decision to do something about an issue may not be followed up with actions aimed at the same thing, and therefore, may not become policy.

In summary, we define policy as the guiding principle behind regulations, laws, and programs; its visible manifestation is the strategy taken by government to solve public problems. In the abortion question there are two opposing principles vying for dominance: One is the notion that an unborn fetus has a right to life, and the other is that a woman should have the right to determine what happens to her body. In 1987, the latter was governmental policy but by 1992 this began to change as a result of new court decisions and administrative rules. (These are described at the end of this chapter.)

CONSTRUCTING POLICY ISSUES

How an issue is characterized is a crucial component of policy making. Those who succeed in defining an issue control the policy approach that government takes because the way an issue is characterized influences the solution or type of policy adopted by government. Once again consider the abortion issue. If it is characterized as a moral issue—where "unborn babies" are murdered—then the only solution is to prohibit abortion and treat it as a crime. If, on the other hand, it is characterized as a question of who should make the decision to abort a fetus—the government or the woman—then abortions should be legal. Finally, if it is characterized as primarily a health issue—where the questions pertain to the health of the mother and the condition of the fetus—then public policy should give medical professionals control over the decision. It also is possible to say that abortion is partly each of the three constructions—each has some validity and thus policy towards abortion should recognize this. However, there is a school of thought, called *strict constructionist,* that takes the position that it isn't our place to determine which construction is valid because one construction is no more valid than any other. Instead, the only thing we should do is describe the claims of each group, who is making the claim and why, in order to come up with a general theory of how policy issues are constructed and their impact on policy.

The relativism of strict constructionists bothers some people and so there is another group called *contextual constructionists* who believe that it is possible to look at the context in which a claim is made and then make a judgment about the validity of each claim (Best 1989). As the reader will see and be able to infer upon reading the rest of this book, I adhere to the *contextual constructionist* position.

POLICY TYPOLOGIES

There are several typologies of policy in existence. One of the most often quoted is that of political scientist Theodore Lowi, which distinguishes among distributive, redistributive, and regulatory policies (Lowi 1972). The first type of policy is one that provides goods and services to citizens, such as recreational, police, or educational services. The second type of policy takes resources or goods from one group and gives it to another, such as tax or welfare policies. The third type of policy regulates what individuals may or may not do, such as environmental protection and public safety policy.

One criticism of Lowi's typology is that it is not mutually exclusive and exhaustive. For example, a policy such as environmental protection can be both regulative and redistributive at the same time. The government in the 1960s adopted a policy to reduce the amount of sulfuric acid in smoke emitted from electrical power generating plants. This is a regulatory policy aimed at reducing air pollution, but it affected eastern plants more than those in the West because the former burn fuel with a higher sulphur content. This gives the western plants an advantage and thus had redistributive effects. So in this case, a regulatory policy is also redistributive.

To date, no one has been able to come up with a completely satisfactory typology of policy. This is in part due to the lack of conceptual clarity about the term *policy.* One problem lies in distinguishing policies from the specific kinds of tools or tactics that may be used to reach their objectives. Borrowing military terminology, we might say that policies pertain to general *strategies* whereas tools of implementing policies pertain to *tactics.* The latter includes things such as levying penalties rather than providing incentives, contracting with private agencies versus direct provision of a service by a governmental agency (as in education), letting a "market" mechanism decide how services will be provided, and letting local option, rather than a state or federal department, provide the service itself.

These various tools, which will be described in more detail in Chapter 4, can be applied to a variety of substantive policy areas. It is these tactics for achieving policy objectives that are important for understanding the conditions of successful or non-successful policy implementation (Salamon 1981). Government regulation is but one way of trying to achieve policy objectives, and such regulatory activity can have a redistributive impact. The impact of a policy should be distinguished from the means used for achieving policy goals, however. While we can categorize the types of tools used to achieve policy goals, we cannot categorize the policies themselves, except in regard to their subject matter, that is, health, education, and so on.

■ WHY STUDY PUBLIC POLICY?

The study of public policy is important because it breathes life into learning about American politics and administration. By concentrating on public policy rather than on governmental institutions, we can gain an understanding of government as a process of complex interactions among a variety of organizations, both public and private. This process affects all of our lives as citizens. Studying public policy is critical to a basic understanding of American government because it allows us to understand the economics of governmental activity. The economic stakes in the making of public policy are enormous. (The combined federal, state, and local government budgets in 1993 were over 2 trillion dollars.) How this enormous amount of money is spent should be of interest to all of us.

Policy often deals with difficult problems that threaten our health (such as the disposal of toxic wastes) and our survival (such as nuclear war). Public policy allows us to understand who receives the benefits of governmental activity and how. Finally, the study of public policy enables us to determine how well the ideals of democracy are upheld in a complex society that is very dependent on public bureaucracies.

There has been a tendency since the New Deal for Americans to turn to government for solutions to many problems. The tendency was reversed somewhat in the Reagan administration. But, over the long haul, contemporary governments are likely to be heavily involved in attempts to find ways of coping with society's problems. Table 1–1 shows that the government's share of the gross national product—the dollar value of all goods and services produced in one year—has been increasing since 1930. By 1985, government expenditures were more than one third of the GNP. Even though President Reagan tried to halt government growth, Table 1–1 shows that total government expenditures grew between 1980 and 1985 but remained about the same from 1985 to 1990.

The enormous sums of money expended by government in the United States benefit some groups more than others. Not everyone receives the same amount

TABLE 1–1 ***Total Government Expenditures as Percent of Gross National Product (GNP)***

Year	GNP	Total Government Expenditures	Percent of GNP
	(billions of dollars)		
1930	$ 91.0	$ 11.1	12.2
1940	100.4	18.5	18.4
1950	288.3	61.4	21.3
1960	515.3	137.3	26.6
1970	1015.5	317.4	31.2
1980	2732.0	889.6	32.5
1985	4014.9	1401.2	35.0
1990	5463.0	1907.1	34.9

Source: *Economic Report of the President,* February, 1986, (Washington, D.C.: U.S. Government Printing Office, 1986) pp. 286, 381.

from government and this maldistribution of public rewards has important political repercussions. Considerable controversy is generated over the distribution of public expenditures somewhat apart from the question of whether the policies themselves are effective.

Due to the growth of government during the past 40 years, public policy has an extensive impact on our everyday lives; from the moment we get up in the morning until we go to bed at night, and from the beginning to the end of our lives, public policy affects what we do and who we are. The food we eat for breakfast has been inspected and graded and its distribution regulated by various governmental agencies from the Federal Trade Commission to the Food and Drug Administration. The water we drink and the clothes we wear are similarly affected by government policy. The vehicles we use to get to work are licensed by government agencies and the streets we travel are provided by government agencies. Most of our children attend public schools, get lunches provided by government, or stay in daycare centers regulated by government. Many of these government activities were undertaken in response to problems that require collective action and were aimed at improving our health and safety. In many cases, our lives are better as a result of these policies that we often take for granted.

But there are limits to what government can accomplish. Some of the problems addressed by government are intractable. The problem of poverty, for example, has been with us since the beginning of history and is likely to remain so. Other problems might be better addressed by government if the legal authority of government and its administrative apparatus were more adequate or better designed. Environmental protection is a case in point. Much more might be accomplished in reducing the chemical pollution of the environment if governmental agencies were more effectively organized. For some problems, such as crime control, there is a need for people themselves to become involved in finding solutions. This notion has been called *coproduction* by some political scientists (Whitaker 1980). It refers to the fact that without the active participation and help of citizens, there is little that government agencies can do to control crime or solve the many other problems facing the country. Understanding the policy making process will give us a better idea about the limits to the government's ability to solve or ameliorate society's problems.

Traditionally, American politics is taught by studying various governmental institutions such as the presidency, Congress, courts, political parties, and interest groups. The traditional questions addressed are: Is the system of government that these institutions constitute very democratic? What amount of participation exists in the system? Is it a good method of governance? What reforms would help improve the system?

There are certain disadvantages to learning about American politics by studying the institutions of government. First, there is a tendency to focus more on the large, glamorous, and dramatic questions such as increased presidential power, the U.S. Supreme Court's landmark decisions, and the results of election campaigns. These are the activities of government that receive the attention of the mass media and thus appear to be important—even crucial—to policy making. But focusing on these institutions and events gives a false impression of how policy actually is made. By focusing on institutions, an inordinate amount of attention is given to the *beginning stages* of policy making. These stages are agenda setting (deciding which problems will be addressed by governmental agencies) and policy formulation (trying to develop ways of coping with the problems). But not enough attention is given to the middle and ending stages, including implementation (devising programs to carry out policies) and evaluation (determining how effective and efficient the programs are). And almost no attention is given in the institutional approach to the question of policy termination (how and why a policy is ended). It is at these latter stages, however, that the most important factors shaping policy have their effect (Meier 1979; Ripley & Franklin 1976; Nakamura & Smallwood 1980). Thus, those who try to follow public policy through the headlines and major news stories are inadequately informed.

The beginning stages are more glamorous and dramatic because there is only one president but millions of bureaucrats, many of whom are at the "street level" (that is, the public officials who have direct contact with citizens, such as school teachers, police officers, and social welfare workers). Every move, mood, and manuever of the one and only president is followed in excruciating detail by the media while the behavior of the millions of street-level bureaucrats is ignored. The president, in comparison to a single street-level bureaucrat such as a social welfare intake worker or a police officer, has a much greater impact on the nature of policy. But the *collective* action of the multitude of street-level bureaucrats is far more important in determining the nature of policy than the president's singular actions.

One of the most influential scholars of American politics and decision making has written that one can look at all of government and politics as a policy making process, and "to understand policy making one must understand all of political life and activity" (Lindblom 1980, 5). This statement could also be put another way: In order to understand political life, it is necessary to understand the policy-making process. And it is the entire policy-making cycle, described next, that is crucial, not just a part of it. What is most critical is to have a balanced view of the total cycle and not to give more attention to one as opposed to another aspect of the institutions involved in policy making.

Focusing on institutions distorts our understanding of American politics because it traps us in the classical politics-administrative fallacy. This is the erroneous belief that policy is made, or formed, by the "political" branches such as Congress and the president, and carried out or implemented by the "administrative branches," and that the administrative branches do not or should not change or make policy. In reality, there is no separation between the two activities. Administrators as well as legislators make policy and legislators as well as administrators are involved in implementing policy, but as long as we focus on institutions, it is extremely difficult to extricate ourselves from this trap.

One of the benefits of studying policy is that it is inherently more interesting to discuss policy issues than political institutions. Should we have national health insurance? Is the negative income tax a more effective approach to ameliorating poverty than welfare payments? Should women be permitted to have abortions on demand? Should marijuana be legalized? Does deterrence stop crime? Should we have a death penalty for certain crimes? Is solar energy a viable energy alternative? Should the drinking age be raised to twenty-one in all states? Should we require people to use seat belts in automobiles? These and a multitude of other policy questions are all very provocative. It should be noted, however, that finding answers to them is not easy, especially when we consider the likelihood that a particular solution will be successfully implemented. Answering these latter questions requires an understanding of the policy-making process and the problems the process is expected to resolve. Thus, a policy studies approach to American politics and administration requires that we address substantive questions in areas such as education, health, public safety, welfare, defense, and the environment.

■ PUBLIC POLICY AND POLITICAL THEORY

One of the most important questions of the last quarter century in political science has been whether or not a power elite, consisting primarily of business interests, makes policy at the national as well as at the state and local levels. This question really has never been answered. The majority of scholars continue to debate whether the American system closely approximates a democratic system in which the people have a large impact on policy or whether policy is made almost entirely by a business elite. The research and discussion about this question have not ended. It is hard to determine empirically if a power elite makes most of the decisions. To do this, we would have to know whether a power elite keeps important items off the agenda as well as if it determines the outcome of social issues that are already on the agenda. What is *not* considered by public agencies is as important as—and maybe even more important than—what becomes a part of the public agenda. Does the elite control which issues will be considered by government as well as how issues are handled? This debate is known as the *elite versus pluralist* debate. It will be described in more detail in Chapter 2.

To some researchers, what gets onto the public agenda is the most important phase of the policy cycle. Political scientists Roger Cobb and Charles Elder (1984) note that:

> pre-political, or at least pre-decisional processes often play the most critical role in determining what issues and alternatives are to be considered by the polity

> and the probable choices that will be made. What happens in the decision-making councils of the formal institutions of government may do little more than recognize, document, and legalize, if not legitimize, the momentary results of a continuing struggle of forces in the larger social matrix. . . . From this perspective, the critical question becomes, How does an issue or demand become or fail to become the focus of concern or interest within a polity? (12)

Compare this statement with that of Michael Lipsky (1980) who argues that, in important ways, policy is made in the "crowded offices and daily encounters of street-level workers" (xii). It is only they whom the average citizen sees and who therefore represent government to the average person. How street-level bureaucrats act, therefore, is what really matters to people.

The two hypotheses expressed by Cobb and Elder and Lipsky point to different kinds of influences on policy making. First, we have the influence of an elite in determining what kinds of issues will become legitimate issues for government decision making, and second, we have the influence of bureaucrats on the policies that do become a matter of government action. These are just two of many theories that exist about the policy-making process. They represent what we will call the *elite* and the *bureaucratic theories* of policy making. The principal theories that exist will be considered in detail in Chapter 3.

Theories are supposed to simplify reality, tell us what events to look for among all of the multitude of activities that take place, and explain how these events are interrelated to produce the final outcome. Some theories do this better than others. A good theory also helps us predict what is likely to happen. Not all theories of public policy making do this equally well. For example, if the elite theory were actually accurate, and if, in addition, people usually tried to further their own self-interest, then we would expect public policy to almost always reflect the interests of the elite. We would predict that any new policy, whether it concerns crime, taxes, welfare, or education, will reflect the interest of the elite. Judge whether or not this is true after reading about the policies described in Part II. Throughout most of this book, we will assume that the bureaucratic theory is the most accurate, and that it is the implementors who are most influential in the making of American public policy. Government bureaucracies are the principal implementors of government policy, but as we shall see in Chapter 4, private agencies also play an important role in implementation.

THE ORGANIZATIONAL IMPERATIVE

One of the most significant developments of the twentieth century has been the growth of governmental bureaucracies throughout the world. This trend has taken place in socialist-oriented countries such as Russia and China as well as in Western industrialized democracies. Although many have attempted to reverse the growth of government—most notably in England with the election of Prime Minister Margaret Thatcher in 1979, and in the United States with the election of President Ronald Reagan in 1980 and 1984—it is unlikely that the trend can be significantly reversed. By 1992, it became clear that government growth had not been halted by either Reagan or Bush. The election of Bill Clinton as president in 1992 guaranteed more government expansion because his policies called for a more active government. According to political scientist Robert Presthus, "I have no illusions that the trend toward size, concentration, and bureaucratic rationalization can be turned aside, given the imperative of economic growth to provide full employment and satisfy the claims of advanced and advancing societies for higher living standards and increased welfare bounties" (1978, viii).

Governmental agencies are not the only organizations that have grown. The global reach of large-scale private bureaucracies—including multinational corporations such as Exxon—is likely to continue in a world whose nations have become increasingly interdependent. The phrase "global factory" characterizes the fact that many modern products, such as bicycles and automobiles, are made in three or four nations rather than just one. Parts of a product may be manufactured in France and Italy and assembled in a third country such as the United States. This is just one facet of this interdependence among large scale private bureaucracies in the world today.

Bureaucracies, therefore, have a pervasive influence on the everyday lives of people in a large part of the world. But what is also important about bureaucracies is that they have a profound impact on the making of public policy. In fact, bureaucracies determine who gets what, where, and when. Legislatures which are, in a legal and constitutional sense, supposed to be the policy-making institutions in American society, now have a much diminished role in the policy-making process. City councils and state legislatures, especially at the local and state levels, often meet only a short time each year and thus have relatively little impact on crime policy, educational policy, welfare policy, or health policy. The urban and state bureaucracies, such as education, police, corrections, welfare, and health departments, are the agencies that really make policy.

City councils, county commissions, and state and federal legislatures make laws, but laws are only part of policy and, as we shall see, not the largest part. In order to get a better understanding of this distinction between laws and policy we will now turn to the policy-making process.

■ THE POLICY CYCLE

We defined policy as the guiding principles underlying the activities of governmental agencies. Policy is what is *intended* to be accomplished by governmental action. But we also can take a realist's perspective of policy. We can assume that no matter what was intended by governmental action, what is accomplished *is* policy. From a realistic perspective, policy is the output of the policy-making system. It is the cumulative effect of all of the actions, decisions, and behaviors of the millions of people who make and implement public policy. Governmental bureaucracies are the largest and most influential of these implementors. There were about 18.5 million people working for federal, state, and local governments in 1992 (see Figure 1–1). Most of them work for state and local governments where the growth in bureaucracies has been most pronounced. In fact, the number of federal government employees has remained relatively stable since 1957, even though the size of the federal budget has increased dramatically in the past decade.

Because policy is the output of the policy-making system, the guiding principles and basic strategies of government are developed at every point in the policy cycle, from agenda setting to policy impact. It is useful to think of policy making as a sequential or chronological process, as shown in Figure 1–2. Thus, we might describe the process in stages: *First,* an issue gets placed onto the policy-making agenda, which means it becomes a problem that is dealt with by a governmental agency, such as a legislature, court, or administrative agency; *second,* the issue is discussed, defined, and a decision is made whether or not certain action should be taken with regard to that issue; this is the policy formation stage; *third,* the action or decision is given to an administrative

FIGURE 1–1 Number of government employees by level of government, 1957–1985.

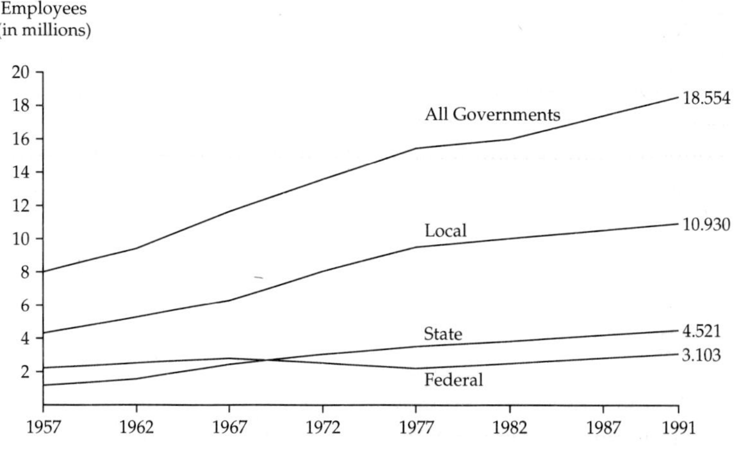

FIGURE 1–2 The policy cycle.

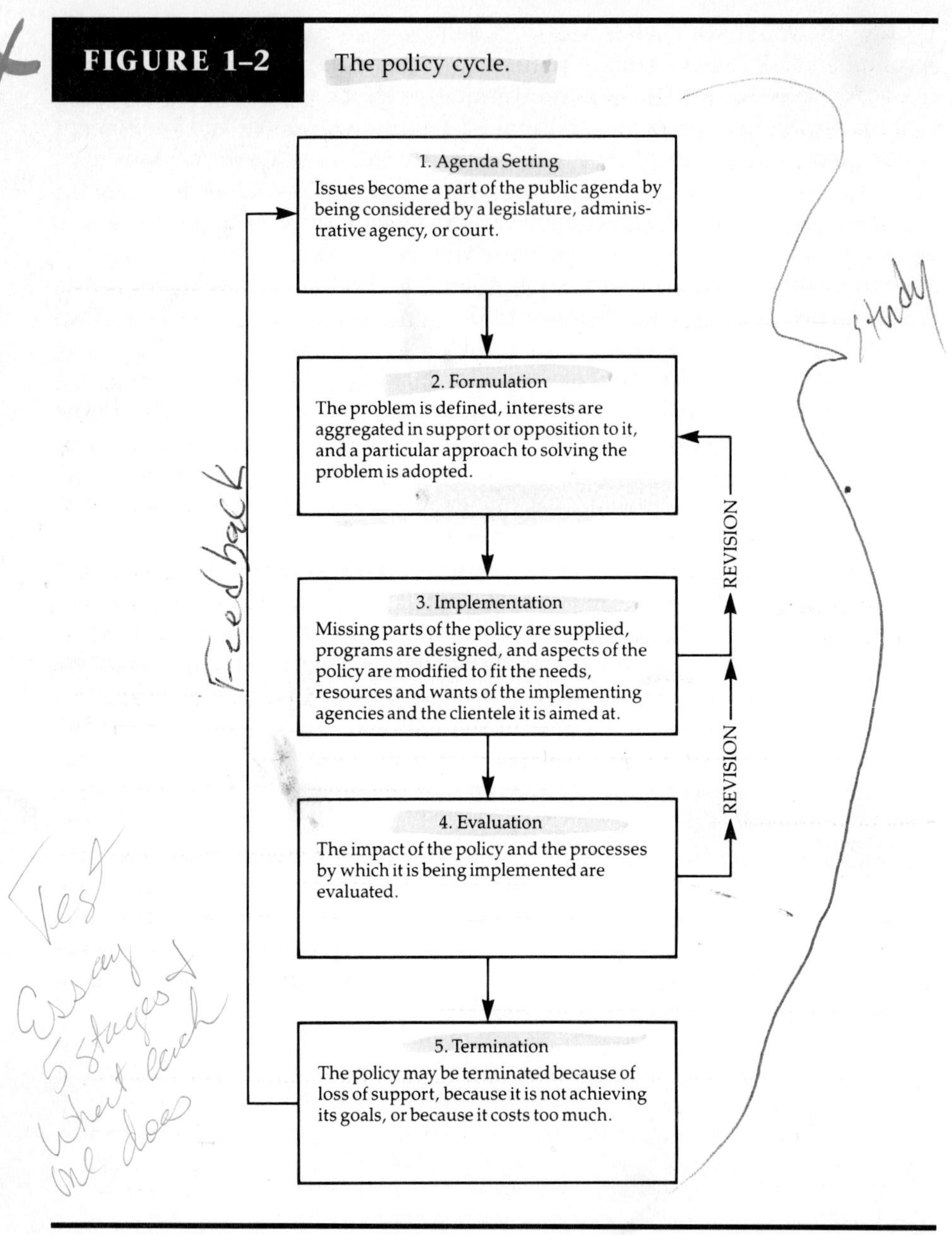

agency to be implemented; *fourth,* the actions taken by the administrative agencies are evaluated to determine what impact they have on the intended audiences and clientele; and *fifth,* policies may be terminated if they lose political support, are found not to be achieving their goals, are too costly, or for some other reason. In addition, there are subloops running from implementation and evaluation to formulation because policies often are adjusted based on knowledge about their actual impact and shortcomings. All five of these stages are described in more detail below.

This view of the policy-making process as involving various stages is useful because it distinguishes important components of a complicated set of behaviors; in short, it simplifies reality. But it also has drawbacks. One is that many components of the process have not been included. For example, the "outputs" of the system might be inserted after the implementation stage. These outputs are all of the actions taken by the millions of government employees who actually implement policy. These activities have significant impact on clientele. In this book we treat outputs as the activities generated at the implementation stage.

Another drawback of this view of policy making is that it is too neat, too logical, and too sequential. In the real world the various stages overlap and intermingle. They sometimes occur at the same time, or out of sequence. For example, agenda setting may lead directly to evaluation because once an item is placed on the agenda, existing policy in that area may be evaluated. Thus, when hunger became a part of the national policy agenda in the late 1960s, existing nutrition and welfare programs were evaluated to see why they were not reaching hungry children. For the most part, policy making is a cyclical process even though it often skips various stages. In addition, policy is always being formed and reformed; it is never a single, clear, and noncontradictory set of objectives but most often a morass of conflicting goals, objectives, and behaviors. It is not made only by "policy makers" at the top, but also by the multitude of street-level bureaucrats who actually deliver the services to people (Lipsky 1980; Prottas 1979). Michael Lipsky, a leading scholar of street-level bureaucrats, asserts:

> I argue that decisions of street-level bureaucrats, the routines they establish, and the devices they invent to cope with uncertainties and work pressures, effectively become the public policies they carry out. I argue that public policy is not best understood as made in legislatures or top-floor suites of high-ranking administrators, because in important ways it is actually made in the crowded offices and daily encounters of street-level workers. (1980, xii)

School teachers, police officers, welfare workers, public health nurses, sanitarians, judges and prosecutors, and the multitude of other people who work in governmental agencies in a very real sense, make policy as they carry out their day-to-day jobs. In this sense, policy is the *output* of the policy-making system.

Conceiving of policy making as a cycle involving stages also has its advantages. The principal one is that it enables us to see the entire process from beginning to end. We therefore can see *policy* being made, not just a single decision, law, or regulation. Laws passed by legislative bodies are only part of policy and, indeed, may be only the smallest part. When a law is passed that has vague and ambiguous objectives—which frequently is the case in American politics—then policy really is formed by the administrative agencies who determine what the real objectives of the law will be. This happens because legislatures, in an attempt to avoid making a choice in controversial situations, frequently will not be specific and clear in the laws they pass. This is a part of the political wisdom that says a smart politician should avoid making enemies which would occur if the legislature took a stand on an issue. It is a part of the advice that former speaker of the House of Representatives, Sam Rayburn, gave to a newly elected congressman when he told him that he should keep his mouth closed because voters will never criticize you for something you *don't* say, only for things you *do* say.

A good example of the way Congress passes the buck to administrative agencies is the Occupational Safety and Health Act of 1970. This legislation confronts two competing interests: Those of workers who may be injured, made ill, or killed by being exposed to hazards on the job, versus the interest of their employers who, in order to reduce the hazards, sometimes would have to undertake rather large expenses. When Congress passed this law, it could not agree on which of these two interests should be given priority. It passed the buck to the Occupational Safety and Health Administration when it failed to specify how the two opposing interests should be balanced. According to Lowi (1972), the act provides only "an expression of sentiments for the desired end results. The OSHA legislation took as its purpose to assure so far as is possible every working man and woman in the nation safe and healthful working conditions and to preserve human resources" (117).

Congress assumed that the agency that was to administer the act would be able to provide the standards of behavior for employers. But in many cases industry has not liked the standards set by OSHA. For example, the only limit set by OSHA on the cost to industry was that it should not have the effect of disrupting an entire industry. In applying this standard to the textile industry, it imposed strict limits on the amount of cotton dust manufacturers could have in their plants. According to OSHA, thousands of workers were suffering from a debilitating, sometimes fatal, upper respiratory ailment known as brown lung disease (byssinosis). The industry disagreed and sued on the grounds that OSHA failed to prove its case for stronger standards. The Supreme Court upheld OSHA and rejected a cost-benefit approach whereby OSHA would be required to prove that the benefits to workers' health outweigh the costs to industry. However, the Reagan and Bush administrations subsequently applied cost-benefit standards to this as well as to other areas of government regulation.

In this case, an administrative agency is really making policy. According to OSHA, the safety and health of workers is paramount and the cost to industry is secondary. The courts have upheld the agency in this matter. Congress sidestepped the issue because it is an exceedingly difficult one. How much is the health and safety of a worker worth in terms of costs to industry? If the standards set by OSHA were to prevent a thousand workers from contracting brown lung disease each year and it costs the textile industry $100 million to achieve this standard (or $100,000 per worker), should the OSHA standard be applied? Whatever answer you give to this question, it is obvious that if you were a congressional representative your answer would make some enemies. A "yes" answer would make industry angry and a "no" would make labor angry. It is what is known as a "no-win" situation, and it is therefore natural for a politician to avoid the issue or to try to keep it off the agenda.

The stages in the policy cycle in Figure 1–2 do not correspond to the institutions and agencies involved in making policy in American government. These institutions and agencies of government are legislatures, courts, administrative agencies, government corporations such as Tennessee Valley Authority, quasi-public bodies such as utilities, the federal system, and regional bodies such as councils of government. There is a tendency to think that policy is formulated by legislatures and implemented by administrative agencies. However, in many instances, administrative agencies formulate policy and legislatures become involved in implementation.

The tendency to think of a formulation being the province of legislatures and implementation that of administrative agencies is due to the doctrine of *separation of powers.* This is the legal doctrine that says that government consists of the legislative, executive, and judicial powers, and that each of these powers is lodged in a separate agency (Congress, presidency, and Supreme Court). Because these powers are derived independently from the Constitution, they must remain separate: Administrative agencies cannot make laws, courts should not make policy, and legislatures should not inject politics into the realm of administrative expertise. But this politics-administration dichotomy, as it is now called, is recognized to be incorrect. While the separation of powers doctrine does exist in constitutional law, the reality is that there is an intermingling of the powers in the day-to-day operation of government.

The policy cycle is an abstract representation of the stages in policy making. As illustrated in Figure 1–2, policy making is a continuous process. Although a policy may become routinized in the sense that it becomes a part of the standard operating procedures of an agency, it is never static or immutable. Changes and modifications will continue to be made throughout the cycle.

The stages depicted in Figure 1–2 illustrate other aspects of the policy cycle. First, policy is made not just at one point in time, but over time (Eulau & Prewitt 1977, 477). The behavior of governmental officials must be repetitive and consistent over time before it can be said that it represents "policy."

According to Eulau and Prewitt, "in reality, policy emerges through time, and it can for this reason only be observed through observing the behavior of governors and governed in time. What the observer sees when he identifies policy at any one point in time is at most a stage or phrase in a sequence of events that constitute policy development" (1977, 481).

The stages depicted in Figure 1–2 are not analogous to stages in child development or economic development where the person or country must pass through one stage before being able to go on to the next. In the policy-making process, some stages may be skipped altogether. For example, a president's decision to recognize the existence of a new country on the world scene is almost self-implementing: It is done when the president signs a decree that says the United States recognizes the legality in international law of the existence of the new country. Thus, in this case, there is no implementation or evaluation stages.

■ ANALYZING AND EVALUATING PUBLIC POLICY

Policy studies is a professional endeavor practiced by a large number of individuals trained in schools of public policy, public affairs, and public administration. A number of academic disciplines contribute to the field of policy analysis, including economics, political science, psychology, education, sociology, engineering, mathematics, statistics, computer science, public and business administration, physics, and geography.

Political scientist Austin Ranney (1962) has identified four reasons for undertaking policy studies. One is purely scientific; that is, the goal of policy study is to add to our knowledge of policy. This might be called a pure scholarly reason when there is no consideration for how the knowledge is to be used. It involves basic research in its purest form; its goal is to add knowledge and theory. Many scholars believe that policy analysis should be restricted to this role. The second reason is professional; that is, the goal of policy study is to improve policy. Social scientists feel professionally obligated to help government find solutions to society's problems. This motive became particularly pronounced in the "experimenting society," which was first described by psychologist Donald Campbell (1969). The hope here is that governmental agencies will set up new programs in a manner that allows them to be tested by social scientists and that these agencies will respond to evaluations of their programs. A third reason for undertaking policy studies is what Alice Rivlin (1971) has called the "quiet revolution." Policy studies have increasingly become a part of government agencies at the federal and state levels. Program evaluation (which is an aspect of policy studies) has been built into government agencies to determine how policies are being implemented and if they are achieving intended objectives (Cronbach 1980). The fourth reason for studying policy mentioned by Ranney is a political one; to advise politicians about what policies they should support in their campaign for office and after they are elected.

Policy studies are a relatively recent phenomenon, dating back to the 1940s. Some of these studies have their origin in World War II, when engineers, physicists, mathematicians, psychologists, and sociologists were recruited in the war effort to help the military. What developed became known as "operations research," so called because it was applied to specific military operations. After the war, these scientists began to apply their tools and techniques to help solve business problems. Their work has evolved into a number of sophisticated mathematical and quantitative methods that are taught in most business schools today. The purpose of this large variety of analytical techniques is to help organizations optimize goals. Given a set of clearly stated goals and objectives, an operations researcher can help find the alternative that will maximize its attainment. Today, this is most often called *policy analysis.*

Although political scientists are interested and involved in doing policy analysis, economists are the main professionals engaged in this kind of policy science. In fact, in government, more policy analysis is done by economists than any other single professional group. Economists tend to be more interested in the front end of the policy cycle—particularly in analyzing alternative ways of achieving policy objectives. Cost-benefit and cost-effectiveness analyses are two of the major techniques used by economists (see Chapter 5).

Another strand of policy studies borrows some of the techniques of operations research and planning techniques, and applies them to the budget-making process in governmental agencies. Known as PPBS (for planning, programming, and budgeting systems), the goal of this form of analysis is to get agencies to state their budgets in the form of program goals rather than in the form of line items. The idea is for agencies to be able to say that they can achieve X units of objectives in program A, Y units in program B, and so on. They must also specify how many resources would be needed to achieve a given unit of objectives in each program. In this way, budget decisions can be based on considerations of how well a program is doing rather than on the political considerations of who it helps and who it hurts.

Most policy studies can be divided into three parts: policy analysis, policy implementation, and program evaluation. These are described as follows:

1. *Policy analysis.* This usually takes place *prior* to making decisions about a particular policy. Its principal aim is to find the most efficient way to maximize goals and objectives. For example, when a number of state legislatures were considering adopting new criminal codes which set specific, minimum sentences for offenses, they asked policy analysts to predict how such a decision would affect the size of prison populations. These predictions were made to anticipate how much money would be needed to build new prisons if the new code was adopted. It

would then be possible to see how much it costs to crack down on criminals. Economics, mathematics, and statistics are the main disciplines involved in this aspect of policy studies. Some of these methods are described in policy analysis in Chapter 5.

2. *Policy implementation or process analysis* This focuses primarily on the process by which policies are translated into programs and how they are administered and managed. The major disciplines involved in this aspect of policy studies are political science and public administration. For example, a legislature contemplating passing a new law that requires children under five to be securely fastened in a childseat while riding in an automobile might undertake an implementation feasibility study. Such a study would describe the various tools that might be used to accomplish its objectives, how many resources would be needed to make the law work and an estimate of how feasible it is to implement. Implementation and methods of evaluating it are described in Chapter 4.
3. *Program evaluation* This is primarily a post-decisional activity aimed at determining whether a program is achieving its goals, what the program is accomplishing, and who is benefiting from it. The principal disciplines involved in this field are psychology and sociology. For example, a new program aimed at improving the educational achievement of underprivileged children may be evaluated to determine if it is in fact accomplishing its objectives. This aspect of policy studies is described in Chapter 5.

PURPOSES AND GOALS OF POLICY STUDY

All forms of policy studies are attempts to inject a high degree of rationality into decision making. Instead of making decisions on the basis of what was done in the past, on the basis of how much support exists for a given program, or on the basis of what administrators or legislators want, decisions are based on how well programs are achieving their objectives.

The major analytical tool of the policy analyst is an abstract representation of complicated decision situations in the form of a model. Elements essential to the achievement of objectives are identified and measured. These become variables whose interrelationships are described in models such as mathematical equations, flow charts, decision trees, and other kinds of models (Stokey & Zeckhauser 1978; Gohagan 1980; McKenna 1980).

These methods have been applied to problems as diverse as health facilities planning, whether or not to seed hurricanes, which bridge to build, how much school busing is needed to achieve integration, man and woman-power planning, and development of vaccines. While these methods often help a decision maker arrive at a better decision, they are not often used in actual decisions. The reason is fairly simple. The policy-making process itself is incremental in nature, nonrational, highly political, frequently disjointed, and loosely coupled (Lincoln 1985). This means that the majority of policy decisions (and other decisions, for that matter) are made in small increments rather than in leaps and bounds, and that thinking does not always precede action; often, an individual or government agency acts first and then analyzes what was done (Palumbo & Nachmias 1984). This does not mean that major changes never are made, only that incrementalism is the norm.Usually a government selects an alternative that "satisfices" rather than maximizes the achievement of policy goals. By "satisficing" we mean that the alternative selected is just a little better than the existing practice. Satisficing includes more than policy goals; it considers political support, organizational strengths, and turf protection, among other things. Policy analysis techniques, on the other hand, are based on the notion that once the best alternative for achieving goals is identified, an organization will implement it eagerly. But in the real world this seldom happens. Organizations are not so flexible as to be able to readily adopt new alternatives no matter how much better they may be in the abstract to what an organization currently is doing. Change comes hard to most organizations. Even when it is possible to get them to change, it is not always possible to predict the consequences of such change. Once these consequences have taken shape, even if they were unintended, it is very hard to reverse them. For example, American agricultural price supports were originally conceived of as a way of helping the average family farm cope with the vagaries of nature. But over the years they have tended to encourage the growth of large, corporate agri-businesses because the large farms can collect high amounts in price support and use these to get bigger. These large, corporate farms became a potent political force and lobby that sought to keep the agricultural price support policy from being changed. This outcome was not intended by those who originally adopted agricultural price supports. However, it is difficult to reverse this policy. In 1985, for example, President Reagan tried to end farm price supports and ran into a storm of controversy.

Nevertheless, there were strong pressures throughout the 1970s aimed at increasing rationality in decision making. Evaluation research gained a strong foothold in many government agencies. Spurred on by a number of political trends to be more efficient and less wasteful and to be more responsive to citizen desires, many government programs adopted evaluation research units. The goal of evaluation research is the same as the goal of policy analysis, although the methods used are slightly different. Rather than developing models of potential decision situations, evaluation researchers look at programs that have been adopted and ask: Have they achieved their intended objectives? How well and how much have the programs been implemented? These two forms of evaluation are known as *summative evaluation* (to see if objectives are being achieved) and *formative evaluation* (to see how the program is implemented).

These and other forms of policy evaluation are described in more detail in Chapter 5.

By the early 1980s, evaluation research was faced with a crisis: Government agencies were not using the results of evaluations when making policy decisions (Palumbo & Nachmias 1984). This gave rise to the development of techniques such as evaluability assessment (which is done to see *if* a program can be evaluated) and utilization-focused evaluation (an approach whereby decision makers help design the evaluation and thereby "buy into" the results). In addition, attention focused on how policies were being implemented. Implementation of policies became the Achilles heel of policy making (Hargrove 1976). For example, evaluators found that a program aimed at improving the way welfare mothers kept their household budgets was not working. When a second team investigated they found that the program wasn't working because it was never implemented (Patton 1979).

The ability of policy studies to influence policy in the future will depend on whether or not we recognize that there are limits to how much rationality can be injected into the booming, buzzing, and confusing world of decision making. Evaluation is political, no matter how scientific it tries to be (Palumbo 1987). Perhaps the best metaphor used to describe the complex, nonrationality of decision making is the *garbage-can model* (Cohen, March & Olsen 1972; Lincoln 1985). In this model, instead of problems looking for solutions, we find solutions wandering around looking for problems to which they can be attached, and techniques looking for solutions to which they might be applied. It is similar to Kaplan's "law of the instrument" which is represented by a small child who first acquires a hammer and finds that everything needs to be pounded.

Policy making, in short, can never be made entirely rational. This does not mean that we should give up all attempts to inject a degree of rationality into decision making. There is a lot of value in *attempting* to be rational, even if complete rationality is not possible. As we proceed through this book, describing the various stages in policy making, and the ways to optimize and evaluate policy, the following questions should be kept in mind:

1. Can the objectives of the policy be achieved?
2. Are there social technologies in existence that enable us to achieve policy-stated goals?
3. Has the policy actually been implemented?
4. How well has it been implemented?
5. Has the policy achieved its goals?
6. What goals has the policy actually achieved?
7. Are there better ways of achieving the same goals?

If you can answer these seven questions for any policy—health, welfare, transportation, defense, environmental protection—you have a substantial amount of knowledge about the policy-making process, the tools and techniques for optimizing policy, and the subject matter of the particular policy in question.

■ SHORT HISTORY OF ABORTION POLICY IN AMERICA

One of the most important points we make in this chapter is that the nature of policy is forever changing and dynamic, at times almost ephemeral. It is a concept whose meaning in any specific context can be known only after its consequences (albeit often unintended) are discerned. The history of abortion policy illustrates this point.

Discussion of abortion and its moral, ethical, and medical implications had begun long before the abortion reform movement gained momentum in the 1960s. Laws regulating abortion were placed on the public agenda in a number of states during the early part of the nineteenth century. These laws permitted abortion during the early stages of pregnancy, before the mother could feel movement of the fetus, and "were not primarily designed to make abortion a crime; they were aimed at unsafe practices, poisonous remedies, and criminally incompetent practitioners" (Rubin 1982, 11). By the mid-1800s, however, state laws had been added or modified so that abortion was effectively illegal throughout the United States, except in unusual cases. These laws remained in effect until the early 1970s.

The medical profession had the greatest influence in formulating and implementing the law on abortion throughout the nineteenth century. In the early part of the century, the medical profession pushed for restrictions on who could perform an abortion in order to increase its professionalism by ridding its ranks of quacks and incompetents. But by the mid-nineteenth century, physicians supported reform for a different reason. Medical science and research had increased in sophistication and evidence was mounting that the development of a human *in utero* was a continuous process from conception to birth. Life did not suddenly "enter" the fetus causing it to move or "quicken." Physicians began to oppose abortion primarily on moral rather than medical grounds. According to Eva Rubin, "Some doctors were indignant that women could or would interfere with life in its early stages and were not particularly sympathetic to the views of the women involved, whom they saw as ignorant of the facts and anxious to conceal the 'fruits of illicit pleasure,' or selfishly determined to put their own interests ahead of those of the unborn child" (1982, 12).

During the twentieth century, the medical profession would once again push for reform, but this time in the opposite direction. Physicians sought to provide appropriate medical service for women needing abortions. Support for abortion reform began to build in the medical profession primarily as a result of the many "hatchet" abortions which often resulted in death. Slowly the topic was discussed in medical journals. The legal profession also became interested. In 1950, through the American Law Institute, a model state abortion law was drafted. Gradually the topic found its way into the printed media. By the late 1960s, the topic had reappeared on the public agenda due in part to the thalidomide-deformed babies (the drug was given to some pregnant women by physicians) and the German measles epidemic that swept the country.

Reform legislation was passed in some states during the 1950s and 1960s. Sympathetic to the argument favoring "therapeutic" abortions, these laws provided for legal abortions only in specialized cases. The newly formed women's movement, on the other hand, maintained that the right to abortion was essential for women to take a fair and equal place with men in the workplace. They argued that if women were not allowed to control their reproductive lives, the greater goal of economic equality would never be achieved.

The entrance of the women's movement into the abortion controversy changed how the issue was defined and thus set the stage for a shift in policy. A new sense of urgency, of immediacy, of need was interjected into the discussions. The argument for repeal of abortion laws rather than reform bubbled to the surface and events were ripe to produce a massive change. But where would the change take place?

Prior to 1970, abortion regulation had been left to the state legislatures. Each state had some form of abortion law on its books. To change the face of abortion policy in the United States it would be necessary to change the laws of each state; but achieving change on a state-by-state basis could be extremely slow and perhaps impossible. However, the likelihood that Congress could be influenced to enact legislation that would supercede state laws was very small. In fact, the abortion controversy was not amenable to a political solution. Eva Rubin writes: "The abortion issue was, however, one particularly unsuited to rational and careful consideration in democratic deliberative bodies, because of its highly charged emotional content, its entanglement with moral and religious issues, and the ferocity of pressure group activity on the subject" (1982, 170).

The pro-choice crusaders decided instead to try a litigation campaign modeled after the civil rights strategy of the National Association for the Advancement of Colored People. The strategy involved carefully selecting and arguing abortion cases before federal courts with the hope that ultimately a case would reach the U.S. Supreme Court. The strategy worked. In late 1971, the Supreme Court heard two cases which had worked their way up from federal appeals courts. The first case, *Roe v. Wade,* challenged a law passed before the Civil War; the second case, *Doe v. Bolton,* dealt with a 1968 Georgia law. The two cases were heard together and the impact of the Supreme Court's decision was immense.

Women were found by the Court to have a limited "right" to choose an abortion. This right had to be balanced against competing interests, such as the protection of the fetus, and the state's right to regulate health. The woman's right is paramount during the first trimester (that is, the first three months of pregnancy), but as the pregnancy continues, the state's right to protect the fetus and to regulate health supercede the woman's right. Therefore, said the Court, states may regulate abortion during the second trimester (four to six months) and prohibit it during the third. (The exception is allowing abortions necessary to preserve the life of the mother.) However, the states may not place undue obstacles in the path of women choosing abortions during the first trimester. The Court found no constitutional basis for holding that the fetus is a person.

These decisions effectively nullified all restrictive state abortion laws and went beyond what even the pro-abortion coalition expected. Because of this, the decisions may actually have been a wolf in sheep's clothing for the pro-choice movement. The Court had interpreted public support for therapeutic abortions perhaps too broadly and assumed the same support for elective abortions.

The reaction from pro-life groups was instantaneous, enormous, and well-orchestrated. At both the state and national levels, pro-choice legislators were identified and campaigns against them were mounted, a few successfully. Propaganda-like techniques were initiated in the media, "baby killer" labels and pictures of nearly formed fetuses appeared. Restrictive state abortion laws were enacted making it difficult for women to obtain elective abortions. The Catholic Church and fundamentalist Protestant religious organizations provided money and support for pro-life campaigns. Attempts were even made to convene a constitutional convention to override the Court's decision through constitutional amendment.

At the federal level, pressure was put on Congress to thwart elective abortion wherever and whenever possible. Riders were attached to foreign aid bills that prohibited use of the funds for abortion or contraceptive programs. A great debate formed and continues over the use of federal health funds for elective abortions. Legislation prohibiting the use of Medicaid funds for elective abortions were introduced yearly from 1973 through 1976, when a Medicaid rider called the Hyde Amendment was finally passed. Immediately, however, a restraining order was issued to keep HEW from implementing the restriction.

In June 1977, the Supreme Court handed down a decision in *Beal v. Doe* dealing with the use of Medicaid funds for elective abortions.* The decision was a stunning blow to the pro-choice forces. The Court held that the federal government was not obliged to finance elective abortions, although the states may choose to do so. The Court ruled that states could not interfere with a woman's right to choose an abortion by making abortion a criminal offense, but it drew

* 432 U.S. 438 (1977).

The Silent Scream

New advances in medical technology that made it possible to save prematurely born babies not much older than fetuses that can be legally aborted changed perceptions of the fetus. Right-to-life groups used another advance in technology—ultrasound imaging—to portray a 12-week-old fetus being aborted. Dr. Bernard Nathanson appeared in the video as a sober, bespectacled, professional narrator, announcing that "we are witnessing the dazzling new science of fetology, which enables us to witness an abortion from the victim's vantage point." Dr. Nathanson points to the suction cannula which he says is going to "dismember, crush, destroy, tear the child apart until only shards are left" (Petchesky 1987, 60). The fetus, he says, tries to escape and then rears his head back in "a silent scream." But what Dr. Nathanson fails to tell the audience is that medical experts agree that at 12 weeks the fetus does not have a cerebral cortex to receive pain impulses and that a scream is not possible since the fetus does not have lungs.

the line at encouraging the choice through the availability of federal funding. Funding for therapeutic abortions, however, was to be maintained. Pro-choice supporters argued that the decision would effectively eliminate elective abortions for indigent women.

From 1973 on, pro-choice advocates found themselves in a defensive position. Tactics and strategies available to the pro-life choices were not available nor appropriate for them. Whereas the pro-life choices could label abortionists and pro-choice sympathizers as "baby killers," describe the death of living fetuses, and generate public emotional support for their cause, it was very difficult to generate emotional support for abortion on economic and convenience grounds. Unlike the pro-life forces that managed to take the offensive and were successful in obtaining passage of restrictive state laws, the pro-choice advocates were forced by these events to continue challenging state laws in court simply to protect what they had gained. However, public opinion remained fairly stable after the *Roe* decision. A large majority favored legal abortions if a woman's health is endangered, if there is a strong chance there is a serious defect in the baby, and if the woman became pregnant as the result of a rape. But only a minority were in favor of abortion if a married woman did not want more children, a poor woman could not afford anymore children, or an unmarried woman did not want to marry the man (see Table 1–2). These figures remained fairly stable into the 1990s. More than 80 percent favored abortion in cases of rape, incest, and danger to the life of the mother, and 60 percent favored abortion if the fetus may be deformed. Also, the percentage

TABLE 1–2 *Public Opinion and Abortions, 1972–84*

Percent of public who agree that abortion should be legal for a pregnant woman:	1972	1974	1976	1978	1980	1982	1984
If there is a strong chance there is a serious defect in the baby.	79%	85%	84%	82%	83%	85%	80%
If a woman is married and doesn't want any more children.	40	47	46	40	47	48	43
If a woman's own health is endangered by the pregnancy.	87	92	91	91	90	92	90
If the family has a very low income and cannot afford any more children.	49	55	53	47	52	52	46
If a woman became pregnant as a result of a rape.	79	87	84	83	83	87	80
If a woman is not married and doesn't want to marry the man.	44	50	50	41	48	49	44

Source: *New York Times,* (October 14, 1984) E3.

who favored abortion as a means of birth control dropped to 19 percent, and to 25 percent if the mother was poor and couldn't afford to support the child.

The pro-choice supporters had forced the abortion issue onto the institutional agenda of the Supreme Court. The *Roe* decision opened up the public discussion and controversy, which in turn forced the issue onto the institutional agenda of the U.S. Congress. The repercussions are unclear. A woman's right to choose an elective abortion was still guaranteed in 1993, but whether in practice all women had this opportunity is doubtful. Many of the state laws passed immediately after the *Roe* decision were extremely restrictive. Some states restricted the sites where abortions could be performed to hospitals which sufficiently increased the cost of an abortion above what a poorer woman could afford. Many states had consent requirements before an abortion could be performed, thus giving husbands and even grandparents veto power over the abortion. In Akron, Ohio, for example, a woman desiring an abortion first had to listen to a description of the development of a fetus and a warning that the fetus is a human life from the moment of conception. Many of these more restrictive laws were struck down by the higher courts, but some were upheld. For example, in *H.L. v. Matheson,* the Supreme Court upheld a Utah law requiring a physician to notify, if possible, the parents of a minor seeking an abortion.*

Like most policy, abortion policy continues to change. The U.S. Supreme Court agreed to hear a number of cases involving state laws in its 1993 session. One such law was passed in Missouri in 1979 but was enjoined from enforcement by the Supreme Court the day after it was enacted. It required that all abortions after the twelfth week of pregnancy be performed in hospitals, and that females under the age of eighteen obtain permission from their parents or a court before an abortion could be performed. Another section of the law required that a second physician be present in all cases where the aborted fetus may be capable of living outside the mother. The Missouri attorney general argued before the court, "The state has an interest in protecting the health of its citizens and can regulate that interest." The opposing lawyer, representing Planned Parenthood, argued that the state's true purpose was not to regulate health but to restrict women's right to abortions.

The Supreme Court struck down the Missouri law on its merits,† but the Court also held that the statement in the 1973 *Roe* decision that a woman could secure an abortion in the first trimester did not really mean there could be no regulation. The Court dealt an even greater blow to the pro-choice forces when it upheld the constitutionality of the Hyde Amendment (passed in 1977), which prohibited the use of federal funds for abortions except where the life of the mother would be endangered if the fetus was carried to term. However, on June 11, 1986, the Supreme Court ruled in *Governor Richard Thornburgh v. American College of Obstetricians and Gynecologists* that states may not enact restrictive laws that "intimidate women into continuing pregnancies."‡ The law in question was a Pennsylvania law that required a woman to receive specified information at least twenty-four hours before she could give "informal consent" to an abortion. The information was to include data on the risks of abortion and alternatives to abortion and a description of the fetus at two-week intervals. The majority decision said that this interfered with the privacy of the doctor-patient relationship. The Court also declared, "We reaffirm once again the general principles of *Roe v. Wade*" (*Arizona Republic,* June 12, 1986, A1).

However, in 1987, President Reagan issued an order proposing a revision of long-standing program rules regarding federally funded family-planning clinics. The new rule prohibited staff of the clinics from mentioning abortion as an option for pregnant women. Pro-choice forces criticized the rule saying that good-medical practice requires that a woman with an unwanted pregnancy be notified of all medical options for handling it so she can make an

* 450 U.S. 398 (1981).
† *Planned Parenthood of Missouri v. Danforth,* 428 U.S. 75 (1976).
‡ 106SCT2169 (1986).

informed choice. But in 1991, the U.S. Supreme Court in *Rust v. Sullivan* upheld the rule against the charge that it violated the 1st amendment's freedom of speech clause (the court sidestepped the abortion issue in this case).

In 1990, President Bush appointed another conservative jurist, David Souter, to the Court, and the Court's decisions began to take a decidedly pro-life turn (although *Roe* was not directly overturned by the beginning of 1993). The direction the Court took was to shift the question back to the state level. In 1989, in *Webster v. Reproductive Health Services,* the Court upheld a Missouri law that imposed new restraints on abortion. The court said that states may (1) ban the use of tax money for encouraging or counseling women to have abortions not necessary to save their lives; (2) ban public employees (doctors, nurses, and other health-care providers) from performing or assisting an abortion not necessary to save a woman's life; and (3) ban the use of any public hospital or other taxpayer-supported facility from performing abortions not necessary to save life. In addition, the Court said states may require doctors to determine, when possible, whether a fetus at least 20 weeks old is capable of surviving outside the womb.

Justice Harry Blackman declared in a dramatic dissent from the bench: "For today, at least, the law of abortion stands undisturbed. For today, the women of this nation will retain the liberty to control their destinies. But the signs are evident and very ominous, and a chill wind blows" (*Arizona Republic* "Roe's Fate May Hang in Balance," July 4, 1989, A5).

Justice Blackman was right for the new conservative Supreme Court seemed likely to continue chipping away at *Roe.*

2

Agenda Setting: What Problems Will Become Subjects for Governmental Action?

Americans have many opportunities and advantages but they also face many problems. For example, some do not have enough food to eat, or adequate housing; some face discrimination when looking for a job and some cannot find a job. Many have to endure traffic congestion, breathe dirty air, and drink poor quality water. Some people cannot lose weight, others cannot find a date, some cannot afford the car they would like to own, and still others have noisy neighbors they do not like.

There is an infinite variety of personal problems and concerns of citizens. Government is able to help relieve some of these but not others. We all recognize that some matters are appropriate for governmental action (such as preventing sex discrimination) whereas others are not (such as finding one a date). There is, of course, an ideological debate in the United States about the legitimate or proper sphere of governmental action. Conservatives prefer to limit government to only a few functions, allowing the private sphere or market to regulate behavior; liberals want to have government more involved in helping achieve social justice. Also, the things we consider appropriate for government policy action change over time. For example, attempting to reduce sexual discrimination in the work place has been a part of the government's legitimate or recognized sphere of responsibility since the 1960s; prior to then, it was not.

Regardless of one's philosophy, it is difficult to get policy makers to put issues on their official agenda. Legislators have a multitude of things that clamor for their attention, including streams of information, mail from their constituents, interest-group pressures, discussions with fellow legislators, media stories, political-party pressures, and research results.

How do policy makers decide which problems deserve their attention and which should be ignored? How and why do some problems become a matter of governmental policy while others do not? What is the public agenda and who has greater access to it? These are some of the questions that will be addressed in this chapter.

■ THE NATURE OF PUBLIC POLICY AGENDAS

Of the vast number of problems that are potential candidates for government attention, only some get onto the agenda. Understanding the agenda setting process will be facilitated if we distinguish between the *systemic* (general public) and the *institutional* (governmental) agendas (Cobb & Elder 1984). The term *agenda* refers to the general set of political controversies that take place in society. The agenda is not written down anywhere; nor is it a book in which things are entered. Rather, the agenda is the set of problems to which policy makers give their attention.

The systemic agenda is the broad set of issues that potentially *can* become the subject of public policy. The institutional agenda is more specific and concrete; it consists of the issues that actually *are* subjects for public policy. Most issues move from the systemic to the institutional agendas. An *issue* is a conflict between two or more identifiable groups over procedural or substantive matters relating to the distribution of resources and rewards in society (Cobb & Elder 1984, 82).

There are numerous systemic and institutional agendas in the United States. Each state, city, and local area has its own systemic agenda. For example, what is considered to be an important issue in Ohio may be different than what is considered important in Utah or Montana. Similarly, the city of Cleveland has a different systemic agenda than Tucson. There is some overlap among the systemic agendas of Cleveland and Tucson (and other cities). Both cities are faced with environmental pollution and slums. But there also will be many systemic agenda items that are different; adequate water supply is a more crucial issue in Tuscon than it is in Cleveland.

In addition to these state and local systemic agendas there is a national systemic agenda that overlaps to some extent with state and local agendas but also is different from most, if not all, local systemic agendas. For example, the issue of what to do about Marxist governments in Central America is a part of the national systemic agenda but not specifically a part of agendas of Mobile, Alabama, or Des Moines, Iowa.

Just as there are different systemic agendas, there also are a number of different institutional agendas. Each legislative body in the country has its own institutional agenda. This includes the U.S. Congress (Senate and House of Representatives), the 50 state legislatures, and numerous city councils and county commissions. The problems that move from the systemic agenda onto the institutional agenda in the New York State legislature, for example, will be different from the problems that become a part of the institutional agenda in the Kansas state legislature or the Chicago city council. Again, there may be some overlap among the institutional agendas of a number of states and even cities. For example, many states and cities are facing the problem of overcrowded prisons and jails and several of them may be considering similar ways of coping with this problem. But most jurisdictions also will be wrestling with their own unique problems and trying their own unique solutions.

In addition to the institutional agendas of legislatures there are the institutional agendas of executive and judicial branches of government at each level of government—national, state, and local. The vast number of administrative agencies and courts in the United States all have their own institutional agendas. For example, the problems that get onto the president's institutional agenda will overlap considerably with the items on Congress's agenda, although they will be very different from the issues that the governor of Arizona or the mayor of Los Angeles faces.

The chief executives at the three levels of American government are the president (at the national level), the governors (at the state level), and the mayors and city managers (at the local level). Each of these levels also have numerous administrative agencies—such as the Department of Defense, State Highway Patrol, or City Health Department. There are many other administrative agencies such as county commissioners and heads of independent governmental bodies such as the Port Authority of New York and New Jersey and the Tennessee Valley Authority.

As if this complexity of institutions was not enough, the courts also are divided among the three levels of government. There are federal courts (headed by the U.S. Supreme Court), state courts (headed by state supreme courts), county courts, and city courts (sometimes called magistrate's courts).

Even though each of these entities has its own systemic and institutional agendas, the *process* by which issues move from the systemic to the institutional agenda is the same in all units at all levels of government. One of the advantages of the public policy approach is that the same process applies to all units and thus it is not necessary to learn how Congress, state legislatures, city councils, and so on, make policy. Hence, in this chapter, we will emphasize the *process* of agenda setting without describing each specific level or agency of government. However, for purposes of illustration, we will focus specifically on the national actors such as the president, Congress, and U.S. Supreme Court.

■ AGENDA SETTING IN THE POLICY-MAKING CYCLE

Although each stage in the policy cycle is important in its own way, agenda setting may be the most crucial. Agenda setting is analogous to gate keeping; the gate keepers decide which issues will get onto the public agenda and which will be shut out. If an issue is shut out, then there is no chance for the legislature, executive agencies, or courts to influence policy in regard to that particular issue. Hence, being able to keep important items off the institutional agenda is a key source of power.

It has been only a decade since political scientists have recognized this important stage in policy making. Prior to then, most analyses of policy started with what happened once a question was considered by Congress. In 1972, Cobb and Elder published the first edition of their book, *Participation in American Politics.* In it they argued that what happens before a question gets to a legislative body such as Congress often plays the most critical role in determining what issues and alternatives are to be considered by government and the probable choices that will be made. What happens in the decision-making councils of the formal institutions of government often does no more than recognize or codify the results of a struggle among forces in the larger social matrix. In other words, a great deal of policy making takes place *before* government becomes formally involved in an issue.

Political conflict is not like an intercollegiate debate in which the opponents agree in advance on a definition of the issues to be debated. The question of what to do about a specific problem such as hazardous waste may be settled before the formal governmental system gets involved. The determination of what does and what does *not* become a matter of governmental action is, therefore, the supreme instrument of power.

■ GETTING ACCESS TO THE INSTITUTIONAL AGENDAS

Suppose you were facing a problem that you felt the government could and should try to alleviate. How would you go about trying to get it onto the institutional agenda of the appropriate governing body? If you were the owner and publisher of the *New York Times*, it would be rather easy: By publishing a big story about the problem, you might be able to get it onto the systemic as well as the institutional agendas. The president of the United States can single-handedly set the systemic and institutional agendas. But if you are an ordinary citizen, your job would be much more difficult, and chances are you wouldn't succeed. But you would have a better chance if you understood the process of getting access to the public agenda.

Much of the agenda-setting literature assumes that an "objective" problem exists that is discovered by groups or by a policy entrepreneur and then moved onto the systemic or institutional agendas (Milward & Laird 1990). In the Cobb and Elder model, a sensational event triggers interest in a new issue and thus propels it onto the agenda. But there is another part to agenda setting that these two models miss: The way an issue is framed is equally important as whether or not it gets onto the agenda at all. For example, the Congress in 1991 considered a Civil Rights Bill that would reverse U.S. Supreme Court decisions that made it more difficult for minorities and women to sue companies or public agencies that practiced discrimination (whether or not the discrimination was intended). President Bush labeled it a "quota bill" and threatened to veto it. The *New York Times* reported that "it has not mattered that the bill includes an explicit rejection of quotas in hiring and promotion. Nor has it mattered that the administration's argument that the bill would lead employees to use quotas has not been buttressed by examples from the past. To many gleeful Republicans and almost as many fearful Democrats, the 'quota bill' label seems pretty firmly stuck." (Clymer 1991, Section 4:1). Even though the label reopened the volatile issue of race relations which were deteriorating rapidly in 1991, the Bush administration was reported to be considering using the "quota" label as a major campaign theme in the 1992 presidential election. Framing the issue as involving quotas rather than as helping overcome discrimination would not only help the Republicans politically among blue collar voters, it would also have an impact on the kind of policy that could be adopted.

It is apparent that understanding the way issues are framed is as important as understanding how issues get onto the agenda; we consider the latter first.

There are several ways an issue can get onto the systemic and institutional agendas. One is where "insiders," usually political elites, initiate a policy proposal by means of a private decision within the ranks of government. A second is when "outsiders" or groups outside of government initiate issues. And the third is where groups, individuals, or government officials mobilize public interest in order to spur the government to do something about an issue (Cobb, Ross & Ross 1976).

There are a number of ways to mobilize public interest. The most frequently used route is for a group of professionals (that is, researchers, public administrators, lawyers, business executives) to become interested in the problem and use their expertise to get the attention of the general public. For example, suppose you lived in an area that was affected by a hazardous waste dump. There are a number of groups identified with such an issue. These include environmental groups, people living in the area, and governmental agencies. A *policy entrepreneur* is someone who helps initiate the process of moving the issue from

CASE 2–1 *Proposition 13*

Cutting government taxes is an issue with broad social appeal, and Howard A. Jarvis is the policy entrepreneur who brought this question to public attention in 1977 when he championed the adoption of Proposition 13 in California. The question was put before the California voters in a referendum. Proposition 13 became part of the California Constitution and it had profound and immediate implications for fiscal administration, and hence affected a wide range of government activity.

In California, more than 300,000 signatures—defined in the California Constitution as 5 percent of the votes cast in the previous election for governor—are necessary to place a proposition on the ballot. The ordinary citizen in California would have a hard time succeeding in using this strategy. However, Jarvis had help from the United Organization of Tax Payers, which was assisted by a political consulting firm specializing in fund-raising through mail campaigns. But it was Jarvis's efforts that began fifteen years prior to the referendum which culminated in the successful passage of Proposition 13. The unpopularity of property taxes in California was another key factor in the proposition's success (Cohen 1984, 96).

To be adopted, Proposition 13 had to win the support of a majority of those voting. To do this, it was presented to voters in simplistic fashion, as a measure against "big government" and "government waste." A major unifying theme behind public support of Proposition 13 was a negative attitude towards welfare (Danzinger 1980). The public wanted to cut welfare spending, which was identified as one of the evils of government. Jarvis was successful in defining welfare as primarily for the benefit of the undeserving poor rather than for the middle class (which was, in fact, untrue). Moreover, because welfare expenditures are financed primarily by federal and state taxes, Proposition 13 would have little impact on welfare expenditures; instead, it was aimed at property taxes, which are the source of local

this *identification group* to the wider, more attentive public. Policy entrepreneurs are often instrumental in building public support for an issue and in shepherding an issue onto the systemic and institutional agendas (Eyestone 1978, 88–96; Milward 1980; Kingdon 1984). They have a knack for sensing the importance of problems before they are widely recognized and making people aware that an issue exists.

Policy entrepreneurs usually have several motives for wanting to get an issue onto the systemic agenda. They may have a genuine concern about helping the public solve a vexing problem—such as hazardous waste, or crime. They may also have a self-interest insofar as they may—and usually do—know how revenue. Thus, Proposition 13 had the impact of cutting expenditures for education, which the majority of its supporters did not intend (Cohen, 97).

Proposition 13 had the support of conservative taxpayer groups, real estate interest groups, Ronald Reagan, and other prominent Republicans. It also had constant media exposure, which portrayed the measure as anti-government, anti-welfare, anti-politician, and anti-taxes. These issues were presented in a highly symbolic way that was easy for the public to understand. The campaign was so successful that Proposition 13 became national news during the last three weeks before the election and local television shows gave Jarvis free airtime. The impact of Proposition 13 was quite different from what was intended, however. It limited property taxes to 1 percent of the market value of property and rolled back the assessed value of real property for tax purposes to the 1975–1976 level. During the first year of its implementation (1978–1979) it cut local revenues in the state by $7 billion, which was over half of what property taxes would have been if it had not passed. School districts lost $3.5 billion, which was over 50 percent of their property tax receipts and 30 percent of their revenues from all sources. Owners of commercial business property benefited (28 percent) as well as owner-occupants of houses (who benefited 24 percent) because their taxes were lowered. However, the state provided more than $4 billion a year from state surplus to bail out local government; thus the impact on local services was not as severe as predicted. The poorest sections of California's communities suffered the most. Even though welfare services remained high, they were hurt by cuts in free services in areas such as zoos, tennis courts, refuse collection, museums, and cultural and recreational services offered by schools (used by daycare services). The biggest cuts were in education and the negative impact on public schools lasted until 1983.

to help solve the problem and expect that their solution will be used (Lewis 1984).

If you were a policy entrepreneur and wanted to get people interested in an issue, you would be wise to be somewhat ambiguous in defining the issue (Cobb & Elder 1972, 112). Ambiguously defined issues enable everyone to find a cause he or she likes about the issue and can identify with. The issue also should have wide social significance—something that is important to a large number of people. An issue will have a greater chance of getting onto the systemic agenda if it extends beyond the present time and is nontechnical and simple. Case 2–1 illustrates these principles.

CASE 2–2 ***The Abortion Controversy***

The triggering event that brought the abortion controversy to the fore in the early 1960s was the Finkbine case. Sherri Finkbine was married and the mother of four children, all of whom were under seven years old. She was expecting a fifth child when she discovered that the sleeping pill she was using was thalidomide, which was known to produce deformities in fetuses. Her doctor recommended that she have a therapeutic abortion because of the strong possibility of her child being deformed.

Because of widespread publicity about her case, the local public hospital cancelled the scheduled abortion. After Finkbine's doctor asked for a court order to perform the abortion, she and her husband became public figures. The Finkbine's doctor was unable to obtain a court order. Finkbine and her husband then decided to go to Sweden to have the abortion. The obstetrician who performed the abortion told her that the embryo was so seriously deformed it would never have survived (Luker 1984, 64).

Prior to the Finkbine case, abortion moved onto the systemic agenda in California in stages. First, small groups and elite professionals in California held discussions in small groups. Included in these groups were physicians, attorneys, and public health officials. Then in 1961 the issue was introduced into the California state legislature. The people who appeared at these hearings on both sides were predominantly members of professional elites. Under existing law, physicians have authority to determine when continuing a pregnancy constituted a threat to a woman. By 1964, the California Committee on Therapeutic Abortions was formed, which organized a support group of

While seemingly clear in its intention, Proposition 13 was actually ambiguous enough to carry different meanings for different groups, and that is why it was possible to form this winning coalition. 'Remote, complex government" was the target, and through Proposition 13, citizens would "gain control of government again." The measure was "a form of generalized emotional release as well as a response to specific grievance for many voters." (King 1978, 393).

The use of symbols is important in moving an issue onto agendas. Individuals try to impose symbols of legitimacy on the policies they like and they do this by creating a catchy phrase. "Law and order," "school busing," "getting control of government," and "right to life" are all symbols that generate emotions. Manipulating the right symbols is crucial. For example, when Cesar Chavez led a strike against California farmers in the late 1960s, he turned the about 2,000 physicians for therapeutic abortions. Between 1964 and 1967, the American Medical Association, the American Bar Association, and the California Medical Association lent their support to reform.

The issue became increasingly emotional after 1967 with the emergence of women's organizations. Many of these organizations argued that abortion was a woman's right because it was essential to her right to equality (Luker, 92).

A bill allowing therapeutic abortions passed the California legislature in 1967. After the bill was passed, the number of abortions in California went up slightly in 1968 to 5,018, then tripled to 15,952 in 1969, and in 1972 the number reached 100,000, where it has remained since. By late 1970, 99.2 percent of all California women who sought an abortion received one, and one out of three pregnancies was ended by legal abortion.

A number of women's organizations and groups of professionals pressed to extend the California policy to the rest of the country. They succeeded in 1973, when the U.S. Supreme Court issued its decision in *Roe v. Wade,* which made it possible for a woman to get an elective abortion during the first trimester of pregnancy. The pro-life groups were caught off guard by this decision. They had not been organized on a national scale as the pro-choice groups were, although this soon changed. The Finkbine case put the abortion issue on the national systemic and institutional agendas and it has remained there ever since.

event into a civil rights issue. He emphasized the minority status of the grape pickers and in so doing, motivated many people to support a grape boycott who would not otherwise have done so.

Thus, a policy issue is not generally centered around facts, but an interpretation of those facts. Kristin Luker (1984) describes the abortion controversy as follows:

> . . . both sides agree that embryos have heartbeats by approximately the twenty-fourth day of pregnancy but they do not breathe until birth. They cannot agree, however, about what these facts mean. For those on the pro-life side, it is important that embryos have heartbeats. They consider the lack of respiration unimportant and argue that in any case it will occur in time. For pro-choice people, the converse is true: because embryos do not breathe until birth, and all babies breathe, the presence of a heartbeat is merely an indicator

> that a baby may eventually be born, and until then the embryo is something else, namely, a fetus. The two sides therefore examine exactly the same set of 'facts' but come to diametrically opposed conclusions about them. (5)

It helps if there is a triggering event that brings the issue vividly before the public. There are a number of such triggering devices, including a natural catastrophe such as an earthquake; an unanticipated human event, such as a riot or assassination; a change in the environment, such as increase in air pollution; an imbalance in the distribution of resources that leads to civil disturbances; or a large demographic change, such as the massive black migration to northern cities in the 1950s and 1960s. These triggering events can create an issue for the systemic agenda. Case 2–2 illustrates a triggering event that put abortion onto the national systemic agenda in the early 1960s.

Triggering events such as the Finkbine case can lead to the development of contending groups with different ideas about how a problem should be solved. A group may try to exploit an issue for its own gain. This may be done by the way an issue is identified. This process has enormous impact on the ultimate solutions that are adopted (Dery 1984). For example, in 1982, the issue of driving while intoxicated was brought to public attention in much the same way as the abortion controversy. Relatives of the victims of drunk drivers constituted the group most identified with the issue. They formed organizations such as Mothers Against Drunk Drivers (MADD) and Students Against Drunk Drivers (SADD). As the issue moved onto the systemic agenda, it was defined primarily as a battle against "the drunk"—the villain responsible for about half of approximately 45,000 highway fatalities each year. This led to harsher penalties for drunk drivers (Nienstedt 1986). Other possible solutions, such as safer cars, were not an important component of what soon became more of a symbolic crusade (Gusfield 1981). The crusade in Arizona is described in Case 2–3.

The way we define problems depends on our beliefs and values, not facts. Thus, issues are never uniquely determined nor completely solved (Wildavsky 1979, 57). They are transformed and superceded by other problems as we learn to live with them. For example, an issue such as drunk driving or abortion is put onto the systemic and institutional agendas and laws are passed that attempt to deal with the issue; however, that seldom ends the matter. Those who oppose the policy will continue their opposition, the law may prove to be inadequate, or new views about the nature of the problem may develop. In all cases, the issue will continue to be a part of the systemic agenda, although it may fade from view for a time and then reappear at the top of the agenda, perhaps in new form. Some issues remain part of the systemic agenda for years and move onto institutional agenda from time to time, usually in changed form. For example, the idea of having health insurance in the United States that would cover every citizen has been in the public spotlight on and off for three quarters of a century. Public discussion of the idea stretches back to the

CASE 2–3 *Drunk Drivers and MADD*

Many of the people associated with Mothers Against Drunk Drivers have personally been the victims of a drunk driver. This probably gives them a zealousness they otherwise would not have. Donna Pickering, the president of the Arizona chapter of MADD, is one such person. Her husband was killed in August 1980 by a drunk driver who ran head-on into their family camper.

Pickering believes that everyone convicted of drunk driving should serve time in jail. In 1986, Arizona law mandated a jail sentence for first offenders only if the percentage of alcohol in their blood is more than 0.20, or if they have caused an accident in which someone also was seriously injured.

In 1985, the Arizona chapter of MADD proposed legislation that would require police to seize the driver licenses of people arrested on suspicion of drunk driving. The license would be returned after two weeks if the driver could successfully defend his or her case in an administrative hearing. Other bills proposed by MADD sought to ban "happy hours" and other discount drink specials in bars, and to grant police permission to take blood samples to be used as evidence against suspects. Several of these measures have potential constitutional difficulties, particularly the possibility that they violate the due process clause of the Fifth Amendment concerning self-incrimination. None of these measures passed the Arizona legislature in 1985 (*Arizona Republic,* January 20, 1985, A-14).

days of President Theodore Roosevelt, but it was President Harry Truman who proposed national health insurance during the 1950s. His proposal was defeated in Congress and it was not until 1964 that Congress finally passed Medicare and Medicaid legislation (described in detail in Chapter 6). The issue was raised again in 1974 and 1975 when Senator Edward Kennedy sponsored a scaled down version of national health insurance together with Representative Wilbur Mills, who was then chair of the powerful House Ways and Means Committee. However, their bill did not get out of Congress. Health became a major agenda item again during the presidential election of 1992 when Bill Clinton made it a major part of his campaign. First lady Hillary Rodham Clinton was given the responsibility of developing a health policy proposal which was introduced in late 1993. It was certain to remain on the institutional agenda because health had become a major concern to Americans, particularly those who lost their jobs and, therefore, their health insurance (see Chapter 6).

Another issue that has been on and off the institutional agenda is child abuse. Barbara Nelson (1984, 5) describes how child abuse became a major issue following the Mary Ellen case of 1874, in which a visitor discovered that a young girl had been regularly bound and beaten by her stepmother. This celebrated case led to the forming of the New York Society for the Prevention of Cruelty to Children. The issue went underground after this, but resurfaced in the 1950s due to the work of radiologists (who are experts at reading X-rays of bone fractures) who alerted pediatricians to the problem. In 1962, two pediatricians published their famous article, "The Battered-Child Syndrome." Within weeks, stories of child abuse were picked up by the mass media and the issue became a part of the systemic agenda. At this time, however, child abuse was narrowly defined as being a problem of individuals with character defects. Nelson (1984) writes, "Favoring the narrow definition during agenda setting had important, long-lasting effects on the shape of child-abuse policy. By ignoring neglect, the connection between poverty and maltreatment was purposely blurred. In fact, strenuous efforts were made to popularize abuse as a problem knowing no barriers of class, race, or culture" (15).

What accounts for these ebbs and flows of attentions to a particular issue? How important are prominent figures such as Kennedy and Reagan in getting ideas to come to national attention? We will address these questions in the following section.

■ WHO HAS GREATEST ACCESS TO AGENDA SETTING?

The Media

The mass media—television, newspapers, and radio—have instant access to agenda setting and, in many cases, push an issue onto the national public agendas of Congress and the courts. The media create as well as reflect issues. In the latter role, the media have been manipulated by clever politicians. For example, in 1961, shortly before President John F. Kennedy was to deliver a major foreign policy address at the University of North Carolina, he instructed his aid, Ted Sorenson, to ask journalists Joseph Alsop and Walter Lippman for their suggestions on how to counter conservative Republican charges that he wanted to appease the Soviets. Kennedy incorporated part of their replies into his speech. This made it difficult for these prominent journalists to criticize Kennedy's policy; after all, part of his proposals came from them. It also made it difficult for Kennedy's opponents to get favorable press coverage.

President Kennedy was an expert at manipulating the public policy agenda through news management. He released information personally to journalists to maximize favorable coverage of his policies. Twenty years later, "the great communicator," Ronald Reagan, also proved to be especially skilled at manipulating the news media. During his 1984 presidential campaign Reagan was so well protected by his aids that all of his appearances were perfectly orchestrated. He did not have to respond spontaneously to reporters' questions. Reagan was also a master at manipulating symbols and turning things to his advantage in the way he defined an issue. For example, in 1985 Congress seemed well on its way to defeating a multibillion dollar appropriation for the MX missile. However, Reagan convinced Congress that he needed the MX missile as a "bargaining chip" in his arms negotiations with the Soviets. Reagan's way of defining the issue, in addition to political pressure on Congress, succeeded in getting approval for the MX.

Another example of this technique is the way Reagan handled his proposal for aid to the contras in Nicaragua in 1986. The contras are the rebel groups who oppose the Sandinista (communist) regime in Nicaragua. In May 1986 Congress turned down Reagan's request to supply the contras with $100 million in military aid. Shortly thereafter, the Reagan administration released a story that Nicaragua had invaded neighboring Honduras. The story hit the media and changed the issue from one in which the United States was trying to overthrow the government of one foreign country to one in which the United States was trying to help a different foreign country protect itself from aggression. Reagan succeeded in achieving military aid, despite the fact that the Sandinistas claimed they were not aggressors (they were in hot pursuit of the contras after a battle in Nicaragua) and in spite of the fact that many similar incursions had taken place in the past that were not as heavily publicized as this one was.

The techniques Reagan used were similar to those used by Kennedy more than twenty years earlier. Kennedy prepared carefully for his news conferences but, unlike Reagan, he used them as a regular and frequent vehicle to publicize his administration's policies. Kennedy also contacted leading editors, publishers, and reporters personally, and punished journalists who criticized him by withholding stories from them (Kern 1981, 2).

The media is one of the most useful instruments for setting the public policy agenda, and both Kennedy and Reagan knew this. Because the press is the principal source for interpreting events, it is one of the main architects of the public policy debate (Hillsman 1971). The media (press, television, and radio) interprets events every day, day after day (Hillman 1971, 114). In many cases, journalists directly set the policy agenda, as illustrated in Case 2–4.

The ability of the media to directly influence the public policy agenda was tested in one study involving a national television program about health care fraud broadcast on May 7, 1981. The researchers interviewed two groups: Those who watched the program and those who did. They found that those who viewed the program saw home health care as more important, fraud and abuse as a larger problem, and more need for government action than those who did not watch it (Cook et al. 1981, 9–10). According to this study, the media is capable of directly influencing general attitudes about a policy issue.

CASE 2–4 *The War in Laos*

In 1961, Laos and its war were entirely unknown to the American public. The only American agencies interested in the issue were the National Security people in the U.S. State Department, who felt that the Laotian government should be anti-Communist. This policy was pursued by the Far Eastern desk in the State Department and by the CIA. To achieve this goal, the United States helped force Laos's Prince Souvanna Phouma out of power in 1958. As a result, political conditions in Laos grew worse. When the Kennedy administration took office in 1960, pleas came from the American Embassy to support the neutralists in Laos, but this was opposed by the State Department, the CIA, and the Defense Department. Being newly elected, Kennedy was still learning his way around the national security bureaucracy, so he did not take a position at first.

Journalist Joseph Alsop was a member of the Washington Press Corps who felt strongly about Laos and he wrote a letter to Kennedy asking him to give personal attention to the impending crisis there. The letter further implied that if the president did not pay personal attention to Laos, Alsop would make things difficult for Kennedy on another sensitive issue (Kern 1981, 21). Thus, Alsop was performing a direct, agenda-setting function.

Kennedy complied with Alsop's request. He owed Alsop a debt since the latter supported Kennedy during his presidential race. Alsop had written extensively about Laos in the *Washington Post* and other newspapers. Kennedy subsequently spent more time on Laos than on any other issue during his first 100 days as president (Sorenson 1966, 722).

By March 1961, the other major newspapers began to pay attention to Laos. On March 3, 1961, the *New York Times* editor alleged that the "Russians plan to take over the area in the near future." This editorial contributed to a highly publicized convening of the National Security Council as well as a flurry of presidential activity designed to warn the Russians of American resolve (Kern 1981, 25). Thus, through the media, the Laos issue had become a part of the institutional agenda of the executive branch.

Government policy makers who watched the program also indicated a change in their attitudes about the seriousness of fraud and abuse in home health care, as well as about whether or not there should be government action. The researchers who conducted the study concluded that it was not the story itself that directly influenced policy makers, but the active collaboration between journalists and policy makers during the investigation for the story. This finding reveals the symbiotic relationship that exists between the media and governmental officials—a relationship that provides politicians access to the media and provides journalists with solutions to the problems presented in their stories.

Simply changing attitudes of policy makers about the seriousness of an issue is not enough. To get the issue onto the institutional agenda, a policy maker must introduce the matter to the legislature. According to one study, members of Congress often initially hear about a given item by reading about it in a newspaper, seeing it on television, or hearing about it on radio; a second way they hear about an issue is through letters that a media story generates (Kingdon 1984, 25–39).

Nelson (1984) suggests that the media played a major role in agenda setting for the child abuse issue. The number of media stories about child abuse increased greatly following the 1962 publication of an article written by two pediatricians, called "The Battered-Child Syndrome." Professional research articles on the issue also grew exponentially, and in 1976, a journal devoted to the issue was created. Nelson concludes that "child abuse achieved the public's agenda because the interest of a few pioneering researchers crossed the bridge to mass-circulation news outlets. Public interest was sustained and grew, however, because the media have both many *sources* of news and many *types* of audiences to whom they present the news" (73).

A Harvard University study based on interviews with 20 policy makers and 16 journalists who were particularly influential also documents the important role played by the media in agenda setting. The study found that the "most significant impacts of the press occur early on the policy-making process, when it is not yet clear which issues will be addressed and what questions will be decided. Officials believe that the media do a lot to set the policy agenda and *to influence how an issue is understood by policy makers, interest groups, and public* (Linsky 1986, 87, emphasis added). The latter aspect of agenda setting is particularly important. As Linsky (1986, 94) notes a little later in his book, "the way the press frames the issue is as important as whether or not it is covered at all. If the press characterizes a policy option one way early on in the decision-making process, it is very difficult for officials to turn that image around to their preferred perspective." For example, when the Reagan administration attempted to reverse a long standing policy of the Internal Revenue Service that denied tax-exempt status to educational institutions that practiced racial discrimination (Bob Jones University in Greenville, South Carolina, is the case in point), the decision was characterized as racist. Reagan was unable to erase this construction of his administration's action.

The media's influence on policy has become more pronounced with the advent of television. Television has replaced political parties as the means of communication between officials and voters, according to political scientist James David Barber (Orren 1986, 10). The specific impact of television according to the Harvard studies (Linsky 1986, 66) are "television diminishes the quality of communication among officials in public settings such as Congressional hearings; forces oversimplification of issues; nationalizes a story and puts it on the policy makers agenda; creates a supportive environment for certain options; and accelerates the policy making process." The last impact changes policy because it forces public officials to respond to an issue much quicker than they ordinarily would. Often, the result is a reversal or a change in policy that was already in place. For example, when journalist Walter Pincus wrote a story about the "neutron bomb" that was being considered by the Carter administration, it "touched off a political explosion that reverberated throughout the United States and Europe," (Linsky 1986, 22). The neutron bomb would kill by radiation rather than by blast or fallout. When it hit a building, it would leave the building intact but kill the people inside. The outraged reaction to Pincus' story caused the Carter administration to cancel plans for the bomb.

The media plays a role in setting the agenda at the state and local levels as well. For example, political scientist Herbert Jacob (1984) found that perceptions about what constitutes the crime problem are shaped primarily by what city officials see in the press and by what reaches them through the official governmental channels. The latter is mainly the crime statistics that police agencies record in the *Uniform Crime Reports.* These are often used in media stories about the rising (or falling) crime rate. During the 1970s and early 1980s, the stories were invariably about a new increase in crime. As a result, fear of crime increased in cities throughout the country and continued to increase even after the actual crime rate leveled off. Moreover, the fear of crime was highest among those least likely to experience crime, such as older, middle-class whites (Skogan & Klecka 1976).

The media, therefore, are a major influence on public policy agendas at the national as well as the local levels. The media create as well as *reflect* issues and the views of others. Reporters as well as policy makers have professional interests in which policies are on the political and public policy agendas. They are engaged in a continuing struggle to control the view of reality that is presented to the American public (Linsky 1986, 36). The relationship between policy makers and reporters is inextricably intertwined, says Linsky (67), "like different colored strands in a single ball of thread."

Government Administrators

Another powerful group with direct access to the public agenda is governmental administrators. Traditionally, administrators have been viewed as neutral experts who hammer out a means of carrying out legislation in an effective and efficient way (Walker 1981, 78). This view underestimates the influence of administrators in the agenda-setting process, however. Administrators often are consulted in the early stages of deliberation when policy makers are just beginning to assign relative importance to various policy problems. It is at this stage that much of the agenda is shaped. The further along the process moves, the more difficult it is to affect the way an issue is defined.

One source of the administrators' power is their expertise (Weber 1949, 232). They know all the technical details about an issue because it is their job, whereas legislators usually do not have the time to devote to such details. This is even more pronounced at the local level where most councilmembers, state representatives, and senators work only part time (Altfield & Miller 1983).

In many cities, legislators give up the right to develop proposals of their own and instead simply approve or disapprove those proposed by the city manager and the administrative agencies directed by him or her (Miller 1981; Romer & Rosenthal 1978). As one student of the power of the bureaucracy put it, "Within its own ranks, public bureaucracy numbers a wide variety of highly organized and technically trained professional personnel, whose knowledge and skills powerfully influence the shape of official decisions" (Rourke 1969, 2).

Administrative agencies are powerful also because they are able to create new interest groups as government becomes larger (Milward 1980, 258). Unlike traditional interest groups that pressure government to create a new program, these groups are created as a result of government programs. Political scientists Colarulli and Berg (1983) call these *imputed interest groups.* For example, when the federal government adopted school lunch programs in the 1930s through the New Deal's Agricultural Adjustment Act, this led to the creation of the American School Food Service Association, which consists of employees who benefit from the school lunch program like the workers behind the counter who serve the food. This group has successfully lobbied for permanent funding of school lunches in low-income areas of the country (Steiner 1976, 190). It is also involved in national discussions about nutrition policy, in the day-to-day implementation of school lunch policy, in training of kitchen employees, and in helping its members attain professional standing. In this way, the group ensures a continued need for the program.

The President and the White House Staff

Although administrators have a great deal of influence in setting the agenda on day-to-day matters, the president and the White House staff are more powerful (Kingdon 1984). The president can veto legislation, fill key policy-making positions in government, and command public attention. By commanding public attention, the president can also put pressure on government officials. This was demonstrated in 1985, when President Reagan convinced Congress that the multibillion dollar appropriation for the MX missile was a necessary "bargaining chip" in his arms negotiations with the Soviets.

The major components of the president's power are the White House staff and the Executive Office. The latter includes the Domestic Policy Staff, Council of Economic Advisers, and the Office of Management and Budget (see Figure 2–1). According to a study by John Kingdon (1984, 28–29), the White House staff and Executive Office are important in agenda setting in a high percentage of cases. But they are more important in working out alternatives for items already on the agenda than in getting new items onto the agenda.

The president's top-level appointees such as cabinet members also play a significant role in bringing new items onto the agenda. For example, in 1978, Secretary of Health, Education, and Welfare, Joseph Califano, initiated a war on smoking. However, because he failed to get President Carter's approval, Califano got into trouble with the initiative, and was subsequently removed from his position. Kingdon (1984, 33) concludes that "with regard to agenda setting, then, a top-down model of the executive branch seems to be surprisingly accurate." This is surprising, perhaps, because of the importance that lower echelon administrators have in what are known as "policy subgovernments." These will be described following a discussion of some of the other powerful actors in agenda setting.

The U.S. Congress and the Congressional Staff

According to Kingdon (1984), Congress is almost as powerful as the president in the agenda-setting process. This power is based in Congress's legal authority to enact legislation and appropriate funds as well as the influence and visibility of some of its key members. Many major policy actors, including the president, try to anticipate what Congress will do about a particular proposal. For example, the president will modify or drop a proposal altogether if it seems there is little chance that Congress will enact it. According to one key presidential aide, "You'd damned well better consult with the Hill, or you're going to be in deep trouble once your proposal gets up there. If you're smart at all you make a point of that" (Kingdon 1984, 39).

Although Congress has a strong incentive to engage in agenda setting, it will dodge controversial issues if it can (Price 1978). At the same time that representatives want to satisfy their districts, they also want to achieve good public policy goals. Hence, they will seek to get on committees that are in their area of interest and expertise as well as deal with problems of importance to the constituents (Walker 1981).

Congressional full-time staff members are also very important in agenda setting because they devote more time and attention to a particular policy area. Many times an idea will originate with the congressional staff because a representative's attention is spread very thin over a number of issues. Representatives juggle a myriad of other activities, such as seeing constituents, holding press interviews, meeting with interest group representatives, and communicating with members of the executive branch. Thus, it is generally

FIGURE 2–1 The government of the United States.

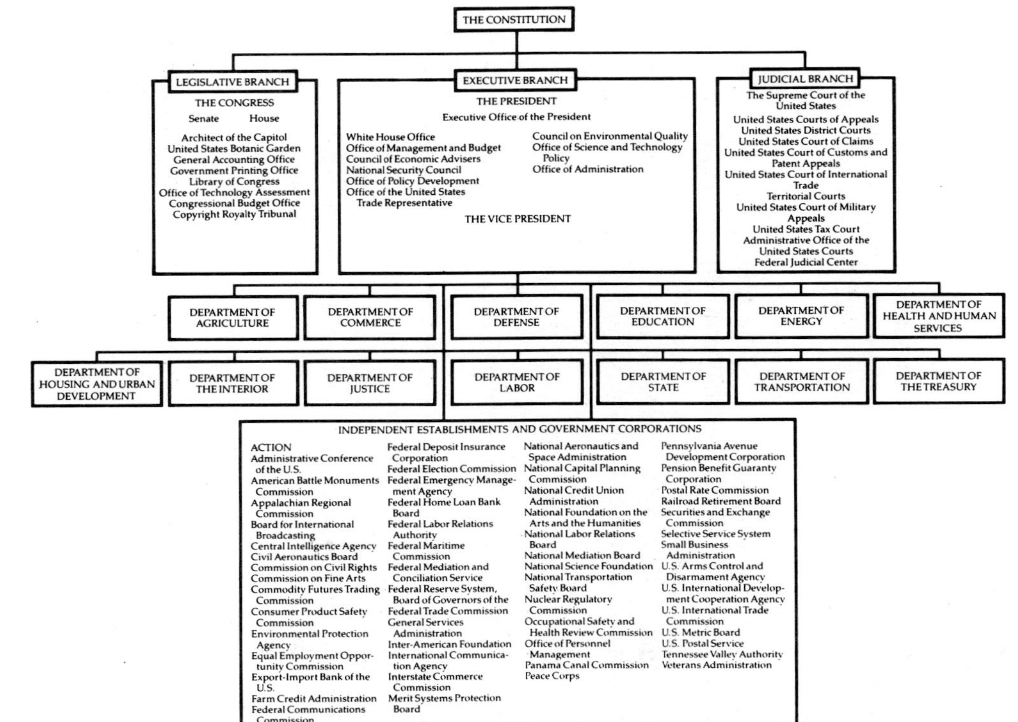

Source: *U.S. Government Manual, 1985–86,* Office of the Federal Register, National Archives and Records Administrator, p. 827.

up to the staff to draft legislation, negotiate the details of agreements among interested parties, arrange for hearing witnesses, write speeches, and prepare briefing materials for their bosses. But, of course, congressional staffers do these things in close collaboration with their bosses, the elected officials (Salisbury & Shepsle 1981).

Interest Groups

Although not as powerful as Congress in agenda setting, interest groups still play an important role. The lower the visibility of an issue, and the less ideological and partisan the debate about it, the greater the influence of interest groups (Kingdon 1984, 49).

Business and industry interest groups are the most influential, followed by professional associations such as the American Medical Association, the American Bar Association, and labor unions, although the power of labor unions diminished considerably during Reagan's two terms.

Much of the activity of interest groups consists of blocking items they oppose rather than in bringing new items to the fore. Their goal is to protect their prerogatives. Interest groups can mobilize the community and initiate a letter-writing campaign, which is their most potent weapon. For example, President Carter's attempt to contain hospital costs in 1978 was effectively blocked by the hospital lobby which encouraged communities to come to the defense of "their community hospitals."

The National Rifle Association (NRA) has been very successful in blocking gun control legislation, although its power was somewhat diminished in 1993 when the Brady Bill was passed by Congress. Named after James Brady, the presidential assistant who was shot during the assassination attempt on Ronald Reagan, the bill required a two-week waiting period for anyone purchasing a gun. Although the NRA lost on this issue, it did not roll over and play dead. After another defeat in New Jersey, which had banned assault weapons, the NRA launched a fierce fight to weaken the Bill. NRA's chief lobbyist in New Jersey said: "This organization does not take things sitting down. It never has. Legislators should know that" (Specter 1991, 14).

Academics and research consultants are also important interest groups. For example, the question of deregulation (that is, ending government controls in an industry such as the airlines) was preceded by a period of sustained attack by scholars in the late 1970s on government economic regulations. As Kingdon describes, "It really was a case of economic theory's direct impact on policy agenda" (1984, 57). Similarly, in health regulation (see Chapter 6), academicians were responsible for generating many ideas about the best way to contain health care costs.

The principal influence of researchers and academicians lies in their ability to affect the general climate of ideas about a policy (Weiss 1981). They do not have a direct impact on a program in the sense of changing or stopping a specific policy; instead, they have an indirect and long-term impact because they influence how government officials perceive issues.

Policy Subgovernments

When combined together, groups of professionals, administrators, and congressional staffers form *policy subgovernments* whose influence on agenda setting becomes very powerful. The policy subgovernments have been called "iron triangles" by political scientists to convey the idea that they pretty much control the policy process. Although subgovernments are not a legally recognized unit of government, they often have a greater impact on public policy than the formal structures of government. In many cases, policy subgovernments will initiate a program before formal legislation is passed (see Case 2–5).

Congressional committee members, interest groups, and bureaucrats represent only a small part of subgovernments. In addition, subgovernments may involve just about anyone interested in the many benefits that flow from a policy domain, including bureau chiefs, administrators of line agencies, university academics, consultants, representatives of resource suppliers, governors, and members of state and local governments. These are referred to as "policy communities" by some political scientists (Milward & Laird 1990).

The lengthy development of an issue by members of a policy subgovernment occurs in many areas. Another example described by Milward (1980) is the process by which public housing programs were created in Ohio. First, a group of professionals and administrators developed the agenda and then mobilized support from others to create the illusion of mass support from government groups, civil rights, and community development organizations. These groups succeeded in creating a constituency of potential producers and builders of housing, developers and realtors, mortgage brokers, and people from the building trades.

Policy subgovernments in education are described by Meltsner and Bellavita (1983) as "policy networks." They define policy networks as "the constellation of actors, institutions, issues, and structures that make up a policy arena, such as health, education, banking, and agriculture. People in, say, a state education policy network deal with more than a single issue. In addition to competency testing, the network is also concerned with textbook selection, financing, special education, curriculum development, and other issues" (44). So far there are no studies indicating how typical this network pattern is but as research on the policy-making process increases, it is likely that subgovernments will be found in almost all areas of public policy making.

Policy subgovernments are able to control the agenda in one of two ways. Either they can make the debate about policy issues unintelligible to outsiders and act as a barrier to broader participation in problem definition, or they can define the issues in ways that favor their interest. According to Hummel (1982), members of a bureaucracy or professions use "bureaucratese"—secret

CASE 2–5 ***Community Corrections***

In many states, community corrections programs have been created by policy subgovernments. Some of these programs have been initiated by groups of professionals—that is, judges, lawyers, criminal justice specialists, probation officers, and reform groups—who are convinced that many nonviolent felons should be kept out of prison because prison conditions make them worse. They believe that as many as 30 percent of those in prison could be handled outside of prison with no lessening in punishment or decrease in public safety. In Kansas, for example, officials began informal diversion programs at the county level in which some offenders were put into treatment programs instead of being sent to prison. These diversion programs were started with the help of federal funds from the U.S. Law Enforcement Assistance Administration. Additional support for these programs came from various private groups and individuals who believed that not enough was being done in the state's prisons to rehabilitate offenders and that rehabilitation may succeed better if they are kept in their community rather than being sent to prison.

These various individuals visited other states and cities that already had community corrections programs in operation. Included in the group were a judge, members of the Catholic Church, and university professors. They returned with a report and recommendations for adopting a similar program in Kansas. They successfully lobbied the state legislature which passed the Community Corrections Act for the entire state. The process took about six to seven years. This same process occurred in a number of other states such as Oregon, where diversion programs were started in a number of counties in the early 1970s with the use of federal funds from the U.S. Law Enforcement Assistance Administration. Oregon finally passed a law in 1977 recognizing the existence of corrections programs and expanding them to other counties (Palumbo, Maynard-Moody & Wright 1984). Several other states (for example, Minnesota, Colorado, and Connecticut), have similar programs and other states are considering adopting alternative sentencing programs to cope with prison overcrowding.

professional languages and jargon—to keep other people outside. "Jargon prevents us from knowing what the jargon users are talking about" (156). The process allows virtually all issues in some areas to be defined as technical ones, or as matters that are best left to the experts (Derthick 1979; Heclo 1978). For example, teachers and school administrators frequently argue that the determination of what constitutes effective teaching is best left to professionals because they are the only ones who know what constitutes effective teaching (see Chapter 7). Medical doctors virtually own the way problems are defined in the health area. The same claim is made by all professional groups.

BIAS IN AGENDA SETTING

The close interrelationships among members of policy subsystems create what is known as institutional bias. Not everyone has equal access to agenda setting. In fact, some groups feel they have a presumptive right to problems, or that they "own" the problem, and that a policy cannot be adopted without their participation—and actual domination. For example, the medical profession in the United States almost exclusively defines the problems of American health care policy. This monopoly on defining problems in health care has not only stifled reform but contributed to escalating health care costs (Alford 1975). The medical profession controls health care policy in several areas: physician care, hospitalization, mental health, aging, alcohol, substance abuse, and, until recently, abortion (Cobb & Elder 1972, 180). Case 2–6 illustrates how and when physicians lost control of the agenda in abortion policy.

The presumptive right to problem definition, like that of physicians and health care, often becomes institutionalized. Many areas of policy are dominated by a limited and relatively stable set of actors operating within a relatively closed communications network. They are by no means representative of citizens in general nor do they necessarily reflect the view of the majority. The "power elite" or power structure in a community maintains its control of the institutional agenda in yet another way; by making sure that certain items unfavorable to them stay *off* the agenda. The distribution of power in society is affected not only by what government does but also by what it *does not do*. Thus, there are "two faces" of power in society: One that determines what issues get onto the public agenda and how the problem will be defined and one that keeps things off the agenda, thus preventing government from acting and upsetting the advantage held by the power elite (Bachrach & Baratz 1970).

This second area of agenda setting has been called *non-decision making*. The concept was invented by a political scientist and an economist who were addressing the question of whether community politics is controlled by a small group such as a power elite, or whether there is fairly widespread participation in decision making throughout a system, called *pluralist democracy*. In the 1950s, sociologists C. Wright Mills and Floyd Hunter did significant research on this question of power. Both concluded that a small power elite (or power structure) controls all major public policy decisions at the national as well as at the local levels. Mills (1956) found that the military-industrial-governmental complex made all important national decisions. The public has relatively little influence on this process. According to Mills, "Administration replaces electoral politics;

CASE 2–6 *Physicians' Ownership of the Abortion Issue*

Until the Supreme Court decision in *Roe v. Wade,* the medical profession controlled abortion policy. Kristin Luker (1984) lucidly describes how physicians gained control over abortion policy in the nineteenth century as a way of increasing their power and legitimizing their position in medicine. Prior to then, the notion that abortion is equivalent to murder was not a prevalent one. In ancient Rome, abortion was frequent and widespread. There was no legal regulation of abortion, and Roman law explicitly held that the fetus was not a person (Luker, 12). Although the early Christian Church denounced abortion, sanctions for abortions were never as severe as the murder of an adult, and abortions before "quickening"—that is, the movement of the fetus—were legally ignored. In the nineteenth century, English common law ruled that since there was no statute on abortion, it was a misdemeanor at worst if performed during the first three months.

Abortion began to emerge as a social problem in the second half of the nineteenth century as newspapers began to run stories about women who died from abortions performed by lay people. Physicians began to focus on the issue and the American Medical Association in 1842 decided to make it a major issue. It used the abortion issue as a way of distinguishing "legitimate physicians" from other medical sects and pressed for licensing laws and moral statutes in a number of states.

As a result of the physicians' campaign, laws were passed that prohibited all abortions except those performed by a physician. After physicians gained

the maneuvering of cliques replaces the clash of parties" (1956, 267). Similarly, Hunter (1953) found that a power structure of about forty people controlled policy in Atlanta, Georgia. These elitists were predominantly business officials and old, established families in Atlanta.

However, another study of decision making in local communities concluded that, while a relatively small group of individuals control policy in each major area—that is, welfare, education, employment, and so on—different groups were powerful in each different area (Dahl et al. 1961). The researchers called this pluralist democracy. While it is not democratic in the sense that average citizens participate in making public policy, according to these researchers, pluralism is as close an approximation to democracy as is realistically possible.

According to Bachrach and Baratz (1970) however, Dahl and his collaborators failed to look at decisions that the government did *not* make—that is, non-decisions. Bachrach and Baratz argue that it is in this area of non decisions that the power structure is most able to protect its interest. Thus, the control over abortion policy, the issue went underground for almost a century (Luker, 39). By 1890, anti-abortion statutes were a standard part of the law throughout the United States. But in the late 1950s, groups of professionals (lawyers, physicians, psychiatrists) and lay people began to agitate for changes. Several states, including North Carolina, Colorado, and California, passed more liberal abortion laws in the 1960s, and in 1973 a landmark Supreme Court decision changed the law throughout the country.

By approaching this issue as they did during the nineteenth century, physicians transformed the abortion debate from a social issue to a technical one which only they had the expertise to solve. In the twentieth century, women's groups succeeded in redefining the abortion issue as pertaining primarily to the role of women in American society (Diamond 1985). As Luker writes, "If the status of the embryo has always been ambiguous, as argued here, then to attribute personhood to the embryo is to make the social statement that pregnancy is valuable and that women should subordinate other parts of their lives to that central aspect of their social and biological selves" (1984, 8). But as women entered the labor force in large numbers in the 1970s and the status and role of women changed, subordination to an unwanted fetus was still considered a barrier to women's economic and social independence that more and more women were unwilling to accept.

greatest bias in the system comes during the agenda-setting process where the rich and powerful are successful in keeping items off the public policy agenda, not during the policy formulation (see Chapter 3) or implementation stages (see Chapter 4).

■ PROCESSES OF AGENDA SETTING

It is as difficult to determine empirically if a group or individual has been successful in keeping an issue off of the agenda as it is to trace the actual origins of an item that gets onto the agenda. This is because at any point in time there is a plethora of ideas floating around on the systemic agenda, and there are many places where they may have originated. Most often, a combination of factors is responsible for getting an issue onto or keeping it off the agenda. Nor is the process a rational one. Rationally, the process of agenda setting should proceed as follows. First, a major problem is recognized to exist by a number of individuals and groups. Second, the problem is discussed and information about it is disseminated to larger groups. Third, government officials—that is, legislators, governors, and administrators—are involved in the process and a national debate ensues about various ways of solving the problem.

The process of agenda setting has been described in numerous ways. Most of these models conceive of the process as moving through stages. The early stages usually involve activity within policy communities that voice concern about an issue. Then the media pick up and dramatize the issue and this propels it onto the institutional agenda (Downs 1972; Peters & Hogwood 1985; Walker 1977; Cook 1981; Nelson 1984).

Instead of this neat logical scenario, the process more closely resembles a garbage can in which ideas are not clearly defined, technologies for solving problems do not exist, agencies operate by trial and error, and participation in the discussion is very fluid. People generate and debate solutions to problems because they have a self-interest in doing so, not because they hope to find an optimal solution to a problem. The political conditions must be ripe in order for an issue to get onto the national institutional agenda. John Kingdon (1984) calls this a "window of opportunity," which opens for only a brief moment. And it is policy entrepreneurs who are able to coordinate the groups in the policy subgovernments in order to take advantage of the brief opening.

Policy entrepreneurs are able to bring a problem into the personal experience of legislators by giving them a first hand look at it. For example, in Seattle, Washington, a pediatrician by the name of Abe Bergman invited Senator Warren Magnuson of Washington to view horrible burn cases in the hospital to highlight the problems of flammable children's clothing (Axelrod 1981). Similarly, in Colorado, Roger Lauen, who ultimately became director of community corrections, brought several state legislators into the Colorado state prison and introduced them to a group of young men who were facing five-year prison terms for using marijuana, not for selling it. This convinced legislators that the prisons were being used for individuals who should not be there and they then supported community corrections.

Policy entrepreneurs like Bergman and Lauen are willing to invest their time, energy, reputation—and sometimes, money—in the hope that there will be a return. That return takes the form of a policy that the entrepreneur would like to see enacted, and perhaps personal advancement. Their major efforts are often focused on those in the policy subgovernments who try to reach a consensus about what should be done.

At the same time, political events are occurring. A change in public mood or opinion, a change in government officials or administration, and perhaps a sensational event may occur, which opens the window of opportunity for the policy entrepreneur and gets the issue onto the agenda. Policy entrepreneurs must have multiple skills. They must not only persuade the

FIGURE 2–2 Systems model of politics.

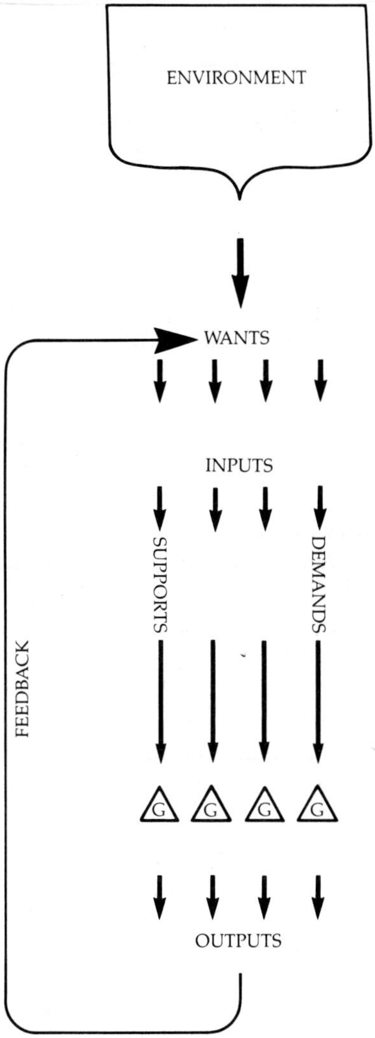

ENVIRONMENT

WANTS

INPUTS

SUPPORTS

DEMANDS

FEEDBACK

G G G G

OUTPUTS

Source: David Easton, *A Systems Analysis of Political Life,* (Chicago: University of Chicago Press, 1965).

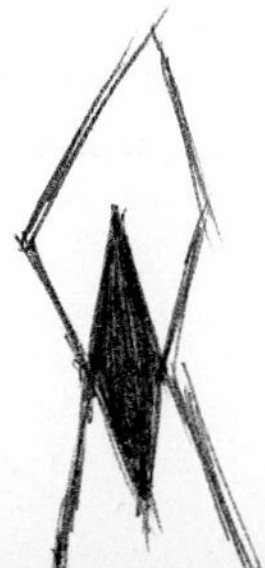

policy subgovernments; they also must be effective brokers, negotiators and make critical couplings among the media, politicians, interest groups, and the public (Kingdon 1984, 192).

■ AGENDA BUILDING AND POLITICAL THEORY

Agenda setting has been recognized as an important component of policy making in American politics since the early 1970s. Prior to then, political scientists did not pay much attention to this important component of policy making. Earlier political theories, such as systems theory, referred to an analogous function, however, called *gatekeeping*. In systems theory (see Figure 2–2), the environment gives rise to wants which are converted into demands by interest groups, the public, or individuals. These demands then proceed through the system, going through check points (marked G in Figure 2–2) where they may be stopped completely from continuing on to other points, and where they can be modified in some way. These check points are occupied by gatekeepers—those who initiate a demand by first voicing it, or those whose actions at some point have the opportunity to determine its destiny (Easton 1964, 86–88).

Traditional democratic theory is based on the notion that the people (that is, voters) determine the direction of public policy. They do this when they elect representatives and senators who stand for the policy positions favored by a majority of the public and who, after they are elected, put these policies into practice. Most political scientists, however, believe that this view is incorrect. The mass public has little knowledge of issues and do not even know the name of their representatives in Congress. In the television age, personality and image are much more important than issues as a determinant of how people vote. And elected politicians do not often put their campaign promises into action once they are elected. Thus, electing people to office is not a very effective way of determining the direction of public policy.

If it is true that electing people to office is not a good way to influence the direction of public policy, then it may be possible to have an impact by determining what gets onto the public agenda. If the process of agenda setting is an open one, then we have widened public participation and increased democracy. But, as we have seen, access to agenda setting is restricted to a relatively few powerful people and groups in the policy-shaping communities. The researchers who have done more than anyone else to analyze the agenda-setting process conclude that the changes in agenda building over the past 20 years have "tended simply to further advantage the already advantaged and to frustrate the many for whom participation is a right and civic duty but not a consuming passion nor a full-time occupation" (Cobb & Elder 1984, 190).

Policy Formulation: Designing Solutions to Public Problems

■ THE NATURE OF POLICY FORMULATION

Defining Policy Formulation

At one time, policy formulation was considered to be the whole of policy making. It was assumed that when Congress passed a law and it was signed by the president the act of policy making was complete. We now know that this stage in policy making is but one step in a process that begins before legislation is enacted and continues afterward. Nor is what happens during formulation the most important part of policy making.

The word *formulation* is a better description of what happens during this stage of policy making than *formation*. According to *Webster's Ninth New Collegiate Dictionary* (1984), formation is "an act of giving form or shape to something or taking form." But policy does not really take form until it is implemented. As policy scientists Hogwood and Peters write, "Policies are abstractions that only achieve substance once they are delivered" (1983, 87). Hence, policy *formation* is not an accurate description of what happens during this stage of the policy cycle. The phrase *policy formulation* is a little more accurate because formulation means putting something into a systematized statement or expression, or reducing it to a formula. Enacting a bill is akin to reducing policy to a formula, or systematized statement. But as we shall see, most legislation is ambiguous, broad, and general rather than systematic.

Another way to characterize this stage is by the phrase *policy legitimizing*. This implies that enactment into law gives policy legal status. In some ways, this description is more accurate than formulation because elements of a policy are often in operation before they are given formal, legal status. (For example, many policies begin at the local level before they become a part of state or national legislative action.) At the same time, legitimation is too narrow a definition because more than ratifying or legalizing a policy is involved during this stage.

Just as policy formulation was considered in classical political science to be the whole of policy making, the reverse idea—that implementation was the key or Achilles' heel of policy making (see Chapter 4)—began to develop in the 1970s. However, by the 1990s, a more balanced view began to develop (Palumbo & Calista 1990). Both policy formulation and policy implementation were considered to be important in making good policy. A poorly designed policy could not be corrected through implementation no matter how well it was implemented.

Policy design is concerned with the tools or combination of tools that government uses in order to achieve its objectives. Public policy almost always attempts to force or enable people to do things that they might not otherwise do. Political scientists Schneider and Ingram (1989) classify policy tools into four categories: (1) *Incentives* consist of tangible payoffs (i.e., money) or sanctions, (2) *Capacity building* provides information, training, education, or other resources to enable people to carry out desired activity, (3) *Symbolic or hortatory* assume that people are motivated from within and will behave in accord with what government wants. Symbolic tools seek to convince people that what government wants to achieve is important, and (4) *Learning* is used when there is no agreement about what should be done to solve a problem, but agencies and target populations can learn what action may be most effective in achieving desired objectives.

Good policy design would use the appropriate tools for a given situation, but as we shall see in this chapter, this is not always easy to do.

Subprocesses of Policy Formulation

Policy, therefore, is not completely and finally formed during the formulation stage. What occurs is that the problem is further defined, information about it is collected and discussed, alternatives for approaching or ameliorating it are screened, and a preferred choice is finally made. The process does not occur in a specific sequence because policy making is not this neat, logical, or rational. It is best to conceive of the activities just mentioned as *subprocesses* that occur during this stage of the policy cycle, not necessarily in sequential order. For example, some members of Congress may have a preferred method for handling a problem even before all the information about the problem is gathered, or the problem itself is fully defined. They may simply be following the dictates of their ideology. For example, in solving a problem, a conservative member of Congress may prefer to eliminate a governmental agency whereas a liberal member may prefer to create a new one. The sequence of activities just described are the steps a completely rational decision maker would take when addressing a problem. But rational decision making is only one view of what actually happens. In this chapter, we will consider the rational theory of decision making along with several others after considering the principal institutions involved in this process.

THE PRINCIPLES OF GOVERNMENT

Policy in the United States is formulated by the legislative, executive, and judicial branches of government at the national, state, and local levels (see Table 3–1). These agencies operate within a system of constraints that was

TABLE 3–1 ***Public Agencies Involved in Policy Formulation***

Level of Government	Legislative	Executive	Judicial
National	U.S. Congress	Presidency and cabinet	U.S. Supreme Court, federal district courts, and other federal courts (that is, customs court)
State	Fifty state legislatures	State governors and state administrative agencies	State appellate courts
Local	Numerous county commissions, city councils, and township councils	County commissioners and departments, city mayors, managers, and administrative agencies	County courts, magistrate courts

built into American government by the U.S. Constitution. These constraints often are referred to as principles of American government; they are (1) separation of powers, (2) checks and balances, and (3) federalism.

The U.S. Constitution limits the power of the national government by placing the three major powers of government—legislative, executive, and judicial—into three separate branches, which are the U.S. Congress (legislative power), president (executive power), and Supreme Court (judicial power). It was not absolutely necessary for the framers to lodge these powers in separate branches; they could have put them all in one branch. For example, in England and in many U.S. counties, the legislative and administrative powers are lodged in the same branch (the Parliament in England and the county commissions in U.S. counties). The framers of the Constitution, having just won a revolution over strong executive power, believed that "the accumulation of all powers, legislative, executive, and judiciary, in the same hands, whether of one, a few, or many, and whether hereditary, self-appointed, or elective, may justly be pronounced the very definition of tyranny" (Hamilton, Jay & Madison 1787, 313).

The framers went a step further, for they actually did not completely separate the three powers but, instead, made each branch share its power with the other branches. This is called the system of *checks and balances.* Thus, the Congress has legislative power but the president shares this through the power to veto acts of the legislature. The Supreme Court holds the judicial power, but the president shares this through his power to appoint judges to the courts and in the power to see that the laws—including decisions of the courts—are faithfully executed. The president was given the executive power, but Congress shares this through its power to create executive agencies and to appropriate money for the execution of laws. Similarly, the U.S. Senate shares judicial power through the constitutional requirement for Senate approval of presidential appointees to the Supreme Court.

These are but a few examples of how power is legally checked and balanced within a system of separated powers. As a result, policy is not made unless by consensus among the branches of government. If one of the branches has an objection, it can usually apply a check to prevent the policy from being given life, or at least slow down its implementation.

Constitutional checks and balances, moreover, are accompanied by political checks. Each branch of government is responsible to a different constituency. Under the original constitutional design, the U.S. House of Representatives was to be responsible to the people (it was, in fact, the only democratically selected branch), the Senate to the states, the president to the electors, and judges to the president with the advice of the Senate. And each branch serves a different term: House members serve two years; senators, six years; the president, four years; and federal judges have life tenure. Thus they all cannot be ousted in one election.

During the 1980s and early 1990s, the checks and balances became magnified because the Congress was controlled by the Democrats while the presidency was controlled by the Republicans. This produced the phenomenon called "divided government" and created a crisis of confidence in government. It was not possible for the people to hold elected officials accountable for the many domestic problems the country faced because the Republicans blamed the Democrats and the Democrats, in turn, blamed the Republicans. The result was more like a stalemate than a system of checks and balances.

The Constitution also limits the power of the national government through two measures: the Bill of Rights and federalism. The Bill of Rights (the first ten amendments to the Constitution) prohibits the government from doing a number of things such as establishing religion; abridging free speech or freedom of assembly; conducting unlawful searches and seizures; depriving people of their life, liberty, or property without due process; imprisoning the accused without a jury trial; and handing out cruel and unusual punishment.

Finally, the principle of federalism restricts the powers of the national government by reserving to the states and the people all powers "not delegated to the United States by the Constitution, nor prohibited by it to the States" (Tenth Amendment). Federalism in the United States has had a long and complicated history that cannot be described here. Suffice it to say that the power of the national government has expanded and that of the states has declined. However, the states and local governments still retain significant powers in areas such as criminal justice, education, and public health, while national power has expanded in areas such as economic regulation, environmental protection, welfare, medical care, and national defense. Nevertheless, in all policy areas the federal and state governments share power; no government has complete control in any area (Godzins 1963; Elazar 1962). Even in areas we normally think of as being exclusively national, such as foreign relations, the states share power with the federal government (Palumbo 1969), and in areas that traditionally have been predominantly local, such as education, the federal government has considerable power. Thus, to adequately describe how policy is formulated in any area, it would be necessary to describe not only the major national actors—that is, U.S. Congress, president, and Supreme Court—but also the state and local governments. This would take up far too much space in this book. Instead, we will consider national actors in policy formulation. Then in Part II we will consider those areas in which state and local governments have significant responsibilities in public policy.

■ THE MAIN POLICY ACTORS

The U.S. Congress: The First Branch

> I don't think they play at all fairly, and they quarrel so dreadfully one can't hear oneself speak—and they don't seem to have any rules in particular: at least, if there are, nobody attends to them—and you've no idea how confusing it is. (Lewis Carroll, *Alice's Adventures in Wonderland*)

To the untrained observer, this quote might seem to aptly describe how legislatures in the United States operate. But while this is the way it appears on the surface, Congress has many rules, and these rules are extremely important to its functioning (Oleszek 1984).

In addition to the rules—some of which are described next—there are precedents and folkways that govern the behavior of Congress. Folkways permit variations in the rules. The major folkways are: Legislative work is important (do not spend time grandstanding with the media); courtesy (members should not make personal attacks on colleagues); and specialization (members should not try to be jacks-of-all-trades). Those who follow these folkways are accepted into the inner group that manages the affairs of the legislature and are rewarded with assignments to prestigious committees. Those who violate them find their legislation blocked in committees or on the floor.

Decision-Making Structure There are certain enduring features of the congressional decision-making process. One is the decentralized power structure. There are numerous specialized committees in Congress—more than 300 in all—a weak leadership structure, and multiple decision points. This means that at each step of a bill's progress through Congress, a majority coalition must be formed to move the measure along. There is a need for bargaining and compromise in order to form the winning coalition at each point and so these become the leading legislative tools.

Congress is decentralized because each member owes his or her election to voters, not to the leadership in Congress. Congress is also specialized structurally among the numerous committees, all of which have overlapping responsibilities. For example, several different committees have responsibility over energy so that a bill relating to energy must be sent to a number of different committees. The committee structure facilitates a form of decentralization that is difficult to upset. This is known as the system of *subgovernments, iron triangles,* or *policy subsystems* described in Chapter 2. A subgovernment forms when congressional committees and subcommittees develop special relationships with pressure groups and executive agencies. Some scholars believe these subgovernments in fact make policy in each specific area and they tend to do this so as to promote and sustain each others' interests. Part II of this book describes some of the subgovernments in policy areas such as energy and welfare.

Legislation must work its way slowly through the committee system. A single bill may go through more than 100 separate steps to get through the process. Thus, it is easy to defeat a bill, but very difficult to pass one. Majority coalitions must be mobilized when the bill is (1) introduced, (2) assigned to a committee, (3) the subject of hearings, (4) sent to the other chamber, (5) on the floor of the House and Senate, and (6) sent to the president. If a bill makes it through these steps, what finally comes out is quite different than what went in.

Many bills are passed during the last few weeks of a congressional session when the pressure of time makes for a hectic process. Compromises that were not possible in July all of a sudden can be made in December. Some issues take years and even decades of deliberation before they finally are enacted into law. Health care for the poor is one example, described in Chapter 6.

Differences between the House and Senate Although both branches of Congress are similar in many ways, they also are very different. The House is more than four times the size of the Senate; senators represent a much broader constituency and serve much longer terms. Because of its larger size, the House operates by more structured rules, and individual representatives are subordinated to the necessities of the entire House. The Senate is more personal and individualistic. Party leaders in the Senate are careful to consult all senators who have an interest in pending legislation; in the House, only the key members are consulted.

Power is more evenly distributed in the Senate than in the House and each senator is more powerful than each number of the House. Because they are elected every six years, senators are less vulnerable to constituency pressure than House members and are more likely to be generalists. The Speaker of the House has enormous power and prestige but there is no counterpart in the Senate. Even with all of these differences, the House and Senate are similar in many ways. They both are decentralized and have numerous committees. Bills must pass through many points before they can be enacted. And if the House and Senate versions of a bill are different, the bill must go to a conference committee consisting of members of both branches before it finally passes.

Influences on Congress In making decisions, members of Congress are influenced by their constituents, the president, the news media, lobbyists, party leaders, and their colleagues. But representatives who are popular back home can defy all other influences. Lobbyists play an important role in policy making and will be described in more detail below. Their importance stems from their ability to act as key sources of information on issues, and to stimulate public debate.

Generalizations about which source of influence is most important are difficult to make, and usually depend upon the particular issue and time. Sometimes lobbyists may be the most important influence, whereas other times it may be colleagues. Two generalizations that apply in most cases are (1) the news media are the most important influence, and (2) the influence of political parties on congressional behavior has declined in recent years. These two ideas are related. As political party and institutional discipline have declined, a new breed of politician has appeared, reared on television, and skilled in its use to establish a power base outside Congress. Former Senate Majority Leader Howard Baker called this the "feisty freshman phenomenon," adding:

"When I first came here it took me a long while to work up to my maiden speech, and I did so with great deference to the institution. . . . But now members hit the ground running. . . . Now, if no one listens, they don't care because they go outside and someone will listen to them with a TV camera" (Dewar 1984, 13). Thus, even freshmen senators such as Phil Gramm of Texas are able to gain national prominence with the budget balancing law that Congress passed in 1985.

The Rise and Decline of Congressional Power The power and prestige of Congress vis-à-vis the president has declined during the twentieth century, reaching a low point after Richard Nixon was elected president in 1972. The approval rate for Congress (that is, the percent of the public who think Congress is doing a good job) fell to 21 percent in February 1974 (Sundquist 1981). Its power was so low that President Nixon openly defied Congress when he impounded $8.7 billion in funds that Congress had appropriated. Nixon took the stance of economizer, and when Congress could not agree on a budget ceiling in 1970, Nixon decided to cut spending on many of the programs authorized by Congress, such as aid to cities and public works. Nixon eventually lost this battle, however, when Congress passed the Congressional Budget and Impoundment Control Act of 1974. Nixon also made unilateral decisions on the Vietnam War, giving orders to mine Haiphong Harbor without consulting leaders of Congress, and withholding information from Congress under the claim of executive privilege.

A little more than a decade later, Ronald Reagan defied Congress when his National Security Staff members sold arms to Iran and then used the proceeds to support the Contras in Nicaragua who were trying to overthrow the Sandanista regime. Reagan did this even though the Congress, in the Boland Amendment to the 1985 Omnibus Appropriations Act, prohibited all funds for the Contras' military and paramilitary operations.

The ongoing battle between Presidents Nixon and Reagan and Congress was not new or unexpected, however; there has been a power struggle between the branches since the inception of the country. It was, as described above, built into the U.S. Constitution through the separation of powers and checks and balances. At times, the president has been the dominant branch, and at other times, Congress has dominated.

Shifts from executive supremacy to legislative supremacy have depended more on who is president than on any other factor. Strong presidents have always been able to outshine Congress. During the nineteenth century there were relatively few towering presidents. There have been many more in the twentieth century and few presidents, if any, subscribe anymore to the view that Congress should make policy and the president carry it out. Thus it is unlikely that the country will ever again see a Congress as powerful as it was in the latter part of the nineteenth century. According to Brookings Institution researcher James L. Sundquist:

> [T]he era of the strong president—strong in aspiration if not always achievement—has unquestionably arrived to stay, carried out on the force of trends as irreversible as anything can be. And the fact limits severely the degree to which even a determined Congress can recapture lost authority. (1981, 20)

Congress has reasserted itself since falling to its low point in its struggle with Richard Nixon. In the 1970s it initiated and enacted a number of measures, including economic stimulus measures, air and water pollution legislation, oil price controls, health, and women and minority rights measures. And, although President Reagan exerted forceful and sustained leadership that was in marked contrast to Jimmy Carter, Congress has attempted to regain some of its lost power, particularly during Reagan's lame duck term.* For example, at the beginning of Reagan's second term, Senate Republicans elected Robert Dole of Kansas as their majority leader. Less than a week after formally taking up the reins of his new position, Dole announced that the Republican senators would ignore the budget drafted by President Reagan. He said they would write their own document and propose cuts in highly sensitive programs, including military spending and Social Security, two areas in which Reagan adamantly opposed cuts (Roberts 1985). Dole, therefore, began his job as a strong majority leader, such as Lyndon Johnson was in the late 1950s. It was symbolic of congressional resurgence even in the face of a president as strong as Ronald Reagan. The Democrats won control of the Senate by a 55 to 45 margin in the 1986 elections, and widened their control in the House. This Democrat control, coupled with the foreign policy scandal involving the sale of arms to Iran and the transfer of money realized from the sale to the Contras in Nicaragua, further weakened President Reagan, indicating that Congress would regain some strength during Reagan's final two years in office.

However, George Bush became president in 1988 and shortly thereafter reestablished presidential dominance over Congress, especially after his forceful leadership in the war against Iraq called "Desert Storm." Bush's popularity soared so high that the Democrats failed to come forth with potential candidates for the 1992 election until late 1991. Things changed again in 1993 when Democrat Bill Clinton was president. American troops were killed attempting to arrest a war lord in Somalia (where the U.S. was cooperating with the U.N. in a humanitarian effort). The sight on TV of dead American soldiers being dragged through the streets of the Somalia capitol caused a public outcry and enabled the Republicans in the Senate to partially restrict the President's power to commit troops to foreign military action.

Congress can never surpass the president because it lacks the capacity to give the country a sense of making progress toward accepted goals. Senator

* Although the term "lame duck" is technically used to refer to the second and final term of a president, Ronald Reagan certainly did not behave like a lame duck during the first two years of his second term.

Les Aspin (D-Wisc) explained the reason for Congress's ineptitude: "Since only the most politically secure congressman [or congresswoman] can afford to offend constituents—and since there are so many ways to offend them—natural survival instincts dictate that a congressman [or congresswoman] will duck any tough issues that he [or she] can. Politically, it is often much safer to let the Executive do the leading" (1974, 73).

According to Representative Joe L. Evins (D-Tenn), a member of Congress is a "special pleader and a sort of super lobbyist for his constituents and his area" (1963). Getting reelected is a representative's goal, not leading the country down new paths. Political scientist Richard Fenno fully supports this view: "That parochialism can immobilize the Congress on more urgent matters is illustrated by the energy deadlock of 1978. The deadlock occurred because the decision lay in the hands of Conference members, particularly Senators, who were evenly balanced between producer and consumer points of view, and who found no incentive for compromise" (1978, 48).

Congress adopted a number of institutional changes in the 1970s to help secure its powers. These changes include:

1. *The Legislative Reorganization Act of 1970* (PL91-510) required all votes, even those in committees, to be made public. To further increase public scrutiny of its affairs, the House in 1973 and the Senate in 1975 decided to hold their committee bill drafting sessions in public, and, in 1979, the House began to televise its floor sessions.
2. *The Congressional Budget and Impoundment Control Act of 1974* established a congressional budget process that encouraged coordination and centralization. It created several House and Senate budget committees and the Congressional Budget Office, which tightened control over backdoor financing methods such as borrowing.
3. *The War Powers Resolution of 1973* compels Congress to arrive at a decision to either affirm or override a president's course of action that utilizes military force.

Congress also attempted to enact a legislative veto as a means of checking presidential power but failed to do so—an indication of its ultimate weakness vis-à-vis the president. In 1976, the House of Representatives came within two votes of a two-thirds majority favoring a bill introduced by Representative Walter Flowers of Alabama to make all rules and regulations of all executive agencies subject to a legislative veto. Over the next two years, House proposals subjecting regulations of various agencies to a congressional veto were killed in the Senate. President Carter vetoed bills containing legislative vetoes where he could and, where he had to sign the bills, he would consider the provisions not legally binding, hoping the U.S. Supreme Court would rule on the matter. The Supreme Court finally did in 1983 when it rejected the legislative veto as an unconstitutional breach of the separation of powers.

Thus, the situation remains as it has been: the two branches of government will continue to battle, and the president will continue to win the battles, particularly when the office is occupied by a strong leader. Congress will never completely recover or return to the golden era of congressional power. Today the Senate still suffers from some of the same problems that the various reforms of the 1970s were supposed to correct. Republican Dan Quayle of Indiana, chairman of a select committee appointed in 1984 to help rescue the Senate from itself, said: "We are witnessing the atrophy of the Senate" (Dewar 1984). Political scientist Norman Ornstein of the American Enterprise Institute said the Senate was facing an identity crisis, one that had reached an acute stage: "It never was supposed to be efficient; it was supposed to be creative. But it isn't creative; it's scattershot. It doesn't just bend over backwards to protect the intense feelings of its minorities, it lets individuals run roughshod over any semblance of institutional process. It has neither a broad perspective nor a narrow capture of detail" (Dewar 12).

Senator Barry Goldwater of Arizona blamed the "enormous proliferation of congressional staff" for the problems of Congress. Referring to this as the tail (staff) wagging the dog (Congress), he said that in 1984 there were 7,500 staff employees for House members and 3,700 for Senators. Appropriations for the operation of Congress went from $77.7 million in 1973 to $1.5 billion in 1984 (Goldwater 1985). While some of this increase was necessary to make Congress less dependent on the executive branch for information, most, said Goldwater, was for "the all-consuming aim of most members for reelection."

Goldwater went on to say that a great many of the legislative staff do nothing but dream up legislative initiatives that they sell to their superiors. In effect, the senator said, the staff tell the members when and where to be each step of the way until legislation is passed. More staff are on the floor and attend committee hearings than are members of Congress; this leaves members free to devote their time to campaigning for reelection, said Goldwater.

Congress members devote a lot of time to reelection efforts because of the incredibly high cost of campaigning. Their combined campaign spending in 1984 exceeded $1 billion. The constant search for campaign finances forces members to schedule long absences and puts them at the mercy of Political Action Committees (PACs). In columnist George Will's terms, Congress has become a giant Burger King where everybody has it his or her way to the greatest extent possible.

Thus, more than a decade after enacting various reforms in order to recapture some of its power, Congress is still suffering from a case of extreme inability to take concerted action.

The President

The U.S. president sets the policy direction for the country in the presidential leadership model, proclaiming the policies and programs that he or she contends will move the country forward (Burns 1978, 18). According to James Sundquist:

> The president has become the prime center of legislative initiation not merely because he heads the vast apparatus of the executive branch but perhaps primarily because he is given a mandate by the people as political leader of the country. By midcentury, what may be called the presidential leadership model was firmly in place. The president was accepted even as the legislature's own leader, expected to set the goals for the legislative sessions, to assemble the agenda, to plan the strategy for the passage of individual bills, to negotiate the necessary compromises, and then even to round up the votes for their enactment. (1981, 418)

Presidential Resources Whether or not the president will be able to lead the country in the direction he wants depends on the resources available and on how he uses those resources. The principal resources of the president are time, information, expertise, and energy.

Time is constant. The president has a four-year term, but really only about two years in which to get his program through. Time is needed for him to select issues, draft alternatives, and decide on priorities. As the term proceeds, the president becomes mired in detail and the chances of getting his program through Congress diminishes. Thus, the president must move rapidly and early in his tenure in order to get his program through. This is especially true of a second-term or lame duck president. Because the Constitution prohibits a third term, a second-term president has even less time to get programs through Congress (Spitzer 1983).

To make informed choices, the president must be at home with a staggering range of information. However, there never is enough time to get all the necessary information, so most decisions are made without it. Also, the president is at the mercy of his administrative agencies that may withhold vital information or give him incorrect data if it opposes the president's program. For example, when President Nixon sent his Family Assistance Plan to Congress in 1973, his staff did not have the time and resources to check if it would work. The deputy undersecretary of Health, Education, and Welfare and the other welfare experts in the department were aware when they sold the welfare program to Nixon that the bill contained defects that could cause its defeat in Congress (Anderson 1978, 143–44). The House passed the bill, but when it reached the Senate Finance Committee, members of that committee knew enough to ask the questions that defeated it.

The job of president is extremely demanding; the constant stress and time pressures require a lot of energy. The president must act fast for his resources decline with time and can only be replenished if it looks as if he is likely to win a second term. The first year in office is crucial in the first term and there even is less time in a president's second term.

Choosing Agenda Items Presidents are free to choose their own agenda and usually come to office with an agenda in mind. Personal beliefs and hopes for reelection are strong factors in a president's choices. Also important is the desire to attain high historical standing—which is why some presidents, like Richard Nixon, have their office conversations taped.

The presidential agenda, from Kennedy through Reagan, reflects each president's personal persuasions. For Kennedy, the principal domestic issues were aid to education, medicare, unemployment, area redevelopment, and civil rights. He was not able to get any of these through Congress. Lyndon Johnson took office promising to carry out Kennedy's unfinished domestic agenda but this agenda changed somewhat. Medicare and aid to education were two of Johnson's four top agenda items; the other two were poverty and civil rights. Richard Nixon came to office with a totally different set of domestic priorities; his top objectives were welfare reform, revenue sharing, crime reduction, and energy. The latter continued to be a top priority for President Ford, along with inflation and regulatory reform. President Carter's agenda priorities strangely enough resembled those of his predecessors; his top items were energy, inflation, welfare reform, and hospital cost containment (Light 1982, 70). President Reagan came to office with a completely different set of priorities. Top on his list were increases in defense spending and cuts in other government programs, particularly social welfare and deregulation. President Bush came to office saying he wanted to be the education and environmental president, but found after he was in office that he spent most of his time in foreign policy, especially after the spectacular collapse of the Soviet Union in 1991. He came under severe criticism for spending almost all of his time in foreign affairs (and much in traveling) and neglecting pressing domestic issues. By 1992 when the economy was in a deep recession, President Bush's approval rating plummeted to the lowest point in his term.

The principal sources of a president's agenda are campaign promises, the executive branch agencies, Congress, and the media. Issues circulate for years before finally making it onto the president's agenda, and some issues seem to have a momentum of their own; they become hot, and then cool down. For example, civil rights was high on Kennedy's and Johnson's agendas but receded into the background during Nixon's presidency; education as an issue declined from its height after the Johnson years and then resurfaced somewhat in 1984 under Reagan, with a very different emphasis.

A crisis such as the oil embargo of 1973 will catapult an issue onto the agenda. Still, executive branch agencies are one of the most important sources of agenda items because they have all the advantages: "the information, manpower, the Congressional support, and the expertise" (Light 1982, 92). More recently, presidents have sought out public opinion through polling as a way of setting their priorities. President Carter had a regular polling operation and this is likely to remain the case for future presidents.

Political parties, interest groups, and the media are minor sources for the president's agenda. Since the president *is* the party, he decides what the party agenda will be rather than the other way around. Interest groups channel their items through Congress and the bureaucracy rather than the president, and the media reflect more than initiate issues.

Choosing among Alternatives On any given issue, the first thing the president must do is decide whether or not to act. Doing nothing is a choice and is often an advisable course of action. In making choices among alternatives, the president must weigh the political and economic costs as well as their technical feasibility against the political capital at his disposal. A new program costs more than expansion of an old one, and large scale programs cost more than small ones. Some presidents have more political capital than others and some are willing to spend a lot for a particular program. In contrast to economic capital, political capital is intangible. It is the amount of power a president has, which is a function of his popularity, personality, and party support in Congress. For example, during his first term, President Reagan had more political capital than President Carter, and he decided to spend a lot of it on a greatly increased defense budget. This actually increased Reagan's capital among some groups, but was costly to him during his second term. For the most part, once political capital is expended, it can be only partly replenished (Greenstein 1978).

Political costs include the effort required to get congressional cooperation, the cooperation of the bureaucracy, and public acceptance. The first question the president's staff usually asks about a bill is: Will it fly on the Hill? Lyndon Johnson tried to get congressional cooperation by letting key members of Congress help create and draft bills. But he also ran the risk of exposing his plans to congressional opposition before the bill even saw the light of day (Kerns 1976, 232).

Economic costs are another factor in decision making. President Carter emphasized economic costs as the most frequent reason he rejected or asked for redrafting of potential programs (Light 1982, 139). Lyndon Johnson was less concerned with economic costs and actually believed that he could have both "guns and butter" (that is, defense and domestic programs). His economic advisers supported this idea, arguing that taxes would increase as the economy expanded and that the economy was likely to expand sufficiently to provide large defense expenditures for the Vietnam War as well as for domestic programs.

Over time, the built-in increase in the federal budget has grown to the point where it is no longer possible to adopt many new programs. The amount of controllable expenditures in the budget decreased between 1975 and 1993. Figure 3–1 shows that the mandatory portion of the federal budget expanded faster than the discretionary portion between 1967 and 1993. The mandatory portion increased to about $767 billion in 1993 ($980.6 billion including

FIGURE 3–1 "Mandatory" programs are taking over the budget (Outlays in 1993 Dollars).

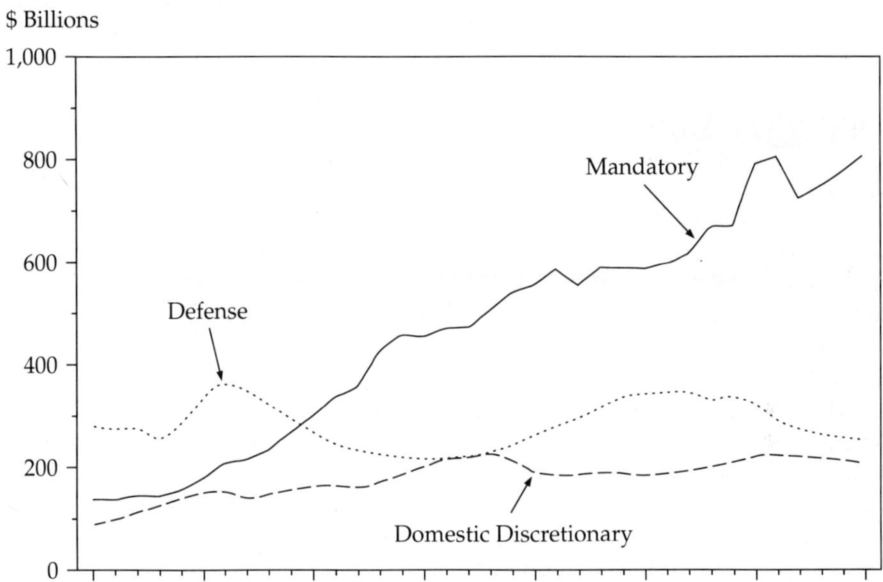

NOTE: Includes deposit insurance and pension guarantees on a cash basis; excludes undistributed offsetting receipts.

Source: Budget of the United States Government, Fiscal Year 1993, (Washington, D.C.: U.S. Government Printing Office, 1992).

interest). They amount to over 50 percent of the budget, compared to 23 percent in 1961. Hence, the current increment in the budget is already claimed by past commitments and the battle must rage over next year's share (Schick 1980, 57). This is due in part to entitlement programs; the benefit payments going to individuals are established by Congress and, when a new budget is passed, these payments are automatically made. They cannot be changed unless Congress changes the laws themselves. In 1992, the budget deficit was so large that the principal problem was deciding what to cut rather than where to increase spending.

Political scientists Brian Hogwood and Guy Peters (1983) believe that the table of existing laws is so crowded that most policy making is actually policy *succession* rather than adoption—that is, the replacement of existing policy, programs, or organizations by others. The government has expanded its activity so much, and the budget deficit is so large, that completely new activities are rarely adopted. For example, in health care, 90 percent of all medical care expenses are covered by the public sector. Any "new" policy would probably be only an incremental change on this. This does not mean that the new programs are never adopted or that major changes are never made. For example, Social Security was adopted in 1935 and space exploration in the 1960s. But most often it is existing policy that gives rise to new policies. As a result, contemporary politicians have little latitude except to try to pay for the commitments made by their predecessors.

Technical feasibility pertains to whether or not the program will work. This is the last question that is asked, and even if there is a negative answer, it is often ignored (Light, 145). Presidents often find it necessary to assume a program will work, even if the White House staff does not have time to confirm this. Program effectiveness is not as important as the symbolic aspects; in fact, both Carter and Reagan ran on platforms that criticized the bureaucracy. Because public opinion about government has been low since the late 1960s, more political mileage can be gotten by deriding the bureaucracy than by saying it is very effective.

The president is often at odds with the permanent civil service officials who run executive agencies and are just below the level of presidential appointees. President Nixon attempted to appoint his loyal followers to these key administrative posts. In 1984, the conservative research agency, the Heritage Foundation, published a plan to ensure that the president's mandate is carried out. The *Mandate for Leadership II: Continuing the Conservative Revolution* (Sanera & Butler 1984) was considered the blueprint for the second Reagan term. Charging that the top-level bureaucrats in federal agencies were well to the left of the American public, author Michael Sanera contended that career government officials are an elite, "influenced through an interlocking network with professional schools and to professional associations, exercising substantial control over policy decision making in the agency" (*Public Administration Times,* Jan. 1, 1985, 12). These officials, said Sanera, will sabotage the president's program by leaking materials to the press and to Congress and by inciting lobbying by client groups. In order to prevent them from doing this, Sanera recommends "jigsaw puzzle management." This is where career staff never have enough of the pieces of information to be able to put together the entire picture of the policy being made. In addition, troublesome career personnel can be shipped to less sensitive policy areas or to another agency.

The potential conflict between the president and the permanent civil service officials makes it difficult for presidents to get information on technical feasibility. It is the bureaucracy that has control of this. Moreover, it often is not possible to determine the technical feasibility of a program before it is implemented. A program such as the Comprehensive Employment Training Act, for example, may take years before its technical feasibility can be known (see Chapter 7).

The president cannot wait for an ideal program to come along; they just do not exist. Thus, he is likely to take the first feasible alternative that is available, which usually is one that has been suggested by an executive branch agency. (See the discussion of satisficing on page 90 for a theoretical discussion of this.)

Setting Priorities Because of the limited time available, the president must have a list of priorities. Congress expects the president to provide leadership. President Carter's agenda was perceived as massive by Congress—and the president as arrogant and inept—because he did not set priorities (Light 1982, 162). Presidential priorities are based on a program's legislative potential and whether or not a crisis exists. The potential for getting a program through Congress is crucial. If a program will not fly on Capital Hill, the president generally will not make it a high priority. But a crisis can overrule this. For example, the Birmingham riots of 1963 allowed John Kennedy to introduce civil rights legislation much sooner than he would have had they not occurred (Light, 162).

A president's decision-making style will greatly influence the outcomes of decisions. It affects who participates, how many ideas will be considered, and the timing of decisions. For example, President Carter wanted all arguments to be written out in memos, whereas Kennedy and Johnson preferred to hear the protagonists in person. Thus, if one could not get an idea on paper in the Carter administration, it never was considered. Moreover, the intensity with which views are held cannot be determined by written memos. And, because Carter demanded written memos, fewer ideas reached him.

Internal rivalries are common among members of the White House staff. For example, Carter's staff had great conflicts over how to handle the so-called energy crisis in 1979. In July of that year, Carter held a domestic policy summit meeting at Camp David to deal with the issue, and, after an unsuccessful meeting he asked all White House staff as well as his cabinet members to resign. This created a number of problems for Carter. Vice-President Walter Mondale and White House aide Stuart Eisenstadt vigorously opposed the resignation of HEW secretary Joseph Califano, whereas White House staffers Jody Powell, Hamilton Jordon, and Patrick Cadell supported it. The liberal wing lost and Califano resigned but this did not improve Carter's image with the electorate (Shull 1983). Such infighting also existed in the Reagan administration. For example, the State and Defense Departments feuded over the extent to which the State Department supported the president's hard line stand toward the Soviets. Those in the State Department's Special Arms Control Policy groups who did not support Reagan's Strategic Defense Initiative were considered outcasts. Thus, some Defense Department officials felt that they had to battle those who wanted to "sell out Reagan's dream" (Pincus 1985, 6).

The Decline and Rise of Presidential Power After the Watergate hearings, when Nixon was near impeachment, there was a decline in presidential power and a resurgence of congressional power. The president's frustration

increased in the mid and late 1970s, as it became more difficult to get legislation through Congress. There were so many people the president had to corral that efforts had to be doubled even for routine decisions. In the past, when Congress had strong leaders such as Sam Rayburn in the House and Lyndon Johnson in the Senate, the president could rely on these leaders to deliver the votes. This was not as easy for Ford and Carter, however (Valenti 1980). The reforms that Congress underwent in the 1970s (described above) greatly decentralized power; in addition, the increased power that today's junior members of Congress have because of the changing role of the media, makes it difficult for strong leaders to develop.

During his first term, President Reagan was able to refute all predictions about the decline of presidential power. He was able to get almost everything he asked for from Congress, primarily because of the coalition that developed between southern Democrats and Republicans in the Senate and the House. The achievements of Reagan's first term assured that he would be labeled a strong president by historians. The policy changes on which he campaigned in 1980 were all enacted by Congress under his domination in 1981. Within eight months, corporate taxes were almost eliminated for many major firms and individual income taxes were lowered by a quarter. The growth of government programs was cut and massive increases in defense spending were made. "Reaganomics" and the Reagan revolution swept through every state and city. He also restored power to a presidency that had been bent and diminished by a succession of one-term presidents, including two who resigned while in office (Johnson and Nixon), one who was assassinated (Kennedy), and two who were soundly defeated after one term (Ford and Carter). After this, the public seemed to hunger for a heroic figure and Reagan was eager to oblige.

Presidential domination of Congress continued under President Bush, who had the highest approval rating by the public of presidents since these records were kept. Bush's popularity was largely due to his successful leadership in the war with Iraq. During the first three years after his election in 1988, he had a perfect veto record: not one of his vetoes had been overridden by Congress. But by mid-1992, his approval rating plummeted as the economy remained in a stagnant recession. As a result, he lost the 1992 election to Bill Clinton who promised to focus on domestic policy issues, especially economic growth. Since both houses of Congress were controlled by the Democrats after the 1992 election, it was possible that there would be another era of presidential domination. However, the new mood of anger among American voters that surfaced during 1992 promised to force the new president to move cautiously.

The Courts as Policy Makers

At all levels of government, the courts make policy because it is their function to interpret the Constitution and laws. Legislatures do not and cannot express their intentions in language specific enough to avoid ambiguity and broad enough to cover even conceivable contingency. Thus, when one jurist was asked if judges make laws, he replied, "Hell, yes! Made some myself!" Judges make law when they select a specific interpretation of a law, executive order, or constitutional provision as it applies in the particular case before them. This power stems from the very earliest period in American history. It is called the power of judicial review, which was established in 1803.

In 1801, the Federalist faction, headed by President John Adams, was handed a crushing defeat when Thomas Jefferson was elected to the presidency. In the waning days of his term, Adams and the Federalist party, which dominated Congress, moved to entrench themselves in the judiciary. Dozens of federal judgeships were hastily created and filled with loyal Federalist appointees. The Jeffersonian faction was enraged by the court-packing, but it was powerless to take action against a perfectly legal maneuver. Upon taking office in 1801, Jefferson discovered that a number of commissions (a formal, written warrant granting power) for justices of the peace in the District of Columbia were undelivered. Adams had apparently vacated his office before tying up all the loose ends. Jefferson instructed his new secretary of state, James Madison, to withhold seventeen commissions, including the judgeship of William Marbury. As a result, Marbury, joined by three other frustrated appointees, sued in the Supreme Court. Their case was based upon a provision of the Judiciary Act of 1789 which extended to the Supreme Court the power to issue a *writ of mandamus*—that is, an order requiring an official to perform a formal, nondiscretionary act. In other words, Marbury and the others requested a court directive ordering Madison to surrender their commissions, since they had been duly appointed to the posts.

The Chief Justice of the Supreme Court at the time was John Marshall, Jefferson's arch rival. As President Adam's secretary of state, Marshall had not only carried out the court-packing ploy but owed his own exalted position to one of the last-minute, lame-duck appointments by Adams. Many thought Marshall was in a bind. Could he, in view of the plain language of the Judiciary Act and his own background, refuse to issue the writ? The Jeffersonians expected Marshall to grant the order, and in this tense atmosphere there was talk of *impeaching* the Chief Justice of the Supreme Court if he granted the order.

But Marshall's decision confounded both friend and foe, Federalist and Jeffersonian alike. In the first twenty pages of the twenty-seven page decision, Marshall expatiated on the basic justice of the Federalist position, agreeing that the plaintiff, Marbury, had a legal right to the post and castigating Jefferson and Madison for their "rascality." Then, in the remaining seven pages, Marshall, in what seemed like a reversal, informed Marbury the Court could not provide a remedy. While Marbury was entitled to a place on the bench, the provision of the Judiciary Act under which the suit had been brought violated the Constitution. Article III of the Constitution carefully delineates the original jurisdiction of the Supreme Court. Since the Judiciary Act attempted by mere act of Congress rather than by amendment to broaden the Court's original jurisdiction, it was unconstitutional.

In his brilliant decision, Chief Justice John Marshall eloquently gave the Supreme Court the power to overturn a law of Congress:

> It is emphatically the province and duty of the judicial department to say what the law is. Those who apply the rule to particular cases, must of necessity expound and interpret that rule. If two laws are in conflict with each, the courts must decide on the operation of each. So if a law be in opposition to the Constitution . . . the court must determine which of these conflicting rules govern the case . . . this is the very essence of judicial duty. (*Marbury v. Madison,* 1CR.137, 1803)

Fifty years later, the Supreme Court reasserted its power against Congress when it struck down a legislative measure in the Dred Scott decision of 1857.* Since then, the Court has often used its power mainly against legislation of state and local governments (Birkley 1983). Considerable controversy was generated during the 1930s when the Supreme Court repeatedly struck down New Deal legislation.

As powerful as judicial review is, it is limited by a number of factors. First, the courts cannot initiate an issue but must wait until a case is brought before them. Second, the courts rarely go beyond the specific issues brought by the litigants. The litigants must have standing to sue, present a case or controversy, show that there is an injury for which there is an available remedy, and exhaust state or federal administrative remedies before turning to the courts. These requirements shape how the issue is framed.

Judges are further constrained by the rule of *stare decisis,* which means "let past decisions stand." Precedent rules in the court, unless there is a good reason to set it aside. In addition, the courts are confined by the language of the statute or the constitutional provision under question.

Finally, judges must rely upon the executive branch to enforce their decisions. Thus, even after the courts have made a decision, it may not necessarily be carried out. Moreover, federal judges are aware of the fact that they are not elected and serve during good behavior.† Hence, they are reluctant to come into open conflict with the legislature or president knowing they are at a distinct disadvantage. When it comes to policy formulation, the courts have distinct limitations.

■ INTEREST GROUPS

Interest groups have long been considered to be among the most powerful and least legitimate groups involved in policy making. This view stems in

* In the Dred Scott case, Chief Justice Roger Taney struck down the Missouri Compromise as unconstitutional, thereby refusing to allow the negro slave, Dred Scott, to return to Illinois.
† Federal judges can be removed only by impeachment, a process that is extremely difficult to carry out. Few judges have been impeached over the course of American history.

part from the way interest groups have operated in the past. For example, in the years just preceding the Civil War, the chief Washington representative of the Colt Firearms manufacturer was famous for plying legislators with free food, revolvers, and female companions. Today's lobbyists use different means of obtaining favorable treatment for their causes. With the high cost of getting elected, most people who run for public office must depend on groups to finance their campaigns. By joining Political Action Committees (PACs), private businesses are legally permitted to contribute to the campaigns of aspiring congressmen and women. PACs have become exceedingly important in financing political campaigns. The National Association of Realtors, for example, is one of the largest PACs in the country. It donated $2.3 million to federal political candidates between January 1983 and October 1984 (Grier 1984, 32–33). The NAR endorses Democrat as well as Republican candidates; the NAR also did $10 million worth of volunteer work for candidates in 1984.

It is difficult to determine how successful PACs are, but many candidates could not run for office if they did not receive their support. Political Action Committees support incumbents of both political parties. Incumbents are more likely to win than challengers. Thus, PACs buy good will by supporting both sides of the political spectrum.

A second major strategy of interest groups is to generate mail to representatives whenever an issue of concern to them is being considered. The National Rifle Association, for example, can deluge Capital Hill with letters and postcards every time the issue of gun control is up for debate. This usually succeeds in defeating legislation the interest group opposes.

The third strategy of interest groups is to give representatives information about pending legislation. Interest groups employ experts who know a lot about issue areas. Their input can sometimes offset the large amount of information provided by executive agencies. When interest groups join with administrative agencies and staff members of Congress, they form what is known as an *iron triangle,* or a policy subgovernment. These iron triangles, discussed in Chapter 2, maintain strong control over public policy in particular areas.

Subgovernments may be even more effective after a program is created. This usually gives rise to the formation of new interest groups whose major purpose is to protect the continued existence of the program. Political scientists Guy C. Colarulli and Bruce Berg call these "imputed interests" (1983, 13). Imputed interest groups develop as a result of government action and are created as a direct response to a new government program (see Chapter 2).

Many imputed interest groups, like the American Food Service Association, have been at the forefront of the lobby effort (Colarulli & Berg, 14). The ASFSA, for example, sponsors legislative workshops and offers its members training which leads to certification and professional standing. The implication for policy making is that once established, the imputed interest group develops expertise which is the key to access and influence in policy making.

As part of the subgovernment, these groups lobby for the indefinite continuation of a program. As a result, enacted programs are difficult to undo or change.

■ MODELS OF DECISION MAKING

As noted in Chapter 1, it is difficult to understand policy making by studying the institutions that are formally responsible for making policy. There are too many details and exceptions to generalizations. Thus, it is necessary to put the details into a conceptual framework called the *policy cycle* (see Figure 1–2). However, there also are a number of theories about policy making that we should consider before moving on to the next stage in the policy cycle. These theories, or *models* of decision making, were created primarily to explain policy making in general, thus it will be useful to consider them here.

Americans have a great deal of faith in rationality. Until recently, few people questioned the descriptive or prescriptive accuracy of the rational actor model as applied to the way decisions are or should be made. It was assumed that public officials were, in fact, rational when they made decisions (the *descriptive* dimension) and that rational decision making was a desirable way to make decisions (the *prescriptive* dimension). But since the publication of Herbert Simon's *Administrative Behavior* (1947), there has been increased criticism of the rational model. Graham Allison continued this critique in his analysis of the Cuban missile crisis. Allison (1971) identifies three different models of decision making: (1) *rational actor,* (2) *organizational process,* and (3) *government politics.* The rational paradigm is but one way to view decisions, Allison attests, and it is not necessarily the most accurate.

The *rational actor* is one who clearly defines a problem, searches for all possible alternative ways of handling it, weighs each alternative in terms of its costs and benefits, and selects the alternative that maximizes achievement of goals at the least cost. The second model described by Allison, *organizational process,* is not a rational procedure. Decisions in organizations are based upon the way things have been done in the past—called standard operating procedures—and these are not always the best way to address a problem. The third Allison model, *government politics,* is when decisions are made through negotiation, bargaining, and compromise. This model is not rational either in the sense that it does not maximize achievement of goals and objectives but instead seeks to achieve a solution that is satisfactory to all groups affected by the decision.

There are many other models of policy making in addition to these three. Some were developed by economists, some by political scientists, and still others by organizational theorists. In the following section, we will consider the rational actor model in more detail as well as the following models: incremental, public choice, politics, systems, garbage can, and Marxian analysis.

Before we begin, however, it is important to remember that no single theory is better than any other; each provides a different view of reality. A better understanding of what actually goes on in policy making is possible if it is viewed from the perspective of many theories rather than just one.

The Rational Actor

Cost effectiveness, efficiency, and economy all are highly cherished values of American administrative history. If a public agency is not efficient, if its policies are not cost-effective, or if it does not try to get the greatest "bang for the buck" then it will not be looked upon with great favor by the American public. All of these values derive from economics, and they are part of what we normally think of as rational.

Many policy analysts consider the rational actor model an accurate way to describe how policy choices are made. According to Graham Allison (1971), this model of decision making is one way to look at the decision made by President Kennedy and his advisers during the Cuban missile crisis of 1962. This event is described briefly in Case 3–1.

According to Case 3–1, the president and his advisers surveyed all possible options, weighed each, and selected the one that was best. But is this really how the decision was made? Was it as rational as this? The beauty of Allison's analysis is that it points out other equally plausible explanations. The theory we bring to understand a decision determines what evidence and events we find. This in turn supports the theory with which we began. If we begin with the assumption that Kennedy's decision was a rational one, we overlook other events and evidence that would support an alternative explanation. The organizational process model directs us to different facts. For example, as a result of a squabble between the CIA and the Defense Department over whose responsibility it was to send a U-2 intelligence flight over Cuba, a ten-day delay occurred before the existence of missiles in Cuba was verified. This delay constrained the options available to President Kennedy. So, while the rational actor model is a plausible one, it is not the only way to describe how Kennedy's decision—or any other decision—was made.

Incrementalism

A major criticism of rational choice theory is that it makes unrealistic assumptions about the capabilities of human beings. It assumes that it is possible to identify all possible alternatives when in fact most people have only time and ability to search for a limited set of alternatives. The theory called *incrementalism* takes the position that public policy decisions involve only modest changes in the status quo rather than rational inspection of all options. According to this theory, the search for an alternative solution ends as soon as we find one that represents a slight improvement over existing practice.

CASE 3–1 *The Cuban Missile Crisis*

In October 1962, the United States and the Soviet Union stood eyeball to eyeball for thirteen days when the Soviet Union tried to put intermediate range missiles into Cuba. The missiles were capable of hitting targets in the United States, although Cuba and the Soviet Union claimed that they were defensive weapons.

The confrontation was a major watershed in the Cold War between the United States and the Soviet Union. It also was a test of President Kennedy's resolve. Some observers say that the wily old Soviet Premier, Nikita Khrushchev, was trying to see how the newly elected young president would react when the two superpowers stood on the brink of nuclear war.

A rational person would react to such a situation as follows: The United States could not tolerate offensive missiles in Cuba. This information was clearly transmitted by President Kennedy to the Soviet Union. The goal of the United States in this situation was quite clear: To remove the missiles that already were in Cuba and stop the Soviets from shipping any more there.

A number of approaches could be taken to attain this objective. In making his decision, President Kennedy assembled his most trusted advisers and told them to set aside all other tasks in order to make a "prompt and intensive survey of the dangers and all possible courses of action" (Allison 1971, 57).

Six courses of action were considered by the group. The first was to do nothing. This decision would have instantly doubled the Soviet's missile capability and perhaps even reversed the strategic balance of power between the two countries. Thus it was rejected. The second alternative was to apply diplomatic pressure through the United Nations, or to approach the Soviet Premier directly. This option held little promise since the Soviet Union could veto any action in the United Nations. Moreover, Premier Khrushchev might

Incrementalism maintains certain assumptions about the way individuals and groups interact in a decision situation. It assumes that each individual or group will pursue its own interests and goals. But because people's interests are likely to conflict, it is not possible to achieve or satisfy everyone's interests simultaneously. Each person will be faced with the conflicting interests of others, and the only way for each person to achieve his or her goal is to compromise or be satisfied with less than what he or she hoped to get. This results in incremental, rather than major, changes in the existing situation.

Incrementalism is said by some scholars to be better than a system in which a centralized source considers all options and then imposes a solution on use the United Nations to seize the diplomatic initiative, charging that the United States was about to invade Cuba. Since Kennedy had already authorized the Bay of Pigs fiasco, this was not a remote possibility. Thus, this alternative was also rejected. The third alternative was to approach Fidel Castro secretly and persuade him to split off from the Soviet Union. But since the missiles belonged to the Soviet Union, the decision to withdraw them depended on the Soviets, not on Castro. Thus, this alternative would be ineffective as well.

The fourth alternative was to invade Cuba. But this would simply play into the Soviets' hand by reinforcing their claim that they were putting defensive rather than offensive weapons into Cuba. Hence, it was also rejected. A fifth option was a surgical air strike designed to knock out the missiles. This option was advocated by the military advisers. However, it was rejected because of the possibility that such a strike would destroy more than the missile sites, kill Soviets in Cuba, and cause Cuba and the Soviet Union to retaliate.

The final alternative considered by the group was to blockade Cuba and prevent the Soviet Union from sending more missiles and equipment to Cuba. This action had problems: Vice-President Johnson said it would be an act of war, that the Soviets might react by blockading Berlin, and if the Soviet ships did not stop, would the United States sink them?

Despite these problems, the blockade was selected because it was a middle course of action; it put the ball in the Soviets' court so that they would have to make the next move. And a naval blockade could be effectively implemented because of the U.S. Navy's great strength in the Caribbean. The blockade worked. The missiles were withdrawn and President Kennedy had perhaps his finest hour as president.

the contending interests. Economist Charles Lindblom (1959), who originated the term, calls this latter system *synoptic rationality* because it assumes that rational individuals can get a synopsis of all the relevant facts. Incrementalism is said to be better because a number of individuals, each surveying options, can consider more information than a single individual.

In making a policy decision, incrementalists do not consider all possible alternatives. Instead, they examine options that are close to current practice one by one until they find one that is slightly better than the existing approach. Unlike rational choice, incrementalism does not seek an optimal policy. It is not a value-maximizing choice system but one that looks only for improvements over the status quo. For this reason, it is described as the "science of muddling through" (Lindblom 1959).

One version of incrementalism that describes administrative behavior is called *satisficing*. Originated by Nobel Prize winner Herbert Simon, satisficing challenges the assumption that people are capable of maximizing; they simply do not have the resources or time to engage in a comprehensive search for alternatives. Instead, they search the immediate environment until they encounter an alternative that is good enough (Simon 1957, 204–205). The rational person will accept this even if it does not maximize goals. Thus the theory of satisficing is not a rejection of rational choice but a modification of it.

There is empirical evidence that satisficing is a more accurate description of actual decision making than rational choice. For example, in a study of zero-based budgeting in the Department of Agriculture, Wildavsky and Hammann (1968) found that officials were unable to survey all alternatives before making a decision. (Zero-based budgeting requires an agency to assume each year that its budget has to be completely justified as if it were starting from zero.) Because they did not know how to make calculations of costs and benefits required by the zero-based budgeting they were asked to follow, they were not able to act in the synoptic rational way that zero-based budgeting requires.

Economists David Braybrooke and Charles Lindblom (1963) argue that incrementalism allows an organization to learn by its mistakes. It gives the agency time to reconsider its objectives and return to its previous practice. Political scientists David Paris and James Reynolds support this view:

> By not trying to solve the problem once and for all but by permitting us to consider a policy issue again and again, the strategy allows us to employ our changing, experienced-based empirical and normative outlooks as we make new meliorative policy adjustments. For example, instead of aiming to eliminate poverty or solve the problem of crime, this strategy will ask what specific, limited policies can yield some reduction of the harmful effects of poverty or crime. (1983, 128)

On the other hand, incrementalism has been criticized as being a defense of the status quo. Critics contend that the theory does not tell us how to make good or fair decisions because it looks only to "satisfice" or reach a slight improvement over the status quo. Finally, not all people or groups involved in the decision process have the same ability to protect their interests. Instead of achieving a compromise satisfactory to all interests, incrementalism will be biased in favor of the more powerful interests.

Public Choice

Economists have dominated the literature on decision making, and public choice theory is no exception. Most contributors to this theory are well-known economists, such as Kenneth Arrow, James Buchanan (who won the Nobel Prize in economics in 1986), Gordon Tullock, and Anthony Downs. However, a number of political scientists also have contributed to public choice theory, including William Riker, Vincent Ostrom, Elinor Ostrom, Peter Ordershook, and Robert Abrams.

Public choice theory, like economic theory, assumes that people who are rational will pursue their own self-interests. Consequently, people are not likely to pursue collective interests unless given proper incentives. Thus, the principal problem in decisions is how to aggregate individual preferences into a collective choice that is not harmful to all people involved. Kenneth Arrow (1954) discovered one of the most important paradoxes of individual choice and collective action. The paradox is that even though each person may rationally pursue their own interests, the collective choice that results may be non-rational and harmful to all participants.

To illustrate this paradox, consider the crop production of farmers. It is in the self-interest of each farmer to hold down production of farm products because if supplies are kept down, the price for the crops will be higher. However, each farmer will reason that his or her production will not greatly affect the total crop production because each farmer comprises only a small portion of the total agricultural output. If each farmer follows this line of reasoning—and it is perfectly rational for them to do so—then they all will produce a large amount of crops, thereby driving the prices down and harming all farmers. In this case, then, choices that are rational for each person have non-rational collective consequences.

Public choice theory explores various ways of solving the dilemma of non-rational collective choices. In doing so, it contributes to a better understanding of public policy. The greatest contribution of public choice theory illuminates the problem of getting people and groups to work toward collective ends or goals that will benefit the entire society—that is, the public interest. The pure individualist would argue that there is no collective or public interest that is different from the sum of each person's self-interest. This issue has still not been completely settled.

Politics

In the political model, each individual or group is a player in a competitive game. Bargaining is the principal means by which decisions are made (Cyert & March 1963). Individuals share power and differ about which action should be taken. Analyzing the Cuban missile crisis through a political model Allison writes, "to explain why a particular formal governmental decision was made or why one pattern of governmental behavior emerged, it is necessary to identify the games and players, to display the coalitions, bargains, and compromises, and to convey some feel for the confusion" (1971, 146).

The games and players in the area of forest management are described by journalist Perri Knize (1991, 104) as follows:

> The National Forest Management Act of 1976 stipulates that those who are most intimate with the national forest—the public and the local Forest Service team—should work together to decide how they should be managed. But in practice the forests are ruled by competing and complementary agencies in Washington, D.C. Forest Service administrators are concerned with maximizing their budgets, holding on to their jobs, and preserving the status quo. Congressmen want jobs in their districts and continued timber-industry support for their reelection campaigns. And the White House wants to take care of its friends. All use national-forest timber as a means to achieve their aims.

Participants in government have independent bases of power, therefore power in government is shared by a number of groups and people. Each participant sits in a seat that confers separate responsibilities (Lindblom 1959). To get what they want, each participant must persuade others to work with or support him or her. Persuasion, rather than command, is the key strategy in the game of politics. In trying to persuade others, each person uses whatever influence they have. Each person, of course, has a different amount of influence.

There are several sources of influence, including friendship, rational persuasion, or coercion. According to Ed Banfield:

> the actions of many persons, each of whom has independent authority, must be concerted for a proposal to be adopted; the proponents of the proposal try to concert these actions by exercising influence—by persuading, deceiving, inveighing, rewarding, punishing, and otherwise inducing. Meanwhile the opponents exercise influence either to prevent the actions from being concerted or to concert them on behalf of some alternative proposal which they prefer. (1961, 30)

The majority of political scientists probably subscribe to the political model as the best way of explaining how legislators act when they are considering a bill. This classical and traditional view of Congress is still a powerful theory of public policy making in the United States.

Systems Theory

Systems theory sees the political system as one of several subsystems that make up the overall social system. Political scientist David Easton (1965) has done more than anyone to advance systems theory. Easton sees the prime function of the political system as the *authoritative allocation of values.* By this he means that the political system has the power to make authoritative decisions, because it has a monopoly on the legal use of force to back them.

A political system consists of inputs (demands and support), outputs (decisions and actions), and a "black box" that converts the inputs into outputs (see

Figure 3–2). It is referred to as a black box because not much is known about what goes on inside it, and because it is difficult to observe directly.

Demands are generated from the wants of various citizens and groups. Most demands do not get into the political system, although some will become a part of the institutional agenda by being converted into issues. This mobilizes support groups which give greater weight to the particular demand.

The process by which demands are translated into issues is called *gatekeeping* (Easton 1965, 133–37). Gatekeepers selectively restrict inputs and therefore perform one of the most important functions of the political system. In the American political system, each of the relevant agencies—that is, Congress, president, administrative agencies, and courts—has its own agenda. Only a few members of the body politic have access to these various agendas. According to Easton, "the fundamental fact confronting all societies is that scarcity of some valued things prevails. It leads to disputes over their allocation" (1965, 53). This includes not only material things, but also power, prestige, and respect.

Systems theory became popular among political scientists during the late 1960s and 1970s. It still has a large number of adherents—as well as some

FIGURE 3–2 Simplified model of a political system.

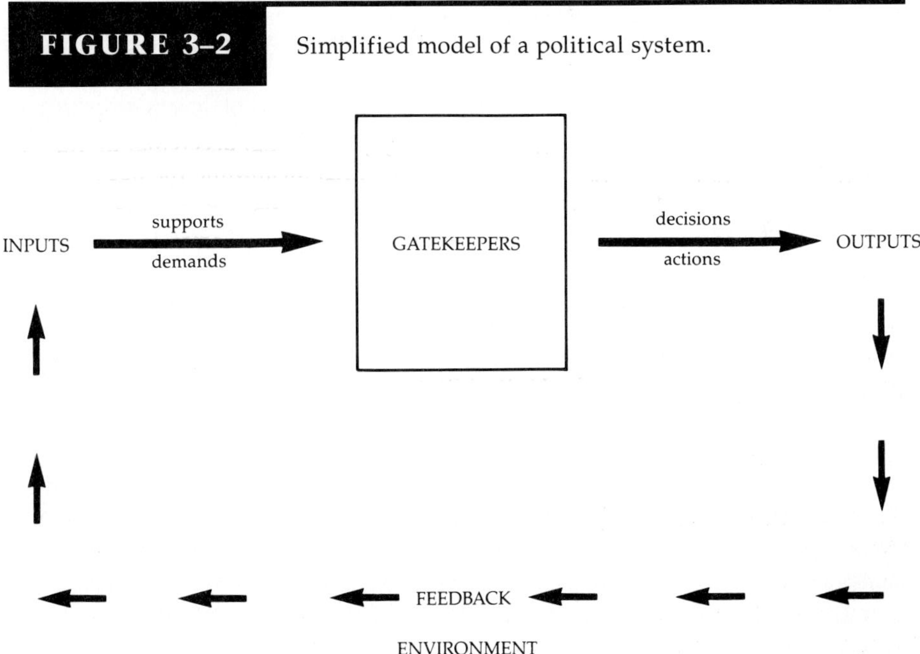

Source: From David Easton, *A Systems Analysis of Political Life,* (Chicago: University of Chicago Press, 1965).

critics—and it has left its mark on political science because many of its concepts, such as inputs, demands, and feedback, have become a standard part of political science.

The Garbage Can Model

The garbage can model stems from organizational theory; it is at the opposite end of the continuum from the rational choice model. According to the garbage can model, organizations such as legislatures, administrative agencies, courts, universities, or corporations do not have consistent and well-defined preferences. The technology by which they try to accomplish their goals is unclear; instead, they operate on the basis of trial and error, the residue of learning from the accidents of past experience, and pragmatic inventions and necessities (Cohen, March & Olsen 1972). There is no internal consensus in organizations and constant conflict about which goals to pursue. Coalitions form to support particular interpretation of goals, and the strongest coalition usually wins.

The garbage can model is similar to the political model in that it emphasizes groups in conflict, coalitions, and the use of bargaining (Cyert & March 1963). It differs from the political model, however, in that the decision cycle may move from solutions to problems, rather than the reverse. What this means is that an administrator may act in a given decision situation without analyzing it first, and then search for the best rationale for the action that was taken. Rather than look for the one best way or most efficient alternative for solving a problem, organizations search for support for actions already taken, and for support that serves the interests of the subgovernments or policy subsystems in which they operate (Palumbo & Nachmias 1984, 108).

Marxian Analysis

In contrast to theories that focus primarily on how decisions are made *within* organizations, Marxian analysis focuses on the interrelationship between the economic and political systems. One cannot study the Marxian view of public policy apart from the underlying economic structure of capitalism and the class conflict it engenders. According to Marxism—named after the nineteenth-century German political philosopher—public policies are designed to serve the interests of the owners of capital and the political officials who serve them. Laws in the capitalist system are the principal means for maintaining the social and economic order: Law is the instrument of the ruling class.

It is tempting to dismiss Marxism as being so broad and deterministic as to be implausible. But there is some empirical evidence that supports the theory that an economic elite dominates government in the United States. For example, more and more millionaires are being elected to Congress. In 1980, at least 20 senators and 17 House members had assets in excess of a million dollars, and 31 other senators and 55 representatives had at least half a million dollars in assets (*U.S. News & World Report*, June 2, 1980, 46). But because lawmakers are not required to reveal their assets precisely, the actual holdings of U.S. senators and representatives could be much higher. *U.S. News & World Report* reported in 1980 that at least 27 senators and representatives (in addition to the 123 mentioned above) might be millionaires. Moreover, two out of three senators and one out of four representatives supplemented their congressional pay with outside incomes of $20,000 or more a year. The *Congressional Quarterly* reported that in 1983 one-third of the Senate's 100 members were active or potential millionaires when their salaries were combined with income from speeches, outside income, and the value of their nonresidential real estate and other holdings (November 26, 1983, 2563). Two of the wealthiest were Senator H. John Heinz (R-Penn), who listed his assets as $21.3 million in 1980, and Representative Frederich Richmond (R-NY), who had assets of at least $22 million. And six of our past seven presidents (Bush, Reagan, Carter, Nixon, Johnson, and Kennedy) were millionaires.

The situation was essentially the same 100 years ago. In 1880, the Senate was called the millionaires' club (Josephy 1975). It contained people such as Leland Stanford, the California railroad mogul; Nelson Aldich, the Rhode Island wholesale grocer and banker; Philetus Sawyer, the Wisconsin lumber tycoon; and George Heart, Horace A. W. Tabor, and James G. "Bonanza" Fair, the western mining kings. Almost half of the Senate's members were millionaires (Rothman 1966). An eminent midwestern newspaper cogently described the situation in 1884:

> Behind every one . . . of the portly and well-dressed members of the Senate can be seen the outlines of some corporation interested in getting or preventing legislation, or of some syndicate that has invaluable contracts or patents to defend or push . . . Once, great men went to the Senate to work for their principles and ideals; now rich men go there to work for their interests or to aid their purses. (Eisenstadt, Hoogenboon & Trefousse 1979)

The Marxian perspective on public policy gained a number of adherents during the 1960s with the rise of "the new left." The new left placed great emphasis on equality, had little confidence in electoral politics, no particular faith in law, and emphasized conflict rather than consensus as a strategy for change (Dolbeare & Dolbeare 1973, 188–89). The groups espousing a new left philosophy arose to prominence through their resistance to the Vietnam War, support of civil liberties, fight against poverty, and philosophy of community control.

Although it did not have a coherent ideology, the new left was clear in its opposition to technology and materialism ("tune in, turn on, and drop out"). New left thinkers also believed that large scale bureaucracies—both corporations and governments—were not responsive to public control. According to the new left, the military-industrial complex combined to create a war economy in order to steer off the collapse of capitalism (Ham & Hill 1984). Thus, defense spending was required to shore up the capitalist system which would collapse without it. Powerlessness and alienation were the fate not only of the poor and minorities under capitalism, but of the middle class as well. The reason for alienation is that the middle-class worker takes part in a mechanized process that he or she cannot understand or control (Jessop 1982).

New left theories did not survive the turmoil of the 1960s and by the end of the 1970s were almost totally eclipsed. While they were not pure Marxists, the new left agreed with most of the fundamental tenets of Marxism. Among these are (1) the American economy can be characterized as a system of monopolies; (2) capitalism is a system in which huge corporations dominate entire sectors of the market, rendering the economy bureaucratized, hierarchical, and totally controlled by the few (Milward & Francisco 1983); and (3) the exploitation of workers generates huge surpluses, so large that even technological innovations are unable to absorb them (Baran & Sweezy 1968, 79).

Instead of creating more growth, the huge surpluses generated by capitalism cause its stagnation and collapse. If government directed this surplus toward the poor, the system might be saved. But the government is responsive to the preferences of corporations and the ruling oligarchy who do not want greater benefits for the working class. Broader education, for example, would threaten the existence of the class structure and make it difficult to obtain low-wage, menial employees. Thus, national support for education is kept low and government financing is channeled disproportionately to elite private schools and colleges. Foreign investment is another means of disposing of the surplus, but this leads to conflict and a need for military spending. This is not an undesirable result, however, because defense spending is undertaken not for actual defense but for the high profits it produces (Jessop 1982; Wolfe 1980).

According to Marxian theory, the capitalist government is a major channel through which economic activities are carried out and profits made (O'Connor 1970). The government supports the defense establishment because it serves both as a source of profits and as protector of overseas ventures (Williams 1968). Capitalism generates greater poverty and what progress is made for the average person is constantly threatened by cycles of inflation and recession. Not only does capitalism produce less material affluence for the poor and the middle class, it creates alienation, subjection to machines, and meaninglessness.

■ CONCLUSION

In his book, *Essence of Decision: Explaining the Cuban Missile Crisis* (1971), Graham Allison does not conclude that one of the three models of decision making is better than any other. Instead, each contributes something to our knowledge of how decisions are made. The same can be said about the seven models of policy formulation we have just described. Each explains some part of decision-making reality and each is useful.

Still, it is true that the principles of government described above and the institutional structure of American government make rational choices in policy making rather unlikely. The rational actor model as well as public choice are valuable more as prescriptions of how we should act than as descriptions of how we do or can act. Systems theory is an analytical model for organizing the events that surround policy making, while incrementalism, politics, the garbage can model, and Marxian analysis are primarily descriptive—and perhaps somewhat realistic—views of how policy making actually proceeds.

No matter how they go about making decisions, legislators often take positions on an issue more for its symbolic value than because of a firm commitment to principles. Thus, most legislators will oppose crime and favor a tough stance toward criminals or the Soviet Union because this will win votes, rather than because they are convinced of the soundness of these policy orientations. This further enhances the opportunity for administrators to make public policy as they fill in the intricacies of the laws passed by legislatures.

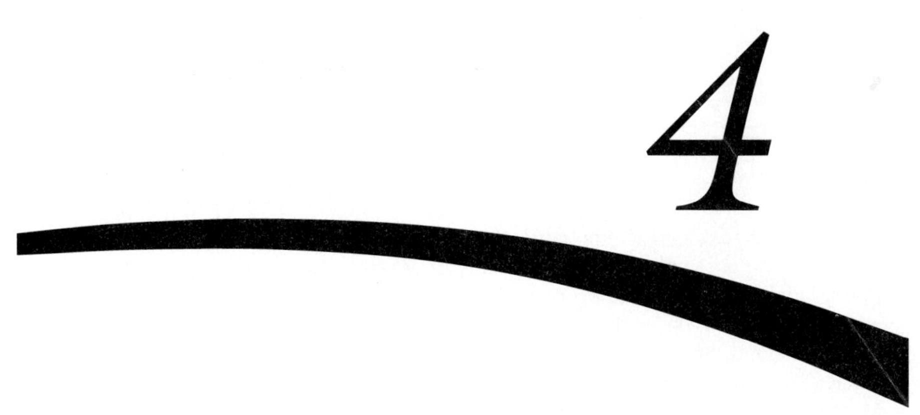

Implementation: Filling in the Gaps of Public Policy

WHAT IS IMPLEMENTATION?

The study of implementation has grown enormously in importance in political science. In the early 1970s, before the appearance of the path-breaking book by Pressman and Wildavsky (1984), very little research was conducted on policy implementation as such. In the mid 1970s implementation was still being called a "missing link" in the study of public policy (Hargrove 1976). But by 1980, as research grew in this area, implementation failures had become the Achilles heel of the Great Society programs of Lyndon B. Johnson (Williams 1980). In this short period of time, implementation became recognized as the key to the success or failure of public policy. Today, researchers and policy makers agree that much of public policy is made *while* it is being implemented, not before. In the second edition of the *Policy Making Process* (1980), Yale economist Charles Lindblom writes: "In principle some administrative acts merely implement a prior policy decision. If so, we can forget them as part of policy making. Most, perhaps all, administrative acts make or change policy in the process of trying to implement it. For all such acts, we must analyze implementation as part of policy making" (64). G. Ronald Gilbert, an associate professor of management, describes the role of administrators in policy making as follows:

> It has been argued on the one hand that the administrator's role is to develop and carry out the will of those who set policies (essentially maintaining the classic policy/administration dichotomy). On the other hand, there is recognition that administrators are actively involved as are other elites, interest groups, and the like, in the making of policy in its formative as well as its implementation stages. In fact, in the regulatory area the role of administrative agencies has been fused to the extent that administrators formulate, implement, and even adjudicate public policies. Public administrators are able to influence policy in its early formation stages through active campaigning, selective interpretation of technical information, and through their own program designs, strategies, and tactics. They are often able to rearrange or modify the intent of legislature enactments as a program is formed and structured, or they can extend or reduce the policy terrain upon which their programs rest. (1984, 1–2)

If implementation is so important in policy making, what is it? We defined implementation in Chapter 1 as a *stage* in the policy cycle. But by using the term *stage,* we do not want to imply that it is a distinct and separable stage that comes *after* policies have been formulated. To many people, implementation means carrying out decisions made *prior* to implementation by some person or agency other than the one that has to implement them. This meaning of the term implementation can be illustrated with a story usually told at conferences called the "boil the ocean syndrome."

The story goes as follows. During World War II, American and British military officers were at a loss as to how to stop the German submarine attacks on allied military ships. In exasperation they turned to an operations researcher and asked him if he could come up with a solution. He thought for a moment and then responded: "That's easy, all you have to do is boil the ocean." The military officers exclaimed: "But how do we do that?" To which the operations researcher responded, "I don't know, I only make policy, it's your job to implement it." Implementation, in this story, and in everyday language refers to the carrying out of goals or plans. It refers to a *stage* in decision making that occurs after a decision has been made about what goals are to be sought.

A number of things should be emphasized about this definition of implementation. First, it implies that one can distinguish between means and ends, and that implementation refers only to the means of achieving given ends. Yet at times it is impossible to make a sharp distinction between means and ends. Therefore, implementation should *not* be defined as the means of achieving goals. In selecting means, implementors often determine which goals will be achieved and which ones will be ignored. To illustrate this point, recall the Missouri law we discussed in Chapter 1 concerning abortions. The law specified that after the first trimester, abortions must be performed in a hospital. This ostensibly refers only to the *means* by which abortions are to be done. But in fact, as the counsel for Planned Parenthood noted, this provision has the effect of restricting the *number* of abortions because fewer people have access to or can afford a hospital abortion.

In other contexts, implementation implies an automatic or mechanistic procedure. Implements are tools, as in the phrase "farm implements." But as most researchers have noted, implementation of public policy is not simply a technical matter of constructing a machine that punches out an end product. It is instead "a process of interaction between the setting of goals and actions geared to achieving them" (Pressman & Wildavsky 1984, XV). According to Erwin Hargrove, we often revise our goals according to the availability of means: "If we find it is going to be very difficult to accomplish something then we try to do less" (1976, 4).

In this book, we will define implementation as the part of the policy-making process during which politicians, bureaucrats, private interest groups, and the public at large vie for control over the direction of a program. In this broad sense, implementation is a continuing effort to raise the capability of organizations to carry out projects (Williams & Elmore 1976, 3). It deals with how to "bring together communications, commitment, and capacity so as to carry a decision into action" (Walter Williams 1980, 3). It concerns how we "lead subjects to comply with policy mandates" (Brigham & Brown 1980, 8). It is, in essence, a continuation of the policy-making process in an arena involving federal, state, and local government agencies and private agencies, firms, interest groups, and individuals (Palumbo & Harder 1981).

Macro- and Micro-Implementation

There are two different aspects to the implementation stage of policy making. One is the *macrolevel*, which refers to the interaction among government agencies. For example, the implementation of federal government policy often requires the interaction and cooperation of federal, state, and local governmental agencies as well as private organizations. The jobs program of the Comprehensive Employment and Training Act is a good example of this. It requires the collaborative efforts of the U.S. Department of Labor, state governmental agencies such as departments of human resources, city agencies, including city councils and offices of employment opportunity, private business firms, and voluntary neighborhood and community groups.

The second level of implementation is the *microlevel*, which refers to the interaction of individuals and divisions *within* a department. Specifically, the microlevel of implementation concerns the interactions among an agency head, department chiefs, supervisors, and the street-level workers. The questions at this level include how to select and train personnel, what style of leadership and management works best, how an agency should be structured, what budgeting procedures should be used, and numerous other questions involved in traditional public administration. We shall discuss some of these in a moment. Note that all implementation involves both macro- and microlevels of behavior. In carrying out any significant policy, most agencies interact with other agencies and organizations (macro) as well as with units within the agency (micro) to carry out the policy directions.

■ PLAYERS IN THE GAME

The implementors of policy include a wide variety of agencies and individuals. Over 14.5 million individuals implement public policy within the United States government (federal, state, and local). Many private agencies are also responsible for carrying out government policy. For example, much of health policy in the United States is implemented by private, quasi-private and public hospitals, nursing homes, insurance companies, physicians, and other health facilities and agencies. In any policy arena, public bureaucrats represent only part of the implementation process, and, frequently, not the most influential part.

Perhaps one of the most significant contributions made by implementation research is to call attention to the variety of different agencies involved in carrying out a particular policy. As an example, Pressman and Wildavsky (1984, 103–107) describe the many agencies involved in carrying out the federal jobs program (an attempt to create jobs for minorities) in Oakland, California. The program included nine federal agencies, two city agencies, one state agency, two interest groups, and two private firms; it also included thirty separate decision points involving different combinations of these agencies. The number of agencies involved in the Oakland jobs program is not unusual; most federal programs are implemented by a large number of separate agencies.

Not all policies will involve such a large number of different types of agencies. But almost invariably a program will involve several different types and levels of agencies. Some policies, such as the jobs program, involve federal, state, and local government agencies as well as private business firms. Other policies may involve only the interaction of a federal agency and private business firms. Such is the case with the Federal Food and Drug Administration's activities. State government policies may involve the interaction of state, county, city, and private non-profit agencies. Such is the case with community corrections policies, which involve the state department of corrections, county commissioners, judges, sheriffs, prosecuting attorneys, and private and volunteer counseling and social service agencies. Almost every policy area has its own unique organizational arrangement. A number of these will be described throughout this book, particularly in Part II.

One additional concept that we will refer to in this chapter is the *street-level bureaucrat*. This expression was first coined by political scientist Michael Lipsky (1976). It describes those individuals who have direct contact with citizens; they are the people who actually *are* government as far as a citizen is concerned because they interact with citizens and interpret government laws, rules, and regulations for them. They include the millions of school teachers, police officers, judges, prosecutors, probation officers, social welfare workers, nurses, physicians working in public health departments, driver license examiners, internal-revenue auditors, high-school principals, housing authority managers, and unemployment office workers who supply government services and enforce government regulations.

Street-level bureaucrats are not all lower-level employees in public/private organizations. In fact, many of them are rather high level and/or autonomous individuals such as judges, prosecutors, teachers, university professors, and public health physicians. Even though many street-level bureaucrats occupy a fairly low-level position within the organization, they nevertheless have an enormous impact on the direction of public policy. This has greatly influenced our ideas about administration, and changed many of our beliefs about how agencies are and should be run.

■ TRADITIONAL PUBLIC ADMINISTRATION AND IMPLEMENTATION

The study of implementation, along with current research in organization theory, has literally revolutionized the way we think about organizations (Lincoln 1986). These new views stand the study of organizations on its head: Instead of policy being made by the top levels in an organization, we now view policy as being made largely by people at the bottom levels (Lipsky 1980; Prottas 1980; Ham & Hill 1984). Instead of being goal directed, rational instruments, organizations are viewed as "organized anarchies," garbage cans (Cohen, March & Olsen 1972), or as loosely coupled systems (Weick 1976).

Traditional public administration—abbreviated TPA throughout this chapter—is based in the belief that there is a technical administrative solution to problems. It emphasizes centralized control of decision making and the belief that the goals or objectives of the top level policy makers should be faithfully carried out by those lower down in the organization.

Traditional public administration theory, also called the scientific theory of public administration, holds that (1) organizations should be centralized; (2) there should be a sharp line between politics and administration; (3) perfection in organization is attained in a hierarchically organized and professionally trained public service; and (4) that efficiency is the principal value to be served by administrative organizations (Gates 1980). In short, the ideal public organization is the ideal bureaucracy described by German sociologist and economist Max Weber (Gerth & Mills 1949).

There have been a number of counter trends in the study of public administration, including the human relations movement that began in the 1930s (Mayo 1933), the works of Dwight Waldo (1948), Paul Appleby (1952), and Herbert Simon (1957) in regard to the political realities of organizations, and the works of Chris Argyris (1963, 1965) in organizational development and self-actualization. Later theorists recognize the psychological needs and satisfaction of workers as keys to successful administration. The human relations movement emerged from a series of experiments that were conducted in the Hawthorne plant of the Bell Telephone Company during the early 1930s. The experiments were an attempt to see if worker productivity could be improved by making changes in the physical environment, such as in the amount of lighting. The experimenters found that productivity improved no matter what amount of illumination was provided. Although puzzled by this at first, the experimenters soon discovered that workers were reacting positively simply because they felt that management was concerned about them. This subsequently has become known as the "Hawthorne effect." The revisions in organization theory that culminate in the current view of organizations began with the human relations movement.

Misunderstandings about Implementation

According to Arthur Schlesinger, Jr., Franklin Roosevelt's favorite administrative technique was "to keep grants of authority incomplete, jurisdiction uncertain, charters overlapping" (Schlesinger 1959, 528). In this way, Roosevelt was able to keep the power to make decisions to himself. He loved to know everything that was going on and have a finger in every pie. He violated every cherished principle in the text. But he was still deemed a successful administrator.

As the Roosevelt technique illustrates, there is more than one way to implement a program successfully (Lewis 1984). This runs counter to TPA theory, which holds that there are scientific principles of administration that apply in all management contexts. Principles such as unity of command, matching authority with responsibility, centralization, and span of control, are supposed to be applicable to *all* management situations. Thus, a person should receive orders from one superior only, otherwise there may be conflicting orders to follow. An individual who is given responsibility to carry out a particular program should be given the authority to make the decisions needed for successful implementation. As part of the unity principle, all organizations should be hierarchical, with one person at the top, and all orders should flow from the top to the bottom of the pyramid. The theory also holds that there is a limit to how many individuals a superior can effectively supervise, thus, there should be a limit to how many persons one should have under his or her direct supervision. The ideal span of control was never precisely identified, but the general belief was that the average person could effectively supervise only between six to eight individuals. With a larger group, the average person could not closely observe and keep track of what people are doing.

Another principle of TPA is the delegation of authority. To avoid the mistake of trying to do everything themselves, supervisors should delegate authority to subordinates so that they are able to effectively carry out their responsibilities. The failure to delegate—the attempt to keep your fingers in every pie as President Roosevelt did—was often cited as the principal reason for management failure.

Many of these principles accord with common sense and are no doubt practiced by many managers. But others are contradictory (Simon 1957). For example, the principle of unity of command contradicts the delegation principle; one cannot maintain unity if authority is delegated to a number of subordinates. Nevertheless, the principles of TPA have some practical value. The situation is somewhat analogous to the principles of Euclidean geometry: While inadequate for dealing with space in the entire universe, Euclidean geometry is still useful when we want to build a bridge here on earth. Likewise, the principles of TPA are useful when we face the practical need of getting a job done, even though they do not describe how organizations generally are run.

Modern management theory, on the other hand, is based on the notion that contingency theories are better than the quest for universal principles (Perrow 1978). Contingency theories hold that there is more than one way to administer an agency. The way an agency is managed depends upon the nature of the environment in which it operates and the kind of problems it faces. Thus, whether or not authority should be centralized depends somewhat on the task environment (that is, the kind of job the agency does). In an uncertain task environment, decentralization may be better than centralization (Perrow 1972). Similarly, whether or not orders should be directed from the top down or whether individuals at the lower levels of the organization should participate in decision making depends on whether or not their agreement with the goals of the policy is necessary (Vroom 1960).

The differences between contemporary management theory and TPA run still deeper than the question of whether or not it is possible to use universal principles of administration for all situations. There is a fundamental disagreement on at least four tenets. We shall label these the *technology fix*, the *anthropomorphic view*, the *illegitimacy of change view*, and the *upside-down perspective*.

The Technology Fix The technology fix is similar to the liberal fix, or the "there ought to be a law" syndrome. This is the view that whenever society is faced with a problem, whether it be in the area of poverty, health, crime, pollution, transportation, education, employment, inflation, or culture, all we need to do is pass a law and the problem will somehow be solved. As a result, we have seen a proliferation of laws in these areas over the past generation, but the problems have not gone away. We assume that these laws will be translated into programs automatically (Ostrom 1974). Relatively little thought is given to whether or not we actually have the social technologies for solving problems in these areas, or how these policies should be implemented. Thus, many of the policies adopted in these areas produce effects quite different from what was intended. Sometimes, as in urban renewal, the policies ended up benefiting the community power structure rather than the poor. Sometimes, as in the War on Poverty, initiated in 1964 by the Johnson administration, the policy was deemed to be a failure. (There is, of course, continuing debate about whether it was a failure. See Chapter 7.) In almost all cases, the policy efforts wound up costing much more than was anticipated.

Administration, we now know, is not just a technical matter, and policies are not automatically translated into program reality. Instead, some thought should be given to the question of implementation feasibility (Hargrove 1976; Lewis & Wallace 1984; Gilbert 1984). Among the questions considered in implementation feasibility are: Does the program require space, facilities, or resources that are not easily available? Do the existing staff have the professional capability to perform the work that is required? Does the program require different behavior on the part of street-level bureaucrats and how realistic is the expectation that they will do it? What cooperation of agencies and groups is likely to be needed to carry out the program? Are there existing support and client groups whose interests will be adversely affected by the program? Does the program threaten the status or jobs of those who must implement it? How much and what opposition exists toward the program? (Williams 1976; Weatherly 1979).

In order to cope with these questions, organizations should be open and flexible systems so that they can learn as implementation proceeds (Wildavsky 1979). Likewise, management should not be viewed as a technical problem whose goal is to get the most out of employees. Instead, it should be viewed as an experimental process in which hypotheses are tested and probed and then changed when it becomes apparent that the approach is not working (Landau & Stout 1979; Stout 1980). Flexibility is the key to organization success in contemporary implementation theory (Elmore 1979; Williams 1980; Lewis & Wallace 1984; Bresnick 1982).

The Anthropomorphic View The view that decisions are made by individuals at specific points in time is known as the *anthropomorphic view.* In TPA, there are decision makers who set policy, and the employees in a bureaucracy who carry out these decisions. But, in fact, decisions are not discrete events. According to Palumbo and Wright, decisions are "part of a process that extends over time, that is affected by many variables, and that no single individual or group of individuals actually can be identified as having made" (1981, 1170). There is no doubt that certain individuals will be held *responsible* for what happens in particular circumstances, as indicated by Harry Truman's famous statement "the buck stops here." And, if things go right, there will be no shortage of people who will claim that they "made" the decision, as indicated by President Kennedy's famous statement that "success has many parents but failure is an orphan." But, in fact, decisions accrete over time; they evolve and are continuous. Carol Weiss (1980) found that most decision makers do not believe that they actually make decisions. They write memos, answer inquiries, give their opinions, edit drafts of regulations, and the like, but they do not formulate decisions in response to a specific event such as the Cuban missile crisis.

The term "policy" refers to consistency in behavior with respect to *what* is being done or *how* it is done in a given domain of public activity (Eulau & Prewitt 1973, 477). Policy behavior is characterized by repetition; it occurs not just at one point in time but through time. Eulau and Prewitt (1973, 481) describe policy as follows: "Whether the outcome of slow accretions, of spectacular actions, or of governmental inaction, it seems clear that policy at any one point in time is necessarily partial and time-bound for one does not in that case really know whether it is a standing decision." Thus, since policies evolve over time—rather than "made" at one point in time—they are bound to change during implementation.

The Upside-Down View The *upside-down view* is the belief that directives, orders, and policies in an organization should flow from the top to the bottom. According to TPA, an ideal organization is a centralized hierarchy with control emanating from the top (Nakamura & Smallwood 1980). As a result, a very large proportion of research and writing in TPA is directed at the question of how to make the directives and orders of those at the top become the behavioral principles of those at the bottom. Merit systems, effective communications, training, and the artful use of sanctions and rewards are all considered techniques and ways for manipulating the behavior of street-level bureaucrats.

But communications are distorted and changed as they are transmitted down the organizational ladder. "The members of a hierarchy do not, in fact, think of themselves as mere messenger boys, faithfully transmitting the reports of the superior" (Tullock 1964, 139). Subordinates add to and subtract from the messages they receive. They decide what parts of general policy directives affect their part of the hierarchy. They prepare orders and pass along to their subordinates only those parts of the directives they consider relevant. By the time the directive reaches the lower level, there are major differences among the versions received by comparable bureaucrats in different parts of the organization (Meltsner & Bellavita 1983). Hence, the policy that develops is an outgrowth of each bureaucrat's own motives, and the processes of a particular office rather than what the center of power wants in an organization. According to Anthony Downs, "at every level, there is a certain discretionary gap between the orders an official received from above and those he issues downward, and every official is forced to exercise discretion in interpreting his superior's order" (1967, 134). This constitutes what Downs calls "leakage of authority."

In the contemporary view of implementation, this leakage is sometimes desirable. For example, when the street-level bureaucrat is the only "boundary spanner" in the organization—the only person who knows what the clients are like and what may work with them—the street-level bureaucrat can help determine which policies actually work and why they work (Prottas 1980). Discretion is desirable, therefore, because it enables the organization to adopt policies to local needs and conditions. This "reinvention" of policies helps make them work.

We should not assume that all modifications of policies will be beneficial; it is possible—even likely—that some modifications will be harmful (Calsyn, Tornatsky & Dittmar 1977). In fact, if street-level bureaucrats are motivated primarily by self-interest, it may well be the case that modification of policies will tend to serve the interests of bureaucrats rather than the clients they are supposed to serve. According to the economic theory of rational behavior (Downs 1967; Olson 1971), we should expect individuals to serve their self-interests when they choose a particular course of action. Modification of policy is undesirable to the extent that it benefits the street-level bureaucrat or groups other than those for whom the services originally were intended.

Additional problems are created by inadequate flow of information from the bottom upward. Often the executives at the top do not know what people lower down in the organization know. Charles Peters, editor-in-chief of the *Washington Monthly,* recalls his days working for the Peace Corps, "I would find that a problem that was well-known by people at low and middle levels of the organization, whose responsibility it was, would be unknown at the top of the chain of command or by anyone outside" (1986, 27). This is because the people at the lower ranks are fearful of giving their bosses bad news, especially when there is a tendency to punish the bearer of bad tidings.

The Illegitimacy of Change View This view holds that the goals stated in policy documents—including laws, court orders, and regulations—should be carried out "to the letter," which stems from the need for accountability (Davis 1972). This means that administrators should not make policy because they cannot be held accountable for it; they are not legally or constitutionally charged with the responsibility for making policy, only for carrying it out. They cannot be replaced at the next election if the people are dissatisfied with what they do. The problem with this view is that it assumes that the goals stated in policy documents usually are clear and unequivocal and that it is possible to control the discretion of street-level bureaucrats who carry out policy. Neither of these assumptions is true.

As explained earlier, the goals stated in policy documents, particularly those in legislation, are seldom stated clearly and unequivocally. This is due to the nature of the legislative process. In order to get a bill passed it is necessary to make it appeal to as wide a group of supporters as possible. This requires compromise and watering down goals and objectives. For example, Medicare began in the Truman administration as a bill aimed at providing comprehensive health care for the poor, but by the time it was passed almost twenty years later, it provided only certain hospital care for most (not all) of the elderly (Marmor 1973). No bill would have been passed if the goals had not been watered down.

Such compromising in legislation is not unusual. Many laws are passed more as symbolic gestures than as realistic attempts to solve social problems (Edleman 1964). Bills often are passed because of the votes they will garner and to satisfy the claims of interest groups, and little, if any, thought is given to how they actually will be implemented. As a result, top-level administrators charged with the responsibility of implementing the bill must use discretion in determining exactly what the bill will [accomplish] in practice. This discretionary function of administrators exists all down the line in administrative agencies. Many street-level bureaucrats—those who actually deliver the services to the people—also have a great deal of discretionary power in determining which policies, services, and programs will be delivered and which individuals actually will get them. The cumulative effect of their actions amounts to public policy, and it is often quite different from what is stated in policy documents themselves.

This discretion of street-level bureaucrats, in the view of TPA, should be controlled, channeled, circumscribed, and, if possible, abolished (Davis 1972). However, there is a difference between controlling and channeling discretion. The former refers to the control superiors exercise over subordinates, and the latter is the control that individuals exercise over their own actions. It is undesirable to try to control discretion. Although rules and regulations constrain what street-level bureaucrats do, they do not control that behavior. This is because there are often numerous and conflicting rules that operate and bureaucrats can use the particular ones they want to support the action they take. Rules become an instrument for protecting street-level bureaucrats from their supervisors rather than the other way around (Crozier 1964).

Another reason why it is impossible to control discretion completely is because it is impossible to supervise street-level bureaucrats as they are delivering services or performing their jobs. Police on the beat, teachers in the classrooms, nurses in clinics or out making home visits, sanitarians out checking restaurants, probation officers working with offenders, prosecutors negotiating with defendants, and the multitude of other street-level bureaucrats most often work without direct supervision. For the most part, this is unavoidable because there are never enough resources to provide close, frequent, and direct supervision, and because they often are physically separated from their superiors. This does not mean that some attempts to limit discretion have not been successful. For example, Eugene Bardach and Robert Kagan (1982) describe how the discretion of food inspectors has been restricted:

> An inspector's judgment always is at work in fitting a rule to the details of what he sees, in deciding, for example, whether a dirty rail on a conveyor in a meatpacking plant poses a risk of "remote product contamination" or "direct product contamination," the latter requiring a tougher response. But discretion

for inspectors to overlook obvious or clear rule violations, to grant extended time for abatement, to "forget" citations after they have been written up, seems by all accounts to have been restricted. (76)

Finally, there are no exact performance standards in existence that specify exactly how street-level bureaucrats should do their jobs. It is therefore difficult or impossible to define how a street-level bureaucrat should behave or what constitutes good behavior in all situations. For example, it is difficult to specify exactly how police officers should handle a domestic disturbance, how nurses handle a patient, or how a teacher should deal with a difficult child, because each case is different. There are some general rules that can be specified, but how they should be applied in a specific case must be left up to the individual (Elmore 1976).

If lower-echelon workers do not want to cooperate with established standards, there are many tactics they can use to avoid or negate them. They can use aggression, develop negative attitudes, or engage in slowdowns. Michael Lipsky notes that "the management challenge . . . at the heart of the problem is how to make the worker's need for personal, material, or psychological gratification mesh with the organization's needs" (1980, 17). If management fails to do this, street-level bureaucrats are likely to use their discretion to defeat what top-level management wants to achieve. But even if it were possible to appeal to workers' needs, it is still questionable whether or not their behavior *should* be completely restricted.

The Importance of Implementation in the Policy Cycle

Implementation is now recognized as one of the most important aspects of the policy cycle (Nachmias & Rosenbloom 1978; Meier 1979; Ripley & Franklin 1982; Nakamura & Smallwood 1980; Gilbert 1984; Lewis & Wallace 1984). This is a rather stunning conclusion, especially since for many years it was generally believed that only the legislature made policy, while administrators merely carried it out. Still, this view has not been totally rejected by researchers and participants in the policy-making process.

Why is implementation such an important stage in the policy-making cycle? One reason is primarily political; legislators tend to make laws that are vague and ambiguous because such laws are less likely to generate intense opposition than laws that are clear and specific. An example of this situation is described in Case 4–1.

To avoid sticky issues, legislators engage in what is known as symbolic politics (Edleman 1964). They will take a stand on the general issue, such as being generally in favor of federal aid to education, but they will avoid the specific question of whether aid should be given to parochial as well as public schools, or whether such aid is to be used only for disadvantaged children. The symbolic value a legislator gets by being identified with an issue

Title I of the Elementary and Secondary School Act

Title I of the Elementary and Secondary Education Act of 1965 involved the federal government more deeply in elementary and secondary school education than any other legislation in American history. Ninety-five percent of the school districts in the United States receive funds from the federal government under Title I. The problem that Title I meant to address is the disparity in educational achievement between poor and middle-class children.

Various groups have been opposed to the federal government providing aid for elementary and secondary education: Catholic groups such as the National Catholic Welfare Council opposed such legislation unless it was given to parochial schools as well as to public schools; public school groups such as the National Education Association opposed giving aid to parochial schools. Thus, legislation that clearly and unambiguously stated that aid was going to be given to both kinds of schools for the express purpose of improving the education of disadvantaged children would suffer certain defeat.

To get around this problem, Congress dreamed up the concept of "child benefit," which allocated aid to children rather than to the schools. Since the aid was to benefit all children, it was not clear whether such aid was to be used only for disadvantaged children or as general aid for whatever purpose desired by local school districts (Stoner 1978). The concept of child benefit made the law acceptable to parochial as well as public school officials, but it created implementation problems. During implementation, the U.S. Commission of Education attempted to persuade most school districts to use the funds for disadvantaged children. But because the legislation was so general, many states used the funds for general purposes and the federal government was unable to stop them.

is often more important than the substantive question of whether or not the law's goals can be implemented.

Another reason a great deal of policy making occurs during the implementation stage is because it is not possible to specify the details of a law in advance; these can only be filled in at the time they are being applied at the local level. For example, a law aimed at improving the education achievement of disadvantaged children cannot spell out in detail precisely how this should be done in all communities. Legislators do not know the skills of educators in every community, nor do they know the most effective educational techniques for a particular mix of students. In order to permit local adaptation of the laws, a number of gaps must be left in the law. Policy making occurs when these gaps are filled in by the public administrators and private agencies responsible for carrying out the law (Elmore 1976).

A third reason a great deal of policy making occurs during implementation is that, in many cases, there are few established techniques for accomplishing policy goals. For example, there is no quick technological fix for improving the educational performance of disadvantaged children. Because of this, agencies experiment with different methods of achieving policy goals. Sometimes the methods used to achieve one set of goals accomplish something unanticipated by legislators or administrators. Unintended consequences are the result. For example, the method of "maximum feasible participation" that was used to reduce poverty in the 1960s (see Chapter 7) had little effect on the level of poverty although it helped create a leadership corps among minorities and the poor.

A fourth reason policy making occurs during implementation is that implementors do not always agree with policy objectives specified in the laws. As a result, they may resist carrying it out. They may resist because they believe the objectives of the law are unrealistic. For example, decriminalization of public drunkenness was designed to rehabilitate problem drinkers and to provide them with emergency services, including food and shelter. Police and health administrators realized that these objectives were not appropriate for all classes of problem drinkers. Street drunks were poor clients for rehabilitation, but needed emergency care. Public health agencies in some states decided to devote their resources to problem drinkers who had the greatest potential for rehabilitation—a process known as "creaming." As a result, police were left with no facilities to handle problem street drunks, the clientele for whom the laws were originally designed, and they simply stopped arresting and referring drunks to the detoxification centers. In this case, legislatures failed to consult with the relevant agencies when they wrote the legislation (Aaronson, Dienes & Musheno 1984).

Resistance may also occur if legislation upsets the established routines of a bureaucracy. Bureaucrats can resist carrying out policy they do not agree with by dragging their feet or by outright sabotage. A favorite technique for the latter is to leak information to friendly reporters which, when published by the media, can kill a program before it gets started. If implementors do not agree with the goals of policy, they can engage in games that result in the "classic symptoms of underperformance, delay, and escalating costs" (Bardach 1977, 5). These games result in the diversion of resources away from their intended use, the deflection of policy goals, the resistance of efforts to control behavior, and the dissipation of personal and political energies in game-playing that might otherwise be channeled into constructive, programmatic action (Bardach 1977, 66). Note, however, that administrators who change the goals of policy during implementation are not necessarily neglecting their jobs. Instead, they may be attempting to find ways of making a vague or bad law work.

The fifth and perhaps most important reason policy making occurs during the implementation stage is that Congress and the courts are both unable or unwilling to monitor or control the agencies responsible for implementation. Although Congress and the courts have some power to influence implementary agencies, they seldom use it. The first way Congress can control implementation is by manipulating the resources of federal agencies. If it does not like the way an agency is administering a law, it can cut the agency's appropriations. A second way Congress can exercise control is by determining *which* agency will implement a program. Sometimes Congress places the responsibility for administering a new program on an agency that is hostile or lukewarm about that program. For example, Medicaid was placed in a new division in the Bureau of Family Services of HEW and given a meager allotment of personnel (see Chapter 6). As a result, it quickly attained the stigma of being a welfare program rather than a health program.

Although Congress can coerce a federal agency by withholding funds from it, it should not be assumed that Congress will actually use this power. It takes extraordinary events for Congress to take such concerted action. For example, when President Richard Nixon impounded money that was appropriated for programs he did not like, Congress forced the president to spend the money. But it takes extraordinary events for Congress to do something such as this. For the most part, the details of implementation have relatively low priority for congressmen and women, except to intervene on behalf of a constituent or on projects in their districts. Politically, there is little to be gained from interfering with the way federal agencies are implementing policy and almost nothing to be gained by trying to influence state and local or private agencies involved in implementing federal policy. Moreover, most representatives are not willing to take the time that would be required to monitor how well a program is being implemented.

The courts have even fewer powers than Congress and are even more limited in their ability to control implementation. They cannot appropriate or withhold money from federal agencies nor determine which agency will implement a policy. Moreover, the courts must wait until a case is brought to them before they can act; they cannot initiate a case themselves. When a case is brought to them, they are limited to the issues in the case. The courts technically cannot go beyond these issues in their rulings. For example, during the 1983 term, the Supreme Court decided it would hear cases on the issue of abortion. One case involved the question of whether or not a teenage girl seeking an abortion needed the permission of her parents before she could get the abortion. In this case, the Court could rule only on the specific issue of parental consent, not the legal right to abortions in general.

These limitations do not mean that the courts have no impact on implementation at all. They do. For example, the courts have had a significant impact on how federal and state prisons and local jails in the country are run. They have ruled that many state prisons violate the Eighth Amendment's prohibition against cruel and unusual punishment of the U.S. Constitution. This is because some prisons are vastly overcrowded with two or three times as many prisoners as they were built to hold. Still other prisons and local jails have been cited for not providing adequate health care facilities. The courts have ordered that these conditions be corrected. As a result, the condition of prisons and jails in the United States has improved (Levine, Musheno & Palumbo 1986).

The Supreme Court's greatest influence on policy derives from two separate but related issues. The first is the Court's ability to get an issue onto the public agenda. Chapter 1 described how the pro-abortion groups used the courts to get a ruling on the abortion issue. Their strategy was patterned after the NAACP's strategy in getting the issue of segregated schooling before the Court in *Brown v. Board of Education of Topeka et al.** The second way the Court influences policy is through the power of judicial review, which is the power to determine if a particular law does or does not conform to the U.S. Constitution. This power often leads to landmark cases such as *Roe v. Wade* that greatly influence the direction of policy.†

It should be added that Congress can and sometimes does reverse the Court's decisions. More important, however, the Supreme Court does not implement its own decisions. As President Andrew Jackson reputedly said about a decision made by Chief Justice John Marshall, "Marshall made the decision; now let him enforce it." Jackson's statement reveals the inherent weakness of the courts to affect implementation. They must rely upon the executive branch and ultimately, state and local agencies (both public and private) for enforcement. Sometimes this enforcement does not occur. For example, in *Brown v. Board of Education*, the Supreme Court ruled that segregated schools violated the equal protection clause of the U.S. Constitution. Yet thirty years after the 1954 ruling, many schools in the United States—particularly those in the Northern and Eastern cities—are more segregated than they were when the Court handed down its decision (Bullock & Lamb 1983). For further discussion of the desegregation case, see Chapter 9.

As a result of the relative inability of Congress and the courts to influence implementation, implementors are fairly autonomous. They therefore have a greater impact on the making of public policy than other branches of government. It would be difficult to measure just how much influence they have, however. Certainly implementors far outnumber legislators or judges. If it is true, as we shall argue next, that those who carry out policy on a day-to-day

* 347 U.S. 483 (1954).
† 410 U.S. 113 (1973).

basis actually make the most policy, then it is true that the overwhelming majority of all policy is made during implementation.

Several Definitions of Successful Implementation

Soon after he was sworn in as the first commissioner of the New York Citywide Parks Department on January 19, 1934, Robert Moses, in a surprise move, fired the park commissioners of the city's five boroughs, their superintendents, secretaries, and an assortment of deputy commissioners. By the end of that year, a year in which New York City was suffering financial crises, Moses had made such amazing accomplishments in creating new parks that he was dubbed the "Hercules of the parks." The *New York Times* called his achievements nothing short of miraculous: "It is almost as if Mr. Moses had rubbed a lamp, or murmured some incantation over an old jar, and actually made the genie leap out to do his bidding" (*New York Times,* March 20, 1934).

By December 7 that same year, Moses succeeded in restructuring Central Park Zoo in a way that so impressed Governor Al Smith that he was moved to tears and commented, after a long pause during the opening ceremonies, "When Mr. Moses was appointed Park Commissioner, I used all of the influence I had with him to get him to work on a new zoo. And now look at him! In less than eight months, we've got a zoo that's one of the finest of its kind in the world" (Caro 1975, 382).

These were really the smallest parts of Robert Moses' accomplishments. What he is most noted for are the numerous bridges he built. The Triborough Bridge was the next big accomplishment; it is a bridge so big that its anchorages—the masses of concrete in which the cables are embedded—are as big as the biggest Egyptian pyramids. Overcoming amazingly complex obstacles to build this bridge, Moses' solutions were triumphs of imagination. A whole series of bridges followed: the Bronx-Whitestone, the Throgs Neck, the Cross Bay, the Robert Moses Twin Causeway, the Alexander Hamilton, the Henry Hudson, the Marine Parkway, the Brooklyn Battery, and the Verrazano-Narrows.

While some have been critical of Moses' tactics—he did not let legal niceties restrain him and he stepped on anyone who got in his way—he was acclaimed for knowing his way through the mazes of the law. He moved swiftly, and the state would belatedly catch up with him. But whether or not Moses' achievements represent great accomplishments or great disasters depends upon whether or not one agrees with the end result—a result that catered to the use of the automobile and suburbanization of New York City. Some planners believe that this contributed to the destruction of New York (Jacobs 1965). There is no doubt, however, that Moses could get things done. He was a successful implementor.

There are probably numerous other examples of implementation success in history. But the more typical scenario is one of implementation failure, such as that described in Case 4–2.

CASE 4–2 *Operation Breakthrough*

In 1969, the Department of Housing and Urban Development initiated "Operation Breakthrough" as a way of providing some twenty-six million housing units for the country in ten years. The program involved assembling already manufactured modules of housing at the housing site rather than traditional on-site construction.

Operation Breakthrough had all of the ingredients that strongly augur for success: able, committed leadership in the persons of George Romney, the secretary of HUD, and Harold Finger, the assistant secretary for Research and Technology; clear objectives in the form of a specific ten-year goal of building twenty-six million units; and a good beginning. But by 1974 the program was judged a failure. Among the reasons for this were (1) inertia in the construction industry; (2) a diffuse and self-protective group of building contractors, architectural and engineering firms, and financial backers; (3) weak congressional support; (4) inadequate funds; and finally, (5) a loss of leadership when Romney was not reappointed in 1972 by President Nixon (Ingram & Mann 1980, 175–77).

The two opposing examples of Robert Moses on the one hand and Operation Breakthrough on the other raise a number of questions about implementation success or failure. Are there more examples of implementation failure in American history than there are of success? What are the causes of successful and unsuccessful implementation? Is it necessary to have a dynamic leader such as Robert Moses in order to have successful implementation? What, in fact, is implementation success?

It is difficult to answer these questions because it is difficult to measure implementation failure or success (Ingram & Mann 1980). From one perspective, the many accomplishments of Robert Moses might be said to be eminently successful (Lewis 1984). But Moses has also been criticized by many. The monumental book about Moses written by Caro concludes that, in the end, his achievements were not really appreciated by the public.

While it may be difficult to measure implementation success or failure, several researchers have tried to identify the conditions of effective implementation. Sabatier and Mazmanian (1979, 484–85) have identified the following five conditions for effective implementation:

1. The program is based on a sound theory relating changes in target group behavior to achievement of the desired end-state (objectives).

2. The statute (or other basic policy decision) contains unambiguous policy directives and structures for the implementation process so as to maximize the likelihood that target groups will perform as desired.
3. The leaders of the implementing agencies possess substantial managerial and political skills and are committed to statutory goals.
4. The program is actively supported by organized constituency groups and by a few key legislators (or the chief executive) throughout the implementation process, with the courts being neutral or supportive.
5. The relative priority of statutory objectives is not significantly undermined over time by the emergence of conflicting public policies or by changes in relevant socioeconomic conditions that undermine the statute's "technical" theory or political support.

Sabatier and Mazmanian recognize that it is difficult for all of these conditions to be present. Good social theories and technologies are not always available, the legislature often passes laws with ambiguous and conflicting goals, implementation is sometimes assigned to a nonsupporting agency, and support for the program may wane during the long period of time it sometimes takes to implement it. The authors recommend ways of trying to deal with these problems and their recommendations generally are attempts to find ways of approximating the five conditions. For example, they say that if the legislature "insists on passing legislation with only the most ambiguous policy directives, then supporters of different points of view can initiate litigation in the hope of finding a court that will invalidate the law as an unconstitutional delegation of (legislative) authority" (1979, 503).

It is difficult to meet the five criteria for effective implementation because they make unrealistic demands of legislatures and top-level administrators. Sabatier and Mazmanian ask that legislators be absolutely *clear* in what they want, but this is not easy to do. Other researchers make similar assumptions. For example, Edwards and Sharkansky argue that "those responsible for carrying out a decision must know what they are supposed to do. Orders to implement a policy must be delivered to the appropriate personnel, and they must be consistent, clear and accurate in specifying the aims of the decision makers." (1978, 295). The authors' second condition refers to resources. If personnel lack the resources, "policy makers will be disappointed in the results" (303). Their third condition, which is similar to Sabatier and Mazmanian's, states that implementors must desire to carry out the policy (Edwards 1980).

One seldom meets these conditions for effective implementation. Although not explicitly stated, Sabatier and Mazmanian view effective implementation in an instrumental way. Their conditions imply that success or failure is a function of how well goals are carried out. Implementation success is measured in terms of efficiency, economy, and effectiveness. The goals of policy, in this view, are treated as givens, and successful implementation is measured in terms of whether or not these goals are achieved. Implementation deals only with means, not ends. The question to be answered is, "Did the agency achieve the goals intended by the policy in the most efficient and economical way possible?"

This view of implementation is called the *rationalistic approach*. The rational policy analyst assumes that the only *raison d'etat* for the policy process is to achieve certain substantive ends—to improve health, reduce crime, or build more roads, for example. When these ends are not achieved, we have what is known as "the implementation problem" (Elmore 1979). When this occurs, we employ traditional means of trying to improve implementation. That is, we write more specific legislation, tighten regulations and procedures, centralize authority, and monitor compliance more closely. But, instead of increasing control, these methods often increase the complexity of programs. Instead of improving them, this approach often makes them worse (Elmore 1979; Landau & Stout 1979; Wildavsky 1979). In addition, the rationalistic approach leads us to expect too much, and thus fosters the conclusion that government is incapable of doing much good. Implementation feasibility analysis becomes a conservative process inhibiting necessary political innovations (Dror 1984, 195).

Because implementation is a continuation of policy making, it partakes of all of the other elements of policy making. Effective carrying out of goals or the achievement of specific objectives is but one aspect of that process. Policy making is also a way for individuals to obtain power, to acquire the substantial rewards and benefits available through government, and to get and hold public jobs. In this broader sense, implementation is a part of a political process. Thus, in the classic definition of politics and policy making, it is a way of deciding who gets what, when, and how (Lasswell 1936).

Another way to look at implementation success is in terms of the extent and process of implementation (Palumbo & Maynard-Moody 1991). The extent refers to whether the right clients have been reached as well as a sufficient number. Process refers to whether sufficient resources are being used and adequate organizational arrangements and communications exist. This defines implementation success as existing independently of whether the activities and tasks being undertaken achieve the outcomes specified that may be beyond the control of the implementing agencies. As political scientist Ann Schneider (1982, 718) notes: "If the quality of implementation is judged in terms of whether the tasks and activities achieve the goals of the policy and if these goals are not achieved, then there is no way to determine whether policy failure was due to defective implementation or inadequate theory."

There is no single definition of successful implementation. How we define successful implementation depends upon what theoretical perspective is used to analyze the decision-making process (Palumbo 1985). There are four distinct definitions of successful implementation: rationalist, incrementalist, bureaucratic, and adaptive. To the complete rationalist, successful implementation is carrying out the goals specified by the legislature. To the incrementalist, successful implementation is doing something that is just a little better than what was done before. The incrementalist eschews finding the optimum or best solution and believes instead that the most that is possible is a "satisfactory" course of action. This is a modified form of rationalism (Lindblom 1979) because it assumes that organizations exist to achieve goals.

In the bureaucratic definition, implementation is successful when the power and status of the implementing agency increases (Bardach 1977; Williams 1980). According to this view, success in achieving an agency's goals can actually be detrimental to the agency. For example, if a police department could eliminate all crime, it would go out of existence unless, of course, it could find a different mission. The best known example of this is the March of Dimes. Once polio had been conquered in the 1960s, this agency turned its attention to eliminating birth defects. Successful implementation in this rather cynical view is frequently the opposite of successful policy. According to this definition, a welfare agency does not want to eliminate poverty or even to decrease it because it would either lose some of its personnel and budget or cease to exist altogether.

The fourth definition—adaptive implementation—is a more recent view of successful implementation. This defines success as the adaptation of policy to local circumstances (McLaughlin 1976; Berman 1980; Palumbo, Maynard-Moody & Wright 1984; Lewis & Wallace 1984). The argument here is that, because most policy is couched in general terms, it must be modified in order to be able to fit local circumstances. If the policy *and* the implementing agency are not mutually adaptive, the policy will not be successfully implemented.

In reality, successful implementation is a combination of all of these definitions. Achievement of at least a portion of a program or a policy's goals must occur in order to say that a policy has been successfully implemented. The question, however, is one of *perceived* rather than actual achievement of goals, and ideology often is a factor in determining how successful an agency has been in achieving goals. For example, those who are ideologically disposed to governmental welfare programs will believe that a program has been more successful in increasing welfare and reducing poverty than those who are ideologically opposed to governmental involvement.

Successful implementation usually involves only incremental changes from what had occurred prior to the introduction of the policy. Major radical changes, such as those initiated by New York City Park Commissioner Robert Moses, will usually invite opposition from those hurt by the changes. As a result, major changes usually will not be perceived as having been successful, at least not by those involved at the time the changes are occurring. History, of course, may judge Robert Moses differently.

Because social problems cannot be solved or completely conquered, successful implementation will generally enable the agency in charge to survive and grow. The successful implementing agency will find ways of dealing with a problem that not only ameliorates the worst effects of the problem, but also increases its own power.

Finally, successful implementation almost always requires that the policy or program be modified and adapted to fit the local circumstances. Few policies can be completely designed beforehand, or implemented in all locations in exactly the same way. The physical conditions, the people involved, resources, timing, and a number of other factors will affect the way a policy can be implemented.

■ THE LIMITS TO SUCCESSFUL IMPLEMENTATION

One of the founding fathers of America, James Madison, wrote in *The Federalist* papers: "The structure of government reflects the nature of man: If men were angels, government would be unnecessary." The same thing could be said of implementation. If we knew clearly what we wanted to accomplish with a particular government program, if this message were clearly transmitted to the people who carry it out, if we were fully capable of doing it, and if those who carried out the programs agreed with its goals, then we would always have perfect implementation. This also would be somewhat akin to having angels as public officials, which we know is highly unlikely. As a result, there are a number of limitations to successful implementation. For example, the people who implement programs—that is, street-level bureaucrats as well as upper-level administrators—may not know what their superiors want them to do; second, they may not have the means to implement a program; and third, they may disagree with the policy and therefore resist carrying it out.

It is impossible for those who implement policy to know at all times exactly what it is that their superiors want. Not only is there always a certain amount of information leakage whenever a message is transmitted downward in an organization, those at the top often do not want to be perfectly clear about what they want.

One of the favorite phrases of Richard Nixon when he was president was "Let me make one thing perfectly clear." He used the phrase so often that it began to backfire on him. Cynical observers felt that Nixon usually said this when he, in fact, wanted to confuse the issue even more. Most presidents and, for that matter, governors, mayors, senators, chief executives, heads of departments, directors, and other top managers, do not like to be "perfectly clear" in what they say about a particular policy. President Eisenhower felt that presidents should not get into the details of decision making. This often is referred to derogatorily as "micro-managing." Still, there is a tendency among presidents (and top management) to believe that their subordinates will fully understand what they want and carry out their wishes. However, decisions are not self-executing; they set a process of decision making in motion. This process is one of interpreting what the decisions mean for each person in the organization (Meltsner & Bellavita 1983).This phenomenon of not knowing what those at the top want is sometimes referred to as leakage of authority. Messages transmitted through an organization lose some of their meaning during their journey and pick up new meanings every time they are relayed from one person to the next. Economist Gordon Tullock (1965) tried to calculate how much change occurs in messages in the transmission process. He concluded that in a small organization of only forty people, individuals at the bottom will wind up devoting only about 40 percent of their time doing things those at the top want. As the organization grows larger the amount of leakage increases geometrically, so that in a large organization there is quite a large gap between the desires of those at the top and the behavior of those at the bottom. However, the more successful those at the top are at getting the street-level implementors to support and accept program goals, the better the organization performs (Palumbo, Musheno & Maynard-Moody 1985).

Individuals in an organization who interact with people at the street level face a complex job, one that forces them to adopt coping mechanisms. These coping mechanisms lead to policy behavior that varies with what those at the top of the organization want. The street-level bureaucrat is asked to make changes in the behavior of individuals over whom he or she has relatively little control (such as students, criminals, welfare recipients, and sick people). Since the resources supplied to implement these goals are never adequate, the street-level bureaucrat may develop stereotypes to make their clients easier to handle; they may also invent shortcuts, or simply find ways to make their jobs easier (see Case 4–3). For example, during implementation of special education programs in Massachusetts during the 1970s, educators were not given sufficient resources. Instead of attempting to assess each child individually, they developed informal categories that enabled them to routinely and rapidly assess children (Weatherly & Lipsky 1977).

Another drawback to successful implementation is that we often lack the means to carry out policy goals. One of the principal means for carrying out policy is a large organization. Such organizations are not readily adaptable to new circumstances. They often fight new wars with the same techniques and methods used in previous wars (see Case 4–4).

The first U.S. troops sent to Vietnam performed as if they were fighting a large-scale military battle on the plains of central Europe. This is what they had been trained for but the Vietnamese soldiers were quite different. The United States had a difficult time adapting to a war in which the soldiers wore black pajama-type uniforms, used sharpened bamboo snare traps, and blended into the jungle. Likewise, the War on Poverty in the 1960s was fought with the techniques and methods used during the Great Depression. It was assumed that poverty was caused by economic malfunctioning. It became clear, however, that we did not really know how to fight the poverty of the 1960s. The social technology simply was not available. And, although we improved our strategies, we never did fully master the problem.

CASE 4–3 ***The Use of Deadly Force by Police***

The first example of policy making by street-level bureaucrats involves the question of when the use of deadly force by a police officer is justified. Each year police kill anywhere from 300 to 600 civilians. Over 50 percent of these civilians are black and another large percent is Hispanic. The laws in each state regarding when deadly force should be used vary significantly. In some states, the law says it should be used only when there is a felony crime involved or when a felon is trying to flee; in other states, the laws are less restrictive and allow the use of deadly force whenever an officer feels his or her life is threatened. But police officers are almost never punished when they use deadly force, even when the conditions under which it is used are questionable. The case of Mrs. Love in Los Angeles is not unusual. On January 3, 1979, two police officers responded to a request for assistance from a bill collector who had been threatened by Mrs. Love. When the officers arrived, Mrs. Love was standing in front of her home holding an 11-inch boning knife. The officers drew their guns as they approached her. A series of pleas, orders, and threats ensued, followed by Mrs. Love throwing the knife. The officers then fired a total of twelve rounds in rapid-fire sequence, hitting Mrs. Love eight times and killing her. Were they justified in using deadly force in this case? How might this kind of policy making by police be controlled?

When we fail to carry out policy because we lack the social technology to do so, the responsibility lies with those who designed the policy, rather than with the bureaucrats (Robertson 1984). Policies are supported by legislators because of the symbolic benefits they derive; they are often passed even when legislators know their goals cannot be achieved. For this reason, it is not at all fair to judge implementation by how well the policy achieves goals (Dror 1984).

The third limit to successful implementation is resistance by implementors who do not agree with the policy's goals. President Truman recognized that career officials in government (that is, those who have civil service status and therefore cannot easily be removed) have views of their own, which often vary with those of the elected officials. In his memoirs, Truman wrote, "Too often career men seek to impose their own views instead of carrying out the established policy of the administration. Sometimes they achieve this by influencing the key men appointed by the president to put his policies into operation. It has often happened in the War and Navy Departments that the generals and the admirals, instead of working for and

CASE 4–4 *The Crackdown on Drunk Drivers*

In 1982, a nationwide effort was launched to reduce the amount of deaths and accidents caused by people who drive while intoxicated. Many states passed harsh laws in an attempt to deter drunk driving. The laws carry automatic jail sentences of forty-eight hours for a first offense plus fines, revocation of the driver's license, and other punishment. But these laws were not implemented the same way in every jurisdiction. For example, the county district attorney in Douglas County, Kansas, implemented the law differently than the city district attorney of the largest city in the county. The city district attorney allowed first offenders to be "diverted" from court. This meant that the offender could avoid the forty-eight hour jail sentence if he or she agreed to pay the court $200, pay for and attend the Alcohol Information School, perform 100 hours of community service work, voluntarily restrict the right to drive between 10 P.M. and 7 A.M., and obey all state driving laws for a year. The city district attorney argued that this practice of allowing diversion was in accord with the law. The county district attorney disagreed. He believed that the law intended that first offenders should receive the forty-eight hour jail sentence as well as the punishment given to those who were diverted. A state senator involved in getting the law passed in Kansas admitted that the state legislature had left the decision about whether to prosecute or divert first offenders up to the individual judges and prosecutors in different courts.

under the secretaries, succeeded in having the secretaries act for and under them" (1956, 40). Just how often subordinates disagree with superiors is not known and has not often been studied. But it is certain that it must happen in a large percentage of cases.

Federalism and Implementation In addition to these three major limits to implementation, American public policy has another limitation because of the unique form of government called *federalism.* The American federal system gives independent powers to the two major levels of government—the national and the state. Many federal policies are implemented through state governments. Federal officials are not free simply to carry out national policy themselves; for political, practical, and legal reasons they must work with state and local governments. This poses additional hazards for implementation.

The implementation we have been discussing up to this point is called *micro-implementation* because it deals with the problems within organizations. In contrast, implementation through federalism is called *macro-implementation* (Van

Horn & Van Meter 1976). Macro-implementation is concerned with implementation *among* organizations, called interorganizational problems. In fact, the first studies of implementation focused strictly on macro-implementation (Pressman & Wildavsky 1984; Berman 1980). Similarly, most of the new perspectives on implementation research have stemmed from macro-implementation studies.

The limitations that federalism places on implementation are similar to those involved in micro-implementation, except they are more pronounced. Lack of a clear understanding of what the federal policy is, inability to carry it out, and resistance to the policy, all occur when policy is carried out through the system of federalism. The end result is that what actually gets carried out varies greatly from one state and locality to the next. Instead of uniform policy throughout the nation, there is wide local variation. From one perspective this is a highly desirable result, because it gives freedom and autonomy to the localities. The "new federalism" of President Nixon is an example of this.

The switch from categorical to block grants under the Nixon administration was made expressly for the purpose of giving greater freedom and control to local areas over the making of policy. *Categorical grants* are grants made by the federal government to a local area to carry out a specific program, such as improving the educational achievement of disadvantaged children. Categorical grants received a great deal of criticism in the late 1960s and early 1970s because they allegedly involved too much federal control over local policy. They also were criticized for involving too many regulations, too little flexibility, and for offering piecemeal solutions to complex problems. *Block grants,* on the other hand, were designed to correct these deficiencies because they provide funds that localities are free to spend for general purposes as they wish. Two examples of block grants are illustrated in Cases 4–5 and 4–6.

In summary, macro-implementation has many of the same limitations as micro-implementation. The principal difference is that in macro-implementation the variations in policy that occur are expected and desired, especially in the block grant programs. In micro-implementation, the variations are not expected, at least when organizations are viewed in the classical, top-down, bureaucratic sense. But advances in implementation research and in organization theory suggest that this is the wrong way to view organizations. According to this newer view, described next, variations in policy from office to office within an organization are desirable.

■ A PROCESS MODEL OF POLICY IMPLEMENTATION

Implementation research has changed our understanding of how organizations do and should operate. It is an important step in the development of the study of public administration, one that reflects changes that have been going

CASE 4–5 *The Community Development Block Grant Program*

The Community Development Block Grant Program enacted in 1974, consolidated seven of the Housing and Urban Development's categorical grants into a single block grant program. Under CDBG, cities were free to select their own projects without having to compete for money as they did under the old categorical grant approach. Grant money was allocated through a "needs formula" based on the size of a city's population, the amount of overcrowding in its housing stock, and the extent of poverty in the city. The block grants for the program could be used either for physical construction or for social service projects such as child care, health, or recreation services.

A study of CDBG by Kettl (1982) found that there was wide variation in the way cities used the grants. The poorer neighborhoods more often chose social service projects rather than physical improvements which they ostensibly needed more. The study also shows that the selection of projects was based more on their political support than on whether they fit into long-term planning goals. "In the end, it was bargaining—among elected officials, citizens, city bureaus, and neighborhood agencies—that was the most prominent feature of local decision making" (1982, 201).

The bargaining process produced scattered, short-term, neighborhood-based projects. But they also provided physical improvements in neighborhoods and jobs for neighborhood residents through the social service projects. Although the projects were uncoordinated, and there was no attempt to identify important needs, they did provide a major rehabilitation of housing, waterfront development, and downtown revitalization in some cases. Still, because there were no specific goals against which to evaluate the program, Kettl was unable to conclude whether the block program was a success.

on in the field for at least a generation. Walter Williams (1980) lists eight major tenets of the implementation perspective. In abbreviated form, these are:

1. The complexities involved in the delivery of social services means that considerable modifications will be made in programs as they are implemented.
2. The determinant of the path that these modifications will take is the *process* by which the program is implemented.
3. The discretion of implementors is irreducible.
4. The central concern of management must be *commitment* to program objectives and the *capacity* to provide the services.

CASE 4–6 *The Comprehensive Employment and Training Act*

As is typically the case with public policy, the Comprehensive Employment and Training Act of 1974 was designed to achieve multiple goals which could be in conflict. One goal was to provide counter-cyclical fiscal policy. This means that if employment was down, more money was to be spent on CETA to try to take up some of the slack. Another goal was to provide training and jobs for the economically disadvantaged. These two goals could conflict during times of high employment because counter-cyclical policy would call for a cut in spending even though some economically disadvantaged people were out of work and needed training.

Although more than $2 billion was appropriated for CETA in 1974, it produced only a total of 185,000 jobs. A high proportion of these jobs were in city and county departments as local officials used CETA funds to rehire city workers who were previously laid off by the city. The cities hired a high proportion of laboring and service workers, while the counties hired clerical workers. The typical public service employee under CETA was white, male, between the ages of 22 and 44, with a high school diploma, and who was *not* seriously disadvantaged. Very little attention was given to placement of the economically disadvantaged.

Was CETA a failure? Whether a program has failed may be difficult to determine, especially when the goals of that policy are stated in ambiguous terms. If we measure success or failure by the extent to which a policy meets its intended goals, then CETA was a failure, because it did not act as a counter-cyclical force (185,000 jobs was only a small percentage of the unemployed at the time). Nor did CETA help the hard-core unemployed significantly. However, by giving local areas freedom to select their own projects, CETA may have accomplished more than if the federal government had restricted the program and attempted to help only the economically disadvantaged (Pincus 1976).

5. Implementation generally takes a long time.
6. Only broad direction of social policy is possible so implementors should have flexibility.
7. The information managers need for implementation should provide details about the capacity of the organization to cope with its environment.
8. In a federal system, local entities occupy a central role because of the local power base they have.

Implementation is an evolutionary process (Majone & Wildavsky 1984) and a part of the process set in motion by a new policy or program (Palumbo

& Sharp 1980). If an administrator wants to carry out a program, he or she must fit it into an existing structure. The structure of an organization is given, and "anyone with a job he wants doing must adapt purpose to structure rather than the other way about" (Dunsire 1979, 78). The traditional model of administration does not recognize this. Instead, it sees the process of implementation as a progression from the general to the particular, a narrowing of the field of view or of thought, a limiting of choice or discretion, in which each stage is more pragmatic and closer to hard facts than the previous one. Dunsire (1979) contrasts this model with a network model in which the stages are interconnected. In the network model, we make assumptions about the ordering of the links, their nature, and how they relate to establishing links (that is, communications) between separate bodies.

The key notion in this network or process model is that an organization has a number of skills and structures already in existence that can be combined in various ways to get something done (Fleming 1980). Each organizational unit can be included in many different chains, and each is independent of the other. Pressman and Wildavsky (1984) use this model to identify individuals and groups involved in the federal jobs program in Oakland, California, and to describe decision points that had to be completed in order to get the end result. In their description, they use the metaphor of a Rube Goldberg machine which has numerous delicate parts intricately linked to each other in order to produce a specific outcome. In a mechanism this complex something is very likely to go wrong, and according to Murphy's Law,* it usually does. The end result is therefore often very different from that expected at the beginning.

One hopes that the outcome will not always be negative, as Murphy's Law indicates. Delegation of control to the lower echelons, the street-level bureaucrats, is essential if the capacity to deliver services is to be increased. This will produce a great deal of variability depending on how implementors respond to policy. But, according to Richard Elmore (1979), this variability will produce valuable information about more and less successful practices: "If some mechanism exists for capitalizing on variability at the delivery level, then complexity operates to raise the level of knowledge required for successful implementation" (41). If, on the other hand, there is an attempt to reduce this variability and to control the activities of street-level implementors through enforced compliance and monitoring, the result is likely to be greater complexity and a greater "implementation problem."

A process perspective of implementation contains some other components as well. One is the importance of leadership or entrepreneurship in getting a program successfully implemented (Yin 1979; Lewis 1984; Palumbo, Musheno & Maynard-Moody 1985). Administrators must be committed to the goals of the program and able and skilled in creating conditions for achieving them. The importance of commitment was recognized by the Reagan administration

* Formulated by the aerospace engineer, Edward A. Murphy, Jr. In succinct form the law says: If there is a wrong way to do something, then someone will do it.

in a negative way when he attempted to cut back certain programs. Instead of attacking these programs outright, he appointed people to administer them who did not truly support them. According to Garry Wills (1982), "a man who believes in book banning was put in charge of the Education Department, and a dentist was put in charge of Energy." The tactic worked in some cases but not others.

Another important element in the implementation process is the tools used to accomplish goals. A theory of implementation must explain which tools are likely to persuade the target groups to behave in the desired manner. The target groups include not only the citizens or that part of the public at whom the policy is aimed (that is, criminal offenders, students, welfare recipients, and so on), but also the members of the organizations who deliver the services or perform the functions required in the policy (that is, street-level bureaucrats, top-level administrators, and supervisors).

The tools used to channel implementation in desirable directions can be classified either as incentives or penalties (Brigham & Brown 1980). These are the "sticks and carrots" that may be applied to get people to change or adopt desired behaviors. According to Brigham and Brown, "Incentives include grants, exemptions, and facilitative measures . . . which seek to induce a 'voluntary' change in behavior. Penalties, on the other hand, are sanctions that involve unpleasant consequences imposed by a legally constituted authority for violation of the law" (1980, 9).

Under what conditions are incentives likely to be more effective than penalties? At times it may be necessary for government to use negative or heavy handed techniques to get a policy implemented. According to Max Nieman, "it is useful to adopt, as at least a working, devil's advocate-like assumption, the proposition that the heavy, visible, and coercive hand of government is in some respect desirable—that coercion from our public institutions has its virtues" (1980, 20).

Some argue that noncoercive methods work better than penalties. Charles Schultze (1968, 6–7) has written that when government intervenes "we ought to maximize the use of techniques that modify the structure of private incentives rather than those that rely on command." This, in essence, is a call to rely more on market mechanisms and less on government control as a more effective implementation approach.

Whether an approach is more effective may also depend upon the *type* of goods or services that are being supplied by government (Savas 1977). A collective good or service, for example, might be provided more effectively and efficiently using coercive tools such as regulations and penalties for anyone who violates the regulations. A *collective good or service* is one from which individuals cannot be excluded from partaking in and which cannot be consumed by a single individual. Examples are national defense and the air we breathe. If government provides national defense or clean air for the country, particular individuals cannot be excluded from benefiting from it, even if they do not make a contribution toward its supply. Collective goods are to be distinguished from *private goods and services* which are provided only to those who pay for them, and, once consumed, are gone. Examples are food and haircuts.

Some economists and political scientists believe that coercive incentives are needed to get people to provide collective goods because of the "free rider" problem. This refers to the fact that a person can enjoy a collective good such as clean air even if that person does not help produce it. For example, if the government adopts regulations that result in clean air no one can be excluded from partaking of the benefits whether or not they pay for or contribute toward this good. Thus, the only way to get people to pay for the production of this collective good is through coercive means such as taxation and penalties.

The distinction between collective and private goods is useful for determining when different types of implementation tools may work. However, it is not always easy to classify all goods and services into one of these two categories. For example, a city park is both a collective and a private good. Individuals can be excluded from a park by erecting a fence around it. Clean streets are a collective good in that everyone can use them if they are provided by a city. But some streets and roads are private and individuals can be excluded from them by fences and gates. Public safety is a collective good in that if the streets are made safe by police patrols, everyone can enjoy this benefit. But we know through research that police patrols alone are not sufficient to make streets safe. Individuals must participate in helping provide this good through means such as keeping watch on a neighbor's house, turning on lights, locking their houses, installing burglar alarms, and taking safety precautions.

The process model of implementation tells us that the kinds of tools used to accomplish the goals of policy are related to the kind of policy goods or services involved. However, this describes the model only at the broadest level. It has yet to be worked out as a guide for specific circumstances. In Part II of this book, we will see how the process model can be used as a way of determining why policies fail and how they can be improved.

5

Evaluation: Determining the Effectiveness of Public Policy

■ POLITICS AND PUBLIC POLICY EVALUATION

> The experimenting society will be one which will vigorously try out proposed solutions to recurrent problems, which will make hard-headed and multi-dimensional evaluations of outcomes, and which will move on to try other alternatives when evaluation shows one reform to have been ineffective or harmful. (Campbell 1971)

Thus begins Donald Campbell's optimistic vision of program evaluation. Campbell wrote this statement in a 1971 paper, two years after his milestone paper, "Reforms as Experiments" (Campbell 1969). But evaluators soon recognized that public agencies didn't often "move on to try other alternatives when evaluation shows one reform to have been ineffective or harmful." The issue of how to improve utilization of evaluation soon became the major concern of the profession during the 1970s. Several major works focusing on this question appeared including Michael Q. Patton's *Utilization Focused Evaluation* (1978) and Weiss's "Measuring the Use of Evaluation" (Weiss 1981).

Evaluation seldom can conform to the ideal model that Campbell originally assumed. Evaluating is a part of policy making. As such, it is a political, as well as a technical matter. It is political because those who are ideologically in favor of a public program such as welfare benefits and who sponsor such a program are likely to say that it has succeeded, whereas those who are ideologically opposed are likely to say the program has failed. Consider, for example, Republican President Reagan's "supply-side economics" of the 1980s. The Reagan administration in its 1984 reelection campaign asserted that his policies had succeeded: Reagan pointed to the improvement in the unemployment rate (which had dropped from a high of 12.5 percent nationwide in 1982 to 7.8 percent just before the election), the economic upturn in 1982 and 1984, and the low inflation rate as evidence of success. The Democrats, on the other hand, said the policies had failed. They pointed to the huge budget deficits, which were produced, they said, by Reagan's tax cuts and large increases in defense spending. They also cited the big trade deficits of 1984 and continuing high interest rates as additional evidence of the failure of Reaganomics. This same debate continued unabated into the 1990s.

Medicare and Medicaid, discussed in Chapter 7, are also evaluated differently by different groups. From the perspective of ideal health policy, these programs can be seen as failures. They provide health care only for the elderly and a small portion of the indigent. They do not provide comprehensive health care to all citizens who need it, as those who pushed for health care legislation originally wanted (Marmor 1973). Also, the costs of these programs skyrocketed, exceeding all original expectations of what they ultimately would cost. On the other hand, the programs have provided medical care for a large number of older Americans and have contributed greatly to improved medical technology in a number of areas.

Thus, in both of these examples, it is not clear whether the policies have succeeded or failed. This is because success and failure are slippery concepts that are "often highly subjective and reflective of an individual's goals, perception of need, and perhaps even psychological disposition toward life" (Ingram & Mann 1980, 12). Regardless of the objective impact of a particular policy, its success may be judged more on the basis of the political ideology and personal values of the evaluator rather than on whether the policy actually increases the general welfare.

This does not mean that it is impossible to be somewhat objective in evaluating public policies. In fact, the purpose of evaluation is to inject a large degree of objectivity into evaluating public programs. And professional evaluators who formally evaluate a program are supposed to be objective. Although government programs have always been evaluated, professional evaluation research began around the latter part of the 1960s with the hope that an experimenting society would be able to rationally and objectively determine if programs were succeeding or failing (Campbell 1975; Rivlin 1971). But as the field evolved, this optimism diminished. Questions were raised by critics as well as by evaluation researchers about the most appropriate methods for evaluating programs, the role of evaluation research in public policy decisions, and about the utilization of evaluation research (Palumbo & Nachmias 1984). We will consider these and other issues in this chapter.

HOW EVALUATION RESEARCH BEGAN: FROM PPBS TO THE EXPERIMENTING SOCIETY

The 1960s were tumultuous and revolutionary years for public policy and evaluation in the United States. It was a decade buffeted by changes of many kinds: advances in civil rights, women's liberation, anti-war protests, riots in the streets, black liberation, white backlash, the rise and fall of the Black Panthers, takeovers of universities by students, non-negotiable demands, confrontation politics, defiance of all authority, the generation gap, flower children, hippies, the greening of America, the War on Poverty, attacks on bureaucracy, community control, power to the people, and the deinstitutionalization of people in mental hospitals, prisons, and schools.

In support of and leading many of these developments were new coalitions among groups that had never worked together. These coalitions brought about changes that in less turbulent times would not have occurred. Middle-class white college students protesting the "immoral war" in Vietnam, chanting slogans such as "Hell, no, we won't go!" marched hand-in-hand with blacks and Hispanics who demanded "freedom now!" Middle-class women, demanding liberation from sexism and domination by male chauvinism, joined these groups in a coalition that looked as if it might give rise to a new political party and a new generation of politics. The coalition was powerful enough to discourage President Lyndon B. Johnson from seeking reelection. This was the first time in American history that an incumbent president had made this decision.

The ferment hit university campuses in a number of ways. At some schools, students chained themselves to the dean's door and presented the dean with a list of "non-negotiable" demands. One of these demands was that students be given a larger role in the governance of universities and in evaluating the performance, selection, and promotions of their professors. Their demands were similar to those being made by blacks, women, the poor, tenants, and citizens in general of all authority; they were asking for more democracy and for a greater voice in the making of policy. Within the halls of academe, university professors were told that their research and teaching must be "relevant" to the problems of the times. No longer could they engage in research simply for the sake of seeking knowledge; it was their responsibility to help find solutions to social problems.

The list of problems seemed endless, and the government responded by adopting a barrage of laws aimed at trying to end poverty and discrimination, improve the education of disadvantaged children, end police brutality, and clean up the environment. Many of these programs had questionable success at best. The perception that the programs were failing, coupled with the demand that ways of solving social problems be found, provided fertile ground for the beginning of evaluation research.

It was in this social and political climate that program evaluation first began outside of education. There are three separate streams of evaluation. The first is evaluation of educational programs which began early in the twentieth century and was aimed, at first, primarily at testing student performance and then, later, evaluating curricula and programs (Guba & Lincoln 1989, 22–38).

The second major type of evaluation that began in the early 1960s applied scientific methods to help administrators improve or optimize their decisions. This was known as *operations research.*

In the early 1960s, program budgeting techniques were introduced into the Defense Department by President Kennedy's Secretary of Defense, Robert McNamara. In contrast to many of the "whiz kids" that Kennedy had brought into government from universities (primarily Harvard), McNamara had been Chairman of the Ford Motor Company before his defense position. When he arrived in Washington he brought with him the business decision techniques of operations research to try to improve defense decisions. These techniques were called Program Planning and Budgeting Systems (PPBS). They were an attempt to get department heads to think in terms of the concrete objectives that programs were supposed to accomplish and what types and amounts of resources would be needed to accomplish them. Prior to PPBS, managers prepared budgets in terms of the number of new positions, how much new equipment of various kinds, and what supplies they would need to run their department. This traditional method is known as "line-item budgeting," because items such as supplies, personnel, or equipment occupy lines in the budget. Under PPBS, managers would have to show what their programs were supposed to achieve and how much of these objectives they would be able to achieve with various levels of resources. Decisions about how many and what combinations of resources would be needed to achieve a greater number of units of program objectives were made through sophisticated techniques such as mathematical modeling and computer simulation.

When Lyndon B. Johnson succeeded Kennedy as president, he was so taken with PPBS that he encouraged all federal departments to adopt it. But

these attempts at sophisticated, rational decision making by federal government agencies all failed (Brewer 1973), and by the late 1960s, attempts to extend and routinize PPBS were abandoned.

However, the attempt to make policy decisions more rational was not abandoned. Late in the 1960s, Northwestern University psychology professor Donald Campbell wrote an article entitled "Reforms as Experiments" (1969) in which he argued that we ought to treat government programs as "natural" experiments and test the degree to which they work. He recommended using techniques that are similar to the ones psychologists used in experiments on students and mice in university laboratories. The major difference, said Campbell, is that government programs do not take place under the controlled circumstances of a university laboratory; they take place in the real world where complicating events make it difficult to isolate the effects of the "treatment" from other factors. In order to control for these, Campbell helped create a new set of methods for studying government programs called *quasi-experimental design*.

A new wave of optimism spread through universities and governmental agencies. It was again hoped that rationality could be injected into policy decisions through "natural" experiments that could be tested through quasi-experimental design. The "experimenting society," as it came to be called, might make it possible to discover why programs were not working. The operating premise was that if programs were not working, we could find out why, and perhaps adopt ones that worked.

Evaluation research took off rapidly in the early 1970s. Several new books appeared (Weiss 1972; Caro 1971), the Evaluation Research Society was formed in 1971, and the federal government began to require that a certain portion of funds for programs be devoted to evaluating them. At the end of the Johnson era, the federal government spent about $24 million on program evaluations. By 1977, this sum had increased to over $243 million.

Evaluation became a more routine function of the federal government throughout the end of the 1970s and into the first half of the 1980s. The Program Evaluation and Methodology Division (PEMD) of the U.S. General Accounting Office (GAO) was created in 1974. It was charged with the responsibility of conducting program evaluations and helping other GAO divisions in their program evaluation. The GAO has over 5,000 employees and its major responsibility is to assist Congress by providing information for its legislative activities and oversight of the executive branch.

In 1982, the PEMD conducted a survey of executive branch evaluation activities. It defined evaluation as "a formal assessment, through objective measurements and systematic analyses, of the manner and extent to which Federal programs (or their components) achieve their objectives or produce other significant effects, used to assist management and policy decision making" (IPE 1982, 3). There were 228 agencies conducting evaluations according to this definition. The survey found that in 1980, the nondefense cabinet departments and agencies spent in excess of $177 million for program evaluation. A total of 1,353 full-time professionals conducted 2,362 evaluations, 60 percent of which were under contract with external organizations.

A number of state governments also began to develop an interest in evaluating programs and policies. Until the late 1970s, most states audited but did not evaluate government programs. Legislative *post-audits* are the traditional method of evaluating policies at the state level. A post-audit is aimed at determining whether funds are properly disbursed and accounted for. It looks only at how money is handled. Program evaluation, on the other hand, emphasizes program *outcomes* instead of *inputs* (that is, funding).

By 1980, almost all states had adopted a new approach to evaluation. Between 1976 and 1979, 34 states had adopted "sunset" laws (Henry & Smiley 1981). These laws required that an agency prove that it was accomplishing its objectives, otherwise the "sun would set" and the agency would be eliminated. The sun did not set on many agencies, however, and state legislatures turned to the more modest goal of program evaluation as a way of trying to improve programs. By 1980, 40 state legislatures had accepted a commitment to program evaluation. This new approach to evaluating government programs was not simply an extension of the defunct PPBS; it was different in several ways. First, it was developed mostly by psychologists and educational psychologists rather than by economists, statisticians, and business administrators. The latter group provided the intellectual apparatus for operations research and PPBS. Second, evaluation research is primarily a post-decision activity rather than a pre-decision activity as operations research and PPBS are. Using the techniques of quasi-experimental research design, program evaluations are conducted after the "intervention" is introduced, not before. For example, a new law to crack down on drunk driving, or the new "negative income tax" laws were evaluated after they took effect and had been in operation.

Another difference between PPBS and evaluation research lies in their goals. The goal of PPBS was to analyze different ways of achieving *given* objectives whereas the goal of evaluation research is to determine if the intervention has produced the desired impact. Although PPBS could be conducted after a program was adopted, it generally was conducted *prior* to program adoption. Its purpose was to determine which of a number of possible different alternatives worked best. For example, we could use policy analysis to evaluate what method would be most effective in reducing automobile fatalities. (We describe such an analysis later in this chapter.) Evaluation research on the other hand, is conducted after a program has been in operation and concerns the impact and implementation of that program.

Finally, evaluation research differs from policy analysis in the research techniques it uses. Whereas PPBS used cost-benefit and cost-effectiveness analyses as its major techniques, the principal methodology for program evaluation is the interrupted time-series analyses. Both are described below. Part of the reason for this is that each type of evaluation stems from different disciplines; psychology is the principal core of evaluation research, whereas economics is the core of operations research and PPBS. Traditionally, each of these disciplines uses different research methods. Whereas psychology relies more on experiments and experimental design, economics uses mainly cross-sectional and longitudinal designs. The latter method attempts to identify cause and effect by controlling for the influence of other variables mathematically and statistically rather than through control and experimental groups.

■ TYPES OF EVALUATIONS

Evaluation research, as we have seen, is different than policy analysis in several ways. Still, there is no single type of evaluation research. In fact, there are at least a half-dozen different types, all of which are described below. The first type of evaluation used was *impact* or *summative.* It is still the dominant paradigm, or model, in the field.

Summative Evaluation

The main question in a summative evaluation is "What difference does the program make?" Summative evaluation focuses on the extent to which policy outcomes contribute to the achievement of goals and objectives (Dunn 1981, 356). Lee J. Cronbach (1980), one of the leading evaluation researchers, defines evaluation as follows: "By the term evaluation, we mean systematic examination of events occurring in and consequent on a contemporary program—an examination conducted to assist in improving the program and other programs having the same general purpose" (14).

In order to conduct a summative evaluation, it is necessary to clearly identify the goals or objectives that the program is meant to achieve. For example, a government program aimed at drunk driving has the specific objective of reducing the number of injuries and deaths caused by drunk drivers on highways and streets. Several methods of trying to do this can be adopted. The results of these methods, called *program outputs,* are evaluated to determine if highway fatalities were in fact reduced. As long as it is possible to specify the objectives of a program, the principal challenge in evaluation is to see if the impacts of the program outputs can be isolated from any other factors that might contribute to those impacts. Because social programs take place in the world rather than in a controlled laboratory setting, it is much more difficult to isolate and attribute the impacts to the program efforts rather than to other factors. As we shall see in the next section, this is not always possible.

Often it is not possible to specify the goals or objectives that are intended by the program. As indicated in earlier chapters, most government policies, laws, and programs have vague and ambiguous goals. Under these circumstances, the more difficult problem is not trying to see if the program achieved its objectives, but trying to determine *what* objectives the program is supposed to achieve.

To clarify program goals, evaluation researchers have developed goals clarification methods such as *evaluability assessment.* In evaluability assessment, first developed by a federal government program evaluator (Wholey 1983), researchers take specific steps before conducting an evaluation. These are as follows:

1. Identify those program components that are well defined and *can* be implemented. If the program's overall goals are vague, then determine which aspects of the program should be included in the evaluation. Include only those aspects of the program whose goals can be made specific in the evaluation.
2. Prepare a "flow model" of how all the goals of the program are linked to the various program components from documents describing the program.
3. Interview program personnel to verify the model, to see if any goals are missing, and to determine how to measure their achievement.
4. Compare this program manager's model with the document's model and revise the linkages as necessary.
5. Develop the evaluable program model (Ruttman 1977, 1980).

Evaluators soon began to realize that it is not always easy to establish a clear set of goals that all program participants agree on. One evaluation researcher referred to this process as the "goals clarification game"; a game that the program staff hates to play because the evaluators always win (Patton 1978, 98). It also is a nonsense game, Patton adds, because there seldom is a simple set of goals in an organization and different groups within the organization will prefer different goals.

Attempts to clarify goals may involve complicated techniques such as the *Delphi method.* In this method, a questionnaire is distributed to program managers and the results are summarized and discussed by managers in a group session with the hope that differences can be reconciled. According to Patton, this only "postpones the war until data are gathered to be used as additional ammunition in each side's fight" (1978, 105).

Goal-Free Evaluation

The problems encountered in an impact evaluation have prompted researchers to seek other types of evaluation. One of the earliest alternative types to be created was *goal-free evaluation,* which was developed by Michael Scriven

(1972), a philosopher working with the Evaluation Network out of San Francisco State University. In goal-free evaluation, the evaluator avoids specifying what the program goals are a priori; instead, the evaluator attempts to determine just what the program actually is achieving, and then decides the extent to which these achievements are fulfilling important societal needs.

For example, the Head Start program that began in the late 1960s was supposed to give educationally disadvantaged students an early start in school so that they could compete with other students when they entered first grade. The hope was that these children would be able to do as well as other students in subsequent years. Thus, a specific goal for this program might be to make the average grades of program students equal to those of all other students.

In 1969, a team of Ohio State University researchers who evaluated the program concluded that the Head Start program was largely ineffective in producing any cognitive or affective results in students. In other words, students in the program did not perform as well as all students in the grades they received. Opponents of the program rejoiced and pronounced it a failure. But critics said that the evaluation failed to consider the health, nutrition, resources redistribution, cultural, or community goals of the program (Williams & Evans 1969; Evans 1971; Patton 1978). The fact that it was serving some of these socially useful goals was sufficient to sustain the Head Start program for years even though many had assumed it was a failure. A goal-free rather than a summative evaluation would have been better in this particular case because it would have pointed to some of the positive accomplishments of the program. In any case, the program continued even though the evaluation concluded it was not working. The reason was that it was supported by some key stakeholders which, as we will see next, is often much more important than an objective or scientific evaluation in determining whether or not a program will be continued. A subsequent study showed that the program actually did improve the cognitive abilities of student participants, although it took years for this to show up.

Critics of goal-free evaluation contend that it does not avoid the problem faced in the goal-clarification game. Instead, this method simply replaces the staff's goals with global goals that only the evaluator knows. According to Michael Patton (1980), "[Michael] Scriven's goal-free model eliminates only one group from the game—local project staff. He directs data only in one clear direction—away from the stated concerns of people who run the program . . . I am unconvinced that the standards he applies are other than his own preferences about what program affects are appropriate and morally defensible" (111).

Utilization-Focused Evaluation

Patton has proposed a different type of evaluation to solve the goals-clarification game called *utilization-focused evaluation.* According to Patton,

this type of evaluation "does not depend on clear, specific, and measurable objectives as the *sine-qua-non* of evaluation research. Clarifying goals is neither necessary nor appropriate in every evaluation" (1978, 117). Utilization-focused evaluation (UFE) uses an open systems approach, which emphasizes disjointed incrementalism, muddling through, and satisficing in contrast to the rational, goal-maximizing perspective of summative evaluations. (See Chapter 3 for a discussion of these concepts.)

There is a need to give some credence to goals in UFE because it is the accepted way of talking about organizations and because different people have different perceptions of what the program's goals should be. But what goals are to be used is a subjective matter. In order to determine which goals to use in UFE, it is necessary to identify the relevant decision makers and use *their* perceptions as the principal criteria. The purpose of a UFE is to provide information that the relevant decision makers—not the evaluation researchers—want.

The focus in UFE is on identification and organization of relevant decision makers and information users. This means locating people who "have a genuine interest in research data—persons who are willing to take the time and effort to interact with evaluators about their information needs and interest" (Patton 1978, 70). These people are not always upper-level personnel; in fact, an evaluator may accomplish more by working with street-level personnel. The questions that the evaluation should address are those that these relevant decision makers specify. The personal factor, says Patton, is thus the key to a successful evaluation because it is based on the assumption that decision making in government is largely a personal and political process rather than a rational and scientific process.

In addition, UFE focuses attention on how the program is being implemented rather than on its impact. Patton (1979, 318–19) describes an evaluation in which researchers used a one-group, pre-test/post-test design on a program designed to teach welfare recipients the basic rudiments of parenting and household management. A sample of welfare recipients were interviewed before and after the program was formally adopted. Since there was no difference, the researchers concluded that the program was ineffective. But Patton investigated further: "As it turned out, there is a very good reason why the program was ineffective. . . . As a result of . . . political battles the program was delayed and further delayed. Procrastination being the better part of valor, the first parenting brochure was never printed, no household management films were ever shown, no workshops were held, and no case workers were ever trained. In short, *the program was never implemented—but it was evaluated*" (1979, 319).

Utilization-focused evaluation avoids this kind of error. Still this type of evaluation has a number of drawbacks. Perhaps the most important involves deciding *who* are the relevant decision makers. Because these people define the objectives of the program, they are crucial to its evaluation. Patton does not give us explicit guidelines for making this decision. How do we determine which members have a "genuine interest in research data"? Should they include the clients of the program—that is, students, welfare recipients, and offenders? Most evaluation researchers interact primarily with middle- and top-level management and are not likely to reach out to the street-level bureaucrat or program clients to include them in the process.

A second problem of utilization-focused evaluation is the possibility that evaluation researchers will be co-opted by those at the top. Evaluation researchers might get most, if not all, of their information about the program from those at the top and come to accept their view as the only legitimate one in the organization. Their reports, therefore, may simply rationalize and legitimize the position of upper-level agency managers.

Formative Evaluation

Evaluating whether and how well a program is implemented is often called *formative evaluation.* Patton (1978) identifies three different types of implementation evaluation as follows: (1) effort evaluation, where the purpose is to determine how much activity has occurred and how well it is done; (2) process evaluation, where the purpose is to determine how the parts of the program have been put together; and (3) treatment specification, where the purpose is to identify just what activities are supposed to have an effect.

Some scholars (Dunn 1981) refer to process evaluation as program monitoring. Monitoring answers the question: "What happened, how, and why?" Dunn characterizes this as "pseudo-evaluation" and distinguishes it from formal, or summative, evaluation, which has the production of information about policy outcomes as its goal.

Whether it is called program monitoring, utilization-focused, process, or formative evaluation, the questions raised when the implementation of a program is evaluated are: What do the clients in the program experience? What services are actually provided to clients? What does the staff do? What is it like to be in the program? How is the program organized? (Leithwood & Montgomery 1980).

Formative evaluation addresses some of the problems that summative and goal-free evaluations overlook. Not only can formative evaluation tell the manager something about how the program is being implemented; it also may be able to identify what is going wrong. This kind of information should be more valuable to program managers since it may help them improve program performance. Formative evaluation overlaps with the concerns of public administration because it attempts to improve program management. For example, it may address the question of whether or not program supervisors are using the right management style or getting the support of those at the lower echelons of an organization.

At the same time, formative evaluation leaves a number of evaluation problems unsolved. Most important, formative evaluation cannot reconcile the fact that different groups within and outside the implementing agencies have different goals or expectations about what the program should be accomplishing (Attkisson & Nguyen 1981). For example, community corrections programs (see Chapter 8) are usually implemented by a number of different agencies such as a state department of corrections, county commissioners, prosecuting attorneys, county corrections directors, probation officers, sheriffs, mental health counselors, and a number of private groups such as volunteers and nonprofit agencies such as the YMCA and churches. Each of these groups have different perceptions about what community corrections is supposed to accomplish. The legislature passes the law because it believes that it will help relieve overcrowding in state prisons and perhaps even alleviate the need to build additional prisons. This was the argument used in many states that adopted community corrections programs. The county commissioners agree to join the program because they believe that it is a way for counties to obtain additional funds for the county. Reform groups believe that such programs will be more successful in rehabilitating offenders, particularly the less serious felony offenders. Judges believe that the program will give them more control over offenders because they can more carefully monitor offenders in the community and determine how long they will have to serve their sentences (Palumbo & Sharp 1980).

These different groups are sometimes called *stakeholders*. Each has a different stake in the program and different expectations about what it will do for their interest. Evaluations that take into account the differing interests of each major group involved in a program are called *responsive evaluations* (Stake 1975; Guba & Lincoln 1981). The failure to consider the interests of stakeholders can seriously impair an evaluation. For example, the director of the Denver Urban Observatory recounts how the Denver City Council rejected a sophisticated cost-benefit analysis of their fire department because it recommended that the city shut down several fire stations. Had evaluators considered the views of citizens beforehand, they would have discovered that most citizens would rather *not* save money if it means closing down a fire station in their neighborhood (Heiss 1974).

A process evaluation has advantages as well. For example, it can help determine whether a program has failed because it has not been adequately implemented. This is illustrated in Case 5–1, which describes a program implemented in Lawrence, Kansas to increase the self-esteem of elementary school children.

Process evaluations also can be used to determine which of several different ways of implementing a given program is better. There are a number of different ways to achieve a given outcome and some may be better than others. For example, community corrections programs rely heavily upon halfway houses to provide various services (such as individual counseling, psychiatric help, alcohol and drug abuse treatment, and help in finding employment) for nonviolent offenders. These halfway houses can be run by state agencies or by private, nonprofit organizations. These two different ways of implementing

CASE 5-1 *The Tribes Program*

In 1982, in Lawrence, Kansas, a new program was introduced in the elementary schools. The purpose was to increase the self-esteem of elementary school students. The program was based on the theory that because children who do well in school have high self-esteem, we should be able to improve the grades of poor children if we improve their self-esteem. Self-esteem was to be increased by putting the children into groups (or "tribes") and allowing them to participate in problem-solving exercises. At the beginning or lowest level, the teacher participated in the group discussions. When the groups reached the highest level, they operated without a teacher. Because they gained confidence in such a setting, their self-esteem also was supposed to increase.

Parents objected strongly to the program, arguing that the values specified in the program were the province of parents, not teachers. They also objected to some of the examples that were being used. They objected particularly to a triage exercise in which a group of children was asked to pretend it was in a lifeboat at sea and one of its members had to be sacrificed so that the others could live. The children who were selected to be sacrificed quite naturally were not happy, nor were their parents.

An impact evaluation at the end of the school year showed that there were no changes in the self-esteem of the students who participated (Palumbo & Wright 1982). However, a process evaluation of the program found that it really had not been implemented by most teachers. Teachers were apparently fearful of the parents' strong objections to the program and decided not to use it. Without this process evaluation, administrators might have concluded that the program was a failure when in fact a more accurate conclusion is that is was never properly implemented.

the same program can be evaluated through a process evaluation to determine which works better, that is, which is more successful in getting the offender reintegrated into the community and finding him or her a job.

A process evaluation of community corrections programs in Oregon, Colorado, and Connecticut found that the private agencies did better than the public agencies (Palumbo, Musheno & Maynard-Moody 1984; Palumbo, Maynard-Moody & Wright 1984). One of the reasons is that the public agency employees who implemented the program in one state did not support it as much as the private agency individuals in the second state. Probation officers in Oregon, where the program was run by public agencies, were lukewarm in their support because of the problems the program posed to their union. Since the program was run by counties, all probation officers in a county that adopted it had to become county employees and give up their state position. This threatened to balkanize the union and greatly weaken it. Thus, the union opposed it and the program was not implemented as well as in the state that used private agencies to implement the program.

Constructionist Evaluation

Social Constructionism is a conceptual orientation that has been used in sociology, criminology, political science, and the humanities. It completely rejects traditional, positivist ontology, epistemology, and methodology. It rejects the positivist ontological belief that there is an empirical "reality" that can be uncovered by research. In evaluations, this means that there isn't a simple program reality concerning whether or not the program has achieved its goals; instead, there are multiple "realities" and the purpose of an evaluation is to discover what these are in the hope that a consensus can be reached among stakeholders. Epistemologically, social constructionism rejects the subject-object duality, or the belief that it is possible for the evaluator to stand apart from the program being evaluated and be objective. Finally, and perhaps most importantly, it rejects the notion that it is possible to reach nomothetic generalizations about programs. Instead, all evaluations are idiographic: each program is unique, and the goal of an evaluation should be to completely understand the context in which the program operates. Thus, case studies are the best method to use. Quantitative methods that focus on "variables" and attempt to statistically analyze relationships among variables, distort knowledge because it strips programs of their context. Moreover, participant observation is the best way to understand programs because it is the only way to see the program as those involved in or affected by the program see it.

■ A CRITIQUE OF SUMMATIVE EVALUATION

The alternative evaluation methods discussed above were developed mainly because of problems encountered in summative evaluations. In this section, we will consider six major drawbacks of summative evaluations. These include: (1) inability to be objective; (2) use of evaluations as political ammunition; (3) vagueness of policy goals; (4) incongruence with the way organizations make decisions; (5) changes in goals during implementation; and (6) the difficulty of controlling for other factors that affect program impacts.

Inability to Be Objective A study conducted by the George Washington University Center for Social Policy Studies, after an in-depth analysis of the federal government's evaluations of social programs, concluded that the much-touted, objective, scientific conclusion of evaluations are too often found to be based on hidden political and social value judgments or personal interests. No matter how hard they may try, evaluators have values that cannot be completely suppressed. A summative evaluation applies scientific methods to objectively determine whether a program is achieving its intended goals. But data do not speak for themselves; they must be located first, and then interpreted. Consciously or not, the evaluator's own preferences and values concerning a program's goals will influence what data will be found and how they are interpreted. An evaluator with conservative leanings is less likely to find data that show government welfare programs are working than one who has liberal predilections. Moreover, the type of research methods used by the evaluator influence the kinds of data found; quantitative methods focus on different kinds of data than qualitative methods. Thus, one major problem with summative evaluations is that they cannot be completely objective, even though the assumptions made in summative evaluations is that they can discover "the truth."

Use of Evaluations as Political Ammunition Summative evaluation is not always what policy makers actually want. According to [F. Williams] Heiss (1974), a former director of the Denver Urban Observatory (a federally-sponsored agency aimed at analyzing and finding solutions for urban problems), "the rational methodology of evaluation poses serious threats for the local government policy maker. . . . Officeholders want to reduce conflict, to keep things calm before elections while opponents need cannon fodder to gain headlines. An evaluation report produces just that kind of cannon fodder that political opponents can use" (40). Heiss describes how an opponent of the mayor of Denver, in a successful campaign to unseat the mayor, used evaluations of programs conducted *with the mayor's support.* This kind of experience makes politicians somewhat leery of using evaluation research. Heiss quotes Governor Walker of Illinois in a speech as follows: "Very rarely does one see anything in the medium about government program evaluation unless it has to do with scandal" (1974, 40).

Vagueness of Policy Goals There is good reason why program goals usually are vague. As pointed out in Chapter 4, legislators often write legislation with vague goals in order to get the support from stakeholders needed to pass legislation. Legislation that has clear goals is more likely to alienate those who do not agree with the goals. Second, the legislature may not know exactly what it wants to achieve and may pass the problem on to the executive branch. Third, there is political advantage in being vague because it is easier to avoid criticism when there is flexibility in what a particular policy means. As a result of these and other factors, much of the legislation initiating new programs lacks clear goals. This leaves evaluators with the task of attempting to clarify goals when they evaluate a program, which they often do unsuccessfully (Patton 1980).

Lack of Congruence with Organizational Decision Making A fourth problem with summative evaluation is that it is not congruent with the way an organization actually makes decisions. Summative evaluation assumes that organizations really try to identify goals and find ways to maximize their achievements. But most public agencies are not so rational (Palumbo & Nachmias 1984). This is not because public agencies are inefficient or incompetent, but because the problems they work with are very complex and difficult to define in a single quantitative index such as profits. According to Heiss, "The process of identifying goals, establishing measurable criteria, and collecting program data are techniques designed to eliminate ambiguity when ambiguity may be what has given the program its genesis and sustained its continuity" (1974, 41). William Dunn argues in the same vein: "Many of the most important policy problems . . . are sufficiently complex, messy, and ill-structured for the 'problem-solving' model of policy analysis. They are problems for which this model is inappropriate or simply inapplicable" (1981, 356). Policy making is a complex phenomenon involving numerous individuals and agencies pursuing diverse and often competing goals. It is not often possible to characterize this process in the form of a rational model.

Changes in Goals during Implementation The rational model does not allow for the possibility that goals may change during implementation. But changes are almost inevitable in all public programs (Majone & Wildavsky 1984;

CASE 5–2 *Medical Education in New York*

In the late 1970s, the state of New York tried to increase the proportion of medical doctors entering primary care specialties and reduce specialization, encourage location of physicians in rural (small town) areas, and improve the clinical experience of students (Cingranelli, Hoffebert & Ziegenhagan 1981). To this end, the state opened a new regional campus and appointed a dean to head it. As he wrestled with the conflicting pressures from the local community, health-system agencies, hospital administrators, and local physicians, the dean developed new, more operational goals and downplayed the original goals. The immediate objectives adopted by the dean were to recruit personnel, establish working relationships with the hospital in the area, help local physicians enhance teaching skills, and develop the budget (Cingranelli et al. 1981, 41). The reasons for the shift in goals according to the authors of the study were: (1) the original policy was formulated without clearly specified goals, thereby giving administrators considerable discretion to decide what specific goals would be emphasized; (2) local administrators disagreed with the originally stated goals; and (3) the community resisted the original goals.

Palumbo & Harder 1981). Cases 5–2 and 5–3 illustrate this point. Neither of these cases is unusual.

Inability to Control for Other Factors In order to be able to say that a program produced a specific outcome rather than other factors, it is necessary to control for the other factors. This may be difficult—or even impossible—however, if a true laboratory experiment cannot be conducted (Tittle 1985).

The crackdown on speeders is a good illustration. For example, suppose a public official orders a crackdown on all speeders on the state's highways in order to reduce the level of fatalities, which had been increasing rapidly. After much fanfare, the program is begun and shortly afterward there is a drop in highway fatalities. The public official who began the program announces with even greater fanfare that the program is a tremendous success. Was she justified in claiming credit? Did the crackdown work? Not necessarily. A claim

CASE 5–3 ***Blind Vendors in California***

In 1945, the state of California began a program under federal legislation that placed blind persons as vendors in stands and snack bars in federal buildings through its Business Enterprise Program (BEP), operated by the Department of Rehabilitation. The program was looked upon as sheltered employment for those who could not participate in the competitive market. By 1973, the policy goals had changed. They shifted from a narrow focus upon employability as a rehabilitation objective toward a broader concern with mainstreaming the rights of disabled persons in society (Kress et al. 1981, 24).

Policy makers in the California Department of Rehabilitation began to believe that the program was rehabilitating very few disabled persons and that it isolated vendors from the competitive market, thereby discouraging independence and self-help. Confusion developed over whether the program's actual purpose was rehabilitation or developing independent business persons. Interest groups for the blind sought to emphasize the policy's success in providing opportunities for blind persons in business. In the early years of the program, most blind vendors operated small tobacco-stand locations that offered a limited variety of items. But by 1970, more people took to eating meals away from home, and by the 1980s, a number of blind vendors operated large, full-service cafeterias that grossed over half a million dollars in annual sales (Kress et al. 1981, 25).

Thus, following an evaluation of the program, the administrators decided that the BEP was a business enterprise aimed at providing opportunities for blind persons, not a rehabilitation program.

that it did could be justified only if all of the other variables that could have led to the drop in accidental fatalities were controlled. There might have been a change in weather that reduced the number of miles driven, and therefore, the number of fatalities. Or the number of accidents may have experienced a *regression effect*, meaning that the number may have already peaked, and was experiencing a natural, expected decline.

The problem with summative evaluation is that it is not possible to control for all variables unless we use experimental designs. Since this is seldom possible, most evaluations cannot reach unequivocal conclusions.

As a result of these six major drawbacks, summative evaluations have somewhat limited utility. It would be wrong to conclude they have no value at all. But unless they are accompanied by a process or formative evaluation, they can actually be misleading (Palumbo & Sharp 1980). Of course, rigorous methods can help overcome some of the problems associated with summative evaluations. But there always will be some doubt that all factors have been controlled and most practitioners want and need more certainty in order to be able to defend their programs.

PROGRAM EVALUATION AND POLICY ANALYSIS METHODS

There are numerous evaluation methods and techniques. The policy analysis techniques used by economists are quite different from the evaluation research methods pioneered by psychologists. Both are so numerous and complex that it would take a rather large volume just to describe them. Thus, we will only describe a few of the major techniques from each area. Before proceeding, however, we will briefly consider where these techniques fit into the broader picture of research methods.

Research methods can be divided into two main categories: *quantitative* and *qualitative*. Quantitative techniques are numerical, and require that the phenomena being studied be expressed in mathematical terms. Qualitative techniques are nonnumerical and rely upon personal familiarization with the behavior being studied. The latter is usually obtained through participant observation. A scientific study is often equated with quantitative methods such as those employed in mathematics, statistics, and computer science. More recently, however, there has been a recognition that quantitative methods are compatible with qualitative methods as well, especially in the social sciences (Palumbo & Musheno 1984).

The principal quantitative techniques used in policy analysis come from economics. They include linear and dynamic programming, decision trees, numerous statistical methods, cost-effectiveness, and cost-benefit analysis. The latter two, which we will describe next, are used extensively in public policy.

The principal quantitative techniques used in evaluation research come from the disciplines of psychology and sociology. They include interrupted time-series analysis, which we describe below, and a host of statistical techniques. Policy analysis and program evaluation are both based on numerical data, thus it is necessary to measure program variables with some degree of precision in order to use these techniques.

Qualitative methods, on the other hand, are based on data such as detailed, narrative descriptions of situations, events, people, interactions, and behavior. These are collected through open-ended questions in order to try to capture the point of view of those involved. Case studies are the principal way that qualitative research is presented. The principal assumption of the qualitative method is that an understanding of program activities and outcomes will emerge from personal experience with the program (Patton 1978, 41).

Sometimes quantitative and qualitative methods are combined in an evaluation (Cook 1985). Called *triangulation,* it combines the two methods in four ways (Denzin 1978). One is to have both numerical (hard) and non-numerical (soft) data pertaining to program activities and outcomes. The second is to have one investigator use quantitative methods and another use qualitative methods and compare their results. A third is to use alternative theories on the same data and see which one fits best. The fourth is to use quantitative combined with qualitative data collection methods.

The following two sections outline two major techniques, one from evaluation analysis and another from policy analysis. Neither of these methods involves extensive quantification; they are among the simpler quantitative policy analysis and program evaluation techniques.

Time-Series Analysis

The first program evaluation technique we will describe is *time-series analysis.* This technique was used to analyze a program aimed at reducing the number of people who drive after drinking alcoholic beverages through general and specific deterrence. By passing and enforcing stiff laws, the program aimed to prevent people from driving after drinking. The stiffest laws against driving while intoxicated are in European countries, particularly Sweden and Norway. The laws of both these countries are much harsher than the laws in the United States.

In all laws, drunken driving is defined in terms of the amount of alcohol in one's blood. In Sweden, anyone having .5 or more *pro mille* alcohol (milligrams of alcohol per milliliter of blood), or .05 percent blood alcohol content (BAC) in American notation, is considered to be drunk. The permissible blood level in the United States is 1.0 *pro mille* or .10 percent BAC. Thus, a person has to drink considerably more in the United States than in Sweden in order to be considered drunk. Moreover, in Sweden, finding that one has .5 or more *pro mille* is conclusive evidence of drunk driving, while in the United States it is merely presumptive evidence. The sentences in Sweden also are harsher. In Sweden, a person with between .5 and 1.5 *pro mille* is defined as "driving while intoxicated," and a fine is imposed equal to two months pay, plus suspension of driving privileges for six or more months. For over 1.5 *pro mille,* called "drunk driving," the penalty is a prison sentence of one month and suspension of driving privileges for one year.

An extensive analysis of whether such stiff laws deter drunk driving was done by Larry Ross (1982). After examining the impact of such laws in Sweden, Norway, and France, Ross concluded that they in fact deter drunk driving, but only temporarily. After an initial decline over a short period of time, the amount of fatalities due to drunk driving increases again. Ross believes that what occurred in Norway and France is that the initial publicity surrounding the adoption of drunk driving laws had the effect of reducing drunk driving, but the effect soon dissipated as drivers learned that the probability of being caught was in fact very low. However, in Sweden, the chance of being caught remained high and, as a result, the law there is more effective. The chance of being charged with drunk driving in Sweden is one out of every 200, whereas in the United States, it is one in 2,000. The probability of receiving the full sentence when caught is very high in Sweden. Of the 5,808 Swedish motorists convicted of driving while intoxicated in 1975, 99 percent were given the two months salary fine and one percent were imprisoned. Of the 5,571 convicted of drunk driving, 70 percent were sent to prison, 14 percent were fined, and 12 percent were given conditional release (Snortum 1984, 27).

The deterrent effect of stiff laws can be illustrated with the following example. In 1978, the French Parliament adopted a strict law that provided for breath-testing of all drivers passing through roadblocks set up for this purpose. The law was passed after strenuous debate. The beverage industry and automobile clubs opposed the law. The debate focused on the balance between personal liberty and the public interest. The latter won, and the law was passed on July 12, 1978.

The law provided for roadblocks in which every driver stopped could be required to submit to a screening test for alcohol. Failure to submit resulted in immediate suspension of driving privileges and penalties. If a person has more than .8 *pro mille,* the penalty was revocation of driving privileges for six months and a stiff fine.

Shortly after the law was passed, the automobile accident figures declined, which was said to be due to the law. The Interministerial Committee for Road Safety—equivalent of the U.S. National Highway Traffic Safety Administration—declared in its newsletter: "Towards a record year for highway safety—thanks to the Alcotest law, an exceptional summer" (Ross 1982, 36).

The beverage industry attacked the law as a declaration of war on the traditional beverage of the French people. The controversy stirred up by the law ensured that the majority of the population knew about the law. A survey of adults taken in August of 1978 found that 97 percent knew about the law's existence, and 66 percent could specify what the legal blood alcohol content was to qualify for drunk driving.

As a result, the crash-related injuries showed a sharp drop—one that is statistically significant (see Figure 5–1). The drop in 1978 was about 12.5 percent of the average crash rate. But the trend moved back up as deterrence dissipated over the next eight and a half months. However, the campaign *did* avert 11,000 injuries and 700 deaths during the period it was effective (Ross 1982, 39).

Interrupted time-series analysis is the statistical method used to test whether or not the drop in alcohol-related fatalities is due to chance fluctuations or due to a new program or law's intervention. It is an elegant method for testing the effects of an intervention such as the adoption of the stiff law in France in 1978. However, many problems are associated with such analyses. The principal question is whether the drop in fatalities is

FIGURE 5–1 Crash-related deaths in France with seasonal variation removed.

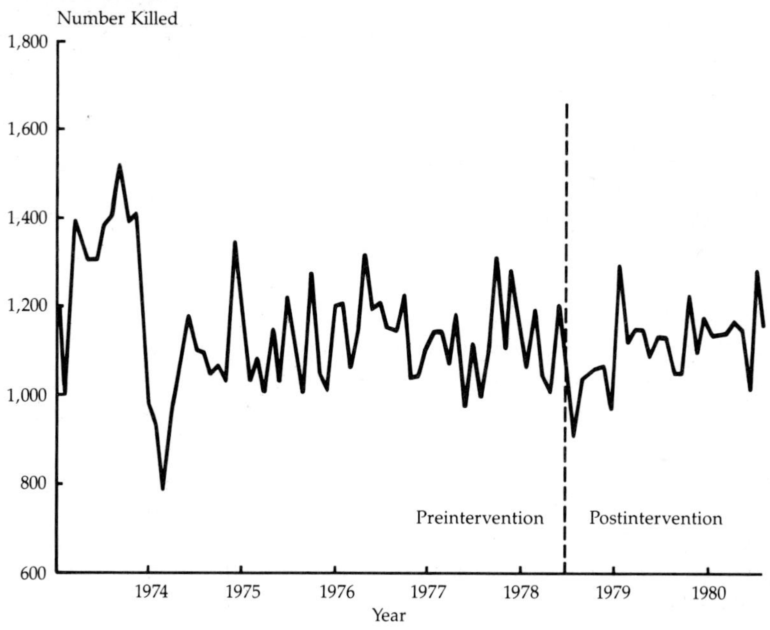

Source: Reprinted by permission of the publisher, from *Deterring the Drinking Driver: Legal Policy and Social Control* by H. Laurence Ross, (Lexington, MA: Lexington Books, D.C. Heath and Co.) Copyright 1984.

actually due to the intervention and not to other factors. Social interventions are often introduced when a number of other things are occurring, and it is sometimes difficult to determine if the drop is due to the intervention or to these other factors. For example, suppose we introduce the law concerning drunk driving at the same time that there is a great deal of publicity about the law which increases drivers' awareness of the risks and reduces the social acceptability of driving while intoxicated. It would be difficult to determine whether the drop in the number of accidents was due to the stiffer drunk driving law or to these other factors.

Statistical techniques can be used to tell if the drop is a chance phenomenon rather than a real one. Because the crash rate normally shifts from year to year, a slight drop may be due to this normal, chance shifting. Statistical methods can be used to determine what the probabilities are of this occurring. Usually, if the probability of a drop of a particular magnitude occurring by chance is less than 5 out of 100, we reject the notion that it is a chance phenomenon. We would then try to statistically eliminate any fluctuations that occur during particular seasons. For example, it may be the case that fatal crashes increase during the summer because more people drive then. We can account for (that is, control) these seasonal fluctuations statistically and inspect the remaining drop to see if it could be due to chance.

Once we have completed the statistical analyses, we must eliminate other possible explanations. For example, part of the drop in the number of crashes in France after the introduction of the 1978 law might be due to changes in drinking habits. However, wine sales and consumption per capita remained the same after 1978; thus this could not account for the drop. The number of miles driven in 1978 is another possible explanation, but this did not change either. Other factors that might account for the drop are a change in weather, changes in the amount of enforcement by police, and other things that we do not know about. In this particular example, corroborating evidence pretty much eliminated many of these other known and unknown explanations. This evidence is based on roadside inspections conducted after the law went into effect that found that the proportion of drivers with illegal concentrations of blood alcohol dropped from 3.4 percent before the law took effect to 1.8 percent after. The drop of 1.6 percent is too large to be due to sampling error, and thus seems to confirm that the law, or the publicity that accompanied it, reduced the number of people driving while intoxicated.

Another difficulty in determining whether an intervention has an effect is that a particular law such as the 1978 drunk driving law in France is just one in a series of laws dealing with the same problem. For example, in 1965, France passed a law requiring that persons suspected of drunk driving be given breath tests, and this was made stiffer in 1970 when blood tests were made compulsory for certain accidents. The 1970 law also defined drunk driving as driving with a blood alcohol content in excess of .8 *pro mille,* and increased the penalties. Thus, the 1978 law was an extension of earlier laws.

We might, therefore, expect that the drop after the 1978 law would only be an incremental one if these earlier laws had any lasting deterrent effect.

In many cases, the social intervention may simply codify changes that had been occurring prior to the introduction of the law. The community corrections law in Oregon is such an example. The law was passed by the legislature in Oregon in 1977, although community corrections programs had been introduced in several counties as early as 1972 through federal funds provided by the Law Enforcement Assistance Administration. In these counties, community corrections programs were well under way before they were officially adopted by the state. As a result, we should not expect to observe a large change in these particular counties after the law was introduced.

One final problem in determining whether an intervention really has had an effect is establishing exactly when the intervention was implemented (Musheno 1981). As in the Oregon example, laws are not always implemented immediately after they are passed. They may be implemented incrementally before they actually are passed, or they may never be fully implemented. For example, from the time the drunk driving law was passed in France, from July of 1978 to January of 1979, only 1,100 roadblocks were authorized throughout France, and only 1,416 positive results were found (Ross 1982, 42). This indicates that there was official diffidence to enforcement of this law. Hence, the drop in fatal crashes that occurred was probably more of a result of the publicity given the law than a result of its enforcement (Legge & Webb 1982).

Similarly, Ross (1982) found that the drop in fatal crashes in Sweden after the introduction of a stiff law in 1974 was not significant, indicating that deterrence had little effect. However, an analysis of the data by another investigator shows that there was a small proportion of alcohol-impaired drivers on the road, and a lower rate of alcohol-related traffic deaths among Scandinavian drivers compared to American drivers, but this was due to a variety of legal, social, psychological, and cultural variables rather than to deterrence alone. John Snortum (1984) found that 61 percent of Swedes endorsed the .5 *pro mille* standard of the law, 25 percent felt it should be even stricter, and only 6 percent felt it was too harsh. Americans do not show as great an endorsement nor believe that drunk driving is as serious an offense as Swedes. For example, when asked to rate the seriousness of various crimes, Americans in Baltimore gave bank robbery a rating of 8.02 and drunk driving 6.55, whereas Swedes rated bank robbery 8.56 and drunk driving 8.59. This difference in attitudes about seriousness of drunk driving led Snortum to conclude that the moral endorsement of a law strengthens its effectiveness. Hence, specific implementation of the law may be less important in determining how much effect it has than public endorsement.

These difficulties in unequivocally sorting out the effect of a program are a major reason why it may be difficult for policy makers to place much of their decision weight on formal evaluations. Equivocation and debate are standard fare in academic research. The replication of studies that question the findings of previous research contribute substantially to advances in knowledge. But decision makers cannot base their decisions on things that only *may* be true lest they come under heavy criticism for adopting policies they should not have adopted. If they claim that they believed there was a good chance that they were right when they made the decision, they may be severely criticized. Policy makers are supposed to be certain, not just 90 percent confident, in their decisions.

Cost-Benefit Analysis

Policy analysis can be helpful in reaching a decision as long as it is not the only factor being considered. As we shall see, however, nonrational factors—such as the power of those opposing a "rational" solution, or the cultural beliefs of people—often play a more important role. This second example illustrates the policy analysis technique of *cost-benefit analysis.* Formal cost-benefit analysis has its intellectual roots in nineteenth century utilitarianism and neo-classical economics. It was first used by the federal government in 1936 through the U.S. Flood Control Act which specified that the federal government should improve navigable waters and their tributaries "if the benefits to whomsoever they accrue are in excess of the estimated costs." Cost-benefit studies subsequently were conducted for most federal water projects. By 1950, the procedures for such analyses were standardized and became widespread not only in the water resources field, but in transportation, health, and defense. By 1973, cost-benefit analyses began to consider not only simple objectives but trade-offs between competing objectives. For example, in water resources, these competing objectives were economic development versus environmental quality. Many people criticized cost-benefit analysis because of the difficulty of translating the benefits of many public programs into dollar amounts. For example, what are the dollar benefits of a health policy such as Medicare? As we shall see in Chapter 6, this is not easy to measure.

In order to use cost-benefit analysis, one must be able to quantitatively measure the benefits of a specific alternative. The use of restraining devices in automobiles in order to reduce injuries and deaths seems to fit this prerequisite. Thus, we will use it to illustrate this technique.

Automobile Safety Considerable controversy has dominated the issue of automobile safety. About 45,000 people are killed in automobile accidents every year, and hundreds of thousands are injured. The total cost of these accidents is in the billions of dollars. There is no doubt that society has an interest in trying to reduce this huge cost, even if it means encroaching somewhat on the private interests of those who would be affected by governmental regulations in this area.

There have been virulent debates in Congress, the executive branch, and the courts over this problem. The principal themes raised during these debates pertain to consumer choice, free enterprise, the effectiveness of different safety devices, the benefits derived from regulations, and the consumer's willingness to pay for greater safety.

American public policy is far behind Europe in this area. Several European countries have adopted laws that require people to use their seat and shoulder belts or be fined. Several states in the United States have also enacted mandatory seat belt laws. In 1955, the Ford Motor Company was the first company to make lap belts optional in its cars; by 1964, 14 states required that cars sold in their states have lap seat belts. The auto industry soon responded by making lap seat belts standard in all cars. This was codified in 1968 through the Federal Motor Vehicle Safety Standards Act (FMVSSA), which required all automobiles to be equipped with lap/shoulder belts. Except for a few changes, including an unsuccessful attempt to force motorists to use the belts through ignition interlock devices, American public policy in 1992 remained much the same as it was in 1968.

During the 1950s and 1960s, the United States conducted research on passive safety devices such as the air bag. Called "passive" because the driver is not required to activate them in order for them to work, air bags were technologically feasible by 1972. Another passive safety device is the automatic seat belt which fastens around the driver and front-seat passenger upon starting the car. However, none of these passive systems was adopted in the United States. Instead, American public policy relies on passengers voluntarily fastening seat belts, but this has not been effective. Only about 10 percent of automobile passengers on the average actually use seat belts. This is tragic because seat belts can reduce injuries and fatalities if they are used. Educational campaigns to get more auto passengers to use their seat belts have had little, if any, effect.

In 1966, Congress enacted the National Transportation and Motor Vehicle Safety Act which created the National Highway Traffic Safety Administration (NHTSA). This agency was responsible for adopting standards to enhance the "crashworthiness" of cars sold in the United States—that is, to try to improve the ability of autos to withstand crashes through better absorbency of shocks and better bumpers. In 1972, NHTSA required that all cars sold in the United States be equipped with passive restraints by 1975. But in 1974, Congress responded to pressures from the auto industry when it passed the NHTSA appropriations bill and required that all regulations proposed by NHTSA be submitted to Congress for approval. In effect, this gave Congress the option to veto standards adopted by NHTSA.

Subsequent attempts by NHTSA to require auto manufacturers to install passive restraints on cars met with such intense controversy that in 1976, the Secretary of Transportation proposed a voluntary passive restraint demonstration program. Under the proposed program, manufacturers were to install air bags in at least 500,000 new cars between 1979 and 1980 for no more than $100 per car. A voluntary agreement was signed with the auto companies that was to take effect in 1980. But the incoming Carter administration decided that the voluntary demonstration program was not strong enough and, instead, mandated that manufacturers install air bags on the phase-in basis so that by 1984 *all* new cars would be equipped with the device.

Congress balked at this and amended the rule to prohibit enforcement by NHTSA unless consumers were offered a choice between air bags and manual seat belts. Before this could take effect, however, the Reagan administration came to power, and on April 6, 1981, the rule was delayed, and then rescinded in October of 1981. The action was praised by the automobile industry and castigated by consumer and safety advocates. Carnegie-Mellon professors of engineering who studied the cost-effectiveness of the issue were disappointed: "It is sad and ironic that, despite over a decade of attention to [automobile] occupant-restraint policy by government, consumer groups, legislators, and corporations, the proportion of motorists protected by any occupant restraint (active or passive) is less today than it was in 1970" (Graham, Henrion & Morgan 1981, 10).

During the next three years of the Reagan administration, delays and court suits dominated automobile safety issues. Despite efforts by Congress to breathe life back into the air bag, the administration's delaying tactics succeeded in preventing action. On July 11, 1984, Secretary of Transportation Elizabeth Dole announced a new version of the passive restraint rule. It ordered all automakers to install air bags or automatic seat belts in all new passenger cars sold in the United States by 1989 unless states representing two-thirds of the population passed legislation requiring the use of seat belts before then. Thus, in 1986, the situation remained as uncertain as it had for the previous 15 years. Eight years later, in 1994, the government still had not required auto manufacturers to install airbags, but many manufacturers began putting them in as standard equipment, primarily on the more expensive cars.

An extensive cost-benefit analysis conducted by Carnegie-Mellon researchers in 1981 found that the existing American policy toward restraint systems is the least cost-effective and has the lowest cost-benefit ratio of the several alternatives it investigated. These alternatives include mandated seat belt use laws, air bags, and air bags combined with mandated seat belt use laws. The following description briefly summarizes these alternatives and their associated costs and benefits.

Costs and Benefits of Mandatory Seat Belt Use About 25,000 front-seat passengers die in crashes each year and over 500,000 more suffer moderate to serious injuries. Many of them die or are injured because they do not buckle their seat belts. It is difficult to explain just why people fail to use their seat belts, but Graham et al. (1981) speculate that it is due primarily to the way people compute the chances of being injured or killed in an auto accident. Most people calculate their chances on the basis of a single trip rather than over the course of their lifetime, and they also tend to believe that their individual chances are better than "the other guy's." On a single trip, the chances of being seriously injured or killed in an auto accident are pretty remote. The chance of being killed is 1.4 in 10 million, and the chance of being injured is 2.5 in a million. But over the course of a lifetime, the chances are much greater. The chance of being killed is 1 in 100, and the chance of a serious injury is 1 in 6. Motorists should use the latter statistics when they calculate their chance of injury or death, but they don't. Moreover, they underestimate their own chances. In a national survey reported by Graham et al. (1981), only 23 percent of the respondents said that their chance of injury or death was greater than the national average and most felt that they were less likely than the average to be injured. When asked if their chances of injury or death were greater, the same, or less than people like themselves, 40 percent said less and 45 percent said the same; only six percent said greater than people like themselves.

In calculating the costs and benefits of a mandated seat belt use law, air bags, and the existing system, Graham et al. (1981) made two major assumptions. One is that all policies could take effect immediately for the entire fleet of cars on the road, and the other is that all other factors (such as a shift to smaller cars, speed limits, miles traveled, and highway improvements) remained the same. They also used the advice of experts, other studies, and what people appear to be willing to pay for safety in getting estimates for uncertain parameters such as the effectiveness of restraints, usage rates, the costs of restraint systems, and the value of human life. Thus, it is obvious that a lot of assumptions must be made just to begin cost-benefit analysis.

The analysis begins with a base-case scenario, a system wherein there are no restraint systems in cars at all, and therefore, no use of restraint devices. Then, based on certain assumptions, the analysis estimates how many lives are saved under the current belt system policy in existence in the United States in 1955. This is depicted in Table 5–1. Assuming that installing seat belts costs $75 per car, and that seat belts are installed in 10 million new cars, annualizing these costs over the life of a car at 5 percent per annum, the total cost of the current seat-belt policy is approximately $900 million. Next, making assumptions about the effectiveness of lap/shoulder harnesses, and about how many injuries equal one fatality (they assume that 70 injuries equal one death, based on costs), the authors of the study conclude that the current system averts a total of 1,670 fatalities a year. Thus, the cost per fatality of the system in use is approximately $538,000—not a very cost-effective alternative.

A similar set of assumptions and analyses can be made for a compulsory seat-belt law and for a combination air-bag/seat-belt law. As Table 5–1 shows, the compulsory seat-belt law is the most cost-effective at a cost of $114,000 per life saved, while the air-bag law is second, at a cost of $220,000 per life saved.

Which policy is best? If cost-effectiveness is the sole criterion for making the decision, then a mandatory seat-belt law is the best choice. But if other criteria are to be used, then this is not the best choice. For example, if the

TABLE 5-1 *Cost-Effectiveness of Policy Options*

	Fatalities Averted				Approximate Economic Costs per Fatality Avoided	
Policy Options	Total	Rank	Incremental	Rank	Total	Rank
Base-Case Scenario	—	—	—	—	—	—
Current Lap/Shoulder Belt Requirement	1,670	(7)	—	—	$538,000	(7)
Educational Campaign for Belt Use	2,660	(6)	990	(6)	380,000	(6)
Compulsory Belt Usage Law	8,430	(3)	6,760	(3)	114,000	(1)
FMVSS 208 (Adams Plan)	3,690	(5)	2,020	(5)	357,000	(5)
Passive Belt Design Standard	7,120	(4)	5,450	(4)	185,000	(2)
Air Bag/Lap Belt Design Standard	12,440	(2)	10,770	(2)	265,000	(4)
Air Bag/Lap Belt Usage Law	15,000	(1)	13,330	(1)	220,000	(3)

Source: John Graham, Max Henrion & M. Granger Morgan, "An Analysis of Federal Policy Toward Automobile Safety Belts and Air Bags," Carnegie Mellon University, 1981, p. 67.

number of lives saved is the principal factor in the decision, as some policy analysts would urge (Nagel 1981), then the air-bag option is the best because it saves about 15,000 lives, whereas the compulsory seat-belt law saves only 8,430. Thus, under the circumstances, the most cost-effective law may not be the most desirable policy option if we consider the total number of lives saved to be more important.

Cost-benefit analysis is yet another criterion that might be used. To do a cost-benefit analysis, it is necessary to translate the benefits—in this case, lives saved—into dollar amounts so that a cost-benefit ratio can be computed. Translating lives saved into dollars is not easy, as it is obviously difficult to estimate how much a human life is worth. Economists use several methods for calculating the value of a human life. These are: (1) expected life-time earnings; (2) awards in court cases; and (3) what people are willing to pay. None of these methods is considered to be without its flaws. Graham et al. (1981) use the third method in their study and calculate that a life is worth $700,000. Using this figure, they compute a cost-benefit ratio and conclude that the compulsory seat-belt law is still the best alternative, with air bags coming in second, and the existing system a very poor third.

A number of assumptions were made in this analysis and, as with any policy analysis, the results that come out are no better than the assumptions that go into it. Changing one or two assumptions can alter the results, and so it is essential to look carefully at how reasonable the assumptions are before the results are deemed credible.

It is unlikely that a policy maker will have the time, inclination, or ability to investigate thoroughly the reasonableness of all of the assumptions made in a cost-benefit analysis. Yet without considering how reasonable the assumptions are, policy makers may be reluctant to place much weight on the conclusions. Of course, policy analysis is not likely to be the only factor in a decision. According to Graham et al. (1981, 10), policy analysis should be only one factor in a decision along with things such as ethics, public acceptance, political feasibility, equity, and justice. Another policy analyst writes: "Policy analysis is not simply a scientific and technical process; it is also a social and political process where the scope and intensity of interaction among stakeholders governs the way that information is produced, transformed, and utilized" (Dunn 1981, 355). Two major factors militating against adoption of more "rational" (that is, cost-effective and cost-beneficial) auto safety policies are the power of the automobile industry, an important stakeholder, and cultural beliefs about the extent to which the government *ought* to regulate in this area. In regard to the latter, many Americans believe that individuals have the right to choose whether or not to use seat belts and the government should not try to force them to do so. The automobile industry has consistently taken the stand that it is drivers who cause accidents, therefore, they should be responsible for their own safety (Tolchin 1984). Thus, a law that mandates the use of seat belts might not be as effective in the United States as it is in Europe. A mandatory seat-belt law may not be as effective in operation as the policy analysts estimate because American drivers may find ways to circumvent the system. Estimates of how many lives a compulsory seat-belt law would save, therefore, could be distorted.

In some cases, cost-benefit analysis may be used to serve political ends. Even though it appears to be an objective and neutral technique, cost-benefit analysis is susceptible to political manipulation. This was demonstrated by the Reagan administration with regard to governmental regulations in health and other areas (Tolchin 1984). On February 17, 1981, shortly after he took office, Reagan signed Executive Order 12291, which established the dominance of cost-benefits principles for the evaluation of all major regulations issued by government. In implementation, the Reagan order was used to emphasize the costs of regulations to business and industry and to ignore the benefits of clean air and water, occupational injuries avoided, auto fatalities avoided, and better informed consumers. Similarly, the cost of installing seat belts and the effect of this on the automobile industry were considered to be more important than lives saved or injuries prevented. Thus, even when cost-benefit analysis supports regulation, as was the case concerning automatic safety restraints, the regulations may be rescinded. In this case, the Reagan administration rescinded the regulation and rejected the anticipated benefits because of the uncertainty about incremental seat-belt use.

■ DECISION MAKING AND EVALUATION RESEARCH

Evaluations are supposed to help decision makers make better decisions, but most decision makers do not actually determine whether or not there should be a mandatory seat-belt law, whether or not women should be permitted to get abortions when they want, or whether busing will be used to achieve integration in a school district. This is because decisions accrete through small uncoordinated steps taken in many places, by elected representatives, interest groups, the media, the public, and administrators (Weiss 1980, 382). Decision makers and program administrators seldom decide at a particular instant in time to adopt or discontinue a program; they seldom decide to restructure organizations; and they seldom decide to undertake new initiatives even though, in all these cases, they may have access to evaluation research that suggest they do just that.

Decisions are not discrete events. They are part of a process that extends over time, that is affected by many variables, and that no single individual—even the President of the United States, or the head of a large corporation—actually makes. Someone may have to acknowledge responsibility for a specific decision as indicated by Harry Truman's famous statement "The buck stops here." And, if things go right, there will be no shortage of people who claim they made the decision as indicated by John F. Kennedy's famous statement that "victory has 100 fathers and defeat is an orphan." Even an important step toward a decision, such as one made by a congressional appropriations committee not to fund a given project, is only one step in a complex chain of events, activities, memos, and the like that continue even after that decision is made.

The type of evaluation research that is used in a particular case will depend upon the kind of decision-making process that is used. It would be appropriate, for example, to use a rationally-oriented type of evaluation such as cost-benefit analysis if the decision-making process in organizations is not rational. A great deal of evaluation research is based on the assumptions of microeconomic theory. That is, individuals and organizations are assumed to be rational, and to behave so as to maximize some identifiable goal or set of goals. Accordingly, the principal job of the evaluator is to identify these objectives, and to estimate the relative effectiveness of different strategies for attaining them. But what if decision makers pay little attention to the relative effectiveness of different strategies for attaining the objectives stipulated in an evaluation? Suppose they are more likely to act first and only then analyze why it is they did what they did (Palumbo & Nachmias 1984). Suppose further that decision makers conduct their analyses intuitively and store them in personal memories, so that when the organization is faced with a similar situation in the future, its members recall previous experiences and try to apply these to the new situation. They do *not* reanalyze, search for alternatives, nor establish desired objectives. Instead, they repeat the cycle of acting first and then analyzing why they acted as they did. Obviously, in such a situation microeconomic methods will be of little help for these organizations.

Microeconomic methods of making decisions are called *synoptic-rational* models. They assume that organizations behave in the following ways: (1) a problem is perceived; (2) information is gathered about the problem; (3) objectives or goals for solving the problem are established; (4) alternative ways of achieving the goals are listed; (5) the alternative that achieves the greatest amount of goals at the least cost is selected; and (6) this alternative is implemented.

If, in fact, organizations act in this rational fashion, then we would observe the following five preconditions for successfully evaluating the program:

1. The program must have clearly stated goals on which all relevant participants agree.
2. An explicit technology for achieving these goals must exist and be implemented.
3. The methodology for determining the extent to which the program produces the outcomes must be available.
4. The managers of the program being evaluated must be committed to working toward achieving program goals through the alternative selected.
5. Decision makers must be committed to utilize the results of the evaluation.

An evaluation cannot be successful unless all of these preconditions are met. But they seldom are. As we have already observed, legislation is often ambiguous because it is politically expedient to be ambiguous. Moreover, goals do not become less ambiguous when they are delegated to administrative agencies for implementation. In regard to Precondition 2, technologies are seldom available for achieving goals. We do not know how to eliminate the causes of poverty and crime, nor how to design the perfect implementing organization. Regarding Precondition 4, the ideal program manager is committed to working toward achieving program goals, but we do not always have ideal managers. Finally, decision makers are not always committed to using the results of evaluation, especially if they are negative. The synoptic-rational model of organizational decision making is based on preconditions that are seldom, if ever, realized. Why, then should evaluations be based on them?

The alternative decision structure can be called the *reverse decision cycle,* or the *garbage can model* (Weick 1976; Dunsire 1978). In this model, instead of organizations trying to find solutions to problems, agency executives have solutions and they look for problems to which these solutions can be attached. Instead of analysis first and action following, the usual pattern is for an organization to act first and then analyze what was done.

The five preconditions for successful evaluation for the reverse decision cycle model are:

1. Some of the activities engaged in by program administrators have positive outcomes valued by some stakeholders.
2. The positive outcomes are related, if only indirectly, to the formally-stated goals of the agency.
3. The evaluation focuses mainly on the positive outcomes.
4. Program managers trust the evaluators.
5. The evaluation may or may not be used depending on the findings.

These preconditions are compatible with goal-free and/or process evaluations, described earlier in this chapter. The evaluator looks at what is being accomplished by the program and identifies positive outcomes. The positive outcomes will be beneficial to some of the stakeholders associated with the program (Stake 1974). Since the agency will have formally stated goals for which it will be held accountable, the positive outcomes must be somewhat correlated with these goals even if they are not identical.

One of the most important functions of program managers is to generate enthusiasm for the program among those who implement it. They cannot do this if an evaluation points out flaws in the way the program is being run. All programs have both positive as well as negative outcomes. To help maintain a high level of commitment from his or her employees, the program manager must emphasize the positive outcomes. But evaluations conducted under the synoptic-rational paradigm invariably turn up negative aspects of programs. This is because programs seldom, if ever, meet their original intentions perfectly. Thus, a program manager has to be wary of—and even downright hostile toward—a synoptic evaluation. Most programs operate in a politically volatile climate. No matter how solid its methodology, a synoptic evaluation cannot help a program manager because parts of it can and usually will be used against him or her.

In order for an evaluator to gain access to data for the program being evaluated, the program manager must be willing to trust the evaluator. The likelihood of trust will increase with the conviction that the evaluation will produce helpful and useful information for the program manager. Thus, according to the reverse decision cycle model, it is impossible for the evaluator to be totally objective and scientific. This does not mean that the evaluation should whitewash or cover up wrongdoing. It only means that evaluators should perform a role similar to lawyers in the adversarial process: they should make the best case they can for the program they are evaluating. Given that values cannot be eliminated from evaluating (Guba & Lincoln 1981), they might just as well become open, explicit aspects of the evaluation.

The preconditions for the reverse decision cycle might be characterized as political evaluation (Stufflebeam & Webster 1981). Political evaluation has the following advantages: it is acceptable to program managers; it helps build a positive image of social programs; it points to those aspects of the program that achieve positive outcomes; and it helps build and maintain constituents' support for the program. At the same time, political evaluation has some inherent problems: it is biased toward emphasizing the positive aspects of programs; it is susceptible to co-optation by program managers; and it is scientifically and professionally less credible than synoptic evaluation. Although it may be inferior to summative evaluation on these grounds, it is more in accord with actual organizational decision-making processes. It is, therefore, more realistic. Ideally, we might like to increase the amount of rationality in organizations, but this is unlikely because the model of rationality was meant to apply to economic transactions, not public programs. Consequently, the political evaluation paradigm is a more realistic alternative for policy evaluation than the synoptic model.

■ THE USE AND ROLE OF EVALUATION RESEARCH

> Practical men, who believe themselves to be quite exempt from intellectual influences, are usually the slaves of some defunct economist . . . it is ideas, not vested interest, which are dangerous for good or evil. (John Maynard Keynes, *The General Theory of Employment, Interest and Money,* 1936)

> Contrary to what their critics often suppose, intellectuals are not usually the authors of particular processes. . . . What intellectuals chiefly bring to policy debates, and what chiefly accounts for their influence is not knowledge but theory. (James Q. Wilson, Harvard University, 1981)

In the late 1970s, evaluators felt shock and dismay when they began to discover that policy makers were ignoring the fruits of their labor. In the 1980s, this developed into a better understanding of what the legitimate role of evaluations should be in policy making. According to early evaluators, utilization occurred only when the findings of an evaluation altered decisions or programs. This definition soon proved to be too restrictive (Weiss 1980; Larsen 1980). A more recent study indicates that utilization most often occurs as a diffuse and indirect infiltration of research ideas into the understanding that policy makers have of the world (Weiss & Bucuvalas 1980, 263). Thus, in order to understand utilization, it is necessary to have a better awareness of "the convoluted ways in which decisions take shape—and the complex interplay of situations, problems, opportunities, and actors" (1980, 274). Political scientist Martha Feldman (1990) in a study of federal transportation policy, found that evaluations changed the perceptions of those involved in the program; thus, she concluded, evaluations affect a policy by changing the way program effects are perceived.

Other researchers have begun to study these "convoluted ways" that decisions are actually made. Eleanor Chelimsky (1986), head of the General Accounting Office's Evaluation Division, believes that different levels of authority in an organization seek different kinds of information, and that utilization is enhanced if the kind of information each level wants is provided. Two evaluation researchers found that most managers are constantly busy and their allocation of time shifts rapidly from one question to the next. They change focus every six to seven minutes, and complete activities on one question in less than nine minutes. About 70 to 85 percent of their day is spent in unscheduled and unpredictable conversations with others; half of these are initiated by others rather than by themselves. Their communications are conducted with people on a casual, personalized, and anecdotal basis. They use shortcuts and simplified representation of things and do not want extensive information. Thus, to achieve greater utilization of complicated evaluation research, evaluators should interact frequently with managers in a way that does not take too much time (Sproull & Larkey 1979; Cronbach 1980; Schulberg & Jerrell 1979; Conner 1979).

Perhaps as important as understanding how decisions are made is understanding the political factors involved in decision making (Palumbo 1987). A number of researchers have found that political factors are critical to utilization or non-utilization of evaluations. Windle et al. (1979) found that evaluations of community mental health centers performed by the National Institute of Mental Health were used only if managers could justify expansion or modification of the program, but not if they recommended reduction of ineffective activities. Similarly, a sophisticated cost-benefit analysis of fire stations in Denver was ignored by the Denver City Council because citizens had no interest in saving money if it meant losing neighborhood fire stations (Heiss 1974).

Evaluators, then, should consider not only external politics, but also the bureaucratic politics of organizations. Policy makers, administrators, and evaluators each respond to their own decision elements from a different perspective. For policy makers, the most important factor in their decision is the expressed demand or support for a program, not its cost or the need for the program. Policy makers rely on interpersonal contacts in reaching decisions whereas evaluators rely on technical standards (Delbecq & Gill 1979). One researcher (Hargrove 1980) describes how three different officers in the Department of Labor each developed their own evaluation plans for the Comprehensive Employment and Training Act (CETA). The type of evaluation each developed depended on the professional background of those in the office. For example, one office was staffed by economists, so they used cost-benefit studies. Another office looked only at whether CETA participants had increased their earnings. The third office argued that a number of different goals should be considered. The three offices finally reached a compromise, resulting in an evaluation that was satisfactory to no one.

Evaluation results are similar to new programs introduced into an organization. Because they arouse uncertainty, they are likely to generate opposition unless properly introduced through group consultation and other organizational development techniques (Stevens & Tornatsky 1980). Not only is it necessary to modify the organization as a result of an evaluation—the evaluation findings *themselves* should be modified to fit the organization's needs if they are to be used (Kiresuk & Lund 1979; Larsen & Weiner 1981).

The Role of Evaluation in Policy Making

Recognizing that policy making is not a rational process in which various groups attempt to maximize goals, evaluation researchers have begun to focus on the question of what role rational evaluations might play. According to Lee J. Cronbach of Stanford University, "We agree with the rationalists that evaluation should contribute to wiser social actions. We do not agree that the one best action will be made crystal clear by a factual study" (1980, 61). Italian policy analyst Giandoemenico Majone (1989) argues that "facts" alone do not change policy; argument and persuasion play key roles.

Evaluators now recognize that there are numerous roles evaluations can play. They can reinforce official commitment to a program, reduce uncertainty, neutralize critics, bolster supporters, shift responsibility for failure to researchers, and legitimize decisions made on other grounds (Weiss & Bucuvalas 1980; Nachmias 1981). Evaluation researchers will continue to believe that the rational solution to problems is the best solution, whereas legislators will continue to believe that the best solution is the one with the greatest amount of support (Brandl 1978). In making policy decisions, legislators consider the effect it will have on their constituents first, its political feasibility second, and the substantive merit of the policy last. Evaluation researchers have exactly the opposite priorities (Chelimsky 1981).

Information is an important source of power, both for individuals and for organizations (Heiss 1974; Rich 1979). Thus, a bureaucrat who knows how effective a program is will be far better off than one who does not. Similarly, evaluations conducted by the executive branch will tend to shift power in that direction. This explains why legislatures at the national and state levels have increased the amount of evaluations they do. Because information is a source of power, evaluation research is likely to continue to be an important activity in the policy-making process. But it is not likely to perform the ideal function for which it was designed; that is, to find out what programs actually work and to deliver criticism with the hope that the solutions will be adopted or supported. Instead, it is likely to perform the more limited function of adding information to the debate and struggle that surrounds the entire complex policy-making process.

■ EVALUATION AND TERMINATION OF PUBLIC POLICIES

Government programs are seldom terminated as a result of an evaluation. They more often are terminated because of political or ideological opposition (de Leon 1983). Termination is the final stage in the policy cycle. However, it is not a typical outcome of policies. More often, a policy or program is modified or changed slightly, or replaced by one that is slightly different (Hogwood & Peters 1983). This is not because bureaucracies are imperialistic and resistant to change but rather because there are enormous human costs involved in terminating a program. To initiate and implement a new policy requires an enormous investment of resources and the commitment and dedication of a large number of individuals. It also often leads to the development of imputed interest groups, discussed in Chapter 3. Terminating a program may require that all of these individuals and groups be abolished or, at least, transferred to a different program. But admitting defeat is not easy, and it is these human factors that often prevent a program from being terminated.

Certainly it is easier to terminate a specific program than it is to abolish the agency that administers the program, or change the policy that gave rise to the program and perhaps the agency as well. And a *function* of government seldom is ended because it may be essential to the continued existence and operation of society—that is, defense, law enforcement, education. Distinguishing among functions, policies, agencies, and programs is useful in understanding the termination or modification process (de Leon 1983; de Leon & Brewer 1983; Bardach 1977).

A function of government is a general activity which may be mandated by the constitution and without which society cannot operate. For example, defense is a necessary function of government as is regulating interstate commerce, law enforcement, public health, education, and maintaining social welfare. It is debatable just how many of these functions must be provided by governmental as opposed to private agencies. However, even the most ardent conservatives would not agree that defense, regulation of interstate commerce, and law enforcement should be turned over to private agencies. These functions—as well as public health, education and provision of social welfare—are likely to remain government functions rather than be terminated.

The *agencies* created to pursue particular policies in each of these functional areas are easier to terminate than functions. Policies usually change when a new administration is elected to office. This may even result in reorganization or even termination of an agency of government, although this is rare. Agencies are the second least likely to be terminated or changed, next to functions of government. When the Reagan administration came to power in 1980, for example, it changed federal education policy (see Chapter 7) and promised to abolish the Department of Education. In 1987, the Department of Education still existed, although with a vastly changed policy orientation.

Programs are the easiest government entity to change or terminate because termination rarely requires major changes in policy or modification of an agency of government. Thus, the Department of Health and Human Services can give up the Comprehensive Employment and Training Program initiated by Congress without greatly affecting the agency itself. Abolishing a particular program signals or reflects a change in policy in that area. If the change in policy is not major and only incremental, which is usually the case, then only the programs that carry out the policy are likely to be affected. If the policy change is major, as happens from time to time, then the agency operating the program may be affected as well. Only during major constitutional changes will functions of government actually be affected.

Part II

SUBSTANTIVE POLICY ISSUES

Part II of this book applies the policy cycle concepts developed in Part I to several substantive policy issue areas—including health, welfare, crime, education, and energy policy. Each chapter will take the policy issue through each step of the cycle after first defining the dimensions of each issue and the events that propelled it onto the government's institutional agenda.

Part I of this book deals with general principles about the policy process. These principles are likely to remain accurate for a fairly long period of time. Because policies do change, sometimes very rapidly, some of the discussion in Part II could be out of date by the time this book is published. For example, in 1984 Health Maintenance Organizations, described in Chapter 6, were rarely used in the United States, but because of rising health costs that affected business corporations as well as the government, there has been increasing pressure on people to use HMOs instead of private physicians. The assumption behind this is that increased competition among health care providers will drive costs down. As a result, HMOs experienced fairly rapid growth in 1986, one that was not fully anticipated by most health policy analysts, even though some analysts advocated their use. By the end of 1992, HMOs had become one of the fastest growing ways that health care was delivered. Thus, any particular public policy can change rapidly, although it rarely does. The extent to which rapid changes occur may affect the timeliness of some of the issues discussed in Part II.

Any policy issue, such as health care, usually is the concern of several levels of government at the same time: national, state, and local. To gain a complete understanding of the policy-making process in a specific area would require that the process and the interaction among the levels be described. In some areas (including health, social welfare, and energy) the federal government plays a larger role than state and local governments, whereas in other areas (such as education and crime) state and local governments are paramount. For these latter policy areas, far more emphasis will be given to state policy making than for the areas that tend to be dominated by the federal government. Thus, there will be a shift back and forth in emphasis among levels of government in Part II depending on the policy area being discussed.

Public policy issue areas such as health, welfare, crime, education, and energy involve large complex questions. There is such a mass of detail in each area that specialists spend years developing expertise in a single area. For example, there are criminal justice experts and, within this area, law enforcement, juvenile delinquency, and corrections experts. The policy process framework enables us to gain a reasonably good understanding of all of these areas without becoming a specialist in each one. Understanding how and why problems get onto the institutional agenda, how they are defined and policy formulated, and so on, through the entire cycle, makes it possible to understand the major dimensions of the issue area, the possible solutions to problems, and the directions that policy is likely to take in the future.

6

Health Policy: The High Cost of Good Health

■ THE NATURE OF HEALTH CARE IN THE UNITED STATES

Almost as soon as surgeons opened the chest cavity of sixty-one-year-old dentist Barney Clark in November 1982 to replace his failing heart with an artificial one, ethical questions about such surgery began to surface. The surgery was indeed a medical triumph, almost a miracle. Many people with heart problems probably thought that the day would not be far off when they too could get an artificial heart to replace their own failing hearts, and if so, the lives of millions could be extended for years.

But that day still is remote—if it ever arrives at all. A number of additional artificial heart transplants were performed after the one on Clark. None of them, including Clark, were considered successful (*Science*, June 1986), which raised a number of ethical questions. From the perspective of health policy, the most important question concerns the cost of such operations. The use of complicated technologies such as the artificial heart is one of the main reasons medical costs have gotten out of control. It is estimated that the cost of the first artificial heart was $200,000 (Altman 1983). Not many people can afford this, although many could use a new heart. A federal panel in 1989 said that the artificial-heart program which was projected to benefit 17,000 to 35,000 people at a cost of $5 billion yearly, extended the average patient's life only 4 1/2 years (Wallinga 1989, 66).

Not only are the costs of an artificial heart very high, such technological breakthroughs increase the demand for medical services, thereby driving the cost of medical services even higher. Many people would like to have an artificial heart, or a pacemaker, or heart by-pass surgery, but the heart is only one of the organs people need. Medical technology makes it possible to replace hip joints, kidneys, livers, lungs, knee and ankle joints, limbs, and a number of other body parts. Unfortunately, not only is the cost of these very high for the individual, the cost to society has gotten so high that we may be forced to engage in rationing to decide who will be given the benefits of this marvelous technology and who will not. (Rationing is discussed in more detail later.)

In 1972, the U.S. Congress sidestepped this difficult issue with regard to kidneys when it decided that everyone on kidney dialysis would be provided with funding for this expensive procedure. Persons receiving kidney dialysis are put on a machine once a month. This machine purifies the blood that the individual's own kidneys are no longer capable of purifying. The procedure costs $25,000 for each patient. The number of people needing such medical treatment increased from 11,000 in 1972 to 59,200 in 1982 at an annual cost of $1.5 billion to the country. Should we continue to provide this expensive treatment to those who need it?

If there are sufficient resources available, the humanitarian answer to the question above seems obvious: All who need such treatment should receive it. No doubt many of the new medical technologies are effective and help many people, but there are not enough resources to handle all the different kinds of patients who need expensive medical technology. Society might be able to afford to provide everyone with any *single* medical procedure such as kidney dialysis, but when all the different types of treatments are added together, the costs are phenomenal. Heart transplants, open heart surgery and kidney dialysis are only some of the more expensive types of medical technology that are needed. Newborn intensive care units are another. These units are used to try to save the lives of premature infants, many of whom weigh less than a pound at birth and who have little chance of surviving. A newborn intensive care unit is aimed at rescuing critically ill newborns with rapid intervention and a heavy concentration of specialized therapies such as intravenous feeding, respiratory support, laboratory facilities, and skilled personnel. About $1.6 billion was spent on this kind of care in 1982 for about 20,000 infants. The average cost of treating a premature baby in intensive care was $80,000, and some individual bills can run as high as $160,000 (Guillemin 1982). Even after treatment, the infant has a high probability of dying, and even if it survives, it often contracts a serious disease such as cerebral palsy.

There are many incentives to provide this type of service. Obstetricians feel compelled to turn to newborn intensive care in response to parental pressure; neonatologists have an interest in furthering the techniques of their specialty; and hospitals find that such units are a boon to their finances. On the surface, we might conclude that this kind of health service should be provided. After all, who could oppose trying to rescue a newborn infant? But there are serious questions about whether the enormous concentration of human time, energy, skill, and emotion invested in a premature infant who has a poor chance of survival is justifiable. Should public tax funds be used for this purpose? Should every premature baby receive this kind of care? Who should make the decisions?

Newborn intensive care units cost about $1.6 billion a year. At the other end of the age spectrum are the elderly who suffer from arthritis and rheumatism. About 162,000 hip joints of such individuals were replaced in 1979 at a cost of $1.1 billion, and it has been estimated that another 122,000 could use them each year at an annual additional cost of $1 billion a year. Aggressive, comprehensive treatment of cancer is another form of expensive care that the elderly require. People undergoing such treatment often have poor odds for recovery. Technologies for sustaining people with chronic digestive disease are also available at a cost of $750 a day in the hospital or $255 a day at home. The total cost to society for all of those who need this treatment is obviously very high.

No one wants to tell a patient who needs an artificial heart, kidney dialysis, a new hip joint, or treatment for cancer or chronic digestive disease that the country cannot afford it. But soon this admission may have to be made. Can society afford the total costs of all of the medical heroics it provides? When the cost of open heart surgery, artificial hearts, kidney dialysis, newborn intensive care, hip joints for arthritic patients, intensive cancer therapy, and a number of other technological developments are added together, the bill is enormous, while the number of people who benefit is relatively small (see Case 6–1).

This latter point, in fact, is the key to the health-care problem facing the country today. Medicine has turned its attention to diseases that strike the elderly in an apparent attempt to forestall the aging process. For example, Dr. James H. Saminous, the American Medical Association's executive vice president, was quoted as saying that "perhaps in no other single year have the strides in medicine received headline attention as often as they have this year" (*New York Times*, January 2, 1983, 121). The advances he singled out were (1) nuclear magnetic resonance, which is a technique that uses magnets instead of x-rays to show chemical imbalances that may precede such diseases as atherosclerosis, cancer, and strokes; (2) medical lasers, which can be used to remove brain tumors and skin cancers; (3) cyclosporin, which improves

CASE 6–1 *Heart Transplants versus Artificial Hearts*

Heart transplants rather than artificial hearts became the new technology for treating people with heart disease by 1987. During the early days of heart transplant operations, the record was rather dismal: of 166 transplants done by Dr. Christian Barnard during the period of 1967–1970, only 23 survived past 3 years. An even worse record was compiled by Dr. Denton Cooley of Houston, all of his 21 patients died shortly after their operations.

By 1987, the five-year survival rate of heart transplant patients of Dr. Normal Shumway of Stanford University Medical Center approached 60 percent, although at a cost of $100,000 for the first year and around $10,000 to $20,000 for each additional year of life. One patient, Willem Van Buuren of San Rafael, California, lived 17 years with a transplanted heart—the world's longest survivor. In 1987, there were 94 medical centers in the United States doing heart transplants, but most required that the prospective patient be a good risk, have medical insurance, and deposit $125,000 before surgery.

In addition, none was able to return to work; they had to take 20 or more pills a day, which weakened their bones, caused cancer, and produced kidney dysfunction. Half of those alive after five years developed coronary artery disease. While technology for heart transplants was still in its infancy in 1992, research on artificial hearts seemed to be advancing, according to the independent research Institute of Medicine. It announced on July 23, 1991, that self-contained mechanical pumps implanted in patients' bodies would be available to replace diseased hearts by the year 2010. But some members of the Institute said the high cost of the artificial heart—about $150,000—might make it unfeasible. And it could not be developed without federal research support. This raises questions about whether scarce federal government money should be used for this as opposed to other programs.

survival rates after organ transplants; and (4) genetically engineering human insulin for diabetics.

But the attempt to forestall the consequences of aging cannot succeed. Daniel Callahan asks, "If death can be forestalled, for how long and in what circumstances should it be? At what point does rehabilitation of the crippled cease to be of benefit to society? If one malignancy can be cured only to set the stage for death by another, just what, if anything, is gained? (1977, 23–24). As if to answer his own questions, Callahan goes on to say, "Medicine has not conquered death, nor is it likely to. But within that limit its power continues to increase, and it is precisely that increase that compels a basic reexamination of our basic ethical attitudes and premises toward it" (23–24).

Rationing Health Care

When we consider that those over sixty-five years old comprise about 12 percent of the population but consume about a third of all health care expenditures, it is no wonder that some begin to question where the limited amount of money should be spent. David Wallinger, a fourth-year medical student, has written: "Justice demands that we divert money from high-tech artificial hearts to public health, from programs that prolong old age to those that nurture the young" (Wallinger 1989).

Aside from the possibility that Mr. Wallinger might change his mind when he gets old (i.e., over 65), he overlooks a couple of important issues about rationing health care. One is that he is placing concerns about collective well-being over individual rights. If the person who needs high tech health care happens to be his mother, he may well be disturbed that it is not available because resources have been transferred to "nurture the young."

But even more important is the question of who shall decide which groups, or which types of health care will be supported? Some advocates for rationing health care feel the decision is obvious. For example, Paul Menzel (1990) believes "Like low-benefit terminal care, life-extending care of the severely demented becomes a first-order candidate for restrictions if we take seriously the task of matching rationing policies with people's actual values." Why does Mengel believe that such policies are obvious? How about the severely retarded or chronic schizophrenics, should medical care be withheld from them also? And where does the list end?

It is true, as medical ethicist Daniel Callahan (1988) argues, that individual demand for health care is virtually boundless. But this does not imply that society should ration health care rather than simply try to limit the total amount spent on health care. Moreover, as will be discussed next, large savings may be possible by eliminating unnecessary services and facilities, thereby making it unnecessary to ration health care (Relmon 1990). Moreover, it is likely that the poor would bear the brunt of any form of rationing (Brennon 1991). In fact that seems to be what happened under Oregon's rationing system. In Oregon, the state first figures out how much money it can spend on health care for the poor and then decides what services will be bought. A commission made up of doctors, social workers, and health-care advocates lists the total number of health services that might be provided (709 in 1991). These are priced and ranked by a mix of social values and actuarial statistics. The total number of people below the poverty line who fall into certain categories receive a standard package of doctor and hospital care and medication, which determines where the line is drawn regarding which illnesses will be treated and which not. In 1991, the line was drawn at swelling of the esophagus. All conditions below that line would not be treated. Immediately below the esophagus was disk surgery; anyone who needed this would not get it. The plan has been criticized as making the

CASE 6–2 *Who Wants Less Than Optimal Health Care?*

The following letter appeared in the *New York Times* on April 4, 1982.

To the Editor:

While it is doubtless true that, as in any industry, there is some mismanagement of resources in the field of health care, several aspects of health-care cost containment are usually glossed over when this subject is discussed in the press.

Whatever regulatory or free-market controls might be imposed on a physician's use of high technology or hospital beds, the consequences of "over-economy," when it occurs, become the physician's burden alone.

Legislative guidelines and regulations invariably deal with groups of patients with classes of medical problems, ignoring the concept of the individual with extenuating circumstances. It is easy for society to prescribe sweeping reductions in the "indiscriminate" use of high technology.

For the patient, however, denial of a diagnostic or therapeutic modality with even modest likelihood of benefit is greeted with anger or, if harm can be shown to have resulted in retrospective analysis, with cries of criminal negligence. Retrospective medical care requires far less training and expertise than the prospective variety.

Second, blame for the high cost of health-care technology is usually placed squarely on physicians or hospitals, the true users of this technology, rather than on the medical-industrial complex, the true providers. The soaring

poor accept rationing, whereas others do not. However, it also is defended on the grounds that it increases access to health services for groups that previously had little or none (Specter 1991). Moreover, under "Managed Care" systems (discussed next) which by 1992 had become the dominent form of health care, rationing already occurs because in these systems insurance companies play a large role in determining what treatments will be covered and how long hospital stays can last. So it is clear that the question is not whether or not we should ration health care because it is already being done. For example, Medicare covered heart, kidney, and liver transplants in 1992, but state Medicaid systems made their own decisions. One could get a liver transplant in some states but not others. When Arizona's Medicaid program dropped liver transplants in 1987, 43-year-old Dianna Brown died because she had no way to pay for the operation. Medical ethicists say that if there is to be rationing it should not be on the basis of ability to pay or age.

profits of these companies and their potential impact on health-care costs are rarely cited.

It is true as well that some of this technology is legitimately expensive and that our ability to advance science is not matched by our ability or willingness to pay for it. No sooner does a technological advance arrive to improve the quality of medical care than we, as physicians, are forced to find ways to restrict its availability and use, a sad irony.

And society itself puts pressure on physicians to raise fees. Malpractice insurance rates for some specialties run in excess of $40,000 a year. In New York, insurance providers recently submitted a request for a rate increase of over 200 percent. Whether justified or not by the size and number of malpractice settlements, these costs are borne by physicians and their patients regardless of how good an individual practitioner's care may be.

The rising cost of health care is clearly a problem beyond simple mismanagement of resources by hospitals and physicians. The people of this country must decide to what extent they will accept less than complete availability of advanced health-care technology but should not then punish their physicians for offering less than optimal care.

Gerald O. Franklin, M.D.
Chappaqua, New York

For most organ transplants, there is a strong bias in favor of young patients. This amounts to a form of rationing and it can be defended. But, since the average time that a person lives after a heart transplant is less than 5 years, what difference does it make if the patient is 40 or 60 years old? More importantly, there is no systematic method of making rationing decisions and there is some doubt that one can be developed. As Joshua M. Weiner, senior fellow at the Brookings Institute says, "All this seems to say is so far, we haven't yet figured out how to play God" (Rich 1991, 7). (See Case 6–2.)

In reexamining our basic ethical premises towards medicine, two very important points should be stressed. One is that medical science contributed very little toward the decline in the mortality rate during the twentieth century, and the other is that medical science can do little to cure the chronic diseases of old age now facing society. Let us now examine these points in detail.

The Contribution of Medicine to the Decline in Mortality

The dramatic increase in expenditures for health care that began in the 1960s is not responsible for the decline in mortality and the concomitant rise in life expectancy that has occurred during the twentieth century (McKinlay & McKinlay 1980; Saward & Sorenson 1980; Brown 1985). Most of the decline in mortality occurred before 1950, due primarily to our ability to control infectious diseases such as tuberculosis, diphtheria, whooping cough, smallpox, typhoid, scarlet fever, measles, flu, and pneumonia. These were all controlled by the sanitary revolution that began at the turn of the century, by better diet, and by the rising standard of living. According to medical researchers McKinlay and McKinlay, "Rather more conservatively, if we attribute some of the fall in the death rates for pneumonia, influenza, whooping cough, and diphtheria to medical measures, then perhaps 3.5 percent of the fall in the overall death rate can be explained through medical intervention in the major infectious diseases considered here" (1980, 14).

A brief look at health conditions at the turn of the century will give us a better idea of how infectious diseases were controlled. (See also Case 6–3.)

CASE 6–3 *Medical Technology: 300 Years Makes Quite a Difference*

The following two examples illustrate how much has changed in medical technology over the past 300 years. The first example takes place in the year 1685 when the royal physicians were treating King Charles II just before he died (Rosengren 1980). First, they extracted a pint and a half of blood from the king. Then they gave him an emetic, two physics, and an enema. A sneezing powder was given to purge the brain, and cowslip powder to strengthen it. When these did not work, the physicians gave him more emetics and more blood was taken from the king, and a plaster of pitch and pigeon was applied to his feet. A multitude of substances were taken internally including melon seeds, slippery elm, black cherry water, lavender, gentian root, nutmeg, and forty drops of extract of human skull. Finally, bezoar stone was employed, but the royal patient died.

The scene now shifts to the year 1982, almost 300 years later. A team of physicians open up the chest cavity of sixty-one-year-old dentist, Barney Clark, to replace his diseased heart with an artificial heart called the Jarvik-7. The operation was a success, but shortly afterwards, Clark developed complications including pneumonia and irregularities in the artificial heart. Another operation was performed to repair a defective valve in the artificial heart. After the twentieth day, Clark was said to be making a steady recovery. He stood up for the first time and was taken off the respirator for seven hours. Clark

The turn of the century, although not very long ago in years, was a long time ago in the development of medical terminology. The year 1900 was a time when many of our grandparents were facing health risks that have now been conquered. Polio then was widespread. Diabetics faced short and debilitating lives. Preventive medicine was unheard of, and the risk factors of heart disease such as obesity, diet, and smoking were ignored. The electrocardiogram was still 20 years in the future. A person who wanted to go into medicine as a career could enter "medical school" after high school, which took two years to complete. Most of these schools operated without state licensure and many were really just degree mills. A person who perceived him or herself ill and went to a physician for treatment had a fifty-fifty chance of benefiting from the encounter.

In 1900, most physicians were in general practice and the hospital had not yet emerged as a key medical institution. The three leading causes of death in 1900 were influenza and pneumonia, tuberculosis, and gastroenteritis. As it had been throughout human history, most people born in 1900 died before they reached the age of five. Only 50 percent of children survived until their fifth birthday. The infant mortality rate was 200 per 1000 live births and the

---

was visited by Dr. Willem Kolff, one of the developers of the artificial heart, who was told by Clark, "Don't quit." By that, said Dr. Kolff, Clark meant that he prefers this "noble experiment to a graceful death" (*Kansas City Times*, 1982, A-5). Twenty-one days after the operations, doctors were surprised by Clark's progress: "He stands and sort of shuffles around and sits down in the chair," a spokesperson said (*Kansas City Times*, 1982, A-4). He spent several hours a day in a reclining chair next to his bed and was learning to speak by placing his finger over the tracheotomy tube running from his throat.

On December 23, 1982, doctors hoped that Clark would be able to leave the hospital and were trying to complete arrangements for a home in Salt Lake City where he could live rent-free after he was well enough to leave the hospital. Compressed-air outlets would have to be provided in the home because Clark's Jarvik-7 heart is drawn by an air compressor. But on his twenty-seventh day, Clark's doctors said they did not know when he would be well enough to leave the hospital. All agreed that it would take weeks for him to gain enough strength to be released.

On February 23, 1982, Barney Clark died as a result of massive circulatory collapse, shock, and failure of all the organs in his body except the artificial heart, which continued to pump even after his death (Altman 1983, 1).

average life expectancy was 36 years for the gentry, 22 for tradesmen, and 16 for laborers. One of the reasons for such short average life expectancy was that so many died during childhood.

Throughout the nineteenth century, the population was swept by many epidemics of smallpox, yellow fever, cholera, typhoid, and typhus. Many of these communicable diseases were transmitted through water and food supplies. Sanitary food handling and storage were not practiced, and drinking water was polluted with human waste. People working in factories did not have fresh, running water from taps but drank from barrels standing in various locations. The barrels into which everyone dipped their cups were also used for cleaning toilets. Most individuals did this because they were ignorant about how disease is spread. (The germ theory of disease was not yet fully developed.)

Sanitation practices improved after 1900 and this, coupled with inoculations against various communicable diseases, accounted for a drop in the major communicable diseases. By 1950, most communicable diseases had been effectively controlled or eliminated and life expectancy increased dramatically; most people could expect to live into their late sixties. By 1982, life expectancy for the average person was 74.1 years, and 25 percent of the population was over 65. But these advances were not made without cost; as people survived longer, they began to suffer from the diseases of old age. These are known as chronic diseases.

The three leading causes of death today are chronic diseases of the heart, cancer, and stroke. These diseases have important ramifications for health policy. First, they are illnesses for which the patient and the medical establishment must assume equal responsibility; one's health rests as heavily on the shoulders of the patient as it does on those of the physician. Chronic diseases can be prevented through better living habits, environments, and diets, but they cannot be cured. Second, chronic disease is not something that a person catches, but is socially and culturally produced. Chronic illness is not entirely a result of something internal to the patient; it is also traceable to external forces in the social and physical environment (Rosengren 1980, 4). For example, although heredity plays a role, many forms of cancer are produced by environmental factors in places where we work, in the water we drink, or from smoking. Heart disease is also strongly related to diet, life style, and smoking.

The third major characteristics of chronic diseases is that they are not curable in the same way communicable diseases are. They require the expenditure of enormous amounts of money for medical services that Lewis Thomas (1974) calls "halfway technologies," because they are applied after the fact in an attempt to compensate for the incapacitating effects of disease whose course we are unable to stop. Heart disease, stroke, and cancer are unpredictable in intensity, duration, and degree of intensity. They are episodic, with acute flareups and remissions. They often involve multiple failures in which the breakdown of one organ (heart) leads to the impairment of others (liver, kidney).

Medical science has made few advances against chronic diseases over the past twenty years. For example, in 1984 the National Cancer Institute released a statistical profile of cancer which showed that 49 percent of cancer victims diagnosed between 1976 and 1981 were expected to live at least five years. That is only 1 percent better than the 48 percent rate for those whose disease was detected from 1973 to 1975 (*New York Times,* December 2, 1984, E-7). In May 1986, a study by Dr. John Bailar of the Harvard School of Public Health and Dr. Elaine Smith of the University of Iowa charged that the huge investment in cancer treatment research has had very limited impact on the "most fundamental measure of clinical outcome—death" (*U.S. News & World Report,* April 19, 1986, 94). The study showed the incidence of cancer increased 8.5 percent between 1973 and 1981 and that cancer mortality increased from 170 deaths per 100,000 Americans in 1962 to 185 per 100,000 in 1982. The only area where mortality has been reduced is among young patients, who account for only 1 to 2 percent of all cancer deaths. Critics of the study say that it is unfair to focus only on mortality, and that lung cancer deaths account for most of the increase in mortality. Nevertheless, the mortality figures show that progress against cancer has not been very great. And a 1987 General Accounting Office report examined progress in survival for 12 types of cancer from 1950 to 1982 and concluded, "For the majority of the cancers we examined, the actual improvements have been small or have been overestimated by the published rates" (*Arizona Republic,* July 22, 1990, A10).

In its annual report in 1985, the U.S. Department of Health and Human Services announced that deaths due to heart disease—the nation's number one killer—declined by 26 percent between 1970 and 1980, and that deaths from stroke plummeted by 48 percent. However, the department's report added that these improvements were due in large part to changes people made in their life styles—less smoking, better diets, and more exercise.

The halfway technologies we use on chronic diseases such as cancer and heart disease may prolong life, but the patient is dependent on those technologies for many years. Thus, although we may extend an individual's life through medical technology, the costs are very high. These high costs are at the heart of the contemporary health problem in the United States.

The High Costs of Medical Services

In 1983, the average American committed more than a month of his or her yearly salary to securing medical protection (Zeckhauser & Zook 1981, 92). In all, Americans spent $357.2 billion for health care in 1983 and $425 billion in 1985. The latter amount was almost 11 percent of the gross national product—more than any other nation has spent on health care.

By 1993, Americans were devoting almost 14 percent of the gross national product ($809 billion) to health care, which was one of every $7 they spent. Still, about 35 million Americans had no health insurance and, as a result, very little health care.

Federal, state, and local governments and private insurance comprised the majority of expenditures for health in 1991; patients' out-of-pocket expenditures were about 20 percent of the total (see Figure 6–1).

Figure 6–2 shows the growth and relative size of national health expenditures and the gross national product from 1966 projected through 2000. Notice that while health expenditures as a percent of the gross national product have increased steadily throughout the period, both national health expenditures and the gross national product have shown wide fluctuations from year to year. What is significant is that the growth in national health expenditures is not parallel to the growth in the gross national product. Thus, there are times, particularly since the mid-1980s, when health expenditures were increasing rapidly while the gross national product was declining. This causes a crisis in financing, because while health costs are increasing the funds potentially available to finance health care are declining.

Figure 6–3 shows the factors responsible for the increase in personal health care expenditures (PHCE) for three periods. The factors causing growth have changed in the three decades. Factors affecting growth are economy-wide inflation, medical price inflation in excess of economy-wide inflation, population, and all other factors, including increases in use and intensity of health care services per capita. Note that about one-half the growth in PHCE was due to increases in use and intensity of health care of the elderly and poor. Inflation caused half the growth during 1970–1980 and this remained a major factor from 1980 to 1990, but increases in medical-specific prices affected health expenditures more during 1980–1990 than the previous two decades. Figure 6–4 gives some idea of what these medical-specific costs are. They consist of hospital room charges and physicians' services, both of which increased far more rapidly than general inflation.

For example, throughout the entire period, the cost of hospital rooms and physicians' services rose more rapidly than consumer prices in general (Gibson & Waldo 1981, 9). Part of the reason for this is the increase in surgical operations from 7.2 operations per 100 persons for 1972 to 8.6 per 100 in 1980. A study conducted at the University of San Francisco Hospital found that the increased use of surgery was largely responsible for the rising cost of medical care. The researchers studied 2,011 patients admitted to the hospital in 1972, 1977, and 1982, and found that the most dramatic rise in expenses was for infants with respiratory distress and those who needed heart surgery. The average cost for those infants who needed heart surgery was $85,368 (*Arizona Republic,* November 7, 1985, C-2).

There are a number of other reasons for the increase in health care costs. One of the more important is increased use of expensive technologies that require very expensive equipment. The Institute of Medicine, a branch of the National Academy of Science, estimates that the use of new technologies and the overuse of existing technologies accounted for as much as 50 percent of the annual rise in health care costs from 1980 to 1990. An example is the electronic

FIGURE 6–1 The Nation's health dollar—sources and destinations: 1991, 1995, and 2000.

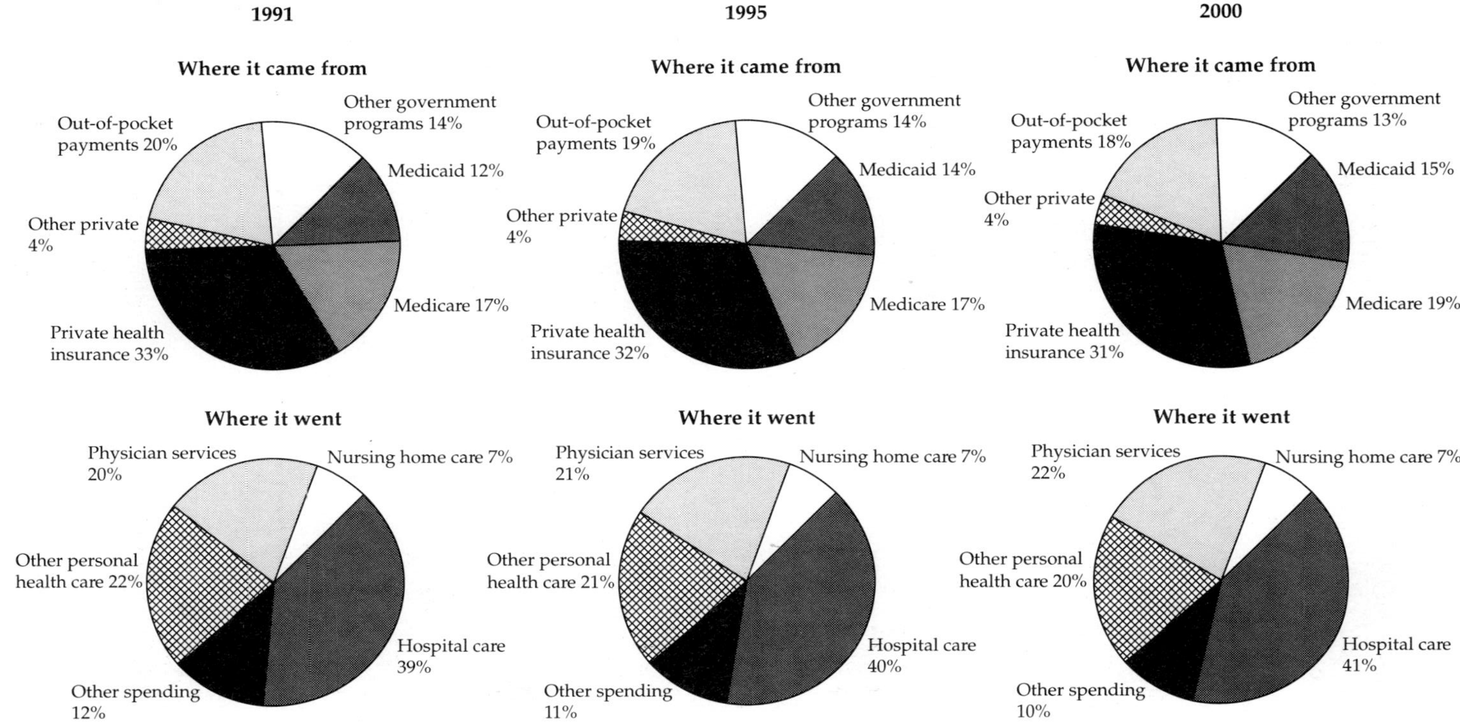

Notes: Other private includes industrial inplant health services, non-patient revenues, and privately financed construction. Other personal health care includes dental, other private professional services, home health care, drugs, and other non-durable medical products, and vision products and other durable medical products. Other spending covers program administration and the net cost of private health insurance, government public health, and research and construction.

Source: Health Care Financing Administration, Office of the Actuary: Data from the Office of National Health Statistics.

FIGURE 6–2 Percent change in national health expenditures (NHE) and gross national product (GNP), and NHE as a percent of GNP: 1966–89 and projections 1990–2000.

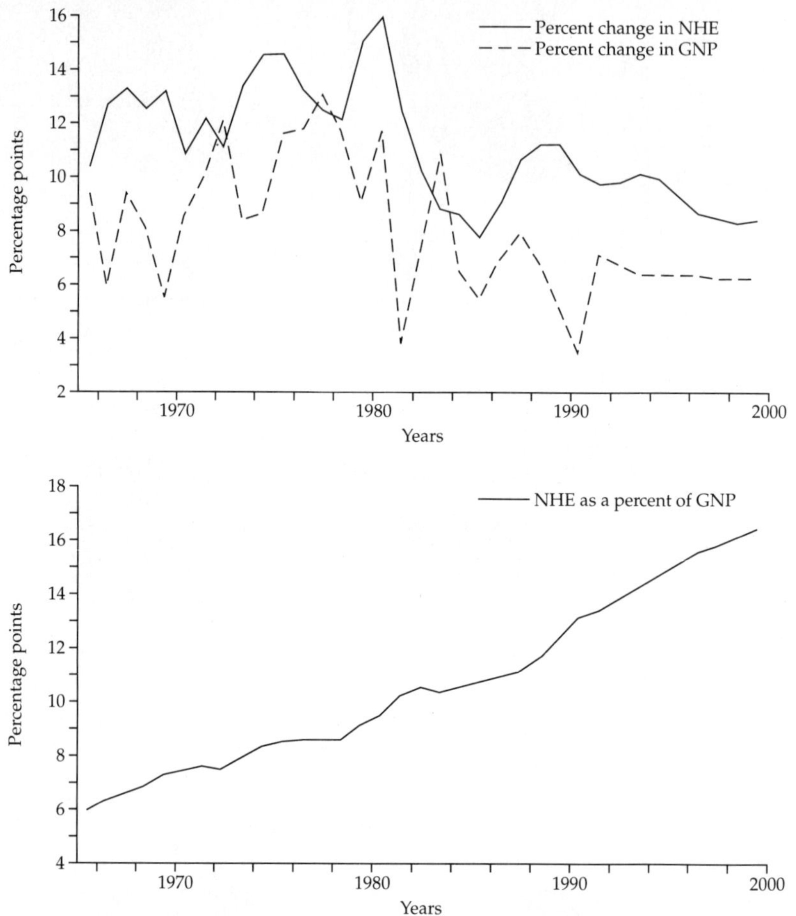

Source: Health Care Financing Administration, Office of the Actuary: Data from the Office of National Health Statistics.

FIGURE 6–3 Annual percent growth in personal health care expenditures (PHCE) and factors affecting average annual growth in PHCE for selected periods: 1960 to 90.

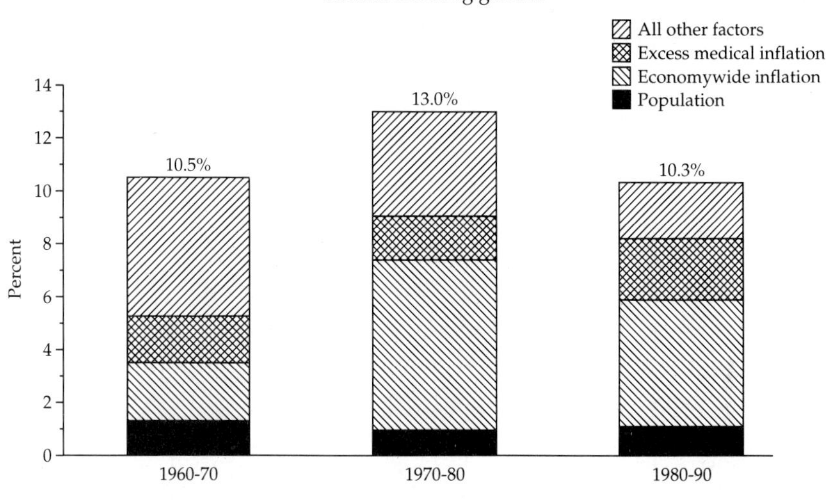

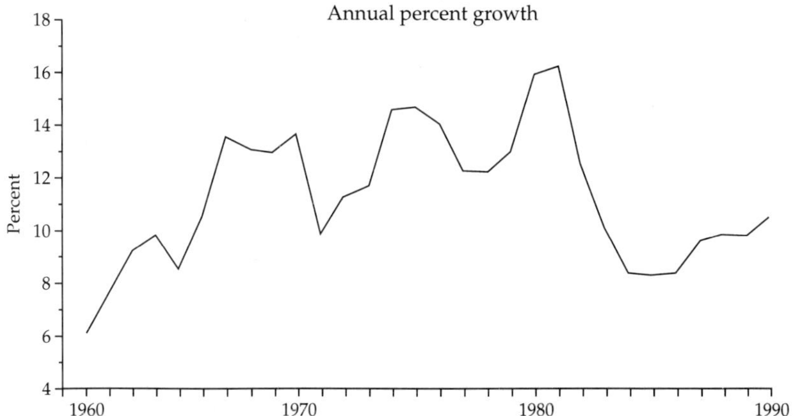

Source: Health Care Financing Administration, Office of the Actuary: Data from the Office of National Health Statistics.

FIGURE 6–4 The rising cost of medical care.

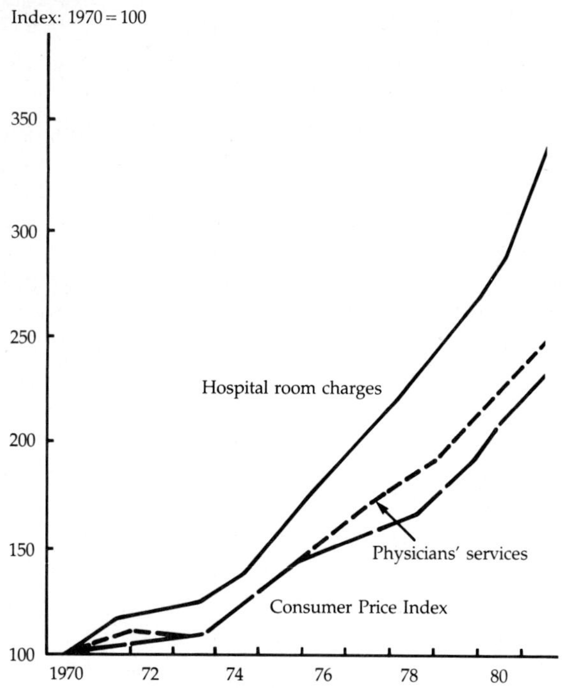

Source: James Fralick, "Rx for treatment of hyper health-care costs," *Across the Board*, U.S. Department of Health and Human Services, Health Care Financing Administration (April, 1987) p. 67.

fetal monitor, which keeps account of the heart beat of babies about to be born. They are used because patients ask for them but also because doctors are worried about malpractice suits if something goes wrong during birth. Use of electronic monitoring can aid in a physician's defense in a malpractice suit. Some experts argue that electronic monitoring is a major reason why Americans have the highest rates of Caesarean sections in the world. Doctors want to avoid being criticized for not doing a C-section and the fetal monitor is used to indicate if the baby is undergoing stress. At the slightest sign of stress, the doctor opts for a C-section.

Another example of how technology increases cost is cataract surgery. It increases demand because the surgery is much easier than previous methods. Journalist Samuelson (1988, 28) remarks, "High-Tech medicine and affordable health care may not be compatible."

Another major reason why health care in the United States is so expensive is the high administrative costs of operating a system in which there are a large number of types of providers and insurance plans. It is estimated that the cost of administering the fragmented system amounts to 20 percent of total expenditures (which were $817 billion in 1992) (Rich 1992, 20).

This is much more than the costs of systems of national health insurance such as Canada's whose administrative costs were 11 percent in 1987. There is considerable controversy about this, primarily about the trade-off regarding the quality of care if the federal government became the single national health insurer. These issues are discussed later when we discuss national health insurance. But some experts say that part of what pushes up billing costs is the exponential growth of different insurance plans, each with constantly changing terms and co-payment rules. Disputing bills, which insurance companies do in order to save money, actually causes an enormous amount of extra paperwork and thus money. Of the estimated $175 billion in administration costs in 1991, $38 billion represented profit and administrative costs of insurers, $43 billion administrative and billing costs for doctors; and about $94 billion administrative and billing costs for hospitals (Rich 1992, 20).

To a certain extent, health care is a luxury good rather than a necessary one. As a society becomes more affluent, it spends more and more on medicine. There is a definite relationship between the per capita income of a country and the percent of the GNP spent on medicine (see Figure 6–2). But the average person in the United States pays for only 20¢ of every dollar that is spent on health care. Private insurance pays 33 percent and the government pays 43 percent (see Figure 6–1). In 1985, the average person paid only 9.3 percent of hospital costs.

The fact that the individual patient has to pay only a small portion of the bill out of his or her pocket creates the illusion that the person is getting something for nothing, which drives up the cost of health care. Because those who pay do not use the service (third-party insurers), there is no incentive to keep costs down. Doctors, for example, follow professional interests when they use the most elaborate treatment available. They are also practicing defensive medicine, with one eye on the possibility of facing lawsuits for malpractice. Thus, they tell the patient he or she must be hospitalized and order numerous laboratory tests more as a protection against the possibility of a lawsuit than because they actually are needed (Stevens 1982). Hospitals are willing to provide the tests because it increases their revenues. And the patients willingly submit to whatever is recommended by the "experts" because they are not in a position to know what they need. Even after the Reagan administration introduced a prospective payment system in 1984 in order to contain hospital costs, profits rose by more than 14 percent (Rich 1985, 32). Under the prospective payment system, hospitals receive a flat fee in advance for each patient based on the diagnosis. If the person has heart failure, for example, the fee might be $2,790, no matter how long the person is in the hospital. Thus, it pays for hospitals to cut the length of stay of patients, which they did in 1984 and 1985. But they made up for this by handling more patients, increasing their total revenues and profits.

Another reason health care costs are difficult to control is because they are hidden. For example, in 1990, business paid $139.1 billion in insurance premiums as a part of the benefits to workers. This is paid to insurance companies which in turn pay the hospital or doctor when the employee receives medical services. Since the employee does not have to pay for the services directly, there is no incentive to seek the cheapest possible care. In fact, an employee's incentive may be just the opposite. Likewise, the doctor and the hospital receive their money from the insurance company, which also provides no incentive for the least expensive and minimum amount of service (Olson 1982). Until 1983, the hospital, in effect, was given a blank check. The government and the insurance companies paid whatever bill they presented. Insurance companies also benefit from the system because they can raise premiums and get more profits, thus they have no incentive to hold down costs. Increased premiums are simply added to labor contracts when they are negotiated.

Blue Cross and Blue Shield are two of the largest insurers who provide insurance for health care, and they have a special relationship with hospitals that give them a distinct advantage. Blue Cross contracts with the hospital and pays them directly for the services provided, whereas most other insurance companies pay the patient who, in turn, pays the hospital or doctor. The former arrangement simplifies billing and thus hospitals give Blue Cross a discount of 10 to 30 percent. But this also contributes to rising costs because Blue Cross administrators are less likely to challenge the hospitals. Thus, whenever hospitals raise their rates, Blue Cross increases its payments without questioning the need for higher rates, and then turns around and raises its premium rates to the insured (Salmans 1982).

One last reason for rising health care costs should be mentioned here. This is the large amount of fraud and abuse that exists, particularly in regard to government programs. In March 1982, a House of Representatives Select Committee on Aging concluded that from $2.5 to $6.2 billion is siphoned off improperly each year by hospitals, doctors, nursing homes, and pharmacies from Medicaid. This is enough to pay for all the kidney dialysis, newborn intensive care, and hip-joint replacements performed in the United States in one year, and still have a considerable amount left over. The abuses are in the form of kickbacks and rebates to clinical laboratories and pharmacies. Attempts to stop it were called an "unmitigated disaster" by a Congressional House Committee on aging. Very few individuals are ever caught and convicted. The national average in fraud cases is 1.5 convictions per state each year and twenty states in 1983 had not even set up the federally funded Medicare fraud units (*Kansas City Times*, March 27, 1984).

Managed Health Care

The majority of Americans who have health care insurance (68%) are covered through their work; it is one of the benefits that employers offer employees (along with retirement and other forms of insurance). Health care costs have risen so rapidly, however, that employers in 1990 began "managed health care" programs as a way of trying to reduce costs. By 1991, companies spent $3,161 per employee to cover medical costs, which amounted to one-fourth of their net earnings.

Managed health care programs are essentially health maintenance organizations set up by companies; there are a number of variations, but the basic plan requires employees who choose the plan (and about a third did in 1990) to select from a list of primary care doctors who contract to provide treatment for a set fee. The physicians are picked because they agree to change fees at specified rates that are set by the insurance company and the corporation. The choice of hospitals also is limited. In the plan for employees of Marriot Corporation, employees must pay a monthly premium as well as 10 percent of their medical bills up to an annual maximum of $1,500. Employees who do not enter the program must pay a higher premium plus 30 percent of their medical bills up to a maximum of $5,000.

There are other versions of managed care. The plan for Allied-Signal Corporation, which covers 48,000 of the company's 76,000 U.S. employees, pays the doctors in advance a set annual amount for each employee no matter how many trips they make to the doctor. Those who do not participate pay high deductibles and co-payments (Swoboda 1990, 20).

Companies do not want to change the system because it is something they have done traditionally. It is likely that any changes will build on the system rather than scrap it. But several of the problems of the system would also have to be fixed. These include (1) the system depresses take-home pay; (2) gives large companies advantages over small ones because the latter have to pay larger premiums; (3) provides some workers better health care than others; and (4) leaves millions uninsured.

All of the reasons for increasing health care costs add up to a problem that is unlikely to be readily resolved because of the nature of the problem itself. We will discuss the various policies that have been aimed at containing health care costs later in this chapter.

The Aging of America

Because of the successes we have had in conquering infectious diseases, and because of better diets, Americans are living longer than ever before. From

1940 to 1984 life expectancy rose from 62.9 to 74.1 years for an average American, and infant mortality dropped from 26 per 1,000 live births to 12.5. In 1992, 12 percent of the population was sixty-five or older, and it is estimated that by the year 2020, 50 percent of the population will be over sixty-five. As people live longer, the rate of chronic diseases increases because such diseases are most likely to afflict older people. As a result, the use of elaborate halfway technologies is also increasing.

Health care costs for the elderly have risen from $8.2 billion in 1966 to $174 billion in 1992. This latter figure was 29 percent of the total health bill, even though the elderly (people seventy-five years and over) comprise only 3 percent of the population. Medical care for the 5 percent of Medicare enrollees who die each year requires between 25 and 35 percent of Medicare dollars. Thus, the elderly absorb proportionately the largest share of the health care expenditures.

A large percentage of the elderly are in nursing homes or in hospitals. Nursing homes are institutions without exits. Once admitted to a nursing home, patients lose their options; in most cases, they have arrived at their last place of residence (Hochbaum & Galkin 1982). A survey of residents of nursing homes in Kansas found that 95 percent felt that their move to the home was permanent (Maynard-Moody 1982). In New York State, only 9 percent of the residents are ever discharged to their homes; the rest die or are discharged to hospitals or other nursing homes. But almost a third of those living in nursing homes are physically and socially capable of living on their own outside a nursing home (Maynard-Moody 1982). Persons usually are admitted because they are unable to take care of themselves, but many improve and could be discharged. Unfortunately, most cases are not reviewed after they have been admitted to a nursing home.

Most elderly people are admitted to a nursing home from a hospital after a precipitating event such as a broken hip. Many of them enter a nursing home because they lack the ability to live independently or are unable to piece together from an unorganized and fragmented health care system, a solution to their needs (Hochbaum & Galkin 1982, 59). Furthermore, there is an incentive for them to enter a nursing home because Medicaid covers only a small portion of their care if they stay at home, but a larger portion if they enter a nursing home. But even after a patient improves, nursing homes do not have mechanisms for discharge planning. Thus, most of those who enter never leave.

One of the reasons the elderly seldom are discharged from a nursing home is that there is no place for them to go after discharge. Most have given up their homes and would have to be taken in by relatives if they were discharged. General housing trends in the nation tend to isolate the elderly. Over two-thirds of American homes are the single family, detached suburban type (Woodward 1982). Such homes are ideal for the nuclear family (husband, wife, and children) but not for the grandparents. Only 8 percent of the elderly in 1980 said they lived with their children, although 42 percent said they depended on their children for support.

Most elderly people live in a retirement community, a nursing home, alone at home, or in a home for the aged. In essence, they are separated from the rest of society and this may well be a factor in their health care needs. There is some evidence indicating that if the elderly continued to be productive and valued by society, their health would not deteriorate as rapidly.

AIDS

Although many communicable diseases in the United States have been conquered and the major health focus has been on the chronic diseases of aging, in 1981, a major new communicable disease appeared, caused by the Human Immunological Virus (HIV). The virus, which is transmitted through sexual contact or blood, causes Acquired Immune Deficiency Syndrome (AIDS), which is a breakdown in the immune system, leaving the victim vulnerable to a number of illnesses which are fatal.

By 1991, it was estimated that 10 million people worldwide carried the HIV virus and 1 million in the United States had it. Over 126,000 Americans had died from AIDS caused by the HIV virus and another 196,000 had developed AIDS and would likely die (see Figure 6–5).

But the general public's attitude about AIDS treated it as a moral issue believing it to be a direct result of liberal and permissive attitudes of the 1960s and 1970s; they tended to believe that people who get AIDS bring it on themselves as a result of the way they behave. For example, a 1988 Times/CBS News Poll found that only 39 percent said they have a lot or some sympathy for people who get AIDS from homosexual activity, and only 30 percent said they had sympathy for people who get AIDS from sharing needles while using illegal drugs (Kagay 1991, B8). In the early 1980s, AIDS was identified as a "gay plague" because it was homosexuals who most often got AIDS. This perception prevented resources from being directed into a fight against the disease. The Reagan and Bush administrations refused to give high priority to a fight against AIDS. But as male homosexuals took corrective steps and the rate of AIDS among homosexuals fell, the rate among minorities accelerated, primarily due to intravenous drug use. The proportion of AIDS cases who were IV drug users reached 30 percent by 1993, up from 17 percent in the mid-1980s. Of all the AIDS cases in 1992, 53 percent were Anglos, 30 percent African-American, 17 percent Hispanic, and less than 1 percent Asian and Native Americans. A commission appointed by Congress recommended in 1992 that prevention efforts and treatment programs more effectively address the special needs of minorities who bore a disproportionate share of the disease. It argued that socioeconomic factors—particularly poor access to health care and substance abuse brought on by poverty—had a powerful influence on how they behaved and thus the government had an obligation to help them. But public support for the AIDS effort could fade if it was seen as another infection of the underclass. Minorities do not have great power in American politics, especially IV drug users.

FIGURE 6–5 AIDS: Its deadly 10-year history—Cases reported as of Sept. 30, 1991.

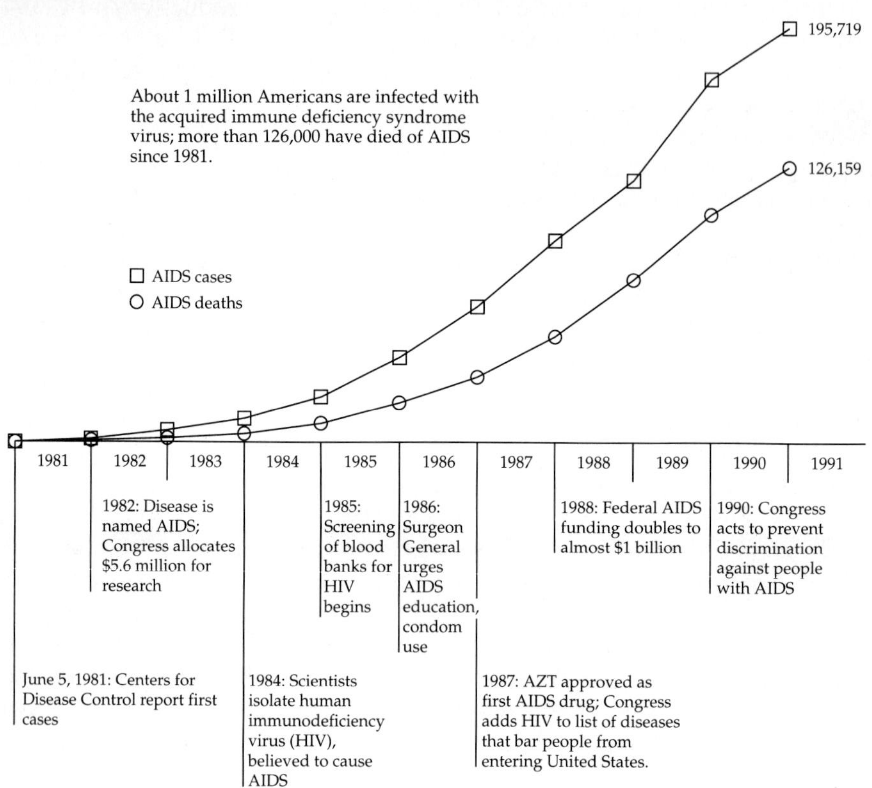

Source: Gay Men's Health Crisis; AIDS Action Council; Centers for Disease Control; Knight-Ridder Tribune News, National Weekly Edition, Nov. 18–24, 1991, p. 10.

How the AIDS problem is defined thus has a big impact on what public policy will be. A large part of the public, particularly conservatives, looked at it as a moral issue. People bring it on themselves as a result of how they behave, in this view, and thus the solution is for them to stop their "immoral" behavior (that is, having homosexual relationships and using IV drugs). Social scientists on the other hand, see it primarily as a sociocultural problem for which the solution is prevention and treatment programs such as providing free clean needles to addicts and providing condoms to sexually active youth. Moralists see this as condoning and encouraging immoral behavior and thus oppose it. The medical community see AIDS as a biomedical problem and want resources channeled into medical research in the hope of finding a cure and better ways to treat it.

The hopes of finding a cure are very low because of the long period in which no symptoms appear and the impracticality of testing everyone. Even more important is the complexity and mutability of the virus. It is good at camouflaging its intentions. It lies dormant for years and then all of a sudden flares up. It lives so deep in the interior of one's own genetic mechanism that it is hard to kill it without killing the patient.

Some experts believed that AIDS peaked in 1991. Most of the 1 million people who carried the virus were infected years before, and the number of new infections every year were steadily dropping, from 100,000 in the early 1980s to 40,000 in 1991. But some argue that the epidemic had peaked only among gays and IV drug users, not in the heterosexual population to which it had spread in 1992. Others doubted whether it would spread as rapidly among the heterosexual population because it is very difficult to transmit through regular sexual intercourse. It also is difficult to tell if the disease had peaked because it is difficult to estimate exactly how many people actually have the HIV virus. Since it is asymptomatic for a long period, people may not know they have it and continue to infect others. Moreover, researchers do not know how many people actually are inflicted but not yet ill.

Activists have tried to have AIDS treated the same as any other disease because they believe it must be stripped of its stigma in order to combat it. But at the same time, they argue that it is special in order to maintain high public support for fighting the disease. The fight against AIDS depends on the public recognizing that it is not a gay, underclass, Democrat, or Republican disease, but an equal opportunity disease.

Inequities in Health Care Services

Although there has been a vast improvement in the availability of health care provided to the poor, many inequities still exist. The improvements that have occurred since 1940 in the distribution of services have been dramatic. In 1940, only 9 percent of the poor were covered by hospital insurance; by 1970, that figure had increased to 78 percent, and in 1980 it was 85 percent. In 1930, the high income groups had one-third more hospital admissions and twice as many physician visits as the poor. By 1970, the poor had more hospital admissions per 100 persons than the rich, and more physician visits as well. However, discrepancies still existed between whites and blacks. In 1970, 14 percent of whites visited a physician as compared to only 3.5 percent of blacks. In addition, about 38 million Americans had no health insurance at all in 1992, and only half of those with incomes between $5,000 and $10,000 a year had adequate insurance protection. By 1992 this situation had gotten worse; although 38 million Americans could not afford private health insurance, they were not poor enough to qualify for Medicaid. Another 15 million had inadequate insurance coverage. The poor were twice as likely as those with middle incomes, and three times as likely as those with upper incomes, to be unprotected by health insurance (Bayer & Callahan 1985). During the 1992 recession, millions of people lost their jobs and as a result their health insurance also.

Thus, Medicare and Medicaid have had a major impact on the maldistribution of health care services among the poor and the rich. But there still are some inequities in existence, particularly between blacks and whites.

An Ounce of Prevention

The kinds of diseases that afflict Americans today are best dealt with through prevention rather than by medical heroics such as heart transplants. Many studies have shown that the incidence of heart disease, stroke, and cancer can be reduced by things such as exercise and improved diet. About 390,000 new cases of occupational diseases are recognized annually, and more than 100,000 people die each year from identifiable occupational causes. Similarly, the 45,000 automobile deaths that occur each year and hundreds of thousands of injuries could be reduced through preventive measures.

Some of these diseases, injuries, and deaths could be prevented through better design of the work environment and better safety devices for autos. Many, however, require changes in behavior on the part of the individual. For example, if more people would stop smoking, drinking alcohol in excess, exercise more, use their seat belts in autos, and eat more balanced diets, chronic diseases and accidents would be greatly reduced. And if we improved automobile safety devices we could save 20,000 or more lives a year. These are things over which medical technology has little control even though we view the doctor as the key to health. According to Saward and Sorenson, Americans have "bought the importance of seeing the doctor. But upper respiratory infections and gastroenteritis account for most of the calls to a doctor and many more are made by people who have nothing at all the matter with them" (1980, 14).

The most difficult health measures are those that require the cooperation of the individual, or require a person to change his or her personal habits. A large improvement in health and exercise habits occurred in the early 1980s as jogging and physical fitness became popular. But smoking, alcoholism, drunk driving, and poor diet continued to be major problems. Whether government policy can or should try to control this is a question we shall address later in this chapter.

■ SETTING THE HEALTH POLICY AGENDA

Health care has been a part of the institutional agenda since the earliest settlements in America, although in a limited way and primarily at the local level.

In 1639, for example, Massachusetts Bay Colony passed an act ordering the recording of each birth and death, and in 1647 passed a regulation to prevent the pollution of Boston Harbor. In 1701, Massachusetts passed legislation requiring that smallpox patients be isolated from the rest of the population.

After the American Revolution, a number of yellow fever epidemics prompted several states to pass legislation permitting cities to adopt boards of health. Boston established one in 1799, Philadelphia in 1794, and New York in 1796. By the end of the eighteenth century, New York City formed a public health committee that was concerned with the quality of the water supplies, construction of common sewers, drainage of marshes, and interment of the dead.

A number of cities established public health departments in the early nineteenth century. Charleston established one in 1815, Philadelphia in 1818, and Providence in 1832. These concentrated mostly on sanitary nuisances, crowded living conditions, dirty streets, and the regulation of public baths and slaughterhouses. States established health departments later in the nineteenth century. At first, they were concerned mostly with matters such as quarantines in the major ports; subsequently, state departments of health adopted state-wide functions such as planning, intergovernmental relations, and regulations.

At the federal level, the U.S. Public Health Service began as a marine hospital in Norfolk, Virginia, in 1800. It was established by the Marine Hospital Service Act of 1798, which authorized the president to appoint physicians in each division to furnish medical and hospital care to sick and disabled seamen. But the first supervising surgeon for the Public Health Service was not appointed until 1870. In 1890, the Public Health Service was given the authority to provide interstate control of communicable diseases as a result of another devastating epidemic of yellow fever that entered New Orleans and spread throughout the Mississippi Valley. In 1902, the Marine Hospital Service was renamed the Public Health and Marine Hospital Service, and in 1912, it was named the U.S. Public Health Service.

The first major public policy thrusts to improve health focused on sanitary practices. Many infectious diseases are carried through water and food supplies, or by physical contact. Before the turn of the century, many lakes and rivers received the discharge of open and untreated human wastes and sewage, which led to disastrous epidemics. During the nineteenth century, the city of New Orleans alone had thirty-seven epidemics of yellow fever as well as outbreaks of cholera, plague, and smallpox. The public health profession was successful in helping control food and waterborne diseases and in promoting inoculations as a means of controlling infectious diseases such as diphtheria and whooping cough. Coupled with this was legislation aimed at improving sanitation, lighting, and ventilation in the crowded tenement houses in cities such as New York, Philadelphia, and Newark. Although this was designed primarily to improve living conditions for the poor, such tenement housing legislation also had a beneficial impact on their health.

Following successful public health measures aimed at cleaning up water and food supplies, the major focus of the health care agenda shifted to health care financing. Health care financing has been on the public agenda in America since the beginning of the century. In 1912, a campaign issue for Theodore Roosevelt on the Bull Moose ticket was universal health insurance. Since then a number of groups have favored shifting the burden of financing health care from private institutions to the federal government.

A central theme in this argument has been that private financing has produced intolerable inequities in the distribution of medical services in the United States (Marmor & Christenson 1982, 84). Labor unions such as the Congress of Industrial Organizations and United Auto Workers have spear-headed the recurrent demands for national health insurance. These demands failed to get onto the agenda of the federal government until the 1930s when various pressures resulted in the enactment of the Social Security Act (SSA) in 1935. The social reform leaders' primary aim was to provide economic security for the elderly, but this was bolstered by a loose coalition of church, professional, and consumer organizations who wanted to get the federal government involved in health care. As a result, the Social Security Act of 1935 greatly expanded public health services in the United States. Title VI of the SSA assisted states and other political subdivisions in establishing and maintaining adequate public health services, including the training of personnel for local health work. Grants-in-aid were provided to the states, which in turn strengthened and expanded their health programs.

However, President Roosevelt did not have national health insurance high on his list of priorities. Opposition by physicians, hospitals, and insurance companies to what they called "socialized medicine" effectively stymied movement toward any form of national health insurance during the 1930s. Opponents of national health insurance argued that the private market produced high quality health care in the United States and that "socialized medicine" as proposed in national health insurance would destroy this. They had allies from business groups such as the U.S. Chamber of Commerce, the National Association of Manufacturers, and Young Americans for Freedom.

Demands for national health insurance were revived during the Truman presidency. The principal argument was that medical services were inequitably distributed and that the rich were getting better medical services than the poor. For a time it appeared that national health insurance might pass; in 1948, public opinion favored federal financing of medical care, and the democrats gained control of Congress. But even with the support of President Truman, national health insurance still was blocked in Congress.

In 1950, the Democrats lost control of Congress and the American Medical Association stepped up its campaign against national health insurance. The debate over health insurance was intensely ideological. According to sociologist Paul Starr, "The interest groups opposed to health insurance repeatedly found it useful to cast the issue in ideological terms. By accusing the supporters of health insurance as being agents first of German statism and then of Soviet communism, they meant to inject a meaning into health insurance that the reformers deeply resented" (1982, 187).

The issue was moribund from 1952 to 1960, partly because it was not high on President Eisenhower's list of priorities and partly because of the American Medical Association's effective campaign against it. Supporters of national health insurance then decided to shift their strategy to one of incrementalism. They pared down their goals and agreed to accept more limited legislation aimed at helping the elderly and the poor. They argued that the United States was the only Western industrialized nation that did not have a government program of providing support for health care for the poor and the elderly. In fact, many European countries had established health insurance programs. The first country to establish a national system of compulsory sickness insurance was Germany in 1883; Austria followed in 1888, Hungary in 1891, Norway in 1909, Serbia in 1910, Britain in 1911, Russia in 1912, and The Netherlands in 1913.

The mid-1960s were ripe for resurrecting the financing issue and placing it on the agenda again. According to Marmor and Christenson, "A constituency supported such efforts, welfare economics provided some intellectual justification, and a healthy economy provided the means" (1982, 85). A crucial congressional shift occurred when the House Ways and Means Committee Chairman Wilbur Mills decided to support a program aimed at providing hospital and physician services for the elderly. Leading advocates of the legislation included groups such as the Committee of One Hundred, chaired by Walter Reuther, head of the United Automobile Workers union. Using a rhetoric of crisis, breakdown, and chaos, they were able to convince Americans that action was needed. Surveys showed that a large percentage of Americans agreed, even though they did not regard the crisis as their own. But the issue was firmly implanted on the institutional agenda, and beginning in 1965, a host of policies aimed at improving the health of Americans were formulated and adopted.

However, the issue of national health insurance died down until 1992 when Harris Wofford won election to the U.S. Senate from Pennsylvania with his proactive stance on health care as a major factor. And, with the election of Bill Clinton in November 1992, the prospects for major health reform brightened, although none of his election proposals involved a national health insurance system.

■ FORMULATION AND ADOPTION OF HEALTH POLICY

The period between 1965 and 1978 blossomed with a host of health-care policies. More than seventy separate acts were passed, ranging from the Air Quality Control Act of 1972 to the Saccharin Control Act of 1976. For purposes of discussion, we will divide this legislation into five major categories: (1) hospitals; (2) the elderly and the poor; (3) controlling costs; (4) health-care personnel; and (5) preventive health measures. Each of these categories is described below.

Hospitals

Prior to the surge of new legislation beginning in 1965, Congress passed a watershed act for health care in the United States. This was the Hospital Survey and Construction Act (HSCA) of 1946, also known as the Hill-Burton Act. Although unanticipated, this legislation had a greater impact on health care costs and services in the United States than any other single piece of legislation. The purpose of this act was to encourage the construction of hospitals, particularly in rural and poor areas.

As we shall see, most health-care legislation passed after 1965 was a bundle of compromises tied loosely together by a coalition of opposing forces, each of which expected something different from the law. As a result, most legislation has vague and ambiguous goals, which the implementing agency has the task of making specific and concrete. This was *not* the case with the 1946 HSCA. There were no conflicting goals in the act; it was given sufficient funding, and the social technology for accomplishing its goals was available. Thus, it contained all of the potential for success and was very popular politically. It was supported by the states because it would feed money into them for construction. It also was supported by interest groups, including the powerful American Medical Association and the American Hospital Association. The public also was very supportive since it believed that availability of hospitals was essential to improving health. It was, in short, ideal "pork barrel" legislation yielding rich political benefits.

The legislation took off rapidly. There was little attempt at the federal level to monitor the states, and hospitals with as few as twenty-five beds were approved. By the mid-seventies, the legislation was so successful in stimulating hospital construction that the number of hospitals had grown to excess. Congress began searching for ways of cutting back construction because hospitals, by engaging in unnecessary surgery, were threatening the lives of the patients they were supposed to serve. In 1947, the value of hospital assets was $5.88 billion, and by 1974, this had increased to $52 billion. The use of hospitals almost doubled during this same period. This alarmed Congress and raised questions about the need for much of the surgery being performed. For example, only half of the surgeries to remove ovaries and half of appendectomies could be justified. Support for the HSCA began to crumble. By 1975, congressional appropriations declined by 25 percent. In 1974 the poor complained that they were not being served by HSCA, and in 1978, the Department of Health, Education, and Welfare issued new regulations aimed at improving access to hospitals by the needy.

Attempts to contain the growth of hospitals began as early as 1964 with amendments to the HSCA. These amendments established local health facilities planning councils. In 1966, comprehensive health planning agencies were created which were supposed to survey local needs and decide whether additional hospitals were needed. But neither the councils nor the health planning agencies were effective. So, in 1974 Congress passed the Health Planning and Resources Development Act (HPRDA). However, this time Congress chose not to specify the precise objectives of the planning agencies; instead, it tossed the issue into the laps of the local Health Systems Agencies (HSAs) (Thompson 1981).

Under the 1974 HPRDA some 200 HSAs were established to assemble and analyze data, assess the adequacy of health resources in their areas, prepare five-year health plans, and establish priorities among objectives. The HSAs could issue certificates of need and recommend approval or disapproval of any hospital action that would increase total bed capacity or entail the expenditure of over $100,000 for equipment. The HSAs could freeze a community's hospital capacity, or refuse all requests for equipment purchase and modification. National health planning guidelines for 1975 contained a planning standard of four hospital beds per 1,000 persons as a maximum for a community, accompanied by an 80 percent occupancy rate.

Some experts believed that such direct action strategies could not work, and indeed, they have not worked to date. Although HSAs wielded both "sticks and carrots"—that is, sanctions and rewards—health care providers payed little attention to HSA plans. More than 90 percent of the requests for hospital facilities submitted to HSAs have been approved. The sticks—called "limp spaghetti" by one HSA director—allowed the agencies to stymie or delay projects deemed to be inconsistent with health plans. But, as one expert noted, asking professionals to control the growth of things that benefit them is a little like asking the fox to guard the hen house (Olson 1982). It did not work. And so, over a period of forty years, public policy on hospitals has done a complete about-face; it began by encouraging the growth it was now attempting to control.

In 1982, hospital room and board fees were rising 14 percent, almost triple the inflation rate for that year. Under the system existing in 1982, hospitals were paid according to the bills they submitted. As a result, there was extremely wide variation in what was paid; some hospitals charged $1,500 to treat a heart attack patient whereas others charged $9,000 for the same treatment.

In 1983, the Secretary of Health and Human Services recommended a prospective payment plan aimed at controlling hospital costs. Under the plan, hospitals would receive a predetermined fee regardless of the length of the patient's stay or the kind of service rendered. The prospective payment plan was adopted at the end of 1983. The plan set fees in advance for some 467 different treatments. Hospitals could not bill patients for what the government did not pay. Efficient hospitals were rewarded; if their fee was lower, they could keep the difference between their actual costs and the fee.

Hospitals fared well under the system. Profit margins on Medicare operations rose 14 percent in 1984 during the first year of the plan (Rich 1985). This led to criticism that hospitals were discharging patients too early and delaying treatment to the poor in order to maximize profits. The prospective payment system radically changed the relationship between hospitals and patients, hospitals and doctors, and doctors and patients. Fierce competition developed among hospitals, requiring them to keep an eye on costs. Some believed that the quality component would inevitably be sacrificed. However, a critical review of the system completed in 1991 concluded that the prospective payment plan "appears to have saved Medicare money without causing systematic, documented harm to patients or the health care industry" (Coulam & Gaumer 1991, 73).

Hospitals vigorously oppose any attempt to regulate costs. For example, in 1983 attempts were made to control hospital costs in Arizona. The Arizona Hospital Association announced it was prepared to spend $3 million on a public relations campaign to quash these efforts. Ronald Krause, president of the association said, "We will resist every piece of legislation aimed at hospitals" (Seper et al. 1983, A-10). Of course, there was good reason for the opposition. Americans were spending $817 billion a year in 1992 on health care, which made it a very lucrative business indeed. As a result, the number of private hospitals and health care companies in the United States increased dramatically. Hospitals and doctors found ways of getting around government attempts to control costs. After the 1983 controls on payments for in-hospital care, doctors shifted many services to out-patient clinics which are not covered by the controls. From 1985 to 1990, Medicare spending for outpatient services grew three times as fast as spending for patients admitted to hospitals (Pear 1991, 1). This was changed in 1991, but it did not halt the steady rise in health care costs. It is like pushing on a balloon, said Representative Pete Stark of California. The 1991 bill provided lump-sum payments that would give hospitals an incentive to provide outpatient care more efficiently. But such proposals did not attack the more fundamental issue of whether it was time to completely overhaul the way health care is financed, an issue that will be discussed next.

The Elderly and the Poor

It took more than a quarter of a century to reach the point where conditions were ripe to provide hospital services for the elderly and the poor. On July 30, 1965, President Lyndon Johnson signed the Medicare and Medicaid bills in Independence, Missouri, where Harry Truman was born. Johnson chose Independence to mark the fact that twenty years earlier, President Truman tried to get similar legislation passed. Reflecting on the two decades that finally culminated in Medicare, Johnson said that the surprising thing was not that the bill had passed, but that it had taken so many years to pass.

Title XVIII of the Social Security Act established the Medicare program to provide health insurance benefits for the aged and disabled. Title XVIII is divided into two sections: Part A, Hospital Insurance, and Part B, Supplementary Medical Insurance. Part A pays for part of the cost of inpatient hospital care and related care provided by skilled nursing facilities. Part B provides coverage for a variety of medical services and supplies furnished by physicians or other health care professionals, outpatient hospital services, and home health services. Part A of Medicare is financed through a payroll tax on employers and employees. Part B is financed through premium payments (32 percent) and general revenues (68 percent).

Medicaid was established in 1965 by Title XIX of the Social Security Act as a joint federal-state program to provide medical assistance to certain categories of low-income persons. The program is state administered and provides federal matching funds for a portion of the cost of providing medical benefits to the categorically eligible. Those eligible for Medicaid are those who receive assistance under various titles of the Social Security Act, including poor families with dependent children, permanently and totally disabled persons, blind persons, and certain individuals among the elderly poor. The federal share of Medicaid payments in a given state is based on the state's per capita income. The federal share ranges from 50 to 78 percent, averaging 54.5 percent in 1980. Medicaid has a stronger orientation toward long-term, non-acute, institutional care than does Medicare. Long-term care includes nursing facilities, home health agencies, and mental hospitals. Long-term care benefits comprised half of Medicaid expenditures in 1980. Government nursing home payments comprised about 50 percent of total spending for nursing homes in 1980 (Gibson & Waldo 1981).

Both laws got off to a quick start. By July 1, 1966, over 90 percent of the 200 million Americans had signed up for Medicare. Medicaid was a bit slower, but by July 1968, thirty-seven states had adopted programs, and by 1971, every state except Arizona had signed up. (Arizona still was not a participant in 1987.) In their first full year of operation, the two programs cost the federal government $4.5 billion dollars. But by 1980, Medicare and Medicaid together cost $60.6 billion, financing nearly 28 percent of all personal health care expenditures and accounting for over two-thirds of all public spending for personal health care. In 1983, about one-fifth (51 million people) of the American population was covered by Medicare and/or Medicaid and by 1986, Medicare expenditures *alone* reached $60 billion.

Medicare and Medicaid have dramatically altered the nature of public spending for health care since 1965. Twenty years ago, the federal government share of public spending was 13.2 percent and the state and local government share was 13 percent. By 1986, the federal portion increased to 29.6

percent, while the state and local share dropped to 10 percent (Gibson & Waldo 1981, 13). Because a large percentage of Medicare and Medicaid expenditures covers hospital care, public spending for hospital care jumped from 38.9 percent to 54.8 percent between 1965 and 1967, and remained at that level through 1985. The public share of spending for physicians' services went from 8.5 percent in 1965 to 27.9 percent in 1983 (Gibson & Waldo 1981, 8).

The supporters of Medicare and Medicaid believed that these laws actually would be short-lived and would soon be replaced by broader legislation such as national health insurance. But by 1992, these laws had been in existence for twenty-seven years.

Both Medicare and Medicaid are typical products of the policy-formulation process in that they attempt to achieve more than a single goal. They are intended to improve the health of Americans, but at the same time, they are aimed primarily at the elderly, poor, and disabled rather than at the majority of Americans. These policies are supposed to achieve both health and social welfare goals while at the same time keeping costs within reason. But since the elderly suffer from chronic diseases that require expensive halfway technologies, the Medicare and Medicaid policies have not been very successful in accomplishing their goals.

Controlling Costs

As the cost of health care continued to rise, public policy focused more on ways of trying to control it. In 1973, Congress passed the Health Maintenance Organization Act. By introducing competition into the health services delivery system, it was hoped that health costs might come down. In addition, it was assumed that Health Maintenance Organizations would be more efficient and economical in providing services than the traditional solo practice system. A Health Maintenance Organization (HMO) is a group practice plan in which members are treated by any of the physicians employed by the organization. In solo practice, the patient sees his or her own doctor in a private office.

Health Maintenance Organizations come in various types. The traditional *staff model* employs a number of different physicians. The patient must use one of the physicians who is employed by the HMO. Thus, the patient technically cannot choose his or her physician in this type of HMO. The Kaiser Plan in California and Hawaii operates on this principle.

The staff model is one of three acceptable forms of HMOs. In the second type, the organization contracts with a medical group to provide services on a salaried basis or in terms of a fixed amount per HMO member. In the third type of HMO, called the *individual practice association,* the organization contracts with physicians to provide service on a fee-for-service basis. The 1973 act also specified what types of services should be provided by HMOs. Enrollment was to be broadly based, including various age, social, and income groups. The organizations were also required to hold open enrollment for thirty days each year.

The HMO Act overturned state laws that prevented the establishment of prepaid group practices. It required all employers of more than twenty-five employees to offer the choice of an HMO if one was available in their area. However, the requirement that HMOs hold open enrollment for thirty days each year put them at a competitive disadvantage with traditional solo practice. Open enrollment forced them to accept the most difficult cases and biggest risks, whereas other plans could be more selective in what risks they would take. The HMO Act thereby tried to satisfy two sets of concerns at the same time: those who favored competition, and those who felt government ought to ensure services to those for whom services are not usually available. The 1976 and 1978 amendments to the act tried to change this by modifying the open enrollment requirement and by limiting the scope of benefits. By 1978, membership in HMOs was about 7½ million people and by 1987 it had reached 29 million (Gloderell 1988, 23).

Health Care Personnel

Another goal of health care policy in the United States has been to increase the number of physicians available, particularly in regions where the shortages are the greatest such as rural areas and small towns. Most physicians practice in large cities and metropolitan areas where facilities and patients are more plentiful. In 1963, the Health Professions Assistance Act was passed, requiring medical schools to expand enrollment before they would be eligible for federal funds for construction. The legislation was supported by the medical profession. A number of other bills passed by Congress have sought to increase the supply of physicians, particularly those in general practice (which declined from 64 percent in 1940 to 27 percent in 1970) and in rural areas. The 1971 Comprehensive Health Manpower Training Act, for example, provided capitation grants to medical schools based on the number of students enrolled.

In 1973, the Emergency Health Personnel Act was passed in an attempt to increase the number of physicians locating in critical shortage areas and the percentage going into general practice. This was done through special project grants to bring about improvements in medical school curriculums. However, the act did not specify a target number of physicians, nor did it define what it meant by "critical shortage areas." As a result, it had a negligible impact on the distribution of physicians. It was followed up in 1976 with the Health Professions Educational Assistance Act which continued the capitation grants of the 1971 CHMTA, but which no longer emphasized increasing the number of physicians; it focused more heavily on trying to correct the geographical imbalance in the supply of physicians and on increasing the number of physicians in general practice. As we shall see in the next section, these laws had only partial success in achieving their objectives.

Preventive Measures

The late 1960s and early 1970s were boom years for laws aimed at preventing accidental injuries, fatalities, and environmental threats to health and safety. The Traffic Safety Act was passed in 1966, Clean Air Amendments in 1970, the Occupational Safety and Health Act in 1970, Consumer Product Safety Act in 1972, Noise Control Act in 1972, Hazardous Material Transportation Act in 1974, and the Safe Drinking Water Act in 1974. All of these were part of what was known as the "new social regulation," which required administrators to identify and define pertinent threats to health, create standards to reduce them, and assure compliance by firms.

This surge in governmental regulatory activity brought cries of anguish from those who were affected by it, which included a large number of individuals. But governmental regulation is nothing new to American public policy. The government has been involved in regulating economic activity in the United States ever since the passage of the Interstate Commerce Act of 1887 and the Sherman Anti-Trust Act in 1890. And, as described above, state and local governments also were involved in regulating building construction and land use as well as public health. But the surge of regulations of the late 1960s and early 1970s were more extensive, covering more areas than ever before.

There are a number of reasons why government became involved in these areas. One reason is precipitating events such as the discovery of toxic and hazardous wastes dumped at Love Canal, New York, which forced an entire town to close down. Events such as this helped stimulate demand for governmental regulation in hazardous waste disposal. A second reason for increased government involvement is greater knowledge about the link between risk factors such as toxic chemicals and various diseases (Bardach & Kagan 1982). A third reason was the surge in automobile fatalities in the 1960s and an increase in occupational diseases and accidents. Fourth, the affluence of society in the late 1960s inspired the belief that society could afford the cost of creating safer and healthier environments. The strategy adopted by government was to pass the cost on to industry by requiring them to adopt safety devices or add pollution-reducing equipment. The only cost to government was that of setting up a new regulatory agency, which was indeed acceptable, and even desirable.

Initially, the regulatory approach was relatively easy for policy makers because the real cost of carrying out the regulations fell on the shoulders of business firms. Auto manufacturers were required to install seat belts and pollution reduction equipment on cars; industrial firms were required to make their businesses safer and less of a threat to workers' health; and electrical power utilities were required to install costly, pollution-reduction equipment on their power plants. Eventually, however, these costs were passed on to consumers. As the costs mounted, fueling an ever-increasing inflation, opposition to the "new social regulations" grew. The main problem was in determining when the regulations were reasonable and when they were excessive. The principal question was: Are the benefits to society derived from the regulations worth the costs? We have already considered this question with regard to automobile safety (see Chapter 5). In this section, we will consider the risk to health and safety of an unsafe and unhealthy working environment.

The Occupational Safety and Health Act of 1970 (OSHA) was passed primarily due to the lobbying efforts of organized labor. It aimed at fostering a healthful work environment "so far as feasible." It did not, however, set specific targets or time tables for achieving reductions in the rate of injuries or occupational diseases. The law gave the Occupational Safety and Health Administration the difficult task of making tradeoffs between the costs to industry of adopting new practices and the health benefits derived.

The new agency rushed to implement the law, fearing that a long delay would cause it to lose support. But its efforts at aggressive regulation led to considerable opposition in the business community. Business firms argued that OSHA had consistently failed to adopt reasonable cost-effective rules. In November of 1974, President Ford issued an executive order that required OSHA to accompany proposals for new regulations with statements about their economic benefits as well as costs. Both Congress and subsequent administrations pressured OSHA to consider the costs to industry of its regulations. But OSHA considered only whether or not a standard was feasible and the costs reasonable. The agency consistently declined to place a value on human life (Thompson 1981).

Valuing Human Life The issue of whether it is possible to place an economic value on human life comes up in a number of areas in health policy. It has been estimated, for example, that providing sprinklers in nursing homes costs about $86,000 for each year of life saved, and that maintaining coke fume standards in the steel industry costs over $4 million per worker life saved (Rhodes 1980). These costs raise thorny questions not unlike those which we opened with in this chapter. Should we spend $86,000 per life to help save the lives of thousands of eighty-six-year-old residents of nursing homes who may not live much longer anyway and who are totally dependent on others in order to perform simple bodily functions? Before questions such as this can be answered, a distinction must be made between saving a specific, known person whose life is threatened (for example, little Jimmy Smith trapped in a cave, or your mother) and saving the lives of thousands of unidentified people whose lives *may be* harmed some time in the future if we do not take action now. In the former case, the societal response invariably is to do everything possible to save the person. In the latter case, it is a matter of whether or not we have sufficient resources to take the necessary action, whether the amount of resources required is reasonable, and whether or not it would be better to invest the same resources in other, perhaps better purposes. In policy analysis, we are concerned with whether we should take certain present action to possibly prevent some future injuries or deaths. We know, for example, that about 45,000 people will be killed next year in auto accidents. But we do not stop people from driving to avoid this almost certain outcome. Instead, we take some reasonable steps—not all we rationally know could be taken—to try to reduce the number of people who will be killed. But how do we define what is reasonable?

Obviously, there is a point at which expenditures to save lives become excessive. What we need is a means for deciding when this point has been reached. The principle is unassailable. Ethical and moral considerations lead to the conclusion that there are times when it becomes necessary to end a specific life. In 1985 it became legally accepted in New Jersey that it is appropriate to "pull the plug" on someone who is not much more than a "vegetable," being kept alive only through machines. Medical heroics to maintain the life of a patient who is almost completely gone are discontinued after a certain time, especially if there is no hope that the person will be able to recover enough to live without the aid of machines.

The problem is not whether or not we should place value on human life, but *how* to do so. Currently, there are three different ways of placing value on human life:

1. Estimating the future expected income of the person. When this is done, the figure tends to range between $100,000 and $400,000, depending on the group of individuals involved. If this method is used, young men's lives, on the average, are worth more than young women's lives.
2. The willingness to pay principle. This can be done through a survey in which individuals are asked how much they would pay to save a life, or by considering the decisions made by individuals who take high-risk jobs.
3. The average amount courts award to surviving relatives in accident cases. In 1982, the average amount was about $400,000.

Economists cannot agree on which of these three methods of valuing human life is best. In principle, they tend to favor the second method, because they prefer a "market" solution to the questions. The second method is a form of a market solution. However, it has its flaws. For example, individuals who do high-risk work such as washing windows on skyscrapers, or descending into nuclear power plants to clean them out are paid extra for this. The amount they are paid extra might be used to determine how much they value their own lives. Still, this does not consider the possibility that economic necessity forces some of these individuals to take jobs they would not ordinarily take.

None of the three methods of valuing life is without its flaws. The first and third suffer from the fact that the life of a young man in a profession is worth more than that of a young woman. Thus, there is no perfect method for determining the value of human life.

Political scientist Steven F. Rhodes (1980) argues that, as difficult as it is to place value on human life, it is necessary to do so because striving for too much safety in one area drives up the cost of doing business and prevents us from spending money in other areas. It is not possible to have a completely safe environment, thus it is necessary to make choices. When we make a decision to force the steel industry to spend money to reduce the amount of coke fumes in the air, we are implicitly putting a value on human life. Why not make it explicit?

Even though there is no perfect method for valuing human life, accepting a reasonable method helps us make more rational decisions. For example, the study by the Carnegie-Mellon Institute discussed in Chapter 5 (see page 147) used the willingness to pay principle to estimate the cost of a human life. Even though one may dispute the accuracy of the actual figures used, the study enabled us to compare the cost-effectiveness and cost-benefit ratio for several different auto safety policy options. The results show clearly that the incremental policy now in existence for automobiles (that is, lap and shoulder belts) is far less cost-effective than other options. Thus, the study is useful for making decisions about policy in this area.

National Health Insurance

National health insurance has been on the institutional agenda of the United States for a number of years, but so far no bill has been passed. Such a policy, if adopted, would require a major shift in health care policy. Therefore, it is important enough to merit some consideration.

Several basic types of proposed bills now dominate the debate on national health insurance. Each of these proposals reflects different ideological orientations. One type involves minimum governmental intervention. A representative of this approach is the American Medical Association's proposal called Medicredit, which proposes that a federal tax subsidy for health insurance premiums be given directly to taxpayers. Instead of the deductions people take from their income taxes under current law, they would be given a subsidy. Their credit would be graduated inversely with an individual's income; the higher the income, the lower the subsidy. Such subsidies would increase the purchasing power of consumers, leaving the rest of the health-care delivery system much as it is. Other proposals falling into this category are major medical insurance plans, which frequently offer a high deductible (for example, $5,000), and pay bills that exceed 10 percent or more of a family's income.

A second type of proposal involves major government intervention. Most of the proposals in this category would give the government a monopoly on health insurance. One such proposal is contained in the 1974 Kennedy-Corman bill. Under this proposal, every American would be eligible to receive benefits.

The program would be financed entirely through payroll taxes and general revenues, and there would be no cost-sharing by patients.

The third major type of proposal follows a mixed strategy, combining greater government involvement than the current system with increased patient costs. The Ford administration's Comprehensive Health Insurance Plan (CHIP) falls into this category. Under this proposal, employers would offer alternative health plans to their employees, patients would pay a larger share of the cost than they now do under Medicare, and states would be required to control costs. Similar to this is the 1974 Kennedy-Mills proposal which differs from CHIP in that it would be run by the Social Security Administration and financed by a 4 percent payroll tax. The cost of the Kennedy-Mills bill has been estimated at $77 billion a year, whereas the cost of the CHIP plan has been estimated at $43 billion, and the cost of the Kennedy-Corman bill at $103 billion a year (Marmor & Christenson 1982).

Throughout the 1970s a number of these proposals have been debated in Congress and in 1974, it looked as if a bill might be passed when President Nixon introduced his Comprehensive Health Insurance Plan. The plan is similar to the CHIP described above. Hearings were held by the Ways and Means Committee on the bill for three months, but the bill was watered down so much in these hearings that it lost many of its supporters. Labor unions objected to the proposed expansion of private insurance, and medical groups objected to the compulsory enrollment feature and to the financial regulations. On August 21, 1974, Chairman of the Ways and Means Committee Wilbur Mills announced that he would not go to the floor of the House with a bill that was approved in the committee by only a thirteen to twelve vote. Several other bills were introduced in 1975 but died in the committee for lack of consensus.

When Bill Clinton was elected President in November 1992, prospects for major reforms in health care increased. However, although there was widespread consensus that the system was "broken" as former Surgeon General C. Everett Koop said, the Clinton proposal for "managed competition" fell far short of total reform. Under managed competition, businesses would buy health coverage through giant coops that would negotiate with networks of doctors and hospitals for a comprehensive benefit package.

During 1992, there was a great deal of talk about the Canadian system of universal health care. Under this arrangement, all citizens are entitled to care that is mainly funded by the government from taxes. People can choose their doctors who are paid by the government. Costs are controlled by limiting the total pot out of which doctors, hospitals, and other caregivers are paid. However, critics argued that such a system would be very costly. Moreover, the Canadian system had major problems, including rising costs, less high-tech care such as open heart surgery and hip replacements, and complaints by doctors that the government was acting like a military dictator. The physicians claimed the government was trying to make them the scapegoats for their budget woes.

Unlike the British system in which doctors are government employees, in the Canadian system doctors are not employed by the state. But because the government limits the amount it will spend each year, it has a mighty leverage over doctors' fees and hospital costs. This is anathema to American doctors, who charge that the system "rations" health care. But the executive director of the Ontario Ministry of Health says, "So do you. The fact that sick Americans have access to distinguished medical services, so that millions have none, seems like rationing to me. I have never understood why Americans stand for it" (Specter 1989, 31).

It is unlikely that a national health insurance proposal will be enacted in the near future unless a number of unusual events occur simultaneously as was the case for Medicare. These events include, for example, major changes in the public's perception about the need for national health insurance, unusual economic conditions that increase the gross national product, and political circumstances conducive to greater government involvement, such as Democratic Party control of the presidency and Congress. In 1993, only the last event existed, but there wasn't consensus among the Democrats about what policy should be adopted and a continuing depressed economy. Whatever direction health policy takes, it is most likely to involve incremental changes rather than a large step forward—or backward. The most likely course in the future will be a mixture of increased government involvement along with more patient cost sharing and the promotion of competition in the delivery of health services.

The Health Policy Formulation Process

Much of the legislation described in this chapter was passed in the usual way policy is formulated in American politics. Many of the bills attempt to achieve several different goals simultaneously, and several of the goals are conflicting. Such is the case with the Health Maintenance Organization Act of 1973. This policy was aimed at trying to increase competition in the delivery of health care services, thereby driving down costs. At the same time, the act provided comprehensive services and required a thirty-day open enrollment period. It could not both reduce costs and still provide comprehensive services, thus the range of services and number of individuals eligible had to be restricted.

Many of the bills passed between 1961 and 1974 were the result of compromises that led to undesirable consequences. Such was the case with Medicare, particularly with regard to the decision about how hospitals and physicians were to be reimbursed. The law decided that hospitals would be given their "reasonable costs" and physicians should be paid their "customary fees." Instead of deciding to reimburse hospitals for actual expenses and set the fees to be paid for physicians, Congress accepted the compromise approach fearing that the bill would be killed if these provisions were not written into the law. As a result, health-care costs have skyrocketed, and the principal beneficiaries have been physicians and hospitals. In October of 1965, *Medical World News* described Medicare as a bonanza for physicians (Thompson 1981). According to economist Mancur Olson, "these programs [Medicare and Medicaid] have . . . been designed and administered in such a way as to generate vastly increased incomes for physicians and some other relatively well-to-do providers" (1982, 9).

Medicaid and Medicare are excellent examples of *interest group liberalism* (Lowi 1964), in which the government simply responds to pressures from organized interests rather than establishing its own priorities. The legislation was designed and controlled by the major interest groups who benefited from it. A large number of the elderly and the poor gained access to medical services under the legislation at the expense of the public and to the great benefit of those who provide health services.

In addition to multiple and conflicting goals and compromises, another major characteristic of the health policy formulation process is *incrementalism.* None of the legislation that we have described initiated a radical shift in health care services and none radically altered the means by which health care is delivered, or provided broad and comprehensive care to a large proportion of the population. None of the bills was formulated in a rational way in the sense that specific goals were identified and the best or most cost-effective means was adopted for achieving those goals.

Incrementalism, multiple and conflicting goals, and compromises are characteristic of most of the health care legislation when we consider each bill individually. When we consider the bills as a group, we can see that health care policy is formulated in a disjointed and uncoordinated manner. Thus, while some bills were aimed at increasing the supply of doctors, others were aimed at encouraging physicians to engage in general practice, promoting construction of hospitals, helping finance care for the aged, increasing services for the poor, and trying to contain the skyrocketing costs generated by all of the other bills. Instead of an overall plan to guide policy, we have a series of separate, uncoordinated, incremental steps that often lead to unanticipated and undesirable consequences.

The final characteristic of health care policy to be considered here is that it often contains large gaps to be filled in by administrators. The Occupational Safety and Health Act is a good example of this. This legislation was mainly the result of the lobbying efforts of organized labor. The law stressed the need to foster healthful working conditions "so far as feasible," but it did not specify targets or time tables for achieving reductions in the rate of injuries or occupational disease. Most importantly, the law tossed the bureaucracy the difficult issue of tradeoffs between worker health and safety and costs. Hence, OSHA has played a large role in determining the direction of policy with regard to worker health and safety. As we shall now see, this is rather typical of health care policy in general; those who implement policy have a great deal of influence in determining the direction it takes. This includes both governmental administrators and private organizations and individuals.

IMPLEMENTING HEALTH CARE POLICY

At least a dozen different federal government agencies and a large number of state, local government, and private agencies are responsible for implementing health policy. The largest federal agency in terms of dollars spent is the Health Care Financing Administration of the U.S. Department of Health and Human Services. This agency implements Medicare and Medicaid.

Although not the largest agency in terms of dollars spent, the U.S. Public Health Service has the largest number of separate agencies under its command, including the following:

- *National Institutes of Health*—responsible for conducting health research.
- *Health Services Administration*—provides health services to low income families through grants.
- *Alcohol, Drug Abuse and Mental Health Administration*—supports research, treatment, and demonstration programs.
- *Health Resources Administration*—administers health planning and manpower programs.
- *Food and Drug Administration*—administers laws regarding dangerous drugs, food, medical devices, and cosmetics.
- *Center for Disease Control*—responsible for prevention and control of communicable diseases.
- *Office of the Assistant Secretary for Health*—manages the Public Health Service and the HMO program.

Other major federal agencies that implement health care are the Veterans Administration Medical Program, which operates VA hospitals and nursing homes; the Occupational Safety and Health Administration in the Department of Labor, which enforces health and safety standards; and the Mine Safety and Health Administration in the Department of Labor, which inspects mines and enforces health and safety requirements.

During the implementation stage, numerous interest groups try to influence a program's impact. A few examples are the National Governor's Conference, the Council of State Governments, and the National Association of Counties, which pressure the Department of Health and Human Services to change its regulations. Other important interest groups include the American Medical Association, American Hospital Association, and organized labor, all of which have a large stake in the billions of dollars spent on health care during implementation. In addition to government agencies and private interest groups, health care policy is implemented by hospitals, private insurance companies, physicians, private nursing homes, medical schools, and innumerable private business firms. New legislation often requires the cooperation of the individuals and private agencies in order to succeed. The following discussion describes some of the intricate and complex interrelationships that are created during implementation of health policies.

Medicaid and Medicare

Medicaid policy was implemented rapidly. Legislation was signed in 1965; by July 1968, 37 states had Medicaid programs, and by 1970, every state had a Medicaid program except Arizona. Medicaid is a joint federal-state cooperative program in which the states determine the amount of coverage available. As a result, implementation varies from state to state; some have very liberal benefits, whereas others do not. New York State, for example, adopted eligibility standards that entitled about 45 percent of the state's population to medical benefits (Thompson 1981, 129). Southern states provide much more limited coverage and a much smaller percentage of the poor receive benefits.

At the federal level, Medicaid was launched in a somewhat hostile administrative environment. It was initially placed in a new division of the Bureau of Family Services in the Department of Health, Education, and Welfare, where it became identified with social welfare rather than health. At the state level, 60 percent of Medicaid programs are administered by welfare departments (Loeb 1979, 12). This creates an identity problem for the program: Is it a health or a welfare program? A welfare program has more negative connotations than a health program. Being not clearly one or the other is even worse. Plagued by soaring costs and controversy, Congress did not move rapidly to beef up the program's meager personnel allotment. As a result, it took several years for federal officials to gain control over the states which were intent on moving rapidly.

Medicare exemplifies a public policy whose implementation was—and still is—completely controlled by the providers of health-care services, including physicians, hospitals, and insurance companies. Blue Cross and Blue Shield dominate the insurance system for hospital and physician services. In 1979, there were sixty-nine Blue Cross plans and sixty-nine Blue Shield plans. These programs enrolled 85.4 million persons for hospital care and 73.5 million persons for surgical services—37 and 38 percent of the population, respectively. Blue Cross and Blue Shield represent 47 percent of the hospital market for the elderly and 38 percent of the under-age-sixty-five market. For surgical care, they represent 67 percent of the elderly market and 35 percent of the market for workers and their families. Blue Cross and Blue Shield plans dominate the market for nursing home care, particularly for the elderly, where they hold 76 percent of the market (Carroll & Arnett 1981, 57).

Through Blue Cross, the hospitals have "created a system whereby almost everyone who [is] insured could choose the most costly hospital without paying extra, thereby tending to eliminate price competition among hospitals"

(Olson 1982, 9). The American Hospital Association supports this arrangement as do physicians and the insurance companies, because they all benefit from it. Physicians have worked to perpetuate this system. Mancur Olson cites one example in Oregon: "By encouraging partiality toward their own insurance company and resistance to the offending commercial insurance companies, the organized physicians were able to eliminate cost-cutting and competition-inducing insurance practices" (1982, 12). Physicians are able to control Blue Shield because every plan has at least one physician on its board. Thus, concludes Olson, "Because some of the providers have selected incentives that enable them to organize, and because the typical citizen has no incentive to gather detailed information on health policy, the details of health policy are mainly determined by providers" (1982, 14).

Note that the implementors of Medicare are mostly private agencies and individuals, not governmental agencies. Thus, although Medicare was passed mostly to improve the health of the elderly, it has been implemented in a way that increases the income of providers. This has occurred through vast increases in the costs of services being provided. The amount paid for Part A (hospitals) and Part B (physicians) claims under Medicare were about eight times higher in 1980 than in 1967, and the increases in benefits paid per individual rose by over 400 percent. In 1989, median doctor income rose 12.8 percent three times the rate of inflation. (Reagan 1992, 65) The medical service component of the Consumer Price Index during this period rose by 170 percent while the overall index increased by only 107 percent. The price index for physicians during this period rose by 150 percent (Thompson 1981, 182).

Health Service Agencies

As costs mounted, Congress made several attempts to control them. But most legislation aimed at controlling costs was unsuccessful. One example is the National Health Planning and Resources Development Act of 1974, which established 200 health service agencies throughout the country. These agencies were to assemble and analyze data, assess the adequacy of hospital resources in their areas, prepare five-year health plans, and establish priorities among objectives. The health service agencies had both sticks and carrots to command the attention and cooperation of providers. They could allocate technical assistance and planning funds to groups that agreed to cooperate with plan objectives, or they could stymie or delay projects deemed inconsistent with their plans by denying them a certificate of need. These sanctions, however, had little impact.

Health service agencies did not receive widespread support during implementation. The public was only dimly aware of their existence. Both the American Medical Association and the unions opposed them, and several presidents were cool toward the idea. As a result, they were not very effective in promoting efficiency and economy in the delivery of health care services.

Health Maintenance Organizations

Health Maintenance Organizations, established in 1973, were another attempt to control skyrocketing health-care costs. They also had mixed implementation results. To promote their development, the Department of Health, Education, and Welfare could make grants or issue contracts to public or nonprofit private entities. It could defray planning costs and subsidize development costs by providing federal loan guarantees. Sufficient funds were appropriate to help plan HMOs, and no hostile groups attempted to veto their development. But delays were encountered in making initial loans and the Health Services Administration, which administered the program, was not fully supportive of the idea. In 1978, President Carter moved the program to the Office of the Assistant Secretary for Health, but was unable to increase appropriations for the program (Thompson 1981). It was not until the latter part of the 1980s that HMOs were successfully implemented. By 1984, HMOs were growing rapidly and reached almost 29 million in membership by 1987.

Legislation aimed at increasing medical personnel enjoyed more successful implementation conditions. The Emergency Health Personnel Act of 1973 was backed by the American Medical Association, Congress, and the president. The scholarship program authorized by the legislation bestowed over 22,000 awards annually from 1973 to 1980 and many of them went to minority students and schools. However, as we shall discuss in the next section, this legislation had only mixed and limited success in achieving its goals.

Occupational Safety and Health Act

By far, the legislation that faced the most difficulty during implementation was the Occupational Safety and Health Act. Implementation was delegated to a newly created assistant secretary directly under the Secretary of Labor. Four hundred new positions were created for the program in the first year and 600 were added the second year (Thompson 1981, 35). But OSHA did not have substantial public support and soon developed a bad image. Although they had two years to adopt safety standards, implementors adopted a long list of standards about nine months after OSHA became effective and four months after the standards were published for public comment. In rushing to adopt these standards, OSHA officials wanted to avoid the image of being uncommitted to the program or unsure in their handling of it. They knew that organized labor would be quick to criticize any implementation delays. Rapid implementation, they believed, would win the general respect of the unions (Ashford 1976, 232).

According to the report of the presidential task force appointed by President Ford in 1975, OSHA adopted the same standards as the American National Standards Institute and the National Fire Protection Agency, changing the "shoulds" in each standard to "shalls," and deleting what was obviously unrelated to safety (MacAvoy 1979, 5).

The problem was that OSHA did not take the time to decide which of these many standards were effective and which were not. Thus, it adopted many standards from other agencies that did not in fact contribute to greater safety. The standards took up nearly 250 densely packed pages of the *Federal Register* and covered a wide range of subjects from ladders, guards for machines, and electrical wiring, to limits on concentrations of toxic substances. Some of these standards were excruciatingly detailed, like those requiring that toilets have hinged, open front seats.

Initially, OSHA focused on safety standards rather than health hazards because the former were easier to assess. Health hazards are risks that result from long-term exposure to toxic substances such as asbestos. The research required to assess these risks is costly; it requires a large data base and elaborate research techniques. But even with this kind of effort, assessing the risks of exposure to certain substances is still difficult. The usual procedure is to test the substance on laboratory animals and, with the aid of a computer, estimate what level of exposure would cause risks of disease in humans. But in the end, many uncertainties remain. Dr. Sorell L. Schwartz, Professor of Pharmacology at Georgetown University Medical Center, says that estimating health risks from laboratory-based studies is probably not as good as weather or economic forecasting (Shribman 1982). Safety hazards are much easier to identify. To make a risk assessment, researchers examine the number of accidents among those who work in a particular risk area, and then decide if the risks are great enough to take preventive measures. But even here, the techniques require subjective judgments.

Officials at OSHA used two different strategies to enforce safety hazards standards: *facilitative* and *enforcement*. Facilitative strategies include disseminating information to industry on how to comply, and grants of money to entice cooperation. Enforcement strategies involve levying fines on a company that does not comply with a standard. Officials at OSHA have relied heavily on facilitative rather than enforcement strategies (Pettus 1982).

In 1979, the average proposed fine for nonserious infractions was one dollar per violation for small businesses and \$2.84 for large firms, and the average penalty for serious violations for all businesses in 1979 was \$495 (Pettus 1982, 603). These are not the principal costs of complying with OSHA standards. Compliance costs include expenses of redesigning production space, modifying production processes, purchasing new equipment, hiring additional staff for record-keeping and training, and beginning an industrial medicine program. These costs can be significant and can affect the competitive position of an industry that tries to comply with them. Because of these costs, criticism of OSHA mounted early.

Soon after it promulgated its standards, OSHA encountered an avalanche of complaints. The principal complaint was that the standards were petty, unrelated to increased job safety or health, and too costly to implement. For example, Bardach and Kagan (1982, 4–5) recount the experience of Al Schaefer, the director of worker safety for a major aluminum manufacturing company.

He complained that OSHA inspections—some 30 to 50 a year in the corporation's numerous plants—made little positive contribution to safety in the company. The problem, said Schaefer, is that OSHA mandates safety standards that are not in the highest priority risk area in a plant. He gave as an example the requirement that plants provide alternate exits from the restaurants located in the middle of the company's smelting plant. At that time, the only lunchroom exits at the plant opened onto side corridors which were connected to the rows of furnaces along which crucibles of molten aluminum are transported. OSHA required that Schaefer's company install rear exits in case the molten aluminum spilled and flowed into the side corridors, starting a fire, and trapping workers in the lunchrooms. Schaefer complained that the chances of this occurring were very remote—even less likely than the chance of an earthquake. Nothing like that had happened in the fifteen years the plant had been in operation. He estimated that it would cost $6,000 per lunchroom to install the rear exits, and for the ten lunchrooms in the plant, it would cost the company $60,000.

This seemed unreasonable to Schaefer. Officials at OSHA disagreed. They argued that the inspectors must operate according to rules set down by the agency and that the company could file for a variance if it felt the rule was unreasonable. While the procedure for applying for a variance is cumbersome, it should be, OSHA officials said, because this protects the company against manipulation and bribery. Moreover, if the system is to err, it is best to err on the side of safety.

Was this particular OSHA regulation unreasonable? To answer this we must first define what we mean by "unreasonable." Inevitably, one's definition depends upon his or her ideology. Bardach and Kagan define regulatory unreasonableness as follows: "A regulatory requirement is unreasonable if compliance would not yield the intended benefits, as when installing a government-mandated safety device would really not improve worker safety because of the operating conditions in a particular factory. Further, a regulatory requirement is unreasonable if compliance would entail costs that clearly exceed the resulting social benefits" (1982, 6). The problem is: How do we measure the resulting social benefits?

Whether or not OSHA's regulations were in fact unreasonable is a difficult question. Political scientist Frank J. Thompson (1981) argues that OSHA made many errors in its initial few years and took too long to correct them. We shall consider this question in more detail in the next section on evaluation.

In summary, much of the legislation dealing with health care was implemented in a hostile atmosphere or by those who benefited from the policy. Opposition by numerous groups and waning support by Congress and the pubic seems to be the rule for a great deal of health care legislation. This may account for why much of health care policy suffers a bad image, and perhaps also why many policies have not been entirely successful. We will consider this further in our next section on evaluation.

EVALUATING HEALTH CARE POLICY

Very few scholars and researchers who have studied the health care system believe that it has been successful; most conclude that health care policy is not working well at all. Marmor and Christenson, for example, conclude that "public policy in the past has not achieved satisfactory results because it has not been comprehensive" (1982, 21). David Mechanic (1976; 1978) argues that the health care delivery system is too complex to be influenced by the piecemeal efforts characteristic of public policy; others fault the governmental agencies for inefficiency, resistance to change, and for giving in to health care providers (Olson 1982). According to Thompson (1981), our health care policy goals are inconsistent and unrealistic; they try to achieve cost containment, quality care, and equal access all at the same time.

By 1992, the chorus of condemnation had risen to include the former Surgeon General who said "Band-Aids will no longer do . . . I think we have to sink further into the crisis, maybe even toward chaos, before people begin to scream but when mad enough, they will demand the changes that need to be made" (Quoted in Cohn 1992, 6).

In this section, we will concentrate our evaluation in three areas, beginning with hospital care.

Hospital Care

There have been some successes in health care policy. The Hospital Survey and Construction Act of 1946, discussed earlier, was enormously successful in accomplishing the goal of stimulating construction of hospitals. It provided support for 11,225 projects; half of these were general hospitals, the rest were long-term facilities, outpatient clinics, and related facilities. But wealthier communities received a disproportionately large share of the project. Although construction was spurred in communities with 50,000 or more people, the middle class was the prime beneficiary along with the providers (Thompson 1981). The availability of hospitals helped heart patients and expectant mothers. An increasing number of patients of all types were hospitalized, thereby increasing access to hospitals for the poor, but this also added services. The use of hospitals doubled between 1950 and 1980, but much of this did not actually improve health. Many unnecessary surgeries were performed, particularly appendectomies and hysterectomies. It has been estimated that only half of such surgeries could be justified on health grounds (Thompson 1981, 48).

According to Marmor and Christenson, "the reduction of hospital capacity in the U.S. became a major policy goal because excess hospital capacity is widely believed to contribute to excessive increases in hospital costs" (1982, 125). It has been estimated that a 20 percent reduction in the nation's hospital capacity could save over $6 billion annually—enough to pay for all the kidney dialysis, hip joint replacements, and newborn intensive care units together

(McClure 1976). In 1929, hospitals accounted for 14 percent of the health dollar; in 1960 it was 26 percent; in 1970, 38 percent, in 1980, 45 percent, but it dropped back to 38 percent by 1990.

Attempts to control hospital growth through various laws have all failed. Instead of lowering hospital investment, they have shifted emphasis from building more bed space to purchasing additional and expensive equipment (Marmor & Christenson 1982). Some researchers believed that the certificate of need approach adopted in the 1974 HPRDA Act would not work because hospital employees, physicians, staff, trustees, and local constituents resist attempts to limit hospital growth (Marmor & Christenson 1982; Steinwald & Sloan 1981). Instead, a number of studies showed that mandated rate-setting was more successful. Steinwald and Sloan conclude that "increases in expenses per admission, per patient-day and total expenses were considerably lower in 1977 and 1978 in states with mandated rate-setting than elsewhere in the U.S." (1981, 298). States that have mandated rate systems specify what can be charged for various hospital services. One form of mandated rates is called *capitation*, which provides cash payments per eligible patient to the service provider. By contrast, the usual *fee-for-service* system reimburses the provider for the cost of the medication plus a fixed professional dispensing fee. One study (Yesalis et al. 1981) comparing the use of drug services between fee-for-service and capitation found that drug use was similar among control and experimental counties with the exception of nursing home patients; use in this category decreased under capitation and increased under fee-for-service. The study also found that (1) the average cost of a day's drug therapy, (2) the average drug cost per recipient, and (3) the average Medicaid expenditures for drug services per recipient were 16 percent lower under capitation than under fee-for-service.

Beginning in 1984, hospitals operated under a system of set fees according to 467 diagnostic related groups, or DRGs. The intent of this system was to control costs. By establishing a set fee, it was hoped that hospitals would reduce the stay of a patient. Although the system reduced stays, the total revenues for hospitals went up because the number of hospital admissions increased. The average stay of Medicare patients dropped from ten days in 1981 to less than eight in 1985 (*U.S. News & World Report*, April 14, 1986, 61). While the upward spiral of medical costs dropped from 9 percent per year in 1981 to 6.2 percent in 1985, it still was increasing. Moreover, the poor were being harmed under the system, particularly the 33 million people who could not afford private health insurance but who were not poor enough to qualify for Medicaid. Many of these people were literally dumped from private to public hospitals in large cities. In addition, the post-hospital network of nursing homes was swamped as hospital discharges to nursing homes jumped 40 percent in the first eighteen months of the DRG system.

Public policy in regard to hospitals has failed in other ways as well. Although the Hill-Burton Act stimulated construction of community hospitals, the average hospital built under the legislation has only 100 beds. These hospitals were built on the assumption that the hospitals should be a community institution, responding to community needs. But a 100-bed facility is not very cost-effective because of the high cost of equipment. A cobalt machine, hemodialysis facility, kidney transplant equipment, or a CAT Scanner each costs $1 million to install. Hence it is not cost-efficient for every hospital to be equipped with these units.

To try to solve this problem, regional medical centers were established. These centers were meant to be sophisticated hospitals with the latest equipment, linked to the smaller community hospitals that did not have such equipment. This system has been successful only in large metropolitan areas, however (Rosengren 1980).

The acquisition of expensive equipment is only one factor in the high costs of hospitals. Another is medical personnel, who account for over 60 percent of all hospital costs. In 1960, hospitals employed about 114 persons for every 100 patients. In 1974, this increased to 250 employees per 100 patients, and by 1986, it had reached 366 employees per 100 patients.

The growth in the use of hospitals did not just happen; it was stimulated by physicians. Patients do not usually volunteer to go to a hospital, they are told they should or must go. Physicians are quick to order patients into a hospital somewhat as a protection against malpractice suits. But there is another factor involved as well. The growth in medical specialization requires numerous back-up personnel that a physician cannot afford to provide. Hospitals provide these back-up personnel. The growth in medical personnel over the past four decades—to 5.3 million health professionals and workers in 1982—has been mostly in areas other than physicians. In 1982, there were 844,000 health practitioners (medical and osteopathic physicians, dentists, and pharmacists), 223,000 health administrators, 650,000 health technologists and technicians, 1.6 million nurses, dietitians, and therapists, and almost 2 million health service workers—that is, nursing aides, practical nurses, health aides, and dental assistants (Waldo 1982, 18). In 1986, there were 3,023,000 hospital personnel working in 5,814 general hospitals.

By 1993, the role of hospitals was influx. As a result of cost-cutting measures more and more care was being shifted to care facilities outside of hospitals.

The evaluation of health policy with regard to hospitals, therefore, is mixed. While there has been a great increase in the number of hospitals, there is now excess capacity and little success in controlling growth of hospital equipment, beds, and costs.

Medicare and Medicaid

The evaluation of Medicare and Medicaid also is mixed. According to Marmor and Christenson, "The dissatisfaction with Medicaid stems primarily from its high costs and secondarily from its shortcomings in delivering services to target groups" (1982, 17). The program operates very unevenly from one state to the next. Medicaid is the largest single program in terms of public outlays for the poor. Much of the dissatisfaction with Medicaid is due to its high costs, which results from its success in reaching eligible individuals. In 1967, 5.2 million individuals were enrolled in the program, and by 1980, 25 million were enrolled. In 1986, about 41 percent (about 13.5 million people) of the nation's poor were in the program.

Medicaid has improved the health of the poor as indicated by infant mortality, flu, cervical cancer, and diabetes rates, all of which declined from 1965 to 1982. Before Medicaid, people with low incomes saw physicians far less often than middle class people, but by the mid-1970s, this inequity had been erased. The reduction in out-of-pocket costs to the poor has been an important reason for their increased utilization of physicians (Anderson & Newman 1980). Of those who use Medicaid, 34 percent receive aid to dependent children and are under twenty-one years old; 21 percent are adults in families receiving aid to dependent children; 25 percent are over sixty-five; and 13 percent are totally disabled (Loeb 1979, 17). More than 60 percent of the Medicaid dollar is spent on the disabled or aged. However, 40 to 50 percent of the poor are not covered by Medicaid because each state can define its own eligibility rules.

In the South, low-income individuals are at a disadvantage compared to those in other states; and, within states, urban whites receive a disproportionately large share of Medicaid benefits. Medicaid permits each state to set its own standards and southern states have regressive policies; twenty states extended no coverage to the medically indigent. In Texas, Alabama, and Tennessee, a family of four with an annual income above $2,000 did not qualify for Medicaid in 1985 (Bayer & Callahan 1985, 539).

In large cities "medicaid mills" have sprung up. In New York City, such mills are housed in shabby, nondescript storefronts along the most desolate blocks in the city. Doctors grind routinely through dozens of patients in a single hour in order to maximize their income. The medical coordinator for the state Health Department's office of professional conduct called the mills a "continuous obscenity." "It isn't that we treat poor people worse than animals," he continued, "It's that the incentives are all designed to give the biggest rewards to the biggest criminals. No real doctor would spend a day there" (Specter 1991, 9).

Many of the most committed doctors refuse to participate in Medicaid because of the low fees. For example, in 1991, doctors in New York received $15 through Medicaid for a routine electrocardiogram, whereas Medicare paid $45 for the same service and, if the patient had private insurance, the fee was $100. In a 1991 survey, the New York City Health Department could identify only six private physicians willing to provide a full range of service in the city's most ravaged neighborhoods containing over a half million people eligible for Medicaid.

Medicare has been successful in boosting access to medical services among the elderly (Thompson 1981) and in reducing disparities in hospital care based on race and socioeconomic status. According to Bayer and Callahan, "Not only has the program provided a crucial, albeit limited, source of financial support for those in need of medical care, its existence has also made possible an extraordinary expansion in the technological basis of medicine's response to the health needs of the elderly" (1985, 533). Still, Medicare covers only 40 percent of the per capita outlays for health care of the elderly.

The most persistent criticism of Medicare is that its costs have gotten out of control reaching $110 billion dollars in 1990, accounting for 9 percent of all Federal spending that year. The principal reason for this is that neither the patient, the physician, nor the hospital have an incentive to keep costs down. University of Maryland economist Mancur Olson contends that Medicare and Medicaid were "designed in such a way as to generate vastly increased income for physicians and some other relatively well-to-do providers" (1982, 4). Because the costs are covered by insurance, patients think that they have freedom of choice. But, says Olson, this is only the "freedom to choose the most expensive of available alternatives without having to pay extra for it." According to some researchers (Ruby, Banta & Burns 1985), Medicare has had a major influence on the adoption and use of technology in the treatment of a number of diseases such as end-stage renal disease (that is, kidney dialysis and transplants). The increased use of these technologies and use of surgery has been the major reason for the rising costs of medicine. In particular, these researchers say, surgery on heart attack patients and infants with respiratory or delivery problems have had a dramatic impact on rising expenditures (Ruby, Banta & Burns 1985). The largest growth in Medicare costs were in physicians fees which were over $1 billion in 1990. Growth in the volume of physician services completely offset the effects of a Federal law that froze their fees in 1984.

Physicians are not the only ones who benefit from Medicaid; insurance companies also benefit. Blue Cross, in particular, has a big advantage under the system. As a result, Blue Cross has been able to dominate the hospital insurance business. (See discussion earlier in this chapter.) This arrangement is supported by physicians as well as by hospitals because they can eliminate cost-cutting. Olson (1982) states flatly, "The physicians, hospitals, and other organized providers (such as unionized hospital workers and pharmaceutical companies) have profited disproportionately from Medicare and Medicaid" (13). Olson believes that this problem cannot be remedied through current measures such as professional review or certificate of need. He writes, "I suspect that anyone who understands the freedom of choice arrangements that physicians and hospitals have worked out for themselves, and who still believe that professional review will prevent excessive costs, will believe anything" (17). Instead, Olson believes that the government should promote price competition among providers and give patients an incentive to seek value as well as quality and convenience in health care. He recommends a voucher system as one way to accomplish this. Under such a system, eligible individuals would be given vouchers that they could use where they choose. The assumption is that this would promote competition among providers.

In order to increase incentive to shop around for value, some have proposed that Medicaid should increase a patient's share of the bill. However, according to a study by the Congressional Office of Technology Assessment, "Fewer people would be willing to pay the additional cost of a physician visit or a hospital admission. This reluctance would lead physicians to use less expensive settings and technologies such as ambulatory centers or nonhospital surgery" (*Kansas City Times,* November 4, 1982, A-16). The result, the study says, would be that fewer people who need medical services would receive them and the quality of services would decline.

The assumption that increased competition among providers would reduce costs has never been empirically tested (Steinwald & Sloan 1981). The major argument against the assumption is that most consumers are not able to make enlightened choices among health plan options. Carolyn Wiener supports this view: "Buying a health plan, unlike buying a television set, does not lend itself to consumer cost-benefit analysis" (1982, 2). In health care, the patient usually knows less than the provider about what services he or she needs and how much the provider is likely to profit from them (Mead 1982).

A 1983 study estimated that the Medicare Hospital Trust Fund would be depleted by 1987, and by 1990, it would be expending $24.2 billion more than it took in (Congressional Budget Office 1983, 2). How might this be remedied? A 1984 survey of 1,000 leaders in the health field concluded that a means test (a determination of what economic resources the person has) would have to be implemented by 1990. A survey of the general population that same year found that 54 percent would support a limitation on Medicare (Bayer & Callahan 1985). Researchers Bayer and Callahan conclude that the survey "suggests a fundamental unraveling of the moral and social arguments that led to the establishment of the present age-based Medicare program" (543). They also believe that some cost-sharing was inevitable but that it would likely hit the poor hardest. This would be undesirable because Medicare "preserves, if in a stunted form, a vision of a more general societal commitment to meeting health care needs on grounds other than relative economic advantage. Given the recent (that is, 1985) regressions from the goal of equity in health care, the importance of Medicare extends beyond those it serves directly as beneficiaries" (546).

Programs aimed at attracting physicians to rural areas have "met with less than anticipated success" (Eisenberg & Cantwell 1976). The National Health Service Corps, established in 1970, provided loans to medical students if they agreed to practice in rural areas upon graduation. But only 2 percent of those in the program remained in rural areas beyond the required two years. Hence programs aimed at attracting physicians to rural areas did little to rectify the unsatisfactory level of services in these areas (Marmor & Christenson 1982).

Occupational Safety and Health Policy

Occupational safety and health policy is much more difficult to evaluate. It met with limited success in reducing industrial accidents, although the reduction in the first ten years of its existence was only 4 percent. At the same time, strong opposition to OSHA regulations aroused suspicion of the agency in general and a reluctance toward having any government involvement (Thompson 1981). If the amount of opposition generated by a policy is any indication of its success, then OSHA has been a resounding failure. No doubt OSHA made many errors in implementing regulations during its first few years. Instead of giving local inspectors discretion to determine if a violation was trivial, it centralized enforcement and adopted the approach that a citation must be issued for any violation. But 95 percent of its citations in the early years were for nonserious infractions (Thompson 1981). After only a year of operation, members of Congress were so bombarded with complaints that they introduced numerous bills to amend and even repeal the law.

It took OSHA almost ten years to correct the errors it made. In December, 1977, it finally proposed revocation of some 1,100 safety regulations. These regulations were tailored further in 1978, 1980, and 1981. In 1981, for example, OSHA cut back on its safety standards so that its regulations were reduced from 250,000 to about 15,000 words (Thompson 1981, 9). Thus, although OSHA ultimately corrected some of its initial errors, it was still unable to shake its former image and regain much credibility as a rational enterprise worth continuing.

In summary, existing health care policies are not clearly successes or failures. They fall into the gray area of having accomplished a great deal, while having many defects as well. Because they benefit powerful groups in society, the major flaws in the policies are not likely to be corrected in the near future. Rather than being terminated, these policies will probably undergo incremental changes that are not completely satisfactory to anyone, but which continue to benefit the providers of health care more than they improve the health of the country.

■ TERMINATING HEALTH POLICIES

Health policies are seldom terminated. Certainly, the government's presence in the health area will continue for some time. Particular policies are likely to change direction, rather than be terminated. The most likely candidates for termination are particular programs that have failed and whose termination does not upset implementing agencies. For example, the neighborhood health centers and regional medical programs adopted in the 1960s were terminated.

Sometimes entire agencies are terminated, but those are much rarer events. For example, state mental hospitals were closed in some states such as California between 1970 and 1973 (Cameron 1978). However, it took a coalescing of a number of large scale changes for these hospitals to be closed. First, there was a change in the conception of mental illness. Beginning in the early 1960s, more and more mental health professionals accepted the notion that mental illness is not analogous to other physical illnesses which could be ameliorated or cured through treatment in a hospital. Instead, the belief was adopted that mental illness was caused more by the environment of the individual, and the hospital was conceived of as a malignant environment. Hospitals were considered malignant not only in a medical sense but also because they violated the individual's freedom of choice. Stories and movies such as *One Flew Over the Cuckoo's Nest* helped popularize these ideas. When coupled with changes in government as well as increasing shortages of finances, it became rather easy to decide to close state mental hospitals in favor of community mental health centers. But the termination of the hospitals was done with little planning. Individuals were simply dumped into communities. Many of them wound up living lonely, isolated, and alienated existences (Cameron 1978). In New York City, for example, a number of such individuals could not find homes and wound up living in cardboard boxes in the subways.

Major terminations such as this are not characteristic of health policy. More characteristic are changes in direction or emphasis in specific policies or programs. For example, beginning in 1964, the federal government tried to contain hospital costs by establishing local health facilities planning councils. When these proved ineffective, comprehensive health planning agencies were created in 1966. These agencies were also unsuccessful. Congress passed additional legislation in 1974 and in 1983 aimed at controlling hospital cost increases, yet none of these programs have been effective either. Hence, rather than abandon the policy that produced a proliferation of hospitals, health care policy is more likely to continue the search for ways of controlling costs.

We noted in Chapter 5 that functions of government are hardest to end, with policies next, then agencies, and finally, programs. Promoting health has been a function of federal, state, and local governments for more than a hundred years in the United States. Its role in this area has grown rather than receded, and this growth is also likely to continue.

Government involvement in health policy took place for two reasons. First, in regard to communicable disease, these were truly collective concerns that could not be taken care of in any other manner. Cleaning up polluted rivers or preventing them from becoming polluted and providing adequate sewage systems can only be done by the collective effort of government. There is no way that private enterprise would or could have become involved in these areas.

When the threat of communicable diseases diminished, government involvement shifted to the area of chronic disease, because of what was perceived to be market failures in this area. Private medical practice did not provide adequate medical services for the poor. Thus, government policy began with, and continues to have, a social welfare justification as much as a health justification.

In the 1980s, the election of Ronald Reagan pointed to another possible shift in the direction of health policy. The principal change promoted by the Reagan administration was to diminish the role of government in health care and move toward a means-test and cost-sharing system. Underlying this latter thrust is the philosophy that reliance on government will not work because government cannot resist political pressures to preserve bankrupt hospitals, or to apply budgetary caps on expenditures. Some agree that government regulation will fair because "the bureaucrat doing the regulating is less competent to determine how the institutions should be managed than the managers currently running the institutions" (Atkinson & Cook 1982, 212).

However, by 1993, with the election of Bill Clinton, conditions seemed to be ripe for a major shift in policy. Clinton repeatedly said during his transition that it was impossible to promote economic growth and reduce the huge federal budget deficit without first controlling health care costs. He promised to have a major health care proposal before Congress during the first 100 days of his administration. This did not happen. Many observers believed that it would take a lot longer to get new legislation because of the complexity of the issue. Moreover, Clinton had a reputation for responding to pressures from various groups. Given the power of the insurance industry and medical and hospital groups, it was not likely that major reforms on the order of the federal government becoming the single insurer for health care would take place. In fact, the plan unveiled by Clinton in late 1993 was not even close to being major reform. It still relied heavily on insurance through one's job and on health maintenance organizations for delivering medical services. Neither of these are significant changes and although the plan called for making sure that every American would have health insurance, specifics about how it would be done and how it would be financed were lacking. By the time these specific details are worked out in 1994, and the compromises made due to high pressure lobbying by medical, hospital, and insurance groups, there would not likely be a major shift in health care in America.

Social Welfare: Who Gets What from Government?

THE NATURE OF SOCIAL WELFARE PROBLEMS

Timothy Sipes used to earn about $1,120 a month in a shop that repaired steel mill equipment in Ohio, but he lost his job during the 1982 recession and had to go on welfare. "To be truthful," Sipes said, "I used to think that only blacks and hillbillies were on welfare. I threw a lot of stereotypes around about welfare. Now that I'm on it, my view has changed. . . . I no longer consider people on welfare white trash. They're people trying to survive" (Coleman 1985, 31).

The stereotypes about welfare to which Timothy Sipes refers are that poor people and those on welfare are lazy, degenerate, and perhaps even genetically unfit; they are considered to be shirkers rather than unfortunate victims of technological or economic change. These stereotypes are deeply engrained in the American ideological conscience. Poverty has always been viewed by

Americans as the consequence of personal inadequacies, physical frailty, mental deficiencies, or moral and behavioral defects. And, although Americans have never been particularly generous or sympathetic toward the poor, in the mid-1980s, the United States entered an exceptionally anti-egalitarian mood. As political scientist Benjamin Page wrote, "contempt for the poor is expressed in high places. America's sympathy for the underdog seems to have dried up" (1983, 2).

In the first half of the 1980s, hundreds of thousands of formerly middle-class people wound up on welfare. Between 1979 and 1984, the number of people in traditional two-parent households receiving Aid to Families with Dependent Children (AFDC) more than doubled throughout the United States and tripled in the "rust belt" states such as Ohio. Many newcomers to AFDC roles were put there by the recession of 1981–1982.

These people are not lazy, "ne'er-do-wells" looking for a free handout. A 1984 Interchurch Council of suburban hunger center clientele found that seven out of every ten people were high school graduates, four out of ten had applied for at least 20 jobs in the last year, and three out of ten had worked six years or more on their last job (Coleman 1985, 32). This group in a suburban center is not representative of all people on AFDC, but it does indicate that poverty began to include groups not stereotypically considered vulnerable.

The most dramatic and saddest statistic is the rise in the poverty rate among children. From 1979 to 1983, there was a 63 percent increase in poverty among white children in two-parent families. About 17 percent of all white children were in poverty in 1985, but about *one-half* of all black children and a third of Hispanic children were in poverty. There were 13 million people on welfare in 1992, 9 million of whom were children.

Poverty also became a predominantly female affliction; half of all poor children lived in female-headed, single-parent families, according to a study by the Congressional Research Service and Congressional Budget Office (Rich 1985, 33). In female-headed white families, the overall poverty rate for children was 47.6 percent, 68.5 percent in the black female-headed families, and 70.5 percent in Hispanic families.

The increases in the number of people in poverty in the first half of the 1980s was due to a combination of a deep recession from 1981 to 1983, and huge cuts in government expenditures for the poor. Cash and food stamp benefits available per poor child as measured in constant 1983 dollars dropped from a high of $1,446 in 1976 to $1,156 in 1983. The number of people receiving food stamps dropped from 22.4 million in 1981 to 19.9 million in 1985. In addition, from 1971 to 1985, state governments failed to raise welfare benefits sufficiently to keep pace with inflation. As a result, the purchasing power of combined welfare and food stamp benefits for families without other income dropped by about 22 percent.

By 1990, a new wrinkle in the poverty statistics developed—an ominous one for the future; poverty was hitting young families worse than other age groups.

Getting married and having children was no longer compatible with the American dream. Maybe that is why almost 40 percent of adults over 18 were single in 1993. The poverty rate for young families under age 30 with children doubled from 20 percent in 1973 to 40 percent in 1990 while the proportion of young families with children who owned homes fell from a peak of 47.4 percent in 1980 to 31.5 percent in 1991.

The common conception of the "welfare system" is of the system that helps those below the poverty line, and that is what this chapter focuses on. But it should also be noted that the greatest beneficiaries of government "welfare" are the middle class and wealthy. According to one analyst, benefits and services for the poor account for only 16 percent of the "welfare state." The rest is comprised of social security and Medicare benefits for the nonpoor, deductible home mortgage interest, and tax exclusion of pension contributions (Sherraden 1991).

Criticisms of the welfare system focus almost exclusively on the system aimed at helping the poor. The most popular construction of the system during the 1980s was the conservative argument that welfare benefits provided by the federal government create dependency among the poor and destroy the incentives of people to work. One of the principal conservative books to advance this thesis was Charles Murray's *Losing Ground* (1984). In his book, Murray claimed that a self-appointed intellectual elite had shifted the blame for poverty, crime, and low achievement from the individual to "the system," thereby destroying all sense of individual responsibility for self-improvement. According to Murray, the elite has imposed its views on poverty in direct conflict with widely shared popular preferences, instilling a trend in poverty and dependency that began with the Great Society of the Johnson administration.

The Great Society is what President Johnson said would result from the policies of his administration, which extended the role of the federal government in helping the poor. One of these policies was known as the War on Poverty. Created in 1964 by the Economic Opportunity Act, and administered by the Office of Economic Opportunity, the War on Poverty was supposed to eliminate poverty in America. It included a number of separate programs, most of which no longer exist. Head Start, Upward Bound, and student loan programs were aimed at improving the education of the poor; Job Corps, Neighborhood Youth Corps, and the Manpower Development and Training Program were attempts to provide job skills, good working habits, and jobs for the poor; Model Cities and Community Action Programs were designed to rehabilitate poor neighborhoods, organize the poor for self-help, and give them a voice in the decisions affecting them. Conservatives like Charles Murray argued that these programs *caused* rather than cured poverty. The solution, they maintain, is to eliminate government programs which will lessen dependency. Coupled with economic growth, this will eliminate poverty.

But if empirical evidence were used, the theory that welfare creates dependency and an increase in economic growth will lessen dependency was not supported during the 1980s. Although there was economic growth during the 1980s, the welfare rolls did not decline and the poor got poorer. Federal welfare rolls hit their highest level in history in early 1991. At the same time, the purchasing power of the typical AFDC benefit nationwide decreased by 42 percent as a result of state and federal funding cuts. The "safety net" became more hole than net, and the "welfare system" continued to be a problem as the country moved towards the twenty-first century.

What Is Poverty?

Poverty has been measured by the U.S. Government's Social Security Administration since 1964, based on the cost of a minimum diet. Each year, the threshold is adjusted for changes in the level of consumer prices, for family size, and for the age of the persons in the household. In 1984, the federal government's threshold for a family of four was $10,609.

This way of measuring poverty has many flaws and, in 1985, the government began to consider ways of improving it. First, the income measure does not allow for regional variations in the cost of living. It costs more to live in California than Mississippi and the national index does not reflect this. Second, it does not recognize the difference between living in a central city, where prices are high, and living on a farm, where a small vegetable plot can supplement one's diet. Third, the income definition fails to account for in-kind benefits—such as food stamps, health care, and subsidized housing—and other assets. In 1985, about three fifths of all federal aid to the poor was provided through in-kind benefits. If we add the monetary value of these benefits to a person's income, we would find far fewer people in poverty in 1985 than the 17 percent of the population estimated by the federal government. If both cash and in-kind assistance are included, incidence of poverty in 1985 could be as low as 10 percent.

The most serious criticism of the government's definition, however, is that it measures only the *absolute* level of poverty, not the *relative* level. Some would argue that the latter is more important, and that poverty is a relative rather than absolute matter. For example, America's poor are many times better off than the poor in the rest of the world, yet they still are considered to be poor.

The relative measure of poverty is based on the sociological concept of *relative deprivation.* This derives from a study conducted by Samuel Stouffer of American soldiers during World War II. Among other things, he found that college-educated officers were less satisfied with their rate of promotion than those who did not have a college education, even though the former were promoted at a faster rate. He explained this as being due to their expectations rather than to objective reality. They were not being promoted as rapidly as they expected to be promoted, whereas those without a college education were.

As the standard of living in society changes, our definition of poverty changes. For example, the standard of living has consistently improved for the average family in the United States. As a result, the gap between the average income and the official poverty level has grown wider. In 1960, the median family income was about twice that of the poverty line for a family of four, but by 1984 it was almost 2.5 times that of the poverty line. According to Sar Levitan, "a flexible or relative poverty index pegged to a median family income would reflect productivity gains as well as changes in the cost of living. For example, if the poverty threshold were set at 50 percent of the median family income, the poverty line for a family of four would be one-fifth higher than the current official level" (1985, 4). This would place a lot more people into the poverty category than were so classified in 1985. However, a relative measure would fail to show any progress in fighting poverty because the low income groups have not increased their share of the national income for the past fifty years (Page 1983). Moreover, if a relative measure is used such as 50 percent of median income, we can never show any improvement since the percent in poverty will always remain the same.

Hence, there is no perfect measure of poverty; both the absolute and the relative definitions have flaws. But *how* we measure poverty is important from a policy perspective for it determines how many people are considered to be poor. For example, if we measure it only in terms of income, as the government does, then the incidence of poverty declined markedly in the 1960s, from 22.2 percent in 1960 to about 12 percent by the end of the decade, where it approximately remained during the 1970s until it increased in the 1980s (see Figure 7–1). By this measure, the War on Poverty was a success. But if we measure poverty in a relative sense, there was almost no change from 1965 to 1978; it remained between 14.6 and 15.6 percent throughout this period (see Table 7–1).

Finally, if we measure poverty by income *plus* in-kind benefits, adjusted for direct taxes and the underreporting of cash benefits, the *changes* in the percent of people in poverty are similar to those in Figure 7–1, although the percent is much lower (see Figure 7–2).

Who Are the Poor?

In 1962, Michael Harrington painted a grim picture of the various categories of poor people, which he estimated to be somewhere between 40 and 50 million people. They included:

1. The economic underworld who were concentrated in the urban areas and included 16 million Americans denied coverage by the Minimum-Wage Law of 1961. They included domestic workers, hotel employees,

bus boys, and dishwashers whose wages were so low that they lived in poverty.

2. The rural poor such as small farmers, migrant workers, and those living in economically depressed areas such as Appalachia, Virginia, West Virginia, and South Carolina as well as other southern states.
3. The blacks in northern cities such as Chicago, New York, and Philadelphia.
4. The alcoholic poor on skid row, the bohemians and beatniks, and the urban hillbillies.
5. The elderly, who constituted about 8 million people, or 16 percent of the total poor.

By 1985, these categories had changed somewhat. Although the elderly constituted 14 percent of the total poor, the number of elderly poor dropped from 4.7 million in 1970 (down from the 8 million estimated by Harrington in 1962) to 3.7 million in 1985. By 1989, the poverty rate of those 65 & over dropped to 11.4 percent. Thus, the incidence of poverty for those over sixty-five was slightly lower than that for persons under age sixty-five (Levitan 1985, 9). The drop was due mainly to more generous social security benefits,

FIGURE 7–1 Number of poor and poverty rate: 1959 to 1990.

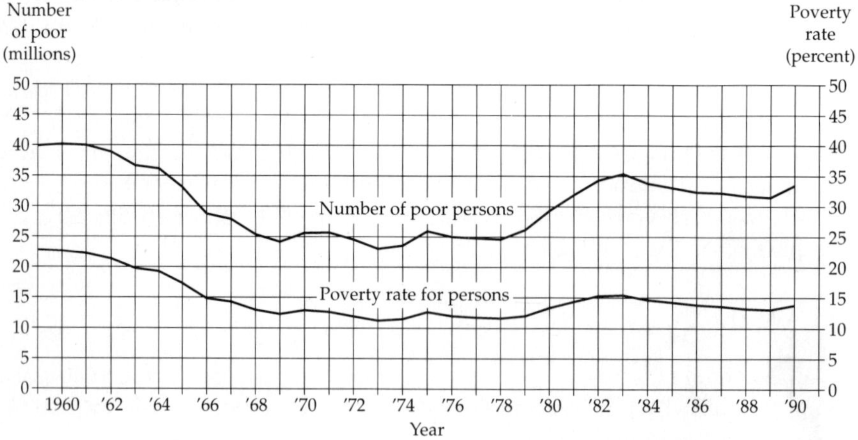

Note: The data points represent the midpoints of the respective years. The latest recessionary period began in July of 1990.

Source: Poverty in the United States: 1990 P-60, No. 175. U.S. Bureau of the Census, U.S. Department of Commerce.

TABLE 7–1 *Incidence of Poverty Measured in Relative Terms**

Year	Percent in Poverty
1965	15.6
1968	14.6
1970	15.1
1972	15.7
1974	14.9
1976	15.4
1978	15.5

* The relative poverty measure here is the proportion of families whose ratio of current income fell below the median income of the whole population.

Source: Sheldon Danziger and Robert Plotnik, "The War on Income Poverty: Achievements and Failures." In *Welfare Reform in America: Perspectives and Prospects,* edited by Paul Sommers (The Hague: Martinus Nyhoff, 1981).

FIGURE 7–2 Trends in the incidence of poverty among all persons according to three measures of income.

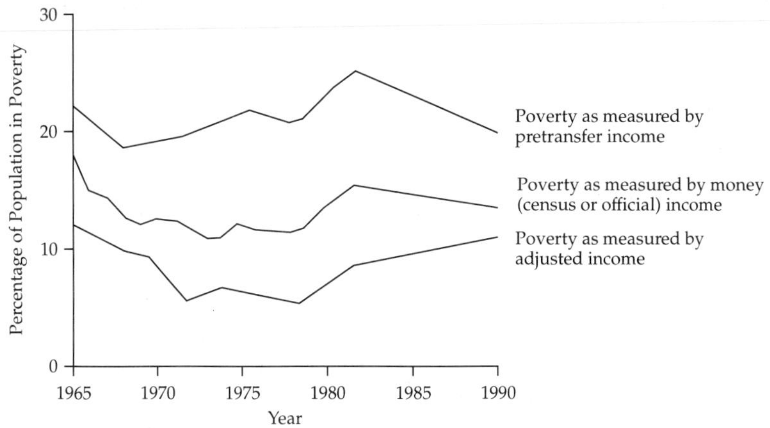

* This definition of income includes in-kind benefits and adjusts for direct taxes and the underreporting of cash benefits.

Source for 1965–1985: Reprinted by permission from the Institute for Research on Poverty from *Focus,* Vol. 7, No. 1 (Winter 1984) p. 2. Copyright 1984 by the Regents of the University of Wisconsin on behalf of the Institute for Research on Poverty.

Source for 1990: U.S. Bureau of the Census, U.S. Department of Commerce, *Measuring the Effect of Benefits & Taxes on Income and Povert,* p. 11.

which were indexed for inflation, and the growth of private and veterans' pensions. However, there were still a large number of working poor in 1985; almost half of the 7.6 million family heads who were poor in 1985 worked. So the economic underworld still existed in 1985 and included the unemployed (like Timothy Sipes, mentioned at the beginning of this chapter) as well as those working in restaurants, hotels, and small businesses.

There have also been major changes in the categories of the poor since the 1960s. One is the so-called feminization of poverty. Increases in the number of single-parent, female-headed households during the 1970s and 1980s accounted for a large part of this. In 1985, about half of all poor families were headed by women, and female-headed families with children were nearly five times more likely to be poor than other households. Many female heads of households had no hope of earning enough to lift their families out of poverty, even if they could find full-time work. This particularly was a problem among black families. The situation among blacks was so bad that Roosevelt University Professor Pierre de Vise told a gathering of the Chicago Urban League in 1985 that the black family was "disintegrating to the point of absolute collapse" (Raspberry 1985, 8). In Chicago's black ghettos, the number of black children living in female-headed households reached 66 percent. "For an increasing number of Chicago's black underclass," de Vise said, "welfare motherhood has become the role model for girls, and drug-dealing and pimping the role model for boys" (8).

Since female heads of families were in poverty, so also were their children. In 1985, one of every five American children under eighteen years and one in four children under six years lived in poverty. The most dramatic rise in poverty—63 percent between 1979 and 1983—has been among white children in two-parent families (Williams 1985, 8). Even more startling was the fact that one of every five American children were homeless, and 37.8 percent of all poor were children. Table 7–2 shows the distribution of poverty by family characteristics. Note that persons in female-headed families living in central cities are most likely to be in poverty.

No matter how poverty is measured, a growing number of Americans were poor and living in poverty in the 1980s. This seemed especially incongruous in a rich nation where, in 1985, more than $1 billion per day was spent on health care and $1 billion a day on military defense.

■ SETTING THE WELFARE AGENDA

Social Welfare in History

The problem of poverty has always been with us. Yet prior to the Great Depression, the problems of the poor had not been on the institutional agenda of the federal government in the United States. Before the New Deal in America,

TABLE 7–2 *Family Characteristics and Poverty, 1990*

Characteristic	Percent in Poverty
All persons	13.5
In families	12.0
related children under 18 years	19.9
in female-headed family, no husband	33.4
in all other families	10.7
Unrelated individuals	20.7
under 15 years	21.4
15–24 years	16.1
25–44 years	10.4
45–54 years	7.8
55–59	9.0
60–64 years	10.3
65 & older	12.2

Source: U.S. Bureau of Census, *Statistical Abstract of the United States, 1990* (Washington, D.C.: U.S. Government Printing Office, 1990).

and throughout the western world, the only policies for the poor were punitive and repressive. America inherited its values and attitudes about the poor from Great Britain. In England, the Statute of Laborers of 1349 forbade giving alms to beggars, and later amendments restricted the geographical mobility of servants and laborers. Between 1722 and 1782, the English implemented a system of workhouses. The poor were put into workhouses where they were required to toil for a meager subsistence. Calvinist theology legitimized these repressive policies, preaching that poverty was a sign that a person was damned and undeserving in God's eyes. These attitudes persisted in England with the passage of the Poor Law of 1834, which regarded poverty as an indication of the moral fault in a person who is poor and in need of help (Waxman 1983). These repressive attitudes were transferred to the United States in the nineteenth century.

Prior to the New Deal, welfare was the responsibility of local governments in America. Poorhouses existed early in the nineteenth century, and churches and religious groups also tried to aid the poor. By the 1860s, complex relief networks developed in the more densely populated states. The states ran some institutions and regulated poor laws. A number of states established boards of state charities that gathered statistics, visited institutions, and collected other forms of evidence used to make recommendations to state legislatures. These boards were the precursors of state departments of public welfare established in the early decades of the twentieth century.

Prior to the 1930s the role of the federal government was limited to publicizing issues through conferences such as the White House Conference on Children in 1909. The federal government also established the Children's Bureau in 1912 and passed the Sheppard-Towner Act in 1921, which funded the establishment of community health centers for women and children.

In 1913, a movement for the creation of municipal departments of public welfare began in Kansas City and spread throughout the country in the next several years (Katz 1983). Women had especially serious problems. Until the late nineteenth century there were almost no pensions or life insurance. Because the poorest men held the hardest and least healthy jobs, they died young, leaving behind their wives and children. Without social security, paid work, or welfare, the plight of women and children was especially pathetic.

A poor family seeking help in the nineteenth century came into contact with an amazing variety of agencies and officials, including charitable agencies such as the Society for Organizing Charity, the Society for the Prevention of Cruelty to Children, the St. John's Home, the local church, and the local bureau of health or charity. Private agencies provided some groceries as well as medical care—which was inadequate—and short-term relief. Often an impoverished family would break up and the children would wind up in an orphanage.

Poorhouses were the most important public residential institution during the nineteenth century. They served more people than reformatories or mental institutions. For example, in 1900 in New York State, almost 90,000 people were supported in city and county almshouses. They were provided with cheap provisions, cheap doctors, and cheap medicines; cheapness was the rule. As a result, the death rate was higher in poorhouses than in hospitals. In 1848, one in every six persons received in a poorhouse died, whereas in the New York hospitals it was one in twelve (Katz 1983).

The principal residents of these poorhouses were children (until 1875, when the Children's Act was passed), the elderly, women, and unemployed males between twenty and thirty-nine years old (particularly during depressions). Dependence was an almost normal aspect of working-class life. Many paupers were old, working-class people who lacked families to care for them and many others were young men temporarily out of work. Most tramps were men on the road searching for a job (Katz 1983).

By the turn of the century, a system of welfare capitalism began to develop. American businesses attended to the social needs of workers through an assortment of medical and funeral benefits as well as provisions for recreation, education, housing, and social services. Their principal motive was to help mold a class of disciplined workers and to forge a link between workers and the company (Gilbert 1983).

However, these practices were never very extensive and were jettisoned with the stock market crash in 1929. With the onset of the depression, the problem of unemployment and poverty moved onto the institutional agenda of the federal government for the first time in U.S. history. With the passage of the Social Security Act of 1935, welfare became a national public concern. The welfare state was born, offering a communal safety net for casualties of the market economy.

Thus, it took a major economic collapse in the United States to push poverty onto the national institutional agenda. However, it was not until the 1950s that the problems of the poor resurfaced on the public policy agenda. World War II effectively took the country's attention away from the problems of the poor. Representative Leonor Sullivan (D-Mo.), elected to her late husband's seat in 1952, became an important advocate for the poor and she pushed hard to get the issue of poverty and hunger onto the national policy agenda. By 1956 she succeeded in persuading Congress to request a food stamp feasibility study from the U.S. Department of Agriculture. However, a subsequent report by the Eisenhower administration was not enthusiastic, and proposals that reached the floor of the House in 1957 and 1958 were defeated. But Representative Sullivan persisted, and in 1959 a food stamp bill was passed. The legislation was not mandatory, however, and Secretary of Agriculture Ezra Taft Benson, a Republican, made no attempt to carry it out.

The food stamp debate was rekindled in 1960 after the election of John F. Kennedy. At Kennedy's request, the U.S. Department of Agriculture set up a task force in 1960 to study the feasibility of using food stamps for the poor. Three members of the task force had been involved in the first food stamp program during the 1950s, and they became the program's most important administrators. On February 2, 1961, Kennedy directed his Secretary of Agriculture, Orville Freeman, to proceed as rapidly as possible with the establishment of a pilot food stamp project. Howard Davis, a member of the 1960 task force, was given formal authority over the program.

In 1962, Michael Harrington's *The Other America* was published. It was a grim account of the extent of poverty in the United States. The book helped crystalize Kennedy's determination to initiate an anti-poverty program in 1963—something that never came to fruition because he was assassinated, but which President Lyndon Johnson picked up later as part of his War on Poverty.

Poverty remained on the national systemic agenda throughout most of the 1960s. Hunger captured the public imagination again in 1967 when Robert Kennedy, the deceased president's brother, went to Mississippi to examine the effectiveness of the poverty programs there. Upon his return to Washington he held a series of hearings that dramatized the extent of hunger. By the end of 1967 the Citizen's Board of Inquiry, a liberal advocacy group, published *Hunger, USA* (1968), a 100-page book of statistics and other data that detailed the extent of hunger and malnutrition in the United States, along with dramatic photographs of starving children and adults.

Television also got into the act in 1968 when it broadcast "Hunger in America" on its *CBS Reports* program. In the opening segment, reporter Charles Kuralt described a baby who was dying of starvation. Kuralt criticized the U.S.

Department of Agriculture for its ineffectiveness in combatting hunger. In addition, a reporter for the *Des Moines Register,* by the name of Nick Kotz, wrote numerous articles about hunger for which he won the Pulitzer Prize in 1968. He also wrote *Let Them Eat Promises,* an all-out attack on Congress and the executive branch for their failure to end hunger.

At about the same time, a number of public interest lobbies emerged and focused on the hunger issue; they became known as the "hunger lobby" (Berry 1984). Working together, they finally stimulated the poor to lobby for themselves, which led to the Poor People's March on Washington in the spring of 1968 led by the Reverend Ralph Abernathy, Martin Luther King's successor as head of the Southern Christian Leadership Conference.

Thus, through the efforts of journalists, legislators, social activists, USDA administrators, lawyers, and the poor themselves, the hunger issue was forced onto the national systemic agenda in the late 1960s. This effort finally paid off, although it took some time. By the mid-1970s, both concern about poverty and the prevalence of poverty diminished.

The welfare issue resurfaced in the late 1970s, this time through the efforts of conservatives who focused on the large increase in the number of people getting food stamps and on allegations of widespread cheating and fraud. They succeeded in turning public opinion against the program. By 1976, welfare's image was one of a program run amok, rife with welfare cheats. The issue returned to the systemic agenda again in 1986, when a Harvard University physicians' group reported that hunger in America was more widespread and serious than it had been in fifteen years (Herbers 1986). The report claimed that while the need for food assistance had increased the use of food stamps, the government's main nutrition program had declined. It blamed restrictive regulations, pride among the eligible, and frequent changes in regulations.

Defining the Problem

Between 1970 and 1976, the public's view of the social welfare problem changed completely from one that portrayed poor people as unfortunate, suffering people who needed and should receive government help to one that portrayed them as lazy, deficient, and crooked people. There are several reasons for this. Following Watergate and the Vietnam War, Americans' confidence in government had plummeted. Consequently, many were convinced that the welfare bureaucracy was incompetent. In addition, the nation's economic performance continued to deteriorate in the 1970s with inflation spiraling upward and rising unemployment producing a situation called "stagflation." These factors laid the groundwork for the campaign launched by neoconservatives and corporations. They publicized allegation after allegation about the inefficiency of government. "They did so through television, newspaper and magazine advertising, by way of think-tank publications, and in political action committee advertising for conservative political candidates" (Schwartz

1983, 121). Intellectuals also, perhaps unwittingly, contributed to the image of inefficient government when they published analyses of government programs such as the War on Poverty which concluded the programs had failed.

Neoconservatives argued that welfare was harmful rather than beneficial because it made people dependent on government. For example, because Aid to Dependent Children was given only to female-headed families where no husband was present, critics claimed that it contributed to the further destruction of welfare families because in order to become eligible, husbands who could not find work would have to abandon their families.

Whether or not these portrayals of the welfare system are accurate will be considered in the Evaluation section of this chapter. Here, we want to emphasize that the way a problem is defined when it gets onto the public agenda is crucial for determining how the issue ultimately will be handled during policy formulation. In the case of welfare, the definition of the problem changed completely from one that looked favorably upon government efforts to ease poverty to one that looked unfavorably upon these effects.

FORMULATING WELFARE POLICY

Who Are the Formulators?

Following the New Deal, the federal government became the main formulator of social welfare policy, and has continued to be, even though President Reagan attempted unsuccessfully to turn the entire responsibility over to the states during his first term. At the federal level, all three branches play a role in formulating social welfare policy. Although Congress initiates policy through new legislation, federal administrative agencies often play a major role in policy formulation. For example, during the life of the food stamp program, the U.S. Department of Agriculture determined who was eligible to receive food stamps, what the benefit structure would be, and the amount of coupons that would be available to each family. The USDA made the majority of policy decisions about this program for more than a decade because the members of Congress were apathetic about these questions, and because liberals and conservatives in Congress were unable to reach a consensus (Berry 1984).

In Chapter 3, policy subsystems were characterized as the principal policy formulators in a number of areas. These policy subsystems consist of members of interest groups, congressional representatives, and administrators in charge of a specific program. However, such policy subsystems do not always exist. For example, in the food stamp area, a policy subsystem did not develop because Congress was apathetic about the program and because there were no interest groups supporting the program. Instead, there was an issue network consisting of public interest advocacy groups and experts who moved from one job to another in the network. Political scientist Jeffrey Berry (1984) describes several individuals in the network. One person moved from the USDA to the House Agriculture Committee; another went from a public interest advocacy group to the House Agriculture Committee; two others left Congress to start their own lobbying and consulting firm on food and nutritional issues; and several others divided their time between the public advocacy groups and the USDA. According to Berry, "Issue networks are still relatively small worlds where personal familiarity and professional reputations lead to job offers within the subsystem" (1984, 134). Moreover, issue networks are not autonomous like the "iron triangles"—that is, administrators, interest groups and congressional staff—which are beyond even the control of the White House (Cater 1964; Heclo 1978). The issue network in food stamp policy making was not beyond the influence of the White House nor public opinion. Presidents and their appointees, as well as public opinion, were able to influence food stamp policy as we will illustrate later in this chapter.

Designing Welfare Policy

Once an issue gets onto the institutional agenda of the policy formulators, two major things happen: first, the problem is defined by the formulators and, second, a program is designed that attempts to begin to deal with the problem.

As cited earlier in regard to agenda setting, our definition of an issue greatly influences the design of policy. Thus policy formulators, particularly legislators, expend a great deal of effort to influence how a problem is defined. In welfare policy, the crucial consideration is whether benefits should be provided to everyone in a particular category, called *universalism*, or only to selected groups, called *selectivism*. If welfare benefits are provided to everyone as with Social Security, there is less likelihood the program will be stigmatized (Gilbert 1983). According to Chaim Waxman, "So long as programs are given in aid of the poor, thus calling attention to the recipient's primary role and status as poor, these programs will continue to be seen as programs that burden the non-poor, that the non-poor are forced to *give* to the poor and for which the non-poor receive no return" (1983, 116). The poor then become scapegoats whenever there is an economic downswing. The solution, Waxman believes, is to create and implement policies and programs that will lead to the integration of the poor with the non-poor, rather than their further isolation.

The United States incorporates both universalism and selectivism in its approach to social welfare. Some social services are given specifically to the poor, aimed at correcting their defects, and at reducing or preventing economic dependency rather than improving the general quality of life for all citizens. These programs include food stamps, housing, Medicaid, Aid to Families with Dependent Children, and various job creation and training programs. Other social welfare programs such as Social Security and unemployment insurance operate on the principle of universalism and are available to all citizens: still others such as Medicare and veterans' benefits are aimed at citizens in certain categories such as everyone over sixty-five or all veterans, regardless of their economic status.

Middle-class opposition to social welfare stems from the view that welfare recipients are somehow disreputable (Gilbert 1983). The "dole" has always been considered to be bad by liberals as well as conservatives. President Franklin Roosevelt observed in 1935 at the very time the Social Security Act was passed that "the federal government must and shall quit this business of relief. To dole out relief is to administer a narcotic, a subtle destroyer of the human spirit" (Woodroofe 1966, 165). This definition of social welfare has persisted ever since.

This definition affects in a very direct way the design of social welfare policies. Many social welfare policies are designed specifically for the poor and they often attempt to distinguish the "deserving" from the "nondeserving" poor with the goal of driving the latter off the dole. These programs tend to receive constant criticism and scrutiny. As typical of American policy making in general, social welfare policy has both universalistic and selectivist components, although the majority of programs fall into the latter category because of American cultural beliefs that some people are lazy and prefer welfare over work.

Contemporary Welfare Programs

Because there is a wide variety of social welfare programs at the federal, state, and local levels, it is difficult to categorize them. The principal distinction is among: (1) cash supplements, (2) in-kind aid, and (3) job training and employment aid (see Table 7–3). Cash supplements and in-kind aid comprise what is known as the *social safety net,* which is designed to help individuals who suffer personal misfortune—such as physical disability—or who experience economic dislocation. There are two tiers to the safety net: the upper tier is comprised of insurance programs, and the lower tier is comprised of the means tested programs for those who have no social insurance at all, or who are not adequately protected by social insurance programs. Employment and job training aid includes a whole range of programs adopted in the 1960s. These programs address particular problems of the poor such as access to adequate health care and promotion of equal opportunities.

Social welfare spending went from less than 2 percent of the gross national product (GNP) in 1929 to about 15 percent in 1985. Much of the growth occurred in entitlement (that is, cash supplement) programs that provide direct support for individuals and families. Most of these programs are universal and not targeted at the poor. Growth in these programs has been more rapid than programs specifically aimed at the poor (Bowden & Palmer 1984, 181). In fact, lower tier programs such as food stamps, Medicaid, child nutrition, subsidies for housing, and AFDC benefits were cut during the Reagan administration.

TABLE 7–3 *Social Welfare Programs*

	Cash Supplements	In-Kind Aid	Job Training and Employment Aid
Upper Tier	Old Age, Survivors, and Disability Insurance (OASDI) Unemployment Insurance (UI) Workers' Compensation (WC)		
Lower Tier	Aid to Families with Dependent Children (AFDC) Supplemental Security Income (SSI) Rent Subsidies General Assistance (state governments) Veterans' Compensation	Food Stamps Medicaid Medicare Veterans' Benefits Public Housing Community Maternal and Child Health Native American Aid Child Nutrition	Educational Programs Employment and Training Programs Equal Employment Opportunity Economic Development

Cash Support Programs The Social Security Act, passed in 1935, is by far the most significant income maintenance program in the United States. It consists of social insurance (Old Age, Survivors, and Disability Insurance and Unemployment Insurance) and public assistance programs for the blind, disabled, and families with dependent children (Supplemental Security Income). Figure 7–3 shows that the greatest portion of government outlays for income security cash payments is in social security. Social security also has shown the greatest growth of any welfare program, particularly since 1970. Social insurance programs account for a larger share of GNP than *means-tested transfers;** they rose from 3.3 percent in 1966 to 7.8 percent in

* A *means-tested transfer* is a program that transfers income from one group, through taxes, to another group. To be eligible for the benefits, the recipients must show that they are needy and have income and assets below a stated amount.

FIGURE 7–3 Government outlays for income security cash payments.

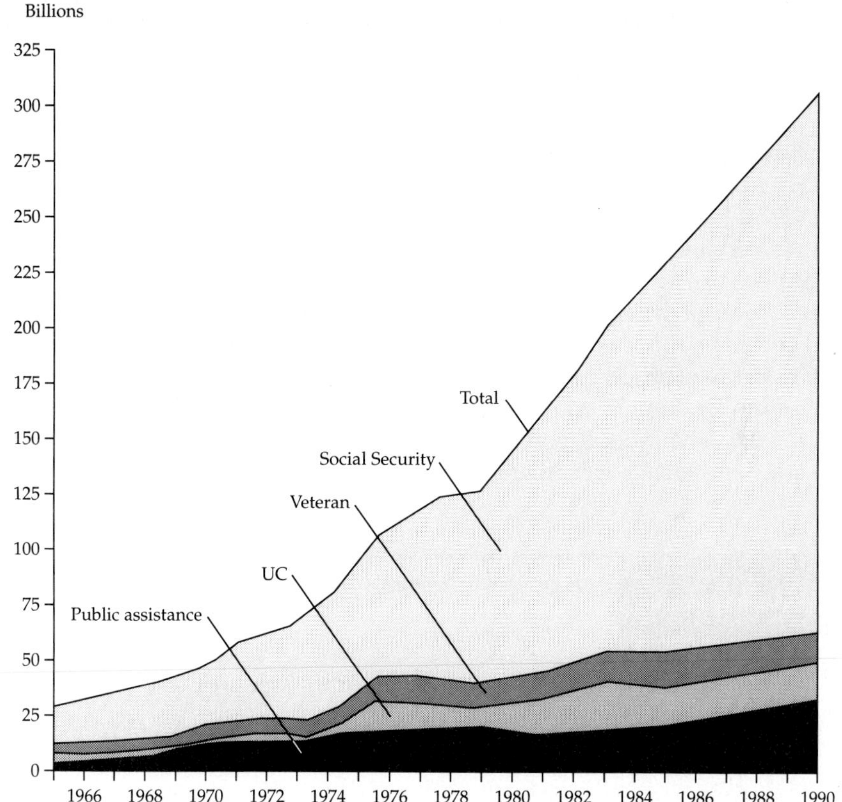

Source: Budget of the United States Government, Fiscal 1990.

1983. None of these programs is designed to eliminate poverty; their goal is to protect workers and their dependents against earning losses from retirement, death, or disability, and to protect the elderly and the disabled from extraordinary health costs.

Social security obligations totaled $193.8 billion in 1987 and over 36 million people received regular cash payments from the system. Coverage is almost universal. Of those who reached age sixty-five in 1984, only 6 percent were not eligible. Individuals must be insured to receive benefits, and people who contribute payroll taxes for at least ten years are permanently insured. The benefits are related to a person's age at retirement, and to the level of covered earnings. In 1987, the average payment for someone who retired at age sixty-five and had earned the maximum during his or her career was $488 a month for a single worker and $883 for a couple. If the person worked beyond age sixty-five, the benefits were reduced $1 for each $2 earned above $7,320. The system also pays an insured worker's surviving children under eighteen, dependent parents of a deceased worker, dependent widows or widowers, and severely disabled adults, ages eighteen to sixty-four, who are unable to engage in substantial gainful employment. In 1985, 37 million people received OASDI benefits and 123 million people contributed taxes to the system (see Figure 7–4). The total outlays in 1985 were $242 billion.

The Social Security Act also provides Aid to Families with Dependent Children (AFDC) and aid to the elderly, blind, and disabled through the Supplemental Security Income (SSI) program. The AFDC program is what people usually think of when they refer to welfare because it is the major means-tested income support program. It is the costliest and the most controversial public assistance program. In 1985 there were almost 11 million AFDC recipients, including about 6.9 million children. Over $16.6 billion in benefits were paid in 1986. The federal government pays about 55 percent of AFDC costs, while state and local governments pay the remainder. (Local governments pay

FIGURE 7–4 Social Security contributors and recipients.

Fewer workers to support retirees

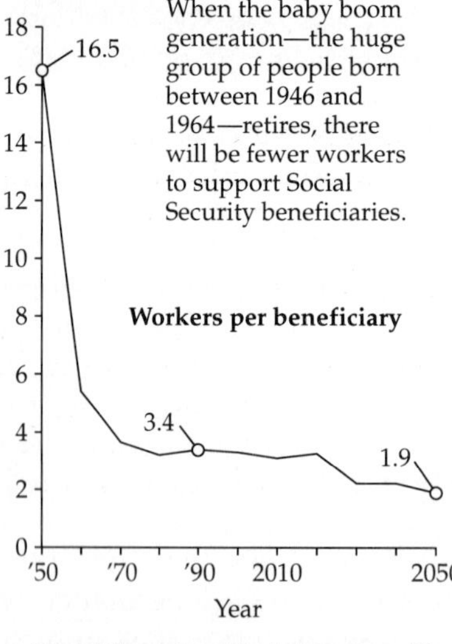

Workers will be retiring later

Retirees now get full benefits at age 65, but longer work lives are ahead as a result of a 1983 law that ultimately delays retirement to 67.

Year of birth	Social Security retirement age
1937 and before	65
1938	65, 2 mo.
1939	65, 4 mo.
1940	65, 6 mo.
1941	65, 8 mo.
1942	65, 10 mo.
1943–54	66
1955	66, 2 mo.
1956	66, 4 mo.
1957	66, 6 mo.
1958	66, 8 mo.
1959	66, 10 mo.
1960 and later	67

Source: Social Security Administration, House Ways and Means Committee.

less than 5 percent of total costs nationwide.) States administer the program, determining eligibility and the level of benefits. Thus there is wide variation from state to state in the amount of benefits paid. For example, in 1984 the monthly cost of basic needs for a family of four ranged from $201 in Texas to $911 in Vermont. The average was $470. None of these benefits was high enough to keep an AFDC family out of poverty in the absence of other income or in-kind assistance.

Supplemental Security Income has less variation than AFDC because the federal government plays a larger role in administering this program (Albritton & Brown 1986). It provides a basic monthly benefit for the aged, blind, and disabled. In 1985, the monthly benefit rate was $325 for an individual living in his or her own household with no other comparable income, and $488 for a couple. But, to be eligible, the assets—that is, auto, property, and insurance policies—of elderly, blind, or disabled public assistance recipients cannot exceed $1,600 for an individual or $2,400 for a couple. In 1985, public assistance expenditures were about $9.5 billion. The typical recipient of SSI is elderly, white, female, and living alone without other support. Only 13 percent of SSI recipients had unearned income other than social security benefits and the average income was $73 a month (Levitan 1985, 14).

Most states provide additional coverage and benefits which vary widely in amounts and types of assistance. These do not generally amount to very much, however; only a handful of states provide substantial benefits.

Another major cash assistance program is *veteran's benefits.* Compensation and pensions were provided to about 28 million veterans and their 60 million dependents and survivors at a cost of $13.9 billion in 1984 (Levitan 1985, 42). About 71 percent of this goes to veterans who have an injury, disability, or death incurred during service. The remaining 29 percent goes to war veterans whose annual income is below a specified level and who are permanently and totally disabled.

Two other cash assistance programs not designed for the poor are *unemployment insurance* and *workers' compensation.* The former is a protection earned by workers against joblessness; to be eligible, one must have lost a job and benefits are based on past earnings. Established by the Social Security Act, unemployment insurance is supported through a payroll tax. Because the program is state-administered, benefits vary widely from state to state. Workers' compensation is meant to protect individuals and families during a period when wages are reduced due to work-connected injuries. Temporarily as well as totally disabled persons receive benefits, and the benefits are generous. In most states, the weekly benefit for a totally disabled worker equals the average weekly salary in the state.

In-Kind Aid Since 1965, the in-kind component of means-tested transfers has risen steadily while the cash transfers have declined. Table 7–4 shows the expenditures for both kinds of assistance. In-kind benefits rose from

TABLE 7-4 *Per Capita Cash and In-Kind Assistance for the Poor, 1965 and 1984*

Year	Total $	Cash %	In-Kind %
1965	1097	81	19
1984	2368	43	57

Source: S. A. Levitan, *Programs in Aid of the Poor,* (Baltimore, MD: John Hopkins Press, 1985) p. 60.

19percent of per capita assistance in 1965 to about 57 percent in 1984, while cash assistance declined from 81 percent to 43 percent over the same years. The market value of noncash benefits for low income people in 1984 totaled $113 billion, or nearly four times the value of cash assistance to the poor. The rise in in-kind programs reflects the skepticism among policy makers about the moral character of the poor. Rather than provide cash benefits to be spent at the discretion of the recipient, these programs provide services for specific needs. The merits of each kind of assistance will be considered in the Evaluation section of this chapter.

One of the main services that the poor need is medical care. With the passage of Medicare and Medicaid in 1965 the federal government has assumed the major responsibility as the provider of health care for the elderly and the poor (see Chapter 6). Medicare is a universal program designed to help the elderly, regardless of income. Only about 10 percent of Medicare expenditures benefit the elderly poor. Medicaid is more specifically aimed at the poor. It offers reimbursements to states for a portion of the medical costs of low-income persons. Each state administers its own programs, and the federal share of expenses is between 50 and 83 percent. About 23 million people received Medicaid benefits in 1983 at a cost of about $33 billion.

As discussed in Chapter 6, the principal problems associated with Medicaid and Medicare are the escalating costs. Part of this is due to the method of delivering health care. Under the Great Society programs, the federal government tried to improve the delivery system by creating community health centers in low-income neighborhoods. The principal goals of these centers were to develop relationships with community service agencies and hospitals and foster participation of the population in decision making. Although the program was funded at a very small level compared to Medicaid, over 800 neighborhood health centers were developed serving over 4 million people.

Housing is the next major in-kind aid provided for the poor. In 1985, 4 million households received government subsidies of $15 billion (Mariano 1985, 20). The various components of housing programs include: (1) public housing for low-income families; most occupants of these units are minorities and elderly; and (2) rent supplements. The federal government pays the difference between the tenant's payment and the actual rent.

Because of the high cost of building new housing, subsidized housing has grown rapidly, surpassing public housing as the principal form of housing assistance for the poor. At the same time, the number of new public housing units financed by the government has declined dramatically since 1981 (see Figure 7–5). The government also subsidizes housing for middle-income people through tax deductions—$23 million in 1984—but very little of this has trickled down to the poor. Figure 7–6 shows the amount of housing subsidies received by various income groups.

Next to medical care and housing, food is the third largest need of the poor. Originated during the New Deal in the 1930s as a way to help bolster farm income, food stamps became an in-kind assistance in 1961. By 1984, the federal spending for food stamps ($12.1 billion) and child nutrition ($5.6 billion) amounted to $17.7 billion. The food stamp program is designed to increase the food purchasing power of the poor. Households receive monthly allotments of food stamps based on their income and household size. All public

FIGURE 7–5 Yearly additions to housing assistance in thousands of units. The Reagan administration proposed no new housing assistance in 1986. Congress approved about 100,000 new units, but 80 percent of those are vouchers or Section 8 certificates used as cash for rental housing.

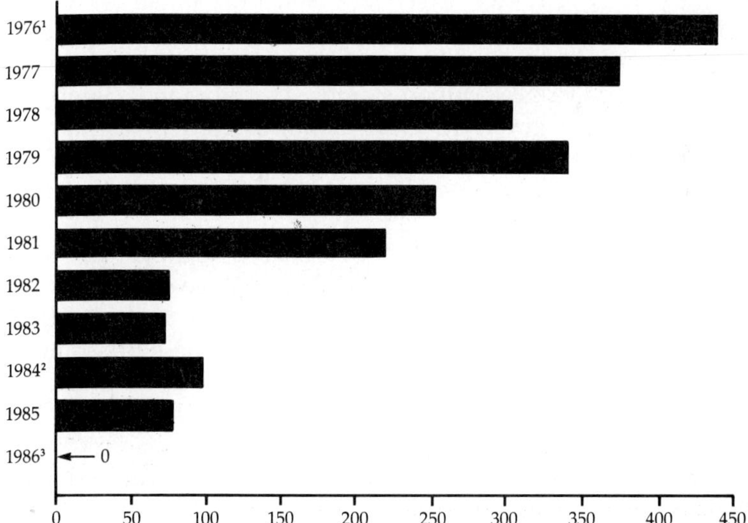

[1] Extra quarter because of change in fiscal year
[2] Election year
[3] Proposed

Source: © 1985 *The Washington Post.*

FIGURE 7–6 Housing subsidies by income group, direct and tax breaks, based on 1980 census.

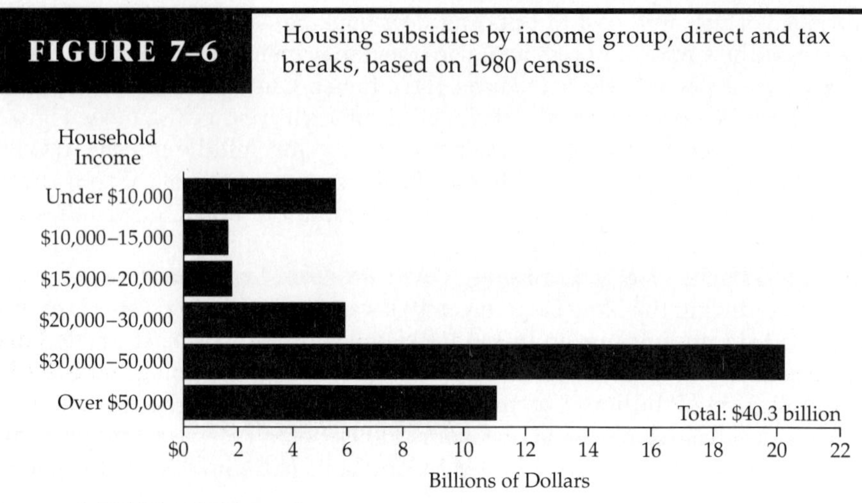

Source: © 1985 *The Washington Post.*

assistance recipients are eligible as well as households with incomes at or below the poverty level. In 1984, the maximum monthly allotment for a family of four was $264, or $.73 per meal for each person. This amount is reduced by 30 percent of a household's net income based on the assumption that a family spends 30 percent of its income on food. Thus, if a family has a monthly income of $600, it receives $64 in food stamps. The program is jointly operated by the federal and state governments and administered by the states. The program grew rapidly, particularly in the early 1970s, but because of escalating costs, in 1977, Congress put a spending cap on the program; the cap was $13.9 billion in 1985.

Child nutrition programs provide breakfast, lunch, and milk to 24.6 million children in private and public schools and daycare centers. Specially targeted at low-income children, the program is administered through state agencies; the school lunch program is the largest of these programs. In 1984, about 10.4 million children from poor homes received free meals at an average federal subsidy of $1.36 per meal (Levitan 1985, 81).

Employment and Training Programs President Reagan was fond of using the following proverb in his 1984 presidential election campaign, "Give a man a fish and you feed him for a day. Teach him how to fish and you feed him for life." Programs aimed at making able-bodied poor independent through training and employment are popular with members of all political persuasions. Thus, there is a wide range of self-help programs for the poor. Some attempt to improve the skills of the poor and make them more employable, some aim to increase the demand for labor, and some try to match the two.

Skill training through vocational education dates back to the Smith-Hughes Act of 1917. As of 1984, the federal government spent about $698 million on this program, distributed in grants to state governments, which then parcel out the funds to local school districts. While the federal government has tried to channel the money to disadvantaged students, most states define "disadvantaged" broadly.

The skill needs of poor adults were the target of the Manpower Development and Training Act of 1962. Skills centers were established in about eighty communities to provide institutional training in a variety of occupations. This was superceded by the Comprehensive Employment and Training Act (CETA) of 1973. Under CETA, states were given more flexibility to develop employment and training services in response to local labor market needs. The program reached a peak of 750,000 enrollees in 1978, but was discontinued and replaced by the Job Training Partnership Act (JTPA) in October 1983. This program puts greater reliance on private sector placement, low training costs, and local autonomy.

In 1964, the Great Society initiated the Job Corps through the Economic Opportunity Act (EOA). This program provided vocational training and basic education to youths fourteen to twenty-one years old who were poor, out of school, and out of work. The Job Corps set up residential training centers in rural areas based on the assumption that young people must be removed from their debilitating home environments before rehabilitation is possible. Enrollees received basic education, vocational training, room, board, health care, recreation, and a monthly allowance ranging from $40 to $100. The total cost of services was estimated at $15,150 per person in 1984, but the benefits also were high. About 80,000 youths were served in 1984 and 36,000 of these were placed in jobs, entered school or the military, or engaged in further training.

Although it was the recipient of much criticism and attempts to do away with it, the Job Corps survived, and, in 1991, was still registering some successes. A costly program—it cost slightly more than $15,000 per student to offer a combination of vocational, academic, and social skills—it trained 66,000 students in 1991. It survives even at this cost because a study conducted by Mathamatica Policy, Inc., of Princeton, New Jersey, found that it returns $1.46 for every $1.00 it spends. It does this because its graduates work longer, spend less time on welfare, and are less likely to be arrested or incarcerated or have a child out of wedlock. And it does this without "creaming" (that is, taking only the ones most likely to succeed). Its typical student is an 18-year-old high school dropout who reads at the seventh-grade level, comes from a poor, minority, one-parent family, and has never held a full-time job. But they volunteer for the program which shows that they are motivated to succeed.

In 1977, the federal government passed the Youth Employment and Demonstration Projects Act (YEDPA) aimed at reducing youth unemployment. In the first year of existence, the program cost $1.7 billion and served about 450,000 youths between sixteen and twenty-one years old (Levin 1983, 3). Eligible families could have incomes of no more than $9,350. Youth unemployment always has been higher than the adult rate, but in the 1980s it reached new heights, particularly for black and minority youths. The objectives of the YEDPA were straightforward: to provide youths with job training, work experience, and job placement. Over 80 percent of the youths in YEDPA were from low-income families and half were black or hispanic. Most had poor academic backgrounds, lack of discipline, and poor work habits. In an economy that just about required a high school diploma, this lack of academic training was a serious handicap. In 1950, about a third of all jobs did not require a high school diploma, but by 1970 this dropped to only 8 percent. A large percentage of the unemployed youth are black high school dropouts; in 1985 they accounted for 58 percent of the unemployed youth and are concentrated in central cities.

Training in the YEDPA involved remedial reading, practical arithmetic, and on-the-job experience. It consisted of four programs: (1) youth community conservation and improvement (which involved repairing homes of low-income people); (2) Youth Incentive Entitlement Pilot Projects (to demonstrate the efficacy of guaranteed employment to youths who resume or maintain attendance in secondary schools); (3) Youth Employment and Training Programs; and (4) Young Adult Conservation Corps (which involved conservation work on public lands and waters).

Such federally-funded job creation programs were eliminated by President Reagan, with two exceptions. One is the summer youth employment program funded under JTPA, which allocates grants to states to subsidize minimum wage, public-sector summer jobs for youths between the ages of fourteen and twenty-one. It gave 718,000 youths such jobs in 1984. The only other employment program remaining provides part-time public service employment for older Americans. Authorized under the Older Americans Act, this program creates job contracts with public and private nonprofit national service organizations. In 1980, 63,000 subsidized jobs of about twenty hours per week each were provided for low-income persons fifty-five years of age and over. Finally, federally-supported vocational rehabilitation programs include poverty as a disabling handicap. While few persons are selected on the basis of poverty alone, many of the disabled in America are poor. Almost 1 million individuals were handled in 1984 under this program and about a quarter of these were rehabilitated.

Economic Development Programs In addition to these programs, the federal government spent more than $14 million in 1984 for economic development of specific areas such as central cities, Appalachia, Indian reservations, and rural areas. Administered primarily by the U.S. Department of Housing and

Urban Development, the money is distributed through block grants to local and state governments for a variety of urban renewal and community development activities as well as for improving housing for the poor. In addition, the Urban Development Action Grant program uses public funds to encourage private investment in redevelopment projects in poverty areas. About $480 million was allocated in 1984 for this program.

Extensive aid to economically depressed rural areas is provided by the Department of Agriculture, authorized by the Rural Development Act of 1972. The Farmers Home Administration is in charge of a major business and industrial loan program to businesses in rural areas. The federal government also has spent over $3 billion since 1965 through the Appalachian Regional Commission. Much of it has been used to construct a major highway system and access roads in a thirteen-state area from New York to Mississippi under the assumption that Appalachia's economic problems are due to its geographical isolation.

Changes in Welfare Capitalism

President Johnson's Great Society programs were based on the notion that government had the responsibility to help the poor and to equalize incomes of the poor and rich. Social engineering expanded under the Great Society as social scientists joined the federal government in an effort to design and administer social policies in compensatory education, job training, and nutrition programs.

These goals were rejected by President Reagan whose main policy thrust was to shrink the public's responsibility for the poor. Under Reagan, the least needy were removed from the welfare rolls. Although he was thwarted by Congress in many of his benefit reduction efforts, Reagan was successful in greatly reducing the social welfare responsibility of the federal government.

A second major shift in welfare goals under President Reagan was the use of private agencies as a part of government policy efforts. This reflected the new meaning of welfare capitalism, based on a view of the welfare state as an untapped market with profit-making potential (Gilbert 1983). Between 1930 and the mid-1960s, the private sector of social welfare was relatively separate from government; it consisted of the moral and charitable agencies that tried to help the poor. But since the 1970s, the distinction between the private and public sectors of social welfare has faded. Through purchase of service agreements, private agencies contract with government to provide social welfare services. This has led to an influx of profit-making organizations into the private sector of social welfare, primarily in nursing homes and child care.

As the federal funds for AFDC were cut, the "new Federalism" of the Reagan administration shifted a lot of the responsibilities for welfare to the states. But the states were facing budget deficits by 1991 and began cutting their welfare payments which hit the poorest of the poor. Even though cash safety-net programs for the poor accounted for only about 5 percent of a typical state budget, this was the area that was politically easiest to cut. Benefits for AFDC which had fallen 42 percent in purchasing power from 1970 to 1991, dropped further in 40 states for fiscal 1992. In California, the governor argued that the proposed cuts would help decrease dependency on the government. Other states used welfare payments as a carrot or, more often, stick to force recipients to change their behavior. In Wisconsin, for example, a welfare mother was docked if her child was truant from school. In Arkansas, a parent was fined $50 for missing a parent-teacher conference. The argument in these cases was that this would give recipients the drive to break the "cycle of dependency." One major way to do this was to make recipients (mostly women) participate in job training and take a job. However, *New York Times* reporter Jason De Parle (1992, E3) writes:

> The problem with many current reform proposals is that they assume that small incentives—cuts or bonuses of $50 or $100 a month—will cause big changes in behavior. But three decades of experimentation show the opposite to be true: that benefit levels have little impact on decisions to work, marry, or bear children.

■ IMPLEMENTING WELFARE POLICY

The description of social welfare policy in the previous sections reveals a hodgepodge of different programs run by various agencies at the federal, state, and local levels of government and by private nonprofit and profit-making agencies. It is no wonder, then, that implementation problems plague liberal and conservative programs alike. According to Martin A. Levin and Barbara Ferman, "Bright ideas often are distorted and delayed in the process of implementation. It seems that more is needed to achieve effective policies than good intentions or even good program designs . . . in the past two decades, implementation has become the single most problematic aspect of policy making" (1985, 2). In the social welfare area, the implementation of programs depends on many different people and organizations, opening up numerous possibilities for disagreement, delay, and resistance.

Types of Implementation Tools Because most programs are built on existing ones, administrators who implement existing programs need to adopt the new work routines and goals. There are various ways of doing this. Levin and Ferman (1985) classify the three basic ways to get implementors to accept the new programs as *enforcement, inducement,* and *benefaction*. Enforcement is done by setting new standards, field-level monitoring to see if the standards are being met, and applying sanctions if they are not; inducement relies on such things as contracts with attached financial rewards; and benefaction involves enhancing the wealth or status of certain classes of individuals through tax benefits.

George Balch (1980) uses a slightly different classification scheme, although the general ideas are the same. According to Balch, we can make people *aware* of the existence of the new programs by providing information about them. For example, one of the reasons many people who are eligible for food stamps do not take advantage of them is that they do not know about them or how to apply. Second, we can make it *easier* for people to adopt new behavior. Third, we can *require* them to adopt new behavior under threat of penalties. Fourth, we can offer *positive* benefits to those who change their behavior in the desired direction.

But even with the best of tools, it is often difficult to accomplish goals because of the numerous agencies and individuals involved in any program. For example, in implementing the Youth Employment and Demonstration Projects Act (YEDPA), administrators faced a number of disorganized interests in which a coordinating mechanism was lacking (Levin & Ferman 1985). Hundreds of agencies and actors were involved in the YEDPA programs, including the local program staff, the prime sponsor (most often the mayor's office of youth employment), city and county governments, schools, unions, public-sector worksites, private businesses, community organizations, and past program employees. Political scientists concluded that steps for effective implementation failed in about half of the YEDPA programs around the country. There were delays, youths were not recruited, worksites were inadequate because they provided too little work, or there was inadequate supervision (U.S. General Accounting Office December, 1980). The result was a multitude of influences that interacted in unforeseen ways. Despite the savings they would receive, some employers in YEDPA would not hire eligible youths because they felt that they were too much trouble; and some unions did not regard the program as being in their interest.

However, in some cities, implementation of YEDPA was successful. Its goals were modest and specific, and the executives in these cities were able to bring the group's interests together (Levin & Ferman 1985). These successful programs were built on the existing infrastructure of programs left over from the Great Society's War on Poverty. The individuals and organizations comprising this infrastructure were alumni of Great Society programs, and their foundation spin-offs. For example, in San Antonio, Texas, the YEDPA program was based on the Great Society's Community Development Corporation formed in 1967 and the network of persons and organizations involved in that program; this led to personal trust among the agencies and individuals. The Community Development Corporation became involved in a broad range of community development projects, including a major role in the financing of large downtown conservation projects. "Fixers" (Bardach 1977), or public sector entrepreneurs (Palumbo, Musheno & Maynard-Moody 1985), jumped into the details of the program and built coalitions among the various groups.

Implementation as Red Tape When implementation fails, it can be disastrous for those on the receiving end—the welfare clients. For example, the Aid to Families with Dependent Children (AFDC) program requires extensive and continuous documentation by recipients. This was made more complex by numerous revisions during the Reagan administration. Recipients must document their income, expenses, and family makeup, all of which is monitored by caseworkers. The case of Anna Burns, whose eligibility had to be recalculated fourteen times in a three-year period, is a good illustration of this (see Case 7–1).

When the Burns case is multiplied by the 3.8 million other families receiving AFDC throughout the United States, the complexity of and paperwork

CASE 7–1 *AFDC and Anna Burns*

Anna Burns is a twenty-eight-year-old mother of three living in Georgia. She was married at the age of fifteen and divorced at twenty; her oldest child is in the sixth grade. She supports her three children below the poverty level with wages from various jobs, Aid to Families with Dependent Children, and occasional support from her ex-husband.

To receive her AFDC check—$193 a month in 1980—she had to document her earnings, taxes, travel, and childcare costs, and the costs of the uniform she must wear at work as a nurse's assistant. To determine her eligibility and her payment amount, the caseworker compared Anna Burns' income to the state need standard.

Because Burns took a new job in 1980, which put her above the eligibility standard, she was informed in December 1980 that she would no longer receive AFDC. However, she remained eligible for Medicaid and food stamps; though the latter was reduced. Her monthly income then was $673.

In December 1980, the federal government mandated changes in the food stamp program which slightly increased Burns' allotment, making her total new monthly income $708. But in February 1981, Burns was required to reduce the hours she worked. Her benefits were then recalculated, and she was once again eligible for AFDC monthly payment of $126 which she received as of March 1981. Her food stamp allotment also was increased from $162 to $171 per month. Then in June 1981, Georgia increased its AFDC payment standard, which increased Burns' grant from $126 to $140, effective in July. This reduced her food stamp allotment back to $160.

required by the program become staggering. Yet Burns' case is typical of the many families who find their benefits constantly fluctuating in response to unexplained and little understood policy changes. The problem is that AFDC policy is based on selectivism, which is aimed strictly at the poor. It attempts to remove the "undeserving" poor from the rolls, assuming that many recipients will cheat if they are not carefully watched. But the costs of administering such complex changes may well offset what is saved in removing individuals from the welfare rolls.

Thus failure during implementation may be the result of poor policy design rather than poor implementation. Following the case study on Anna Burns, the Center for the Study of Social Policy concluded:

> If anything, the blame for this failure must go to the policy makers who enacted the changes without an adequate understanding of how they would be

---

In August 1981, the U.S. Congress mandated additional changes in AFDC and food stamp programs. Burns' allotments were reviewed in September 1981 and even though her monthly income had increased, she remained eligible, but her grant was reduced from $140 to $18 in AFDC while her food stamp allowance was increased to $183, effective October 1981. In November of that year, the caseworker recalculated Burns' eligibility based on the Omnibus Budget Reconciliation Act of 1981 and found that Burns was no longer eligible for AFDC or Medicaid and would have to be terminated as of February 1982. Her food stamp allotment was also cut back, reducing her total family income (including AFDC and food stamp allotments) to $621. In February, Burns' income (without AFDC and food stamps) increased to $511 a month and she failed to document her rent, utilities, and childcare expenses. Consequently, the government reduced Burns' food stamp allotment to $133.

These fluctuations in eligibility and allotments continued throughout this case study. Further adjustments were made in June, August, September, and December of 1982 and March and June of 1983 when this study ended. In October 1984, a new set of AFDC policies were enacted by Congress which required further changes in Anna Burns' allotment.

Source: Adapted from *Through the Briar-Patch: a Case in Point*. Washington, D.C.: Center for the Study of Social Policy, September, 1984.

> implemented and to policy analysts who similarly failed to demonstrate an understanding of how the many technical changes would be applied to individual families. . . . With hindsight, we can now see that the 1981 policy changes both reduced benefits *and* further complicated an already complex system. (CSSP 1984, 26)

Implementors as Policy Makers

Although Congress has a big impact on the direction of public policy, as when it passed the Omnibus Budget Reconciliation Act, administrative agencies often have an even greater impact on policy. The food stamp program described earlier in this chapter is a case in point.

During the life of the food stamp program, USDA administrators made crucial decisions regarding who would receive food stamps and how much they would get. They also created and changed the benefit structure, and determined the amount of coupons that would be available to each family. Administrative regulations like those established for food stamps are fashioned through specified administrative procedures under direct grants of statutory authority. Administrative rule making is a quasi-legislative method of formulating regulations which has the force of law. Such authority has been delegated to administrative agencies since the beginning of the twentieth century because Congress cannot deal with all of the decisions that government must make each day. Although Congress interacts with administrative agencies on these matters, full control by Congress of administrators is not possible (see Case 7–2).

The food stamp program is only one example of welfare policy shaped by administrators. During his first term, President Reagan used administrative rules extensively as a way of cutting 500,000 AFDC recipients from the rolls. He also removed 1 million food stamp recipients through an administrative limit on the allowable income level of participants (Bowden & Palmer 1984, 193). The Reagan administration also used the courts and administrative rules to cut Social Security Disability Insurance (SSDI) benefits for the totally and permanently disabled. By 1975, the SSDI program was making 3 million disability determinations a year. In 1981, the Reagan administration increased federal review of state decisions and adopted a vocational grid to reduce discretion in determining eligibility. By 1982, the termination rate for the program increased to 47 percent and the approval rate was cut to 21 percent, down from the 40 percent level it had been in 1979. In June 1983, Congress imposed a six-month moratorium on the reversals and state governments suspended the disability investigations. According to Social Welfare Professor Donald Chambers:

> there is considerable public policy mischief here. Severely disabled people have been told that they are eligible for benefits one year, receive them for a year

> only to be told the next year that somehow they have become "not disabled." This, despite no apparent change in their outward physical condition, as far as they themselves can tell. (1985, 237)

Private Agencies as Implementors Private agencies have been involved in welfare programs mostly with regard to job training. Under Title I of the Economic Opportunity Act (EOA) of 1964, about twenty-five of the 110 Job Corps Centers were run by the private sector. For example, the Job Opportunities in the Business Sector (JOBS) program of 1973 was run by the National Alliance of Businessmen. It sought to create jobs and training opportunities in the private sector for those who were put out of work by shifts in economic structure such as the closing of steel mills. Business firms were reimbursed for the costs of counseling, transportation, health services, day care, and training. However, few employers actually participated in the program and there were numerous conflicts between the National Alliance of Businessmen, local employers, labor department officials, and local government officials.

Nine years passed before a similar partnership between government and private industry was approved. Help through Industrial Retraining (HIRE), passed in 1982, was to be implemented through the help and support of the nation's largest corporations. It was aimed at unemployed Vietnam veterans, economically disadvantaged youth, and those who had been unemployed for a long time. Its goal was to train 100,000 people at a cost of $140 million, but it failed to meet this goal and was replaced by HIRE II, which also failed to elicit support from the business community (Goodman 1984).

The Private Sector Initiative Program of the Comprehensive Employment and Training Act gave private industry a significant role in decision making through private industry councils at the local level. These councils were successful in involving private sector employers in the design and operation of training programs; they made use of performance contracting, and used service deliverers who were new to the employment and training field. Still, there was poor cooperation between the private industry councils and CETA staff, which harmed morale, drained energy, and alienated the private sector.

Two years after the program began, there was conflict over program goals; the private industry councils wanted autonomy to develop innovative training and to increase involvement of profit-making firms in delivering manpower services. But the autonomy produced conflict when it threatened to take power away from the mayors. Finally, there was conflict over whether or not money should be spent at the end of a budget year: CETA officials took the attitude of "spend it or lose it" while the private industry councils wanted to spend money only if there was a good reason.

On October 7, 1982, the Job Training Partnership Act expanded the private sector partnership concept. Private industry councils were given equal decision-making authority over all employment and training funds in a locality rather than over just some of the funds. Private industry councils and local

CASE 7–2 *Implementors as Policy Makers: The Food Stamp Program*

The food stamp program, initiated in 1939, was an attempt to deal with several problems created during the Great Depression. The program helped farmers at the same time that it fed poor people.

During the 1930s, large farm crops were driving down farm prices at the same time that people were starving.

The food stamp program directed government to purchase commodity surpluses and distribute them to local relief agencies which in turn gave them to families in need. Within two years as many as 4 million Americans were receiving food through this program. Before the program ended in 1943, almost 1,500 counties had instituted it and it was considered a great success. However, World War II reduced the unemployment and crop surpluses that had made the program necessary and the decision to terminate it met little opposition.

In the 1950s, Representative Leonor Sullivan (D-Mo.) attempted to revive the program, by persuading Congress to request a food stamp feasibility study from the USDA. The study was done by the same officials in the USDA who had administered the earlier commodity distribution program. Although the program never got off the ground in the 1950s, a pilot program was initiated in the 1960s by the Kennedy administration. Officials who administered the original commodities distribution program were put in charge of the program making all the decisions about how much to give and to whom. Amidst publicity, the pilot program was an immediate success. According to one official in Fayette County, Arkansas, "Deliveries of fresh milk are way up, meat sales have increased and canned goods are being bought by the case again. I've seen gratitude in the eyes and voices of these people. It makes my job worthwhile" (Berry 1984, 28).

Due to the program's success, the USDA officials continued making all policy decisions with few constraints on their authority. However, the tight

elected officials were to decide policy jointly. This resulted in increased business involvement in job training programs, but conflict between private industry councils and government administrators remained, and the program was slower than anticipated in getting started. The program lacks clear direction and is administered in such a way that it seeks to serve conflicting constituencies. More importantly, because contractors are paid on the basis of their success in placing people in jobs quickly and employers are seeking good workers, the program encourages "creaming." Thus, it may not be serving rules adopted by the administrators drastically cut participation from what it was under the earlier commodity distribution program. Administrators insisted that participants pay for the stamps and because many welfare recipients did not have the money, they could not participate. However, the administrators felt that the stamps should be earned.

Because the president and Secretary of Agriculture were satisfied with the program's progress, no one questioned the decisions of the administrators. The task force program became law on August 31, 1964, when Lyndon Johnson signed a food stamp bill saying, "The food stamp program weds the best of humanitarian instincts of the American people with the best of the free enterprise system" (Berry 1984, 34).

Passage of the law did not change much. Administrators pursued the same policy and guidelines and the program remained under the direction of the same administrators from 1964 to 1967. But in 1967 and 1968, the hunger issue returned to the top of the systemic agenda, culminating in the Poor People's March on Washington. As a result, Congress was forced to liberalize program benefits. The cost of the stamps was lowered and the number of participants increased.

By 1972, controversy subsided and the USDA administrators continued to make policy unrestricted by Congress. But between 1974 and 1976, controversy again developed, this time by conservatives who were alarmed at the escalating costs of the program. By 1975, 19.4 million individuals participated at an annual cost of $4.3 billion. However, the food stamp program survived the Carter years, only to be cut back after Reagan's election.

Source: From Jeffery M. Berry, *Feeding Hungry People: Rule-making in the Food Stamp Program*. Rutgers University Press, New Brunswick, NJ, 1984.

those most in need who are harder to train and place. Jeff Faux, president of the Economic Policy Institute, said that JTPA is obsessed with "very, very short-term goals—placing people very quickly in jobs they would have gotten anyway" (Victor, 1990). The general conclusion about JTPA is that, while it is greatly needed, it does not seem to be reaching those most in need of help, and no one knows exactly what the return on investment is (Chelf 1992, 91). Never-the-less, the Congress increased the appropriation for JTPA in FY 1991 by $318 million, allocating $3.76 billion for the program.

Criteria for Effective Implementation In evaluating the implementation of the youth employment programs in several cities, Levin and Ferman (1985) used the following criteria: the program delays were held to a reasonable level, financial costs were held down, and the original objectives were met without significant alteration or underachievement. Since the goals of youth employment programs seem to be fairly straightforward, it would seem easy to do this. But many government programs, particularly those in social welfare, do not have very clear goals. Thus, requiring that implementors not significantly alter original objectives seems unrealistic. Even in the job training aspects of welfare programs, the problem of "creaming"—that is, taking only the easiest, most employable cases—makes it difficult to determine if goals are being met. To what extent do the more successful implementors take the easy rather than the hard-core cases, and if they do, have they met the "original" objectives of the programs? Some researchers argue that creaming was build into the design of these job training programs (Robertson 1984). And very few social welfare programs have specific, easily measured goals. Gilbert (1983) argues that the private, competitive market cannot work in implementing social welfare programs because it is difficult to measure effective implementation of many social welfare programs. For example, how do we determine the effectiveness of marital counseling programs, planned parenthood, or nursing homes? "Social welfare programs often serve objectives that are impalpable and multiple," says Gilbert, and they defy precise measurement (1983, 10).

■ EVALUATING SOCIAL WELFARE POLICY

When the Social Security Act was signed on August 14, 1935, 20 percent of the nation's workforce was unemployed. Millions of elderly citizens had watched their savings vanish in a tidal wave of bank failures and the collapse of the stock market. Before social security, the poorhouse, with all of its horrors, was the expectation of most elderly; more than half of the elderly had incomes below the poverty level.

By 1986, most of the elderly poor were raised out of poverty—a great achievement—and social security is primarily responsible (Page 1983, 63). The Institute for Research on Poverty at the University of Wisconsin reports that the elderly are the major success story in the War on Poverty. Over 43 percent of this group have pretransfer incomes (that is, incomes before they receive social security benefits) below the poverty line, but after money transfers through social security, their poverty rate falls to 14.6 percent, which is slightly less than the rate for all persons. If we take into account their assets and in-kind transfers—that is, Medicare and food stamps—and favorable tax laws, the economic status of the elderly relative to the non-elderly is even better (Institute for Research on Poverty 1984). In fact, of the $641.7 billion spent in 1983 on social welfare programs, the elderly received $330.6 billion (Taylor 1986, 24). As noted above, by 1989 the poverty rate among those age 65 and over declined to 11.4 percent.

Thus, we have made progress in the battle against poverty in the United States. But how much progress, and in what direction?

How Are We Doing in the War on Poverty? In the early 1960s, Michael Harrington's book, *The Other America,* estimated that 40 percent of Americans were in poverty although the official statistics put the figure at 22 percent. The book helped crystalize President Kennedy's determination to initiate an anti-poverty program in 1963 which culminated in President Johnson's War on Poverty. As shown in Figure 7–1, the number of Americans in poverty declined sharply from 1964 to 1968 from 19 to 12.8 percent, and then declined further in 1972 to 11.9 percent where it remained throughout the 1970s until it increased in the early 1980s. By 1985, it had returned to 19 percent—the same as when the War on Poverty began. The poverty rate declined again in the latter 1980s as economic conditions improved, but rose against to 14.2 percent by 1992.

These figures show that progress was made in the War on Poverty, but they leave some important questions unanswered. For example, How much of the decline in poverty was due to government transfer payments as opposed to improved economic conditions? And what does the trend look like if we include in-kind transfers as well as money transfers?

In regard to the first question, there is no doubt a growing economy in the late 1960s and again in the latter part of the 1980s helped eliminate some poverty, but the principal reduction was accomplished through government programs (Schwartz 1983, 33). The Institute for Research on Poverty estimates that in 1982 cash social insurance transfer payments by government removed 33.8 percent of poor persons from poverty; cash public assistance transfers removed an additional 3.8 percent; and in-kind transfers removed an additional 25.8 percent. Hence a total of 63.3 percent of poor persons benefited from government payments (Institute for Research on Poverty 1984, 8). Although economic growth eased some of the poverty of the 1960s, only about 10 percent of the total reduction in poverty was due to economic growth;* many did not benefit or were excluded from such benefits (Schwartz 1983). "The circumstances of the 1960s and early 1970s demonstrate that while a prosperous economy may benefit the stronger economic groups, its impact on weaker groups can equally be nonexistent, reducing some to even more dire situations" (33). The ones

* Schwartz (1983) computes this by taking the difference between those who would have been in poverty in 1965 (21.3 percent) if we consider all income except that transferred to individuals through government programs and those who would have been in poverty in 1972 (19.2 percent) if we consider all sources of income except government transfers. The difference (2.1 percent) reveals about a 10 percent reduction in poverty when government programs are left out.

reduced to more dire situations were families headed by women under sixty-five who were worse off in the 1980s.

When we include in-kind transfer payments to measure reduction in poverty the results are even better; by 1977, only 6.9 percent of Americans were below the poverty level (see Figure 7–2). With this figure, the War on Poverty might have been won "except for perhaps a few mopping up operations" (Anderson 1978, 37). But even with in-kind transfers included, the rate of poverty rose again in the early 1980s and again in 1991–1992.

The food stamp program has made the greatest impact of any in-kind program for reducing poverty. Since its conception, the program's goals have changed considerably from a commodities distribution program to an unintended welfare reform legislation (Nathan 1976, 64). The program lessens the inequities of the widely varying state AFDC benefits because the less a family receives in AFDC benefits the more it gets in food stamps. It is an income floor for all Americans, and it is the one welfare program to which a person without income can turn. As many as one in six Americans has been a recipient of food stamps at one time or another during a single year (Berry 1984, 145).

In general, the middle-class has benefited more from the social welfare expenditures of government than the poor. Food stamps and AFDC benefits go almost entirely to people who are below the poverty line, but Social Security, which accounts for the largest percent of social welfare expenditures, has grown at the greatest rate since 1975. Although it was not specifically designed to eliminate poverty, Social Security has helped those in the middle-income ranges most (Page 1983, 88).

Successes and Failures in Job Creation and Training Programs Because the "dole" is viewed as bad, a great deal of American social welfare policy is aimed at creating jobs and training unemployed people. A number of studies have evaluated the effect of employment and training programs on subsequent employment rates and earning levels of participants. Some consistent findings have emerged across these different studies. First, women have benefited more than men in terms of increased earnings. The CETA programs, which provided jobs and training, produced no significant earnings gain for men at all, but women benefited because the programs increased the number of hours worked rather than the wages per hours, and women have generally worked fewer hours than men. The CETA programs have also helped prepare candidates for entry-level positions, mostly women and young men rather than older men. In addition, youths benefited from Job Corps. Studies found that the program increased employment and earnings, and reduced welfare dependency, unemployment, criminal activity, and out-of-wedlock births (Institute for Research on Poverty 1985).

However, even during their most successful period, employment and training programs did not cover a very large number of disadvantaged workers. The programs thus made little dent in the unemployment or poverty problems of those able to work. While the programs were cost-effective, they were too small to make much difference. CETA, in particular, came under intense criticism in the late 1970s, primarily from conservatives. The program's implementation was plagued by tension, goal displacement, and bad press. Instead of benefiting the hard-core unemployed, the program benefited better educated, older, white clientele, many of whom took public service jobs. But these jobs lacked adequate supervision, were rife with political favoritism, and turned into "do-nothing jobs" (Levin & Ferman 1985).

Youth training jobs under YEDPA fared better; half of the programs were effectively implemented. Those provided with training were from lower-income families; 51 percent were black or Hispanic and had poor academic backgrounds. However, in half the sites, the programs were inadequate because of insufficient useful work or inadequate supervision (U.S. General Accounting Office, December 1980, 10).

The Job Corps program administered in partnerships with private agencies also received mixed reviews. According to political scientist Garth Magnum, who studied such partnerships, "Private employers often proved to be useful advisers to employment and training programs where they were listened to on significant issues. They often cooperated in the public interest as long as it was not seriously in conflict with the interests of their own firms. They did not prove themselves capable of *managing* public programs. Public administration is simply more complex and difficult than business administration" (Magnum 1982, 24).

The Conservative Revolution and Social Welfare In his 1982 State of the Union address, President Reagan said he inherited a system in which "available resources are going not to the needy but to the greedy." He cited some $44 billion in cuts already achieved in social programs and announced his intention to cut another $63 billion over the next several years. Federal spending on civilian programs was reduced from 9.9 percent of GNP in 1980 to 7.6 percent in 1990; much of the cut was in social programs (Chelf 1992, 14).

Fueled by the conservative attack in the 1970s, welfare clients were depicted as lazy, good-for-nothings who could work but preferred to take welfare handouts. By 1980, the number of Americans embracing the belief that government was incompetent climbed to a solid 63 percent, up from 27 percent in the early 1960s (Schwartz 1983, 26). The image popularized by conservatives was that Americans were being overtaxed to support welfare cheats and that the market could generate enough prosperity to help anyone who wanted to work. Moreover, the conservatives argued, government programs simply increased the dependency of those who were taking "the welfare fix."

Thus, the thrust of the conservative social welfare policy was to force those who could work off the welfare rolls by stringent means tests and severe cutbacks. The Reagan administration tried a number of workfare programs in which it required welfare recipients to work in order to receive benefits. Various alternatives to government welfare also were tried, such as increased reliance on volunteers and the use of vouchers that enabled people to make their own choices in education and housing.

Under the Omnibus Budget Reconciliation Act (OBRA) of 1981, states were allowed to establish a "community work experience program" whereby a recipient must work for minimum wages in public service jobs in order to earn AFDC benefits. Those who did not cooperate were removed from the rolls. A number of studies indicate that the OBRA did not significantly reduce AFDC rolls, however (Goodwin 1978; Englander & Englander 1985). A study of the 1972 Work Incentives Program (WIN) by social welfare professor Mildred Rein (1982) concludes that the program had been ineffective in promoting work effort, reducing caseloads, or moderating the growth of welfare costs. The WIN program provided comprehensive services—education, skill training, and child care—in the hope that this would lead enrollees to economic independence. A study of the New Jersey workfare program found that although the program reduced the welfare rolls, it amounted to harassment because it discouraged those with a legitimate AFDC claim from filing (Englander & Englander 1985). Thus, it reduced the rolls by elimination rather than by finding work for those on welfare.

A similar program set up by Senator Daniel Moynihan of New York—called the Family Support Act—was passed in 1988. It requires an increasing percentage of welfare mothers to enroll either in work or training programs as a condition of their aid. But since most of these women had children, day care would have to be made available for them to participate, and the amount of money appropriated for it was not enough to move many people off of welfare even if day-care was available (Palumbo & Calista 1990).

One of the reasons that workfare programs are unsuccessful is because a large percentage of those on welfare are women without husbands, who have one or two children, little education, and no car. Most have been on welfare for less than two years. In Arizona, for example, of the 21,600 welfare mothers who were physically able to work in 1985, only 3,900 found jobs through the state's three job-training and placement programs. About half of these welfare mothers could not find work because of health problems, drug addiction, lack of transportation, or pregnancy. Of those who were able to find work, many did not because the kind of work available paid less than their AFDC benefits. In addition, many recipients were illiterate, and it cost more than the government had available to train them for more than simple food service or maintenance work (La Jeunesse 1985). Barbara Blum, President of Manpower Demonstration Research Corporation, said, "I don't know what the answer is. These people live terribly complicated lives, and several states have tried different approaches with mixed success. But it remains an issue this nation has to answer" (La Jeunesse 1985, A-11). However, a study conducted by the Manpower Demonstration Research Corporation of eight states concluded that "work programs make a difference. They increase employment and earnings of recipients, and they reduce welfare dependency" (Rasberry 1986, A-13). The study estimated that earnings increased 10 to 20 percent and welfare grants decreased 5 to 10 percent.

Is There a Permanent Underclass of Poor People? In the 1960s, the culture of poverty theory became fashionable with the publication of anthropologist Oscar Lewis's book *The Children of Sanchez* (1961). The book's main thesis is that the poor are different from the nonpoor with regard to their behavior. They transmit these behaviors to their children who, in turn, remain poor for generation after generation. The inability to take a long-range view and plan for tomorrow, low regard for education, the need for immediate gratification, and mental illness all were popularized as aspects of the "culture of poverty" which government or other programs could not change (Banfield 1968).

The facts, however, contradict the culture of poverty theory. A study by Harvard University researchers Mary Jo Bane and David Ellwood found that over a ten-year period, "the same poor people are not always with us—even though the same numbers seem to be" (Stockman 1983, 2). According to the study, many of those who become poor experience short periods of poverty lasting one or two years; only a small number remain poor for a long time. These long-term poor eventually consume a large portion of welfare expenditures. They are the underclass, the hard-core, the most difficult to reach. Another study conducted by University of Michigan researchers showed considerable upward mobility across generations of poor families, "Most of today's poor children are not tomorrow's poor adults" (Hill et al. 1983, 10).

But the changing family structure in America has had an effect on poverty, primarily through the feminization of poverty. From 1960 to 1990, the proportion of women in the labor force went from 18 percent to over 55 percent. An increasing divorce rate led to increases in poverty as one income was split into two and as divorced mothers took low-paying jobs. About one of every five children in 1985 lived apart from one parent, and because of increasing divorce rates, separations, and out-of-wedlock births, it is estimated that almost one of every two children born in 1985 will spend part of his or her first eighteen years in a family headed by a single mother (Moynihan 1981, 8). The problem is even greater among black and hispanic families. The number of poor black families headed by single women more than doubled between 1969 and 1985. Female-headed black families accounted for 44 percent of all black families and female-headed white families comprised 13 percent of all white families (see Figure 7–7).

The breakdown of the black family and the changing structure of the urban economy account for the high rate of poverty among urban blacks and hispanic families. Unlike ethnic groups in the past, they are unable to take manufacturing jobs that offer decent wages because such jobs no longer exist. Instead, the better jobs require relatively high education and are in the suburbs and few blacks or hispanics are able to take these jobs. In the cities,

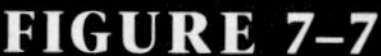

FIGURE 7–7 The growing black underclass.

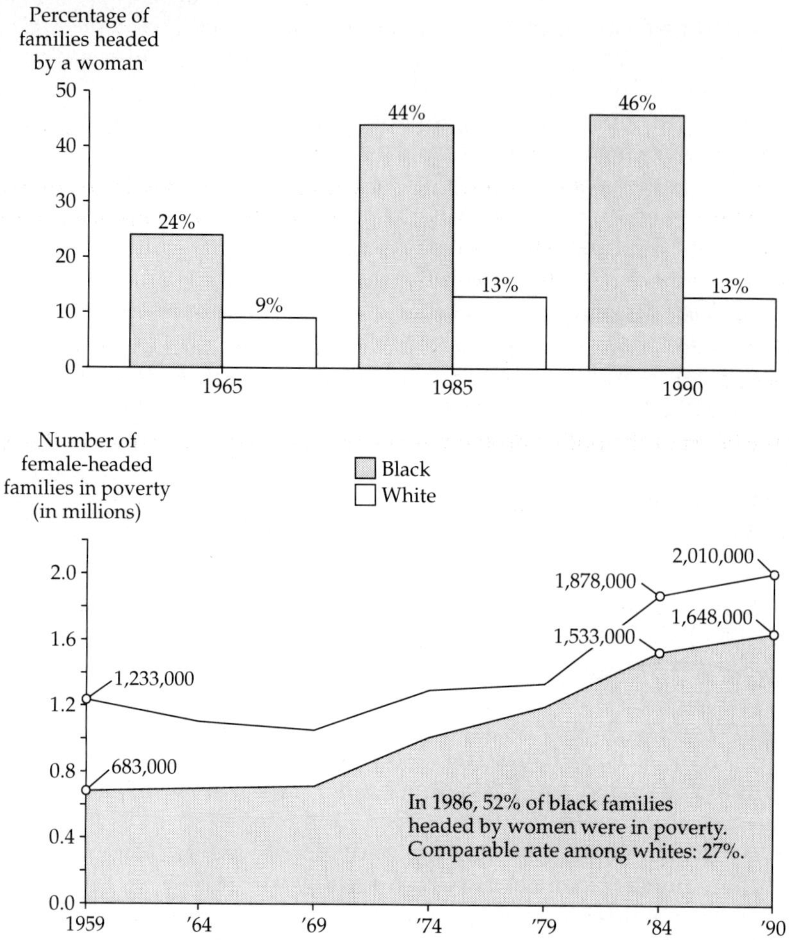
Percentage of families headed by a woman
50
40
30
20
10
0
24%
9%
44%
13%
46%
13%
1965
1985
1990
Black
White
Number of female-headed families in poverty (in millions)
2.0
1.6
1.2
0.8
0.4
0.0
1,233,000
683,000
1,878,000
1,533,000
2,010,000
1,648,000
In 1986, 52% of black families headed by women were in poverty. Comparable rate among whites: 27%.
1959
'64
'69
'74
'79
'84
'90

Note: Except for unemployment chart, most data for blacks before 1968 include "black and other" races. On unemployment chart, data before 1985 include "black and other" races.

Source: Reprinted from *U.S. News & World Report* issue of March 17, 1986. Copyright, 1986, U.S. News & World Report.

Source for 1990: Poverty in the United States: 1990 P-60, No. 175. U.S. Bureau of the Census, U.S. Department of Commerce.

there are low-paying service jobs—for example, janitor or busboy—that do not compensate for the loss of manufacturing jobs. In 1986, half of the 9 million working-age black men were out of work, and the prospects for improvement were rather dim.

One of every three black residents of America's cities was officially poor and 34 percent of black children born in the inner city will remain poor throughout the first decade of their lives. Hispanics are not much better off as Figure 7–8 shows. In 1990, 28.1 percent of Hispanics were at poverty level compared to 33 percent of blacks.

The problems of poverty are so complex that they never will be completely solved. More likely, there will be cycles during which the situation will improve and then worsen. The extent to which poverty is a function of family structure will be difficult to improve. Attempts to change family structure will be met with strong opposition. Yet, according to some experts, "Either systematic intrusions into the family would be required to equalize developmental conditions . . . or the whole liberal focus on equal opportunities—as distinct from outcomes—would have to be abandoned" (Fishkin 1983, 6).

At the heart of the policy problem is the way poverty programs are designed. When we aim welfare benefits explicitly at the poor, and, through means tests determine who is eligible, we attach a stigma to welfare, and blame the poor themselves for their condition rather than economic or other conditions that

FIGURE 7–8 Percentage of each group living below the poverty level.

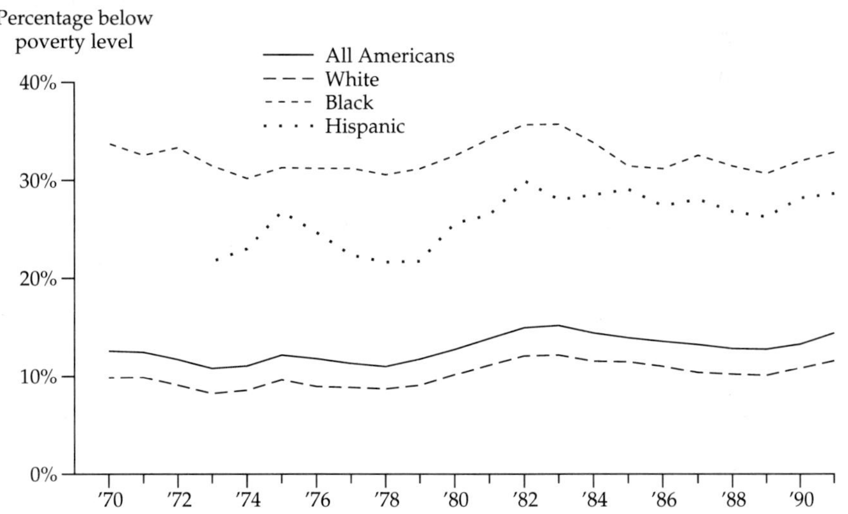

Source: Census Bureau.

may be responsible. We see the poor as a burden for the nonpoor because the latter are required to give them aid for which they get no return (Waxman 1983, 116). Hence, under selective programs, the poor become scapegoats. Programs based on universalism, however, have much greater support. Social Security is politically sacrosanct; it is defined as an "insurance" program or an "earned right." In fact, recipients in 1986 received three dollars for every dollar they put into the system. The system really is one in which taxes are taken from the young and the money transferred to the elderly. It is a form of welfare for the elderly but it is not seen in the same way as welfare for the poor. If the latter were perceived in a universal sense, there probably would be more support for it. Chaim Waxman writes, "the most effective means of breaking the vicious cycle, the stigma of poverty, is by creating and implementing policies and programs that will lead to the integration of the poor with the nonpoor, rather than to their further isolation" (1983, 116). Such a policy requires getting rid of means tests, and extending services to all. For example, child welfare could be paid in the form of a benefit for *all* single adults caring for one or more children; the benefit would be equal to the amount of child-support paid by the absent spouse, or a minimum amount, whichever is larger (Garfinkel 1980).

The British welfare system is based on the principle of universalism:

> One fundamental historical reason for the adoption of this principle was the aim of making services available and accessible to the whole population in such ways as would not involve users in any humiliating loss of status, dignity, or self respect. There should be no sense of inferiority, pauperism, shame or stigma in the use of publicly provided service; no attrition that one was being or becoming a "public burden." (Titmuss 1968, 129)

Yet in 1985, Prime Minister Margaret Thatcher adopted policies similar to those of the Reagan administration, pushing for stricter testing of claimants' financial means, making citizens responsible for their own pension arrangements, and eliminating supplementary benefits. Hence the policy problem is one involving political ideology and political support. A welfare system that is too generous tends to lose public support. There is also a tendency to try to discourage excessive use of services, reduce demand, and reassure the nonpoor that their tax money is not being wasted on "laggards." Welfare policy in the United States in the late 1980s seemed to be firmly committed to this direction.

8

Crime and Justice: Law in Action

■ THE NATURE OF THE CRIME PROBLEM

Crime as a Political Phenomenon

America's crime rate is very high—higher than almost any other Western nation. Approximately 22,000 murders are committed each year in the United States, which is almost half of the total number of Americans killed in the entire Vietnam War (Levine, Musheno & Palumbo 1986). Certain parts of American cities are almost like combat zones. Murder is the leading cause of death for young, black males. Compared to other nations, America is very violent; 11,522 murders with handguns were committed in the United States in 1980, but only 77 were committed in Japan, 8 in Great Britain, 8 in Canada, 8 in Sweden, 24 in Switzerland, 23 in Israel, and 4 in Australia.

America's approach to fighting crime by imprisonment is more aggressive than most other nations. For example, the United States incarcerates twice as many people on a per capita basis as Canada, three times as many as Great

Britain, and four times as many as West Germany. The United States has the highest incarceration rate among industrialized nations, higher even than Russia and South Africa.

Although the percent of households experiencing crime during the 1980s decreased from 30 percent in 1980 to 23.7 percent in 1990, the criminal justice system (or, actually, "non-system") was not functioning very well in 1993 and crime, especially violent crime, was on the rise again; it rose 4 percent from 1990 to 1991 (Bureau of Justice Statistics, July 1992, 2).

Part of the reason why the justice system was not functioning very well is the structural imbalance among criminal justice agencies. For example, in 1990 police received 42.8 percent of total criminal justice expenditures while judicial and legal received only 22 percent, and corrections 33.6 percent (see Table 8–1). Hence, although police may arrest a large number of offenders, courts and prisons are not able to handle them all and they become overloaded and clogged so that the total system does not function efficiently and effectively. The improper functioning of the system results in disrespect for the law and, in some cases, a complete breakdown in some of its components.

When the system does not operate properly it can actually *cause* crime (Gorecki 1983). It does this in several ways. First, a poorly operating criminal justice system actually lowers sanctioning levels—even though harsher laws are passed—by "taxing the limited resources of the justice system" (Pontell 1984, 34). Because the courts become overloaded and the prisons overcrowded, punishment is less swift, certain, and severe. The result is a revolving-door justice, deplored by many. Such a system cannot effectively fight crime. As political scientist Jim Levine correctly notes: "To the extent that potential criminals correctly perceive the limitations of the [system], the credibility of legal sanctions is diminished and the deterrent capacity of the criminal justice system is undermined" (1975, 531).

The growth of crime results in spreading fear and anger. Even though most people will not directly experience violent crimes themselves, they develop a fear of crime vicariously by information disseminated by the mass media—television, movies, and newspapers. Crime makes good news. A day does not pass that bizarre crimes are left unreported in the press. A man is fatally stabbed by his neighbor's teenage son; a vagrant's throat is slashed on a city street; a five-year-old girl is molested with a stick and then bludgeoned to death. These kinds of stories are reported to the public every day.

The average person's reaction to events such as this is fear, anger, and hatred. It does not matter that those who are least likely to be victims of crime—that is, older, white females—also have the greatest fear of crime. The reality of this fear is what produces policy results as candidates for office appeal to the fear, promising even tougher laws if they are elected. Little wonder, also, that the public generally favors the use of harsh punishments such as the death penalty (Levine, Musheno & Palumbo 1986) and that juries mete out harsher sentences than judges (Levine 1983).

TABLE 8–1 ***Distribution of Justice System Direct Expenditure, by Activity and Level of Government, Fiscal 1990***

			Judicial and Legal Services					
Level of Government	Total	Police Protection	Total	Courts Only	Prosecution and Legal Services	Public Defense	Corrections	Other Justice Activities
Percent by level of government								
All governments	100.0%	100.0%	100.0%	100.0%	100.0%	100.0%	100.0%	100.0%
Federal	12.6	12.6	21.0	16.7	27.6	23.3	5.8	40.3
State	34.2	14.8	30.3	34.0	23.6	31.5	61.6	34.8
Total local	53.2	72.5	48.7	49.3	48.8	45.2	32.6	24.9
County	23.5	17.2	35.6	39.5	29.3	34.6	23.6	19.7
Municipal	29.7	55.3	13.1	9.8	19.6	10.6	9.0	5.2
Percent by activity								
All governments	100%	42.8	22.3%	12.5%	7.4%	2.3%	33.6%	1.3%
Federal	100	43.1	37.3	16.6	16.3	4.3	15.6	4.0
State	100	18.6	19.7	12.5	5.1	2.2	60.5	1.3
Total local	100	58.4	20.4	11.6	6.8	2.0	20.6	.6
County	100	31.4	33.7	21.1	9.2	3.5	33.8	1.1
Municipal	100	79.8	9.9	4.1	4.9	.8	10.1	.2

Source: Bureau of Justice Statistics, *Justice Expenditure and Employment, 1990,* p. 3. Sue A. Lindgren, Sept. 1992. U.S. Department of Justice, Office of Justice Programs.

A malfunctioning criminal justice system causes crime in yet a second way. As society calls for harsher penalties and a get tough approach, it turns away from rehabilitation and from trying to correct the social conditions that may be a contributing factor in crime, like poverty and ignorance. As these social conditions get worse, it takes even harsher punishment to deter crime because people living in poverty have less and less to lose. The threat of a prison term of one year would be more effective if applied to a person who has a substantial income as compared to a person who is living in poverty. Hence, stiffer punishment is needed for offenders in lower socioeconomic groups than for middle- or upper-class groups. Unequal social conditions also produce more crime; as social conditions get worse, crime goes up, and more severe punishment is needed as an effective deterrent. But as the severity of punishment increases, the system gets overloaded, which leads to more crime because there is insufficient capacity to implement harsher punishments.

If harsh punishment and a get tough approach by themselves are ineffective, then why are they emphasized as the best way to control crime? Primarily because of the political advantages that accrue to elected officials who advocate a tough stand on crime. For example, political scientist Bernard Bray writes, "Prosecutors in the American South commonly favor the death penalty. They tend to develop prosecutorial strategies based on their understanding that having capital punishment statutes under which capital trials are conducted, and under which the state imposes death sentences, is essential to their political interests" (1983, 4). Politicians engage in symbolic politics where crime is involved. They find that favoring and supporting harsh punishment are sound political investments because both serve their political interests and move their political careers forward. Political scientist John Culver quotes one observer of state politics as saying, "There have been quite a few votes in the legislature . . . in favor of capital punishment measures by those who actually oppose it. These lawmakers can please their constituents without fearing that the executioner is about to go into business again" (1983, 21).

Police also benefit when crime policy takes a get tough approach because they receive the largest share of expenditures for criminal justice. This is because they are politically more powerful than other members of the criminal justice system such as judges or corrections officials. Thus it is in their interest to publicize crime.

How Much Crime Is There? Although it may sound strange, law enforcement agencies do not know how much crime actually is committed. We are accustomed to seeing reports about crime on television and in the newspapers and we assume that these figures accurately measure crime, but they do not. These statistics are a count of the number of crimes *reported* to local law enforcement agencies, which are then sent to the Federal Bureau of Investigation in its *Uniform Crime Reports.* These data are published annually by the FBI in

Crime in the United States and they receive much attention by the media because of the public's concern with crime.

The FBI uses a two-part reporting form. Part I of the report contains the more serious crimes, referred to as *index offenses.* These are homicide, rape, robbery, assault, burglary, larceny-theft, motor vehicle theft, and arson. Part II offenses are primarily property crimes such as forgery and counterfeiting, fraud, embezzlement, buying and receiving stolen property and gambling, offenses against family and children, driving under the influence, liquor law violations, drunkenness, disorderly conduct, vagrancy, and a long list of other offenses, such as possession and sale of obscene material.

The *Uniform Crime Reports* are not accurate for several reasons. First, many crimes go unreported by the public. Of the approximately 35 million victimizations reported in household surveys in 1991, only 37 percent or 13 million were reported to its police. The former estimate is from the National Crime Survey, which is conducted twice yearly for the Bureau of Justice Statistics. In 1991, the survey included over 60,000 households in all parts of the United States. About 128,000 people were interviewed to find out whether they had been victimized by crime within the past six months. The 60,000 households are a representative national sample. The 35 million crimes are an estimate based on the responses of this sample. These "victimization" surveys, initiated in the early 1970s, are considered a more accurate measure of crime, although they too have their defects which will be discussed below.

The amount of underreporting of crime that takes place also depends upon the type of crime. Personal thefts such as purse snatching, pocket picking, and larceny are the most underreported; only 26 percent of these crimes are reported to police, 37 percent of the household crimes such as burglary, and 48 percent of violent crimes of rape, robbery, and assault are reported (see Figure 8–1).

Another limitation of reported crime data is that there is wide variation in the way police in different areas record their data. McCleary and colleagues (1982) studied three separate police departments and found marked changes in reported crime due to organizational changes within the departments. The discretion of individual police officers and departments often determines whether crimes are reported. Police officers do not always record all crimes reported to them, and police departments may fudge data—that is, report less crime than actually comes to their attention—in order to make the department look good. On the other end, more efficient departments will uncover more crime because they respond sooner and work more effectively. Thus a city with a higher crime rate does not necessarily have a less effective criminal justice system; the police may in fact be doing a better job, which shows up in a great number of arrests.

O'Brien (1985, 36) concluded after a study of reported crime, "thus, it is not, in general, safe to consider changes in official crime rates over time as changes in the rate of offending." He also (1985, 35) states, "UCR crime rates

FIGURE 8–1 Trends in reporting selected crimes to the police, 1973–1984.

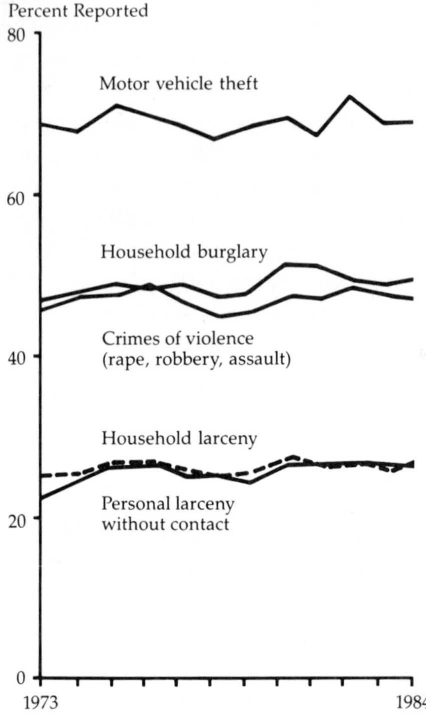

Source: U.S. Department of Justice, Bureau of Justice Statistics Bulletin, *Criminal Victimization 1984,* Washington, D.C. (1984) p. 4.

should not, in general, be used to compare the relative rates of crimes across jurisdictions."

The advantages of victimization surveys are (1) they make reporting easier for victims because the interviewers go to households rather than requiring victims to report to them, and (2) the responses are kept confidential. To minimize some of the errors in reporting, the sample of households is scientifically selected to represent the entire nation. The interview schedule has been tested and is valid and reliable. The interviews are conducted by trained interviewers. Nevertheless, there are errors in victimization data although fewer than in reported crime data. Criminal victimization surveys show that all crimes have declined since 1981, but that property crimes such as larceny and burglary have declined at a more rapid rate (see Figure 8–2). Although declining, a large number of crimes are committed each year in the United States.

FIGURE 8–2 Number of victimizations per 1,000 persons or households.

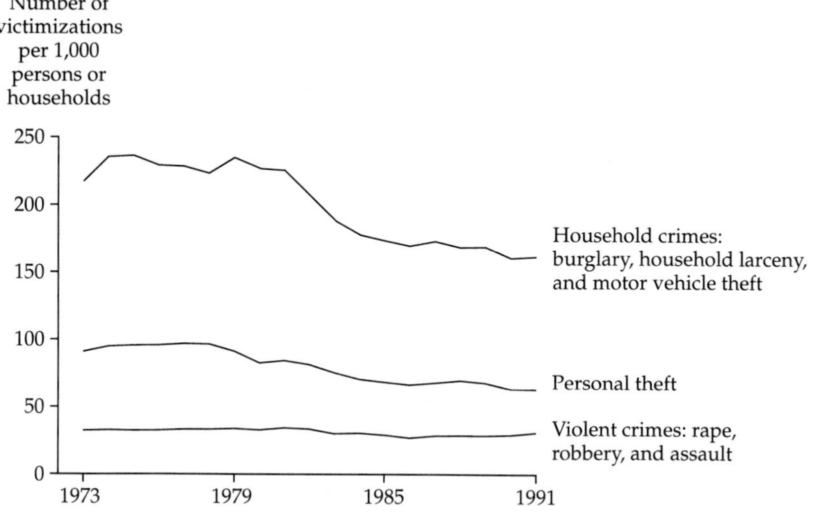

Source: Bureau of Justice Statistics, *National Update,* July 1992, Vol. 11, 1, p. 1.

About 35 million total victimizations were reported in 1991. But what does this mean to the average person? First of all, only a small percentage of citizens are ever victims of a crime. For example, only 5.7 percent of the adult residents of cities such as Chicago, Philadelphia, and San Francisco were attacked by anyone in a personal crime and only 3.2 percent reported an injury (Skogan & Maxfield 1981, 45). Crimes of high concern—a new category included in Bureau of Justice Statistics bulletins—which are rape, robbery, or assault by a stranger or a burglary, comprised only 7.2 percent of all victimizations reported in 1991. The most likely victims of these crimes are young, poor blacks. Street thieves, including purse snatchers and robbers, usually victimize poor and working-class citizens. Thus, while the average citizen is not likely to experience crime, crime has been a big issue in public policy for some time.

The criminal victimization surveys themselves are seriously flawed. Levine (1976) notes that respondents may mistake for crime incidents that are trivial personal annoyances, or they may mistake when the incident occurred. Respondents may exaggerate their experiences, or even lie outright to make themselves seem more important. They may give what they consider to be the socially desirable response. Levine believes that ". . . while police reports no doubt suffer from crime underreporting, surveys may be flawed by crime overreporting, which leads to inflated crime rates" (Levine 1976, 309–10). He concludes, "Only an omniscient deity would be capable of providing an exact tabulation of crime . . . " (Levine 1976, 326). Chambliss (1984) makes a similar argument in an article entitled, "Crime Rates as Crime Myths." According to Chambliss, 40 percent of the 37 million victimizations reported in 1973 were for personal larcenies where there was no contact; items were reported stolen from an unlocked desk, open car, and so on. About 60 percent of the victims said that they did not report them to the police because nothing could be done, or that it was not important enough. These "crimes," therefore, were rather trivial and make crime seem worse than it is. More importantly, however, is the fact that victimization surveys provide no data on white collar crimes such as fraud, embezzlement, and forgery. The questionnaire used in the survey only asks whether the respondent has been a victim of a personal or property crime and does not refer to "white collar" crimes. People do not know when they are the victim of crimes, such as being over charged due to price fixing if companies or charged for services not delivered, such as from auto mechanics.

White Collar Crimes The crimes we have been discussing thus far are those the public usually thinks about when considering public policy issues. But when measured in terms of economic losses to society, white collar and corporate crime far exceed street and predatory crime. White collar crime consists of violations committed by individuals or small groups in connection with their occupations (Clinard & Quinney 1973). These include violations by physicians, pharmacists, lawyers, auto or appliance repairpersons, bank tellers, and small businessowners. The crimes involved are tax evasion, embezzlement, fraudulent repairs of autos, televisions, and other appliances, check kiting, and violations in the sales of securities.

Corporate crime is crime committed by large business firms. There is evidence that such crime is extensive. Nearly two-thirds of the Fortune 500 corporations were charged with violations of corporate law over a two-year period (Clinard 1983). A more recent study found that 115 of the Fortune 500 corporations had been convicted between 1970 and 1980 of at least one major crime or had paid penalties for serious illegal behavior (Clinard 1983, 15). Their illegal practices included price-fixing, false advertising, marketing of unsafe products, environmental pollution, political bribery, foreign payoffs, disregard of safety regulations, evasion of taxes, and falsification of corporate records to hide illicit practices. The public has increasingly come to regard white collar and corporate crime as serious offenses. But while there is increasing recognition and disapproval of its existence, less attention is given to white collar and corporate crime in public policy than to street and predatory crimes. This is largely because street crimes are violent and frequently involve physical harm to the victims.

There also is an intellectual rationale for emphasizing the dangers of street crime. For example, political science professor James Q. Wilson argues that "predatory crime, in particular crime committed by strangers on innocent victims, causes the kind of fear that drives people apart from one another and thus impedes or even prevents the formation of meaningful human communities. Predatory crime violates the social contract" (1985, 5). Notice the use of the term "predatory" and the phrase "committed by strangers on innocent victims." (Are there other kinds of victims?) Such terms are value laden inasmuch as everyone would be afraid of "predators." But the question of whether street crime is worse than white collar crime is not an "objective" reality; it is a socially constructed one, and a particular construction reflects a specific political ideology. Why, for example, does "predatory crime" violate the social contract any more than corporate or occupational crime? Jeffrey Reiman, for example, notes that when mine workers are killed because of unsafe working conditions, it is called a "disaster" rather than "murder." He says that we wear blinders when we do this. If someone is held responsible for the death of mine workers, he may be fined, Reiman writes, "but will he be tried for murder? Will anyone think of him as a murder? *And if not, why not?*" (1984, 66; emphasis in the original).

Reiman answers as follows:

> The reality of crime as the target of our criminal justice system and as perceived by the general populace is not a simple objective threat to which the system reacts: *It is a reality that takes shape as it is filtered through a series of human decisions running the full gamut of the criminal justice system*—from the lawmakers who determine what behavior shall be in the province of criminal justice to law enforcers who decide which individuals will be brought within that province. (1984, 67. Emphasis in the original)

We usually do not define wrongdoing by corporate executives, doctors, mechanics, bankers, and others as crimes. When the Ford Motor Company went ahead and continued to sell Pinto automobiles when it knew that some people would be incinerated because of faulty gas tanks, and when the Robbins Company sold the Dalkon Shield contraceptive to women when it knew that they were harmful, these were not considered crimes, and certainly not "murder" (Cullen, Maakestad & Cavender 1987).

Nevertheless, white collar crimes are far more costly, both in lives lost and money than all the street crimes listed in the UCR. Tens of thousands of people are killed and hundreds of thousands injured each year by unsafe products and working conditions, but these are not contained in the *Uniform Crime Reports.* The amount of money stolen by insider trading on Wall Street or by savings and loan executives during the 1980s far exceeds the money stolen by all the crimes reported in the UCR. But these are not listed in the UCR or reflected in victimization surveys. Reiman (1991, 78) says, "The criminal justice system is a carnival mirror that presents a distorted image of what threatens us." We are doubly deceived, says Reiman. We are deceived about what really threatens us; occupational or white collar crime is more dangerous than street crime, but official crime data do not reflect this. And we are deceived into believing that the criminal justice system will protect us by locking up those who commit street crimes.

■ AGENDA SETTING IN CRIMINAL JUSTICE

Only a small percentage of the social problems in the country become candidates for public policy. Why do some issues come to the attention of policy makers while others do not? There are a number of different ways that an issue may become part of the public agenda. Some of these are listed below, in order of importance:

1. Pressures by interest groups, including professional associations and public bureaucracies.
2. Desires of important people in the community.
3. Attention given to a problem by the mass media.
4. Triggering events such as a sensational murder.
5. Personal interests of legislators.
6. Pressures of public opinion.

Often a combination of these factors is needed to get something onto the agenda. In order for crime to get onto the national public agenda, it usually takes a number of years, pressure from various groups, and certain triggering events.

Crime became a part of the national policy agenda only in the mid-1960s. Until then, crime, for the most part, was strictly a local matter. The process by which it got onto the national policy agenda began with the rise of the civil rights movement in the early 1960s. The techniques used by civil rights advocates during this time gained national attention; they included freedom rides, sit-ins, and mass demonstrations. These groups were met by police repression using techniques such as fire hoses and police dogs.

Alarmed by these events, the public began to demand law and order. Liberals and conservatives split over the causes of crime and how to deal with it. Conservatives blamed a breakdown in the respect for law and order; lenient judges; moral decay in the church, school, and family; and the liberal decisions in favor of defendants by the U.S. Supreme Court. For example, in his 1964 presidential acceptance speech before the Republican National Convention, conservative candidate Barry Goldwater said, "Tonight there is violence in our streets, corruption in our highest offices, aimlessness among our youth, anxiety among our elderly, and there's a virtual despair among the many who look beyond material success toward the inner meaning of their lives" (Cronin, Cronin & Milakovich 1981, 18). Liberals, on the other hand, believed that crime was symptomatic of other social problems such as poverty and lack of education. This position was represented by President Lyndon Johnson. During the 1964 presidential campaign, Johnson responded to Goldwater, saying, "I feared that as long as these citizens were alienated from the rights of the American system, they would continue to consider themselves, outside the obligations of that system" (Cronin et al., 24).

Crime thus became a part of the national political agenda and has remained so ever since. The triggering incidents that put it there—civil rights protests and police repression—are not the most common route by which items get onto the agenda. The more common route is through the pressure of interest groups. The most powerful of these are the various law enforcement groups such as the International Association of Police Chiefs, the National Sheriffs Association, the Police Foundation, the Police Benevolent Association, the Fraternal Order of Police, and the National Troopers Coalition. Their power comes from several sources. First of all, police control all of the crucial information used to identify the nature and scope of crime in the United States. And police budgets grew substantially throughout the 1960s and 1970s, an era when reported crime grew as well. In 1990, local, state, and federal governments spent nearly $31.8 billion on police protection. Compared to other institutions of the criminal justice system, law enforcement dominates criminal justice expenditures and employment in the United States (see Table 8–1). A second reason law enforcement interest groups are powerful is the influence of police in local politics. Police organizations have their greatest influence on local policy rather than the national agenda. Since crime policy is made primarily at the local level, this local influence is important.

Local Policy Agendas Crime has been a core issue of city politics in almost every city for a generation. One study found that law and order dominated urban elections over the entire 31-year period 1948 to 1978 (Heinz, Jacob & Lineberry 1983, 3). Crime is a major public concern; it occupies a large portion of media coverage, is crucial to a city's image, and critical to the electoral fortunes of local politicians. During the 1960s when crime rates were rising rapidly across the country, crime became a part of the local policy agendas in almost every city. Although the crime rate rose throughout the country at a rate unprecedented in America's history, the *fear* of crime rose even more rapidly. Debilitating fear gripped many cities. Entire areas were abandoned at night as citizens locked themselves behind closed doors.

Crime was a crucial issue in numerous city elections, particularly during the 1960s. In Newark, New Jersey, riots and a police campaign touting "Fear City" marked city politics. In Philadelphia, the mayor used the police to intimidate ward committee members to support his election; later a police commissioner became mayor. In Minneapolis, a police lieutenant shook the political establishment by defeating the incumbent mayor with a campaign emphasizing law and order. In Phoenix, the police became the largest part of the city's budget, absorbing 28 percent of all city expenditures. Thus crime was used by political entrepreneurs as a means of gaining power; politicians were quick to respond to, and even exploit, the rising fear of crime (Wilson 1975). In this way, politicians themselves helped shape the policy agenda.

■ THE MEDIA AND CRIME

Crime is given a great deal of emphasis by the media, especially newspapers and television. Crime and justice topics averaged 25 percent of all offerings in the newspapers in Chicago during a one-year period (1976) studied by political scientist Doris Graber (1980). Television was a close second with crime occupying 20 percent of all offerings on local television, and 13 percent on national television. The coverage of crime ranked ahead of most other topics; it was three times as much as coverage of Congress, the presidency, or the state of the economy (Graber 1980, 26). In addition to crime news, prime time television featured twenty crime drama programs weekly, comprising 63 program hours per week, or 33 percent of total program time. This amount of time devoted to crime news and dramas in Chicago is similar to what other studies have shown in other locations (Terry 1984). The time devoted to crime remains the same regardless of changes in crime statistics reported by police.

Given this heavy emphasis on crime, what kinds of crime and criminals do the media construct? The two crimes audiences see most often on prime time crime dramas are murder and robbery (Estep & Macdonald 1984). A persistent emphasis is overrepresentation of violent crime as compared to property or white collar crime. Estep and Macdonald (1984, 122) write, "this exaggerated focus on murder, robbery and assault on television, we argue, maximizes the fear of crime within the public." Moreover, women are usually murder victims on these shows and this may heighten female viewers' sense of vulnerability.

The emphasis on violent crime is often coupled with an image of the criminal as a young male, usually black or belonging to other minority groups (Graber 1980, 55). However, Graber writes that she found there were some differences between the media and the public, with the public more often than the media perceiving criminals as largely flawed in character, nonwhite, and lower class, "It is the public, rather than the media, that thinks of crime almost exclusively in terms of street rather than white-collar crime" (1980, 68).

Barrile (1984) sums up the television messages in two perspectives: the personalized crime perspective and the retributive justice perspective. In the first, crime is seen as a failure of the individual rather than due to social causes such as poverty, unemployment, or discrimination. In addition, great emphasis is placed on acquisitiveness and private profit. In the retributive justice perspective presented by the media, the individual is culpable and deserves strict punishment such as the death penalty in order to teach others a lesson.

The media's motivation is to attract and entertain its audience rather than confront crime realistically. But in doing this, the media's images are "often inaccurate and uniformly fragmentary, providing a distorted mirror reflection of crime within society and an equally distorted image of the criminal justice system's response to such behavior" (Bortner 1984, 16). The distortion is in favor of depicting street crimes, which receives the greatest coverage by far, while business crimes receive little coverage. "When the emotional effect of subject matter is added to other prominent factors," Graber (1980, 37–38) writes, "the balance in favor of street crime impact is overwhelming." For example, in the late 1970s, the media got involved in a program that lifers in Rahway prison had been conducting. Called the Juvenile Awareness Project, it involved having juveniles be confronted by fierce looking prisoners with the intent of scaring them so that they would not want to be sent to prison. The Golden West Broadcasting Company made a documentary of it, which caught on, and was then picked up by other media organizations. However, the documentary was greatly distorted depicting the juveniles as "animals" and "punks." One editorial was accompanied with a picture of a juvenile with pointed, devil-like ears. An evaluation of the program, however, found that none of it was true; the juveniles who were involved were not criminals for the most part (some mothers sued the Golden West Broadcasting Company for saying their sons were criminals); and the project had little impact on the juveniles future behavior (Cavender 1984), but it had a large impact on the way the public perceived crime and criminals.

How the Media Constructs Crime Images

The media acts as "gatekeepers" that allow certain events and their interpretations to reach public attention while others remain unreported. They do this in two ways: (1) news editors look for "themes" that they will emphasize in the day's news; and (2) crime reporters have regular "beats" that causes them to look for certain events and ignore others.

The use of themes by editors is illustrated beautifully by Mark Fishman (1984) in his description of how a television station in New York in 1976 created a crime wave against the elderly. A local television station reported a "crime wave" against the elderly in which the muggers, rapists, and murderers were usually black or Hispanic youths and elderly whites the victims. The public outcry was immediate. The mayor criticized the juvenile justice system, saying it was responsible for allowing the crime wave to occur. The Senior Citizens Robbery Unit (SCRU) of the New York Police Department (NYPD) was given more manpower and money as a result, and new, tougher legislation for juvenile offenders was introduced into the state legislature. However, says Fishman (1984, 161), "It is doubtful that there really was a crime wave or any unusual surge of violence against elderly people. No one really knows, least of all the journalists who reported the crime wave." Fishman notes that the NYPD data did not show a crime wave and even showed that the murder of elderly people had dropped by 19 percent. However, as we will discuss next, there was no "reality" about crimes against the elderly; there was only the "reality" that the television station had created and which the other media immediately picked up and repeated.

The way the crime wave story developed is that the editor of the television station (which Fishman refers to by the pseudonym WAVE), faced what he felt was a "slow news" days. When he came to work in the morning, he scanned the wire services and the police wire (which is separate from the other news wires) looking for a theme in order to impose some order on the huge number of unrelated events coming over the wires. Coming across stories about the robbery of an elderly woman and a report about a police educational meeting with a group of senior citizens that focused on self-protection, he found a theme. The events were stripped of their contexts by the editor and put into the theme of a crime wave against the elderly. Other media picked up the stories because media organizations always watch what is going on in other media organizations. Fishman (1984, 169) writes, "When journalists notice each other reporting the same crime theme, it becomes entrenched in a community of media organizations." As the story spread, the reality of the theme was confirmed by the media organizations who first reported it.

The police then began to feed similar stories to the media over the police wire. The police are thus important contributors to the construction of crime stories and crime waves because they are the *sole* suppliers of information to the media. Police try to supply incidents they think the media is interested in, provided the police want to promote the particular theme. Police tend to supply stories to the media where they have the most success, which underscored the seriousness of the crime problem, and which demonstrate a need for their services—namely, violent, face-to-face crimes (Terry 1984). In this case, it was certainly to their advantage to supply stories about crimes against the elderly. The SCRU of the NYPD had an important interest in this because they felt they were under staffed and that this would help them. It did. More resources were given to the SCRU of the NYPD after the stories broke.

Elected officials then picked up on the crime wave story seeing in it the chance to get attention and, possibly, some votes by being champions of the "helpless" elderly. They added additional credibility to the notion that the crime wave was real by calling attention to it and not questioning its validity. This is not unusual because public officials get their knowledge of crime through the media or from the police departments. They do not offer a contrary or independent view about the nature of crime (Jacobs 1984).

In addition to news editors, crime reporters contribute to constructions of crime. They also emphasize violent, predatory street crime committed by minority people because it makes good stories, but also because of the way news reporting is institutionalized. Crime reporters have "beats" that tend to become routinized. News from the beats are allotted space and time according to fairly regular patterns. Events remote from these beats are ignored (Graber 1980). The media looks for what is *newsworthy,* but, in doing so, it selects "events which are atypical, presents them in a stereotypical fashion, and contrasts them against a backcloth of normality which is overtypical" (Hulsman 1986, 32).

Thus, crime becomes what is constructed in the newsrooms instead of outside of them. The process of constructing a social problem described by Spector and Kitsuse (1987) fits the creation of the 1976 crime wave against the elderly in New York. The four-part model is as follows:

1. A group or groups attempt to assert the existence of some condition, define it as harmful, publicize these assertions, and create a political issue. (In the WAVE case, it was the media and the police.)
2. Official organizations recognize the legitimacy of the claims and the groups (the mayor and elected officials in New York).
3. The claimants do not like the remedy and express dissatisfaction with how it is being handled. (The mayor criticized the juvenile justice institutions' handling of the problem.)
4. Attempts are made to create alternative solutions. (New legislation was introduced in the state legislature that would transfer a juvenile who was involved in a crime against the elderly to the adult courts. The legislation died when the "crime wave" subsided.)

The juveniles in this case were "suitable enemies" (Christie 1986). They were seen as dangerous. They were powerful and their victims were frail and old. This made for good drama and the stuff that the media and politicians love. But it was a social construction of reality, not reality itself.

Defining the Crime Problem Crime has meant different things in different cities, depending on which groups were defining the issue. In Newark, it meant the looting that accompanied civil disorder, as well as robbery and mugging. In San Jose, it meant prostitution that was rampant in the city in the 1960s. In Minneapolis, crime was defined mostly as vice, and in Philadelphia, references to crime by Police Commissioner Frank Rizzo were thinly veiled references to crimes by blacks (Heinz, Jacob & Lineberry 1983).

Crime policy faces competition from other local issues such as transportation, budgets taxes, and urban redevelopment. While crime was fairly high on the agenda of city governments from 1962 to 1974, it did not reach the number one position until 1974. Beginning in 1974, it outpaced budget and tax problems (number 2), the economy (number 3), race and ethnic relations (number 4), and a number of other issues (Jacob 1984). Thus crime became the number one item on city agendas at the very time crime rates, as measured by the *Uniform Crime Reports,* had peaked and were beginning to level off or decline. Political scientist Herb Jacob explains why crime became more salient on the policy agenda at a time when "objective" indicators showed that it was leveling off:

> The appearance of crime as a salient issue may have been related to the public's attention to school desegregation, race relations, and civil disorders, matters that some persons linked to crime. These last three issues muddied the waters for those seeking more vigorous law enforcement policies. More aggressive policing, for instance, was seen by many black and Hispanic leaders as aggravating already hostile race relations. (1984, 23)

Policy makers tended to define crime in terms of violent and property crime, no matter what the official crime rates showed. Police corruption and police-minority relations also were high on policy makers' agendas between 1948 and 1978, but violent and property crime remained the top items. According to Jacob (1984), the prominence of these crimes is a product of the ways in which public officials learned about crime. They obtain knowledge via secondhand reports through bureaucratic channels and the media (Jacob 1984). They were therefore basing their decisions about how many resources to allocate to fighting crime on unreliable information because they could not be sure that crime itself was increasing or if the changes simply reflected changes in reporting methods. Newspapers as well as high-ranking police officials acted as "if they knew how many crimes had been committed in their city and the direction of the trend," but "comparisons between individual cities were hazardous, because small differences were often the result of variations in the reporting and recording practices" (Jacob 1984, 45–46). In addition, the media emphasizes violent crime, adding to peoples' fears. One reaction of the public has been to demand stronger punishment, which is reflected in the percent of people who favor using the death penalty. In 1966, 38 percent of the public favored using the death penalty; by 1974 this had increased to 63 percent, and by 1985 to 72 percent.

The attitude of most policy makers and of the public in the 1980s tends to exclude anything but a get tough approach to solving the crime problem. However, certain interest groups and professionals succeeded in getting other approaches onto the agenda. For example, a number of judges, court personnel, and representatives of church and social service groups succeeded in getting the state of Kansas to introduce community corrections—an alternative to putting offenders in state prison—onto the state policy agenda in the late 1970s. Their attempts were successful even though the state's Republican governor was in favor of building additional prisons. However, few states were receptive to such a "soft" approach to crime. Instead, most crime policy during the first half of the 1980s took a hard line approach.

■ FORMULATING CRIME POLICY

Criminal law is found in constitutions, legislation, judicial decisions, and administrative rules. A variety of agencies and institutions help shape crime policy. All three levels of government are involved in making criminal law. And agencies in each of the three branches—legislative, executive, and judicial—help formulate these laws. Interest groups are also heavily involved. They include groups such as the National Rifle Association, American Bar Association, and American Civil Liberties Union at the national level; the probation officers union, state bar associations, and sheriffs associations at the state level; and the Police Benevolent Association, homeowners associations, and local newspapers at the local level.

Like public policy in other areas, crime policy is shaped not only by the legislatures but by implementing agencies such as the police, courts, and corrections agencies. The formulation of criminal justice policy may be especially influenced by triggering events. For example, in Phoenix in 1976, crime became a major public policy issue when a reporter investigating land fraud was killed. Burton Barr, the majority leader of the Republican-dominated House of Representatives, said that this killing had the greatest single impact on the legislature of any event of the previous twelve years. The incident triggered the passage of a major anti-crime package in the Arizona legislature and a total revision of the Arizona Criminal Code. The revision represented a shift in justice philosophy to get tough on crime by increasing the penalties for a variety of crimes and installing mandatory sentencing for many offenses. The latter revision took discretion away from judges in many decisions. For example, a second-time offender who used a weapon on committing the second offense was automatically sentenced to twenty-five years in prison. Judges could not lessen this sentence no matter what the circumstances of the crime.

The revised Arizona law reflected a general shift in policy across the country away from rehabilitation and toward retribution. A California corrections official summarized this trend as follows:

> In California, the population has made it clear that it wants people locked up for a long time. Alternatives to incarceration no longer are the focus of debate. The issue now is to build more prisons as cheaply as possible. California voters don't want a Cadillac prison system. They simply want criminals out of their lives. (Levine, Musheno & Palumbo 1986, 470)

The Four Policy Goals in Criminal Justice

There have been four areas of emphasis in criminal justice policy over the course of American history. These are:

1. *Retribution* This is the belief that a person who commits a crime should be punished. It is based on the concept of "an eye for an eye," and punishment is considered to be the major goal of policy. In recent years it has been called "just desserts."
2. *Deterrence* This is the rational notion that punishment will deter not only the individual who commits a crime but other potential offenders as well. There are two types of deterrence: *Specific deterrence* is aimed at preventing the person who committed a crime from committing future crimes by teaching him or her a lesson. *General deterrence* is meant to prevent others from committing a crime under the assumption that the one being punished will serve as an example. For deterrence to work, punishment must exceed the gains one obtains from crime. For example, a two-year prison sentence for stealing $2 million is unlikely to deter anyone if the person who commits the crime is able to keep the money.
3. *Incapacitation* While specific deterrence aims at preventing a person from committing a crime after that person is released from prison, incapacitation aims at prevention by placing criminals in prison.
4. *Rehabilitation* This policy is based on the idea that a person who commits a crime can be treated and once again become a law-abiding citizen.

Policy formulators have shifted among these four policy orientations over the course of American history. Retribution was the main goal of corrections policy in early American history. Early corrections techniques were as inhumane as the worst offenses committed by criminals. Mutilation, including whipping and branding, was common. Spies lost their eyes, perjurers lost their tongues, rapists were castrated, and thieves lost their hands.

It was not until the Age of Enlightenment that corrections policy changed. The English utilitarian philosopher Jeremy Bentham (1748–1832) and Italian philosopher Ceasare Beccaria (1738–1794) helped spread the idea that humans are rational beings who calculate the costs and benefits of their actions before committing a crime. If the benefits are greater than the cost, a person will commit a crime. Late in the eighteenth century, deterrence became the basis of correctional policy until the end of the nineteenth century.

Rehabilitation became popular with policy makers in the twentieth century. Prison administrators were quick to adopt rehabilitation because it fit their administrative convenience. As a management tool, it gave them the power to decide when a prisoner was rehabilitated and thus ready for release, or when a prisoner would have to stay in prison longer. At the same time it made prisons seem more humanitarian since it replaced the older practices of physically punishing prisoners. Although rehabilitation was supported by prison administrators, it never was adequately tried.

Rehabilitation was replaced by retribution as a policy goal in the late 1970s. A number of scholars concluded that rehabilitation was not working (Martinson, Lipson & Welks 1975), and public officials were quick to pick up on this theme because it supported the argument that it was time to get tough on criminals. Given the roundabout way in which information about crime comes to policy makers, it is little wonder that the general trend in policy shifted toward retribution.

■ CRIMINAL JUSTICE AND THE POLICY-MAKING PROCESS

Although retribution became the primary thrust of criminal justice policy at the national level and in most state and local areas in the late 1970s, it has not been the sole and exclusive policy thrust. This is because there is a multiplicity of agencies and jurisdictions involved in formulating criminal justice policy, each of which pursues different needs that do not always correspond to those of other agencies. At the state level, there are courts, attorney generals, bureaus of investigation, state highway police, and prisons. At the county level, there are county sheriffs, deputies, jails, attorneys, courts, and court services agencies. At the municipal or town level, there are local jails, attorneys, courts, police, and a host of private security agencies.

Each of these agencies is autonomous. For example, a county attorney may pursue a policy of incapacitation, while a judge may pursue a different policy. There are judges who will impose the most lenient sentences possible no matter what the legislature or prosecuting attorneys do. It is not possible to make all levels and units in the system follow the same policy.

Many professional organizations and interest groups, such as police associations, corrections officers, and citizen advocacy groups take a keen interest in the work of criminal justice agencies. They lobby at the legislative and executive level for their policies. Some interest groups are very powerful. The National Rifle Association is a case in point (see Case 8–1).

The federal influence on criminal justice policy is another complicating factor. Through the now defunct Law Enforcement Assistance Administration, the federal government tried to influence the direction of local law enforcement policies through a number of innovative programs. From 1969 to 1981, the Law Enforcement Assistance Administration spent almost $8 billion on numerous programs aimed at controlling crime. This money was given to states as block grants (that is, general purpose grants) through state planning agencies, to be spent on projects approved by the state agency. But criminal justice has a strong tradition of local control. Even though there was a strong push in the mid-1980s toward retribution by the federal government, several states (Minnesota, Kansas, Oregon, Colorado, and Connecticut) adopted community corrections laws running counter to these national trends. Thus, in formulating criminal justice policy, various institutions—that is, law enforcement, prosecution, courts, and corrections—have their own interests and needs which do not all follow common policies. The discussion of the courts and crime policy in the next section will illustrate this.

CASE 8-1 ***The National Rifle Association and Gun Control***

The National Rifle Association (NRA) almost invariably gets its way on issues relating to gun control. In 1986, it was able to get Congress to virtually rewrite the Gun Control Law of 1968, which was passed after the assassinations of Reverend Martin Luther King, Jr. and Senator Robert Kennedy. Even though its traditional ally, the police, opposed the bill, the NRA was able to get an overwhelming vote in its favor. Opponents such as the International Association of Chiefs of Police argued that the bill would add to the problem of violent crimes because it would eliminate record-keeping requirements. According to the executive director of the International Association of Chiefs of Police, "We've said all along that this will add to the problem of rising violent crimes. We'll see more and more guns used by criminals" (Curry 1986, Sec. 5, 1).

The arguments and evidence in favor of strong handgun laws seemed to be overwhelming. Countries that have strong handgun control laws all have very few handgun murders. For example, in 1980 there were the following number of handgun murders in each of the countries with strong laws: Japan, 77; Great Britain, 8; Canada, 8; Sweden, 18; Switzerland, 23; Israel, 23; and Australia, 4. That same year, there were 11,522 handgun murders in the United States.

The Courts and Crime Policy

Although the major duty of the courts is to apply the laws passed by legislatures to specific cases, they also make policy. The vagueness of legal concepts and the impossibility of determining in advance all of the situations to which the law might be applied give the courts many opportunities to formulate policy.

First of all, courts must interpret the meaning of various terms and phrases in a law. They may try to define the law narrowly or arrive at a broader definition based on the spirit of the law. Courts often follow the latter approach and in so doing help make policy. For example, the Mann Act of 1910 makes it a federal crime to take a woman across state lines for the purpose of prostitution or debauchery or for "any other immoral purpose" (Levine, Musheno & Palumbo 1986, 448). What constitutes debauchery and immoral purposes? In 1971, the U.S. Supreme Court ruled that having a mistress was immoral, and taking her from one state to another was a federal crime.*

* *Caminetti v. U.S.* 242 U.S. 270 (1971).

The NRA takes the position that owning a gun is a constitutional right and that government should not interfere with this right. Moreover, its members believe that strong gun control legislation would interfere with the millions of sports enthusiasts who own guns for hunting, skeet shooting, and marksmanship, while doing little to prevent criminals from obtaining weapons. The NRA also disputes the argument that private ownership of handguns increases murder or crime.

The NRA used a combination of campaign contributions and letter-writing campaigns as a way of trying to get its goals in 1986. For example, Common Cause, the Washington-based citizens lobby, said that in 1985, the NRA spent $1.5 million on political action committees and on buying newspaper space and broadcast time in pursuit of getting the federal law changed (Curry 1986). It gave money to senators and representatives who supported its positions. In addition, the NRA succeeded in tripling its membership from 1 million in 1978 to 3 million in 1986. This is a lot of votes, which helps explain the NRA's success.

The most important means of making policy is in the courts' use of *judicial review.* Judicial review is the courts' ability to determine whether or not a law is constitutional. This power was first asserted early in American history in the *Marbury v. Madison* case of 1803, described in Chapter 3. Judges ever since have had the power to decide not only what the words in the Constitution mean but also whether a particular law violates the constitutional provisions. For example, is capital punishment cruel and unusual punishment in violation of the Constitution's Eighth Amendment? In 1972, in *Furman v. Georgia,** the Supreme Court addressed this issue—at least in regard to the way capital punishment statutes were then written and implemented.

The Court's decision in *Furman v. Georgia* actually contained three different policy positions. Two justices felt that the death penalty was cruel and unusual punishment per se and favored total abolition. Their position did not win. Three other justices felt that the death penalty was cruel and unusual punishment in particular cases involving discretionary application with no set

* 408 U.S. 238 (1972).

standards. Their views prevailed. The other four justices who were in the minority did not believe the death penalty was cruel and unusual punishment.

Executions were halted in all states for a while after the Supreme Court's *Furman* ruling. But soon afterward, states passed new statutes that eliminated the discretionary components the Court objected to. Then in 1976, the Supreme Court made it clear in *Gregg v. Georgia** that the death penalty was not unconstitutional as long as the statute under which it is imposed does the following:

1. Places information about the defendant before the trial court to assist it in reaching a decision.
2. Places special emphasis on mitigating or aggravating circumstances affecting the defendant's blameworthiness.
3. Reviews every death sentence by a state appellate court.

The courts have had considerable impact on criminal justice policy in the areas of defendant's rights as well as prisoner's rights. Still, the Supreme Court does not have the final word in any policy. Its rulings can be overturned by the legislature, and it must depend on administrators to implement its decisions. Thus, in the area of prisoner's rights, many of the Court's rulings have had little impact because they were not implemented.

■ IMPLEMENTING JUSTICE POLICY

The Implementors

Implementing criminal justice policy involves four distinct elements: (1) investigating crimes and arresting those accused of committing crimes; (2) prosecuting the accused; (3) adjudicating guilt or innocence; and (4) correcting or punishing those found guilty. In order for a particular policy, such as reducing drunk driving, to be effective all four elements must work in harmony. The police must arrest the right people and make "good arrests" in the sense that there is sufficient evidence the person actually committed the crime. The accused must quickly be brought before a judge for a preliminary hearing to see if there is enough evidence to hold the person for a trial. Prosecutors must prepare their cases properly. A speedy trial before a jury of one's peers also is required. Finally, for those convicted, adequate and appropriate corrections programs and institutions must be available.

The people who are employed by the agencies in each step in this process are the implementors of justice policy. A wide variety of professions and

* 428 U.S. 153 (1976).

occupations are involved, including police officers, attorneys, clerks, judges, counselors, probation officers, parole officers, corrections officers, wardens, psychiatrists, psychologists, researchers, computer experts, secretaries, and filing clerks. All of these individuals have a great deal of *discretion,* which means they can change or form policies while they are being implemented. Discretion is one of the major factors influencing the implementation of justice policies. There is no hierarchy of authority in the Weberian sense but only a loose organization of separate offices, each with a certain degree of legal authority and each operating somewhat autonomously. According to sociologist Henry Pontell, "It is clear that individual authorities have their own goals and needs—there is no 'goal' or 'goals' of criminal justice in practice but only formal goals in the strictly legal-traditional sense" (1984, 28). What, then, are the factors affecting the way justice policy is implemented?

Factors Affecting Implementation

According to political scientists Van Horn and Van Meter (1977), there are eight general categories of variables that affect policy implementation. These are:

1. Policy resources (for example, money).
2. Standards for implementation.
3. Communication of the standards.
4. Methods used to enforce the standards.
5. The disposition of people who work in the implementing agency.
6. Characteristics of the implementing agency (for example, staff competence).
7. Characteristics of the political environment (for example, public and elite opinion).
8. Economic and social conditions.

The influence of some of these factors seems obvious. Without adequate resources a policy cannot be fully implemented. To a certain extent, this is what happened in regard to retribution policy during the 1980s. Harsh laws were passed and more criminals were arrested. But most states did not provide enough money for constructing the prisons that were needed. Thus, retribution was much less harsh in implementation than was the case of the law on the books (Pontell 1984).

Standards for implementation must be clear to implementors in order for a policy to be effectively carried out. This is not often the norm in American policy making, however. Vague standards generally are the rule and a great deal of discretion is left to the implementing agencies. The disposition of implementors often determines how this discretion will be used. For example, in states that decriminalized public intoxication during the 1970s, police failed to cooperate with the treatment centers to which they were supposed to bring street drunks. This is because they had a disdain for "social work" as opposed to police work. Police officers felt that the problem had a low organizational priority. Their fellow officers did not look kindly on the law; they were hostile toward the treatment centers to which they were supposed to bring the drunks, they felt drunks were belligerent and repulsive, and they felt it had nothing to do with preventing crime (Aaronson, Dienes & Musheno 1984).

Characteristics of the Implementing Agencies Among the characteristics of organizations that affect implementation are the degree of decentralization and participation in decision making. Some argue that a decentralized structure will produce better results. The so-called bottom-up school emphasizes the discretion of street-level bureaucrats, like the police officers. These individuals are closest to the actual problems and thus are in a better position to determine what will work (Elmore 1980). The problem is that these individuals may pursue their own self-interests rather than that of the organization. There are times when the self-interest of individuals and that of the organization conflict, as when police use patrol cars to run household errands or visit their friends. Prosecutors also adopt shortcuts and deviations in order to meet their production norms. These shortcuts tend to undermine the formal adversarial system and replace it with a system of mutually advantageous exchanges (Feeley 1973; Blumberg 1967; Nardulli 1978). Thus, prosecutors place a premium on speed rather than due process. In order to dispose of cases rapidly, they presume the defendant is guilty, thus plea bargaining rather than trials becomes the rule. Judges, defense lawyers, and prosecutors participate in this process because it serves all of their self-interests. Prosecutors choose only the most favorable cases where a plea of guilty can be obtained easily and quickly. Thus, they usually file felony complaints on only half of felony arrests. They do this in order to build good conviction records. Prosecutors are elected officials, so their track record of convicted defendants strongly influences their future political careers. Therefore, convictions take precedence over due process, social justice, or deterrence (Reiss 1974).

A second school of thought maintains that the only way to make an organization work is to appeal to the self-interests of its members. According to political scientists Musheno, Palumbo, and Levine, "The extent to which public interest goals can be reached depends entirely on how well they serve the self-interests of those who are responsible for executing the policies in question" (1976, 266). These self-interests include the desire to expand one's power or authority, get promoted, receive a salary raise, or improve interpersonal relations. For example, the attempt of the federal government to stimulate prosecution of economic crimes by local prosecutors failed to appeal to the self-interests of implementors. The policy grew out of national pressure by consumer-oriented interest groups. However, it was not implemented for several reasons: Economic crime is seldom an issue on which local prosecutors can build political careers; judges are not heavily involved in controlling economic crime; and police officers find it difficult to ferret out economic crimes such as tax evasion, fraudulent repairs, or check kiting.

There does not always have to be a conflict between organizational and individual self-interests. Public sector entrepreneurs can help bridge individual and organizational interests by building agreement among members of an organization about the goals that should be achieved. In a study of community corrections in Colorado, Oregon, and Connecticut, Palumbo et al. (1985) found that when entrepreneurs were able to build agreement between top and street-level implementors about the goals of community corrections, implementors were more successful in achieving program goals. These goals included reducing the commitment of nonviolent felony offenders to state prisons without increasing the threat to community safety. Other studies also have found that goal consensus is important in order for implementation to be successful. Wycoff and Kelling (1978) found that a lack of goal consensus thwarted efforts to introduce change in personnel policy in a major city police department. Similarly, lack of consensus has affected the acceptance of team policing and other projects (Green 1981).

Another characteristic of the implementing agency is the degree of support the staff has for the program. Palumbo et al. (1985) found that agencies in which the implementors supported the program were most effective in achieving goals. Program managers were important in building internal support since they often acted as philosophical proponents for the program they directed.

The Political Environment Agencies do not work in a vacuum but interact with a number of other agencies. For example, implementing community corrections programs involves judges, prosecutors, sheriffs, counselors, community representatives, nonprofit agencies, halfway houses, employers, and religious institutions. Successful implementation requires collaboration and cooperation among these agencies and individuals. It usually requires considerable political skill to get agencies to work together. The extent to which they succeed will determine whether support for the program will be forthcoming from the legislature. In a study of an attempted sentencing reform in Austin, Texas, Charles W. Grau makes the following conclusion:

> At the systemic level, the planned sentencing reform in Austin threatened prosecutorial hegemony over sentencing, which was reinforced by the interests of the courts in maintaining fine revenues, of the judges in promoting career advancement, of the bar in protecting the sentence and plea negotiation

> process and minimizing clients' sentences, and of the probation department in maintaining the flow of revenue from its caseloads. (1981, 96)

Hence political problems mitigated against sentencing reform, which was an attempt to get judges to use community restitution as a sentencing option.

Other studies support the importance of political factors in the organization's environment. In a study of Michigan's policy for mandatory sentencing of criminals who use guns, Bynum (1982) found that clear policy directives and the commitment of key individuals were not sufficient; the prosecutors applied the policy selectively, particularly against minorities. The political factors that helped determine when the gun law would be used pertain to the prosecutor's need to work with other criminal justice agencies and to pursue particularly heinous crimes. Said Bynum, "Since prosecutors are elected officials and many have further political aspirations, they are particularly sensitive to public sentiment about crime" (1982, 49).

Relationship among Factors Affecting Implementation Many factors are related to successful implementation, although the information on which variables have the most influence is sparse (Morash 1982, 18). According to Morash, ambiguous and inconsistent standards are likely to be important, as are self-interests of implementors and interorganizational politics. But few studies have included a large number of variables in an attempt to identify which are most important. A study of community corrections implementation in three states by Palumbo et al. (1985) is one exception. This study considered the following implementation variables:

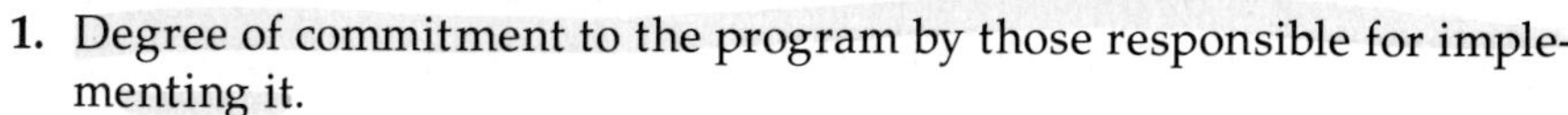

1. Degree of commitment to the program by those responsible for implementing it.
2. Degree to which the program has been routinized.
3. Amount and types of changes made in the program.
4. Efforts of entrepreneurs.
5. Amount of coordination achieved among the numerous implementing organizations.
6. Amount of support given to the program by elected officials, service providers, and the community.
7. Amount of access to decision making that implementors have.
8. Amount of influence over decisions of various groups such as judges, sheriffs, prosecutors, and advisory boards.
9. Amount and type of training provided.

Before describing how these factors were related to successful implementation it is necessary to briefly describe community corrections. Community corrections is a way of mobilizing community resources and restructuring criminal justice agencies in order to make nonviolent felons pay for their crimes while at the same time reintegrating them back into the community. Community corrections can be used as a sentencing alternative to prison for convicted, nonviolent felons or as a transitional program for individuals who are within six months to a year of being released from prison.

The programs studied in Oregon, Colorado, and Connecticut were administered in completely different ways (Palumbo et al. 1985). The Oregon program was a county option program run by the State Department of Corrections, whereas the Colorado program was run by the State Judicial Department through judicial districts. Both of these were sentencing alternatives to prison. The Connecticut program was run by the State Department of Corrections as a transitional program for people within a year of being released from prison. The study found that states, counties, and districts that were most successful in implementing community corrections had (1985, 11):

1. A higher level of commitment to the program by those who must implement it, particularly by the street-level implementors.
2. An emphasis upon the principles of community corrections and particularly rehabilitation rather than just taking advantage of available funds.
3. Greater agreement among implementors and between the upper- and street-level implementors about the goals of community corrections.
4. More modification of the program to fit local needs and job structures.
5. Greater access to decision making by those who implement the program.
6. Greater perceived support by legislators, service providers, and the community.
7. "Entrepreneurs" or catalysts who are strong philosophical proponents of the program, who help get it established and who promote agreement between upper- and street-level implementors about what the goals of the program should be.
8. More training for program implementors.

While the study did not quantitatively identify which of these variables was the most important, the major factors seemed to be the level of commitment to the program, agreement about the goals, and the work of "entrepreneurs." The latter factor was particularly crucial since it was entrepreneurs who promoted agreement about goals, increased the commitment of street-level implementors, and encouraged the diffuse agencies—police, prosecutors, judges, sheriffs, advisory groups, legislators, advisory committees, service providers, wardens, state and regional administrators, halfway house staff, and probation officers—to work together toward common goals. As one sheriff remarked:

"Before Lou [the director] took over, none of us even got together, much less talked to each other. Now we have a common denominator" (Palumbo et al. 1985, 74).

In summary, criminal justice policy is greatly influenced and changed during implementation. This is partly because criminal justice statutes and directives are vague and ambiguous, partly because implementors have a great deal of discretion, and partly because there are a large number of independent and autonomous local agencies involved in implementing policies. As a result, a particular policy thrust such as retribution will not necessarily be implemented by all agencies and if it is, it will be different in each agency in which it is implemented.

EVALUATING CRIMINAL JUSTICE POLICY

In order to determine if a law or program has had the expected impact, we would conduct a summative evaluation. If we found that the program was not achieving its objectives or was not working properly, we might expect that the program would be terminated or changed. But this does not always happen. For example, in Kansas City, Missouri, the Police Foundation conducted a year-long experiment beginning in 1972 that was aimed at testing the effectiveness of the routine patrol function of police. The goal of the patrolling program was to help deter crime. Three similar areas of the city were selected for the experiment. In one area, the number of routine patrols was quadrupled; in the second area, the number of patrols remained at the normal level; and in the third area, no routine patrols were used. Because the experiment was conducted for a full year in similar areas, any differences in crime rates could be attributed to the differences in patrol. The experiment found that there were no differences in crime rates, citizens' attitudes toward the police, reported victimization rates, citizen behavior, or the number of traffic accidents. With such clear results, we might expect that cities throughout the country would discontinue routine patrols which, after all, are expensive. But they have not.

The reasons why this and many other evaluations are ignored are numerous. One is that it takes more than one study to convince people that the results are correct. Another is that evaluations are but one factor in decisions about a program. Political factors, rather than "rational" information, are often more important. A third reason is that studies often cannot control for all of the other variables that may contribute to a particular outcome. Therefore, they are not very reliable as guides for practical action. These and other problems will be considered in the next section on deterrence.

Deterrence: What Is Cause and What Is Effect? Even though retribution has been the principal orientation of criminal justice policy in the 1980s, a large number of officials still justify their actions and proposals in terms of deterrence. For example, on Saturday, October 22, 1983, two experienced correctional officers were brutally murdered and two others seriously injured during separate assaults in the control unit at Marion Federal Prison in California. One officer was murdered a short time after 10:00 A.M. while he and two other officers were returning an inmate to his cell from a shower. Using a homemade knife, the inmate stabbed the officer about forty times in full view and without regard to staff and inmate witnesses.

Marion is the most stringent maximum-security facility of the forty-three institutions in the U.S. federal system. It opened in 1963 to replace Alcatraz. The 330 inmates housed there are the most violent and dangerous of the 30,400 offenders in federal custody. There is no federal death penalty for the crimes committed at Marion. Prisoners already serving life sentences are, in effect, immune from any further sanction in their actions. The Director of the Federal Bureau of Prisons, Norman Carlson, argued that cases such as the one at Marion illustrated the need for a federal death penalty: "For those who must come in contact with these individuals for the rest of their lives there is no safety because there is no deterrence. . . . In my opinion, inmates who murder, then murder again, must be held accountable for their violent actions" (1983, 7). Carlson justified his call for the death penalty in terms of deterrence. Other government officials often use the same argument. An example is the Attorney General of Arizona who, in 1986, argued that the crime rate in Arizona was rising because not enough criminals were being jailed. The Attorney General said, "In 1981 we were increasing our imprisonment rate by 25 percent, substantially faster than the rate of national increase. As a consequence, our crime rate was falling much faster than the national rate" (Sitter 1986, B-3).

Are these policy makers correct? Does deterrence reduce crime? Perhaps these questions can be answered with another: Would you be tempted to commit crimes such as armed robbery, rape, theft, or assault if you knew that there was a very small chance that you would be arrested? Most likely your answer is no, because it is much more than the law that keeps most of us in line; guilt, shame, conscience, and superego have been internalized within us by our families, schools, churches, and peer groups. The law is only a last resort (Stone 1976).

Little empirical research existed on the effect of deterrence prior to 1970. Since then a considerable amount of research has shown that there is indeed a correlation between certainty and severity of punishment and deterrence of criminal behavior, with certainty playing a greater role. However, there is a question about which way the causality runs. According to one argument, low crime rates lead to more certain and severe punishment rather than the other way around. This is because when crime rates are low, the system is not overburdened and is able to handle the cases it has. As crime rates go up, there are political pressures for harsher penalties and greater law enforcement, which causes structural imbalances in the system (for example, more police than prosecutors, judges, or prisons), and the system gets overloaded. As a result it is not able to deal effectively with its work load and punishment becomes less certain and severe (Pontell 1984).

A second reason why findings about deterrence and crime rates are unreliable is that many research studies do not adequately control for other contributing factors. For example, if citizens in a particular area are morally repulsed by crime, then they are likely to not only support more severe sanctions but also to become involved in law enforcement. The association between sanctions and crime rates may thus be primarily due to a third variable—the cooperation of citizens with police—rather than the sanctions themselves (Tittle 1985). Other variables that might intervene are citizens taking greater precautions to avoid being victimized or altering their life styles.

Finally deterrence theory is unreliable because it makes a dubious assumption about the process by which it works. It assumes that potential lawbreakers have an accurate perception of what the sanctions and their chances of being caught are. In fact, no research has demonstrated that this is true.

Several leading researchers have concluded that the deterrence hypothesis has not yet been proven empirically and, because of the difficulty and expense of conducting good studies, the hypothesis may be impossible to prove or disprove. Sociologist Charles Tittle has concluded, "It appears that methodological, theoretical, practical, and contextual hurdles may forever prevent social science from answering questions about deterrence in a confident way. . . . Every issue bearing on deterrence is currently controversial, and every empirical finding is contradicted" (1985, 289).

Hence, we do not know if deterrence in fact does work. More significant from the evaluation perspective is the fact that it may be impossible to determine unequivocally whether or not deterrence works. Too many complex factors are involved to do more than reach conclusions about the *probability* of deterrence working. Public policy makers are more likely to base their decisions about deterrence on political factors rather than empirical research. Thus, prosecutors, attorneys general, and law enforcement officials are likely to support deterrence policy because it is good politically and because it serves their organizational interests. They can always find studies and so-called experts to legitimize their position and to give their arguments the aura of scientific respectability.

The controversy surrounding gun control and deterrence is similar except that because it is such an emotional issue, it generates even more political support. The evaluations conducted on gun control legislation often come to opposing conclusions. For example, consider the following two conclusions:

> The data indicate that gun control legislation is related to fewer deaths by homicide, suicide and accidents by firearms. (Geisel, Roll & Wettick 1969, 666)

> On the basis of these data, the conclusion is, inevitably, that gun control laws have no individual or collective effect in reducing rates of violent crime. (Murray 1975, 88)

Both of the studies quoted above were of state-level crime rates. Consequently, they suffer from the same methodological problems described above with regard to deterrence. Each study used slightly different control variables; because they are aggregate, ecological rather than experimental studies, the variables that account for differences in crime rates have not all been controlled. An ecological study measures events at a specific point in time and tries to control for the influence of other variables statistically. Experimental studies use a control and experimental group and attempt to eliminate other, compounding variables through random assignment to each group. Thus, it may be some unidentified third variable rather than the gun control laws themselves, that are the cause of the differences in crime rates.

For example, it may be that gun control laws work better in one state as compared to another because of cultural attitudes towards guns. Southern states are less likely to support gun control laws than northern states. Aggregate, ecological studies cannot control for all possible variables and thus are true only until more accurate studies come along. But studies that use methods such as experimental design do not do much better. Even with the best of studies, it is difficult to say whether or not gun control laws work because their impact is not large enough to detect. According to two leading researchers, "if there are crime reduction effects to be obtained from these kinds of gun control laws, they are just at or somewhere beyond the threshold of detectability through present-day social research methods" (Rossi & Wright 1985, 324–25).

There are several reasons why the impact of gun control laws is hard to measure. One is that each state or city has its own laws; a state with strict laws may border on one with lax laws. The effect of the state with strict laws is diminished because guns can easily be obtained in a neighboring state. Another is that there are over 1 million guns in circulation already; about half of all households in the United States have a gun. Most of these are used legitimately, perhaps as many as 90 percent. Gun control laws that require registering guns and licensing ownership are usually opposed by these individuals and by the National Rifle Association. For gun control laws to be effective, they should be aimed at the small percent of abusers, not the entire population.

In the end, political factors are more likely to determine gun control policy than empirical evaluations. The NRA, for example, has been extremely successful in preventing strict national gun control legislation from being passed. In April, 1986, when it succeeded in getting Congress to modify the 1968 Gun Control Act, the NRA contributed huge sums of money to the senators who voted in favor of their bill. The act was passed even over the opposition of various law enforcement groups that normally are their allies. In this case, legislators were more attuned to the votes that the NRA might control than to evaluations of gun control policy.

The death penalty is the third policy question that serves to illustrate the political and ideological nature of criminal justice policy. Rational evaluative information plays a very small role in this area. The theory behind capital punishment is straightforward. Death represents the ultimate punishment; it is feared by even the most downtrodden. Because it is irreversible it allows no hope of a reprieve, unlike life imprisonment. Therefore rational people will stop short of some crimes if they believe that death will be the penalty. But the research about the deterrent effect of the death penalty leaves the question unresolved. Researchers face the same dilemmas as those studying gun control laws, or the impact of deterrence in general. The studies that have been conducted all have methodological flaws, thus none is fully valid (Levine, Musheno & Palumbo 1986).

Since the deterrent effect of the death penalty is unclear, then the principal justification must be retribution. This certainly seems to be a valid reason for using the death penalty. Take the case of James Lee Gray who was convicted in 1976 of murdering a three-year-old girl after kidnapping and sodomizing her. At the time, he was on parole from Arizona where he had served seven years of a twenty-year sentence for the 1968 slaying of his sixteen-year-old fiancee. According to law enforcement officials, Gray took the three-year-old to a wooded area, sodomized her, pressed her face into the mud to suffocate her, and then threw her body off a bridge. It certainly seems that Gray is a perfect case for capital punishment. His own mother asked the state of Mississippi, where he committed the crime, to execute her son. Retribution seems to be in order.

The problem is that because only a small percentage of murderers receive the death penalty, it is imposed in an arbitrary and capricious manner. There are many other murderers who commit heinous crimes who do not receive the death penalty. There are about 22,000 murders committed a year in the United States. About 250 offenders receive the death sentence each year and even fewer are executed. When the death penalty was being used at its height in the early 1900s, only 100 people a year were executed. In addition, blacks are executed in far greater proportions than whites, and if the victim of murder is white, the murderer is more likely to get the death penalty than if the victim is black. Thus, it is used in a discriminatory manner. To use the death penalty in a just and equitable manner, it would be necessary to execute thousands of offenders each year. This is very unlikely to happen. Hence, we will continue to use the death penalty in an arbitrary way unless it is completely abolished. This is not very likely given the state of public opinion—72 percent of the public favored its use in 1985—and past U.S. Supreme Court rulings (Bedau 1982; Van Den Haage & Conrad 1983; Gorecki 1983).

In regard to capital punishment, then, political factors and ideology are more important in policy making than empirical evidence or rational arguments. Is this the case for all criminal justice and other policy issues? Are all of them as emotional as gun control or the death penalty? There is no well-researched answer to these questions as no one has yet compiled a complete list of policy issues to determine how emotional each one is. However, political factors are often more important than scientific evaluations in public policy making (Shotland & Mark 1985). Policies and programs seldom are terminated or changed on the basis of evaluation studies alone.

The Future of Criminal Justice Policy The political factors that gave rise to the get tough policy of retribution in the late 1970s are still present in the 1990s. Fear of crime is still an important issue on the public policy agenda in many states and cities; the public mood still remains strongly in favor of the use of the death penalty and retribution; and states continue to spend large sums of money on law enforcement and corrections. Although the crime rate began to decline in the mid-1980s, there was little support for a change in policy. For example, given the fact that prisons were severely overcrowded in many states, more emphasis on alternatives to incarceration—that is, intensive probation or community corrections—might be pursued.

The high cost of prisons forced policymakers to support alternatives to incarceration during the 1980s. But the new policy was labeled "intermediate punishments" rather than alternatives to incarceration, partly because it sounded like something that would be more acceptable to the public, but for other reasons as well. The principal one is the argument that more than just two options—prison or probation—are needed in order for officials to better "fit the punishment to the crime," for example, achieve "just deserts." Criminals, the argument goes, don't fall into just two categories and so punishments also should form a continuum from the least onerous—probation—to the most onerous—prison.

A number of intermediate punishments were developed during the 1980s to fit this new rationalization:

- *Intensive probation,* where offenders are supervised very closely by two different probation officers;
- *Electronic monitoring and home arrest,* where nonviolent offenders are restricted to their homes except for certain approved reasons such as going for medical care or shopping;
- *Shock incarceration,* where first time offenders are put into a boot camp type facility and subjected to military-like marching and discipline for four months and then released onto probation for the remainder of their sentence.

- *Community corrections,* where offenders are placed in halfway houses and provided with counseling and treatment for their substance abuse problems, given help in finding jobs, and provided with educational and job training.
- *Community service and fines,* where offenders are fined and/or sentenced to work in the community, such as cleaning litter on highways or working in hospitals.

All of these intermediate sanctions provide more options for court officials, and they are supposed to alleviate prison overcrowding and reduce costs (because they are assumed to be cheaper than prison). But they have been criticized for widening the net of social control (which is bringing more people under the state's authority and increasing the severity of sentences) and also for actually adding to rather than reducing the costs of corrections (Palumbo, Clifford & Synder-Joy 1992).

Major changes in the direction of public policy do not occur often. This is partly because a particular policy thrust, once established, generates a number of interests and beneficiaries who attempt to see that the policy is maintained. Law enforcement and corrections officials, whose numbers increased dramatically in the late 1970s, strongly support the shift to retribution. They are a politically powerful force in agenda setting and problem definition in criminal justice. Any large shift in policy away from retribution would negatively effect their organizational and personal interests. Unless major political changes occur in the United States, retribution and deterrence policies are likely to dominate criminal justice policy throughout the 1990s.

9

Educational Policy and the Goal of Equal Opportunity

THE NATURE OF THE EDUCATION PROBLEM

For more than a century, education in the United States has been dominated by liberal ideology. Schools are seen to have two major functions in this view: (1) to provide equality of opportunity for jobs, and (2) to develop a common political community among the diverse groups that make up American society. Common public schools were developed in the middle of the nineteenth century in order to instill a common set of values among the diverse groups that make up the American population. In the absence of public education, liberals believe that the accident of birth would determine whether a person grows up rich or poor. Schools are supposed to overcome this by giving children of the middle and lower classes a chance to advance on merit. One of America's leading philosophers, John Dewey, believed that "the office of the school environment is to balance the various elements in the social environment and to see to it that each individual gets an opportunity to escape from the limitations of the social group in which he [or she] was born" (Lukas 1985, 105). Horace Mann, the founder of common public schools, felt that schools were the great equalizer of the conditions of human beings—the balance wheel of the social machinery. Merit is thus an important principle in liberal ideology.

In the 1980s, this ideology was challenged from both the left and right. On the left, neo-Marxists maintained that the schools do not really overcome the social class structure of society; they simply reflect the unequal social structure and legitimize existing capitalist institutions (Apple & Weis 1983, 7). For example, French scholar Pierre Bourdieu (1973) supposes that elite knowledge is a form of symbolic capital similar to monetary capital. Inequality in monetary capital is reproduced as inequality in culture (that is, symbolic capital), which is then transmitted through the schools (Anyon 1983). As a result, children from lower-income groups tend to be placed in the lower-ability groups and in the noncollege preparatory tracks in school, whereas those from the upper-middle and upper class are placed in the better schools and in college preparatory tracks. Lower socioeconomic class children also score lower on standardized tests such as the Scholastic Aptitude Test (SAT), which have a large impact on who goes to college and on which college they will attend (Sexton 1961; Spring 1985).

The left also charged that the schools failed to educate the blacks in urban ghettos who demanded to be given greater control over the education of their children. The poor were not asking for the abolition of public education, only a larger role in school policy. They did not succeed in this. By the mid-1980s, minorities were losing ground in education in yet another way. Minority enrollment in colleges and universities declined: "The urgency of the 1960s and the steady growth of the 1970s are gone," said the Reverend Timothy Healy, President of Georgetown University. "Increasing minority access is no longer a front-burner issue" (Fiske 1986, 7). Black enrollment in four-year colleges reached a peak of 10.3 percent in 1976; by 1982, the proportion had declined to 9.6 percent. Increases in tuition costs, cuts in student financial assistance, and tightening of academic standards were the main reasons for the decline.

During the Reagan presidency, the bigger challenge to liberal ideology came from the right. The conservative position reflects an ideology that was common at the time of the American Revolution. Many of the intellectuals in the Revolution believed that government should minimize its involvement in education. They feared that government-operated schools would seriously abridge the free development of ideas, particularly in regard to religion. Therefore, the separation of church and state required the separation of schools from the state.

John Trenchard and Thomas Gordon, writing in the *Cato letters** at the time of the Revolution, believed that government schools would create uniformity of thought and hinder the development of scientific, technological, political, and social ideas. This position lost support with the development of common public schools in the 1830s. These schools were meant to "Americanize" the immigrants who began pouring into American cities around 1840. They were also meant to provide a trained work force, which was why American industry supported the concept of common public schools.

Common public schools have dominated American education ever since. Private schools comprise only a small percentage of all elementary and secondary school education. But support for expanding the role of private schools increased under the Reagan administration. In addition, there was a crisis of confidence in public education. The public believed that the schools were failing to do their job. The Gallup national opinion poll reflects this changing attitude: The percentage of respondents who gave the schools in their communities an "A" or "B" rating decreased from 48 percent in 1974 to 31 percent in 1983 (Gallup 1983, 39). Standardized test scores such as the Scholastic Aptitude Test also declined during the 1970s. Schools were facing a financial crisis as well, which was reflected in low teacher salaries. During the mid-1970s, teachers suffered a decline in their salaries of 1.7 percent per year so that by 1990 they were one of the lowest paid professions. Student confidence in education also was low and school violence was high. During the 1980s and first half of the 1990s most schools in large cities had a police officer on patrol. It was estimated that as many as 100,000 students carried weapons to school. Absenteeism was as high as 30 percent on any given day and even as high as 50 percent in New York City schools (Everhart 1982, 2). A pattern of "getting by" seemed to be the norm for most students. The fact that the average grades of students was increasing at the same time that standardized national test scores were declining was indicative of serious problems. All of this provided grounds for the argument that there should be increasing involvement of the private sector in schools.

The Privatization of Schools

Advocates of private schools are motivated by several factors. One is a desire to curtail the growth of government bureaucracies. Because expenditures on education comprise the largest budget item of state and local governments, turning over a large proportion of educational responsibility to private agencies would greatly reduce the size of government. In addition, these advocates believe that free choice in schooling would improve education. Their theory is that public schools will get better if they do not have a monopoly. A third argument in favor of private schools is that parents who send their children to

* The *Cato letters* were political tracts that were distributed among the general populace.

private schools will no longer suffer the double burden of paying taxes for the public schools as well as tuition for private schools.

Opponents of private schools argue that parents who send their children to private schools do so by choice and thus the double burden is not an unfair one. They further argue that public support of private schools would increase the stratification of schools along racial and class lines and thereby damage society's commitment to disadvantaged groups. Public schools would become the last resort for those who cannot get into private schools; therefore, they would degenerate in quality. Finally, opponents contend that public support of private schools is unconstitutional because 85 percent of these schools are church-affiliated and the U.S. Constitution prohibits government support of religion. Whether or not this interpretation is valid will be considered later in this chapter.

The Nature of Private Schools Private schools in the United States generally are small and relatively autonomous; they are governed through boards of trustees or church organizations, funded primarily through student fees, endowments, and philanthropy, and are primarily religious. Catholic schools made up the majority (53 percent) in 1991. The number of Catholic schools reached a high point in 1969–70 with 11,771 schools and declined to 8,587 in 1991. In 1991, about 12.6 percent of elementary and secondary school children were in private schools. Enrollments in public as well as private schools peaked in the mid-1970s and have been declining by about 2 percent every year since then. Since 1975, school expenditures have declined as a percent of the gross national product while non-Catholic private schools have proliferated, especially fundamental Christian day schools. In the 1990s, private school enrollments were declining less rapidly than public school enrollments. Hence the percent of the student population attending private schools has become slightly larger.

The Development of the Common Public School

Although they comprise only 11 percent of all elementary and secondary schools in the United States today, private schools provided almost the only type of education available early in the nineteenth century. Most children did not attend school in the early 1800s: The main forms of education were apprenticeship and learning through experience. Farming, artisans, and the commercial trades could be learned with only the rudiments of literacy.

Massive immigration into the United States beginning in the 1840s set the stage for the establishment of the common public school. The government-supported schools established in some states, such as Massachusetts, represented exactly what the libertarians feared: They stressed a religious and moral orthodoxy and produced citizens who would be obedient to the government and the church (Spring 1982, 82). These schools were not prevalent in all states, however. Some citizens favored a national system of schools aimed at creating a sense of nationalism. One was Noah Webster, whose *Blue-Backed Speller,* completed in 1783, sold 1.5 million copies by 1801, 20 million by 1829, and 75 million in 1875. The *Blue-Backed Speller* contained a "Federal Catechism," which required memorization of specific answers to questions such as "What are the defects of democracy?" The answer was: "In democracy where the people all meet for the purpose of making laws, there are commonly tumult and disorders. . . . Therefore, a pure democracy is generally a very bad government" (Cohen 1974, 769–71).

Thomas Jefferson also proposed a federal system of education, but only to teach children reading, writing, and arithmetic, which he calculated would take three years. This was sufficient for citizens to be able to read the newspapers and vote. Since the Constitution guarantees a free press, Jefferson believed that this would be sufficient for democracy to function.

Not until Horace Mann did the common public school begin to receive significant support. Mann is considered to be the father of public education; he was Secretary of the Massachusetts Board of Education from 1837 to 1848. He believed that common political creed had to be instilled in all citizens. He lived during a period of great political tension and feared that the extension of the suffrage to the immigrants would lead to mob rule. To prevent this, he advocated the creation of common public schools that would teach the same political values to all children. If families were left to their own choices about schooling, said Mann, the common experience considered so crucial to the development of the nation would have been lost. Schooling would be sought strictly for personal and private interests rather than those of the larger society.

Political Socialization and Common Public Schools Democracy requires that citizens participate in policy making. Such participation cannot happen without a common language, knowledge of the purposes and procedures of government, an understanding of the role of the citizen, and exposure to varying points of view. Political socialization is the process by which citizens acquire this knowledge and experience. Horace Mann correctly saw that a major portion of political socialization takes place in schools. Political scientist David Easton has said that one means of generating diffuse support for a system entails recognition of a common good that transcends the particular good of individuals or groups (Easton 1965, 125). Easton and Hess (1961) argue that no system can attain or remain in a condition of integration unless it develops among its members a body of shared knowledge about political matters as well as a set of shared political values and attitudes. Public schools are the primary means of doing this. They are the most powerful institution in socialization. They give content, information, and concepts that expand and elaborate on the early socialization that occurs in the family (Hess & Torney 1965).

Through political trial and error, a compromise was reached in American education in which diversity was combined with uniformity in American education. Families were free to choose private schools if they had the resources. Moreover, schools were considered to be local institutions that served local communities that were highly homogeneous with respect to occupation, wealth, income, race, ethnicity, and religion. Because public schools were financed by property taxes, schools differed greatly in the amount of support they enjoyed. Even in large cities, schools differed by wards. Immigrant groups were allowed to have schools that stressed their native language, customs, and religious practices. However, most teachers were drawn from Yankee—that is, English—stock.

Throughout American history, right up until the 1950s, public schools were infused with religious practices, reflecting the dominant, local school clientele. Bible reading, religious instruction, religious pageantry, and other religious practices were exceedingly common. In some areas, the public schools were indistinguishable in curriculum and religious influences from the parochial schools that served the same populations (Levin 1983).

Catholic schools were formed because Catholics believed the public schools were dominated by Protestants. As a result, Catholics demanded self-determination. The battles that ensued between Catholics and Protestants were vituperative and occasionally violent. They fought over which version of the Bible was to be used in public schools. The public schools were dominated by native-born Yankee Protestants. And in the eyes of Catholics, public schools represented the maintenance of a secularized core of Protestant values.

By the 1990s, new problems surfaced. One was the increase in the number of children living in single-parent households. One estimate was that 60 percent of three-year-olds in 1990 would live in one-parent households before they turn 18. Such households are more likely to be in poverty. By 1993, almost 20 percent of all children lived in poverty. These children are much more likely to be at risk. In 1987, as many as a third of the nation's school-aged children were at risk either of failing in school, dropping out, or falling victim to drugs, teenaged pregnancy or chronic unemployment.

The crises these children faced became problems the schools had to deal with. Children come to school hungry or wearing only sandals and their sweaters in the winter. Children lack health care and move frequently. New York City School Chancellor Joseph Fernandez said, "We have overwhelmed our classrooms with sociological indoctrination. Education is in a mess because society, unwilling to take on problems of poverty, teenaged pregnancy, drug addictions and other ills directly, pushes them on to the teachers. When schools are required to run the gamut from safe driving to safe sex, it may be the case that we expect too much from them" (Wolfe 1993, 26).

A second major problem schools confronted is the changing ethnic makeup of their students. The percentage of minority students in public schools increased from 24 percent in 1976 to 28.8 percent in 1984, and was projected to be 38.4 percent by the year 2000 (Vobejda 1987, 8). Such changes increased pressures for the schools to teach multi-culturalism and tolerance for all groups. A proposal to teach tolerance for all groups including gays and lesbians in the New York City schools stirred up controversy that led to the firing of the chancellor who introduced the curriculum. What caused so much controversy was the curricular materials mandating that classes should include references to lesbians and gays as real people to be respected and appreciated and instructing that schools begin such lessons in the first grade.

Multi-culturalism and diversity issues confronted education at every level, from kindergarten to college. This greatly complicated the overall issue of whether or not the schools and education were getting worse. Some disputed this and argued that condemnation of public schools was almost a conspiracy to promote use of private schools. For example, the percent who graduated high school increased from 24.5 percent in 1940 to 76.2 percent in 1988; the percent who dropped out decreased from 11 percent in 1970 to 12.6 percent in 1989; and the percent of students who scored above the 1965 national average on the Iowa Test of Basic Skills increased at the third and sixth grade levels. Moreover, the comparisons of scores that students in other countries set is not valid because the United States has a much larger percent of its children in high school.

The Decline of Private Schools

Private, independent schools enrolled about 73 percent of all students at the secondary level by 1879. A mere ten years later this fell to 32 percent, and by 1920 it declined further to 7 percent. From the turn of the century onward, private academies became elite schools serving the well-to-do. Following World War I, there was an attempt to force private schools out of existence. In 1922, Oregon approved a referendum that would have required parents and guardians to send every normal child between the ages of eight and sixteen to a public school in their district. The law was instigated by the Ku Klux Klan, which capitalized on a wave of nativist and anti-Catholic sentiment. Under the guise of attempting to Americanize its citizens, the Grand Dragon of the Oregon Klan said, "Somehow these mongrel hordes must be Americanized: failing that, deportation is the only remedy" (Tyack 1968, 74–98). The U.S. Supreme Court struck down the Oregon law in 1925 in its decision in *Pierce v. Society of Sisters.** The Court upheld the claim that forcing Catholic schools to close would deprive them of their property without due process of law in violation of the Fourteenth Amendment. At the same time, the Court upheld the right of the state to regulate private schools.

* 268 U.S. 510 (1925).

The Decline of Standardized Test Scores

Opponents of public schools cite declining standardized test scores as additional evidence of the failure of public schools. Between 1963 and 1990, Scholastic Aptitude Test (SAT) scores dropped from 478 to 422 on the verbal segment of the test and from 502 to 474 on the mathematics segment (see Table 9–1). However, it is difficult to say how much of this decline is due to the public schools. Studies of the decline in standardized scores point to a number of factors other than the schools. Declines during the 1960s are at least partially due to changes in the composition of students taking the tests. Proportionately more students were going to college during the 1960s than in earlier years. Many of these students were from the lower socioeconomic ranks and they tended to score lower on the SAT than traditional college-bound students. One expert estimated that as much as three-quarters of the

TABLE 9–1 *SAT Scores*

	SAT Mean	
Testing Year	Verbal	Math
1952	476	494
1954	472	490
1956	479	501
1958	472	496
1960	477	498
1962	473	498
1964	475	498
1966	471	496
1968	466	492
1970	460	488
1972	453	484
1974	444	480
1976	431	472
1978	429	468
1980	424	466
1982	426	467
1984	426	471
1986	430	476
1988	427	476
1990	422	474

Source: For 1952–1966, Gilbert Austin and Herbert Garber, *The Rise and Fall of National Test Scores,* (Orlando: Academic Press) p. 13. For 1968–1985, The College Board, Admissions Testing Program, *National Report on College-Bound Seniors, 1985.*

decline during the 1960s was due to compositional changes in those taking the SAT (Eckland 1982).

In the 1970s, the composition of those taking the tests did not change as much as in the 1960s, so only a smaller proportion of the change in that decade could be attributed to this factor. More pervasive forces were at work, although it is not clear just what these forces were. The College Examination Entrance Board (CEEB) and the Education Testing Service (ETS) appointed a twenty-one-member panel to investigate this question. Its report, issued in 1977, pointed to a decline in the number of students taking traditional English courses and an increase in students taking electives such as science fiction, radio/television/film, mystery and detective stories, and "executive" English. The committee speculated that this may account for some of the decline. Other factors mentioned were the increase in absenteeism, grade inflation, social promotion,* reduced homework, and a drop in the level of difficulty of textbooks. The panel blamed families and communities as much as the schools for the rise in absenteeism. Grade inflation could have caused a decline in motivation and effort on the part of students; social promotion made it harder for teachers to deal with classes that had too many students who are not at the same level; and a smaller percent of the more competent undergraduates were entering education as a career.

Indeed, students reported studying less in 1970 than they did in 1960. Perhaps this was due to an increase in watching television. By the time a child graduates from high school, he or she has spent as many hours watching television as in school. Some of this is no doubt at the expense of reading and homework (Austin & Garber 1981).

Although the decline in student performance cannot be attributed to schools alone, public education became the target of a number of groups. In the 1960s, schools were attacked by the movement for community control. These groups charged that the schools were not responding to the needs of ghetto children. In particular, the black community attacked the fact that the teachers in ghetto schools were almost entirely white, middle-class individuals. This argument was similar to that of the Catholics 100 years earlier, who said the school teachers and administrators were mostly Yankee Protestants and this was detrimental to Catholics. Conservatives joined the attack on public schools in the 1970s and 1980s centering their displeasure around the issue of prayer and the lack of discipline in the classrooms. By the 1980s when the Reagan administration proposed vouchers and tax incentives for private schools, the future of public education became bleaker than it had been for over 100 years. We will delve more deeply into these issues in the next section as we trace government's response to the attacks on public education.

* This refers to advancement of students who have been in a particular grade for the requisite time, regardless of how they perform on exams.

AGENDA SETTING IN EDUCATION

The attack on public schools in the 1980s was certainly not the first one. At the end of the nineteenth century, the public schools came under attack by two major groups. One was the economic elite who wanted to control the schools themselves. Another was the well-intentioned reformers who wanted to correct some of the real problems that existed. Both groups claimed that the schools were being used by politicians to dispense favors and strengthen their political power. In order to get appointed as a teacher in many cities, for example, an individual had to be approved by the ward politician; contracts for school construction were given out on the basis of political loyalty. School board members were political appointees. In the large cities, a decentralized, ward-based committee system for administering the public schools had developed. In 1905, Philadelphia had 43 elected district school boards and a total of 539 school board members. At the turn of the century, 16 of 28 cities with a population of 100,000 or more had 20 or more board members (Wirt & Kirst 1972, 7).

Reformers charged that these boards advanced parochial and special interests at the expense of the needs of the school district as a whole. They also charged that political corruption and partisan politics—the result of the decentralized nature of the school system—were responsible for the inefficiencies of education in large cities. "Indeed, many politicians at that time regarded the schools as a useful support for the spoils systems and awarded jobs and contracts as political favors" (Wirt & Kirst 1972, 6). Reformers further charged that such boards provided inefficient management because they worked through numerous subcommittees. They claimed that no topic was too trivial for a separate subcommittee, ranging from ways of teaching reading to the purchase of doorknobs. At one time, Chicago boasted seventy-nine subcommittees and Cincinnati had seventy-four. As a solution, the reformers suggested elections at large, rather than the ward system and the centralization of power in a chief executive, who had considerable power over the board. Reformers sought to separate schools from politics with nonpartisan elections to school boards. They also recommended that board members be elected at large and that the board have a small number of members.

School administrators were depicted by reformers as dedicated professionals whose sole goal in life was to serve students. The model for school administration they adopted was the corporate board of directors. The superintendent of education was to be the managing head and the school board was to act as if they were stockholders:

> By 1910, a conventional educational wisdom had evolved among the schoolmen and leading business and professional men who spearheaded the reforms. The watchwords of reform became *centralization, expertise, professionalization, nonpolitical control,* and *efficiency.* The governance structure needed to be revised so

> that school boards would be small, elected at large, and purged of all connections with political parties and general government officials, such as mayors and councilmen. (Wirt & Kirst 1972, 7)

Tucker and Ziegler suggest that "it is possible to view the reform movement as a reaction against the excesses of a period with too much citizen control. Educational governance under political machines was responsive to citizen preferences but was also extremely corrupt. Reformers saw mass citizen participation and government corruption as causally related and sought to eliminate both" (1980, 146).

Reformers were rather successful in their endeavors. By the 1930s, there were even suggestions that school boards be eliminated entirely. Political scientist Charles Merriam argued that the professionalization of *all* administrative services of government would lead to a new era of political competence (Everhart 1982). By the 1930s, most states were licensing teachers. This contributed to further expansion of the power of professional educators. By 1970, nearly all school districts had adopted a superintendent-board form of governance and about 75 percent of school boards were elected on a nonpartisan basis and about 75 percent on an at-large basis (Tucker & Ziegler 1980).

Influence of the Educational Professional

Evidence suggests that the change in governance initiated by reformers created a shift of power and control away from the public and into the hands of education professionals. Reformers intended that policy-making functions should be the responsibility of elected board members and administrative functions the province of the superintendent, thus preserving direct citizen input into the operation of the public school. But according to Tucker and Ziegler (1980), this did not occur. Instead, school board members deferred to the expertise of the professional administrator (superintendent), and the administrator, having been trained to accept such deference, took the policy initiative at all times. Most school board members today do not view themselves as representatives communicating constituent preferences to administrators. They view their tasks as legitimizing decisions made by administrators, publicizing administrative decisions, and generating public support for these policies (1980, 150). In their research, Tucker and Ziegler note that:

> two-thirds of school boards delegate the agenda-setting function solely to the administrators . . . three-fourths of all items considered by school boards at public meetings were discussed at the initiative of the superintendent and his staff . . . administrative recommendations were adopted in 99 percent of decisions made by formal vote, and nearly 85 percent of school board votes were unanimous. School board members did as they were told. (1980, 155)

With almost total control of agenda setting in their hands, professional educators came to define the public interest in education. The schools became the vehicle of social mobility, determining where people would fit in society because they not only defined the tracks that schools would have—that is, vocational versus college preparatory—but also who would go into each track. The doctrine of equality of opportunity helped legitimize the increased power of professional educators by allowing them to claim to be a friend of the poor (Everhart 1982).

Although normal agenda setting remained in the hands of school administrators, every so often a major incident would push new items onto the agenda. In the 1950s, for example, education became a part of the Cold War after the Soviets launched their first space missile, Sputnik I. Critics of American education pointed to this as evidence that the schools were failing in their job and even were the central source of anti-intellectualism in American life. For the first time, professional educators became the villains rather than heroes. For example, Admiral Hyman Rickover said that the schools were the weakest link in America's defense. Such attacks led to the passage of the National Defense Education Act in 1958, described in the next section of this chapter.

The schools next became a major item on the national agenda during the War on Poverty of the 1960s (see Chapter 7). Assuming that poor schooling perpetuated poverty, the Johnson administration attempted to expand and improve educational programs for educationally deprived children. The Head Start program, for example, attempted to reach educationally deprived children by preparing them before they entered elementary school. The assumption was that improved educational programs would give the poor a better chance of improving their status. In some cities, this assumption was used by local communities to take the schools out of the hands of professional educators and place them in the hands of parents in the community. Charging that the central board of education was not responsive to the needs of ghetto children, community control advocates felt that education would be improved if locally elected boards in each district set the agenda for education. The bill that finally passed in New York in 1968 divided the city school system into thirty-three separate districts. However, because many people failed to vote for school board members, organized groups such as the churches and teachers' unions controlled the election outcomes. Thus, control of the school agendas remained in the hands of professional educators.

Beginning in 1975, church groups and private schools repeatedly brought up the issue of tuition tax credits as a means of supporting private education. President Reagan supported the proposal beginning with his first term in 1981. But education was not a prominent issue in 1981 or 1982. Few would have predicted that it would become a front page story in every major newspaper in the country in 1983 and move to the top of the policy agenda in a majority of states.

Because state finances were seriously constrained in 1981 and 1982, state policy makers showed little interest in education policy. Professional groups that came together to lobby for increased funding no longer had a united front. Teacher unions opposed administrators and school boards. Minority groups and special education groups disagreed with those representing the general education program, and moral issues such as religion and sex further splintered the interest groups. Public displeasure with the schools was reflected in declining support for public school bond issues, which dropped from a high approval rate of 74.4 percent in the mid-1960s to 55 percent in the late 1970s (National Center for Education Statistics 1981).

By 1983, the picture changed dramatically and education moved to the top of the national policy agenda. It began with the release of the 1983 report, *A Nation at Risk,* issued by the National Commission on Excellence, an eighteen-member panel of university presidents and other educators and policy makers. The report received wide attention not only because of the message it conveyed, but because President Reagan used it to advance his administration's education philosophy. This report was followed by several others, including *Action for Excellence* by the Education Commission of the States, *Academic Preparation for College* by the College Board, *Making the Grade* by the Twentieth Century Fund, *America's Competitive Challenge* by the Business-Higher Education Forum, and *Educating Americans for the 21st Century* by the National Science Board. Along with all of these reports, a number of books focusing on education were published in 1983. Education had suddenly become a major agenda item.

A Nation at Risk identified education as a major factor in America's position in international trade. The report declared, "If only we keep and improve on the slim competitive edge we still retain in world markets, we must rededicate ourselves to the reform of the educational system for the benefit of all" (Spring 1985, 21). Warning that the educational foundations of American society were being "eroded by a tide of mediocrity that threatens our very future as a nation and a people," the Commission noted that "if an unfriendly foreign power had attempted to impose on America the mediocre education performance that exists today, we might well have viewed it as an act of war" (National Commission 1983, 5). The report by the Education Commission of the States also linked education and economic development. *Action for Excellence* claimed that the future success of the nation depended on its ability to improve education and training.

A variety of groups defined the educational agenda in the 1980s and, as a result, professional educators lost some of their control over this aspect of policy making. The main items on the agenda were the issues of public support for private schools, prayers in school, the teaching of creationism, and "secular humanism." The latter was a catch-all condemnation of things such as the teaching of values by schools which critics claimed should be taught in the home. The principal sources of these agenda items were the right-wing conservatives and religious fundamentalists led by television evangelists such as Reverend Jerry Falwell and Pat Robertson. None of these issues actually became a part of the system of policy formulation.

FORMULATING EDUCATIONAL POLICY

Professional educators control not only the agenda regarding educational policy, but policy formulation as well. Although they do not pass the state or federal laws that set broad educational policies, they strongly influence what laws are passed. Even more crucial, professional educators *interpret* the laws during implementation, which comprises a large portion of the total educational policy. Before considering the issues professional educators formulate, this next section describes just who the policy formulators are.

The Cast: Educational Policy Formulators

Education is the most locally controlled of all policy areas in the United States. When measured by revenue sources for elementary and secondary education, local areas—that is, cities, counties, and school districts—accounted for 44.6 percent of total revenues in 1982 and 1980 (see Figure 9–1).* In no other policy area do local revenues account for this large a proportion of total revenues. The proportion of the total accounted for by local governments has been declining since 1971 and 1973, and the proportion for which states are responsible has been growing. While the influence of the states over educational policy also has increased, localities remain the predominant influence in policy formulation. This is because of the structure of educational administration. The U.S. Constitution delegates responsibility for public education to the individual states and they in turn have traditionally delegated this responsibility to the approximately 16,000 school districts. The state's have been supplying an increasing proportion of the funds, as Figure 9–1 shows, but this has mainly been in response to court challenges concerning inequality in financing education.

As will be described in more detail later, school districts in poor areas have a much smaller property tax base on which to rely than those located in richer areas and consequently, they spend less. States have tried to equalize spending by passing laws that give more state aid to the poorer as compared to the richer districts. This accounts for some of the increase in the state portion of total revenues that has occurred since 1977 and 1978, but, as we shall see, state influence in policy formulation has not increased commensurately.

In most American communities, an appointed or elected board of education has the formal responsibility for making educational policy. There is great variation from community to community, but, in general, boards of education are supposed to formulate educational policy, and superintendents of schools and school staff are supposed to implement it.

* According to a *New York Times* report (December 2, 1984), the total expenditures for education in 1984 were $144.5 billion, with 6.8 percent from the federal government, 48.1 percent from state governments, and 44.7 percent from local governments. The remaining .4 percent went to private schools.

FIGURE 9–1 Who pays for public education: revenue sources for elementary and secondary schools, in percentages, 1971–1983.

	1971-72	'72-'73	'73-'74	'74-'75	'75-'76	'76-'77	'77-'78	'78-'79	'79-'80	'80-'81	'81-'82	'82-'83	'90
Federal	8.9%	8.7%	8.5%	9.0%	8.8%	8.8%	9.4%	9.8%	9.8%	9.3%	7.4%	7.1%	6.4%
State	38.3	40.0	41.4	42.2	44.6	43.4	43.0	45.7	46.8	47.4	47.6	48.3	48.6
Local	52.8	51.3	50.1	48.8	46.5	47.8	47.6	44.5	43.4	43.3	45.0	44.6	44.9
Total Spending (in billions)	$50.0	$52.0	$58.1	$64.4	$71.2	$75.3	$81.4	$88.0	$96.9	$106.0	$110.2	$117.0	$206.0

Federal
State
Local

Source: National Educational Association, Washington, D.C., *Estimates of School Statistics,* annual (copyright); and unpublished data.

Most boards of education are elected. They tend to be composed of white male business or professional persons who have a college education and are in the upper income category. In 1984, 64.9 percent of school board members nationally had four or more years of college; 55 percent held professional or managerial positions; 93.1 percent were white; 62.9 percent were male; and 53.2 percent had family incomes of $40,000 or more (Spring 1985, 140). The percentage of women on school boards increased from 28.3 percent in 1982 to 37.1 percent in 1983. Still, women remain a minority on school boards and in administrative positions, although they constitute the majority of teachers in elementary and secondary schools. Southern states have the most elite school boards, whereas those in the western states have the least, as measured by income.

Public participation in educational policy formulation is limited. Very few eligible voters participate in local school board elections. At-large, nonpartisan elections make it difficult for minority groups to get elected and give school boards a partisan bias in favor of Republicans and business interests. Local school board members, therefore, tend to be a part of or closely related to the community power structure. But, as indicated above, school boards have relatively little power, and that power has been eroding due to increasing federal and state involvement in education. School boards usually only get involved in policy issues when a crisis arises over such matters as desegregation, sex education, or religion. For example, in the 1970s, fundamentalist groups in various parts of the country demanded that the schools ban certain books, such as those by Kurt Vonnegut and J.D. Salinger. School boards invariably get involved when this happens. In 1986, the Silver Lake, Massachusetts School Board voted to drop a summer reading program that included the works of Mark Twain, John Steinbeck, and Charles Dickens. One board member who voted against the list said she had not heard of half the books on the list. The board revised its vote later after heavy public criticism (Hechinger 1986).

This kind of intervention among school boards is unusual, however. As early as 1960, researchers concluded that educational policy formulation had been taken over by professional educators (Koerner 1968).

Superintendents of education and the central office are more influential in policy formulation than school boards. They often argue that the power of school boards should be further reduced. Albert Shanker, president of the American Federation of Teachers, contends that school boards should meet only once a year to review what has happened and that they should leave decisions such as those about reading courses to qualified educators (Hechinger 1986, 20).

The central office of education in a school district is usually composed of an administrative staff which deals with the overall organization of the school system's curriculum, financial matters, personnel policies, and programs that affect all schools within a district. The central office is a very important source of control because it controls the lines of communication among principals, teachers, and the superintendent of education. The school staff can determine the degree of freedom of political expression that exists within the school and the quality and variety of educational programs. The actions of the local district school staff can affect the options made available to a student and the degree of emphasis placed on vocational and academic programs (Spring 1985). Thus, they formulate key educational policy.

Growth in State Power in Educational Policy

Education became an important item on the agenda of most states by the middle of the 1980s. It made good politics and was looked upon as a way of improving faltering state economies. State governors used the issue to show that they were actively involved in the state's economic development. Some governors and candidates tried to build their political careers on proposals to improve the quality of teaching. Half of all governors made education the top priority in the 1984 "state of the state" messages. In 1986, many governors boasted about the gains they made in education, which they linked to reforms in school programs and improved financing in their states. State legislatures enacted hundreds of new laws to improve the quality of schools. Requirements that students study more subjects to earn high school diplomas, statewide testing, and new standards for teachers were included among these laws. For example, Texas passed sweeping laws in 1984 including detailed lists of what must be taught in specific courses at each grade and how much time teachers must spend on each subject. Kentucky passed a law that permitted the state to take control of school districts that do not meet certain standards, including those with a high school dropout rate of more than 30 percent, an absentee rate of more than 6 percent, and a failure rate on basic skills tests of more than 15 percent. Florida passed a law that required local school districts to obtain prior approval of any experimental courses and to provide the State Education Department with written explanations if they choose textbooks not on the state's approved list. According to the Education Commission of the States, which monitors education legislation, by 1984 at least forty states increased the number of academic courses required for a high school diploma, and thirty-two adopted changed curriculum standards or adopted new procedures for choosing textbooks (Fiske 1984, 18).

Part of this increase in state control is a result of policies initiated by President Reagan. The Reagan administration worked for a reduction in federal responsibility in education. States realized that the federal government was no longer going to step in as a last resort so they began to get more active in educational policy matters. Critics complained that the states were moving into an area for which they were not equipped and that the laws would be difficult if not impossible to implement because of the way state boards operated.

Although similar to local boards, state boards are much less active. They usually are elected or appointed by the governor as is the state superintendent of education. State *departments* of education are the real policy formulators. They are comprised of educational professionals who work closely with the state legislative committee on education. Professional educators in state departments of education, legislative committee members, and interest groups comprise the subgovernments that formulate most state educational policy (see Chapter 2). The interest groups involved include state teachers' associations, teachers' unions, school administrators' associations, and parent organizations. Others, such as the American Legion and various farm, religious, or labor groups, are ad hoc interest groups that become involved only on specific controversial issues such as desegregation or prayer in school.

The Federal Role in Policy Formulation

The federal presence in public education can be traced to the Northwest Ordinance of 1787 which required that one section of land be set aside in each township in the Northwest Territory for the support of education. Federal aid from then until the mid-1900s was modest and took the form either of land grants for the development of land-grant colleges under the Morrel Act of 1887, or grants-in-aid for specific educational objectives which were subject to limited federal controls. For example, the Smith-Hughes Act of 1917 promoted vocational education in high schools. The Vocational Rehabilitation Act of 1920 and the Social Security Act of 1935 provided vocational rehabilitation for the handicapped. Commodities and funding for nutrition subsidies were made available to local school districts through the National School Lunch and School Milk programs in 1946. All this aid was tangential to the general purpose of education, which left the responsibility for public elementary and secondary education with local and state governments.

After World War II, a rapid increase in the birthrate resulted in an increase in public school enrollments. Unfortunately, the states were ill-prepared at this time to accommodate increased enrollments. Capital expenditures for school construction had been greatly reduced during the Depression and had been all but eliminated during the war. The need for new construction was exacerbated by economic conditions after the war as inflation had severely reduced the purchasing power of the dollar. To compound all this, teachers were leaving the teaching profession in pursuit of higher paying jobs and funds were desperately needed to bolster salaries.

The states and localities responded heroically to these pressures (Bailey & Mosher 1968, 11). Revenue receipts of state and local governments for education jumped from just over $2 billion in 1939 and 1940 to over $5 billion in 1949 and 1950, $7.5 billion in 1953 and 1954, and $11.7 billion in 1957 and 1958. But the demands for new buildings, equipment, staff, and services continued to outrun revenues. Pressures continued to mount and a number of pieces of general aid to education legislation were introduced in Congress between 1940 and 1965. None was successful.

The federal government passed three major pieces of legislation during this period. This helped ease the problem indirectly, though none of these bills was general aid to education and all three were expediential responses to specific problems. Two of these bills were direct results of World War II effects: the proliferation of military establishments throughout the country and the realization that science and technology were inextricably bound to our future.

The Federal Impacted Areas Aid program of 1950 was perhaps the closest to general aid for education. Intended to lessen the impact of federal installations and their large number of federal employees on local school districts, this bill authorized federal funds on the principle that the federal government had an obligation to make payments in lieu of taxes to local communities because federal property is nontaxable. This legislation has remained popular with Congresses ever since because it is easy to administer, does not impose federal controls on local districts, and because it is widely distributed among congressional districts.

The second major piece of legislation during this period was the National Science Foundation Act of 1950. This act recognized the importance to national security of scientific research and development and of the training of scientific personnel at the graduate and undergraduate levels. The National Science Foundation created by the act was authorized to "promote scientific research, correlate and evaluate research supported by other government agencies, improve the teaching of science, mathematics and engineering . . . co-operate in international scientific exchange, and disseminate scientific information" (Thomas 1975, 22). Though initially established to aid higher education, the Foundation has benefited elementary and secondary schools by providing training institutes for science teachers and curriculum revision projects.

The third major legislative effort affecting education during this period was a direct congressional response to the successful Soviet launch and orbit of Sputnik I in 1957. In order to improve education in science, mathematics, and foreign language, Congress passed the National Defense Education Act of 1958 with very little controversy. Its passage was linked to an air of crisis which permeated the Congress and the nation. Many felt that the Soviet success threatened America's national security and that a strong educational system was needed for a strong national defense. The act authorized "the expenditure of federal funds to improve the training of teachers, to strengthen programs in the areas of science, mathematics, and foreign languages, and to establish a system of direct loans to college students. These provisions were designed to insure continued American scientific dominance" (Cochran et al. 1986, 267).

Although these three legislative efforts provided substantial sums of aid to the public schools, they did not come close to providing the amounts of general aid needed by the schools for construction and salaries. The three categorical programs passed were "limited solutions to specific problems" (Cochran et al., 267) which "directly benefited some sectors of education and neglected others. Adopted under emergency if not crisis conditions, it [the federal effort] was based on criteria other than achieving an overall qualitative improvement in American education and aiding directly those educational areas in which the needs were greatest" (Thomas 1975, 25).

The fight for general federal aid to education was unsuccessful largely because it became embroiled in battles over aid to parochial schools—which brought up the constitutional issue of separation of church and state—and segregated schools. Clouding the issue of general aid further was the old legislative bugaboo, fear of federal control. "Against the ideological argument that federal aid would lead to federal control, the practical arguments over whether aid should be for construction alone or for construction and salaries, and the economic argument over whether aid should be limited to loans or should include grants as well as loans, were juxtaposed the religious and racial controversies" (Thomas, 21).

The general aid bills introduced in Congress between 1945 and 1960 were of three types: (1) aid to education with no restrictions as to religion or race; (2) aid to education limited to public schools with no restrictions for segregated schools; and (3) aid to education with no restrictions on aid to private sectarian schools, but denied to segregated school systems (Thomas, 21). Interest groups played a prominent role in these battles. In support of general aid to education were the major education groups, including the National Education Association (NEA), the American Federation of Teachers (AFT), and the labor groups such as the American Federation of Labor-Congress of Industrial Organizations. Their support was based on the belief that federal dollars would not only improve the quality of education, but would also help solve the problem of inequity across districts in educational spending. "Districts would no longer be tied to limited local financial resources. Thus per pupil expenditures could be equalized across geographic regions" (Cochran et al. 1986, 268).

Among those opposed to increased federal aid were traditionally conservative groups such as the National Association of Manufacturers, national and local chambers of commerce, and the Daughters of the American Revolution. Such groups were opposed to federal aid on ideological grounds. They viewed federal aid as an intrusion into the traditional sphere of local control that could only lead ultimately to the loss of parental control over their children's education.

The conflict over aid to segregated schools was a major obstacle to passage of any general aid bill. Many liberal groups opposed federal aid to segregated schools on moral grounds. The most active of these groups was the National Association for the Advancement of Colored People (NAACP). The educational system in the South was still segregated in the 1960s despite the 1954 Supreme Court decision in *Brown v. Board of Education of Topeka et al.*, which found "separate but equal" school systems unconstitutional.* The NAACP argued that, in the South the proposed aid would end up in the white school districts at the expense of the black schools. They therefore opposed general federal aid until all school systems were desegregated.

Support for this position in Congress came from Representative Adam Clayton Powell of New York who, with the support of Northern Democrats and conservative Republicans, managed to amend the proposed bills so they would provide funds only to districts that did not engage in racial discrimination. The conservative Republicans supported the bill as a strategic maneuver since they knew that Southern Democrats would then oppose the bill, thereby helping defeat it. Their strategy worked, for Southern congressmen opposed any federal aid bills to withhold funds from all-white schools, and, when such bills came up for a vote on the House floor, they were joined by the same Republican conservatives who supported the

* *Brown v. Board of Education of Topeka, Kansas,* 347 U.S. 483 (1954).

Powell amendments and defeated the bill. This strategy insured the defeat of all general aid bills during this period.

Even if race had not been an issue, however, general aid bills would have been difficult to pass because of the religion issue. The National Education Association and the National Council of Churches refused to support any legislation that included aid to parochial schools, while the National Catholic Welfare Conference refused to support legislation that did not include it.

The domination of these three issues spelled the death knell for general aid-to-education bills during this period. Said Cochran, "When President Kennedy introduced aid-to-education legislation in 1961 that excluded aid to sectarian schools, the bill was defeated through the combined efforts of Catholic groups, conservatives who feared expanded federal control, and Southern Democrats who were opposed to integration pressures" (1986, 289).

Federal Aid for Federal Purposes As noted earlier, the federal aid-to-education bills passed by Congress between 1945 and 1960 were categorical programs targeted at specific problems. The bills were often measures of expedience and always left the principle of local control of education intact. For the most part, these measures played a supporting role for educational activities already undertaken and defined by the states. But the 1960s saw a shift in the aims of federal aid to education. Instead of supporting states in efforts they had already undertaken, the federal government encouraged states to pursue national objectives, which often ran counter to state and local attitudes and priorities (Sundquist 1981). This shift corresponded to a strengthened sense of purpose at the federal level. Propelled by social reform movements, social science research, and Supreme Court decisions, the federal government was taking a more active role in designing policies directed toward redressing social inequities. The schools became a key component of these policy strategies. This surge of purpose was particularly notable with regard to issues of race and poverty.

Inequities because of Race As early as the 1930s, the NAACP had begun to challenge discriminatory practices in education through the court system. These efforts, however, were aimed at graduate school education. As late as 1954, twenty-one states still had segregated school systems (Chelf 1981). In that year, the NAACP's Legal Defense Fund filed suit in *Brown v. Board of Education of Topeka, Kansas,* asking that segregation in the public schools be held unconstitutional. In 1896 the Supreme Court established the "separate-but-equal" doctrine in *Plessy v. Ferguson.** Using this concept the states had established separate school systems for blacks, but in most cases they were far from equal. In *Brown v. Board of Education of Topeka, Kansas,* the Court reversed its former decision and concluded that "in the field of public education the

* *Plessy v. Ferguson,* 163 U.S. 537 (1896).

doctrine of 'separate but equal' has no place. Separate educational facilities are inherently unequal." In a second *Brown* decision in 1955, the Court ordered a "prompt and reasonable start toward full compliance," although the actual implementation was left to the supervision of the federal district courts.*

In reaching this important decision, the Court relied heavily on evidence from the social sciences which argued that racial segregation in the school systems was stigmatizing black children—that is lowering their self-esteem—which adversely affected their ability to learn and ultimately to obtain social goods available to whites. The Court declared:

> Segregation of white and colored children in public schools has a detrimental effect upon the colored children. The impact is greater when it has the sanction of law; for the policy of separating the races is usually interpreted as denoting the inferiority of the negro group. A sense of inferiority affects the motivation of a child to learn. Segregation with the sanction of law, therefore, has a tendency [to retard] the educational and mental development of negro children and to deprive them of some of the benefits they would receive in a racially integrated school system. . . . In these days it is doubtful that any child may reasonably be expected to succeed in life if he is denied the opportunity of an education. Such an opportunity, where the state has undertaken to provide it, is a right which must be made available to all on equal terms. (*Brown v. Board of Education of Topeka, Kansas,* 1954)

The *Brown* decision has had a long-lasting and significant impact on the social mores of our nation and on the social institution of education. But its most immediate effect in the late 1950s was to publicize the plight of black education in America and "thereby highlighted the social and economic costs and consequences of prejudice, cultural deprivation, and poverty" (Bailey & Mosher 1968, 8).

Once the issues of unequal opportunity and racial discrimination were firmly implanted on the national agenda, civil rights legislation began to emerge from Congress. Particularly important was the Civil Rights Act of 1964 which "required administrators to cut off federal grants-in-aid for any state programs administered discriminatorily . . . By outlawing discrimination in all federally-aided programs, the Civil Rights Act of 1964 added full presidential and congressional authority to the Supreme Court's school desegregation mandate of 1954" (Bailey & Mosher, 30–31). The Civil Rights Act became a powerful weapon in the move to end segregation, particularly in education. It eliminated the danger of attaching a "Powell Amendment" to federal aid-to-education bills and helped ease the passage of significant federal education bills. Senator Sam Ervin of North

* *Brown v. Board of Education of Topeka, Kansas,* 349 U.S. 294 (1955), known as *Brown II.*

Carolina said that "no dictator could ask for more power than Title VI [of the Civil Rights Act] confers on the President" (Spring 1985, 187). It completely reversed the relationship that existed between the federal government's Office of Education and local school districts. No longer was the Office of Education the public servant of each local district; it was the interpreter and enforcer of the law.

Inequities Due to Poverty During the early 1960s, Congress enacted a number of laws aimed at upgrading the job skills of the unemployed in both urban and depressed rural areas. All of these bills stressed the need for job training and vocational education, and, because a large number of the unemployed were educational drop-outs, these bills had direct relevance for public education. Like the massive federal programs initiated during the Johnson administration's War on Poverty, these bills were in part a response to mounting social science evidence that "ignorance, unemployment, and dependency were interrelated and self-perpetuating" (Bailey & Mosher 1968, 8) and that those caught in this trap were victims of a "cycle of poverty."

The Economic Opportunity Act of 1964, for example, was enacted by Congress to mobilize "the human and financial resources of the nation to combat poverty by opening to everyone opportunity for education and training and opportunity to work" (Bailey & Mosher 1968, 32). The Office of Economic Opportunity, which was created by the act, implemented a series of programs and coordinated efforts with a number of already existing agencies and programs. "At least 15 Federal agencies and 156 separate Federal programs were involved. These programs dealt with education, manpower training, health, welfare, social security, housing, urban renewal, migrants, and economic development" (Bailey & Mosher 1968, 32).

By the end of 1964, the federal government had firmly established its intention to address serious social inequities within the nation and identified public education as a key element in this effort. Though unable to pass badly needed general aid to education legislation, Congress would soon pass a categorical aid bill for education so far reaching that some would interpret it as general aid.

The Elementary and Secondary Education Act of 1965

The Elementary and Secondary Education Act (ESEA) of 1965 established a major federal role in American public education (see Case 4–1, page 103). This act remains the hallmark of a new form of education legislation, one that supports education in pursuit of a social cause. The act provided funds to all but 5 percent of the nation's school districts and authorized the spending of $1.3 billion in federal funds. With these funds came a new education buzz word, "compensatory education." The passage of this far-reaching legislation is attributable to the following factors:

1. *Targeting the poor* One of the major obstacles to education legislation had been the conflict over aid to parochial schools. By specifically targeting students from low income families as the recipients of the aid, supporters of the legislation were able to reconcile the long-standing conflict over aid to parochial schools between the National Education Association and the National Catholic Welfare Conference. By casting this legislation as an "anti-poverty" bill, the framers made it difficult for anyone to oppose helping poor children even if they were enrolled in parochial schools.
2. *Passage of the Civil Rights Act* A second major obstacle to education legislation had been the conflict over aid to segregated schools. With the passage of the Civil Rights Act of 1964 the conflict became moot. Racial prejudice was no longer a manipulable political issue in Congress. Conservative Republicans could no longer support Powell Amendments with the hope of securing defeat of the bill with the help of Southern Democrats. And Southern Democrats were faced with the possibility of losing large sums of federal money if they continued to oppose desegregation of their public schools.
3. *A shift in the congressional balance of power* President Johnson's landslide victory in the 1964 presidential election carried with it a democratically controlled Congress. In the Senate, the Democrats gained two seats creating a majority of sixty-eight seats to the Republican's thirty-two, a comfortable margin. In the House, Democrats gained thirty-eight seats and in so doing increased the number of liberal votes to be counted on in legislative fights over aid to education. According to Bailey and Mosher, "this enabled the majority party to curtail the coalition of conservative Southern Democrats and Republicans which had so frequently thwarted the passage of key legislation between 1960 and 1964" (1968, 38).
4. *Congressional passage is streamlined* In an astute political move, the Johnson administration managed to get this legislation through the Senate without amendment. This effectively short-circuited the normal legislative route, avoiding many of the stumbling blocks of previous legislative battles. President Johnson eliminated three steps normally taken by proposed legislation: Senate committee, Senate floor action, and the conference committee.

The ease with which ESEA sailed through Congress was attributable to the extensive groundwork that the administration had completed before introducing the legislation in Congress. In addition, the administration engaged in a bill-drafting strategy that secured the cooperation of major interest groups before congressional enactment.

Bailey and Mosher (1968) identify five pivotal controversies that ESEA successfully accommodated. These were: (1) the purposes and distribution schemes for federal school aid funds; (2) the inclusion of parochial school students in federally aided programs; (3) the respective responsibilities of federal, state, and local authorities; (4) the special problems of urban schools; and (5) the reform and improvement of educational practices. Each of these issues required separate negotiations with a variety of interest groups. Framers of the legislation used a package format for the bill which granted "a variety of benefits, while denying to each protagonist his full range of demands. At the same time, viewed as a whole, the product was a closely woven tapestry of educational objectives and program proposals that Congress could not greatly alter without a serious impairment of the substance of political appeal" (Bailey & Mosher 1968, 42).

How was this accomplished? The answer to this question requires a closer look at the specific provisions of the act. The ESEA contained six separate titles, each dealing with different aspects of the relationship between education and poverty. Note that each of these titles contributed in some way to the accommodation of the five pivotal issues identified above:

- *Title I* This is the major categorical program in the act. It provides federal funds to areas with heavy concentrations of economically and educationally deprived children. In this regard, it borrows heavily from the Federal Impacted Areas Aid legislation that preceded it. The funds were to be provided to local education agencies but were targeted for the education of children from low-income families. The formula used to determine the amount of funds each local school district received multiplied 50 percent of the state's annual educational expenditure per child times the number of children from families making less than $2,000 per year.
- *Title II* This program provides aid to develop school libraries and the acquisition of textbooks and other instructional materials.
- *Title III* This program authorizes federal funding for the development of supplemental educational centers and services.
- *Title IV* This program authorizes funding for educational research and training.
- *Title V* This program sets aside money to be used by state departments of education to strengthen their own administrative agencies.
- *Title VI* This program outlines and defines the terms of federal regulations and requirements for receiving grants.

During the 1960s and 1970s, Congress added two new titles to ESEA. Title VII provided funds for the education of handicapped children and Title VIII provided for bilingual programs to redress educational inequities caused by unfamiliarity with the English language. Both amendments reflect the federal government's continued commitment to redressing social inequities of national scope.

Amendments passed in 1967 and 1974 affected the distribution of funds through ESEA. The original funding formula favored wealthier states since it relied heavily on the state's average per pupil expenditure. The wealthier the state, the higher the average per pupil expenditure, and the greater the amount of funds received under Title I. In 1967, this was amended in order to increase funding to poorer states. The 1967 amendment made it possible for states to use either the mean state per pupil expenditure as originally required in the 1965 Act, or the national mean figure. States which had average expenditures greater than the national mean continued to use their average expenditure for the formula. States which had average per pupil expenditures lower than the national mean substituted the national mean in the formula and thereby increased the amount of funding they were receiving under Title I. Whereas the 1965 Act promoted greater equalizations among the rich and poor *districts* of each state, the 1967 amendment promoted equalization among rich and poor *states.* In addition, the amendment changed the definition of low income families from families earning under $2,000 to those earning under $3,000 a year. This served to increase the number of eligible low-income children in a state and further increased the benefits to a state.

The 1974 amendments complicated the funding issue still further. Under these amendments, states with average per pupil expenditures greater than the national average could use only 120 percent of the national average per pupil expenditures. Those with less than the national average were required to use the state figure unless it was less than 80 percent of the national average, in which case they could use 80 percent of the national average in computing their benefits. These changes favored rural and southern states. In addition to these changes, the number of children from low income families were measured in a more complicated manner.

Although ESEA was presented as an anti-poverty bill, and structured as a categorical program of aid, the dollar amounts were so large, the distribution of funds so wide, and the categories of aid so inclusive, that its impact was felt in nearly every school district in the nation. In light of the fact that general aid to education was so badly needed, many school districts initially used the funds as general aid and, after a few years, many opposed the categorical nature of the act. But support for ESEA has remained strong, particularly for Title I. Only recently has the life of this legislation been threatened. But even as restructured under the Reagan administration, ESEA remains the centerpiece of an array of measures that extended federal concern to other previously excluded groups: migrant workers, Indians, the handicapped, and those who speak limited English. Through ESEA and its amendments, education became the principal domestic cause of the time.

Education for All Handicapped Act: Public Law 94-142

Although Public Law 94-142 was not enacted until 1975, its roots can be traced to the Johnson administration and the Great Society era (see Chapter 7). In fact, its earliest precursor, Public Law 89-750, the first federal education program for handicapped children, was passed in 1966 and became Title VII of the ESEA. Operating much like a block grant, Public Law 94-142 authorized grants to states to create and improve special educational programs for the handicapped. Although it provided financial incentives for states to enroll and educate handicapped children, it carried no penalty for not doing so. The Education Amendments of 1970 created a separate Education of the Handicapped Act which authorized several small categorical programs, but it was not until 1974 that specific protections for handicapped children became a condition of receiving funds. The conditions required that the states provide due process procedures, a method of locating handicapped children not being served, racially non-discriminatory testing, and education in an environment that is least restrictive and appropriate to the handicapped child's needs.

Section 504 of the Vocational Rehabilitation Act Amendments in 1973 eliminated discrimination of handicapped individuals under programs receiving federal funds. Testimony at public hearings prior to the enactment of Section 504 clearly described the plight of the handicapped child in education. Over 60 percent of all school-aged handicapped children in the United States were excluded from public schools, and, at that time, forty-eight states and the District of Columbia had statutory exemption in their compulsory attendance laws for children who were physically, mentally, or emotionally handicapped or who could not profit from an education.

One particularly disturbing fact revealed during the testimony had to do with the misclassification of large numbers of black students with learning problems. They were being misclassified as mentally retarded and placed in special education classes for "educable mentally retarded children" at a rate three times that of white children. Unfortunately, these classes were often of poor quality and grossly inadequate, and were frequently the dumping ground for difficult students.

As court cases on behalf of handicapped children increased and improvement of services among the various states lagged, Congress passed the Education for All Handicapped Children Act only fifteen months after the 1974 reauthorization of the Education of the Handicapped Act. The law required that free appropriate public education be provided to all handicapped children. It also required individualized treatment so that the special education and related services that make up each child's education program be determined individually. The process for doing this includes extensive professional and parental involvement, the opportunity for formal hearings to challenge school district decisions, and other procedural safeguards.

Changing Educational Priorities of the Reagan, Bush, and Clinton Administrations

The Reagan administration came to office in 1980 promising to reduce the federal role in education and to eliminate the Federal Department of Education.

Within a year after Reagan's election, his Secretary of Education, Terrel Bell, revoked thirty sets of federal rules governing nineteen federal programs and switched from categorical to block grants administered by state governments. This latter move reflected Reagan's goal to reduce if not completely eliminate the federal presence in education. As Figure 9–1 illustrates (p. 286), Reagan was successful in reducing the federal role and in increasing state responsibility. These policy thrusts were embodied in the 1981 Education and Consolidation Improvement Act which simplified the requirements of Title I of ESEA, gave administrative authority to the states, and program authority to local school districts. In addition, less funds were used for the educationally disadvantaged and for desegregation, which is a step backward for those who believe there is a national interest in promoting desegregated education.

The Reagan administration also made attempts to limit and reduce the degree of federal civil rights enforcement in education. In the U.S. Supreme Court decision in *Grove City College v. Bell* (1984),* the administration succeeded in persuading the Court to limit enforcement of Title IX of the Civil Rights Act to specific programs rather than entire institutions. In addition, the administration did not file any school desegregation cases until 1984, and when it did, it emphasized voluntary rather than mandatory desegregation. The Reagan administration supported limiting the power of the Internal Revenue Service to deny federal tax exemptions to two private schools in the south, both of which followed overt policies of racial discrimination. President Reagan's justification was that administrative rules should not be used for policy purposes. However, as illustrated in other chapters, Reagan did not hesitate to use administrative rules to achieve policies he considered desirable.

Finally, the Reagan administration proposed various bills that would make public funds available to private elementary and secondary education through vouchers or tuition tax credits. One version of such a bill would provide a tax credit of $500 to the parents of each child enrolled in a private elementary or secondary school. An alternative version proposed that a certificate be given to parents in the form of a voucher that could be applied to the tuition costs of a school of their choice. This is not the first time that policy makers have attempted to use public funds for private schools. The intermingling of funds for public and private schools has existed throughout American history and only since the 1950s have the courts made an attempt to keep the two separate.

The Bush administration continued the Reagan policies concerning education, especially the proposal to use vouchers and give parents a choice of schools they could send their children to. However, the vouchers policy met with little success.

The Clinton administration that came to office in January 1993 put education high on its policy agenda. The main argument was that in order for

* *Grove City College v. Bell,* 465 U.S. 555 (1984).

America to compete in the new global economy it would be necessary to have a highly trained and educated work force. One of the major parts of the Clinton policy was the national service program. Under this program, eligible youth would receive federal support for attending college which they would pay back through community service, such as working with municipal police departments, teaching in inner cities, and working with the elderly. However, the initial proposal was for a very small number of youth instead of a universal program as was implied during Clinton's presidential campaign. The principal reason for the meager beginning was the high cost of a full program. Given the huge budget deficits in 1991 and 1992 and the Clinton desire to reduce the deficit by $500 billion by 1995, the administration reduced this program.

The Courts and Policy Formulation

The concept of equity in education is derived from the equal protection clause of the Fourteenth Amendment. From the American Revolution until the mid-twentieth century, the courts ignored education, leaving it entirely to state and local governments. In *Roberts v. The City of Boston* (1849), for example, the Court ruled that education was a state matter and that there was no right to a public education.* Then in 1896, in *Plessy v. Ferguson,* the Court propounded the idea that separate but equal facilities satisfy the equal protection clause of the Fourteenth Amendment to the U.S. Constitution.

Beginning in 1940, the main thrust of educational jurisprudence has been with the constitutional right of individuals to receive education on equal terms, irrespective of their race. In *Sweatt v. Painter* (1950) the Supreme Court ruled that the state was obliged to provide education for blacks equal to that of whites.† This set the stage for the *Brown* decision four years later in which the Court held that segregation on the basis of race denies black children equal protection under the law. The distinction the Court made in this case between *de jure* segregation (that based on law) and *de facto* segregation (that based on factors other than law) has plagued schools ever since (see Case 9–1). The *Brown* decision applies only to situations in which segregation is supported by law. The Court has not yet ruled that de facto segregation violates the Fourteenth Amendment. For example, in *Swann v. Charlotte-Mecklenburg County Board of Education* (1971) the Court said, "We do not reach in this case the question of whether a showing that school segregation as a consequence of other types of state action, without any discriminatory action by the school authorities, is a constitutional violation requiring remedial action by a school desegregation decree."‡

* *Roberts v. The City of Boston,* 59 Mass. Rpts. (5 Cushing) 198 (1849).

† *Sweatt v. Painter,* 339 U.S. 629 (1950).

‡ *Swann v. Charlotte-Mecklenburg County Board of Education,* 402 U.S. 1 (1971).

CASE 9–1 *The "Integrated" Northern Schools in Boston in 1965*

The *Brown v. Board of Education* decision had its greatest impact in the South where segregated schools were supported by laws. Prior to the *Brown* decision, there were separate schools for blacks and whites. In the North, legal segregation did not exist, but the schools continued to be segregated long after the *Brown* decision. In 1965, many black children in Boston described the conditions in their schools as follows:

> [There were] tales of children being beaten with the "rattan," a thin bamboo whip still used then in the Boston schools to discipline recalcitrant children; of overcrowding so severe that classes met in the damp basement, which stank of urine and coal dust, or in corners of the auditorium, where glee club rehearsals drowned out most of what their teachers were saying; of shattered windows, broken desks, three-legged chairs; of chronic shortages of pencils, chalk, and erasers; of outdated textbooks, often with covers ripped off, pages missing or obliterated by ink stains; of racial slurs directed by indifferent white teachers at the black pupils who made up 60 percent of the school; and even reports of one teacher whose classroom was segregated, whites seated in front and blacks in the rear. (Lukas 1985, 100)

Providing public funds to private schools violates the First Amendment to the Constitution concerning freedom of religion. While the U.S. Supreme Court has allowed public support of religious schools under certain conditions, it has consistently rejected direct support of religious schools. The U.S. Supreme Court has upheld the right of parents to send their children to private, religious schools.* It also upheld the right of the Amish to *not* send their children to public school because this would interfere with their free exercise of religious beliefs.† The Amish provide vocational educational training designed to prepare children for life in the Amish community and the Court found this to be an acceptable substitute for public schools.

In 1968 the Supreme Court allowed states to provide textbooks to children in parochial schools, and in 1977,‡ it allowed states to provide standardized tests, diagnostic services, and therapeutic and remedial services for parochial schools.§ But the provision of direct funds is unconstitutional because it

* *Pierce v. Society of Sisters*, 268 U.S. 510 (1924).
† *Wisconsin v. Yoder*, 406 U.S. 205 (1982).
‡ *Board of Education v. Allen*, 392 U.S. 236 (1968).
§ *Wolman v. Walter*, 433 U.S. 229 (1977).

The Boston school principal, Miss Callahan, denied that such racial slurs actually were used. But she did fire Jonathan Kozol, the teacher who was most sympathetic with the black parents' concerns. As described by Lukas, "[Kozol] stood out among the other teachers at Gibson, most of them middle-aged Irish women, veterans of some years in the system, strict disciplinarians who seemed resentful at spending their days teaching ill-prepared black children" (1985, 101). Kozol was fired for allowing the children to read poetry written by a black poet. Callahan said that the only poems acceptable for classroom use were those which "accentuate the positive," "describe nature," or "tell something hopeful."

Source: J. Anthony Lukas, *Common Ground: A Turbulent Decade in the Lives of Three American Families* (New York: Alfred A. Knopf, 1985) pp. 100–102.

involves *excessive entanglement* between the government and religion.* In 1973, a New York State court ruled that a law providing grants, tuition reimbursement, and income tax benefits to parents of children in religious schools was an unconstitutional *advancement of religion* and excessive entanglement.† The Court has also held that compulsory school prayer is unconstitutional even when the child has a right not to participate in the prayer.‡

Thus, the Court has maintained a fairly high wall of separation between church and state in regard to education. This could very well prevent extensive public support of private schools as proposed by the Reagan administration unless the Supreme Court overrules its previous decisions.

■ IMPLEMENTING EDUCATION POLICY

Classroom teachers are the street-level implementors in education policy. They make policy when they teach the classes mandated by state laws or by

* *Lemon v. Kurtzman,* 411 U.S. 192 (1973).
† *Committee for Public Education and Religious Liberty v. Nyquist,* 93 S. Ct. 2955 (1973).
‡ *Engle v. Vitale,* 320 U.S. 421 (1962).

the local superintendent and principals. Due to the professionalization of education, teachers have a great deal of discretion in deciding *how* to teach particular subjects, although what to teach is often decided by committees and groups. In addition, teachers are influenced by their colleagues and their graduate school training. For example, in teaching about government, Wirt and Kirst (1972) found that most teachers proceed from emphasis on symbolic patriotism to explicit but biased use of facts about American history and government. They use symbols and rituals heavily such as saluting and displaying the American flag and singing patriotic songs. Students are taught to comply with rules and to respect authority, and little attention is given to citizens' rights or how to participate in government, particularly at the elementary school level. High school teachers emphasize the legal side of the structure of government. Class and ethnic identity and political allegiances are ignored, as are conflict and controversy. Issues are avoided. In fact, teaching of political values has declined in the United States since 1970. International tests given about knowledge students have of political systems found that among students who had completed high school, test scores were lowest in the United States and Ireland (Tyler 1981). There has been a steady decline among American students in political knowledge and, as a result, Americans are an apolitical citizenry who are not even aware of major political issues (Ehrman 1980).

Most teachers of government are trained primarily as historians and thus historical "facts" are emphasized (Wirt & Kirst 1972, 30). These "facts" are not unbiased, however; they have definite ideological overtones. Jean Anyon (1983) conducted a study of seventeen well-known, secondary school U.S. history textbooks in two large, urban school systems in the Northeast. Anyon looked specifically at the way the books dealt with the conflict over economic and labor union developments from 1865 to 1917. She found that these issues were treated in a biased manner. The textbooks implied that the low wages received by workers was partly their own fault because an oversupply of immigrants created surplus labor. The books failed to treat socialism as if it were a viable alternative, and even to discuss it at all. When they did discuss socialism, they tended to disparage it. The textbooks were also unsympathetic to the more radical segments of the union movement. In addition, they focused only on the strikes that were a setback to workers. The only unions that were favorably depicted were the skilled worker unions that accepted the corporate business form. Another study by Michael Apple and Lois Weis (1983) concluded that the school curriculum in the United States selectively reproduced and approved the cultural and ideological justification of the dominant business groups in the United States.

Another example of bias is described in a study of educational programs conducted by the U.S. National Assessment of Educational Progress (NAEP). According to Paul Olson, most educational programs deemed the following issues as offensive:

> Questions touching family, finances, references to specific minority groups, literary passages with sexual references, and questions dealing with birth control or religion. Exercises dealing with human rights were deemed offensive unless more exercises were added "dealing with . . . responsibilities in a free society." Deleted also were references to sex, unwed mothers, divorce, whisky, the FBI, the president, communism, and specific organizations such as the Ku Klux Klan and labor unions; references to violence or cruelty; exercises with *inappropriate* words or phrases, such as "sportive ladies leave their doors ajar;" exercises that might be interpreted as putting national heroes or the police and other authorities in an unfavorable light; and exercises about the Civil War that suggest the North was better than the South. Senator Joe McCarthy, that demagogue and hate maker of the 1950s, is to be presented, according to the National Assessment, in the light that is neither too critical nor too favorable. (1976, 9–10)

Olson also found that there were no references to the 1 million Americans who come from Japanese and Chinese cultures, Native Americans, Chicanos, and African or Afro-Carribeans. The NAEP recommended works such as *Little Red Riding Hood, Moby Dick, Little Bo Peep, Winnie the Pooh, Charlotte's Web,* and so on, including nothing from Greek, Roman, or Far Eastern culture. When asked why the Navajo Twins, or Quetzelcoetl, or the Bhagavel-Gita were not mentioned, NAEP responded as follows, "The answer is that Africa, South America, and native peoples in North America do not matter, according to the National Assessment. The ancient peoples who created *The Night Chant* lose out to *The Village Blacksmith*" (1976, 13–14).

The type of community in which a school is located also influences the way in which subjects are taught. Schools in lower-class areas tend to be more authoritarian than middle-class schools (Bowles & Gintis 1976). Moreover, children from lower income levels tend to be placed in lower ability groups and in noncollege-preparatory tracks. They also receive lower scores on standardized tests (Sexton 1961). Tracks in a typical high school are college preparatory, general, and commercial. The upper-class children tend to wind up in the first track, middle-class children in the second, and the poor in the third. Thus, in their role of sorting out and tracking students, the schools merely duplicate the social class structure of society. Harvard University professor Christopher Jencks and his colleagues (1972) concluded that a person's social class determined the type and amount of schooling one received and, consequently, the opportunity he or she had. Thus, implementation of the policy of equality of educational opportunity does not result in actual equality of opportunity in jobs or achievement in society.

The Educational Testing Service as Implementor

The standardized tests that students take for admission to college such as the Standard Aptitude Test (SAT) are good predictors of how well students will do in college, who is likely to drop out, and what types of colleges they will attend. These tests have in effect become the gatekeepers for colleges and, as a result, a major factor in the implementation process in American education.

Modern college admissions testing began in 1900, after the College Entrance Examination Board (CEEB) was founded as a membership association by a small number of colleges, universities, and secondary schools. The members of CEEB were concerned with the multiplicity of entrance examinations that existed and the diversity of standards. The CEEB tests were used during the first quarter of the twentieth century in eastern colleges.

In 1926, CEEB introduced the Standard Aptitude Test (SAT), developed by Carl Brigham of Princeton University. It was used initially for selecting scholarship candidates and came into regular use as a part of the college admissions process during World War II. The Educational Testing Service was established in 1948 to consolidate the testing activities of the College Board, the American Council on Education, and the Foundation for the Advancement of Teaching. Other tests were developed in the 1950s by the National Merit Scholarship Corporation. At the same time, the members of the CEEB introduced the Preliminary Scholastic Aptitude Test (PSAT) as an instrument for use in the guidance and counseling of precollege students. In 1971 the PSAT was combined with the National Merit Test to become PSAT/NMSQT.

The American College Testing Program, founded in 1959, serves a similar function as the SAT and is used mostly in the Midwest. Most students who go to college take one or more of these tests. There was a great increase in the number of students taking these tests in the 1950s and 1960s when colleges were expanding very rapidly. At the same time, SAT scores have been declining; they dropped from 478 in 1963 to 424 in 1980 on the verbal test, and from 502 to 466 on its math section (see Table 9–1). A major reason for the drop in the 1960s was the increase in the proportion of students with lower grades who began going to college.

Standardized tests have an impact on educational policy in two ways. First, they make it more difficult for minority students to get into college. Second, one of the principal results of the drop in SAT scores was that a number of states (thirty-eight) enacted laws that required competency tests for candidates for teacher education programs, graduates seeking certification, or current teachers. Such tests have screened out a disproportionate number of teacher candidates among minority groups. In state after state, the results show failure rates among black candidates as high as 60 to 70 percent, while the rate for white applicants is in the 10 to 30 percent range (Fiske 1986, 1). In the South, particularly, failure rates were so high that some believed the black teacher was becoming a vanishing species. In Texas, for example, 1.1 percent of white and 18.4 percent of black teachers failed teacher competency tests in 1986, and in Florida 10 percent of whites failed versus 65 percent of blacks. Many feared that by the year 2000 the percentage of minorities in the national teaching force will be cut in half from 12.5 percent in 1980 to 6 percent. At the same time, the percentage of minority students in public schools by the year 2000 is projected to be about 38 percent.

Some states have gone even further than testing candidates for teaching jobs. In 1986, Texas passed a law that required all teachers and school administrators to take a basic skills quiz. Those who failed in two attempts lost their jobs. The examination consisted of eighty-five multiple-choice questions on grammar, job-related vocabulary, and other areas, plus a written essay. Veteran teachers challenged the test's validity. Said a math and computer instructor in Dallas with twenty years experience and a doctorate, "I've taken harder tests, but it was the idea of knowing I had prepared a number of years for my profession and, with a couple hours' test, I might no longer be employed" (*U.S. News & World Report,* March 24, 1986, 8). The tests were designed to restore confidence in public education. But singling out teachers for such exams seems to demean the profession. Why not doctors, dentists, lawyers, and other professionals? Both Arkansas and Georgia required similar tests of certified teachers in 1986. The U.S. Secretary of Education, William Bennett, predicted that teacher testing would be a national fact of life by the 1990s.

Standardized testing of students and teachers reveals the conflict between the goals of improving educational quality and promoting social equity. Competency tests have the effect of screening people out. President Mary Futrell of the National Education Association, the country's largest teachers' union, said, "If you're going to raise the standards, you have to provide a support system to help people meet them" (Fiske 1986, 14).

Implementing Desegregation Policy

Although desegregation is the law of the land, and the vast majority of Americans acknowledge that school desegregation is a desirable policy, implementing it has been very difficult. Part of the difficulty stems from the fact that it touches on a large number of factors in our lives. It raises new concerns about the quality of schools, and it raises parental concern about interracial conflict. As a means of desegregating schools, busing has engendered a great deal of controversy.

Busing has not been used extensively for desegregation. Only 3 to 5 percent of all students who ride buses in the United States do so for the purposes of desegregation (Rossell & Hawley 1983, 7). Transportation costs for busing are no more than 2 percent higher than they would be without desegregation. Desegregation has improved minority academic achievement while not harming white achievement. Parents who send their children to desegregated schools have been overwhelmingly satisfied with the experience (Harris 1981).

Mandatory plans for desegregation have been more effective than voluntary plans, and *externally ordered* plans (ordered by an agency outside the school system, such as a court) have been more successful than *internally ordered* ones (ordered by the school system itself). Voluntary plans have worked in schools with less than 30 percent minority students but not with more than 30 percent. Desegregation rarely leads to protests, but when it does, protesters are more likely to be from the working-class and are more likely to have feelings of anomie, authoritarianism, and racial prejudice (Rossell 1983, 25). Protests usually occur only if there is a supportive social environment, particularly at the neighborhood level. Protests that lead to demonstrations are more likely to accelerate "white flight"—the movement of whites from the center cities to the suburbs. However, white flight is not a principal result of desegregation. Most of the white flight from central cities began after World War II with suburbanization. It was encouraged more by government mortgage policies that made home ownership easy than by school desegregation. The average loss in white enrollment after desegregation in a particular school district has been from 8 to 10 percent during the first year. White flight is greater if the plans are phased-in rather than immediately implemented. It is also greater if accompanied by significant media coverage and protest demonstrations and if the schools involved have higher achievement levels.

According to Mahard and Crain (1983), desegregation at the lowest grade levels has the most positive effects. These effects include better reading comprehension, improved Intelligence Quotient scores among minority groups, and improved overall racial climate in the school. When desegregation occurs for the first time in secondary schools, however, less than half the schools show a positive effect.

In 1986, the U.S. Supreme Court let stand a lower court ruling that ratified the end of busing in Norfolk, Virginia. The lower court case was based on the notion that better educational opportunities could replace integration as a policy goal. This idea was embraced by the Reagan administration, which defended the Norfolk schools in court as part of the Reagan emphasis on local control. Said William Bradford Reynolds, the Assistant Attorney General for civil rights, "In districts that have sustained good faith compliance with court-ordered desegregation, it's time to restore to local authorities full responsibility for running public schools (*Newsweek*, November 17, 1986, 60). By itself, this particular ruling would not end busing in the United States. However, if combined with other initiatives, the ruling could spell the end to busing as a way of implementing school desegregation.

■ EVALUATING EDUCATION POLICY

In the mid-1970s, students in different parts of the country attempted to sue school systems contending that schools had graduated them without teaching them to read. The courts consistently ruled against the students on the grounds that to do otherwise could constitute judicial intrusion into the educational process. According to judges, students are at least partly responsible for their own education.

Can teachers be held responsible if students do not learn how to read? Some argue that they should, but most believe it is not possible to show a causal link between teaching and learning. The data have many flaws, and, according to some researchers, cannot be used to substantiate claims that our schools are failing to teach reading (Farr & Fay 1982, 4). If we take a long-term view, the reading achievement of the nation's students has improved (Farr & Fay 1982). Schools have succeeded in developing literacy in the population, even though a large segment of the population still is functionally illiterate. Many of the functionally illiterate are recent immigrants, or among the minority poor whose schools are not as good as those of suburban whites. In contrast to other nations, America's schools have had to deal with children whose native language is not English. In spite of this situation, improvements in reading achievement in the lower elementary grades have been continuous throughout the history of education in the United States and have improved considerably since 1969. For example, in 1991 third-grade students scored about 12 percent higher on the Iowa Test of Basic Skills than students in 1969.

In an attempt to assure that graduates of public high schools possess the skills needed to function as members of society and make schools accountable for results, a majority of states have adopted competency testing. For example, in 1983, New Jersey introduced a reading, writing, and mathematics test that was given in the ninth grade. Students who failed took the exam again in the tenth, eleventh, and twelfth grades, until they passed. Those who did not pass, did not graduate (Sullivan 1986).

A second approach to improving schools has been to provide incentives for teachers by instituting merit pay and master teacher programs. A master teacher system is similar to the one used in colleges where individuals advance from assistant to associate and then to full professor if they are able to demonstrate achievement in teaching and research. Merit pay would give salary raises to teachers who demonstrate they have done a good job. The Reagan administration supports the merit pay concept. Teachers' unions, however, have adamantly opposed it for several reasons. One is that it is exceedingly difficult to measure good teaching. As a result, it is relatively easy to abuse merit pay systems and turn them into political tools in which personal friends and supporters are rewarded and enemies are punished. More importantly, it takes attention away from the more fundamental issue: *the salaries of teachers are too low.* As a result, the profession has difficulty attracting the best college students and instead tends to get the poorest students. By 1986, all but one state raised teachers' pay. In California, for example, starting salaries shot up to $20,000 in 1986 compared to $13,000 in 1983 (see Case 9–2).

As if to show that student achievement is not related just to teaching competence, even though few reforms had been instituted by 1985, SAT scores began to improve. Politicians, including President Reagan, were quick to jump on this and claim credit for it. In his 1986 State of the Union address, President

CASE 9–2 *Prescriptions for Education*

On May 16, 1986, the Carnegie Foundation issued a report recommending a number of reforms for education. Four major points were made in the report: (1) higher standards for teaching, including the possibility of a national teacher certification board; (2) merit pay for teachers; (3) greater choice for parents in the schools their children attend; and (4) liberal arts education be emphasized for teachers.

Under the Carnegie proposal, a teacher who had about fifteen years in the profession and who was a lead teacher, the top category, would earn more than $70,000 a year. Such a teacher earned $38,000 in 1986. The report stressed that higher salaries were needed to attract more capable people into teaching.

Not everyone agrees with this. According to Patrick Welsh, who had been teaching English for fifteen years, "money is going to help, and it would draw better people in, let's say brighter people. But it's not going to be the sole solution, because once those bright people get there, if they can't have an impact on their classes, they're just going to be sitting there making money and

Reagan said, "It wasn't government and Washington lobbies that turned education around—it was the American people who, in reaching for excellence, knew to reach back to basics" (Lang 1986). However, there is no scientific evidence to support this. In fact, no adequate explanation is available for why SAT scores were improving except for the psychological model of social psychologist Robert Zajonc of the University of Michigan. His explanation is that intelligence depends upon family size and birth order. The oldest child and children from smaller families are more intelligent than younger children and those from large families. The reason pertains to the intellectual environment to which a child is exposed. An only child is exposed primarily to his or her parents' well-developed vocabulary and adult decision processes. In contrast, a child with five other siblings is exposed mostly to the vocabularies and intellectual processes of his or her siblings. Thus, large family size is related to poorer intellectual growth. Because the SAT is taken by seventeen-year-olds, we should expect increases in the average score if the average family size declined in the 1980s. In fact, it did. This cannot explain *all* of the increase in SAT scores. On the other hand, there is no evidence that the increase in SAT scores can be attributed to the changes in public policy that occurred in the 1980s such as greater state involvement in education, the use of competency tests, or merit pay plans. In fact, SAT verbal scores declined again in the latter 1980s, dropping from 430 in 1986 to 422 in 1990.

then will eventually leave" (Welsh, May 16, 1986). Welsh felt that bureaucratic rules in the schools stifled good teachers.

Mary Futrell, the head of the nation's largest teachers' union, the National Education Association, also had reservations about the merit pay recommendations. Rather than evaluating individual teachers, she felt that an entire school should be evaluated, because the success of any teacher depends upon what other teachers in the school are doing. For example, a business teacher must depend on math, science, English, and other teachers in order to do a good job. Moreover, she added, teachers already are evaluated on an annual basis for union contracts: "These contracts state very clearly how the pay is going to be given. Most of the pay is based on seniority. It is based on experience, and it also is based on what you are teaching in that particular school" (Welsh, May 16, 1986, 12). Thus, changes in how teachers should get paid and recommendations for merit pay conflict with union prerogatives.

The Privatization Issue

Throughout his two terms as president, President Reagan supported public funding of private schools. His administration viewed support as a way of curtailing the growth of government bureaucracy, excessive regulation, and mediocre schools. The Reagan administration felt that free choice in schooling would force public schools to get better and that those who select private schools would no longer suffer the double burden of paying taxes for public schools as well as tuition for private schools. Because private schools clearly serve the public interest in education, the administration felt that taxes for public schools amounted to double taxation for education. These policies continued to be supported during the Bush administration but lost favor when Clinton took office in 1993.

Opponents of choice argue that public support for private schools would further stratify schools by social and economic status, damage the commitment to disadvantaged children, and increase racial isolation. In addition, it would undermine the public interest in providing a common education and harm public schools since they would become a last resort for those who could not afford a private school. Finally, opponents felt that public support of private schools would be unconstitutional because 85 percent of private schools are church-affiliated.

Like many public policy issues, this one is infused with emotion and so not easy to settle. Since public support of private schools already exists in many forms, the issue really is how much support should there be, not whether or not such support should be given at all. In many states not only are there direct expenditures for private schools, but tax exemptions. It has been estimated that the government supports about 26.4 percent of the total income of private schools (James & Levin 1983). Should this be extended through vouchers or tax credits?

The impact of such a plan on education is difficult to predict. However, there is considerable speculation about the possible consequences. Some feel that such plans would lead to a highly-stratified set of schools, each pursuing its own narrow ends with relatively homogeneous sets of students (Levin 1983, 36; Thernstrom 1991, 13). In order to prevent this schools would have to be carefully regulated, which would make the system costly and cumbersome. Others feel that only families with a high enough income would benefit from tuition tax credits because only these families would incur a tax liability (Muller 1983). Vouchers do not have this defect. But once the voucher system is in place, private schools might raise their tuition charges thus keeping private education out of the reach of the poor.

Privatization policies might make public schools worse because public school budgets as well as political support would diminish, particularly from white, middle-class parents. This would remove those families from public schools which are most likely to keep up the pressure for improvements (Breneman 1983). Families that would probably benefit most from privatization are primarily white, upper-income families, whose children have normal educational needs (Catterall 1983). Finally, the constitutional obstacles of the First Amendment make it unlikely that a congressional tuition tax credit program would be held constitutional by the courts (Jensen 1983).

Thus, tuition tax credits or vouchers do not seem to be promising avenues for improving public education in the United States. However, former Secretary of Education T. H. Bell believes that changes in the direction of privatization are inevitable, "Advocates of vouchers and tuition tax credits will at least gain some concessions. Whether you like it or not, it's coming" (Fiske 1986, 19). But it still had not been used in many states by 1993.

Master teacher systems, merit pay, and competency testing have a number of flaws, as indicated earlier. Another problem with these plans is that they detract attention from other, more serious problems in public education. For example, teachers are paid very low salaries and the profession has very low status. The median salary for classroom teachers in 1985 was $23,000, which was lower than the median salary for the population in general for a family of four. By 1990, it had increased to $31,400, but still was below the median salary of the population in general. In addition, elementary and secondary school teachers are primarily female, whereas administrators are mostly

TABLE 9–2 Public school employment by occupation, sex, and race, 1982 and 1990.

[**In thousands**. Covers full-time employment. 1982 excludes Hawaii, District of Columbia, and New Jersey. Based on sample survey of school districts with 250 or more students. 1990 based on sample survey of school districts with 100 or more employees; see source for sampling variability]

OCCUPATION	1982					1990				
	Total	Male	Female	White[1]	Black[1]	Total	Male	Female	White[1]	Black[1]
All occupations	3,082	1,063	2,019	2,498	432	3,181	914	2,267	2,502	463
Officials, administrators	41	31	10	36	3	43	28	15	37	4
Principals and assistant principals	90	72	19	76	11	90	56	34	70	13
Classroom teachers[2]	1,680	534	1,146	1,435	186	1,746	468	1,278	1,469	192
Elementary schools	798	129	669	667	98	875	128	747	722	103
Secondary schools	706	363	343	619	67	662	304	358	570	66
Other professional staff	235	91	144	193	35	227	58	170	187	30
Teacher's aides[3]	215	14	200	146	45	324	54	270	208	69
Clerical, secretarial staff	210	4	206	177	19	226	5	221	181	24
Service workers[4]	611	316	295	434	132	524	245	279	348	129

[1] Excludes individuals of Spanish origin
[2] Includes other classroom teachers, not shown separately
[3] Includes technicians
[4] Includes craftworkers and laborers

Source: U.S. Equal Opportunity Commission, *Elementary-Secondary Staff Information (EEO-5)*, biennial.

male (see Table 9–2). In 1980, 64.5 percent of classroom teachers were female and 35.5 percent were male, while 82.3 percent of principals and assistant principals were male and only 17.7 percent were female. This latter figure was only a slight improvement over 1974, as shown in Table 9–2. However, by 1990, there was considerable improvement in this area: 38 percent of principals and assistant principals were female in 1990. Until teachers' salaries improve, it is unlikely that males will be attracted into the field. An increase in pay would also improve teachers' status which could well be the best way to improve public school education in the United States.

10

Energy and the Environment: The Big Trade-Off

THE NATURE OF THE ENERGY PROBLEM

Pollution of the environment isn't due to evil corporations of rapacious businesses; it is instead the result of the way Americans use energy in order to sustain a high standard of living. Consider air pollution.

There are many days in some American cities when people are told not to go outside during the day if they have respiratory problems, or are old and infirm, because the air poses a serious threat to their health. There are many sources of air pollution, such as electric power industries, automobile emissions, and incineration, but underlying them all is the burning of fossil fuel (oil, coal, gas). If we didn't have electricity or automobiles, we would have a much different and perhaps lower standard of living. On the other hand, as long as Americans continue to burn fossil fuels and emit the resulting gases into the air they breathe, the environment will suffer. That is the trade-off which sometimes also manifests itself as a conflict between the environment (such as owls) versus jobs (such as lumber).

Air pollution is bad enough by itself, but it also is the cause of several other environmental problems as well, including acid rain, ozone depletion, and global warming. Acid rain is formed when sulfur oxide and nitrogen oxide emissions from coal-burning electric power plants and smelting factories rise into the atmosphere and combine with water vapor, falling back to earth with rain. The rain is so acidic that plants and animals die; forests suffer severe loss of trees; lakes and streams lose fish and plant populations. Not everyone agrees that the emissions are the principal cause of acid rain; this will be discussed later.

Burning of fossil fuel also contributes to global warming. It does this through the forming of a shield in the atmosphere that prevents heat from escaping. As is the case with acid rain, there are those who dispute that global warming is occurring or that air pollution contributes to this. Detecting how much warming is occurring and if air pollution is a major cause is a difficult job.

Another problem caused by air pollution is the decrease in the ozone layer in the stratosphere which provides protection from the sun's rays. Some of the gases in air pollution, principally chlorofluorocarbons (CFCs) are believed to be responsible for a general thinning of the ozone layer (Cohn 1987; Graedel & Crutzen 1989). CFC is used in air conditioners and in the production of styrofoam.

Water pollution also is partly a product of the energy sources we use. Major sources of water pollution are acid rain, oil spills, leaking gasoline storage tanks, and untreated human wastes.

While not all environmental problems stem from the use of energy, there is a great deal of overlap between the two. If Americans changed the way they lived, environmental pollution would be greatly reduced. For example, if Americans were to use bicycles, walk, or use mass transit to commute to work instead of automobiles, air pollution in most large cities would decline significantly. Americans are not likely to get out of their cars and ride bicycles (and the way workplaces and housing are situated, they really can't). Instead, changes are more likely to occur when the United States runs out of fossil fuels. First, we discuss this energy policy, then we return to environmental policy.

The End of an Era

In 1956, M. King Hubbert, a young petroleum geologist with Shell Oil Company, informed a meeting of petroleum experts in Texas that U.S. domestic oil production would peak in 1971 and gradually decline thereafter (see Figure 10–1). Shell Oil Company was not happy with Hubbert's figures so it deleted this set of calculations from Hubbert's paper and prepared new graphs that showed peak production would not occur until around the turn of the century.

Shell Oil Company was wrong and Hubbert was right. As shown in Figure 10–2, production in the United States peaked about 1970 and declined

FIGURE 10–1 Hubbert's analysis of the cycle of oil production in the continental United States.

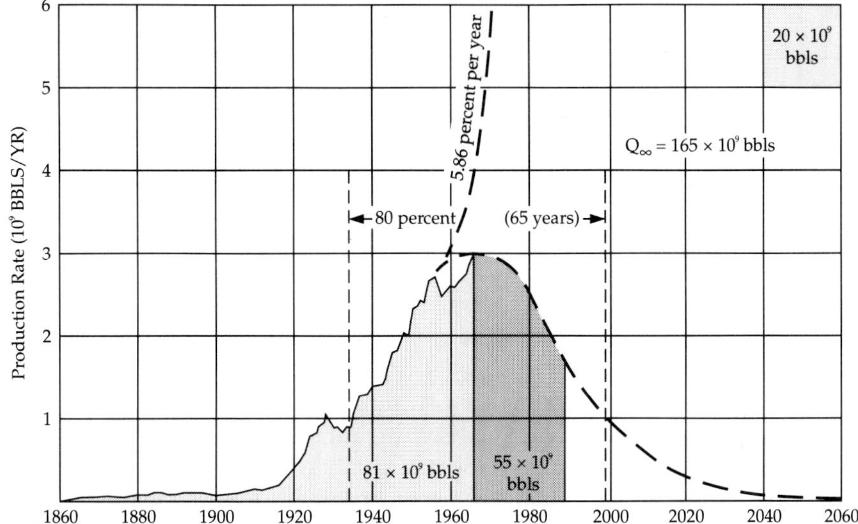

Source: Reprinted from "Resources and Man," 1969, with permission of The National Academy of Sciences, Washington, D.C.

FIGURE 10–2 Crude oil production in the United States, 1955–1980.

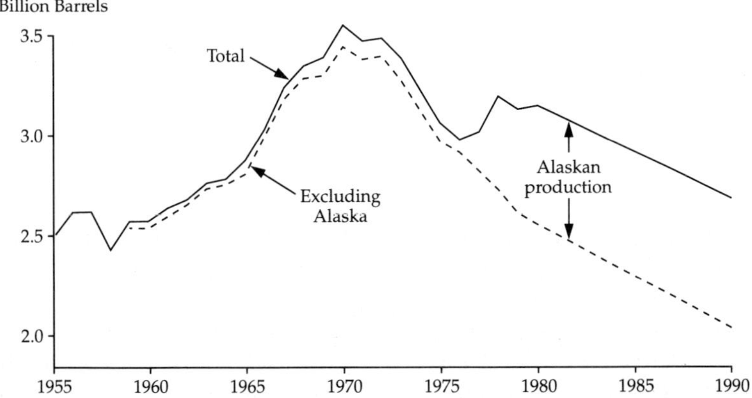

Source: Statistical abstract of the U.S., 1992, p. 697.

thereafter. An oil crisis hit the country a few years later in 1973, when the Arab countries on which the United States depended for most of its imported oil placed an embargo on oil to the United States. They did this in retaliation for America's support of Israel in the seven-day Yom Kippur War. Although the embargo caught the United States by surprise, in fact, there was ample warning. In addition to Hubbert's forecast, others had warned of impending oil shortages. General George A. Lincoln, director of the White House Office of Emergency Planning had warned of an imminent oil shortage as early as the Spring of 1972 (Davis 1982, 105). However, American oil companies and the government refused to believe these warnings.

On October 17, 1973, a new era in American and world history began. Kings, emirs, and sheikhs met in the windswept capital of Kuwait and initiated the oil boycott that caused long lines at gas stations in the United States, skyrocketing oil prices, and the end of energy abundance in America. The energy crisis fragmented American society, alienated large segments of the population, and pitted region against region, interest group against interest group, institution against institution, and business against business. Its ramifications were far reaching. Coming on the heels of the Vietnam War and Watergate, it accentuated the grave doubts that Americans had about their government and even about the country itself. The result was an angry mood among the public and a crisis in energy policy.

The oil crisis, which lasted throughout the 1970s, caused enormous political damage to President Jimmy Carter. In 1979, White House domestic affairs adviser Stuart Eisenstadt told the President:

> I do not need to detail for you the political damage we are suffering from all of this. It is perhaps sufficient to say that nothing which has occurred in the administration to date . . . has so frustrated, confused, angered the American people—or so targeted their distress at you personally. (Greenberger 1983, 8)

Eisenstadt recommended that the Organization of Petroleum Exporting Countries (OPEC) be made the scapegoat in order to take the heat off of President Carter. And the American people were willing to look for a scapegoat. They refused to believe that there actually was an oil crisis but instead felt that the oil companies had created the crisis for their own benefit. In a Gallup survey conducted in 1973 asking "Who or what do you think is responsible for the energy crisis?" 25 percent of Americans blamed oil companies, 23 percent blamed the federal government, 16 percent blamed the U.S. consumer, and 7 percent blamed the Arab nations. By 1979, following the second oil shortage, 42 percent of the public blamed the oil companies for gouging the public. Polls taken immediately after President Carter's austere message in 1977 disclosed that 50 percent of the public refused to believe the United States energy crisis was as serious as the President described (Rosenbaum 1981). By 1979, only 35 percent of the public believed the oil shortage was real.

Oil company profits soared during the 1970s and in many cases, profits rose by 100 percent. There were repeated governmental revelations and accusations of price gouging, manipulation of data, mismanagement of energy reserves, and other actions calculated to sustain energy shortages and increase profits (Rosenbaum 1981). But while oil companies were indeed making excessive profits, it was also true that the Golden Age of Fossil Fuels was dead. The oil and natural gas reserves of the United States will be completely depleted by sometime early in the twenty-first century. In other words, many of the people reading this book will live to see the end of oil and gas production in the United States.

It is not possible to predict the exact time when the United States will run out of oil and gas because the estimates made by various groups vary quite a bit. Experts disagree about how much oil and gas reserves exist, and most estimates must rely upon information that the petroleum industry itself supplies. As we saw in the Shell Oil and King Hubbert case, this information is not always reliable because the petroleum industry has an interest in portraying an optimistic picture. The government's own estimates vary widely and differ significantly from those of industry. For example, the Interior Department estimated in 1982 that American petroleum reserves were between 48 and 130 billion barrels. This is an enormous range of uncertainty. Most forecasts are made by computers and are based on a "fabric of suppositions held together with the glue and paper clips of ifs and assuming" (Rosenbaum 1981, 33).

However long oil and gas lasts, there is no doubt that the world reached its peak of production in 1979 and is now on the decline (Chapman 1983). The U.S. Geological Survey in late 1985 estimated that the world's supplies would last until about the middle of the twenty-first century. Discoveries of oil have been on a decline from a high of 35 billion barrels per year in the 1950s to about 10 to 15 billion barrels per year in the 1980s. According to the study, oil discoveries dropped because of lower-grade prospects available rather than because of the surplus that existed in the mid-1980s. The study concluded, "We have but a few decades to enjoy the convenience of crude oil as our major energy fuel, and while it is found in great supply today, there is every indication that it will become ever more difficult to obtain in years to come" (Associated Press, September 26, 1985). Even more important, most of the reserves and undiscovered oil are in the Middle East. Because of this, more oil shortages and irregularities can be expected. The Arab oil countries are likely to continue to use oil as a political weapon.

Although the use of oil as a component of total energy consumption has been declining since 1975 in the United States (see Table 10–1), it still remained the largest source of energy consumption in the mid-1980s. Americans are profligate consumers of energy as compared to the rest of the world. We use one of every four barrels of oil produced throughout the world and one in every three kilowatt hours of electricity (Chapman 1983, 48). The United States consumes about a quarter of all forms of energy with only 5 percent of the world's

TABLE 10–1 *Energy Use in the United States, 1970–1984*

	Percent of Total Energy Consumption				
	1970	1975	1981	1983	1984
Coal	18.4	17.9	21.4	22.5	23.3
Petroleum	44.5	46.4	43.2	42.6	42.1
Natural gas	32.8	28.3	27.0	24.7	24.5
All other (nuclear, solar, geothermal, etc.)	4.3	7.4	8.4	10.2	10.1
Total energy consumption in quadmillion BTUs	67.8	70.5	73.9	70.5	73.7

Source: U.S. Census Bureau, *Statistical Abstract of the United States, 1986, 106th edition*, p. 556.

population. About a third of American consumption comes from imported sources, and this is likely to continue, unless we drastically reduce our standard of living which we have almost assumed to be a guaranteed right. Most energy consumption is used to maintain the high standard of living, including large, air conditioned, single family dwellings, automobiles, and a multitude of appliances.

With their customary optimism, Americans expect a technological fix to solve this problem. Not too long ago, nuclear energy was seen as the solution, producing non-polluting "clean energy" at little cost. But, as we shall see later, this hope has faded. As Cornell University economist Duane Chapman writes, "Globally, it is impossible that any large region in the world will ever again attain the high level of per capita energy consumption that formerly existed in the U.S." (1983, 318). Therefore, public policy must abandon the impossible goal of sustaining an era of accelerating production and consumption of automobiles, suburban housing, and their related energy-intensive activities.

What Is Energy?

Energy usually is measured in terms of British Thermal Units, or BTUs. A BTU is the amount of heat necessary to raise the temperature of one pound of water one degree Fahrenheit whereas a calorie is the energy necessary to raise the temperature of one gram of water one degree centigrade. On the average, a barrel of oil contains 5.5 million BTUs, a ton of coal about 22.14 million BTUs, and a cord of wood about 22.5 million BTUs (see Table 10–2).

The principal sources of energy can be classified as *renewable* and *nonrenewable*. The renewable sources are all driven by the sun and include wind power, hydropower, geothermal, and direct solar power. The nonrenewable sources

TABLE 10–2 *Energy Units*

Type	Unit	BTU Content
Electricity	Kilowatt hour (Kwh)	3,412 BTU/Kwh
Natural gas	Cubic foot (Cf)	1,026 BTU/Cf
Coal	pound (lb)	11,070 BTU/lb
Petroleum	barrel (bl)	5.5 million BTU/bl
Gasoline	barrel (bl)	5.3 million BTU/bl
Heating oil	barrel (bl)	5.8 million BTU/bl
Wood	Cord	22.5 million BTU/cord
Uranium-225	kilogram (kg)	75 billion BTU/gram

are all derived from fossil fuel: Coal, oil, and natural gas are all remnants of earth's early life forms. They all are finite and limited. Nuclear energy also depends upon a finite fuel—that is, uranium.

PROBLEM DEFINITION AND AGENDA SETTING IN ENERGY POLICY

Who Sets the Energy Agenda?

Rarely does a policy issue get directly onto the government's institutional agenda as it did when the sensational nuclear accident occurred on Three Mile Island in Pennsylvania on March 28, 1979. The incident forced Congress to make a thorough inquiry into the issue of nuclear plant safety. But, as political scientist Walter Rosenbaum writes, "More commonly, issues find their place on the agenda as the result of organized, sustained and skillful activism by issue publics—those segments of the general public that are organized to promote their interests to the government's attention" (1981, 8).

The struggle to get items onto the government's agenda is fiercely competitive. Only a handful of the hundreds of thousands of groups and interests succeed in getting their item onto the agenda. Agenda setting must start anew each year. Each congressional session begins with a determination of the issues to be given priority in that Congress. When an item reaches the agenda, it is almost a commitment to action by the government; officials rarely let an item onto the agenda unless they feel that they can respond (Eyestone 1978).

Energy policy fits as well as any policy can into the category that political scientists call "nondecision making." Prior to the oil crisis of 1973, energy was not on the public agenda. Of course, problems *relating to* specific sources of energy, such as coal, did get onto the public agenda. But after the oil embargo of 1973, "for the first time in its history, the U.S. was forced to think in terms of fuel tradeoffs, and energy was placed on the national policy agenda" (Kash & Rycroft 1985, 434). Prior to the embargo, energy policy was actually a number of distinct, separate policies in the areas of coal, oil, natural gas, nuclear, and electricity. Policy in all of these areas was made through the cooperation of government and producer groups, institutionalized in administrative bureaucracies responsible for implementing and formulating policies in each sector. The producer groups enjoyed informal privileged access or nearly direct participation in policy making through advisory committees set up by the government. The relationship between the Office of Oil and Gas of the U.S. Government and the National Petroleum Council, an advisory committee dominated by the major oil companies, was the most routinized and best known of these arrangements (Chubb 1983). These groups preferred that energy issues be kept off the public agenda. Thus, energy was invisible for over a century prior to 1973 when the Arab oil embargo suddenly brought it to public attention.

The principal issue publics that have a hand in setting the energy agenda are the oil companies, electric utility companies, and environmental groups. In addition, energy items get onto the agenda after a major accident such as the oil spill in the ocean off the shores of Santa Barbara, California, in 1969, or the Three Mile Island nuclear accident in Pennsylvania. As we shall see, environmental groups have much less influence on energy policy than the oil companies and electrical utility companies.

The Oil Companies and the Energy Agenda

American oil companies are huge, multinational corporations that are many times larger than most countries of the world and even bigger than one of the largest governments in the world: the U.S. government. The revenues of Exxon, British Petroleum, and Shell Oil companies in 1980 were $225 billion, and their operations spanned every continent in the world. They sold 27 percent of all of the petroleum products sold throughout the noncommunist world. None of these oil companies is an exclusively American company; they all are multinational. British Petroleum (BP) owns 53 percent of Standard Oil of Ohio, and the British government owns 39 percent of BP. Shell Oil Company is a subsidiary of Royal Dutch Shell of The Netherlands. All of the major companies are partners in a wide variety of enterprises; every company was a partner at least once with every other company on various concessions. Standard Oil of California and Texaco are formal partners in Caltex, and the French company, CFP, nearly always shared concessions with BP and usually shared concessions with Shell Oil. Similarly, Mobil and Exxon were always involved with each other in their seven concessions such as North Sea leases (Chapman 1983, 93).

There always has been a great deal of concentration in the petroleum industry; relatively few companies dominate exploration, production, and marketing. It began with John D. Rockefeller and the Standard Oil Company (see Case 10–1). By 1981, the twenty leading oil companies had revenues that exceeded those of the U.S. government; their revenues were $566 billion, while those of the federal government were $424 billion (excluding social security). The profitability of the oil industry in 1981 was higher than that of any other industry. Petroleum's 17.7 percent return on its assets was significantly higher than the 13.8 percent median return for large manufacturing corporations in the United States. However, since the end of World War II, the oil industry's profits have been equal to or a little below overall industry returns (Chapman 1983).

The typical major American oil company is large, having revenues in the billions of dollars, and is vertically integrated (that is, includes drilling, refining, and distribution), international in operation, and horizontally integrated with other fuels. The twenty major oil companies owned 43 percent of the country's natural gas production in 1980. They also owned coal companies, nuclear power plants, and solar energy companies. The twenty top oil companies control 85 percent of known oil reserves and 72 percent of the refinery capacity.

CASE 10–1 *Rockefeller and Standard Oil*

John D. Rockefeller was born near Richford, New York, in a small rural village. He was born in poverty that was made more difficult by his father's frequent absences and eventual abandonment of his family. Rockefeller began working at age sixteen in Cleveland, Ohio. In 1860, he represented a Cleveland group that sought firsthand information on the financial potential of oil fields in Pennsylvania. The oil fields had been discovered in 1859 by Colonel Drake. Rockefeller visited the oil fields and upon his return, advised the Cleveland group to stay out of the business. They followed his advice. But Rockefeller went ahead on his own and set up a refinery which became Standard Oil Company.

By 1889, Standard had captured almost 90 percent of the market for refined petroleum in the United States. Throughout the period of the Standard Oil Trust, which lasted from 1860 to 1910, oil production in the United States grew rapidly. But in 1911, Standard was found guilty of violating the Sherman Anti-Trust Act and was broken up into its constituent companies. Thirty-three companies were formed where one had existed before. The Sherman Anti-Trust Act, passed in 1890, made it illegal to restrain trade through monopoly practices.

These large oil companies have been able to pretty much set the agenda with regard to oil prices and supplies. During World War I, President Woodrow Wilson initiated government-industry cooperation because oil was recognized to have important strategic military value. After the war, Wilson tried to break up this cooperation, but the oil companies preferred to maintain it since they recognized the values of this cozy arrangement with government. One of the values was the oil depletion allowance that they won in 1926. They also engaged in less legal relations with government, as described in Case 10–2. The oil depletion allowance was passed by Congress in 1926 in an attempt to stimulate oil production. It was based on the assumption that the value of an oil well decreases each year as oil is pumped out. Since an oil well's value declines approximately 27.5 percent each year, oil companies were allowed to deduct 27.5 percent of their gross income from their taxable income.

The origin of the notorious depletion allowance lay in two areas. The first was a fear of an oil shortage in the mid-1920s. The second was a need to standardize the Internal Revenue Service's system of determining the value of a well. Since it is difficult to predict the life expectancy of a well, the IRS could

CASE 10–2 *Teapot Dome Scandal*

The U.S. Fuel Administration that had been set up during World War I by Woodrow Wilson was discontinued in 1919. But the immediate post-war years saw the rise of a threatened oil shortage. The U.S. Geological Survey had predicted that, on the basis of its calculations, the United States would run out of oil in ten years.

In anticipation of a possible oil shortage, President Taft in 1912 set aside large segments of publicly owned lands in California, Montana, and Wyoming on which oil had been discovered. One of these locations was called Teapot Dome. The oil on these lands was to be reserved for future naval needs. In 1922, Secretary of the Interior Albert Fall persuaded President Harding to transfer these reserves to the Interior Department. Fall leased the reserves secretly and without bidding to Harry Sinclair and E. L. Doheny at extremely low rates in return for several bribes. Sinclair and Doheny made their fortunes through oil exploration in Oklahoma. The scandal came to light after Harding died. Fall was tried, convicted, and sentenced to prison. Sinclair was forced to pay the U.S. Treasury over $12 million and Doheny had to pay almost $35 million. They were indicted, convicted, and imprisoned briefly. They did not really suffer much, however. Doheny died at age seventy-nine and left a fortune of $25 million; Sinclair also left a fortune when he died. Interior Secretary Fall, however, died a poor man.

not handle the depreciation of a well in the same way that they depreciated the cost of a machine. Using the depletion allowance, the IRS hoped to standardize this question. Lobbyists for the Mid-Continent Oil Producers Association recommended to the Senate that the oil companies be allowed to deduct 25 percent of its gross income each year from its taxable income, and the Senate accepted. The House of Representatives thought this was not good enough and recommended a 30 percent allowance. A conference committee of the two houses compromised and recommended a figure of 27.5 percent. The figure was accepted.

The depletion allowance permits a petroleum company to deduct 27.5 percent of its *gross* income from its taxable income. However, even with the depletion allowance, the oil industry continues to suffer from booms and busts; as new oil is discovered and becomes more abundant, the price of oil drops and vice-versa. By the end of the 1930s, oil companies sought government regulation as they recognized that such regulation would favor existing companies. This is supported by the fact that during the twenty-seven-year period during which they were regulated by the government, there was little change in the overall structure of the major companies. For example, every major oil company that was in the top twenty in sales for 1954 was still in the top twenty in 1981. Very few even changed their relative position, as shown in Table 10–3. The situation in Oklahoma illustrates the conservative bias of government regulation. When rich oil pools were discovered beneath Oklahoma City in 1929, the drillers in fields outside the city called for government regulation to "stabilize the market." According to political scientist David H. Davis:

> what they were really saying was that with the appearance of serious competition the state of Oklahoma should restrict output, particularly from the newly discovered rival source. Yet only a few years before, the discovery of the Seminole field had brought a similar outcry for curbs on production, and a year later the discovery of the east Texas fields sent the Oklahoma governor to Washington to seek federal government limitations on production. (1982, 74)

There is little doubt that the oil companies have been able to control the policy agenda with regard to oil, primarily by keeping the question off the agenda and making all major decisions themselves. After the Teapot Dome scandal, the question of oil policy went underground until the 1952 presidential election; it was the first time that oil politics had become so open (Davis 1982). The issue was the offshore lands and whether they should be considered the property of the federal or state governments. Democrats supported the position that the offshore lands should belong to the national government, while Republicans advocated that the states should retain them. The Republicans believed this was a good issue with which to wrest control of the government from the Democrats. General Eisenhower in an election speech argued that the question was one of undoing the wrongs of the "power mongers" in Washington. When

TABLE 10–3 *Change in Sales Leadership of U.S. Oil Companies for the Period 1954–1981*

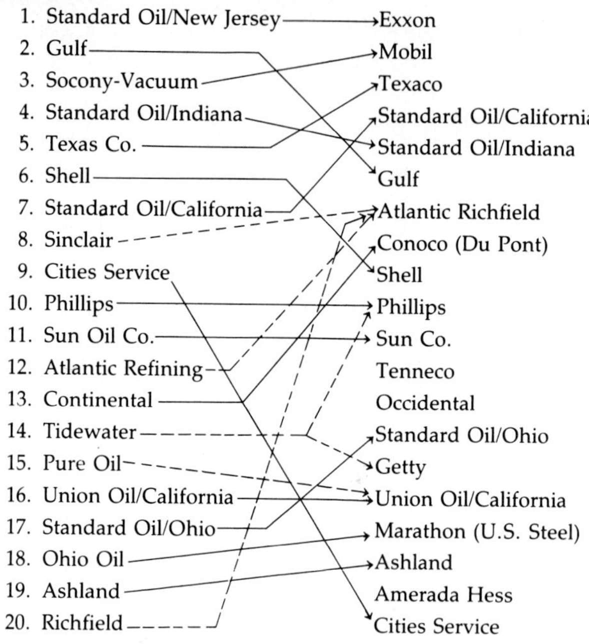

Note: Segmented lines denote mergers and acquisitions. Solid lines indicate changes in relative position.

Source: Duane Chapman, *Energy Resources and Energy Corporations.* Copyright © 1983 by Cornell University. Used by permission, p. 112.

Eisenhower won in 1952, the tidelands oil issue was settled—the lands were given to the states. Oil did not become a part of the national public agenda again until 1969 following a major oil spill in Santa Barbara, California, described later in this chapter.

Electrical Utilities and the Energy Agenda

Oil and electricity have experienced parallel paths of development in the United States. Both were monopolies dominated by a small group of companies in the nineteenth century. Both were dominated by the personality of an individual leader; Samuel Insull played a role in the electric utility industry similar to that played by Rockefeller in the oil industry (see Case 10–3).

CASE 10–3 *Samuel Insull and Electricity*

Samuel Insull became Thomas Edison's private secretary in 1881 at the age of thirty, before the electric utility industry existed. By 1930 he led a corporate grouping that operated electric utilities in more than thirty states. Insull believed that the only sensible way to sell electricity was to have no competition. His thinking was based on the premise that everyone should have electricity at the lowest possible price (McDonald 1962).

Insull was head of the Commonwealth Edison Company in New York City in 1892 at the age of forty-one. The Commonwealth Edison Company was only one of the city's more than thirty electric companies. Insull believed that competition was not beneficial and he set out to eliminate competitive franchises and establish a system of legislative control of rates. At first he did not succeed, but in 1904 he helped form the Committee for Municipal Ownership and argued that unless public regulation of utilities was established, municipal ownership was the only way to secure fair treatment for the public. A report outlining this position was accepted by the National Electric Light Association (NELA) at its convention in 1907. Coupled with a report by reformist groups such as the National Civic Federation, the NELA convinced states that they should regulate rates.

In 1932, Insull, facing charges of fraud and embezzlement, was forced out of the management of these utilities. He fled to Europe to avoid prosecution. The Turkish government seized him on his yacht when he went to Istanbul and returned Insull to the United States where he was tried for using the U.S. mail to defraud investors by sending them what was alleged to be fictitious information about assets and income. Insull was acquitted mostly because his business practices were no worse than normal for that period.

The United States is unique among industrial nations of the world in the degree to which electric utilities are owned by private corporations. Three quarters of the electricity generated in the United States is produced by investor-owned utilities, one fifth by federal, state, municipal, or cooperative organizations, and the remaining small amount is imported.

Electrical utilities are regulated by state governments. Seldom do questions about these utilities get onto the national agenda. There are two things that are likely to bring electricity onto the agenda: one is when utilities request a rate increase, and the other is when there is a major power failure. However, even in these cases a small group of technical experts exercises control, as it does in all aspects of policy making with regard to electricity. The public is in no position to judge whether or not a rate increase is justified, or whether a power failure is due to management inefficiency or to technical factors. The public would not be able to understand the dialogue that occurs at hearings about the need for a rate increase or the reasons for a power failure. Thus, iron triangles—that is, interest groups, regulators, and the industry—tend to dominate the agenda-setting process in regard to electricity.

Electrical utilities welcomed state regulation throughout their seventy-five-year history. Samuel Insull was a leader in the effort to obtain state regulation, as described in Case 10–3. This has been beneficial to utility companies because it has enabled them to control the agenda. According to Harvard University business professor Douglas Anderson:

> consumers of electricity have ignored the regulatory process unless some scandal or political entrepreneur succeeded in making real or imaginal abuses highly visible. Second, it has meant that throughout most of the seventy-five year history of electric utility regulation by the states, the utilities themselves have been free to make all the important decisions regarding the production and marketing of electricity as long as commissioners judged their rates to be fair and reasonable. (1981, 61)

As long as utility rates were stable and service was reliable, about the only people who paid attention to state utility commissions were utility executives (1981, 69). The 1973 Arab oil boycott changed all this as electric costs skyrocketed and threatened the financial position of the companies.

Major Precipitating Events and the Energy Agenda

In 1969, a Union Oil Company well six miles off the coast of Santa Barbara exploded releasing 235,000 gallons of crude oil that spread into an 800-mile long oil slick. It washed up on the city's beaches, killing birds, fish, and plant life. The incident mobilized environmentalists across the nation. Since this oil disaster, environmental groups have had some influence on energy policy. For example, in 1985 they were able to temporarily block an attempt by the Interior Department to lease lands off the New Jersey shore on the grounds that the government failed to file a proper environmental impact statement.

Beginning in 1980, in the ocean west of Santa Barbara, petroleum engineers made the largest American discoveries of crude oil since the oil strikes on Alaska's north slope in the 1960s. By 1985, in a burst of activity, many of the oil producers began erecting offshore drilling platforms and onshore plants to process the oil. However, some environmentalists objected and gathered enough signatures to call for a special election in November 1985 on a petition to impose stricter environmental controls on oil producers. The proposal would require approval of Santa Barbara County voters for any substantive changes in regulations affecting oil companies and add several restrictions opposed by the oil industry. The oil industry raised over $1 million and waged a major campaign against the proposition. Although public opinion was strongly in favor of the proposition at the beginning, the oil industry campaign turned it around and the proposition was defeated by a vote of 43,567 to 26,001.* But even though it was defeated, the Santa Barbara proposition indicates that the oil companies are no longer able to completely dominate the energy agenda. Although not as strong as in the 1970s, environmentalists still maintained some power with respect to energy policy agenda setting.

Environmentalists have even more influence in nuclear energy agenda setting, primarily due to the sensational accident that occurred at Three Mile Island on March 28, 1979. Misled by a faulty instrument, a cooling pump in the reactor at Three Mile Island failed, after which operators on duty mistakenly turned off the emergency cooling system. As a result the reactor heated up dangerously, releasing some radiation and causing the nearby residents to flee. The Nuclear Regulatory Commission (NRC) took charge of the plant and ordered it to be shut down. Human error certainly was a major factor in this accident, but each party blamed others for the problem. Metropolitan Edison, the operators, blamed Babcock and Wilson, who manufactured the reactor; the manufacturers in turn blamed Metropolitan Edison for poor maintenance and operating procedures; and the NRC was blamed for complacency. Following the accident at Three Mile Island, the NRC ordered similar plants shut down, which slowed the development of the nuclear power industry, at least for a few years.

Three Mile Island was not the first nuclear accident to occur in the United States. In 1961, a reactor exploded at the Atomic Energy Commission's National Reactor Testing Station in Idaho Falls, Montana, killing three workers. Similarly, in 1966 a fire broke out at the Enrico Fermi Atomic Power Plant in Detroit when a bit of sheet metal chipped off and blocked the sodium that is pumped through the fuel pile to keep it cool. The safety devices worked and extinguished the fire. Had the controls failed, the result might have been a "meltdown" of the uranium core. If the coolant fails, a nuclear reactor will heat up and the core collapse. The molten mass will burn through the bottom of its container and then through the concrete containment slab under the plant. In 1975, a fire at the Tennessee Valley Authority's Brown's Ferry nuclear plant caused a reactor to overheat and seven of its twelve safety systems failed, but the plant was finally shut down. If the plant were to heat up uncontrollably, causing a steam explosion, it would produce a deadly invisible cloud of radioactivity.

The world witnessed such an event in late April 1986 at the Chernobyl nuclear plant located outside of Kiev. The Soviet nuclear plant overheated and exploded, leaking huge amounts of radiation in the surrounding area, producing a cloud of radiation that drifted over eastern Europe. Hundreds of thousands

* Ken Bolton. Personal communication, December, 1986.

of people were evacuated from surrounding areas and many were permanently relocated since they could not return to their radioactive homes and farms. Although the Soviets were able to burrow under and encase the molten core, they estimated that it would be a long time before the area around Chernobyl would be considered safe and the 92,000 people who were evacuated could return home. According to Yevgeny Velikhov, vice president of the Soviet Academy of Sciences, "if you mishandle that fuel, insulate it too much, it can heat up again and cause some dangers. We have to provide a safe solution for scores of years ahead, and it is a complicated and intricate problem" (*Arizona Republic,* May 27, 1986, F8).

Although few people have been killed by nuclear plant accidents—the Soviets reported that only thirty-one people died following the Chernobyl meltdown—most Americans consider nuclear energy to be dangerous. For example, most Americans consider the chances of their being killed in a nuclear accident greater than that of being killed in an automobile accident, by a hand gun, or by smoking (Allman 1985, 41). In fact, auto accidents and smoking kill far more people than nuclear power mishaps.

Because of public fear, environmentalists have been successful in influencing at least part of the agenda in nuclear power policy, particularly with regard to the siting of nuclear plants. For example, in 1977, demonstrations, marches, and sit-ins were used to protest the building of a nuclear plant in Seabrook, New Hampshire. Two thousand demonstrators marched onto the plant site, set up tents, and refused to leave. State police arrested 1,415 people and bused them to the National Guard Armory. One thousand of the people refused to post bail for their release. Despite the state governor's promise to take a tough stance against the "enemies of nuclear power," he was forced to order their release anyway, because the state could not afford the cost of keeping them locked up.

Problem Definition and the Energy Agenda

As cited in earlier chapters, a crucial part of agenda setting is being able to define the problem. Once defined, this usually determines the direction that policy will take. The National Research Council (1984) distinguishes four different views of energy as follows:

1. *Energy as a commodity* In this view, energy is a collection of commodities such as coal, oil, natural gas, and electricity. But to a physicist, electricity is the only real form of energy. The others are substances that contain potential energy when burned. When defined as a commodity, our major concerns about energy are supply, demand, prices, and the choices that buyers and sellers of the commodities make.
2. *Energy as an ecological resource* This view looks at the relationship between energy use and environmental pollution. Energy use has

implications beyond the interests of buyers and sellers and energy sources are classified as renewable and nonrenewable, exhaustible or nonexhaustible, polluting or nonpolluting. This view assumes resources are finite and interdependent with other resources and that groups other than buyers and sellers are important.

3. *Energy as a social necessity* Energy here is seen as something to which people have a right for home heating, cooling, lighting, cooking, transportation, and other essential purposes of contemporary life. Certain energy needs must be met for society to be viable and private action will not be able to meet these needs; therefore, some public action is essential.
4. *Energy as a strategic material* This perspective became noticeable when oil was used as a political weapon by OPEC in the 1970s. National security is emphasized in this view.

By accepting one of these particular definitions of energy, we set the terms for future political debate; the definition determines who the legitimate participants will be. According to the National Research Council, "Policy choices are often, implicitly, choices among different views of energy, and as such, they legitimize those views of energy most consistent with chosen policies" (1984, 20).

If viewed as a commodity, then the market and producers would be the major policy makers; if viewed as a strategic material, social necessity, or ecological resource, the government's role in policy would increase. If energy is viewed as an ecological resource, the goal of energy policy would be to enhance environmental quality and strengthen local communities. In the commodity view, the powerful oil corporations become the main proponents. The commodity view dominated American history until 1973. After 1973, the social necessity, ecological, and strategic views gained some ground, but were again relegated to the background after Ronald Reagan became president.

At the local level, energy seldom gets onto the public agenda. This is especially true when energy is viewed as a commodity; local governments seldom produce energy commodities. Thus, at the local level, the commodity view leaves energy decisions in the hands of the private sector.

FORMULATING ENERGY POLICY

In 1984, the National Research Council reported:

> In the absence of strong proponents of the social necessity view of energy, or of a community political structure that includes strong representation of consumer interests, energy decisions will tend to be made by the commodity view and by technical concerns and will usually be made by experts and their employees in government and business. (169–70)

According to President Reagan:

> All Americans are involved in making energy policy. When individual choices are made with a maximum of personal understanding and a minimum of governmental restraints, the result is the most appropriate energy policy. . . . Increased reliance on market decisions offers a continuing national referendum which is a far better means of charting the Nation's energy path than stubborn reliance on government dictates or on a combination of subsidies and regulation. (Department of Energy 1981, E-10)

Energy policy formulation in the twentieth century is a perfect case of interest group liberalism, with fragmented institutional arrangements, competing interest groups, and a lack of comprehensive goals. Interest group liberalism allows policy to be made by powerful interests rather than by the people or the market. In one sense, the above quote from President Reagan indicates a desire to return to the nineteenth century.

The principle of laissez-faire characterized energy policy of the nineteenth century. During the latter part of the nineteenth and early part of the twentieth century, there was an attempt to break up monopolies such as the Standard Oil Trust. Although some "trust busting" by government was successful in the early twentieth century, the government was unable to prevent the growth of monopolies in the energy industry. The "free market" hardly existed in this area, so the U.S. government resorted to regulation as a way to control energy supplies and prices. Government became more heavily involved in energy policy in 1926 when it established oil depletion allowances. In 1938, Congress passed the Natural Gas Act, creating the Federal Power Commission (FPC). The FPC was charged with regulating the interstate transportation of gas. In 1954 the U.S. Supreme Court required the FPC to regulate the prices gas producers charged pipeline companies for transporting gas. By the 1960s, all forty-eight states regulated natural gas prices.

Policy Strategies and Physical Constraints

The policy strategies open to government in the latter half of the twentieth century include the following:

1. Increase the production of oil.
2. Replace oil consumption with the use of coal, natural gas, and nuclear power.
3. Conserve energy through the use of more fuel-efficient autos, home insulation, and co-generation.
4. Produce energy from untapped sources such as synfuels, nuclear fusion, and solar energy.

Which combination of these is the best course of action depends somewhat upon the physical constraints under which energy policy making operates. For example, the United States does not have large reserves of petroleum, but it does possess the majority of the world's coal. Thus, a brief description of these principal constraints and resulting policy strategies is in order.

Natural Gas Natural gas did not become an important energy source until the 1940s when pipeline technology permitted economical transportation of gas. Production of gas increased rapidly and reached a peak in 1971 when it comprised 40.2 percent of domestic energy output. Natural gas is the premier petroleum substitute because it is clean burning, easily transported, can be used just as it comes out of the ground, and can be easily substituted for oil. It also does not require much labor for extraction or transportation and thus its industry does not experience labor union problems.

During the 1970s, a large difference between intrastate and interstate gas prices developed because of the way gas prices were regulated. Producer prices for intrastate gas were unregulated, whereas interstate prices were subject to rigid control. The result was a wide discrepancy between the two. In 1976, the average regulated producer price was 48 cents per million cubic feet for interstate gas and $1.60 for intrastate gas (Chapman 1983, 160). The 1978 Natural Gas Policy Act implemented a complicated phase-out of federal regulation of producer prices. This has allowed much of natural gas production to rise to market levels by the late 1980s.

Coal Coal was king in the nineteenth century. Its reign began almost immediately after the Declaration of Independence. The early pioneers in western Pennsylvania and Virginia quickly discovered the valuable energy source that was lying literally underfoot in exposed seams. Coal was easily mined in the early years and could be used just as it was when it came out of the ground. It was a vigorous, expanding industry until 1820 when it reached its peak.

Providence was extravagant in endowing the United States with coal. The United States possesses about one-third of the world' total coal reserves. While it comprises only 22.5 percent of the nation's energy consumption, this percentage is destined to increase. The eastern United States relies more heavily upon coal, accounting for 57 percent for all coal use, compared to 24 percent in the Midwest and 20 percent in the West. Eighty-five percent of coal production is used for electricity. Its use is attractive because it is almost entirely domestic, mostly located on federal lands, has a fairly simple technology for production, and can be substituted for oil in industrial production. But it also has very negative environmental problems and the worst labor problems.

There are several different types of coal, including lignite, bituminous, sub-bituminous, and anthracite. Bituminous is high in carbon and energy content, low in moisture, and usable in continuously operating boilers. It is the most widely used and the most plentiful type of coal in American reserves. But it also is highest in sulfur content and causes the most air pollution. Bituminous coal is produced primarily in the eastern states. Anthracite has less energy per pound than bituminous; it is very hard, which reduces its utility for continuous utility boiler operations. Pennsylvania has 97 percent of the country's anthracite reserves. Lignite is the lowest quality of commercial coal, high in moisture and low in carbon and heat content. It is not easily transported. Its deposits are found mainly in the western states of Montana, North Dakota, Colorado, and Texas. Sub-bituminous coal is between lignite and bituminous in quality. It has more moisture and less carbon and energy content than bituminous. Montana and Wyoming have 93 percent of the sub-bituminous coal reserves.

Coal mining has very high social costs. Coal mining fatalities averaged between 2,000 to 3,000 per year in the early part of the twentieth century. This declined to less than 2,000 per year in 1931 after unionization of the mines, and to 500 per year by 1953. A large part of this latter decline is due to declining production rather than increased safety. With the passage of the Coal Mine Health and Safety Act in 1969, production and fatalities declined even further. The act required better working conditions with respect to roof and wall collapses, dust and methane control, electrical equipment and mechanical safety, more monitoring and sampling, and stricter enforcement of regulations.

Policy in regard to coal has focused primarily on labor. Beginning with the labor strike in 1900, bitter battles between owners and labor unions developed. Major coal miners' strikes occurred in 1902, between 1913 and 1914, and in 1918; some of them involved full scale battles between miners and soldiers. As gas and oil became more attractive, coal production began to decline in the 1920s. With the passage of the National Labor Relations Act in 1934, union strength increased, and in the 1936 election, coal miners shifted their support to the Democrats along with most other unions because they believed that the Democrats were more sympathetic toward labor than the Republicans.

Strip mining—that is, extracting coal from the surface without digging underground shafts—has been favored by the United Mine Workers because it is safer, requires less labor, and is more efficient. However, it leaves the land destroyed unless it is reclaimed—that is, restored to its original condition. (Case 10–4 describes a typical strip mining operation.) The costs of reclamation were passed onto taxpayers until passage of the 1977 Surface Mining Control and Reclamation Act (SMCRA). This long and complex act was the result of years of concern, conflict, and compromise. The law established the Office of Surface Mining (OSM) in the Department of the Interior. But enforcing legislation aimed at making companies reclaim the land is difficult. Still, the Tennessee Valley Authority—a federal governmental body that uses large amounts of coal in providing energy—has encouraged strip mining "of the most destructive sort" in its purchasing policy (Davis 1982, 188). Under Secretary of the Interior James Watt, the policies of the OSM also encouraged strip mining as the

CASE 10–4 *The Rosebud Mine at Colstrip, Montana*

Located on the Montana plains, the Rosebud mine produces over 10 million tons of sub-bituminous coal a year. While its energy value is low compared to bituminous coal, its sulfur content is also low. Extraction of the coal seam, which is twenty-four feet thick and 100 feet deep, begins by removing the topsoil with bulldozers and scrapers and then blasting the next layer of ground loose. Giant draglines with huge buckets strip off the rock and sand down to the coal seam. The coal is dug up with mechanical shovels and loaded onto trucks which take it to the railroad or the electricity generating plant.

The Rosebud mine is owned by the Western Energy Company, which is a joint venture of the Montana Power Company and the Puget Sound Power and Light Company. The mine employs 275 people and it produces about 30,000 tons of coal a day, which are loaded directly into trains that transport the coal to power plants in various parts of the country. The mine is expected to be in operation for forty years.

Local ranchers, Indians, and the people living in nearby towns oppose the mine because it symbolizes a destruction of their way of life. In an attempt to alleviate some of the problems posed by the mine, the owners helped residents build houses, schools, churches, and a shopping center. The state of Montana also enacted a 30 percent severance tax on the coal to offset the added cost for water, sewage, schools, parks, and police that the mine and its employees generate.

Source: Adapted from David H. Davis, *Energy Politics* (New York: St. Martin's Press, 1982) p. 33.

Department of the Interior and OSM did not believe that government should regulate business. Moreover, the OSM was badly managed, according to some observers. The National Wildlife Federation issued a report in 1985 charging that between 1982 and 1984, the OSM collected less than $1 million out of $135 million in fines owed by law-breaking firms (McCarthy 1985, A21). Operators ignored federal government orders to stop their illegal mining and left the land unreclaimed when the coal was depleted. In other words, the OSM really did not enforce the laws concerning strip mining.

Oil Oil replaced coal as the king of energy by 1970 when it comprised 44.5 percent of U.S. energy production compared to 18.4 percent for coal. The

United States became a net importer of oil for the first time in 1947, and by 1953 imported oil comprised 10 percent of American energy consumption. A committee appointed by President Eisenhower recommended oil import quotas to curtail rapidly expanding imports; these recommendations were adopted by Eisenhower in 1959. The quotas limited the amount of oil that oil companies could import to 12 percent of their total distribution. The quotas are estimated to cost the American consumer from $4 to $7 billion a year. From 1959 through 1973 the import quota was the chief jewel in the oil industry's crown of privilege. The industry used political campaign donations as its main tool to secure its position. Counted among their allies were powerful senators from the oil-producing states of Texas, Oklahoma, and Louisiana, including Lyndon B. Johnson of Texas, Russell Long of Louisiana, and Robert Kerr of Oklahoma.

The oil industry's relations with government moved from cozy to constrained after the 1973 oil embargo by OPEC. Petroleum's privileged position already had begun to erode before the oil embargo. Some of the strongest supporters were gone; Senator Robert Kerr of Oklahoma and House Speaker Sam Rayburn of Texas had died. Lyndon B. Johnson was in the White House where he could not provide open support. And, following the Union Oil Company's disastrous oil spill off Santa Barbara in 1969, environmentalists across the nation were mobilized. This spurred the passage of the National Environmental Policy Act of 1969, which established a new federal agency specifically charged with protecting the environment. This gave concerned citizens a weapon with which to battle the oil companies. For example, the act was used to temporarily block the Interior Department's lease of oil lands off the New Jersey shore on the basis that the Interior had failed to provide a proper Environmental Impact Statement (EIS).

The government continued its campaign to bring the oil companies into line in the latter half of the 1970s. The Energy Power and Conservation Act of 1975 put a ceiling on oil prices; the Department of Energy wove a web of regulations in the 1970s; and in 1980 Congress imposed a windfall profits tax on oil profits. The oil companies were making inordinate profits as a result of the skyrocketing price of oil. In 1981, the industry's profitability was higher than for any other industry. Petroleum's 17.7 percent return was higher than the 13.8 percent median return for large manufacturing corporations.

Throughout the 1970s, oil no longer could operate inconspicuously within its own subgovernment, but in 1981, the Reagan administration reversed the trend by decontrolling crude oil prices, not intervening in mergers, opening more federal lands to oil exploration, and setting a tone reminiscent of the 1950s when oil operated inconspicuously within its own subgovernment (Davis 1982, 128).

Even though it is declining as the principal source of energy in the United States, petroleum still supplied the principal source of energy consumption in the United States in 1987. President Carter unveiled a program in 1977 to meet the energy challenge called the "moral equivalent of war." Among the plan's goals was cutting imports in half by 1985. To the surprise of many, the nation did exactly that. Since the spring of 1977 the country has reduced its dependence on foreign oil from a record 8.5 million barrels of oil imported a day—46 percent of its petroleum needs—to 4.2 million barrels a day in 1985. A sharp decline in oil prices in 1986 has raised concern that U.S. imports might increase again, however, paving the way for another energy crisis.

Nuclear Energy Nuclear energy once was thought to be the salvation to the energy problem because it was assumed to be an almost limitless source of energy. In the early 1960s, President John F. Kennedy appointed scientist Glen Seaborg as chair of the Atomic Energy Commission. Seaborg was a superstar who discovered plutonium at age twenty-eight and won a Nobel prize in 1959. He typified the dominant position of the 1960s. Scientists were people who could get things done; they could build bombs to defend the country or launch rockets that could orbit the earth. The vision of the future was one of scientific omnipotence. The Tennessee Valley Authority helped revitalize the economy of the Valley; the Manhattan Project built the A-bomb; and NASA put people on the moon. But by 1970 the faith in science waned as environmentalists charged that scientists were developing nuclear power without regard for the environment. The problem of nuclear waste disposal coupled with the accident at the Three Mile Island in 1979 greatly slowed the development of nuclear energy.

Nuclear energy began as a strict government monopoly with the passage of the 1946 Atomic Energy Act. The argument in favor of complete control by Washington was based on national security. But a breakthrough for civilian reactors came in 1953 when Congress appropriated funds to construct a pilot power plant by the Westinghouse Corporation. In 1954, Congress passed a bill that permitted private industry to construct and operate nuclear plants under regulations of the Atomic Energy Commission, established in 1946. The federal government also continued to support research and the development of nuclear fuels and technology. By 1979 the federal investment in nuclear energy exceeded $12 billion.

However, a series of reactor failures in the 1960s raised public concern and mobilized environmental groups. A 1975 study by Norman Rassmussen of the Massachusetts Institute of Technology concluded that the worst possible accident would be a core meltdown with major radioactive release and adverse weather and population exposure. He calculated the probability of such an accident to be .000000001 per reactor year (or one in a billion), and that it would cause 3,000 immediate deaths plus 45,000 delayed cancer deaths and 26,000 genetic defects (Chapman 1983, 260). However, another study making different assumptions concluded that there is a 25 percent probability of a very serious accident by the year 2000 but only if we have had 5,000 years of reactor experience by then (which, of course, is impossible). Even though the experts cannot agree, they place the probability of a serious accident at a much lower level than the public. Even more problematic is disposing of nuclear wastes. Although many experts feel that the problem is a long way from being solved, this has not stopped the industry from building more plants.

By 1980, the federal government had licensed 71 nuclear power plants, generating 13 percent of the nation's electric power. By April 1986, that number had increased to 101 operating nuclear reactors (see Figure 10–3). However, even with the 101 plants, nuclear energy supplied only 14 percent of the nation's energy.

Most existing nuclear power plants are light-water reactors that are cooled by ordinary water. It has been estimated that the United States has enough uranium fuel to power 375 reactors for thirty years using light water reactors (Rosenbaum 1981, 42). At the current rate of development, this means that

FIGURE 10–3 Nuclear reactors in operation in December of 1985.

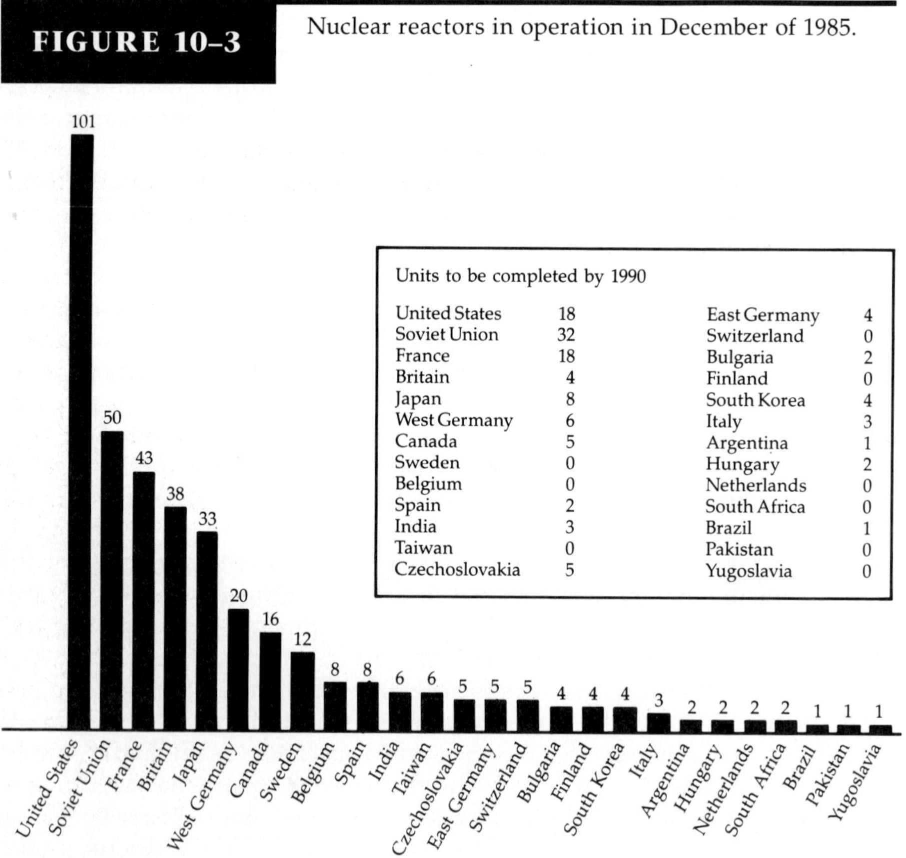

Units to be completed by 1990

Country	Units	Country	Units
United States	18	East Germany	4
Soviet Union	32	Switzerland	0
France	18	Bulgaria	2
Britain	4	Finland	0
Japan	8	South Korea	4
West Germany	6	Italy	3
Canada	5	Argentina	1
Sweden	0	Hungary	2
Belgium	0	Netherlands	0
Spain	2	South Africa	0
India	3	Brazil	1
Taiwan	0	Pakistan	0
Czechoslovakia	5	Yugoslavia	0

Source: Copyright © 1986 by The New York Times Company. Reprinted by permission.

there is enough uranium fuel to last quite awhile, although obviously not an indefinite period. An alternative to the light water reactor is the breeder reactor, which produces fissionable plutonium-238 as it burns uranium-238. Since it produces new fuel as it produces electricity, the new fuel might be used in another reactor. The federal government invested $4.67 billion to create a commercially viable reactor on the Clinch River in Tennessee. But plutonium-238 is lethal and science does not yet have a safe means of disposing of it. As a result, President Carter renounced the use of plutonium and postponed the breeder reactor program indefinitely.

In 1974, Congress passed the Energy Reorganization Act, splitting off the licensing functions of the new Nuclear Regulatory Commission and creating the Energy Research and Development Administration (ERDA), which combined research activities of several agencies. In 1977 Congress abolished the Joint Committee on Atomic Energy in the House and Senate and consolidated ERDA with the Federal Power Commission and the Federal Energy Administration to form a new Department of Energy. In the evaluation section of this chapter we will consider how the series of nuclear accidents has slowed the development of nuclear energy in the United States.

Alternative Energy Sources Solar, geothermal, and wind energy are the main alternatives to petroleum, gas, coal, and nuclear energy. Their development constitutes a soft approach to energy policy in contrast to the hard approach discussed in the next section.* Alternative energy was not very profitable until the oil crisis of the 1970s, which increased the price of oil tenfold and doubled the price of gas and coal. These increases caused the federal government to support research and to subsidize development of the new fuels. During the energy crisis of the 1970s, people turned to the federal government for solutions. The federal government had the money, expertise, authority, and people to develop alternative energy sources. This attitude contrasted dramatically with those of the laissez-faire era in which coal emerged (Davis 1982). Optimism developed about the possibility of using energy from sunlight, geysers, and the wind, all of which are nonpolluting. Of these alternatives, solar and wind power appear to be the most promising.

It is estimated that the heat energy striking the earth's upper atmosphere in thirty minutes exceeds the total U.S. energy consumption in a year. If this energy could be collected and converted to residential, commercial, and industrial use, it could provide all our energy needs. Using existing technology, it is estimated that solar energy could provide up to a quarter of American's current energy requirements. Solar energy can be used to heat water and homes and even to air-condition them. Passive solar energy involves making more efficient use of the sun in the design of homes, whereas active solar energy uses

* A soft energy policy is one that relies more on renewable sources of energy such as solar and wind power; it also prefers a decentralized system for producing energy.

collectors that collect heat and transfer it to a distribution medium such as water. While it is possible for an individual homeowner to install a solar hot water system, the components are expensive and the payback period is too long for the industry to thrive without a tax incentive. In 1978 the National Energy Act permitted homeowners a tax credit of up to $2,000 for installing solar systems, although this was phased out in 1985.

Geothermal energy uses heat from the earth such as steam or the heat deep in the earth. But there are relatively few locations in the United States that have geysers that can be used and there are environmental problems associated with its use.

Wind power has long been used at sea and on land. Until the invention of steam, wind was the whole source of power for ocean travel. As late as World War II, sailing ships could still make a profit carrying wheat from Australia to England. Windmills on land have been used by farmers for years to grind grain, pump water, and generate electricity. Between 1922 and 1952 the Jacobs Wind Electric Company in Montana sold more than $100 million worth of equipment, but sales declined dramatically after 1952 as oil became cheaper. Today a Jacobs windmill costs about $1,500 and generates three kilowatts of electricity. Larger wind generators also are possible. The ERDA and NASA jointly tested a 100-kilowatt generator in Ohio. Blades on these larger windmills resemble airplane propellors, but are usually about 125 to 150 feet across. The Reagan administration has not pushed ahead with alternative energy sources because it prefers a hard energy policy that relies on oil, coal, natural gas, and nuclear power. Thus, tax incentives have been provided by the federal government to stimulate further discovery and production of these fuels.

Synthetic Fuels The U.S. Synthetic Fuels Corporation was established by a federal law in June of 1980. The corporation marked the convergence of faith in science and government. The corporation was to operate like an investment bank. Congress authorized $20 billion to finance the first four years of its activity and further installments of $68 billion were to be made by 1992. The Corporation was run by a seven-member board of highly paid officials, earning between $100,000 and $200,000 a year. The argument was that their salaries should be comparable to those of executives in any large corporation. The Synthetic Fuels Corporation was authorized to finance projects for developing synthetic fuels that would substitute for oil and natural gas. It would guarantee the price of the finished product, enter into a purchase agreement, a loan guarantee, grant a direct loan, or undertake a joint venture with a company that wanted to develop and produce synthetic fuels.

The sources of synthetic fuel are coal, oil, shale, and tar sands. To produce gasoline, for example, coal is crushed, fired, and fed into a vessel where it reacts with steam and oxygen at high temperatures and pressure. Other sources are treated in a similar manner. The cost of developing these fuels has turned out to be much higher than anticipated. And many of its subsidiaries were plagued with problems. For example, the Union Oil Company's Parachute Creek shale-oil project in Colorado was never able to operate for more than a day and a half without clogging occurring in cooling chutes where spent shale enters a water spray (*Arizona Republic* August 23, 1985, F2). The plant had been given $400 million in price supports and gas guarantees. The corporation was crippled when the Reagan administration came to power, and by 1985, was slated for extinction. It began by supporting large plants that could produce 500,000 barrels of gasoline a day. But by 1985 it agreed to support only small-scale facilities that would not become wards of the state. In 1985, the House of Representatives voted to take back $7.4 of the corporation's remaining $7.9 billion.

Agencies and Issues Involved in Policy Formulation

An enormous number of congressional and administrative agencies are involved in energy policy formulation. Fourteen House committees plus twenty-four subcommittees, and ten Senate committees plus twenty-one subcommittees all have some hand in energy policy making. "The results," says energy policy expert Walter Rosenbaum, "are predictable. Congressional responses to energy problems, more often than not, are sluggish" (1981, 73). In addition, there are about fifty-two different federal executive agencies, departments, bureaus, offices, administrations, and White House offices that have some responsibilities in energy policies.

The psychology of abundance still dominates thinking about energy. There is no stable, coherent public consensus on most aspects of national energy issues. According to Rosenbaum, "the voice of the people is nothing more than a confused babble" (1981, 79). As a result, incremental solutions dominate energy policy making in Congress. The public distrusts public officials and the oil companies, partly because they receive contradictory information from them, and partly because of the documented cheating by the oil companies. For example, in April of 1977 President Carter, in a television speech, told Americans that the United States was running out of gas and oil and that it was not possible to substantially increase production. Two years later, Carter's Secretary of Energy announced that "the United States now has an extraordinary surplus of natural gas. For the next six or seven years at least . . . the government will shift its energy policy to emphasize consumption of gas" (*New York Times*, January 10, 1979, 81).

Motivated by environmental lobbies, the public, and the failure of several presidents to present a coherent plan, Congress has increased its role in energy policy formulation. Whereas the president tries—or should try—to represent a single national perspective, members of Congress represent a collection of diverse and competing local viewpoints. Congress can veto or at least paralyze energy policy if it chooses, and it more often reacts to the latest crisis rather than adjusting to long-range national goals. In between crises, public officials in Congress and the executive branch rarely formulate major energy policies without consulting the various energy bureaucracies and private groups that have a stake in a particular issue.

Among agencies, there is continuing conflict and shifting of alliances during energy policy formulation, with little consultation between Congress and the White House. Administrative agencies have their own points of view, which have evolved over the years. For example, the Federal Energy Regulatory Commission, which is responsible for promising abundant, reliable supplies of electricity, and the Environmental Protection Agency, whose legislative mandate includes control of environmental degradation, are usually in conflict.

In addition to numerous interest groups, an energetic public interest movement influences the policy process, including environmental, consumer, product safety, and technology control groups. Their influence was heightened by the passage of the 1966 Freedom of Information Act that requires government to release all but the most sensitive documents to citizens upon request. Additional influence was provided with the 1969 National Environmental Policy Act, which requires all federal agencies to produce environmental impact statements on any program with major environmental impact.

From 1973 through 1983, the impact of interest groups on environmental policy increased, changing the old private industry dominated system of subgovernments. "For the first time in its history, the U.S. was forced to think in terms of fuel trade-offs, and energy was placed on the national policy agenda . . . the structure of the existing policy organizations and processes that managed energy were obsolete and unable to deal with a fundamental change—the substitution of scarcity for abundance" (Kash & Rycroft 1985, 434). The 1973 embargo caught the United States unawares because policy formulation was done by stable semi-autonomous policy subsystems. These subsystems were comprised of industry representatives and the governmental agencies that were supposed to regulate them. The president and Congress were limited to ratifying changes about which a consensus already had developed in the policy subsystems.

The period between 1973 and 1980 saw changes in four issue areas. First, policy goals were changed. Prior to 1973, the principal goals were to achieve energy abundance at the cheapest price possible. This actually was achieved in oil and natural gas, to a large extent because of governmental subsidies and regulation. After 1973, cheapness was abandoned, and efficiency—defined as getting more output with less input—was emphasized along with cleanness and security. Second, energy sources changed. Prior to 1973, petroleum was the principal source of energy. By 1980, petroleum imports had been cut drastically, replaced by nuclear energy, coal, and the search for alternative energy sources. Third, regulations were abandoned as policy instruments. Deregulation and the "market" became the most important instruments for achieving the dual goals of conservation and increased supply. Finally, the number of

participants involved in energy policy formulation expanded exponentially. Everyone from farmers to truckers to homeowners wanted to protect their interests. Many of these interest groups dropped out by 1980, following the decision to deregulate the price of oil.

The Reagan administration disrupted these changes in policy formulation after 1980. In particular, the Reagan administration reduced the number of participants from the federal government, state governments, the private sector, and nonprofit research organizations (Kash & Rycroft 1985). Reagan sought to eliminate the Department of Energy formed under President Carter, but when Congress would not agree, he reduced the department's budget and personnel, which greatly reduced its role in implementing energy policy.

IMPLEMENTING ENERGY POLICY

According to Walter Rosenbaum, "the bureaucracy can interpret, alter, delay, promote, reevaluate, and otherwise shape much of the substance of a policy while implementing it. In effect, bureaucracy is a force separate from Congress or the president that shapes the meaning of policy" (1981, 15). As pointed out in previous chapters, Congress delegates a great deal of authority to executive agencies. For example, in Section 546 of the Energy Policy and Conservation Act of 1978, it instructs the Department of Energy to "establish and publish energy performance targets for federal buildings and [sic] take such actions as may be necessary and appropriate to promote to the maximum extent practicable achievements of such targets by federal buildings." In carrying out these instructions, the Department of Energy has written hundreds of pages of rules and regulations that in effect are laws in and of themselves.

Once Congress passes a law, legitimating a policy, the struggle for policy making shifts from Congress to administrative agencies where it continues unobserved to all but a handful of administrators. For example, Congress has delegated to the Environmental Protection Agency the power to determine which public utilities must scrub their smokestack emissions, what technology must be used, and when controls must be imposed. Under this delegation of authority, the EPA in essence has the authority to determine who will bear the cost for clean air (Rosenbaum 1981).

The Department of the Interior is another agency with substantial policymaking powers in energy. It leases federal land for coal exploration, enforces the 1977 Surface Mining Control and Reclamation Act, determines which coal reserves will be explored and mined, the amount of rent and royalties that coal companies will pay, and the regulations that govern the removal of coal. Under President Reagan, the Department of the Interior has been identified with coal companies and has been accused of giving away public lands and ignoring environmental concerns.

Traditional formulation and implementation of energy policy has been characterized by cooperation between government and producer groups, and institutionalized in administrative bureaucracies responsible for implementing sectional policies on coal, natural gas, and nuclear energy (Chubb 1983). In some cases, producer companies have been able to exert their influence on the administrative agency through participation on advisory committees. The relationship between the federal Office of Oil and Gas and the National Petroleum Council is a case in point. The council is an advisory committee dominated by the major oil companies. It is very influential in energy policy concerning the oil industry. In some cases, the government agency actively encourages, impedes, or otherwise manipulates interest group participation (Chubb 1983). According to Chubb, most interest groups focus on the implementation stage of policy making "because total net benefits controlled by the bureaucracy . . . exceed those controlled by Congress" (1983, 39). In an empirical study of hundreds of agencies and interest groups, Chubb found that 57 percent of the groups concentrated more, or at least as much, on the energy bureaucracies as on Congress. This has been the case throughout history. For example, the National Industrial Recovery Act of 1933 offered oil companies an opportunity to use government authority to end the competition inspired by a tax incentive law. Competition was extensive in the 1920s following passage of the tax incentive laws, which prompted companies to pump as much oil as they could out of a field. The rule of capture* which operated under the tax incentive laws, entitled a company to all the oil beneath its property. When the land beneath their property was next to the property of another company which also could tap into the same pool, there was an incentive to pump as much as quickly as possible. The NIRA offered a solution because its board of directors was dominated by the American Petroleum Institute.

The oil companies were not the only ones to benefit from such cozy triangles; the administrators of government agencies benefited as well. For example, the Department of the Interior had the authority to issue licenses in order for a company to import oil. "Since it paid the companies to get a license," David Davis writes, "the companies paid to get a license" (1982, 81). They did this mostly in the form of political contributions to a representative or senator who had influence within the Department of the Interior. They might also make contributions to a presidential candidate.

Another way in which administrative agencies influence policy during implementation is through delaying action. For example, bureaucratic opponents of the strategic petroleum reserve were able to delay the project for years in spite of repeated endorsements of a large reserve by Congress, two

* The *rule of capture* was first enunciated in a nineteenth-century Pennsylvania case defining the rights to natural gas. Under the rule, the owner of a well is entitled to everything that can be pumped out even if the oil flows from under a neighbor's land.

presidents, and a stream of research findings by academicians and government scientists. Stockpiling oil has been promoted as a cost-effective way to reduce United States vulnerability to another energy crisis since it would give the country a breathing spell when the next shortage hits. The drawbacks are higher prices for oil and the high cost of storage facilities. Oil companies favor this because they benefit from the higher prices that stockpiling produces.

During the battle which began in the early 1970s, the Federal Energy Administration and Department of Energy were on one side, seeking to implement a reserve, and the Office of Management and Budget (OMB) was on another side, criticizing the agencies and supporting a much smaller stockpile. Economists estimated that an optimum stockpile should be between 730 million and 1,460 million barrels. This estimate was approved in the 1975 Energy Policy and Conservation Act, which mandated 1 billion barrels. The OMB estimated that mandating 500 million barrels was more cost-effective. President Carter's chief energy adviser, James Schlesinger, pushed for the higher goal of 1 billion barrels.

In 1979, the OMB issued a study challenging the assumptions underlying the DOE analysis concerning the extent to which supplies would be disrupted by the stockpile. The DOE committed twenty staff-months and $80,000 to an analysis of the problem in 1979 (Jenkins-Smith & Weimer 1985). The OMB countered with its own analysis and cut funds out of the budget for the second 500 million barrels. At that point, DOE decided not to fight anymore. In 1980, new studies were undertaken by scientists at the Massachusetts Institute of Technology that sided with the larger stockpile. The OMB attacked the studies as being so complex and theoretical as to be of no value to policy makers. However, the OMB staffers agreed not to oppose the second 500 million barrels because they anticipated that Ronald Reagan, who had just been elected president, would support the larger reserve. By 1986, the reserve had reached 490 million barrels, costing taxpayers $16.7 billion. Mounting federal deficits in 1986 forced the government to half the reserve at 500 million barrels which represents a 100-day supply of all U.S. oil imports and a two-year supply of the 1986 level imports from the Persian Gulf.

■ EVALUATING ENERGY POLICY

The Role of Analysis in Energy Policy Making

As in all areas of policy making, policy analysis can be used either to provide information to policy makers, or to support a particular political position (Benveniste 1972). Often policy analysis is used as a combination of both. Many different agencies and groups engage in policy analysis, including courts (which must interpret laws), the mass media, organized interest groups, public officials, academic institutions, and private research groups.

In an attempt to strengthen itself vis-à-vis the executive branch in evaluating energy and other policies, Congress increased its staff in the Legislative Reorganization Act of 1970. It reshaped the Library of Congress's Legislative Reference Service into the Congressional Research Service, gave new responsibilities to the General Accounting Office (GAO), added more congressional research staff, and created the Office of Technology Assessment (1972) and the Congressional Budget Office (1974). The Congressional Research Service compiles research done by outside experts rather than conducting its own. The GAO has the largest staff (5,200 in 1986); it began in 1921 as an administrative watchdog with the function of auditing, evaluating, and financial accounting.

All of these steps greatly increased Congress's ability to obtain and process information. However, some experts question whether or not complex energy issues can be solved by analysis. For example, Dan Drefus, who served fifteen years on Senator Henry Jackson's personal and committee staff said in regard to the Clinch River breeder nuclear reactor:

> Clinch River is a good example of an emotional debate. . . . There's no more technical information available . . . and the adversaries have drawn the line in the dust. Even if the thing blew up, some people would still insist it was a good project. The technical answer doesn't matter. (Katz 1984, 234)

Many congressional staff use analysis as a way of promoting the careers of their bosses rather than for providing objective evaluations (Malbin 1980). Thus, much evaluation is used to justify decisions rather than help formulate them. Political scientist James Katz writes, "From this mass of information, much of which is ambiguous, analysts from operational agencies generally select that which legitimizes their agency's performance and allows the policy makers' perspective to be optimistic" (1984, 269). This is not necessarily bad, and in any case, it is unavoidable because, in practice, it is exceedingly difficult to distinguish between policy-relevant analysis of information and policy advocacy. Choices about data interpretation are based on normative criteria and one's values cannot be dissociated from this (Palumbo 1987). Economist Martin Greenberger agrees, "Analysis is inevitably subordinate to the very political process that provides it with raw material. It is itself a component of that process and can only work its influence through it" (1983, 256).

Sudden Shifts in Energy Policy

The election of Ronald Reagan produced a major shift in energy policy—a shift that many analysts argue is potentially dangerous because it does not provide the flexibility needed for the next crisis. Kash and Rycroft (1985) believe that the energy policy developed from 1973 to 1980 widened participation in policy making and made inroads into the iron triangles that had dominated prior to 1973. According to researchers Johnston and Kurtz (1985), national leadership shifted dramatically and virtually abandoned alternative energy research just as researchers in solar, geothermal, and wind power were beginning to make significant advances. Instead of allowing the market—that is, the laws of supply and demand—to make policy decisions, the Reagan administration initiated a return to the pre-1973 situation in which producers made policy. It changed the goals of energy policy to emphasize supply and eliminate conservation. Reagan's Secretary of Energy James Edwards reflected Reagan's position on conservation when he was quoted as saying, "The human body uses least energy when it's asleep or dead" (*Congressional Quarterly* 1982). The only area in which the federal government was seen as having a role in energy policy under Reagan was in bringing the 762 million acres of publicly-owned land into the energy marketplace. In addition, Reagan opposed alternative energy because he did not believe it was cost-efficient, and made massive cuts in the energy research and development budget.

According to Kash and Rycroft, the dominance of the commodity view of energy favored by Reagan restricts policy makers' ability to explore a full range of policy alternatives and it ignores the role of the public in energy because it shifts control to the private sector. According to the National Research Council (1984) this approach leaves people unprepared for changes in world conditions that are bound to occur. Moreover, the commodity view ignores the impact that energy has on the poor. High prices affect poor people far more than the rich. For example, families at the lower end of the income groups spend far more of their income on energy—between 14 and 30 percent—than those at the upper end who spend only 3 to 5 percent (Landsberg & Dukert 1981, 30).

On the other hand, government regulation in the past had a negative impact on energy policy. Most government policies have actually *contributed* to the energy crisis because they stimulated production and drove prices down leading consumers to treat energy as a cheap commodity. This is true of the quotas on oil in 1959, and also of the price controls on natural gas during 1954 and those on oil in 1971 (Mead 1980, 29). But it also is true that most of these policies were what the major producers themselves wanted, and all of this greatly helped the producers in the form of direct and indirect subsidies and higher profits. For example, economist Duane Chapman (1983, 48) estimates that direct federal subsidies to energy production from 1947 to 1977 amounted to $217 billion in 1977 dollars. Add to this the social costs that producers have avoided—that is, air pollution damage, automobile deaths and injuries, hazardous waste cleanup, and black lung disease—and the total subsidy to energy corporations is over $400 billion. These subsidies have not diminished; they actually have increased. In a 1985 report entitled *The Hidden Costs of Energy,* the Center for Renewable Resources, which promotes alternate energy sources, estimated that the federal subsidies to the nation's energy producers cost taxpayers $44 billion in 1984; with the largest share going to utilities. Nuclear power, for example, received $15.6 billion, or 35 percent of the total. The report states, "Perversely, subsidies support rising costs and depletable energy sources and prevent the smooth transition to a sustainable economy. The solution is to gradually phase out all energy subsidies." The next section considers some of the alternatives to the market policy of the 1980s.

Soft and Hard Energy Paths

Amory B. Lovins (1979) has characterized America's energy choices in terms of hard versus soft paths. A *hard path* means a rapid expansion in the use of coal, accelerated searches for increasingly elusive oil deposits and natural gas, and continued growth and subsidization of nuclear energy. A *soft path* would take us toward restrained production of these commodities through a deliberate effort to moderate future demand, increased reliance on solar energy and on other renewable energies, and better use of existing energy sources. It also would entail some changes in life styles—for example, less use of automobiles for transportation—and a more decentralized system of producing energy. A hard path looks upon energy primarily as a commodity whereas a soft path views it as an ecological resource and social need. The Reagan administration opted entirely for a hard path rejecting subsidies for solar or synthetic fuels and conservation.

According to Lovins, the hard path has enormous capital costs, environmental hazards, and technical uncertainties. Most damaging is that it relies on an extremely centralized producer system whose inflexibility was demonstrated several times when entire states and sections of the country experienced blackouts when a single unit in the system failed. The National Research Council study cited earlier (1984) considers this inflexibility one of the biggest dangers in existing policy. To avoid being caught unawares again by a new oil shortage—which is certain to occur—we need to broaden the range of fuels that are used for essential purposes such as transportation, manufacturing, and electricity, increase our capability for fuel switching, do more stockpiling, place greater reliance on mass transportation, and stress conservation policies that promote energy efficiency.

Instead of this, American energy policy making in the 1980s has been turned over to the market. Those in favor of this approach argue that prices will allocate energy resources to their most efficient uses as customers respond to changes in prices. The National Research Council argues against this policy:

> In particular, current policy assumes that the profit motive will encourage producers to develop and market technologies that will save users money at current energy prices and that economic motives will also spur energy users to

> purchase and use those technologies. This belief in the market persists in spite of the evidence that institutional barriers to investment in energy efficiency do not yield to clean market signals . . . and that energy users, even within their range of choice, are often less than fully responsive to price signals or to information about how they can cut energy costs. (1984, 34–35)

Energy costs are not clear to consumers because they cannot tell what their bill is for a given appliance or use, thus they cannot respond effectively to price stimuli. Moreover, there is a great deal of uncertainty about prices which further confuses rational choice. Finally, the energy producer market is not competitive; five companies account for more than 20 percent of the total American energy capital (Rosenbaum 1981). The oil companies also own large proportions of coal, natural gas, and solar energy companies.

Moreover, the social costs of the hard path are enormous. For example, improvements in technology and the use of gargantuan equipment make surface or strip mining of coal very attractive. The beneficiaries of this kind of technology are the Appalachia, Northern Plains, and American Indians (because they own much of the land on where its coal is found), as well as the railroads, who transport 80 percent of the nation's coal. The fifteen companies that account for half of the nation's total coal production, also would benefit. But the environmental hazards of strip mining are enormous. There are thousands upon thousands of ravaged and sterile acres of strip mined land in Appalachia, in addition to contaminated rivers and streams, and decapitated mountain tops and slopes. The 1977 Surface Mining Control and Reclamation Act requires mining companies to restore the land but it is questionable whether they can, even if they have the best intentions. But in fact, mining companies strongly opposed the 1977 act as an unreasonable burden on them. Moreover, the Reagan administration crippled the SMCRA during implementation. To head the Office of Surface Mining, Secretary of the Interior James Watt appointed an Indiana state senator who led the opposition to OSM in Indiana and fought mightily to have SMCRA declared unconstitutional. He failed in this effort but succeeded in just about crippling the Office of Surface Mining. In 1982, about half of the 948 staff members working in OSM were terminated or chose to resign, retire, or transfer. Between 1981 and 1985, the director of OSM was replaced six times, with three different directors in 1985 alone. The effect of this chaotic management was to allow companies to do what they wanted. Less than $1 million out of $135 million in fines owed by law-breaking coal operators was collected by OSM between 1982 to 1984. Of the 4,000 operators who were ordered to stop illegal mining, more than half ignored the orders and left the land unreclaimed after the coal was ripped out (McCarthy 1985). Journalist Coleman McCarthy reported that the attack on OSM would lead, "even by Reagan administration standards, to one of the most ill-planned and reckless schemes in modern politics" (1985).

As the country uses more coal for producing electricity, particularly bituminous coal with a high sulfur content, utilities will have to use scrubbers to remove the sulfur oxide—a yellow, acrid, highly toxic gas released by coal combustion—from their emissions. It poses a health risk to those who are exposed, and has been linked with acid rain production. And the utility industry considers scrubbers to be technologically unreliable and economically inefficient; they break down, do not operate reliably, and add about 15 to 20 percent to the bills of customers. The EPA disputes many of the utilities' claims. In addition to acid rain, such emissions contribute to the "greenhouse effect" which traps the sun's heat in the earth's atmosphere. It has been estimated that this will raise the earth's average temperature by two to three degrees by the year 2000. If it does, polar ice will melt and the ocean level will rise about fifteen feet causing flooding and damage to coastal areas.

A hard energy path also relies on nuclear energy. Since 1980, the percentage of electricity generated by nuclear power plants has increased 14 percent. However, nuclear power still faces significant problems—in particular, the safe disposal of radioactive waste. Environmental groups such as the Sierra Club, Friends of the Earth, and the Union of Concerned Scientists oppose nuclear power and have mounted court challenges that have been very

CASE 10–5 *TVA's Nuclear Problem*

In 1980, the nuclear program of the Tennessee Valley Authority (TVA) was regarded as the pace-setter for the nation. The program envisioned seventeen reactors capable of supplying 40 percent of Tennessee's electric power needs. However, in 1985, TVA was operating only two plants. Eight plants had been abandoned while under construction, three were shut down for safety reasons, and four others were delayed because of safety reasons. In addition, TVA was cited by the Nuclear Regulatory Commission (NRC) for over 1,000 violations of federal regulations. Nuclear engineers and safety officials of TVA say they have so little confidence in TVA management and the regional office of the NRC that they have gone directly to Congress about the TVA's design and construction of its plants (Labaton 1985).

Part of the reason for TVA's problems are the enormous regulatory changes that occurred after the accident at Three Mile Island. For example, the NRC now has precise requirements about safety systems that TVA has been slow in meeting. Second, TVA has not been closely monitored by the government, even though it is a federal agency. Third, the agency has suffered a management crisis as the result of losing its plant managers and operators. In part, the high turnover is a result of morale problems and retaliation costly to the industry. The nuclear industry has also endured numerous regulatory changes and some operational problems. Some of these are described in Case 10–5, regarding the Tennessee Valley Authority's nuclear program. Finally, although nuclear fuel is much cheaper than other types of fuel—about 24 cents per million BTUs as compared to $1.57 for coal, $1.78 for oil, $1.14 for natural gas—it has a higher initial cost due to the cost of constructing nuclear plants, making its total production costs much higher. The price is even higher if we consider the cost of cleaning up a nuclear accident. It cost $1 billion to clean up the Three Mile Island accident, and took about eighty workers a year and a half to complete the job.

Nuclear energy made a comeback of sorts in the 1990s. Although 32 percent of the public opposed building more nuclear power plants in 1991, 40 percent of the public believed that the United States should rely on nuclear power for most of its increased energy needs in the next 10 years (Greenwald 1991, 55). The opposition to building nuclear power plants apparently was due to the NIMBY (not-in-my-back-yard) syndrome; people felt more favorable toward nuclear energy but didn't want it built in their back yard. In addition, environmental groups that had opposed nuclear energy recognized the technology's potential because of global warming and the fact that nuclear plants emit very

---

against those who blew the whistle about safety problems. These have resulted in enormous inefficiency. For example, at one of its plants, the maintenance manuals were outdated, gaskets had rotted, electrical connections were loose, and bolts were missing.

In March of 1985, the TVA stopped all power production at its Brown's Ferry Plant to overhaul its three reactors and bring them into compliance with Federal Nuclear Regulatory Commission guidelines. To meet one NRC regulation, Browns Ferry workers tested every weld, nut, and bolt in the $1 billion plant to make sure it could withstand the shock of an earthquake.

The biggest task, however, for the TVA was finding a top-level administrator; the TVA pay limit of $72,000 was too low to attract qualified and experienced candidates. However, the TVA found a way around this problem and succeeded in hiring an administrator in 1985 who had successfully directed a nuclear plant in Washington. The administrator, William Bibb, said that the TVA was totally dedicated to giving him the time, money, and resources necessary to bring the Brown's Ferry Plant back on line (*Arizona Republic* December 26, 1985, C2). The Plant was finally brought back on line in 1991.

little carbon dioxide. In 1991, the National Academy of Sciences—an independent body that conducted a 15-month federally funded study of the greenhouse problem—called for the swift development of a new generation of nuclear plants to help fight the greenhouse effect.

The problem, however, was developing nuclear plants that are more efficient than the light-water reactors that the United States uses. There are advanced reactor systems being developed that would not burn uranium as fast as the light-water reactor, and they also are safer. But the chances are slim that any major companies will move quickly into the new technology. Billions of dollars have been lost by companies on nuclear plants that were never opened because of public opposition. For example, the Long Island Lighting Companies gave up its completed $5.5 billion Shoreham nuclear facility in 1989 after local authorities refused to approve the firm's plans for an evacuation route for nearby residents in the event of a serious accident. Disposing of nuclear waste also seems to be an insolvable problem. The federal Department of Energy concluded in 1990 that its program to dispose of nuclear waste in Nevada was a technical failure and the government was going to start over (Schneider 1991, E4).

A soft energy path avoids all of the social costs associated with the hard path. Moreover, it is compatible with a decentralized power system, unlike the highly centralized system associated with the hard path. However, critics of the soft path claim a decentralized system implies a fundamental change in the politics and economics of the western industrialized world (Lagassa 1980, 167). Soft energy is laced with tinges of anti-industrialism, anti-urbanism, and anti-technology. According to electric utility representatives, the soft path is an overly romantic vision of an impossible energy future. To be credible, the soft path proponents have to build on the idea of evolutionary change incorporating elements of the soft path gradually into the current systems for dispensing energy resources (Lagassa 1980).

Such incremental incorporation is not utopian as there already exists a well-developed technology for small scale hydroelectric power. Known as the Francis reaction-type water turbine for generating electricity, it was perfected in the latter part of the nineteenth century. By 1932, hydroelectric power supplied 41.4 percent of the total installed electric generating capacity in the United States (Brown, Plitch & Ringo 1980). Today there are thousands of existing small scale hydroelectric (SSH) dams scattered among hills and valleys that were abandoned only since 1950 as a result of the availability of cheap oil. If refurbished, it has been estimated that they could supply the equivalent of 727,000 barrels of oil a day, which is well in excess of the 300,000 to 400,000 barrels of oil a day that was the shortfall during the oil shock of 1979 (Brown, Plitch & Ringo 1980). Law professor Brown and his colleagues believe that "a sizeable proportion of these dams are presently cost-competitive with other more conventional means for generating electric power" (1980, 193). The problem is the cost of meeting the enormous number of regulations and licensing requirements that would be imposed on the development of hydroelectric dams. One example is the fish ladder requirement which would allow fish to swim past the dam. This could cost as much as one half of the construction costs of the SSH project. While this may be a legitimate cost to impose, the multitude of applicable rules affecting SSH, such as acquiring property rights in the water ways, acquiring licenses, and meeting environmental regulations, almost guarantee inefficiency. If these could be removed, then SSH could become a viable alternative energy source. The prospects for a soft path, however, are not encouraging since the United States in the 1980s has chosen a hard path, devoted to economic growth and a centralized delivery system. Alternative energy sources such as synthetic fuels, solar, or small scale hydroelectricity would take about twenty-five years to develop. Most of these things require huge federal subsidies, and in 1987, there was no indication that the United States was about to embark on such a course.

■ TERMINATING ENERGY POLICY AND PROGRAMS

Not all government energy programs are immortal. The oil depletion allowance and regulated gas prices perished in the 1970s, and the Joint Congressional Committee on Atomic Energy, once the evangelist for nuclear power, was abolished by Congress in 1977. And the changes that occurred during the 1970s—increasing the number of participants in the policy process—were halted by the Reagan administration.

It is difficult to terminate programs such as the oil depletion allowance, and it takes major political shifts to terminate the changes in the policy-making subsystem of the 1970s. To do so requires vanquishing the coalitions already arrayed in support of a program, or demonstrating that the program has failed or has dubious merits in order to overcome the reluctance of legislators and administrators. Policy making is a continuous process and no policy is ever completely finished or immutable. There often is interaction among the stages that produce changes in policies. For example, the solar energy program that was passed by Congress in November 1978 was scarcely a year old when it became apparent that tax incentives for homeowners to switch to solar heating were inadequate. Proposals were then sent to Congress to amend it before it had been implemented and assessed. Policy battles are never settled; those who lose at one stage (such as formulation) carry their fight to another stage (such as implementation), or to another time. The only constant in policy making is change and energy is no exception. Another major incident—like the oil shortage that occurred in the 1970s—could force new policy developments and perhaps even a movement in the direction of a soft energy path.

Bibliography

Aaronson, David, C. Thomas Dienes, and Michael C. Musheno. *Public Policy and Police Discretion: Processes of Decriminalization.* New York: Clark Boardman Co., Ltd., 1984.

Albritton, Robert, and Robert Brown. "Intergovernmental Impacts on Policy Variations Within States: Effects of Local Discretion on General Assistance Program," *Policy Studies Review,* Vol. 5, #3 (1986) 524–36.

Alford, Robert. *Health Care Politics.* Chicago: University of Chicago Press, 1975.

Alkin, Marvin C. "Naturalistic Study of Evaluation Utilization." In Larry Braskamp and Robert Brown, eds. *Utilization of Evaluative Information,* 19–28. San Francisco: Jossey-Bass, 1980.

Alkin, Marvin C., Richard Deillah, and Peter White. *Using Evaluations: Does Evaluation Make a Difference?* Beverly Hills, CA: Sage, 1979.

Allison, Graham J. *Essence of Decision: Explaining the Cuban Missile Crisis.* Boston: Little, Brown, 1971.

Allman, William F. "Staying Alive in the 20th Century," *Science,* October, 1985, 31–41.

Altfeld, Michael, and Gary Miller. "Sources of Bureaucratic Influence: Expertise and Agenda Control." Paper presented at the American Political Science Association Meetings, August, 1983.

Altman, Laurence K. "Dr. Clark's Death Laid to Failure of All Organs but Artificial Heart," *New York Times,* February 27, 1983, 1.

———. "Heart Patient: Progress and Treatment," *New York Times,* December 3, 1982, 1.

———. "Health Quality and Costs: A Delicate Balance," *New York Times,* March 30, 1982, 1.

Altman, Stuart H. "The Design of National Health Insurance System for the U.S." In S. Altman and Harvey M. Sapolsky, *Federal Health Programs, Problems and Prospects,* 205–33. Lexington, MA: Heath, 1981.

Altman, Stuart H., and Harvey M. Sapolsky. *Federal Health Programs, Problems and Prospects.* Lexington, MA: Heath, 1981.

Altman, Stuart H., and J.K. Williams. "Federal Involvement in the Development of Health Maintenance Organizations: Competition in the Health-Care Industries." In S.H. Altman and Harvey M. Sapolsky, *Federal Health Programs, Problems and Prospects.* Lexington, MA: Heath, 1981.

Anderson, Cathy D., James Ciarlo, and Susan Brodie. "Measuring Evaluation-Induced Change in Mental Health Program." In James A. Ciarlo, ed. *Utilizing Evaluation: Concepts and Measurement Techniques,* 97–123. Beverly Hills, CA: Sage, 1981.

Anderson, Curt. "TVA Struggling to Get Huge Alabama Nuclear Plant Back on Line," *Arizona Republic,* December 26, 1985, C-2.

Anderson, Douglas. *Regulatory Politics and Electric Utilities: A Case Study in Political Economics.* Boston: Auburn House, 1981.

Anderson, Martin. *Welfare: The Political Economy of Welfare Reform in the United States.* Stanford, CA: Hoover Institution Press, 1978.

Anderson, Ronald, and John F. Newman. "Societal and Individual Determinants of Medical Care Utilization in the United States." In S.J. Williams, ed. *Issues in Health Services.* New York: Wiley, 1980.

Anyon, Jean. "Workers, Labor and Economic History, and Textbook Content." In Michael W. Apple and Lois Weis, eds. *Ideology and Practice in Schooling.* Philadelphia: Temple University Press, 1983.

Apple, Michael W., and Lois Weis, eds. *Ideology and Practice in Schooling.* Philadelphia: Temple University Press, 1983.

Appleby, Paul. *Morality and Administration in Democratic Government.* Baton Rouge: Louisiana State Press, 1952.

Argyris, Chris. *Organization and Innovation.* Homewood, IL: Dorsey Press, 1965.

Argyris, Chris, and Roger Harrison. *Interpersonal Competence and Organization Effectiveness.* Homewood, IL: Dorsey Press, 1963.

The Arizona Republic. "Chernobyl Toll Is 19; New Blast Is Possible," May 27, 1986, E-8.

The Arizona Republic. "High Court Overturns Law Restricting Abortions," June 12, 1986, A-1.

The Arizona Republic. "King Oil's Reign Has Decades Left to Run," September 26, 1985, G-1.

The Arizona Republic. "Rising Medical Costs Linked to Surgery," November 7, 1985, C-2.

The Arizona Republic. "Synfuels Agency Picks 3 Projects for Subsidies While Funding Loss Looms," August 23, 1985, F-2.

Arrow, Kenneth J. *Social Choice and Individual Values,* 2nd ed. New York: Wiley, 1954.

Ashford, Nicholas A. *Crisis in the Workplace: Occupational Disease and Injury.* Cambridge, MA: MIT Press, 1976.

Aspin, Lee. "Why Doesn't Congress Do Something?" *Foreign Policy,* #15, Summer, 1974.

Atkinson, Graham, and Jack Cook. "Regulation: Incentives Rather Than Command and Control." In Mancur Olson, ed. *A New Approach to the Economics of Health Care,* 211–18. Washington, D.C.: American Enterprise Institute, 1982.

Attkisson, C. Clifford Jr. "The Manager as Evaluator," *New Directions for Mental Health Services,* Vol. 8 (1980) 77–90.

Attkisson, C. Clifford Jr., and Tuan D. Nguyen. "Evaluative Research and Health Policy: Utility, Issues and Trends," *Health Policy Quarterly,* Vol. 1, #1, Spring, 1981, 22–24.

Austin, Gilbert R., and Herbert Garber, eds. *The Rise and Fall of National Test Scores.* New York: Academic Press, 1981.

Axelrod, Robert. "The Emergence of Cooperation Among Egoists," *American Political Science Review,* Vol. 75, June, 1981, 306–18.

Bachrach, Peter, and Morton S. Baratz. *Power and Poverty: Theory and Practice.* New York: Oxford University Press, 1970.

Bailey, Stephen K., and Edith K. Mosher. *ESEA: The Office of Education Administers a Law.* Syracuse, NY: Syracuse University Press, 1968.

Balch, George. "The Stick, the Carrot, and Other Strategies: A Theoretical Analysis of Governmental Intervention." In John Brigham and Don A. Brown, *Policy Implementation: Penalties or Incentives?,* 43–69. Beverly Hills, CA: Sage, 1980.

Bane, Mary Jo, and David T. Ellwood. "Slipping Into and Out of Poverty: The Dynamics of Spells." Mimeo, Harvard University (August, 1982).

Banfield, Edward C. *Political Influence.* New York: Free Press, 1961.

———. *The Unheavenly City.* Boston: Little, Brown, 1968.

Baran, Paul A., and Paul M. Sweezy. *Monopoly Capital: An Essay on the American Economic and Social Order.* New York: Modern Reader, 1968.

Bardach, Eugene. *The Implementation Game: What Happens After a Bill Becomes Law.* Cambridge, MA: MIT Press, 1977.

———. "Policy Termination as a Political Process," *Policy Sciences,* Vol. 7 (1976) 123–31.

Bardach, Eugene, and Robert A. Kagan. *Going by the Book: The Problem of Regulatory Unreasonableness.* Philadelphia: Temple University Press, 1982.

Bardach, Eugene, and Lucian Publiaresi. "The Environmental Impact Statement as the Real World," *The Public Interest,* Vol. 49 (Fall, 1977) 22–38.

Bayer, Ronald, and Daniel Callahan. "Medicare Reform: Social and Ethical Perspectives," *Journal of Health Politics, Policy, and Law,* Vol. 10, #3 (Fall, 1985) 533–47.

Beatrice, Dennis F. "Licensing and Certification in Nursing Homes: Assuring Quality Care." In S.H. Altman and Harvey M. Sapolsky. *Federal Health Programs, Problems and Prospects.* Lexington, MA: Heath, 1981.

Beck, John. "New Life-Saving Technology is among Forces Pushing Cost of Health Care Out of Control," *Kansas City Times,* December 9, 1982, 1.

Bedau, Hugo Adam. *The Death Penalty in America,* 3rd ed. New York: Oxford University Press, 1982.

Benveniste, Guy. *Politics of Expertise.* Berkeley, CA: Gendessay Press, 1972.

Berman, Paul. "Thinking About Programmed and Adaptive Implementation: Matching Strategies to Situations." In Helen Ingram and Dean Mann, eds. *Why Policies Succeed or Fail.* Beverly Hills, CA: Sage, 1980.

Berry, Jeffrey. *Feeding Hungry People: Rulemaking in the Food Stamp Program.* New Brunswick, NJ: Rutgers University Press, 1984.

Best, Joel, ed. *Images of Issues; Typifying Contemporary Social Problems.* New York: Aldene de Gruyter, 1989.

Birkley, Robert H. *The Court and Public Policy.* Washington, D.C.: Congressional Quarterly Press, 1983.

Blumberg, Abraham S. *Criminal Justice.* Chicago: Quadrangle, 1967.

Bourdieu, Pierre. "Cultural Reproduction and Social Reproduction." In Richard Brown, ed. *Knowledge, Education and Cultural Change.* London: Tavistock, 1973.

Bowden, D. Lee, and John L. Palmer. "Social Policy: Challenging the Welfare State." In John L. Palmer and Isabel V. Sawhill, eds. *The Reagan Record.* Cambridge, MA: Ballinger, 1984.

Bowles, Samuel, and Herbert Gintis. *Schooling in Capitalist America: Educational Reform and the Contradictions of Economic Life.* New York: Basic Books, 1976.

Brandl, John E. "Evaluation and Politics," *Evaluation,* special issue, 1978, 6–7.

Braskamp, Larry, and Robert Brown, eds. *Utilization of Evaluation Information.* San Francisco: Jossey-Bass, 1980.

Bray, Bernard. "The Death Penalty in the American South: Power, Race and the Human Body." Paper delivered at the 1983 annual meeting of the American Political Science Association, September, 1983.

Braybrooke, David, and Charles F. Lindblom. *A Strategy of Decision: Policy Evaluation as a Social Process.* New York: Free Press, 1970.

Breneman, David W. "Where Would Tuition Tax Credits Take Us? Should We Agree to Go?" In Thomas James and Henry Levin, eds. *Public Dollars for Private Schools.* Philadelphia: Temple University Press, 1983.

Brennan, Troyen A. *Just Doctoring: Medical Ethics in the Liberal State.* Berkeley, CA: University of California Press, 1991.

Bresnick, David. *Public Organizations and Policy.* Glenview, IL: Scott, Foresman, 1982.

Brewer, Garry. *Politicians, Bureaucrats, and the Consultant.* New York: Basic Books, 1973.

Brigham, John, and Don W. Brown, eds. *Policy Implementation: Penalties or Incentives?* Beverly Hills, CA: Sage, 1980.

Brown, Jack H.U. *The High Cost of Healing: Physicians and the Health Care System.* New York: Human Sciences Press, 1985.

Brown, Peter, Laurence Plitch, and Martin Ringo. "Obstacles and Incentives to Small-Scale Hydroelectric Power." In Gregory Daneke and George Lagassa, eds. *Energy Policy and Public Administration.* Lexington, MA: Heath, 1980.

Bullock, Charles S. III, and Charles M. Lamb. *Implementation of Civil Rights Policy.* Monterey, CA: Brooks/Cole, 1983.

Bunker, Douglas R. "Policy Sciences Perspectives on Implementation Processes," *Policy Sciences,* Vol. 3, 1972, 71–80.

Burns, James M. *Leadership.* New York: Harper & Row, 1978.

Bynum, Timothy S. "Prosecutorial Discretion and the Implementation of a Legislative Mandate." In Mary Morash, ed. *Implementing Criminal Justice Policies.* Beverly Hills, CA: Sage, 1982.

Callahan, Daniel. "Health and Society." In John F. Knowles, ed. *Doing Better and Feeling Worse,* 23–24. New York: Norton, 1977.

———. *Setting Limits: Medical Goals in an Aging Society.* New York: Simon and Schuster, 1988.

Calsyn, Robert J., Louis Tornatsky, and Susan Dittmar. "Incomplete Adoption of an Innovation: The Case of Goal Attainment Scaling," *Evaluation,* Vol. 4, 1977, 127–33.

Cameron, James M. "Ideology and Policy Termination: Restructuring California's Mental Health System." In Judith May and Aaron Wildavsky, eds. *The Policy Cycle,* 301–29. Beverly Hills, CA: Sage, 1978.

Campbell, Donald. "Reforms as Experiments," *American Psychologist,* Vol. 24, 1969, 409–29.

———. "Reforms as Experiments." In Elmer L. Struening and Marcia Guttentag, eds. *Handbook of Evaluation Research,* Vol. 1, 71–100. Beverly Hills, CA: Sage, 1975.

Carlson, Norman A. "Murders of Officers at Marion Pen Call for Death Penalty," *Corrections Digest,* Vol. 14, #25, November 30, 1983.

Caro, Francis G., ed. *Readings in Evaluation Research.* New York: Russell Sage, 1976.

Caro, Robert G. *The Power Broker.* New York: Random House, 1975.

Carroll, Marjorie Smith, and Ross H. Arnett III. "Private Health Insurance Plans in 1978 and 1979: A Review of Coverage, Enrollment and Financial Experience," *Health Care Financing Review,* Vol. 3, #1, September, 1981, 55–89.

Cater, Douglas. *Power in Washington.* New York: Random House, 1964.

Catterall, James S. "Tuition Tax Credits: Issues of Equity." In Thomas James and Henry Levin, eds. *Public Dollars for Private Schools.* Philadelphia: Temple University Press, 1983.

Center for the Study of Social Policy. *Through the Briar Patch: A Case in Point.* Washington, D.C.: Center for the Study of Social Policy, September, 1984.

Chambers, Donald. "The Reagan Administration's Welfare Retrenchment Policy: Terminating Social Security Benefits for the Disabled," *Policy Studies Review,* Vol. 5, #1, November, 1985.

Chapman, Duane. *Energy Resources and Energy Corporations.* Ithaca, NY: Cornell University Press, 1983.

Chelf, Carl P. *Public Policymaking in America: Different Choices, Limited Solutions.* Glenview, IL: Scott, Foresman, 1981.

Chelf, Carl P. *Controversial Issues in Social Welfare Policies.* Newberry Park, CA: Sage, 1992.

Chelimsky, Eleanor. "Evaluation Research Credibility and the Congress." In Dennis Palumbo, Stephen Fawcett, and Paula Wright, eds. *Evaluating and Optimizing Public Policy,* 177–87. Lexington, MA: Heath, 1981.

———. "Linking Program Evaluation to User Needs." In Dennis Palumbo, ed. *The Politics of Program Evaluation.* Beverly Hills, CA: Sage, 1987.

Chen, Huey-Tsyh, and Peter H. Rossi. "The Multi-Goal Theory Driven Approach to Evaluation: A Model Linking Basic and Applied Social Science," *Social Forces,* Vol. 59, #1, 106–22.

Chubb, John E. *Interest Groups and the Bureaucracy: The Politics of Energy.* Stanford, CA: Stanford University Press, 1983.

Ciarlo, James A., ed. *Utilizing Evaluation: Concepts and Measurement Techniques.* Beverly Hills, CA: Sage, 1981.

Cingranelli, Daniel, Richard Hoffebert, and E. Ziegenhagan. "Goal Evaluation Through Implementation: The Problem for Policy Evaluation." In Dennis Palumbo, Stephen Fawcett, and Paula Wright, eds. *Evaluating and Optimizing Public Policy.* Lexington, MA: Heath, 1981.

Citizens' Board of Inquiry. *Hunger, U.S.A.* Washington, D.C.: New Community Press, 1968.

Clinard, Marshall B. *Corporate Ethics and Crime: The Role of Middle Management.* Beverly Hills, CA: Sage, 1983.

Clinard, Marshall B., and Richard Quinney. *Criminal Behavior Systems: A Typology.* New York: Holt, Rinehart & Winston, 1973.

Clymer, Adam. "For Civil Rights Bill, the Name's the Game," *New York Times,* May 5, 1991, Section 4:1, 5.

Cobb, Roger W., and Charles D. Elder. *Participation in American Politics: The Dynamics of Agenda Building,* Second Edition. Baltimore, MD: Johns Hopkins Press, 1984; 1972.

Cobb, Roger, J. Keith-Ross, and M.H. Ross. "Agenda-Building as a Comparative Political Process," *American Political Science Review,* 70, March, 1976, 126–38.

Cochran, Clarke E., Laurence C. Mayer, T.R. Carr, and N. Joseph Cayer. *American Public Policy: An Introduction,* Second Edition. New York: St. Martin's Press, 1986.

Cohen, Gaynor. "Cutting Public Expenditures, Proposition 13 in California." In David Lewis and Helen Wallace, *Policies Into Practice, National and International Case Studies in Implementation.* London: Heinemann Educational Books, 1984.

Cohen, Michael, James G. March, and J.P. Olsen. "A Garbage Can Model of Organizational Choice," *Administrative Science Quarterly,* Vol. II, 1972, 1–25.

Cohen, Sol, ed. "Noah Webster's Federal Catechism." In Sol Cohen, ed. *Education in the U.S.: A Documentary History,* 769–71. New York: Random House, 1974.

Cohn, Victor. "How Can We Fix a Broken System?" *Washington Post National Weekly Edition,* February 3–9, 1992, 6–7.

Colarulli, Guy C., and Bruce F. Berg. "Federal Legislation and Interest Formation: The Case of Imputed Interest Groups," *Policy Studies Review,* Vol. 3, #1, August, 1983, 13–22.

Coleman, James. *Equality of Educational Opportunity.* Washington, D.C.: Government Printing Office, 1966.

———. *Policy Research in the Social Services.* Morristown, NJ: General Learning Press, 1972.

Coleman, Milton. "Ohio's 'New Poor'—They Don't Fit the Old Stereotype," *The Washington Post National Weekly Edition,* April 29, 1985, 31–32.

Congressional Budget Office. *Prospects for Medicare's Hospital Insurance Trust Fund.* Washington, D.C.: Government Printing Office, 1983.

Congressional Quarterly. "Energy Issues: New Directions and Goals." Washington, D.C.: Congressional Quarterly, Inc., 1982.

Conner, Ross F. "The Evaluator-Manager Relationship: An Examination of the Sources of Conflict and a Model for a Successful Union." In Herbert C. Schulberg and Jeanette M. Jerrell, eds. *The Evaluator and Management,* 119–37. Beverly Hills, CA: Sage, 1979.

Cook, Fay L., Tom Tyler, Edward G. Goetz, Margaret T. Gordon, and David Protess. "Media and Agenda Setting: Effects on the Public, Interest Groups Leaders, Policy Makers, and Policy." Paper presented at the Annual Meeting of the Association for Public Policy and Management, 1981.

Cook, F.L. "Crime & the Elderly: The Emergence of a Policy Issue." In D.A. Lewis, ed. *Reactions to Crime,* 123–47. Beverly Hills, CA: Sage, 1981.

Cook, Thomas. "Postpositivist Critical Multiplism." In R. Lance Shotland and M.M. Mark, eds. *Social Science and Social Policy.* Beverly Hills, CA: Sage, 1985.

Coulam, Robert F., and Gary L. Gaumer. "Medicare's Prospective Payment System: A Critical Appraisal." *Health Care Financing Review,* Vol. 13, #1, Fall, 1991, 45–77.

Crandall, Robert W. "The Impossibility of Finding a Mechanism to Ration Health Care Resources Efficiently." In M. Olson, *A New Approach to the*

Economics of Health Care, 29–43. Washington, D.C.: American Enterprise Institute, 1981.

Cremin, Lawrence, ed. *The Republic and the School: Horace Mann on the Education of Free Men.* New York: Teachers College Press, 1957.

Cronbach, Lee J., et al. *Toward Reform of Program Evaluation: Aims, Methods, and Institutional Arrangements.* San Francisco: Jossey-Bass, 1980.

Cronin, Thomas E., Tania Z. Cronin, and Michael Milakovich. *U.S. v. Crime in the Streets.* Bloomington: Indiana University Press, 1981.

Crozier, Michael. *Bureaucratic Phenomenon.* Chicago: University of Chicago Press, 1967.

Culver, John H. "The Politics of Capital Punishment in California." In Stuart Nagel, Erika Fairchild, and Anthony Chamnpaign, eds. *The Political Science of Criminal Justice.* Springfield, IL: Thomas, 1983.

Curry, George E. "Pistols and Politics," *Chicago Tribune,* April 13, 1986, 5-1.

Cyert, Richard M., and James G. March. *Behavioral Theory of the Firm.* Englewood Cliffs, NJ: Prentice-Hall, 1963.

Danzinger, J.N. "California's Proposition 13 and the Fiscal Limitation's Movement in the United States," *Political Studies,* Vol. 27, #4, 1980, 599–612.

Davis, David H. *Energy Politics,* 3rd ed. New York: St. Martin's Press, 1982.

Davis, Kenneth C. *Administrative Law,* 3rd ed. St. Paul: West, 1972.

Delbecq, Andre L., and Sandrae L. Gill. "Political Decision-Making and Program Development." In Robert F. Rich, ed. *Translating Evaluation into Policy,* 23–46. Beverly Hills, CA: Sage, 1979.

de Leon, Peter. "Policy Evaluation and Program Termination," *Policy Studies Review,* Vol. 2, #4, May, 1983, 631–48.

de Leon, Peter, and Gary D. Brewer. *The Foundation of Policy Analysis.* Homewood, IL: Dorsey Press, 1983.

Denzin, Norman K. *The Research Act,* 2nd ed. New York: McGraw-Hill, 1978.

DeParle, Jason. "Why Marginal Changes Don't Rescue the Welfare System," *New York Times,* March 1, 1993, E3.

Derthick, Martha. *Policymaking for Social Security.* Washington, D.C.: Brookings Institution, 1979.

Dery, David. *Problem Definition in Policy Analysis.* Lawrence: University of Kansas Press, 1984.

Dewar, Helen. "Is 'The World's' Greatest Deliberative Body Over the Hill?" *The Washington Post National Weekly Edition,* December 10, 1984, 12–13.

Diamond, Irene. "The Development of Family Planning in the American Welfare State." Paper delivered at the Western Political Science Association Meetings, March, 1985.

Dolbeare, Kenneth, and Patricia Dolbeare. *American Ideologies: The Competing Political Beliefs of the 1970s,* 2nd ed. Chicago: Rand McNally, 1973.

Downs, Anthony. *Inside Bureaucracy.* Boston: Little, Brown, 1967.

Downs, Anthony. "Up & Down with Ecology: The Issue Attention Cycle," *The Public Interest,* 28, 1972, 38–50.

Dror, Yehezkel. *Policymaking Under Adversity.* New Brunswick, NJ: Transaction Books, 1984.

Dubnick, Melvin J., and Barbara A. Bardes. *Thinking About Public Policy: A Problem Solving Approach.* New York: Wiley, 1983.

Dunn, William. *Public Policy Analysis: An Introduction.* Englewood Cliffs, NJ: Prentice-Hall, 1981.

Dunsire, Andrew. *Implementation in a Bureaucracy.* New York: St. Martin's Press, 1979.

Easton, David. *A Framework for Political Analysis.* Englewood Cliffs, NJ: Prentice-Hall, 1965.

———. *A Systems Analysis of Political Life.* Chicago: University of Chicago Press, 1965.

Easton, David, and Robert Hess. "Youth and the Political System." In S.M. Lipset and Leo Lowenthal, eds. *Culture and Social Characters.* Glencoe, IL: Free Press, 1961.

Eckland, Bruce. "College Entrance Examination Trends." In Gilbert R. Austin and Herbert Garber, eds. *The Rise and Fall of National Test Scores.* New York: Academic Press, 1982.

Edgmon, T.D. "Organizing for Energy Policy and Administration." In *New Dimensions to Energy Policy,* 81–92. Lexington, MA: Heath, 1979.

Edleman, Murray. *The Symbolic Uses of Politics.* Urbana: University of Illinois Press, 1964.

Edwards, George C. III. *Implementing Public Policy.* Washington, D.C.: Congressional Quarterly Press, 1980.

Edwards, George C., and Ira Sharkansky. *The Policy Predicament: Making and Implementing Public Policy.* San Francisco: Freeman, 1978.

Ehrman, Lee. "The American Schools in the Political Socialization Process," *Review of Education Research,* Vol. 50, Spring, 1980, 99–119.

Eisenberg, B.A., and J.R. Cantwell. "Policies to Influence the Spatial Distribution of Physicians: A Conceptual Review of Selected Programs and Empirical Evidence," *Medical Care,* Vol. 14, June, 1976, 455–68.

Eisenstadt, Abraham S., Ari Hoogenboon, and Hans L. Trefousse, eds. *Before Watergate: Problems of Corruption in American Society.* New York: Brooklyn College Press, 1979.

Elazar, Daniel. *The American Partnership.* Chicago: University of Chicago Press, 1962.

Elmore, Richard. "Backward Mapping: Using Implementation Analysis to Structure Political Decisions," *Political Science Quarterly,* Vol. 94, #4, Winter, 1979–80, 601–16.

———. "Follow Through Planned Variation." In *Program Implementation.* New York: Academic Press, 1976.

———. "Organizational Models of Social Program Implementation," *Public Policy,* Vol. 26, #2, Spring, 1978, 185–228.

Encarnation, Dennis J. "Public Finance and Regulation of Nonpublic Education." In Thomas James and Henry Levin, eds. *Public Dollars for Private Schools.* Philadelphia: Temple University Press, 1983.

Englander, Valerie, and Fred Englander. "Workfare in New Jersey: A Five Year Assessment," *Policy Studies Review,* Vol. 5, #1, August, 1985.

Entereine, Peter F., Vera Salter, Allison D. McDonald, and J. Corbett McDonald. "The Distribution of Medical Services Before and After 'Free' Medical Care—The Quebec Experience." In S.J. Williams, ed. *Issues in Health Services,* 205–14. New York: Wiley, 1980.

Enthoven, Alain C. "A Brief Outline of the Competition Strategy for Health Services Delivery System Reform." In M. Olson. *A New Approach to the Economics of Health Care,* 421–40. Washington, D.C.: American Enterprise Institute, 1981.

———. "Supply-Side Economics of Health Care and Consumer Choice Health Plan." In M. Olson. *A New Approach to the Economics of Health Care,* 467–89. Washington, D.C.: American Enterprise Institute, 1981.

Eulau, Heinz, and Kenneth Prewitt. *Labyrinths of Democracy: Adaptations, Linkages, Representation, and Policies of Urban Politics.* Irvington, IN: Bobbs-Merrill, 1973.

Evans, John. "Headstart: Comments on Criticisms." In Francis G. Caro, ed. *Readings in Evaluation Research,* 401–407. New York: Sage, 1971.

Everhart, Robert B., ed. *The Public School Monopoly: A Critical Analysis of Education and the State in American Society.* Cambridge, MA: Ballinger, 1982.

Evins, Joe L. *Understanding Congress.* New York: Potter, 1963.

Eyestone, Robert. *From Social Issues to Public Policy.* New York: Wiley, 1978.

Farr, Roger, and Leo Fay. "Reading Trend Data in the U.S.: A Mandate for Caveats and Caution." In Gilbert R. Austin and Herbert Garber, eds. *The Rise and Fall of National Test Scores.* New York: Academic Press, 1982.

Feeley, Malcolm. "Two Models of the Criminal Justice System: An Organizational Perspective," *Law and Society Review,* Vol. 7, 1973, 407–25.

Fenno, Richard F. Jr. *Home Style: House Members in Their Districts.* Boston: Little, Brown, 1978.

Fishkin, James S. *Justice, Equal Opportunity and the Family.* New Haven, CT: Yale University Press, 1983.

Fiske, Edward B. "Efforts at Changing Schools in U.S. Entering New Phase," *New York Times,* April 27, 1986, 19.

———. "Minority Enrollment in Colleges is Declining," *New York Times,* October 27, 1985, 1.

———. "Ranks of Minority Teachers are Dwindling, Experts Fear," *New York Times,* February 9, 1986, 14.

———. "States Gain Wider Influence on School Policy," *New York Times,* December 2, 1984, 18.

Fleming, Roy B. "Searching for Process Theories of Bureaucratic Innovation," *Urban Affairs Quarterly,* Vol. 16, #2, December, 1980, 245–54.

Fralick, James. "Rx for Treatment of Hyper Health-Care Costs," *Across the Board,* 64–69.

Frederickson, H. George. "The Lineage of the New Public Administration." In Carl J. Bellone, ed. *Organization Theory and the New Public Administration,* 33–51. Boston: Allyn and Bacon, 1980.

Gallup, George. "The 13th Annual Gallup Poll of the Public's Attitudes Toward the Public Schools," *Phi Delta Kappan,* Vol. 65, 1983.

Garber, Herbert, and Gilbert R. Austin. "Learning, Schooling, Scores: A Continuing Controversy." In Gilbert R. Austin and Herbert Garber, eds. *The Rise and Fall of National Test Scores.* New York: Academic Press, 1982.

Garfinkel, Irwin. "It's Time to Replace Welfare," *New York Times,* January 3, 1980, 19.

Gates, Bruce. "Some Implications of Statistical Analysis for Normative Theory in Public Administration." In Carl J. Bellone, ed. *Organization Theory and the New Public Administration,* 80–105. Boston: Allyn and Bacon, 1980.

Geisel, M.S., R. Roll, and R.S. Wettick. "The Effectiveness of State and Local Regulation of Handguns: A Statistical Analysis," *Duke University Law Journal,* Vol. 4, 1969, 647–76.

Gerth, H.H., and C. Wright Mills, eds. *From Max Weber: Essays in Sociology.* New York: Oxford University Press, 1949.

Gibson, Robert M., Katharine R. Levit, Helen Lazenby, and Daniel R. Waldo. "National Health Expenditures, 1983," *Health Care Financing Review,* Vol. 6, #2, Winter, 1984, 1–29.

Gibson, Robert M., and Daniel R. Waldo. "National Health Expenditures, 1980," *Health Care Financing Review,* Vol. 3, #1, September, 1981.

Gilbert, G. Ronald, ed. *Making and Managing Policy; Formulation, Analysis, Evaluation.* New York: Marcel Dekker, Inc., 1984.

Gilbert, Neil. *Capitalism and the Welfare State: Dilemmas of Social Benevolence.* New Haven, CT: Yale University Press, 1983.

Gladwell, Malcolm. "HMOs: Destined to Succeed in Spite of Themselves," *Washington Post National Weekly Edition,* Aug. 29–Sept. 4, 1988, 22–23.

Godzins, Morton. "Centralization and Decentralization in the American Federal System." In Robert Goldwin, ed. *A Nation of States.* Chicago: Rand McNally, 1963.

Goggin, Malcolm L. "Health Politics, Priorities, and Politics: Two Decades of Experience." Paper delivered at the 1983 annual meeting of the American Political Science Association, September 1–4, 1983.

Gohagan, John K. *Quantitative Analysis for Public Policy.* New York: McGraw-Hill, 1980.

Goldwater, Barry. "Congress Must Stop Letting the Tail Wag the Dog," *The Arizona Republic,* January 6, 1985, C-1, 2.

Goodin, Robert E. *Political Theory and Public Policy.* Chicago: University of Chicago Press, 1982.

Goodman, Michael. "Partners in Conflict: Implementing Public-Private Employment and Training Programs." Paper presented at the American Political Science Association, August, 1984.

Goodwin, L. "Do Work Requirements Accomplish Anything? The Case Against Work Requirements," *Public Welfare,* Vol. 16, 1978, 39–45.

Gorecki, Jan. *Capital Punishment: Criminal Law and Social Evolution.* New York: Columbia University Press, 1983.

Graham, John D., Max Henrion, and M. Granger Morgan. "An Analysis of Federal Policy Toward Automobile Safety Belts and Air Bags," Department of Engineering and Public Policy, Carnegie-Mellon University, 1981.

Grau, C.W. "The Limits of Planned Change in Courts," *Justice System,* Vol. 6, Spring, 1981, 84–99.

Greenberger, Martin. *Caught Unawares: The Energy Decade in Retrospect.* Cambridge, MA: Ballinger, 1983.

Greenstein, Fred I. "Change and Continuity in the Modern Presidency." In Anthony King, ed. *The New American Political System.* Washington, D.C.: American Enterprise Institute, 1978.

Grier, Peter. "Lobbying in Washington," *The Christian Science Monitor,* December 6, 1984, 32–33.

Guba, Egon G., and Yvonna S. Lincoln. *Effective Evaluations: Improving the Usefulness of Evaluation Results Through Responsive and Naturalistic Approaches.* San Francisco: Jossey-Bass, 1981.

Guillemin, Jeanne. "The Price of Medical Heroes," *Society,* Vol. 16, #2, January/February, 1982, 31–38.

Gusfield, Joseph. *The Culture of Public Problems.* Berkeley, CA: University of California Press, 1981.

Ham, Christopher, and Michael Hill. *The Policy Process in the Modern Capitalist State.* New York: St. Martin's Press, 1984.

Hamilton, Alexander, John Jay, and James Madison. *The Federalist.* New York: Modern Library, 1787.

Hanlon, John J., and George E. Pickett. *Public Health: Administration and Practice,* 7th ed. St. Louis, MO: Mosby, 1979.

Harden, B. "Oil and Timber Firms Battle Environmentalists for Forest," *Washington Post,* May 27, 1985, 1.

Hargrove, Erwin C. "The Bureaucratic Politics of Evaluation: A Case Study of the Department of Labor," *Public Administration Review,* Vol. 40, March, 1980, 150–59.

———. *The Missing Link: The Study of the Implementation of Social Policy.* Washington, D.C.: The Urban Institute, 1976.

Harrington, Michael. *The Other America.* New York: Penguin Books, 1962; 1981.

Harris, Joseph P. *Congressional Control of Administration.* Washington, D.C.: Brookings, 1964; 1980.

Harris, Louis. "Majority of Parents Report School Busing Has Been a SatitMsfactory Experience," *Chicago Tribune,* March 26, 1981.

Hechinger, Fred M. "Role of School Boards is Questioned," *New York Times,* May 13, 1986.

Heclo, Hugh. "Issue Networks and the Executive Establishment." In Anthony King, ed. *The New American Political System.* Washington, D.C.: The American Enterprise Institute, 1978.

———. "Review Article: Policy Analysis," *British Journal of Political Science,* Vol. 2, 1973.

Heinz, Anne, Herbert Jacob, and Robert Lineberry, eds. *Crime in City Politics.* New York: Longman, 1983.

Heiss, F. William. "The Politics of Local Government Policy Evaluation: Some Observations," *Urban Analysis,* Vol. 5, 1974, 37–45.

Henry, Gary T., and Walter Smiley. *Legislative Program Evaluation in the States: The Edge that Cuts.* Paper presented at the Midwest Political Science Association Meetings, April 15–17, 1981.

Herbers, John. "Hunger in the U.S. is Widening: Study of 'New Poor' Reports," *New York Times,* April 20, 1986, 1, 17.

Hess, Robert, and Judith Torney. *The Development of Basic Attitudes and Values Toward Government and Citizenship During the Elementary School Years.* Chicago: University of Chicago Press, 1965.

Hill, Martha, et al. "Final Report of the Project: 'Motivation and Economic Mobility of the Poor': Part I, Intergenerational and Short-Run Dynamic Analyses." Mimeo. Ann Arbor: University of Michigan, Survey Research Center, August 1983.

Hillsman, Roger. *The Politics of Policymaking in Defense and Foreign Affairs.* New York: Harper & Row, 1971.

Hochbaum, Martin, and Florence Galkin. "Discharge Planning: No Deposit, No Return," *Society,* Vol. 19, #3, January/February, 1982, 58–61.

Hogan, John C. *The Schools, the Courts, and the Public Interest,* 2nd ed. Lexington, MA: Lexington Books, 1985.

Hogwood, Brian, and Guy Peters. *Policy Dynamics.* New York: St. Martin's Press, 1983.

Hollingshead, August B. *Elmtown's Youth and Elmtown Revisited.* New York: Wiley, 1949; 1975.

Hummel, Ralph P. *The Bureaucratic Experience,* 2nd ed. New York: St. Martin's Press, 1982.

Hunter, Floyd. *Community Power Structure: A Study of Decision Makers.* Chapel Hill: University of North Carolina Press, 1953.

Ingram, Helen M., and Dean E. Mann, eds. *Why Policies Succeed or Fail.* Beverly Hills, CA: Sage, 1980.

Institute of Program Evaluation. *Evaluation Activities of the Program Evaluation and Methodology Division.* Washington, D.C.: U.S. General Accounting Office, 1982.

Institute for Research on Poverty. "Antipoverty Policy: Past and Future," *Focus,* Vol. 8, #2, Summer, 1985.

Institute for Research on Poverty. "Poverty in the United States: Where Do We Stand Now?," *Focus,* Vol. 7, #1, Winter, 1984.

Jacob, Herbert. *The Frustration of Policy: Responses to Crime by American Cities.* Boston: Little, Brown, 1984.

Jacobs, Jane. *Death and Life of Great American Cities.* New York: Random House, 1965.

James, Thomas. "Questions About Educational Choice: An Argument from History." In Thomas James and Henry Levin, eds. *Public Dollars for Private Schools.* Philadelphia: Temple University Press, 1983.

James, Thomas, and Henry Levin, eds. *Public Dollars for Private Schools: The Case of Tuition Tax Credits.* Philadelphia: Temple University Press, 1983.

Jaskow, Paul. "Alternative Regulatory Mechanism for Controlling Hospital Costs." In Mancur Olson. *A New Approach to the Economics of Health Care,* 219–57. Washington, D.C.: American Enterprise Institute, 1981.

Jencks, C., M. Smith, H. Acland, M. Bane, D. Cohen, H. Gintis, B. Heyns, and S. Michelson. *Inequality: A Reassessment of the Effects of Family and Schooling in America.* New York: Basic Books, 1972.

Jenkins-Smith, Hank C., and David L. Weimer. "Analysis as Retrograde Action: The Case of the Strategic Petroleum Reserve," *Public Administration Review,* Vol. 45, #4, July/May, 1985, 485–95.

Jensen, Donald N. "Constitutional and Legal Implications of Tuition Tax Credits." In Thomas James and Henry Levin, eds. *Public Dollars for Private Schools.* Philadelphia: Temple University Press, 1983.

Jessop, Bob. *The Capitalist State.* New York: New York University Press, 1982.

Jick, Todd D. "Mixing Qualitative and Quantitative Methods: Triangulation in Action," *Administrative Science Quarterly,* Vol. 24, #4, 1979, 602–11.

Johnston, Van Robert, and Maxine Kurtz. "Business, Government, and Energy Policy: Controlling the Ideological Pendulum for the Future," *Policy Studies Review,* Vol. 5, #1, August, 1985, 75–81.

Josephy, Alvin M. Jr. *On the Hill: A History of the American Congress.* New York: Simon & Schuster, 1975.

Kagay, Michael R. "Fear of AIDS Has Altered Behavior, Poll Shows," *New York Times,* June 18, 1991, 138.

Kahn, Alfred E. "Health Care Economics: Paths to Structural Reform." In M. Olson. *A New Approach to the Economics of Health Care,* 493–502. Washington, D.C.: American Enterprise Institute, 1981.

Kane, Robert L., and R.A. Kane. "Care of the Aged: Old Problems in Need of New Solutions." In S.J. Williams, ed. *Issues in Health Services,* 3–17. New York: Wiley, 1980.

Kansas City Times. "Artificial Heart Patient Takes First Steps . . . ," December 23, 1982, A-4.

Kansas City Times. "Fraud Battle in Medicaid Called Failure," March 27, 1984, E-4.

Kansas City Times. "Recipient of Artificial Heart Urges Doctor to Continue Work on Device," December 22, 1982, A-5.

Kansas City Times. "Study Says Requiring Patients to Pay More May Hurt Health Care," November 4, 1982, A-16.

Kash, Don E., and Robert Rycroft. "Energy Policy: How Failure Was Snatched from the Jaws of Success," *Policy Studies Review,* Vol. 4, #3, February, 1985, 433–45.

———. *U.S. Energy Policy, Crisis and Complacency.* Norman: University of Oklahoma Press, 1984.

Katz, James E. *Congress and National Energy Policy.* New Brunswick, NJ: Transaction Books, 1984.

———. "U.S. Energy Policy: Impact of the Reagan Administration," *Energy Policy,* Vol. 12, #2 (1984) 133–45.

Katz, Michael B., ed. *Poverty and Policy in American History.* New York: Academic Press, 1983.

Katz, Nick. *Let Them Eat Promises.* Garden City, NY: Anchor Books, 1971.

Kaufman, Herbert. "Fear of Bureaucracy: A Raging Pandemic," *Public Administration Review,* January/February, 1981, 3–15.

Kern, Montague. "The Variables Which Affect Agenda Setting through the Media: Kennedy, the Press, Public Opinion and the Politicians." Paper delivered at the annual meeting of the American Political Science Association, 1981.

Kerns, Doris. *Lyndon Johnson and the American Dream.* New York: Harper & Row, 1976.

Kettl, David. "Can the Cities Be Trusted? The Community Development Experience." In James Anderson, ed. *Cases in Public Policy-Making,* 2nd ed. New York: Holt, Rinehart & Winston, 1982.

King, Anthony, ed. *The New American Political System.* Washington, D.C.: American Enterprise Institute, 1978.

Kingdon, John W. *Agendas, Alternatives, and Public Policy.* Boston: Little, Brown, 1984.

Kiresuk, Thomas J., and Lander H. Lund. "Program Evaluation and Utilization Analysis." In Robert Perloff. *Evaluator Interventions: Pros and Cons,* 71–102. Beverly Hills, CA: Sage, 1979.

Knize, Perri. "The Mismanagement of the National Forests," *The Atlantic Monthly,* October, 1991, 98–110.

Knowles, John H. "The Hospital." In S.J. Williams, ed. *Issues in Health Services,* 3–17. New York: Wiley, 1980.

Koerner, James D. *Who Controls American Education? A Guide for Laymen.* Boston: Beacon, 1968.

Kress, Guenther, Gustan Koehler, and J. Fred Springer. "Policy Drift: An Evaluation of the California Business Enterprise Program." In Dennis Palumbo and Marvin Harder, eds. *Implementing Public Policy,* 19–29. Lexington, MA: Heath, 1981.

Krizay, John. "Medicine and the Market Place," *Society,* Vol. 19, #2, January/February, 1982, 46–51.

Labaton, Stephen. "TVA's Costly Program Riddled with Problems," *The Arizona Republic,* September 1, 1985.

Lagassa, George. "Implementing the Soft Path in a Hard World: Decentralization and the Problems of Electric Power Grids." In Gregory Daneke and George K. Lagassa, eds. *Energy Policy and Public Administration.* Lexington, MA: Heath, 1980.

La Jeunesse, William. "Welfare Moms Trapped in State 'Safety Net'," *The Arizona Republic,* April 28, 1985.

Landau, Martin, and Russell Stout. "To Manage Is Not to Control: Or the Folly of Type II Errors," *Public Administration Review,* March/April, 1979, 148–56.

Landsberg, Hans H., and Joseph M. Dukert. *High Energy Costs—Uneven, Unfair, Unavoidable?* Baltimore: Johns Hopkins Press, 1981.

Lang, Eric L. "To Do Well on the S.A.T., It Helps to Be an Only Child," *New York Times,* February 16, 1986.

Larsen, Judith K. "Knowledge Utilization: What Is It?," *Knowledge: Creation, Diffusion, Evaluation,* Vol. 1, #3, 1980 421–42.

Larsen, Judith K., and Paul Weiner. "Measuring Utilization of Mental Health Program Consultation." In James A. Ciarlo, ed. *Utilizing Evaluation: Concepts and Measurement Techniques,* 77–96. Beverly Hills, CA: Sage, 1981.

Lasswell, Harold. *Politics: Who Gets What, When, How?* New York: McGraw Hill, 1936.

Legge, Jerome S. Jr., and Larry Webb. "'Publicity' as a Problem in the Internal Validity of Time-Series Quasi-Experiments," *Policy Studies Review,* Vol. 2, #2, November, 1982, 293–300.

Leithwood, Kenneth A., and Deborah J. Montgomery. "Evaluating Program Implementation," *Evaluation Review,* Vol. 4, #2, April, 1980, 193–214.

Lessinger, Leon. *Every Kid a Winner: Accountability in Education.* New York: Simon & Schuster, 1970.

Levin, Henry. "Educational Choice and the Pains of Democracy." In Thomas James and Henry Levin, eds. *Public Dollars for Private Schools,* 17–39. Philadelphia: Temple University Press, 1983.

Levin, Martin, and Barbara Ferman. *The Political Hand, Policy Implementation and Youth Employment Programs.* New York: Pergamon Press, 1985.

Levine, James P. "The Ineffectiveness of Adding Police to Prevent Crime," *Public Policy,* Vol. 23, #4, 1975, 523–45.

———. "Jury Toughness: The Impact of Conservatism on Criminal Court Verdicts," *Crime and Delinquency,* Vol. 29, #1, January, 1983, 71–88.

Levine, James P., Michael Musheno, and Dennis Palumbo. *Criminal Justice in America: The Law in Action.* New York: Wiley, 1986.

Levitan, Sar A. *Programs in Aid of the Poor,* 5th ed. Baltimore, MD: Johns Hopkins Press, 1985.

Lewis, Davis, and Helen Wallace, eds. *Policies into Practice.* London: Heinemann, 1984.

Lewis, Eugene. *Public Entrepreneurship: Toward a Theory of Bureaucratic Political Power.* Bloomington: University of Indiana Press, 1984.

Light, Paul Charles. *The President's Agenda: Domestic Policy Choice from Kennedy to Carter with Notes on Ronald Reagan.* Baltimore: Johns Hopkins Press, 1982.

Lilley, William, and James Miller. "The New Social Regulation," *The Public Interest,* Spring, 1977.

Lincoln, Yvonna, ed. *Organization Theory and Inquiry: The Paradigm Revolution.* Beverly Hills, CA: Sage, 1986.

Lindblom, Charles F. *Policy Making Process,* 2nd ed. Englewood Cliffs, NJ: Prentice-Hall, 1980.

———. "The Science of Muddling Through," *Public Administration Review,* Vol. 19, Spring, 1959, 79–88.

Lindsey, Robert. "Santa Barbara to Vote Strengthening Pacts on Oil Drilling," *New York Times,* October 27, 1985, 14.

———. "Integration Plan Disputed in California," *New York Times,* October 13, 1985, 19.

Linsky, Martin. *Impact: How the Press Affects Federal Policymaking.* New York: W.W. Norton & Co., 1986.

Lipsky, Michael. *Street Level Bureaucracy: Dilemmas of the Individual in Public Services.* New York: Russell Sage, 1980.

———. "Toward a Theory of Street-Level Bureaucracy." In Willis D. Hawley, et al. *Theoretical Perspectives on Urban Politics.* Englewood Cliffs, NJ: Prentice-Hall, 1976.

Loeb, Steven. "Medicaid—A Survey of Indicators and Issues." In A.D. Spiegel, ed. *The Medical Experience.* Germantown, MD: Aspen Systems Corporation, 1979.

Los Angeles Times. "Moscow Pays Chernobyl Disaster Victims $1.12 Billion," December, 1986.

Lovins, Amory B. *Soft Energy Paths: Toward a Durable Peace.* New York: Harper & Row, 1979.

Lowi, Ted J. "American Business, Public Policy, Case Studies, and Political Theory," *World Politics,* Vol. 16, 1964, 677–715.

Lowi, Theodore. "Four Systems of Policy, Politics, and Choice," *Public Administration Review,* Vol. 32, July/August, 1972, 298–310.

Lowinger, Thomas C. *Energy Policy in an Era of Limits.* New York: Praeger, 1983.

Luft, Harold. "How Do Health Maintenance Organizations Achieve Their Savings?" *New England Journal of Medicine,* Vol. 298, #24, June 15, 1978, 1337–348.

Luker, Kristin. *Abortion and the Politics of Motherhood.* Berkeley: University of California Press, 1984.

MacAvoy, Paul W. *Regulated Industries.* New York: Norton, 1979.

MacRae, Duncan, and James Wilde. *Policy Analysis for Public Decision.* North Scituate, MA: Duxbury Press, 1979.

Magnum, Garth. *Testimony Before the Senate Subcommittee on Employment and Productivity and House Subcommittee on Employment Opportunities. Examination of the Job Training Program.* 97th Congress, 2d Session. Washington, D.C.: U.S. Government Printing Office, March 15–16, 1982.

Mahard, Rita E., and Robert L. Crain. "Research on Minority Achievement in Desegregated Schools." In Christine H. Rossell and Willis D. Hawley. *The Consequences of School Desegregation.* Philadelphia: Temple University Press, 1983.

Majone, Giandomenico. *Evidence, Argument, & Persuasion in the Policy Process.* New Haven: Yale University Press, 1989.

Majone, Giandomenico, and Aaron Wildavsky. "Implementation as Evaluation." In Jeffrey Pressman and Aaron Wildavsky. *Implementation,* 3rd ed. Berkeley: University of California Press, 1984.

Malbin, Michael J. *Unelected Representatives: A New Role for Congressional Staffs.* New York: Basic Books, 1980.

March, James G., and Herbert A. Simon. *Organizations.* New York: Wiley, 1958.

Marcus, Alfred A. *Promise and Performance: Choosing and Implementing an Environmental Policy.* Westport, CT: Greenwood Press, 1980.

Mariano, Ann. "Does Reagan Want to Kill Housing Aid?," *Washington Post National Weekly Edition,* December 9, 1985, 10–11.

Marmor, Theodore R. *Political Analysis and American Medical Care.* Cambridge, MA: Cambridge University Press, 1983.

———. *The Politics of Medicare.* New York: Aldine Publishing, 1973.

Marmor, Theodore R., and Jon B. Christenson. *Health Care Policy: A Political Economy Approach.* Beverly Hills, CA: Sage, 1982.

Martinson, Robert, Douglas Lipson, and Judith Welks. *The Effectiveness of Correctional Treatment: A Survey of Treatment Evaluations Studies.* New York: Praeger, 1975.

Maynard-Moody, Steven. *The Decision to Place the Elderly in Nursing Homes.* Lawrence, KS: Center for Public Affairs, University of Kansas, 1982.

Mayo, Elton. *The Human Problems of Industrial Civilization.* Boston: Harvard Business School, 1933.

Mazmanian, Daniel A., and Paul A. Sabatier. *Implementation and Public Policy.* Glenview, IL: Scott, Foresman, 1983.

McCarthy, Coleman. "Strip Mining: Milissa Smiddy Leading Confrontation with Appalachia's Most Ruthless Forces," *The Arizona Republic,* November 13, 1985, A-21.

McClure, Walter. *Reducing Excess Hospital Capacity.* U.S. Department of Commerce, Washington, D.C.: Government Printing Office, 1976.

McDonald, Forrest. *INSULL.* Chicago: University of Chicago Press, 1962.

McKenna, Christopher K. *Quantitative Methods for Public Decision Making.* New York: McGraw-Hill, 1980.

McKinlay, John B., ed. *Politics and Health Care.* Cambridge, MA: MIT Press, 1981.

McKinlay, John B., and Sonja M. McKinlay. "The Questionable Contribution of Medical Measures to the Decline of Mortality in the United States in the Twentieth Century." In Stephen J. Williams, ed. *Issues in Health Services,* 3–17. New York: Wiley, 1980.

McLaughlin, Milbrey. "Implementation as Mutual Adaptation." In Walter Williams and Richard Elmore, eds. *Social Program Implementation.* New York: Academic Press, 1976.

Mead, Laurence M. "Health Policy: The Need for Governance." In E.F. Paul and P.A. Russo, Jr., eds. *Public Policy: Issues, Analysis and Ideology,* 165–85. New Jersey: Catham House Publishers, 1982.

Mead, Walter J. "The Performance of Government in Energy Regulations." In Gregory Daneke and George Lagassa, eds. *Energy Policy and Public Administration,* 29–35. Lexington, MA: Heath, 1980.

Mechanic, David. "Approaches to Controlling the Costs of Medical Care: Short Range and Long Range Alternatives," *New England Journal of Medicine,* Vol. 298, February 2, 1978, 249–54.

———. *The Growth of Bureaucratic Medicine.* New York: Wiley, 1976.

Meier, Kenneth J. *Politics and the Bureaucracy: Policy Making in the Fourth Branch of Government.* North Scituate, MA: Duxbury Press, 1979.

Meltsner, Arnold J., and Christopher Bellavita. *The Policy Organization.* Beverly Hills, CA: Sage, 1983.

Menzel, Paul T. *Strong Medicine: The Ethical Rationing of Health Care.* New York: Oxford University Press, 1990.

Miller, Gary J. *Cities by Contract: The Politics of Municipal Incorporation.* Cambridge, MA: MIT Press, 1981.

Miller, James C. III, and Bruce Yandle, eds. *Benefit-Cost Analyses of Social Regulation.* Washington, D.C.: American Enterprise Institute for Public Policy Research, 1979.

Mills, C. Wright. *Power Elite.* New York: Oxford, 1956.

Milward, H. Brinton. "Policy Entrepreneurship and Bureaucratic Demand Creation." In Helen Ingram and Dean Mann, eds. *Why Policies Succeed or Fail.* Beverly Hills, CA: Sage, 1980.

Milward, H. Brinton, and Ron Francisco. "Subsystem Politics and Corporatism in the U.S.," *Policy and Politics,* Vol. 11, #3, 1983.

Milward, H. Brinton, and Wendy Laird. "Where Does Policy Come From?" In B. Guy Peters and Bert Rockman, eds. *The Discipline of Public Administration.* Chatham, NJ: Chatham House, 1991.

Montjoy, Robert S., and Laurence J. O'Toole, Jr. "Toward a Theory of Policy Implementation: An Organizational Perspective," *Public Administration Review,* Vol. 39, #5, Sept/Oct, 1979, 465–76.

Morash, Merry, ed. *Implementing Criminal Justice Policies: Common Problems and their Sources.* Beverly Hills, CA: Sage, 1982.

Morris, Richard B., and William Greenleaf. *U.S.A.: The History of a Nation.* Chicago: Rand McNally, 1969.

Moynihan, Daniel P. "Welfare Reform's 1971–72 Defeat, A Historic Loss," *Journal of the Institute for Socioeconomic Studies,* Vol. 6, Spring, 1981, 8.

Mudinger, Mary. "Health Service Funding Cuts and the Declining Health of the Poor," *New England Journal of Medicine,* July 4, 1985, 44–47.

Muller, Carol Blue. "The Social and Political Consequences of Increased Public Support for Private Schools." In Thomas James and Henry Levin, eds. *Public Dollars for Private Schools.* Philadelphia: Temple University Press, 1983.

Munnell, Alicia. "Paying for the Medicare Program," *Journal of Health Politics, Policy and Law,* Vol. 10, #3, Fall, 1985, 489–511.

Murray, Charles. *Losing Ground: American Social Policy, 1950–1980.* New York: Basic Books, 1984.

Murray, D.R. "Handguns, Gun Control Laws, and Firearms Violence," *Social Problems,* Vol. 23, 1975, 81–93.

Musheno, Michael. "On the Hazards of Selecting Intervention Points: Time Series Analysis of Mandated Policies." In Dennis Palumbo and Marvin Harder, eds. *Implementing Public Policy.* Lexington, MA: Heath, 1981.

Musheno, Michael, Dennis Palumbo, and James Levine. "Evaluating Alternatives in Criminal Justice: A Policy Impact Model," *Crime and Delinquency,* Vol. 22, July, 1976, 265–83.

Nachmias, David. "The Role of Evaluation in Public Policy." In Dennis Palumbo, Stephen Fawcett, and Paula Wright, eds. *Evaluating and Optimizing Public Policy.* Lexington, MA: Heath, 1981.

Nachmias, David, and David H. Rosenbloom. *Bureaucratic Culture: Citizens and Administrators in Israel.* New York: St. Martin's Press, 1978.

Nagel, Stuart. "What is Efficiency in Policy Evaluation?" In Dennis Palumbo, Stephen Fawcett, and Paula Wright, eds. *Evaluating and Optimizing Public Policy,* 71–107. Lexington, MA: Heath, 1981.

Nakamura, Robert T., and Frank Smallwood. *The Politics of Policy Implementation.* New York: St. Martin's Press, 1980.

Nardulli, Peter. *The Courtroom Elite: An Organizational Perspective on Criminal Justice.* Cambridge, MA: Ballinger, 1978.

Nathan, Richard. "Food Stamps and Welfare Reform," *Policy Analysis,* Winter, 1976.

National Center for Education Statistics. *Digest of Education Statistics, 1981.* Washington, D.C.: Government Printing Office, 1981.

National Commission on Excellence in Education. *A Nation at Risk.* Washington, D.C.: Government Printing Office, 1983.

National Research Council. *Energy Use: The Human Dimension.* New York: Freeman, 1984.

Nelson, Barbara J. *Making an Issue of Child Abuse: Political Agenda Setting for Social Problems.* Chicago: University of Chicago Press, 1984.

Nelson, Richard R. *The Moon and the Ghetto.* New York: Norton, 1977.

The New York Times. "Inching Ahead on Cancer," December 2, 1984, E7.

The New York Times. "Many Health Gains Recorded in 1982," January 2, 1983, 124.

Newhouse, Joseph P., Charles E. Phelps, and William B. Schwartz. "Policy Options and the Impact of National Health Insurance." In S.J. Williams, ed. *Issues in Health Services,* 174–203. New York: Wiley, 1980.

Newman, Diana L., Robert Brown, and Larry Braskamp. "Communication Theory and the Utilization of Evaluation." In Larry Braskamp and Robert Brown, eds. *Utilization of Evaluative Information.* San Francisco: Jossey-Bass, 1980.

Newsweek. "The Big Business of Medicine," October 31, 1983, 62–66.

Newsweek. "Busing: The Next Phase," November 17, 1986, 60.

Nieman, Max. "The Virtues of Heavy-Handedness in Government." In John Brigham and Don Brown, eds. *Policy Implementation: Penalties or Incentives?,* 19–43. Beverly Hills, CA: Sage, 1980.

Nienstedt, Barbara. "The Use of Mandatory Sentencing Legislation as Symbolic Statements," *Policy Studies Review,* Vol. 5, #4, August, 1986.

O'Connor, James. "The Fiscal Crisis of the State, Part I," *Socialist Revolution,* Jan/Feb, 1970.

O'Connor, Richard. *The Oil Barons. Men of Greed and Grandeur,* 262–63. Boston: Little, Brown, 1971.

Oleszek, Walter. *Congressional Procedures and the Policy Process.* Washington, D.C.: Congressional Quarterly Press, 2nd ed., 1984.

Orren, Gary. "Thinking About the Press & Government." In Martin Linsky. *Impact: How the Press Affects Federal Policymaking.* New York: W.W. Norton & Co., 1986.

Olson, Mancur, ed. *A New Approach to the Economics of Health Care.* Washington, D.C.: American Enterprise Institute, 1981.

Olson, Mancur Jr. *Logic of Collective Action: Public Goods and the Theory of Groups.* Cambridge: Harvard University Press, 1971.

Olson, Paul. *A View of Power: Four Essays on the National Assessment of Educational Progress.* Grand Forks: University of North Dakota, 1976.

Ostrom, Vincent. *The Intellectual Crisis in American Public Administration.* University: University of Alabama Press, 1974.

O'Toole, Lawrence J., and Robert J. Montjoy. "Interorganizational Policy Implementation: A Theoretical Perspective," *Public Administration Review,* Vol. 44, #6, 491–504.

Page, Benjamin I. *Who Gets What From Government?* Berkeley: University of California Press, 1983.

Palumbo, Dennis. *Evaluating Implementation: Key Issues in Comparative Analysis.* Paper delivered at the International Political Science Association Meeting, Paris, France, July, 1985.

———. "The States and the Conduct of American Foreign Relations." In Daniel Elazar, R. Bruce Carroll, E. Lester Levine, and Douglas St. Angels, eds. *Cooperation and Conflict.* Itasca, IL: F.E. Peacock, 1969.

———. *The Politics of Program Evaluation.* Beverly Hills, CA: Sage, 1987.

Palumbo, Dennis, and Calista, Donald. *Implementation and the Policy Process: Opening Up the Black Box.* Westport, CT, 1990.

Palumbo, Dennis, Stephen Fawcett, and Paula Wright, eds. *Evaluating and Optimizing Public Policy.* Lexington, MA: Lexington Books, 1981.

Palumbo, Dennis J., and Marvin A. Harder. *Implementing Public Policy.* Lexington, MA: Heath, 1981.

Palumbo, Dennis, Steven Maynard-Moody, and Paula Wright. "Measuring Degrees of Successful Implementation: Achieving Policy Versus Statutory Goals," *Evaluation Review,* Vol. 8, #1, February, 1984, 45–74.

Palumbo, Dennis, and Michael Musheno. *New Methodological Perspectives on Process Evaluation.* Paper delivered at the Western Political Science Association, April, 1984.

Palumbo, Dennis, Michael Musheno, and Steven Maynard-Moody. "Public Sector Entrepreneurs: The Doers and Shakers of Program Innovation." In Joseph Wholey, Mark Abrahamson, and Christopher Bellavita, eds. *Creating Excellence: The Role of Evaluators and Managers.* Lexington, MA: Lexington Books, 1985.

———. *An Evaluation of the Implementation of Community Corrections in Oregon, Colorado and Connecticut.* Final Report. National Institute of Justice Grant #82-15-CV-K015, Tempe, AZ, June, 1985.

Palumbo, Dennis, and David Nachmias. "The Preconditions for Successful Evaluation: Is There an Ideal Paradigm?" In Ross Coner, David Altman, and Christine Jackson, eds. *Evaluation Studies Review Annual,* Vol. 9. Beverly Hills, CA: Sage, 1984.

Palumbo, Dennis, and Elaine Sharp. "Process Versus Impact Evaluation of Community Corrections." In David Nachmias, ed. *The Practice of Policy Evaluation.* New York: St. Martin's Press, 1980.

Palumbo, Dennis, and Paula Wright. "Decision Making and Evaluation Research." In Dennis Palumbo, Stephen Fawcett, and Paula Wright, eds. *Evaluating and Optimizing Public Policy.* Lexington, MA: Heath, 1981.

———. *Standing the Utilization Question on Its Head: Utilization of Evaluation Research and the Decision Making Process.* Paper presented at the Midwest Political Science Association Meetings, April 15–18, 1981.

Paris, David C., and James F. Reynolds. *The Logic of Policy Inquiry.* New York: Longman, 1983.

Patton, Michael Q. *Qualitative Evaluation Methods.* Beverly Hills, CA: Sage, 1980.

———. "Evaluation of Program Implementation." In Lee Sechrest, S.G. West, M.A. Phillips, R. Ridner, and William Yearton, eds. *Evaluation Studies Review Annual,* Vol. 4, Beverly Hills, CA: Sage, 1979.

———. *Utilization-Focused Evaluation.* Beverly Hills, CA: Sage, 1978.

Pear, Robert. "1981 Spending for Health Care is Up by 15.1%," *The New York Times,* July 27, 1982, 1.

———. "Government Seeks New Cost Control on Medicare Plan." *New York Times,* June 6, 1991, 1.

Perloff, Robert. "Evaluator Intervention: The Case For and Against." In Robert Perloff, ed. *Evaluator Interventions: Pros and Cons,* 103–17. Beverly Hills, CA: Sage, 1979.

Perrow, Charles. *Complex Organizations: A Critical Essay.* Glenview, IL: Scott, Foresman, 1972.

———. "Demystifying Organization." In R. Sarri and Y. Hasenfield, eds. *The Management of Health Services,* 105–20. New York: Columbia University Press, 1978.

Peters, B. Guy. *The Politics of Bureaucracy: A Comparative Analysis.* New York: Longman, 1983.

Peters, B. Guy, and Brian Hogwood. "In Search of the Issue Attention Cycle," *The Journal of Politics,* 47, 1985, 238–53.

Peters, Charles. "From Ouagabougou to Cape Canaveral: Why Bad News Doesn't Travel Up," *The Washington Monthly,* Vol. 18, #5, April, 1986.

Petchesky, Rosalind P. "Factual Images: The Power of Visual Culture in the Politics of Reproduction." In Michelle Stamworth, ed. *Reproductive Technologies; Gender Motherhood & Medicine,* 57–81. Minneapolis: University of Minnesota Press, 1987.

Pettus, Beryl. "OSHA Inspection Costs, Compliance Costs, and Other Outcomes: The First Decade," *Policy Studies Review,* Vol. 1, #3, February, 1982, 596–614.

Pincus, John. "Incentives for Innovation in the Public School." In Walter Williams and Richard Elmore, eds. *Social Program Implementation.* New York: Academic Press, 1976.

Pincus, Walter. "A Tough Arms Control Team," *Washington Post National Weekly Edition,* October 7, 1985, 6.

Pontell, Henry N. *A Capacity to Punish: The Ecology of Crime and Punishment.* Bloomington: Indiana University Press, 1984.

Pressman, Jeffrey, and Aaron Wildavsky. *Implementation,* 3rd exp. ed. Berkeley: University of California Press, 1984.

Presthus, Robert. *The Organizational Society,* 2nd ed. New York: St. Martin's Press, 1978.

Price, David E. "Policy Making in Congressional Committees," *American Political Science Review,* Vol. 72, June, 1978.

Prottas, Jeffrey. *People Processing.* Cambridge, MA: MIT Press, 1980.

———. *People Processing: The Street-Level Bureaucrat in Public Service Bureaucracies.* Lexington, MA: Lexington Books, 1979.

Ranney, Austin, ed. *Essays on the Behavioral Study of Politics.* Urbana: University of Illinois Press, 1962.

Raspberry, William. "Results, Workfare Works!" *The Arizona Republic,* December 31, 1986, A-13.

———. "Will the Underclass Be Abandoned?" *The Washington Post Weekly Edition,* April 29, 1985, 8.

Reagan, Michael. *Curing the Crises; Options For America's Healthcare.* Boulder: Westview Press, 1992.

Rein, Mildred. "Work in Welfare," *Social Science Review,* Vol. 57, 1982, 212–32.

Reinhold, Robert. "Competition Held Key to Lower Medical Costs," *New York Times,* April 1, 1982.

———. "Majority in Survey on Health Care are Open to Changes to Cut Costs," *New York Times,* March 29, 1982, 1.

Reiss, Albert J. Jr. "Discretionary Justice." In D. Glaser, ed. *Handbook of Criminology.* Chicago: Rand McNally, 1974.

Relman, Arnold. "Is Rationing Inevitable?" *New England Journal of Medicine,* Vol. 322, June 21, 1990, 1808–1816.

Rhodes, Steven E. *Valuing Life: Public Policy Dilemmas.* Boulder, CO: Westview Press, 1980.

Rich, Robert. "Problem Solving and Evaluation Research: Unemployment Insurance Policy." In Robert F. Rich, ed. *Translating Evaluation Into Policy,* 87–110. Beverly Hills, CA: Sage, 1979.

———. *Translating Evaluation Into Policy.* Beverly Hills, CA: Sage, 1979.

Rich, Spencer. "Hospitals May Gripe, But They're Making More Under Medicare," *Washington Post National Weekly Edition,* December 9, 1985, 32.

———. "Growing Up in Poverty," *The Washington Post National Weekly Edition,* June 10, 1985, 33.

———. "The Bottom Line on Organ Transplants," *Washington Post National Weekly Edition,* Sept. 30–Oct. 6, 1991, 7.

———. "If Your Illness Doesn't Kill You, the Paperwork Might," *Washington Post National Weekly Edition,* June 8–14, 1992, 20.

Ripley, Randall B., and Grace A. Franklin. *Bureaucracy and Policy Implementation.* Homewood, IL: Dorsey Press, 1982.

———. *Congress, the Bureaucracy, and Public Policy.* Homewood, IL: Dorsey Press, 1976; 1984.

Rivlin, Alice M. *Systematic Thinking for Social Action.* Washington, D.C.: Brookings Institution, 1971.

Roberts, Steven V. "Dole Ready to Gamble as Budget Realities Clash with Reagan Vows," *The Arizona Republic,* January 10, 1985, A-4.

Robertson, David Brian. "Program Implementation Versus Program Design: Which Accounts for Policy 'Failure'," *Policy Studies Review,* Vol. 3, #3–4, May, 1984, 391–406.

Robinowitz, Francine, Jeffrey Pressman, and Martin Rein. "Guidelines: A Plethora of Farms, Authors, and Functions." In James Tropman, M. Dluhy, and R. Lind, eds. *New Perspectives on Social Policy.* New York: Pergamon Press, 1981.

Romer, Thomas, and Howard Rosenthal. "Political Resource Allocation, Controlled Agendas, and the Status Quo," *Public Choice,* Vol. 33, 1978, 27–44.

Rosenbaum, Walter. *Energy, Politics and Public Policy.* Washington, D.C.: Congressional Quarterly Press, 1981.

Rosengren, William R. *Sociology of Medicine: Diversity, Conflict and Change.* New York: Harper & Row, 1980.

Ross, H. Laurence. *Deterring the Drinking Driver: Legal Policy and Social Control.* Lexington, MA: Lexington Books, 1982.

Rossell, C.H. "Desegregation Plans, Racial Isolation, White Flight, and Community Response." In Christine H. Rossell and Willis D. Hawley, eds. *The Consequences of School Desegregation.* Philadelphia: Temple University Press, 1983.

Rossell, C.H., and W.D. Hawley. "Introduction: Desegregation and Change." In Christine H. Rossell and Willis D. Hawley, eds. *The Consequences of School Desegregation.* Philadelphia: Temple University Press, 1983.

———, eds. *The Consequences of School Desegregation.* Philadelphia: Temple University Press, 1983.

Rossi, Peter H., and Richard Berk. "An Overview of Evaluation Strategies and Procedures," *Human Organization,* Vol. 40, #4, 1981.

Rossi, Peter H., and Walter Williams, eds. *Evaluating Social Programs: Theory, Practice, and Politics.* New York: Academic Press, 1972.

Rossi, Peter, and James D. Wright. "Social Science Research and the Politics of Gun Control." In R. Lance Shotland and M.M. Mark, eds. *Social Science and Social Policy.* Beverly Hills, CA: Sage, 1985.

Rothman, David. *Politics and Power: The United States Senate, 1869–1901.* Cambridge, MA: Harvard University Press, 1966.

Rourke, Frances E. *Bureaucracy, Politics and Public Policy.* Boston: Little, Brown, 1969.

Rubin, Eva R. *Abortion, Politics, and the Courts: Roe vs. Wade and Its Aftermath.* Westport, CT: Greenwood Press, 1982.

Ruby, Gloria, H. David Banta, and A.K. Burns. "Medicare Coverage, Medicare Costs, and Medical Technology," *Journal of Health Politics, Policy and Law,* Vol. 10, #1, Spring, 1985, 141–55.

Ruttman, Leonard. *Planning Useful Evaluations: Evaluability Assessment.* Beverly Hills, CA: Sage, 1980.

———, ed. *Evaluation Research Methods: A Basic Guide.* Beverly Hills, CA: Sage, 1977.

Sabatier, Paul, and Daniel Mazmanian. "The Conditions of Effective Implementation: A Guide to Accomplishing Policy Objectives," *Policy Analysis,* Vol. 5, #4, Fall, 1979, 481–504.

Salamon, Lester. "Rethinking Public Management: Third-Party Government and the Changing Forms of Government Action," *Public Policy*, Vol. 29, #3, 1981, 255–75.

Salisbury, Robert, and Kenneth A. Shepsle. "U.S. Congressmen as Enterprise," *Legislative Studies Quarterly*, Vol. 6, November, 1981, 559–76.

Salmans, Sandra. "Critics Say Lack of Incentives Hurts Insurers' Efforts to Curb Medical Costs," *The New York Times*, March 31, 1982, 1.

Sanera, Michael, and Stuart M. Butter. *Mandate for Leadership II: Continuing the Conservative Revolution.* Heritage Foundation, 1984.

Savas, E.S. "Policy Analysis for Local Government: Public vs. Private Refuse Collection," *Policy Analysis*, Vol. 3, 1977, 49–74.

Saward, Ernest, and Andrew Sorenson. "The Current Emphasis on Preventive Medicine." In S.J. Williams, ed. *Issues in Health Services*, 3–17. New York: Wiley, 1980.

Schick, Allen. *Congress and Money: Budgeting, Spending and Taxing.* Washington, D.C.: The Urban Institute, 1980.

Schlesinger, Arthur M. Jr. *The Coming of the New Deal.* Boston: Houghton, Mifflin, 1959.

Schulberg, Herbert C., and Jeanette Jerrell. "Promises and Pitfalls in the Evaluator's and Manager's Pursuit of Organizational Effectiveness." In Herbert C. Schulberg and Jeanette Jerrell, eds. *The Evaluator and Management*, 7–19. Beverly Hills, CA: Sage, 1979.

Schultze, Charles. *The Politics and Economics of Public Spending.* Washington, D.C.: Brookings, 1968.

Schwartz, John. *America's Hidden Success: A Reassessment of Twenty Years of Public Policy.* New York: Norton, 1983.

Science. "The Artificial Heart: Can It Save Lives?", June, 1986, 10.

Scriven, Michael. "Pros and Cons About Goal-Free Evaluation," *Evaluation Comment*, Vol. 3, 1972, 1–4.

Scriven, Michael, and R.M. Bessone, eds. *Proceedings: Second National Conference on Testing.* New York: Center for Advanced Study in Education, CUNY, 1978.

Seidman, Lawrence S. "Consumer Choice Health Plan and the Patient Cost-Sharing Strategy: Can They Be Reconciled?" In M. Olson. *A New Approach to the Economics of Health Care*, 450–66. Washington, D.C.: American Enterprise Institute, 1981.

Seper, Jerry, Richard Robertson, William La Jeunesse, and Venita Hawthorne. "Health System Changing to Ruin," *The Arizona Republic*, May 29, 1983, A-10.

Sexton, Patricia. *Education and Income.* New York: Viking, 1961; 1976.

Sherraden, Michael. *Assets and the Poor: A New American Welfare Policy.* Armonk: M.E. Sharpe, Inc., 1991.

Shotland, R. Lance, and Melvin M. Mark. *Social Science and Social Policy.* Beverly Hills, CA: Sage, 1985.

Shribman, David. "Calculating the Odds on Accurate Risk Assessment," *New York Times*, January 2, 1983, E-9.

Shull, Steven A. *Domestic Policy Formation: Presidential-Congressional Partnership?* Westport, CT: Greenwood Press, 1983.

Simon, Herbert A. *Administrative Behavior.* New York: Macmillan, 1947; 1976.

———. *Models of Man.* New York: Wiley, 1957.

Sitter, Albert. "Not Enough Criminals Are Jailed, Corbin Contends in Crime Study," *The Arizona Republic*, March 19, 1986, B-3.

Skogan, Wesley G., and William R. Klecka. *The Fear of Crime.* The American Political Science Association, October, 1976.

Skogan, Wesley G., and Michael G. Maxfield. *Coping with Crime: Individual and Neighborhood Reactions.* Beverly Hills, CA: Sage, 1981.

Snortum, John. "Controlling the Alcohol-Impaired Driver in Scandinavia and the United States: Simple Deterrence and Beyond," *Journal of Criminal Justice*, Vol. 12, No. 2, 1984, 131–48.

———. "Alcohol-Impaired Driving in Norway and Sweden: Another Look at the Scandinavian Myth," *Law and Policy*, Vol. 6, January, 1984, 5–37.

Sorenson, Theodore. *Kennedy.* New York: Doubleday Paperback Edition, 1966.

Specter, Michael. "Unhealthy Care for the Poor," *Washington Post National Weekly Edition*, July 15–21, 1991, 9–10.

———. "Assault with a Deadly PAC," *Washington Post National Weekly Edition*, August 12–18, 1991, 14.

———. "Searching for the Best Medical Care Money Can't Buy," *Washington Post National Weekly Edition*, December 25–31, 1989, 31.

Spiegel, Allen D., ed. *The Medicaid Experience.* Germantown, MD: Aspen Systems, 1979.

Spitzer, Robert J. *The Presidency and Public Policy: The Four Arenas of Presidential Power.* University of Alabama Press, 1983.

Spring, Joel. *American Education: Introduction to Social and Political Aspects*, 3rd ed. New York: Longman, 1985.

———. "The Evolving Political Structure of American Schooling." In Robert B. Everhart, ed. *The Public School Monopoly: A Critical Analysis of Education and the State in American Society.* Cambridge, MA: Ballinger, 1982.

Sproull, Lee, and Patrick Larkey. "Managerial Behavior and Evaluator Effectiveness." In Herbert C. Schulberg and Jeanette M. Jerrell, eds. *The Evaluator and Management*, 89–105. Beverly Hills, CA: Sage, 1979.

Stake, Robert. "Program Evaluation: Particularly Responsive Evaluations," unpublished manuscript, 1974.

———, ed. *Evaluating the Arts in Education: A Responsive Approach.* Columbus, OH: Merrill, 1975.

Starr, Paul. *The Social Transformation of American Medicine.* New York: Basic Books, 1983.

Steiner, George Y. *The Children's Cause.* New York: Brookings, 1976.

Steinwald, Bruce, and Frank A. Sloan. "Regulatory Approaches to Hospital Cost Containment: A Synthesis of Empirical Evidence." In M. Olson, *A New Approach to the Economics of Health Care,* 274–308. Washington, D.C.: American Enterprise Institute, 1981.

Stevens, William F., and Louis G. Tornatsky. "The Dissemination of Evaluations, An Experiment," *Evaluation Review,* Vol. 4, #3 (June, 1980) 339–54.

Stevens, William K. "High Medical Costs Under Attack as Drain on the Nation's Economy," *New York Times,* March 28, 1982, 1.

Stevenson, John. "Assessing Evaluation Utilization in Human Service Agencies." In James A. Ciarlo, ed. *Utilizing Evaluation: Concepts and Measurement Techniques,* 35–57. Beverly Hills, CA: Sage, 1981.

Stobaugh, Robert, and Daniel Yergin, eds. *Energy Future,* 2nd ed. New York: Random House, 1982.

Stockman, David. Statement Before the U.S. House of Representatives Ways and Means Committee, Subcommittees on Oversight and on Public Assistance and Unemployment Compensation. Washington, D.C., November 3, 1983, 5.

Stokey, Edith, and Richard Zeckhauser. *A Primer for Policy Analysis.* New York: Norton, 1978.

Stone, Christopher D. *Where the Law Ends: Social Control of Corporate Behavior.* New York: Harper & Row, 1976.

Stone, Clarence. "The Implementation of Social Programs: Two Perspectives," *Journal of Social Issues,* Vol. 36, #4 (1980) 13–34.

Stone, Laurence, ed. *Schooling and Society: Studies in the History of Education.* Baltimore: Johns Hopkins Press, 1976.

Stoner, Floyd. "Federal Auditors as Regulators: The Case of Title I of ESEA." In J. May and A. Wildavsky, eds. *The Policy Cycle,* 199–214. Beverly Hills, CA: Sage, 1978.

Stout, Russell Jr. *Management or Control? The Organizational Challenge.* Bloomington: University of Indiana Press, 1980.

Strike, Kenneth A. *Educational Policy and the Just Society.* Chicago: University of Illinois Press, 1982.

Studer, Sharon. "Evaluative Need Assessments: Can They Make Evaluation Work (Can Anything Make Evaluation Work?)," *The Bureaucrat,* Vol. 9, #4 (Winter, 1980–81) 14–21.

Stufflebeam, Daniel, and William Webster. "An Analysis of Alternative Approaches to Evaluation." In Howard Freeman and Marian Soloman, eds. *Evaluation Studies Review Annual,* Vol. 6. Beverly Hills, CA: Sage, 1981.

Sullivan, Joseph F. "Kean Sticks by Plan for Tougher Test," *New York Times,* March 2, 1986, E-9.

Sundquist, James L. *The Decline and Resurgence of Congress.* Washington, D.C.: Brookings, 1981.

Tarbell, Ida M. *The History of the Standard Oil Company* (2 volumes). New York: McClure, Phillips, 1904; abr. ed. 1969.

Tatalovich, Raymond, et al. *The Politics of Abortion: A Study of Community Conflict in Public Policy Making.* New York: Praeger, 1981.

Taylor, Paul. "Remember the Generation Gap? We Ain't Seen Nothin' Yet," *Washington Post National Weekly Edition,* January 20, 1986, 23.

Thernstrom, Abigail. "Hobson's Choice," *The New Republic,* July 15–22, 1991, 13–16.

Thomas, Lewis. *The Lives of a Cell: Notes of a Biology Watcher.* New York: Viking Press, 1974.

Thomas, Norman C. *Education in National Politics.* New York: McKay, 1975.

Thompson, Frank J. *Health Policy and the Bureaucracy: Politics and Implementation.* Cambridge, MA: MIT Press, 1981.

Titmuss, Richard M. *Commitment to Welfare.* New York: Pantheon Books, 1968; 1976.

Tittle, Charles R. "Can Social Science Answer Questions About Deterrence for Policy Use?" In R. Lance Shotland and M.M. Mark, eds. *Social Science and Social Policy.* Beverly Hills, CA: Sage, 1985.

———. "Crime Rates and Legal Sanctions," *Social Problems,* Vol. 16 (1969) 409–23.

Tolchin, Susan. "Air Bags and Regulatory Delay," *Issues in Science and Technology,* Vol. 1, #1, 1984, 66–82.

Truman, Harry S. *The Truman Administration: Its Principles and Practice.* Greenwood, 1956; 1969.

Tucker, Harvey J., and L. Harmon Ziegler. *Professionals Versus the Public: Attitudes, Communication, and Response.* New York: Longman, 1980.

Tullock, Gordon. *The Politics of Bureaucracy.* Washington, D.C.: Public Affairs Press, 1964.

Tyack, David B. "The Perils of Pluralism: The Background of the Pierce Case," *The American Historical Review,* Vol. 74, 1968, 74–98.

Tyler, Ralph. "The U.S. vs. The World: A Comparison of Educational Performance," *Phi Delta Kappan,* January, 1981.

United Press International. "Alternate-Energy Group Says Federal Subsidies to Utilities Should Stop," *The Arizona Republic,* October 20, 1985, E-10.

U.S. Department of Energy. *The National Energy Plan* (#5-0008). Washington, D.C.: U.S. Department of Energy, July, 1981.

U.S. Department of Justice, Bureau of Justice Statistics. *Police Employment and Expenditure Trends,* 20. Washington, D.C.: Government Printing Office, February, 1986.

U.S. General Accounting Office. *CETA Demonstration Provides Lessons on Implementing Youth Employment Programs.* Washington, D.C.: Government Printing Office, December, 1980.

U.S. News & World Report. "Cancer Survival Data Show Little Progress," April 19, 1986, 94.

U.S. News & World Report. "The New World of Health Care," April 14, 1986, 60–63.

U.S. News & World Report. "No Pass, No Teach," March 24, 1986, 8.

U.S. News & World Report. "Social Security at 50 Faces New Crossroads," August 12, 1985.

U.S. News & World Report. "Wealth in Congress: Where It's At," June 2, 1980, 55.

Valenti, Jack. "The President As Political Leader." In Kenneth W. Thompson, ed. *The Virginia Papers on the Presidency* (Vol. 4), 1–29. Lanham, MD: University Press, 1980.

Van Den Haage, Ernest, and John P. Conrad. *The Death Penalty: A Debate.* New York: Plenum Press, 1983.

Van Horn, Carl, and Donald S. Van Meter. "The Implementation of Intergovernmental Policy." In Stuart Nagel, ed. *Policy Studies Review Annual,* Vol. 1. Beverly Hills, CA: Sage, 1977.

Victor, K. April 14, *National Journal,* "Helping the Haves," p. 901.

Vroom, Victor H. *Some Personality Determinants of the Effects of Participation.* Englewood Cliffs, NJ: Prentice-Hall, 1960.

Waldo, C. Dwight. *Administrative State.* New York: Ronald Press, 1948.

Waldo, Daniel. *Health Care Financing Trends,* Vol. 3, #1, June, 1982.

Walker, Jack. "Setting the Agenda in the U.S. Senate: A Theory of Problem Selection," *British Journal of Political Science,* 7, October, 1977, 430–41.

———. "The Diffusion of Knowledge, Policy Communities and Agenda Setting: The Relationship of Knowledge and Power." In J. Tropman, Milan Dluhy, and R. Lind. *New Strategic Perspectives on Social Policy,* 75–96. New York: Pergamon Press, 1981.

Wallinga, David. "Artificial-Heart Program Drains Health Resources," *The Arizona Republic,* February 2, 1989, C6.

Waxman, Chaim I. *The Stigma of Poverty: A Critique of Policy Theory and Policies.* New York: Pergamon Press, 1983.

Weatherly, Richard. *Reforming Special Education.* Cambridge, MA: MIT Press, 1979.

Weatherly, Richard, and Michael Lipsky. "Street-Level Bureaucrats and Institutional Innovation: Implementing Special Education Reform," *Harvard Education Review,* Vol. 47, #2, May, 1977, 171–97.

Weber, Max. "Bureaucracy." In Hans Gerth and G. Wright Mills, eds. *From Max Weber: Essays in Sociology.* New York: Oxford University Press, 1949.

Weick, Karl E. "Educational Organizations as Loosely-Coupled Systems," *Administrative Science Quarterly,* Vol. 21, 1976, 1–9.

Weiner, Stephen M. "Paying for Hospital Services Under Medicare: Can We Control Hospital Costs?" In Stuart Altman and Harvey M. Sapolsky. *Federal Health Programs, Problems and Prospects,* 135–51. Lexington, MA: Heath, 1981.

Weiss, Carol H. *Evaluation Research: Methods of Assessing Program Effectiveness.* Englewood Cliffs, NJ: Prentice-Hall, 1972.

———. "Knowledge Creep and Decision Accretion," *Knowledge: Creation, Diffusion, Utilization,* Vol. 1, #3, March, 1980, 381–404.

———. "Measuring the Use of Evaluation." In James A. Ciarlo, ed. *Utilizing Evaluation, Concepts and Measurement Techniques*, 17–33. Beverly Hills, CA: Sage, 1981.

———. "Where Political and Evaluation Research Meet." In Dennis Palumbo, ed. *The Politics of Evaluation.* Beverly Hills, CA: Sage, 1986.

Weiss, Carol H., and Michael J. Bucuvalas. *Social Science Research and Decision Making.* New York: Columbia University Press, 1980.

Welsh, Patrick. Quoted on the "MacNeil/Lehrer News Hour," transcript no. 2775, May 16, 1986.

Whitaker, Gordon P. "Coproduction: Citizen Participation in Service Delivery," *Public Administration Review,* Vol. 40, #3, May/June, 1980, 240–46.

White, Sam, John E. Dittrich, and James Long. "The Effects of Group Decision-Making Process and Problem Situation Complexity on Implementation Attempts," *Administrative Science Quarterly,* Vol. 25, #3, September, 1980, 428–40.

Wholey, Joseph S. *Evaluation and Effective Public Management.* Boston: Little, Brown, 1982.

Wiener, Carolyn, Shizuko Fagerhauk, Anslen Strauss, and Barbara Suczek. "What Price Chronic Illness?," *Society,* Vol. 19, #2, January/February, 1982, 22–30.

Wildavsky, Aaron. *Speaking Truth to Power: The Art and Craft of Policy Analysis.* Boston: Little, Brown, 1979.

Wildavsky, Aaron, and Arthur Hammann. "Comprehensive versus Incremental Budgeting in the Department of Agriculture." In F.J. Lyndin and R.G. Miller, eds. *A Systems Approach to Management,* 144–45. Chicago: Markham, 1968.

Williams, Juan. "The Children Who Live in Cars," *The Washington Post Weekly Edition,* June 24, 1985, 8–9.

Williams, Stephen J., ed. *Issues in Health Services,* 3–17. New York: Wiley, 1980.

Williams, Walter. *Government by Agency, Lessons From the Social Program Grants—In-Aid Experience.* New York: Academic Press, 1980.

———. "Implementation Analysis and Assessment." In Walter Williams and Richard Elmore, eds. *Social Program Implementation.* New York: Academic Press, 1976.

———. *The Implementation Perspective: A Guide for Managing Social Service Delivery Systems.* Berkeley: University of California Press, 1980.

Williams, Walter, and Richard F. Elmore, eds. *Social Program Implementation.* New York: Academic Press, 1976.

Williams, Walter, and John Evans. "The Politics of Evaluation: The Case of Head Start," *Annals of the American Academy of Political and Social Science,* Vol. 385, September, 1969, 118–32.

Williams, William A. *The Great Evasion.* Chicago: Quadrangle Paperbacks, 1968.

Willms, J. Douglas. "Do Private Schools Produce Higher Levels of Academic Achievement? New Evidence for the Tuition Tax Credit Debate." In Thomas James and Henry Levin, eds. *Public Dollars for Private Schools.* Philadelphia: Temple University Press, 1983.

Wills, Garry. *The Kennedy Imprisonment: A Meditation on Power.* Boston: Little, Brown, 1982.

Wilson, James Q. "On Pettigrew and Armor," *The Public Interest* (Spring, 1973) 132–34.

———. "Policy Intellectuals and Public Policy," *The Public Interest,* #64, Summer, 1981, 31–46.

———. *Thinking About Crime.* New York: Basic Books, 1975.

Windle, Charles. "The Citizen as Part of the Management Process." In Herbert C. Schulberg and Jeanette M. Jerrell, eds. *The Evaluator and Management.* Beverly Hills, CA: Sage, 1979.

Windle, Charles, Ann Majchrzak, and Eugene W. Flaherty. "Program Evaluation at the Interface of Program Echelons." In Robert F. Rich, ed. *Translating Evaluation Into Policy,* 45–61. Beverly Hills, CA: Sage, 1979.

Winters, John. "Drive Against Drunks: State's 'Tough' DUI Laws Not Enough, Many Say," *The Arizona Republic,* January 20, 1985, A-14.

Wirt, Frederick M., and Michael W. Kirst. *Political and Social Foundations of Education.* Boston: Little, Brown, 1972.

Wise, Robert I. "The Evaluation as Educator." In Larry Baskamp and Robert Brown, eds. *Utilization of Evaluative Information,* 11–18. San Francisco: Jossey-Bass, 1980.

Wolfe, Alan. *The Limits of Legitimacy: Political Contradictions of Contemporary Capitalism.* New York: Free Press, 1980.

———. "School Daze," *The New Republic,* February 8, 1993, 25–33.

Woodroofe, Kathleen. *From Charity to Social Work,* 165. Toronto: University of Toronto Press, 1966.

Woodward, Ann. "Housing the Elderly," *Society,* Vol. 19, #2, January/February, 1982, 52–57.

Wycoff, Martin A., and George L. Kelling. *The Dallas Experience: Organizational Reform.* Washington, D.C.: Police Foundation, 1978.

Yesalis, Charles III, G. Joseph Norwood, David P. Lipson, Dennis K. Helling, Leon F. Burmeister, and Wayne P. Fisher. "Use and Costs Under the Iowa Capitation Drug Program," *Health Care Financing Review,* Vol. 3, #1, September, 1981, 127–37.

Yin, Robert K. *Changing Urban Bureaucracies: How New Practices Become Routinized.* Santa Monica, CA: The Rand Corporation, 1979.

Zald, Mayer. "Trends in Policy Making and Implementation in the Welfare State: A Preliminary Statement." In James Tropman, M. Dluhy, and R. Lind, eds. *New Perspectives on Social Policy.* New York: Pergamon Press, 1981.

Zeckhauser, Richard, and Christopher Zook. "Failure to Control Health Costs: Departures from First Principles." In M. Olson. *A New Approach to the*

Economics of Health Care, 87–116. Washington, D.C.: American Enterprise Institute, 1981.

Ziegler, Harmon, and Kent Jennings. *Governing American Schools: Political Interaction in Local School Districts.* Boston: Duxbury Press, 1974.

Zweig, Franklin M., ed. *Evaluation in Legislation.* Beverly Hills, CA: Sage, 1979.

Index

IRENE AT LARGE

Tor books by Carole Nelson Douglas

MYSTERY

Amberleigh [forthcoming]

Irene Adler Adventures:
Good Night, Mr. Holmes
Good Morning, Irene

A Midnight Louie Mystery:
Catnap

SCIENCE FICTION

*Probe**
*Counterprobe**

FANTASY

TALISWOMAN:
Cup of Clay
Seed upon the Wind [forthcoming]

SWORD AND CIRCLET:
Keepers of Edanvant
Heir of Rengarth
Seven of Swords

*also mystery

IRENE AT LARGE

Carole Nelson Douglas

A TOM DOHERTY ASSOCIATES BOOK
NEW YORK

This is a work of fiction. All the characters and events portrayed in this book are fictitious, and any resemblance to real people or events is purely coincidental.

IRENE AT LARGE

This book has been printed on acid-free paper.

Map by Darla Malone Tagrin

A Tor Book
Published by Tom Doherty Associates, Inc.
175 Fifth Avenue
New York, N.Y. 10010

Tor® is a registered trademark of Tom Doherty Associates, Inc.

Library of Congress Cataloging-in-Publication Data

Douglas, Carole Nelson.
Irene at large / Carole Nelson Douglas.
p. cm.
"A Tom Doherty Associates book."
ISBN 0-312-85223-1
I. Title.
PS3554.O823717 1992
813'.54—dc20 92-1251
CIP

First edition: July 1992

Printed in the United States of America

10 9 8 7 6 5 4 3 2 1

For Richard Adcock,
a good friend
who knew everything
about computers and writers
and made them both work

CONTENTS

FOREWORD

My previous works collated the nineteenth-century diaries of Penelope Huxleigh, a parson's daughter, and recently discovered fragments from the supposedly fictional accounts of John H. Watson, M.D., regarding the activities of Sherlock Holmes, the world's first consulting detective. Readers of these works will know that it violates the scholar-editor's code to intrude into the material at hand.

In previous volumes, I confined myself to the discreet afterword. There I merely smoothed out apparent inconsistencies between the Watson-related accounts of Sherlock Holmes so far published and new revelations from the Huxleigh diaries about the only woman admitted to have outwitted Sherlock Holmes, Irene Adler.

Readers will also know that I have insisted from the first that Sherlock Holmes was no fictional construct, but a historic personage. Additionally, I argued that the Huxleigh diaries—with the details of Irene Adler's life both previous and subsequent to her allegedly fictional meeting with Holmes in the story titled *A Scandal in Bohemia*—support my theory: Holmes was real; Irene Adler was real. Indeed, to my mind the only suspect personage in the Holmes canon is Watson. This may have been a convenient pseudonym for the actual biographer, who has successfully hidden behind the "authorship" of Sir Arthur Conan Doyle for a century.

Now I have uncovered evidence of such a startling nature, an "adventure" of Sherlock Holmes (although it is actually a lost adventure of Irene Adler) that is so linked to documentable historic events that I believe no rational person can read it without admitting that Holmes is far from a figment of anyone's imagination. In addition, this new material sheds fascinating light on a personage later to become a key figure in the Holmes saga.

Because this evidence stems from incontestable historic events in the complex region known as "Afghanistan" only for the past century, I find it imperative to insert a modern section to preface the Huxleigh diaries and Watson fragments and to provide the needed narrative continuity. Rest assured that I have not abandoned the scholar's code. To convey an authentically compelling tone, I have commissioned an unemployed historical novelist and former schoolmate of mine from Forth Worth, who steeped herself in the proper disciplines in order to portray the flavor of the times and the events themselves. Even the Holmes biographer (who may or may *not* have been Sir Arthur) on occasion used the omniscient third-person voice to depict events that none of the principals had witnessed.

So I follow in established footsteps, but beg the reader's pardon and patience nevertheless. Chronology is paramount to the narrative that is about to unfold, which has sinister application to the conflict in Afghanistan in our day, as well as that in the twilight of the nineteenth century.

Fiona Witherspoon, Ph.D., F.I.A.*
November 5, 1991

*Friends of Irene Adler

Oh, Gods! From the venom of the Cobra, the teeth of the Tiger, and the vengeance of the Afghan—deliver us.

—Hindu Saying

N
W
E
S
Malmund
Pass
Sangbur
Maiwand
Khushk-i-Nakhud
Sinjiri
Argandab R.
AFGhANI

MAP KEY: E/B, RHA -- E Battery, B Brigade, Royal Horse Artillery (Maclaine's command)

BoNI -- Bombay Native Infantry

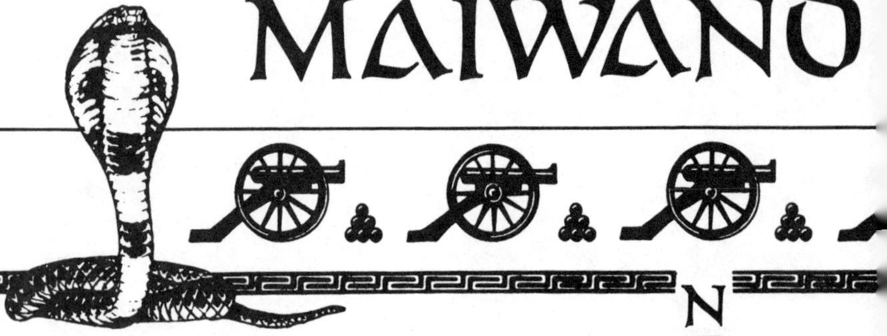

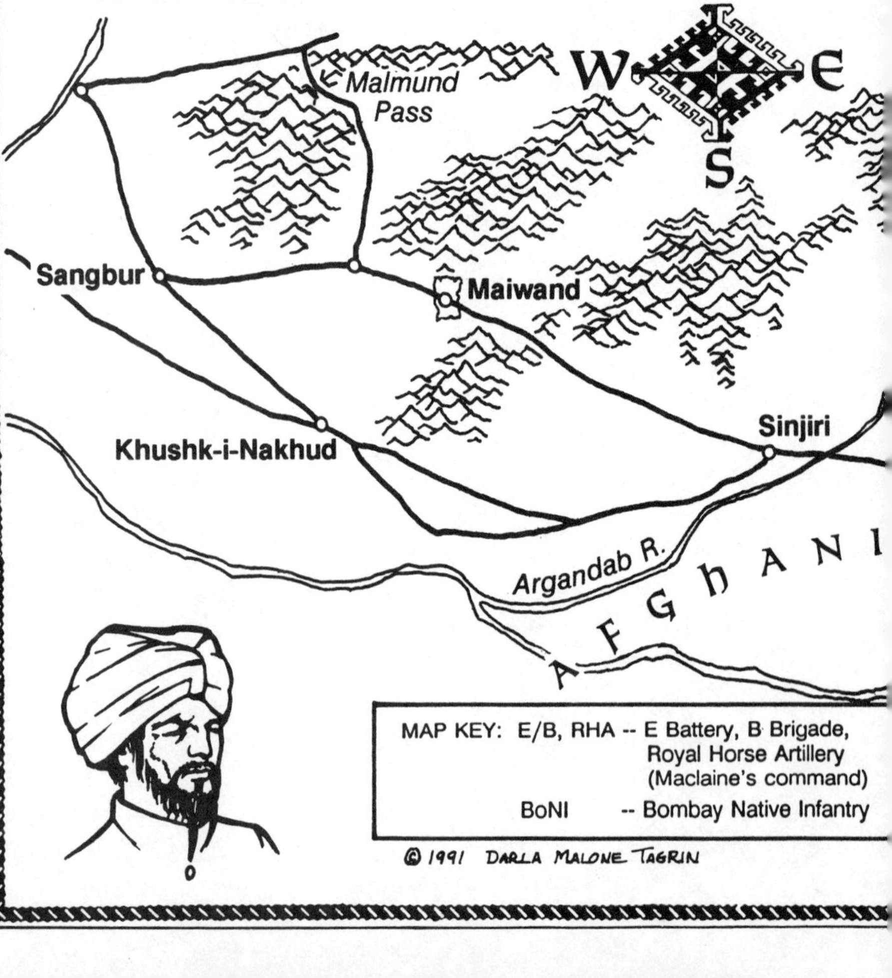

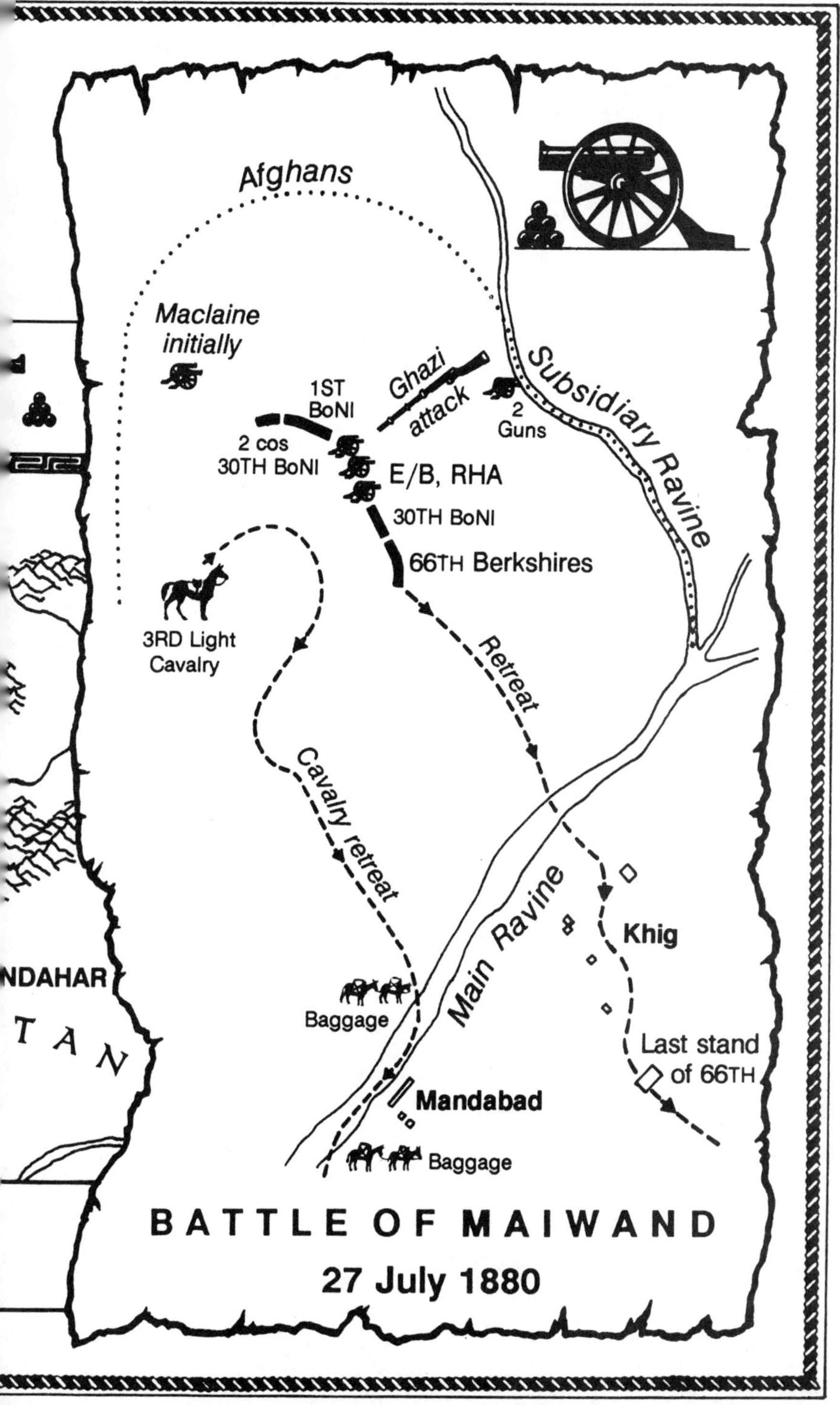

Afghans
Maclaine initially
1ST BoNI
Ghazi attack
2 Guns
Subsidiary Ravine
2 cos 30TH BoNI
E/B, RHA
30TH BoNI
66TH Berkshires
3RD Light Cavalry
Retreat
Cavalry retreat
Main Ravine
Khig
Baggage
Last stand of 66TH
Mandabad
Baggage
BATTLE OF MAIWAND
27 July 1880

IRENE AT LARGE

Chapter One

WHEN TWO STRONG MEN...

Near Sangbur, Afghanistan: *July 25, 1880*

In the very lap of Asia lies a land so fierce and desolate—if not undefended—that were the demons of every faith to collaborate in creating a Hell that would prostrate Christian, Hebrew and Moslem alike in united terror, its name would remain . . . Afghanistan.

Stretching horizontally across the neck of the Indian subcontinent like a hangman's noose, Afghanistan bridges Persia on the west and Tibet and China on the east; British India on the south; and to the north—the great outstretched Russian bearclaw.

Searing in summer and frigid in winter, this unholy landscape huddles behind the scimitar curves of two great mountain ranges—the Himalayas and Karakorum on the east, and on the west the six hundred ridged miles of the Hindu Kush.

Wherever men of adventure and a martial bent gather, the Hindu Kush is spoken of in awed tones. To the timid homebound soul, it is enough to say that the phrase translates as "dead Hindu."

No wonder is it that neither India nor Russia has extended its borders to meet across this dread wasteland. Nor is it any wonder that in the closing decades of the nineteenth century the two great nations of Russia and Britain should nervously dart closer to armed conflict there, like two dogs fighting over the same hideous bone. Possession and advantageous position are the only prizes of what has been called the Great Game between two strong empires. The bone itself is worthless, and bitter gnawing at that.

This is Tartary, ancient road of merchants and conquerors, the no-man's-land separating the northern frontiers of India—Kashmir and the Kush—and the southern fringes of Russia—Tashkent and fabled Samarkand. A lonely wasteland to the unobservant eye, the arid vastness of Afghanistan supports dozens of warring tribes, united only in their devotion to freedom from foreign meddling and their willingness to wreak havoc on interlopers. The traveler, and woe to anyone foolish enough to go solitary into these bleak acres, is never as alone as he may think—or as he may be allowed to think, for a time.

Thus, should a wheeling vulture spy a human form cast lengthwise in a notch atop a bleak ridge, he will not swoop closer to investigate unless he is especially hungry. Such culinary booty is common after the bandits have made their usual forays. Every abandoned traveler is assured of a final, grisly welcome somewhere.

But the lone man visible only to the airborne vulture on this particular summer's day was not lost, or mad, or abandoned. He was present for a purpose, and so was the telescopic spyglass pressed to one eye, its brass carefully darkened so no unnatural twinkle should alert any lurking marauders.

Even a spyglass could barely penetrate the jagged profiles of distance-blued mountain ranges and the tiny camel caravan trickling down a steep incline like a broken string of amber beads. Both men and the tough, two-humped beasts native to these forbidding steppes seemed cloaked in the sere shades of the desolate region, hardly more animate than the darker patches of thornbushes and other scrubby vegetation that punctuate the frozen waves of sand and rock.

The caravan was too immeasurably distant to alarm the watcher, but he rolled over suddenly, aware of the vulture's scant shadow, and turned a dark face to the blazing blue sky. Summer spread its searing, fawn-colored tent over Afghanistan and the heat was horrific, even under the billowing shade of a burnoose.

In an instant, the man collapsed his instrument and tucked it into the leather kit bag belted at his waist beneath the flowing robes. From the bag he pulled something that glinted in the hollow of his hand, a pocket watch, which he consulted. Then he snapped shut the engraved lid and quickly put it away.

The vulture shadow fattened without warning. The man scrambled to his haunches, stretching an arm for the Enfield rifle that lay alongside him, but caution came too late. Another robed man stood motionless below him on the ridge back, a Snider breech-loading rifle slung over one shoulder carelessly enough to be instantly available.

"You are late," the first man said in a language shocking amid that arid wasteland—English.

"I forgo carrying a Burlington Arcade timepiece in Afghanistan," the other said sardonically, moving closer. "One day all of your native dialects will not suffice to talk you out of some tight corner, Cobra."

"Nor will your fabled trick of padding up behind a fellow unheard always save your skin, Tiger," the first man replied with an unamused grin that revealed disarmingly blackened teeth.

Tiger sat on a rock, baggy Turkish trousers ballooning around his knees. He doffed his burnoose's hood, revealing a turban. Under those native wrappings lay a broad, intelligent brow and strong, pugnacious features that indeed boasted the ferocious jaws of a tiger—and unblinking eyes of bright, lapis blue.

"I need that tracker's skill," Tiger said with harsh pride. "I lack your facility for passing among these mountain bandits as one of them. But stealth serves me as well as boldness has served you. We are both yet alive."

Cobra grunted. Unlike the other man, his skin had been toasted to the nut-brown color of a native, and his eyes, if a trifle hazel, seemed almost black in their swarthy setting. Yet beneath it all, and especially in conference with one of his own kind, lurked the aspect of a young English gentleman, no matter how dangerously he played at native tribesman.

"There will be battle," Cobra said, weary of their usual jousting. He did not like Tiger, did not trust the man, though he was an old India hand; Cobra could not say why.

The turban nodded. "Battle, blood and dust. We will have a rare round of it in a day or two. The command underestimates the Amir's forces, as usual. Burrows is a fool."

"He has not seen much action," Cobra admitted with the unease of a young officer discussing the commander. "And Ayub has some crackerjack artillery: two elephant-drawn heavy batteries, twenty-two horse artillery batteries and eighteen mule-drawn mountain batteries, not to mention seven bullock-drawn field batteries."

"The lad can count!" the older man sneered in a way meant to pass as humor-at-arms. "You will soon be heading behind-lines to report all this?"

Cobra nodded. "Not that the command much listens to me."

"The sash-and-sword set never puts much store in the advice of London lads gone native like yourself. You should have stayed in the regiment and clung to your spit-and-polish."

"After the war it is the political chaps who advance," Cobra put in. "And do they heed your reports any more than mine? So is your scouting done?"

"Oh, aye, I have sashayed up the ridges and down the gullies 'til the vultures are sick of the sight of me."

"Better to be seen by them than by the Ghazi fanatics or the Afghan tribesmen."

"Or the women!" Tiger gave a mock shudder. "The Ghazis may kill everything that moves for Allah, but I would rather face one any day. At all costs, do not get wounded and let the village women have at you, boy. They have a real taste for torture, even more than the men. Better to shoot yourself."

"War stories."

Tiger smiled. His teeth were strong and yellow, like a big cat's, leaving no question of why he had earned his *nom de guerre*. "War stories tend to be war truths. Remember that, and remember who told you."

"But you have scouted no surprises for our troops?" Cobra asked.

"No hidden caches of elephant-drawn artillery, no. I have spent two weeks crawling around this bloody dust-laden kiln, and I should know."

"Odd." Cobra got out his spyglass and swept it over the parched landscape below. "Hyena said he had seen you up north recently, in Balkh, near the Russian border."

"Hyena *said*, did he? Like all of his breed, he is much for slinking around after the danger—saying, and little for doing. But he is right, although it was a bit longer ago than that." Tiger leaned inward, his voice so compelling that Cobra lowered his glass to meet the bright blue gaze so ripe with conviction. "That is what I have come to pass to you today. The immediate area is clean as a camel's tooth, but a Russian agent has been doing a mazurka hereabouts to no good. 'Sable' is the code name—vicious, surreptitious beasts they are, too. That is all I've discovered: except for the fact that an officer in our command has been compromised."

"An officer? Will betray us? Why?"

Tiger shrugged. "Could be for gold, or for the rubies in the far Afghan hills—now there is a bribe to make a man's heart clench, a ruby mine! Could be a woman in Simla, with eyes brighter than the Koh-i-noor diamond, but another officer's wife, and blackmail. Oh, my poor lad, the world is rotten with fat fruit, ripe for teasing another's will to one's own. You are such a babe at espionage."

Cobra stiffened in irritation, which no doubt further amused Tiger. "Still, I am the one to report back. What does it matter if the terrain favors us when one of our own may turn? Do you have a name?"

"A name." For the first time, Tiger seemed uncertain.

"Well?" After having his competence challenged, Cobra counterattacked with a vengeance. "What good is it to know the foul deed in advance if you do not know the doer? If you are right, and I happen to think you are, we will engage the Afghans within a day or two. Do you mean to say that all your slinking around on soft cat feet has only turned up a rumor?"

Tiger's mustache bristled like brutal whiskers. "I hesitate to name the man on a matter of such dishonor. But it is . . . Maclaine."

"Maclaine of the Royal Horse Artillery? We need all the artillery we have against the Amir." Cobra stirred, concealing his spyglass. "I had best be making for the plain. This is dire news."

"Wait!" Tiger pulled the burnoose hood over his head, putting his betraying blue eyes into deep shadow. "Let an old game hunter sniff out the trail before you start back. That vulture is still circling. It may spy only carrion, but—"

Cobra nodded. No scout superior to Tiger inhabited all of India. The older man scrabbled sideways across the rocks scorpion-swift, the rifle in his hand cocked like a stinger, until he was out of sight.

Tiger's bag lay on the rocks. Cobra hesitated, as if fearing a sting, but then rapidly unbuckled the straps and studied the contents—quinine pills, a compass and water flask like his own, ammunition, a mustache comb—more likely catch an Afghan with a pocket watch than with one of these! Cobra frowned. He knew not for what he searched, only that he did not trust the bearer.

And then he felt a welt within the leather. His sun-stained fingers probed, working a secret flap loose. A folded document lay in his hand, written on heavy soft paper, so it should not crackle. Odd words. Afghan words. And Russian. Some sort of drawing, a cryptogram.

It took Cobra a moment's work to stuff the paper into his own kit, to replace Tiger's bag in the searing sun as if it had never been touched. He was not as green as Tiger thought. Something in the man's manner today had fanned Cobra's usual dislike into embers of outright suspicion. A British force and the fate of India were at stake. If he were wrong, he would take the consequences. And right or wrong, he would have Tiger to answer to.

He never heard the espionage agent return, but a swelling shadow swooped down suddenly, like a vulture, and squatted near him.

"All clear," said Tiger, smiling . . . smiling like a well-fed big Bengal cat.

Khushk-i-Nakhud, *Evening, July 26, 1880*

On occasion the orchards surrounding Kandahar scented the night air with perfumes that infiltrated even the city's narrow, filthy streets. Here, however, in the British camp midway across the waste that lay between Kandahar and the river Helmond, the only certain fragrance wafted from the plentiful droppings of the beasts of burden needed to transport the baggage and equipment of twenty-five hundred fighting men.

Cobra, now in uniform, slipped unnoticed among the soldiers in the pungent darkness. Horses neighed in answer to ill-tempered bagpipelike brays from the camels. All beasts, native or not, led a brutal life in these parts, and often a short one.

By the muted lantern light of an army soon to go head-to-head with the forces of Ayub Khan, Cobra dodged the shoulder-high wooden wheels of E Battery, B Brigade of the Royal Horse Artillery. The commander of two of these big guns was Lieutenant Hector Maclaine.

Cobra found his man propped against one of the stone enclosures that bracketed the camp, staring into the impenetrable night. Stars sparkled like bright brass buttons above, but no enemy campfires mirrored these hot points of light below. The two men could have been alone in a coal mine with fool's gold salting the ceiling, save for the faint rustles of restless men and animals.

"Stan!" Maclaine greeted the newcomer in surprise. "I doubted you would return before we broke camp."

"Had to report," Cobra said shortly.

"And are we dragging pack and packhorse to greet Ayub Khan tonight, as rumor has it?"

"Perhaps. I merely report to St. John. He carries the news to Slade and the brigadier. Then news becomes rumor."

"Insane that a frontline scout never reports directly. Damn clumsy system."

"Perhaps." Cobra was silent for several moments, as if, used to hurried clandestine meetings, he had forgotten how to converse in other than staccato fashion. "I have uneasy news, Maclaine, and from the look of it, the command will not listen."

"Command lives to order others to listen, not to heed its own scouts' words." The smile in Lieutenant Maclaine's voice was evident even in the dark.

"That is what I fear!" Cobra burst out. "They will not listen, not about Ayub Khan's superior artillery, not about Tiger . . . not about anything."

"What is wrong, old man? Too much time spent in solitary on the boiling sands?"

"Burrows is getting spoiled spy-work, and I know it. I am going out again to scout Maiwand. The previous report sounds too perfect: a long ravine for an attack base and no flaws in the terrain."

"That does not sound like the Afghanistan that has scrubbed our boots raw," Maclaine agreed.

"Just what I thought. I have scoured the ground like a dust devil, and found a secondary ravine to the east no one has reported. If we see action at Maiwand tomorrow, the RHA will be in the vanguard. Keep your eyes and ears open, full-bore," Cobra cautioned him. "You have nothing . . . troubling you?"

"Nothing save dust and heat, a gulletful of quinine pills and a noseful of horse manure. Have I ever struck you as a nerve-ridden man?"

"No, you have not," Cobra answered soberly. "That is what troubles me. Someone who has no notion that I know you has accused you of having a guilty conscience."

"I?" Maclaine leaped up. "Who is this liar? I'll call him out in midbattle, though six dozen Ghazi fanatics charge us."

"This is serious spy-work," Cobra said. "Leave it to me. But for God's sake, Mac, keep a sharp eye about yourself from now on."

"Can you say no more?"

"Nothing until I learn more. God guard you all tonight."

"And you, Stan," Lieutenant Maclaine said. "I vouchsafe we will next meet on a battlefield—or in heaven."

"Just so long as it is not in an undeserved hell," Cobra answered, edging silently into the darkness.

After he had gone, Lieutenant Maclaine stamped a booted foot like a restless horse. Officers of the Royal Horse Artillery were used to chaos, danger, dust and gunpowder. Innuendo and behind-hand dealing, or sinking into the native culture, as Cobra did, was more foreign territory than Afghanistan.

"Odd fellow," Maclaine muttered to the apparently empty and unheeding night.

Cobra was gone by then, eeling through the dark as if it were a silent, immobile sea. He slithered past a wooden wheel and the stolid forms of resting horses, through thinning tents, into the open waste.

Beyond the camp and beside a last solitary stone, Cobra stooped to disinter his native robes, his mind on a jumble of oddities, not the least of which was his friend Maclaine's role in the coming events.

He never heard a sound. All at once the night's opaque ebony curtain dropped upon his head with a tremendous thud. Warm red velvet oozed over his eyes, into his surprised mouth, as he felt his skull split from side to side, a chasm opening into an utter darkness blacker than even the Afghan night.

Chapter Two

... EAST MEETS WEST

The Battle of Maiwand, *July 27, 1880*

Heat haze and dust perform a whirling dervish dance in the distance. But a few thousand yards away, unseen masses of milling men and horses churn as the Ayub Khan's forces move into battle positions.

The hour is early, only nine-fifteen in the morning. Between the two forces lies a flat, merciless Afghanistan plain, already seeming to quiver under the blast-furnace heat, as if viewed in a wavy mirror. A village or two hump carcass-fashion ahead. The only other shelter on the pitiless plain is the ravine previously scouted, fifteen to twenty-five feet deep and fifty to a hundred feet wide, running like a wound toward the northeast.

Brigadier General Burrows rides forward with the general of the cavalry, Nuttall.

"Blackwood!" he orders. "Take Fowell's and Maclaine's sections forward across the ravine under the escort of a troop of the Third Light Cavalry." He watches the sections grind forward into the dusty no-man's-land between the British position at the ravine and the unseen—but not unreported—Afghan hordes arranged into a scimitarlike arc twenty-five hundred yards beyond.

Thus does battle fall upon the British like an afterthought. By ten-thirty A.M. Fowell's two guns open fire from a position five hundred yards northwest of the ravine. Even as the two generals watch with some complacency, for generals expect their orders to be carried out, a sudden spurt, a geyser-burst of dust, erupts on Ayub's front lines.

"What—?" begins Burrows, certain that the Afghan artillery has not yet been drawn into position.

"Must be . . . Maclaine!" Nuttall rises in his stirrups. "Damn fool, he's galloping his guns directly to the front gate of the Afghan position. Why on earth—?"

"Disobeying orders," Burrows roars. "That is why."

The two generals keep a sudden silence, each calculating the advantages and disadvantages of having an artillery section a mile in advance of the regular troops. Soon a mounted messenger, with orders for Maclaine's guns to pull back, is racing into the dust toward his position. Messages from Blackwood are sent as well, telling Fowell's artillery section to move forward where it has a chance of hitting the enemy positions.

In time, by a process of seesawing, Maclaine's position pulls back and Fowell's pushes forward to two thousand yards in advance of the ravine. They form a united front, backed by a half-company of the Sappers and Miners and the infantry, with the Sixty-sixth Berkshires on the far left.

For half an hour only the British artillery pounds the parched Afghan earth. Then Ayub's guns begin heaving, spitting heavy shells into the British lines from breech-loading Armstrongs.

"Ayub has more guns than a battleship," Nuttall shouts into the dusty din as he watches the artillery sections and his cavalry take repeated poundings.

"So Cobra's report said," the brigadier grumbles. "Why are the Sixty-sixth Berkshires so sluggish about holding the line?"

A scout charges up at that moment with the reason: "A shallow ravine joins at right angles to this, sir! Along it the Afghan rifles are harrying our rear baggage section. The men and animals are in disarray, and the Sixty-sixth is forced to deform the line to defend themselves."

"Another ravine? No spy or scout reported this! Then we are in danger of being surrounded, and Ayub has ten to fifteen thousand men to our nineteen hundred field soldiers!" The brigadier grows suddenly quiet. Not until now has it occurred to him that the sun may not set on a British victory.

"Guns!" bawls another officer, riding up. "In the subsidiary ravine. Two artillery guns, pounding the Sixty-sixth."

Dire news comes charging at Brigadier General Burrows after that: the left wing formed by the ambushed Sixty-sixth is steadily being cut down; E Battery, B Brigade of Royal Horse Artillery is ordered to fire one more round, but, ahead of the infantry, is almost surrounded. Maclaine at their forefront fails to retrieve his guns, leaving them to the enemy and retreating under shots fired at a range of only fifteen to twenty yards.

"We need those guns back," Brigadier General Burrows barks.

"Let me order Nuttall to lead a cavalry charge at the captured guns," Leach urges.

Moments later the general watches a saber of dust plough toward the Afghan-surrounded guns, but the charge quickly sputters and retreats.

Nuttall, his face gritty with sand, rides up.

"Charge again," the general orders.

"Impossible, sir," Nuttall replies.

The general eyes the dust storm that is the battlefield. "If another charge is impossible, then so is victory."

Nuttall meets his eyes but says nothing.

By one-thirty P.M. the smoothbore batteries have exhausted their ammunition and withdrawn to the main ravine for restocking. Blackwood, severely wounded, is retiring to the rear also, a gravely wounded Fowell with him. Enemy irregulars harass the coattails of the valiant Sixty-sixth.

An hour and half later, the battle is over; a vast column of

British soldiers and sepoys, native Indian forces, flee south toward Kandahar, mounted Afghans harrying its flanks.

Bodies litter the landscape, thousands of robed Afghans, hundreds of uniformed British troops. The severely wounded fall to the Afghan enemy and die before they can be rescued. Retreat is graceless as well as bitter, punctuated by the bullets of Afghan snipers and the knives of local peasants. Men and animals mill in chaos.

Among them wanders Lieutenant Hector Maclaine, dazed and disillusioned. By now the men have fought for hours without rest or food or water. At dusk, Maclaine ventures into a village in search of the one essential, water. Villagers converge upon him and five Indian soldiers, taking them prisoner. No one notices.

Also among these cheerless, fleeing men is the spy known as Cobra. The cavalry retreat, plunging back through camp, has awakened him from the violent blow to the head. He staggers onward, in the direction the British go: south to Kandahar, sixty miles over the hills and through the mountain passes.

Cobra doubts that he can make such a trek in his present condition, but he must. He must tell the command of Tiger's perfidy. He must reach Kandahar. He must move one foot before the other one more time. . . .

He falls, his face in the familiar dust. He is breathing sand now rather than air, and can feel the earth's hot tremors as running men and hard-hooved beasts bound over this contested ground. Through the seven veils of dust thickening in the setting sun's scarlet train, Cobra sees a figure from a fever dream lurching toward him: a man in uniform carrying a leather satchel.

It is too late, Cobra wants to say, but his dry, heat-blistered lips barely move. The man with the leather bag comes on.

Chapter Three

AFGHANISTAN PERCEIVED

London: *June 1889*

"Well, Watson, you are thinking of Afghanistan again, I perceive."

"I beg your pardon, Holmes?"

"Surely I need not apologize for being observant, Watson?"

"Indeed you should, when you go stealing into a man's thoughts like this."

"Then you admit it?"

"Admit what?"

"Afghanistan, of course."

"I was not aware of dwelling on that unkindly land, but my thoughts may have drifted in that direction. No doubt you soon will tell me how you read them."

Holmes leaned back in the velvet armchair with an expression of satisfaction. "Perhaps *you* would care to tell *me*."

"I do not know why, when you will pull the rug out from under my poor speculations, as you usually do."

"Pshaw, Watson. You underestimate your own capacities. Think, man! It is *your* mind that I have presumed to read. Either refute my conclusion or explain it."

I looked around our too-familiar rooms in Baker Street,

trying to reconstruct the thoughts that had idly streamed through my mind while I had gazed out the bow window on the drizzle of a sullen summer day.

"I suppose," I began, "that I was looking at something incriminating." Yet no souvenirs of my Army surgeon days in Afghanistan decorated the walls. Holmes was the sentimentalist, if I may be so bold as to call him that. At least he was the pack rat, for the domestic landscape teemed with memorabilia of his vocation as a consulting detective, not the least of which was the pointillist pattern of bullet holes punctuating the farther wall with the admirable initials *V.R.*, for Victoria Regina.

"There is much incriminating to observe in these rooms," Holmes said with a smile as he watched me. "Fortunately most of it has incriminated others, not ourselves. Go on."

"Humph." Where exactly had I been staring when Holmes had interrupted my reverie? Out of the window? Not really. Ah. "The photograph of General Gordon has led you in the direction of Afghanistan, has it not, Holmes?"

"How could it? 'Chinese' Gordon campaigned in China and died in Egypt, both sufficiently far from Afghanistan to have no obvious connection."

"Still, I vaguely recall gazing at the old fellow's gilt-embroidered uniform. At least he represents the rough quarter of the globe that Afghanistan shares."

"Very well, Watson, very well! I confess. You were indeed musing on the late general, and a fine-looking subject for contemplation he makes in his fez, with his stars of rank festooning his Oriental tunic. But *you* were my ultimate clue on the direction of your thoughts."

"I said nothing."

"No, but you absently massaged your left shoulder, the site of the wound you took at Maiwand, which caused you to be cashiered out of the Army. Does the damp trouble you?"

"Not so much as the dryness of your deductions," I mumbled, shifting on my chair and only realizing then that the shoulder did indeed ache a bit, as did my leg.

Holmes's quick eyes followed my own to the leg. "A secondary wound, Watson?"

I stirred uneasily, pricked by an annoyance I seldom felt with Holmes, for all his amazing and eternal prescience. "Merely the combined inroads of a damp day and a certain age," said I, "common to inhabitants of our great but fog-bound city. I am stiff from sitting."

"Ah." Holmes commented with the bland skepticism of a physician on hearing a symptom reported by its bearer. "No doubt. Although I have seen you favor the leg before."

"The wound was in my shoulder, Holmes. You know that! The surgeons who treated me in Afghanistan know that! This nonsense of the leg is some sham you have manufactured to explain your deduction. I know what I am thinking and I do not require translations from nearby observers, no matter how brilliant."

"Of course not, dear fellow," Holmes murmured contritely. "I merely wondered why you might be thinking of Afghanistan at this late date. Obviously," he finished insincerely, "I was mistaken."

I said no more. Seldom did my friendship with Holmes tread near the shoals of irritation, but this was one of those rare times. It was ridiculous to suppose that I should care to dwell on Afghanistan after the severe wound and the tedious, long recovery I endured in that unhappy landscape.

The jezail bullet that shattered my shoulder bone and sheared the subclavian artery would have been fatal if my orderly, Murray, had not flung me over a packhorse and rushed me to the British lines. When I was recovering at Peshawar in India, enteric fever hammered me down. For months I lingered on the borderline of death itself. A mere shadow of myself shipped home for England on the troopship *Orontes* in 1881. That was the shade who had met Sherlock Holmes. When we two decided to share rooms, I little guessed what an unforeseen tack my life would take as I became a witness to my friend's astonishing deductive abilities. But I did not always welcome his keen and tireless mind presuming to read mine.

Afghanistan, indeed. For once my detective friend was on a false trail. I had virtually forgotten Afghanistan. Even if I had not been inclined to do so, my months of fever-ridden illness had wiped most details of my wounding and recovery from my memory, thoroughly enough even to baffle the mind-reading abilities of Mr. Sherlock Holmes.

Chapter Four

PEARLS BEFORE PARROTS

''**Araggk. Pieces** of eight. Pieces of eight.'' Casanova peered over my shoulder and cocked his gaudy head.

"You may be able to intone flawless French,'' I said severely, ''but you cannot count in any language. There are only five pieces here.''

The gleam of rubies, diamonds and pearls matched the appetite in Casanova's beady eye. It was fortunate that he was caged, for I suspected that he would have snatched up one of my prizes in a thrice otherwise.

The parrot ambled down his scabrous perch, chortling to himself, while I returned to my self-appointed duty of tending the family fortune.

For a peerless beauty of her era, my American friend Irene Adler Norton had precious few jewels to show for it. She who had introduced Tiffany's spectacular shoulder-to-hip corsage of diamonds to the Milan opera audiences, and who had worn Queen Marie Antoinette's lost Zone of Diamonds around her waist at her wedding (albeit discreetly under her overskirt) had not retained these fabulous treasures, being too poor or too indifferent.

The array that sparkled in her tapestry-covered jewel box was modest, yet each item told a story. On rainy days it amused me to polish my memories along with Irene's jewels, for she herself could never be bothered to fuss over her possessions, no matter how rare or valuable.

So I shined true treasure along with mere souvenir. The outstanding single piece was a twenty-five-carat diamond, the only one Irene had kept from the French queen's long-lost, floor-length girdle of jewels. The next most valuable piece was undoubtedly the diamond choker mounted on velvet. This was a gesture of thanks from Charles Lewis Tiffany, the world-famous jeweler to whom Irene sold the queen's Zone once she had whisked it from under the rather prominent nose of the Baker Street consulting detective Sherlock Holmes.

The most precious article glittered on my palm like a giant dewdrop—a Tiffany piece modest in cost and execution, but the first gift from Irene's husband-to-be, barrister Godfrey Norton. Godfrey, who displayed a legal precision even when under the influence of a romantic impulse, had chosen the perfect insignia for my friend: a diamond-studded musical clef intersecting an equally resplendent key at an angle reminiscent of crossed swords.

"Music and mystery," I can still hear Godfrey saying with that tone of light seriousness that so becomes him. "They are the keynotes of your life, my dear Irene."

Music, I fear, had become a background motif once Irene was forced to leave the Prague opera and to live in virtual anonymity in Paris after the affair of the King of Bohemia's photograph, not to mention the possible pursuit of Sherlock Holmes. Mystery, however, was proving to be a less fragile pastime.

I centered the clef and key on the moss-green velvet within the jewel box and considered the next item. As in a wax museum, the more gruesome exhibits had the more enduring fascination. I picked up the blood-bright ruby brooch shaped like a five-pointed star. It lay on my palm, a glorious stigma, the only gift that Irene had accepted from Wilhelm Gottsreich Sigismond von Ormstein, King of Bohemia. He had meant it to be a consolation prize for relegating Irene from potential royal bride to certain royal mistress after his succession to the throne on the death of his father. Irene, who had refused all jewels during their courtship, accepted this last poisonous symbol of the King's personal betrayal, and fled—with myself—across most of Europe.

To recover the photograph of the two together that Irene took with her as a safeguard, King Willie pursued her to London. When his thugs failed to dent Irene's armor of cool wit, he engaged Sherlock Holmes to recover the photograph, but even that did not help him. The ruby brooch shone like limpid drops of blood under the brisk buffing of my cloth, and I dropped it to the velvet with sudden distaste.

On the Valencia-lace dresser scarf awaiting my attentions lay another loathsome object—not by its associations but by design. This was the work of Charles Tiffany's son Louis—a tortured representation of an anonymous sea slug decked with pearls. Irene insisted that the work was unique, would even one day be valuable, but she was ever an optimist on all fronts. I was sorely tempted to "lose" the ugly thing during one of my cleaning ventures. Certainly the world would not miss a single sinuous and bilious enameled brooch.

Perhaps the most shuddersome of Irene's souvenirs, however, was the plain gold wedding band, which dated from the day she and I met in 1881. She had received it from the hand of a man I shall never forget, Jefferson Hope, an American who drove our first shared cab ride together. When he became gravely ill en route to Irene's humble Saffron Hill lodgings, he confessed a strange tale of perfidy in the American Great Salt Desert involving a woman betrayed and revenge unto the second decade. He was a murderer, that man, though his victims were villains, and he gave Irene the ring of his tragically lost love Lucy.

Only days after that dramatic encounter we read of his capture in the rooms of Mr. Sherlock Holmes, the amateur detective. We were to see Mr. Jefferson Hope no more. He died in police custody shortly after. Mr. Sherlock Holmes proved to be quite another matter indeed.

How Irene had foiled the supposedly peerless detective and the King of Bohemia in the matter of the photograph—and the unsuspected Zone of Diamonds! She had wed, then fled with, a worthier man, Godfrey, with the Zone and the photograph, and most important, with her virtue and integrity intact.

Now the French village of Neuilly near Paris became the newlyweds' home. And now I, Penelope Huxleigh—once Irene's chambermate and Godfrey's typewriter-girl—had joined them. Now, of course, Godfrey required a secretary to manage his correspondence in international law. Since arriving in France the previous summer, I had mastered the language in its written form, though I still stumbled over its spoken cadences.

As an orphaned, unmarried parson's daughter past thirty, it seemed fitting that I should amuse myself by polishing Godfrey's punctuation and Irene's jewelry. One in my social position cannot expect much glamour from life, although my association with Irene first, and now both the Nortons, unfortunately involved me from time to time in a mysterious doing or other. Indeed, had it not been for my sensible counsel on many occasions, my good friends might not be here to enjoy the proceeds of the queen's diamonds. They remained an impetuous pair abroad, even the usually stable Godfrey, when it came to some puzzle in the neighborhood.

Fortunately, all had been quiet after the Montpensier affair, which had begun with a drowned man on Bram Stoker's Chelsea dining-room table in London years before and ended recently in perfidy and lost treasure in Monaco. Yet that resolution had been last fall, and 1889 was now half over, happily with no sign of some new, outré investigation on the horizon. So like any idle sailor polishing brass, I brightened the souvenirs of previous escapades and secretly hoped that they would be the last of their kind. A respectable married couple has far better things to do than to meddle in the affairs of others, especially when those affairs involve theft, murder, unsanctioned relationships and other even more unsavory matters.

Casanova, gargling his consonants and vowels sotto voce behind me, bobbed his red-and-green head in agreement and hungrily eyed the Tiffany squid, his large yellow beak gnashing. I had not thought of *that*, and stopped polishing while I savored—theoretically, of course—the delightful appropriateness of killing two birds with one stone by feeding the repellent brooch to the equally odious parrot.

Chapter Five

A STRANGER IN PARADISE

A wren alit on the back rail of Irene's wrought-iron chair and cocked its meek brown head hopefully at her French pastry.

She immediately paused, tweaked off a morsel and offered it on the platter of her palm. The bird snatched the prize and flitted to the paving stones to consume its treat.

"Truly, Irene," Godfrey said, laughing, "I know that you have been idle too long when you resort to charming the birds out of the chestnut trees. You require more demanding game."

Irene, unlike the bird, refused to be baited, but merely smiled and dusted pastry flakes off her skirt.

Although Paris pouted under unseasonably shrouded gray skies, Irene bloomed like a Holland tulip in her costume of the new Buffalo red, a dramatically dark shade lavished along the high collar, basque, waist and skirtfront with rococo scrolls of black cord passementerie. A Buffalo-red felt hat with ostrich feathers and black velvet ribbon perched on her brunette hair, and lent her the wren's look of pert inquiry combined with an appealing touch of hopefulness, if not outright hunger.

"You do not mean to say, Godfrey," she asked ravenously,

"that you have found some puzzle for me to unravel amongst your exceedingly dull legal documents?"

"I fear my cupboard is bare," he said, hastily sipping the black coffee he had learned to prefer since meeting Irene.

Godfrey, too, looked most debonair, as the French say, attired in a shiny top hat and walking suit and carrying a malacca cane. One sometimes forgot that Godfrey was such a fine-looking gentleman, so royally did Irene's beauty and style command public attention. She always radiated the air of the opera diva she had been—a confidence and intelligence of manner that was most striking in a woman.

No wonder all eyes in the little sidewalk café under the ponderous shadow of Notre Dame fixed on Irene's charming pantomime of feeding the little brown wren, which had flitted back to her shoulder to beg for more.

Speaking of little brown wrens, I suppose that I should mention my disposition and attire that late June day of 1889. My habit of making complete notes in my diary had not failed me that day, and by evening it would prove to be a most astounding date, to say the least. That morning, however, I was innocent of pending revelations, and wore a brown plaid walking suit trimmed in suede velvet cuffs, reveres and collar. My bonnet was suede felt topped by a panache of ostrich tips and wings shaded, like foul coffee soothed by variations of cream, from soft suede to darkest brown. The bonnet had been purchased in Paris at Irene's order, despite my fear that it was frivolous. I need not have worried. I could have worn scarlet satin bloomers and she sackcloth, and I would have gone unnoticed in Irene's company.

Fortunately, I have never been afflicted with the female fault of welcoming personal attention, and Irene's beauty was all the more effective for being unaffected, so we made an ideal pair. I had long since grown resigned, even relieved, to escape public notice when with such a stunning companion.

Some must not only serve by standing and waiting, but by sitting and taking copious notes, and such had been my reluctant role in our previous adventures, such as the Escape from the King of Bohemia, the Distasteful Matter of the Drowned Sailor, the Incident of the Tattooed Heiress, and other intrusive puzzles that flocked to Irene's vicinity like . . . the wrens of Paris.

"You are pensive, my dear Nell." Godfrey leaned toward me with twinkling eyes as gray as the Paris skies. "No doubt you contemplate the likelihood of Irene finding another mysterious matter to investigate. Surely you are safe from such scandals in the saintly shadow of Notre Dame."

"Saintly, indeed," I admitted, "but too tricked-out for my Protestant tastes." I looked up at the gargoyles grinning from the bristling parapets crowning the great cathedral's mass across the street. I had no doubt that these ancient stone guardians were more successful in warding off fiends than I would be at shielding Irene from the temptation of a puzzle.

As my eyes dropped back to earth and half the population of Paris out for a stroll in its Sunday best, they lit upon a disreputable figure—a robed and turbaned man of bearded, dark mien who might have materialized like Beelzebub in Faust's study. I do not like to stare at the less fortunate, or the possibly more predatory, but it was clear that this . . . apparition was gazing toward our threesome.

"Godfrey—"

"Yes?" His eyes left Irene and the greedy little bird.

"There is a man—"

"There usually is on the streets of Paris, and usually several."

"He is watching us."

Godfrey smiled ruefully. "Your use of the plural is kind, but not accurate. He is watching Irene. Most men do."

"You take this sort of thing extremely well, Godfrey. No doubt it is the cool temper required by the courtroom. This man—and I did not look long, I did not wish him to receive any illusions as to my interest—is most savage looking! He does not look a Christian gentleman at all!"

Godfrey looked around with that admirable discretion that Irene is always urging upon myself, to no avail. "Ah. I see.

The bearded Oriental man who looks half beggar and half brigand, and no doubt all infidel to you. But Paris is the crossroads of Europe; men of all races convene here freely."

"But not to look at us! Even at one of us. I find it most disturbing."

"He will likely move on. As we can do ourselves." Godfrey took up his cane and leaned toward Irene, who had been lost in feeding the inordinately tame wren. "We should take our leave," he suggested quietly.

She started, then began to don her dashing, though unconventional black gloves, suitable only for mourning. "Was I ignoring you? Dreadfully sorry. I was wondering if Casanova might not like this precious little one for a companion—although Lucifer would like it too well, I fear!"

Lucifer was the black Persian cat Irene had "given" me on my arrival in Paris the previous August. He was large and lazy and, despite my distaste for cats, often lay across my diary as I wrote or lounged in my lap when I attempted some domestic duty, such as the crochet work that his wicked claws would snarl.

"I agree," said I, gathering up my reticule. "That is the trouble with these so-called 'romantic' sidewalk cafés of Paris; they provide a fishbowl for the sharks that prowl the streets to prey upon. Godfrey, that scoundrel is not moving on. If anything, he is coming closer. Hurry!"

"Oh?" Irene came out of her trance and began to look around in the manner she recommends to me: missing nothing but appearing to overlook everything.

"Do hurry, Irene! Once again you have attracted the attention of some unsavory individual. I will not have our Sunday ruined by an unseemly incident. I knew coming into Paris would be a mistake."

Irene instantly singled out the very man whose demeanor so agitated me. "He is only some poor foreign beggar, Nell."

"Some foreign *rogue* who would see *us* poorer, no doubt. Please, Irene! For once could you refrain from involving us in a public scene? We need only step along to the Left Bank and our coachman will collect us, and we will have had a totally enjoyable outing with not one thing to mar the day."

"Oh, very well." Irene took Godfrey's arm with an indulgent smile at me, but she moved so languidly I feared the rude watcher would have time to bolt toward us and do whatever he so clearly had in mind: beg, beseech, or berate us with some insanity.

Godfrey extended his other arm, which I took, and we threaded through the tables to the street. Most of the passersby were respectable to the point of being fashionable. Top hats bobbled past the blue turban that never left my view, and a tall, blonde woman with golden sable fur burnishing her hem and shoulders brushed past the watching man, oblivious to his unsavory nature. Paris accepts anything. We swung right to escape his view and began crossing the street, forced to pause as a fruit vendor pulled his fragrant cart past us.

I heard no footsteps behind us, but felt such an imperative sense of haste that I crimped my fingers into Godfrey's arm.

"Why, Nell," said he with a reassuring smile. "You are actually worried."

"Indeed. Please, you must whisk Irene away before—"

A presence loomed at our backs. I glimpsed the red-gold pelt of a sable and inhaled a heady foreign perfume—only the fashionable lady but unaccompanied, how odd . . . and then another figure hove to behind me—the mysterious foreigner about to bump into us! We three turned at once, for different reasons: Irene sensing the unknown and rushing to meet it; Godfrey determined to inspect and confront the object of my alarm; I knowing that Fate in bizarre guise was about to enmesh Irene—and Godfrey and me—in another dangerous puzzle.

There he stood, the man who had so unnerved me. And an unnerving figure he was, his skin chestnut-brown, his face and form gaunt beneath garments that were a patchwork of European and Oriental castoffs.

You see! I almost shouted triumphantly in front of all the

Sunday strollers. You *see?* Here it begins again; Irene drawing mystery and skulduggery as a magnet attracts metal.

The fellow, having reached us, fixed us with disbelieving eyes that were—oddly—a shade lighter than his swarthy foreign face. He swayed upon his feet, his pale hazel eyes narrowing, as he stared stupidly at me and intoned in perfect Sloane Square English, "Why, it *is* Miss Huxleigh, indeed."

Then he collapsed to the cobblestones like a sack of potatoes. Irene regarded me inquiringly, even accusingly.

"I do not know!" Staring down at the unconscious man, I could only repeat the obvious. "I cannot speculate how he knew my name, but I most certainly do not know—have never known, never seen—"

"He saw you," she interrupted. "He saw you and could not believe that he knew you."

"The f-feeling is mutual," I stuttered, aware of onlookers gathering around us. "I tell you I have never seen this man before, nor do I hope to again."

Godfrey had bent to examine the creature at the same moment that a waiter from the café rushed over with a glass of red wine. The French belief in the curative value of wine rivals only their conviction in their own cultural superiority. More of that gruesome liquid fell upon the man's barbarously embroidered shirt than on his lips, but he stirred at this bloody baptism, his eyelids fluttering.

"Miss Huxleigh," he murmured as if dreaming.

I stepped back, appalled, my hands clasped at my throat, which was dry. "I have never met the fellow, I swear."

Irene regarded the fallen man from the lofty pinnacle of consideration for a moment; though she was the softest-hearted of women when moved, she was not one to be deceived by false weakness. Then she addressed me dryly.

"Although you pride yourself on strictly abiding by the Holy Writ, Nell, it is not necessary to follow the New Testament example and deny any association yet a third time. Whatever your memory of a connection, this, er, gentleman clearly knows you and your name. Since he has been taken ill—"

"A ruse!" I interrupted, my cheeks hot with anger at the attention the bounder had drawn in my innocent direction.

"A ruse by another name may be a true illness." Irene waited for Godfrey to report on the fellow's condition.

"I am no medical man," he said, glancing up with a sober face, "but it looks like a legitimate illness to me."

Irene nodded briskly, her ostrich plumes bowing faintly to the gesture. "We will take him back with us to Neuilly, then. Our carriage will accommodate him if you ride up with André," she told Godfrey. She gave me a wicked smile. "Or perhaps Nell would prefer to ride with the coachman rather than with our mysterious charge."

My throat felt stuffed with cotton, but I managed to speak. "If you wish to play Good Samaritan to this *stranger*, far be it from me to interfere. But I would never agree to anything so improper as riding with the coachman."

"Good," Irene returned. "I knew I could rely upon you, Nell, to do the proper thing. Godfrey, you must tend the poor man while Nell and I fetch the carriage. Guard him well." With that cryptic instruction, Irene took my elbow and steered me into the crowd milling before the great stone cathedral.

"Paris is unlucky for us," I commented morosely when Godfrey came down the narrow stairs of our cottage at Neuilly after helping the coachman install our mysterious invalid in an upstairs bedchamber.

Godfrey frowned at the chamomile tea our maid, Sophie, had prepared for me, and went to the sherry decanter instead. He returned with a half-full glass and presented it with a bow. "For thy stomach's sake. It has had a turn."

I seldom partake of alcoholic beverages, but my throat was still dry so I sipped the potion, which struck me as no more unappealing than drinking from the perfume flagon Irene kept on her dressing table. "He may have contracted some virulent Oriental disease," I muttered.

"He may have," Godfrey admitted. "We are taking him on faith, given his acquaintance with you."

"You must not! As I told Irene, I do not know—" Footsteps descended the stairs. I paused, loath to subject myself to another reminder from Irene that the wretched man knew me even if I did not know him. Our buxom maid appeared in the hallway.

"You need help?" Godfrey asked in rapid French that I had only lately begun to follow well. "André has gone for Dr. Mersenné in the village."

"*Non, Monsieur,*" Sophie replied, adding—if I understood her correctly—that Madame Norton was having no difficulty disrobing the man!

I turned on Godfrey like an angry goose, so furious I could only hiss my disbelief.

"No, no, Nell. André and I disrobed him for bed. Irene is merely searching his clothing for clues."

"Worse! They might be disease-ridden, vermin-infested—"

"Decently clean, if a bit worn," came Irene's cheery overriding tones from the foot of the stairs. She entered the parlor, her eyes belladonna-bright, though curiosity was her only cosmetic. "Such a puzzle," she added happily, perching on the arm of Godfrey's chintz-upholstered easy chair. "His Eastern outer clothing hides European underwear and his body is sun-browned to the waist, yet his legs are as white as a fish belly."

"Irene!" I remonstrated faintly.

"I am sorry, Nell." Irene sounded genuinely contrite for once. "I should not have said anything so forward as 'fish belly.' "

"You are having fun with me. At least until now your interest in the condition of strange gentlemen's bodies confined itself to corpses."

"We may have one on our hands yet," Godfrey put in a trifle grimly.

"This man may . . . die?"

"But you must not worry, Nell," Irene said. "You do not know him."

"That does not mean I wish him to die, disreputable as he is. He may have had a tragic life . . . have been cast out while a child. He may have contracted a dreadful malady in far-off China while ministering to the heathens."

"Nell is right in one thing," Godfrey told Irene. "It has the look of a foreign fever. Dr. Mersenné may know what, I hope."

Irene nodded, equally grave. "I also hope Dr. Mersenné can diagnose the large puncture wound in his upper right arm."

"The bite of some huge, exotic spider," I suggested.

"More like the injection of some huge, exotic needle," she returned.

"A needle? You mean a syringe? Then he has already seen a doctor."

Irene leaned over and lifted my barely touched glass of sherry from the marquetry table upon which it sat. "I do not think so." She sipped consideringly. "I believe we may have a mortally ill man upon our hands, and one so recently stricken that he did not yet know it himself."

"How recently?" I asked, puzzled.

"Even as he paused to observe us outside the café. In fact, I believe that he has 'fallen ill' because he recognized someone."

"Some . . . one?"

Irene toasted me with my own glass. "You, my dear Nell. I must congratulate you: you have led a most delicious and likely dangerous mystery straight to my doorstep." She eyed Godfrey with rather ferocious jubilation. "To *our* doorstep, my dears. Now we must keep our guest alive so we can learn who is trying to kill him, and why. And we must discover why our formidable documenter Nell does not recall a man who remembers *her* so vividly that the passage of years and a major dislocation in place does not deceive him even on the brink of physical collapse."

"He is not in the least respectable," I protested in explanation of why I should not be expected to recognize such a man.

"That," said Irene severely, "is no excuse."

Chapter Six

A POISONOUS PAST

The cottage at Neuilly was becoming a routine rest-stop for wayfaring strangers. I watched from the front parlor that afternoon as Dr. Mersenné arrived in an officious hush and was rapidly ushered upstairs. I was reminded of Louise Montpensier's arrival on the premises just last autumn: disheveled, wet, hysterical and freshly tattooed.

In Louise's case, there was the evidence of good jewelry upon her person to recommend her. All the turbaned stranger bore in the way of mitigating accoutrements was European underwear, according to Irene, hardly a recommendation in conventional circles!

Still, I shared the anxiety that attends a crisis. My worry was increased by the troubling fact that the man had indeed seemed to know me—or to recognize me, rather. Irene's assertion that the fellow had been attacked in some invisible way right before our eyes—or behind our backs, to put it more accurately—was even more disturbing. It promised that this inconvenient person would not simply vanish from our lives as swiftly as he had appeared, at least not until Irene had satisfied herself as to his identity and discovered the reason for the apparent attack.

I should inject here an architectural note. Although our residence at Neuilly was commonly referred to as a "cottage," this was not the humble, squat dwelling to be found dotting the English countryside. This cottage was two-storied and rambling, like all buildings that date to an assortment of centuries past. It offered narrow stairs, low doorways, and floors paved in slate, stone or broad wooden planks. The place thronged with dormers and unexpected window seats, and the kitchens were a flagstone-floored horror reminiscent of Torquemada's torture chambers, replete with wrought-iron hooks and a massive, man-high hearth perfect for spitting a pig. Numerous bedchambers nestled under the lead-tiled eaves above. The entire arrangement demonstrated that French facility for combining the grand and the cozy. I must admit that I found it amenable.

So we had room aplenty for any unclaimed wretch lucky enough to fall into the path of Irene's curiosity. I kept my own curiosity, which Irene has often accused of being more sluggish than Lucifer after a culinary expedition to the surrounding fields, well reined, despite the hustle and bustle overhead.

At last patience was rewarded. A parade of footfalls on the ancient stairs brought the doctor down first, then my friends. I was reading the *London Illustrated News* with great concentration.

"A most bizarre case," Dr. Mersenné was declaring. "You are correct about the puncture wound, Madame Norton, but no ordinary medical needle made it. A hypodermic needle, no matter how fine, is hollow. Whatever pierced our friend's arm was not. Furthermore, it has taken a rather crude bite of his flesh. Most clumsy. Mademoiselle."

Dr. Mersenné nodded at me as Godfrey gestured him to the chintz armchair and offered him a glass of brandy. I have never known a physician to refuse spirits, and the French especially are no exception.

"Furthermore," he continued as Irene and Godfrey seated themselves before him like attentive pupils, "what is the point of skewering a fellow with a narrow point if one is not injecting some foreign substance? To get his attention?"

"His attention had already been deeply engaged by one of

our party," Irene answered. "You are certain that our guest has not received a recent dose of poison, then?"

"How can I be certain, unless the miserable fellow dies?" The doctor laughed long and easily. "Your own English doctors," he said, like everyone else wrongly assuming that because Irene was married to an Englishman and was friend to an Englishwoman she must be English and not American, "would perhaps nail down the diagnosis with a harder hammer, but my guess is that the man suffers from a chronic fever contracted on the Indian subcontinent."

"India." Godfrey narrowed his eyes and tented his fingers in his best barrister manner. "His dress, of course, comes from that part of the globe."

"I did not see him dressed." The doctor drained his glass and rose, his scuffed black bag again in hand. "But his complexion bespeaks many years in a foreign clime, if he is indeed an Englishman, as you surmise."

"He addressed us in English," Irene put in, "or, at least, he addressed Mademoiselle Huxleigh in that language. His accent was perfect."

"So is your French accent, Madame," Dr. Mersenné said with a bow that was a little too low and a little too long.

"That is true." Godfrey led the doctor to the passage. "Appearances can be deceiving and so can aural impressions." The two men ambled toward the front door.

"Well," I asked Irene, "is it poison or fever, and will he live or die? Like most physicians, Dr. Mersenné was indefinite."

She regarded me closely. Lucifer chose that moment to stalk into the parlor and brush against my skirts. Irene rummaged in a Sèvres box on the marquetry table until she had found a cigarette and one of Lucifer's namesake matches. I found her habit of prefacing the answers to momentous questions with such stage business most annoying.

Irene smiled at me through her veils of smoke, looking like a snake charmer working with a ghostly subject. "He may suffer from both: fever and poison. Doctors are so unimaginative. From my observation, the puncture wound would accommodate any one of a dozen hatpins I have on hand. Or that you have."

"A hatpin?"

"Do not sound so skeptical, dear Nell. I have put a hatpin to good use in my own defense on numerous occasions. Seven to ten inches of sharpened steel is nothing to underestimate, particularly if it is dipped in a toxic substance. Hatpins are miniature rapiers, and often a woman's best defense. Why could they not be a man's downfall?"

"I have never regarded a hatpin as lethal," I admitted, "but then I see the world with the innocent eyes of a parson's daughter." At this announcement, Lucifer narrowed his emerald eyes and leaped onto my lap, there to switch his tail most commandingly. "Why must this creature cast himself upon my skirts?"

"Apparently innocent parson's daughters are as attractive to cats as they are to mysterious strangers."

"Oh, I see I will never live it down," I retorted. "And you still have not said whether the man would live or die."

"I do not know, Nell, any more than Dr. Mersenné does." Irene snuffed her cigarette, then rose and smiled down at me. "All I know is that the swarthy gentleman upstairs requires constant tending. We shall have to take turns nursing him, you, Sophie and I."

"I can stand guard as well," said Godfrey as he returned from seeing the doctor out. "Who will take first watch?"

They stood there, shoulder to shoulder, my handsome friends, and eyed me blandly.

"Perhaps Nell should," Irene suggested at last. "After all, the man is asking for her."

I stood so abruptly—and unthinkingly—that Lucifer thudded to the floor with a furious hiss. The sound was echoed by the parrot Casanova in his cage, but no noise was louder than the oceanic roar of my inner disbelief.

A sickroom always reminds me of a wake to which no one has yet come. My melancholy in the presence of illness is no doubt due to my lot as a parson's daughter. From an early age I made myself useful to my father and his flock, and running sickroom errands was one thing a child could do.

Simply closing the shutters in daylight and putting a dormant form in the bed linens had transformed our cheery upstairs bedroom into a slightly sinister place. A paraffin lamp glowed softly on the bureau, casting enough light to reveal the figure in the bed.

"He looks quite different," I exclaimed, keeping my distance nevertheless.

"A fascinating man," Irene said, her voice vibrant with its most dramatic timbre.

"How can you say that? You know nothing about him."

Her amber-brown eyes fairly scintillated. "Ah, that is what makes him fascinating. Speculation, darling Nell, is always much more exciting than information. What do you think of him now?"

"He will not—"

"Awaken? I cannot say. At the moment he is quiet. You may study him safely."

"I wish Godfrey were—"

"We are better off without Godfrey now."

"Why?"

Irene flashed me a probing look. "You might prefer privacy when you discover who he is."

"You are here, are you not? And I do not require privacy, I require belief. You really think that I know this man?"

"Not . . . yet."

I sighed pointedly and examined this most inconvenient person. Against the pallid bed linens, his profile was etched as sharply as charcoal on canvas. Not even illness could bring pallor to that tea-stained face. Yet his gaunt features were well modeled, and the absence of the turban revealed hair of a lighter brown than his beard, grizzled at the temples.

Drawing nearer, I found myself unable to guess his age. Perhaps the extreme thinness made him seem older. Certainly the sun had tanned his skin until it cracked at the outer eyes into a fan of fine lines.

He moaned and I leaped back, my skirts brushing against my shoes like a swiftly drawn theatrical curtain swaying over the boards. My heart beat in the same breathless rhythm.

"He will not bite, Nell. Quite the contrary. Sophie was unable to get even a leek gruel down him."

"Leek gruel! I can hardly blame the man. An invalid should have barley soup and custards, not some foreign fluid made from disgusting bulbs."

My indignation must have stirred the sick man. I heard another moan from the bed, and then—to my chagrin—my own name was intoned, or slurred, rather.

"Miss . . . Huxleigh."

I leaped backward like a scalded cat, despite Irene's promise that he would not bite. Who was this man? How dare he know me when I did not know him? Was it some kind of dreadful trick?

Irene's warm hand took my icy one in a firm grip, the only grip she ever used. "He cannot hurt you, Nell, but obviously you have inspired some powerful memory. Think! If he has been poisoned and should die, you may be the clue to his past, and to the poisoner. Is there anyone you have not seen in some years?"

"M-my late father."

"Someone alive, or presumed dead, perhaps. Someone from Shropshire?"

I had not thought of the county of my upbringing for many years. "No one from Shropshire would come to such a condition as this."

Irene's grip loosened in disappointment. "Oh, come now. As I remember, you yourself had come to a sorry state in London when I met you, but—what?—three years from Shropshire's genteel safety. You had been wrongly dismissed from your position, had no lodgings, no food . . . indeed, had I not intervened you might have become as hungry and ill as this man."

Her words prodded me closer to the bed. Was there truly someone I knew beyond this intimidating appearance? Someone from Shropshire? Or who had left Shropshire before I did?

My heart stopped. At least my hand, which had come to rest over that organ, could feel no flutter in the general vicinity.

"Yes, Nell?" Irene urged, her voice the intense hiss of a demonic barrister conducting a cross-examination. "What have you remembered?"

"Not . . . what. Who." I whispered, as she did, not because it was a sickroom, but because I hardly dared credit the notion that invaded my mind.

I leaned nearer the semiconscious man. Could this be what had become of my once-attentive curate, the sole man ever to have courted me in any manner, however tentative? Could this be Jaspar Higgenbottom, returned from converting the heathens of Africa, himself converted to sun and turbans and the scent of alien spices?

"Nell?" Irene shook my hand, which she still clutched.

"Er, no. This is no one I remember. The ears are wrong."

She leaned over me to inspect these organs.

"What is wrong with them?"

"N-nothing. These are quite well shaped and discreet. The person of whom I was thinking had far more prominent—and unfortunate—ears."

"Oh. A shame. And did this large-eared person of your acquaintance abandon Shropshire for a foreign land?"

"Yes."

"And why have you never mentioned this interesting globe-trotter from your past?"

"Because he was not! Interesting. I am sorry, Irene, but he was my father's curate for a time, and rather tedious, I fear. I am certain that he is still being tedious in Africa. But he is not here."

The patient reached up a hand of bronze. "Miss Huxleigh," he murmured.

I blushed.

"Most intriguing." Irene sat on the edge of the bed, her brow furrowed in concentration. "Whenever you go on one of your governess tirades he calls your name. Obviously, the sound of your voice as well as your appearance rings a bell with him. Could it be the schoolroom bell? Could this be a former charge?"

"Irene! I may be past thirty, and some of my erstwhile charges may be twenty or so, but I assure you that this man is not one of them."

"No." She regarded him cold-bloodedly. "It is hard to tell, of course, but I would guess him to be our age." She quirked a brow in my direction.

"Perhaps."

The sick man lashed his head from side to side, as fever victims do when trying to elude the heat and pain of their malady. I unthinkingly picked up the damp cloth Sophie had left in a Sèvres basin and dabbed at his forehead.

"Mary," he said suddenly.

I gave Irene a triumphant look and wrung the cloth out over the basin. "You see. Huxleigh is not a unique name. It is *Mary* Huxley, poor woman, who chafes his mind."

"Hmm." Irene looked unconvinced. She rose with a sigh. "Since you are doing nurse duty, you might as well tend him until dinner. Godfrey can stand watch then, and I shall take the first part of the night."

"You have given yourself the bitterest hours. He will be most restless then."

Irene grinned demoniacally. "He will also be most talkative. Call me if his condition should worsen."

She was gone, leaving me with a cloth dripping onto my sleeve cuff and a delirious stranger on my hands.

"I see her game, of course," I told my indifferent charge as I swabbed his face again. I was getting quite used to the sun-darkened skin, despite the man's obvious English origin. No wonder Irene was curious; this man must have quite a tale to tell should he live to murmur more than a few ambiguous names. "She hopes that I will meditate upon your features and recognize you from mere proximity. But I shan't."

I sat back in the straight chair by the bedside to watch and wait. His face had turned toward my voice, although his eyes had remained shut, an arrangement I much preferred. "Mary," he murmured again. A name infinitely more common than Penelope, I reflected smugly. For once Irene the Female Pinkerton was utterly on the wrong track. "Little Mary," he repeated, stirring my sympathy, for the man obviously spoke of a child. "And Allegra."

This name caused me to sit up straighter. Allegra Turnpenny had been one of my charges during my last position of governess a decade before, at the end of the 'Seventies . . . and a Mary Forsythe was one of her little friends who had come to the house on Berkeley Square!

"And Miss Huxleigh," he went on in a mumble that I was thankful Irene was not present to hear. "Berkeley Square."

And suddenly I knew! I leaned forward, studying these altered features for any trace of their original expansive merriment. There was none. Yet, oh, I was grateful for Irene's pragmatic "privacy."

For somewhere beneath this weather-worn mask lay the face of my charges' young uncle, Mr. Emerson Stanhope, who had gone so gaily off to war in a dazzling red uniform. Who had once played a surprise game of blindman's buff with me in the schoolroom and touched my naive heart with a deathless and most inappropriate hope for one who was far above my station.

The door to the chamber swung slightly ajar. I started as if caught filching handkerchiefs. A shadow tumbled in from the passage. Lucifer swaggered over to the sickbed, then bounded onto my lap. For once I felt no urge to instantly unseat the beast, but let him curl into my skirts and proceed to purr and rhythmically dig his claws against the grain of my plaid wool skirt. I drove my fingers into his long hair as into a muff and finally felt warmth tinge my fingertips as shock eased into a kind of stupor.

And so I was when Godfrey entered the chamber an hour and a half later.

"All well?" asked he.

"He has not stirred," said I, picking up the sleeping cat and slipping from the room.

If Godfrey noticed anything odd in my manner and gazed after me, I did not look back to see.

Chapter Seven

DELIBERATE DEATH

"How did your vigil go last night?" Godfrey asked in his most persuasive baritone at breakfast the next morning. He lifted a small crystal jar. "Would you care for some marmalade?"

"Quite peacefully," I replied, taking the marmalade jar. "And how are the sausages this morning?"

"Excellent," said he. "So there was no disturbance to your patient?"

"None at all. Slept like a lamb. Would you care for some ham?"

"No, thank you."

"And did the patient have an episode during your watch?"

Godfrey shook his dark, handsome head almost regretfully. "Nothing. He did not even call out your name."

"How disappointing. Is there any honey? Ah, thank you. And, Irene . . . did she mention anything significant occurring when she returned from her time on duty?"

Godfrey paused in dosing a croissant with a dollop of pale, sweet country butter. "Ah . . . it was rather late. We had other matters than your mysterious gentleman to, er, discuss."

"Truly? I cannot imagine Irene being distracted from a mystery so near at hand for anything."

Godfrey shrugged with masculine modesty. "She was fatigued, no doubt, from her late hours sitting up with the sick man."

"And she did not report any delirious revelations?"

"She reported delirium, but no revelations," Godfrey said at last with the hesitant air of a man conveying the exact truth in an utterly different context from the one under discussion.

"Then it has been a most unproductive night," I summed up, biting as daintily as possible into my condiment-laden roll. I dislike the taste of French baking, which is much overrated by the easily led, and have been forced to resort to disguising the dough with sweets.

"I would not say that the night was unproductive." Irene swept into the small breakfast chamber in a blonde lace combing mantle, her russet hair rippling over her shoulders.

It occurs to me that during the years I have recorded Irene's adventures, or rather, recorded my adventures while living with Irene, that my descriptions of her coloring have varied. For some annoying reason, the exact shade of Irene's hair, even her eye color, shifts with the hour of the day, the hues of her clothing and the range of her moods. Beyond being a gifted actress, she is a human chameleon upon whom the light plays tricks, sometimes painting her hair auburn, at other times brunette. Her eyes have that fascinating tiger's-eye quality of mellowing to orbs of honeyed amber and darkening to coffee-dark brown when her pupils swell with agitation.

That gay, green June morning in Neuilly Irene was nevertheless a walking palette of autumnal hues, as warming as well-steeped tea.

She accepted the coffee cup that Sophie instantly brought her and poured several dollops of clotted cream into it, carelessly stirring the mess with the nearest utensil, a fork. Could the Beauties of Europe watch Irene eat whatever pleased her, there would be more than ground glass in her rouge pot, as happened once in the dressing rooms of La Scala.

"Well, my dears." Irene looked brightly from Godfrey to me, unaware of the current day's aura. "And have you been comparing notes on our patient's progress? What do you think?"

"That you hardly look as if you had sat up half the night," I answered tartly. I had slept barely at all after the strain of fleeing the sickroom and then toying with the dinner that had followed under Irene's formidable scrutiny.

Irene smiled. "Oh, I was up more than half the night at that, Nell, but *I* have not worried about confessions I must make in the morning, as you have."

"What confessions?"

"You might start," she suggested, sipping the scalding coffee with true American bravado, "by telling us the identity of the sunburnt hero upstairs."

"What makes you think that Nell knows?" Godfrey asked.

"Why do you call him a hero?" I demanded simultaneously.

She blinked and stared from one of us to the other. "My, but we are testy this lovely morning. To answer your questions: Nell has always known the man, Godfrey; she simply did not recognize him until last evening." Irene addressed me next. "As for his being a hero, I found a medal concealed in his shoe. What do you say to that?"

I sipped my tea, which had cooled to tepid peppermint consommé. "That I am relieved to learn that the fellow actually *wore* shoes."

Irene laughed delightedly. "You are doing a splendid job of pretending ignorance, but I could tell from your manner last evening that something troubled you. Surely only knowing the identity of the sick man could deaden your palette to Veal Malmaison."

"I suppose he revealed that while you were sequestered with him later?"

"Alas, no. He was as irritatingly mum on the subject then as you are now."

"Perhaps it is a conspiracy," Godfrey suggested, "between our Nell and the mysterious stranger from the East."

"You are a cold-blooded pair," I put in, "to show such

curiosity about a man who may be dying from some subtly administered poison."

"A hatpin is hardly subtle, Nell," Irene corrected me. "And I think that the poison it bore is not fatal to this particular victim. Besides," she added blithely, shaking her napkin free of pastry flakes, "his fever broke in the night. I expect him to be perfectly intelligible this morning."

I could not keep from jumping in my chair. "Why did you not say so the first thing? We must let the poor man know where he is, so he does not panic."

Irene's warm hand covered my icy fist like a tea cozy. "He will not panic. He knows he is among friends."

I was about to ask how this could be, but feared I would not like the answer. So we finished breakfast—or my friends did. I had suddenly lost my appetite, as I had last night at dinner. "I do believe I know him," I admitted at last, "but he has changed so much . . ."

"Perhaps you have as well," Irene said almost consolingly.

"I? Not in the least, I'm sure. After all, *he* recognized me, not vice versa."

"Do you wish to tell us of him?" Godfrey inquired.

"I would rather let him speak for himself," I said firmly. "He has changed so greatly that I dare not speculate on why or how."

"What a shame!" Irene smiled tigerishly. "Speculation is one of the few truly creative entertainments left to our modern times. I have been concocting plots on an operatic scale. I would hate to have our guest destroy them with the simple, dull truth."

We finished breakfast, each in our way, and repaired upstairs to confront the invalid. There he lay, brown upon the bed linens but pale in an inner, spiritual sense. Perhaps the breaking fever had also washed away his resolve.

Sophie made a self-important to-do about fluffing pillows and propping him up against them so he could speak with us. Despite the snowy nightshirt he wore, or because of it, his skin seemed strikingly dark, though his eyes no longer had the unnatural luster of illness.

He spoke in that disconcertingly perfect English while the rest of us studied his remarkable appearance in silence. "I apologize for inflicting myself upon your household. The maid tells me that you plucked me from collapse upon the cobblestones of Notre Dame."

Irene pounced. "Then you speak French, for our servant speaks no English."

He looked taken aback at this challenging response to his apologetic beginning, but added in the language of this land, "Yes, Madame, I speak French. Yet in any language I must apologize for casting myself upon the mercy of strangers. I cannot imagine what weakness came over me."

"Can you not?" Irene did not sound even slightly merciful at the moment. "Come, come, sir. You dissemble."

"D-dissemble?"

"Or, as the plain folk put it, you lie. At the least you mean to mislead us. You have suffered from fever for some time."

"But not in this climate, not so far north. Is this what you mean by deception, Madame?" He was more bewildered than defensive.

"Not at all. There is also your insistence that we are strangers to you."

"But—" He eyed Godfrey and Irene with rather pitiful confusion. "You are."

"And Miss Huxleigh—whose name you have called out not once but several times in your delirium?" Irene pointed to me at a moment when I most would have liked to sift through the floorboards into safe invisibility downstairs. "What is she to think of you now calling her a mere 'stranger'?"

"Really, Irene," I murmured. "The gentleman is quite correct."

The man's gaunt face had stiffened like a soldier's on parade. "I may have said a great deal of nonsense in my delirium. They do not call it 'senselessness' for nothing."

"On the contrary." Irene drew a side chair to the bed the

better to interrogate her victim. "You have not forgotten an iota of what you said while raving. It is merely that with a cool head again, you are prepared to deny it."

"I cannot blame you for thinking me a liar and rogue, considering the circumstances in which you found me. Give me my robes and I'll be gone."

"Oh, I cannot in good conscience do that," Irene murmured. "You are too ill."

"And this is how you treat an ill man, Madame?"

"This is how I treat a prevaricator, sir, well or ill. If you will not answer my questions frankly, I will be forced to bully the answers out of Miss Huxleigh."

The patient's eyes gleamed with fresh spirit. "I do not know what position this unfortunate lady occupies in your establishment, but she does not have to suffer such mistreatment."

"As I thought. You seek to protect her—now, and by your continuing silence about yourself."

A silence ruled the room. Godfrey had watched the exchange with the same sharp attention he would give to a rival barrister's cross-examination, as if more were going on than was evident. I myself was embarrassed by Irene's rough accusations. Yet she had hit a nerve. For the first time I saw color flush that dusky visage.

The man sighed. "You overestimate the chivalry that I am capable of at this point in my life," he said wearily. "It is far more likely that I seek to protect myself."

"And your identity," Irene prodded. She smiled and leaned back in the chair. "My dear sir, you have in the past few hours escaped a horrible and intentional death. Can the truth of your identity be worse than that fate?"

His expression became more bitter than the black coffee Irene and Godfrey consumed so copiously in the morning. "Truth is almost always worse than death, especially to one who has lived on the other side of the veil between East and West."

"Ah." Irene settled happily upon her hard chair. "A story. Begin with who you are."

"Should you not tell me your identity first?"

"A good point. I am a dead woman, sir, but you may call me Madame Norton. And this dashing gentleman is my husband, Godfrey, also presumed dead. Miss Huxleigh you know, and her mortality has never been in question, nor has anything else about her. Miss Huxleigh is of impeccable intentions. Her position in this household is as strict guardian of propriety, and a terrible tyrant she is, too."

"You jest with me," the poor man said.

Godfrey forsook his position lounging against the bureau to approach the bed. "My wife always speaks the serious truth, but often spouts ambiguities, like the Oracle. She means that she and I are wrongfully presumed dead and that we have not sought to correct that mistake. In my case, at least, it does not matter, as I was virtually anonymous before the misunderstanding occurred."

"And"— the man looked into my eyes for the first time— "is . . . Miss Huxleigh in truth the household terror your wife implies?"

"Miss Huxleigh is a stalwart member of the company, but at times her stringent standards do terrify my wife . . . a little, as I believe Irene meant to intimidate you into saying what you may wish to keep to yourself."

"What of this deliberate death she spoke of?"

Irene wasted no words. "Poison," she said. "Borne on the prick of a hatpin. You were infected in the crowd before Notre Dame, but I believe your chronic fever foiled the toxin by forcing your body to perspire it away before it could do its damage."

The man laughed. "Yes, it's hard for civilized toxins to harm a system that has been suckled at the breast of hellish Afghan and Indian plains for over a decade. I have quinine rather than blood in my veins by now."

Godfrey frowned and drew another side chair to the foot of

the bed. "News of this attempted murder does not surprise you?"

Hazel eyes burned in the bezel of that lean, dark face. "Living in India—not as the White Man does, in separate settlements and cool hill-stations, but as the native does—is a form of attempted murder far more serious than poisoned hatpins, sir."

"Oh, you must tell us your story," Irene ordered rapturously, "but first you must explain yourself to poor, dear Penelope. She has suffered enough confusion."

I wanted to die of mortification as those hazel eyes searched mine. He seemed to look only at me, and deeply into me.

"Do you not know me, Miss Huxleigh?"

"I—I believe that I do."

"Do you wish to know more?"

"I believe that Irene is right. I believe that I must know."

He sighed, spread his brown hands on the coverlet and examined them with a kind of weary wonder. "You have before you a dead man, too, Mr. and Mrs. Norton, in everything but the fact of my breathing despite all attempts to end it—my own and others'. In my youth, I was the flower of English gentility, one of hundreds of sturdy blossoms stripped from the bush of England at their peak and exported to a foreign clime. I was sent off to war in a smart uniform with scarlet trousers, with white-gloved hands. With no blood on anything but my morning razor."

"Who were you, in this world of long ago?" Irene wondered.

He studied the figured coverlet, as if its loose-woven hummocks and valleys were an unfamiliar landscape from which he could not tear his eyes.

I found myself answering for him, saying the words he had lost the will to affirm. It has often been my role in life to act for others in this fashion, but at no time has it been more difficult. "Young Mr. Stanhope," I said, my voice remarkably clear, remarkably civilized-sounding, as if I were announcing him to the Queen. "Mr. Emerson Stanhope of Grosvenor Square."

"Stanhope." Godfrey raised a raven eyebrow. "It is an honored name in the Temple."

"And so it shall remain as long as I stay lost and forgotten. But now . . . I must venture from the foreign bolt-holes in which I have hidden for so long." He glanced at me. "And I fear I will bring pain and disgrace upon those who have known me." A flush of color surfaced again in the hollows of those sunken cheeks.

"How do you mean 'disgrace'?" Irene probed.

"That bitter battle is long forgotten. If I survived, others as deserving died that day. Others even more deserving had their reputations tarnished far beyond what the mere metal of medals and history books can honor. I was content to let the dead lie unavenged, coward that I am. Now I fear that a living man will pay the price of my stupidity and my silence, so I must return to England to set things right, if I can. Though nothing can right the perfidy of that day when men and horses died by the dozens in the dust of those brutal plains under the damned, underestimated, relentless thunder of the Ayub's artillery."

"Of what battle do you speak so harshly, Mr. Stanhope?" I asked. I confess that I have never paid much attention to these innumerable skirmishes with outlandish appellations so often fought under foreign skies by my countrymen.

"Maiwand," he answered in loathing tones, as if mouthing the devil's pet name. "A black day for England, and for Maclaine, and for a fool with the youthful hubris to call himself 'Cobra.' "

I barely recalled this engagement, but Irene raised an imperious hand, leaning forward in her chair, her eyes gleaming with dawning intelligence. "Maiwand was nearly a decade ago, Mr. Stanhope. Its name is forgotten except in the military histories, though it was far from England's finest hour. What is the present danger? What is the name of the man you seek, whose life you fear for?"

"A man who saved my own life."

"And who is he?"

Young Mr. Stanhope—and so I still thought of him, despite the lapse of years and his present, much-fallen circumstance—was strangely silent. His sun-darkened face held that inscrutability said to accompany an Oriental turn of mind. This was not the blithe youth who had left Berkeley Square in high spirits but a decade before.

"I know naught of him but those few hectic minutes we shared amid a battlefield dust storm," he finally said, picking at the crochet work—my own—on the bed linens.

Irene leaned back, looking even more inscrutable than he. "Now you truly intrigue me, Mr. Stanhope. You seek a nameless man, whose face must have been obscured when you encountered one another during the heat of battle and whose semblance is certainly time-blurred by this late date. Please tell me at least that he is English! That would narrow the field of search somewhat."

"Why should he not be English?" Mr. Stanhope shot back.

"He might have been an enemy, or an Irishman."

Mr. Stanhope laughed at her quick retort and sardonic wit. Irishmen were frequently soldiers of fortune and ever the enemy to England even as they served under British rule.

"He is European," Emerson Stanhope conceded in a raw voice of weariness, though the cautious fire in his eyes that Irene's questions had lit remained unbanked.

"I am relieved." Irene stood, catching Godfrey's eye. "Then you are in the right place. Perhaps we can help you find your quarry."

"I do not require help, save in your kindness to an ill man."

"An ill man and a hunted one, I think." He made a denying hand gesture but Irene ignored it. "It seems that the life this mysterious gentleman saved is not much regarded by its owner, for that life also appears in fresh and more sinister danger than ever on a battlefield."

"I merely suffer a relapse of fever. It is you who are delirious, Madame, with your hints of poison and conspiracy."

"I am often taken that way," Irene said lightly. "It comes of an apprenticeship in grand opera. Forgive me for harrying you at a time of such weakness. I will leave you to the tender nursing of Miss Huxleigh. No doubt you both have much to discuss."

Her skirts rustled imperiously as she swept out of the bedchamber.

Godfrey paused by the bed. "If you feel strong enough tomorrow, we can move you to the garden for a time; fresh air should do more for fever than anything else."

Mr. Stanhope's hazel eyes crinkled at the corners. "And a smoke, Mr. Norton? I admit that I could use a decent smoke. Outdoors it would not disturb the ladies."

Godfrey laughed at that, no doubt well aware that the activity would never discomfit one lady in particular. "If you hope to hide from my wife's curiosity behind a haze of cigar smoke," he said, "I warn you that it will not do. But the smoke itself can be arranged."

I followed him out to find Irene waiting in the narrow upstairs passage like a governess ambushing a miscreant. "Nell!" Her voice was low and urgent. "You must find out more about Mr. Stanhope's mysterious mission—and his even more mysterious past."

"I must do no such thing! Irene, the man is ill. Have you no shame?"

"He is not so ill that he cannot obscure his motives and plans. Nell, this is for his own good. Mr. Stanhope has obviously been long abroad and is not well suited to conduct the sort of inquiries he intends."

"He is wise enough to dodge your impertinent questions!"

"Then you must put to him some less impertinent queries that he will not avoid. I count upon your impeccable tact, your undying sympathy and your eternal concern for another's own good. You must find out more about your old acquaintance—and soon. For I fear he will not live long to tell anyone more if he is not taken in hand."

Godfrey met my skeptical look with a sober nod. "Irene is

right. There is something odd about the fellow. He has obviously lived outside the pale in India and environs. Englishmen seldom turn renegade in such climes without reason."

I turned reluctantly back to the bedchamber, my mind churning with doubt and fear. And curiosity.

"And while you are at it," Irene added in her best operatic sotto voce, which carried to me even as I opened the door, "you had best find out why he was called by that intriguing sobriquet, 'Cobra.' "

I shuddered, for I have never liked snakes.

Chapter Eight

PILLOW TALK

"**Your** ... friend is a determined woman."

I paused in opening the shutters. If I meant to throw light on my long-ago acquaintance's situation, the actual light of day might draw forth a corresponding candor. Besides, the hushed, dim intimacy of the sickroom made me uneasy, as did the familiar but utterly altered figure upon the bed. I opened the shutters, and the clear morning light poured in.

"Irene has had to be determined," I said, taking the hard chair by the bedside with a false calm. I was not used to playing interrogator.

"Tell me about her," he suggested after a pause. "At first I thought you were employed in some manner in the Nortons' household. Are you actually mere friends?"

"Yes, I am," I said, laughing at his confusion. "And more. I assist Godfrey with certain legal matters, and—although no one can be said to assist Irene; she is far too independent—I make myself useful to her as well. I am not quite employee nor family member. I suppose you could accuse me of idleness and waste."

"You 'make yourself useful,' " he repeated soberly. "That is more than I have done in the years since I last saw you in Berkeley Square."

"Surely the wish to save a man's life is of a high order of usefulness?"

"You have not aged," he said, abruptly changing the subject.

"Of course I have. I am past thirty."

He smiled. "So am I, but a woman should not confess such things so easily."

"I am not the kind of woman who would find any advantage in coyness, Mr. Stanhope. Why would I wish to conceal my age except to deceive someone, most likely myself?"

He eyed me with some perplexity, as if he actually found me—perish the thought—fascinating in some respect. I am not used to being regarded in such a light, although I have often seen its beams showered upon Irene.

"I am quite astounded to find you here in Paris, in such circumstances," he went on.

"Indeed, Mr. Stanhope! You take the words from my mouth."

He frowned again, in the way of a baffled boy. "I do not remember you as being so quick-spoken."

"Ah." The memory of our youthful selves had induced in me a strange tongue-tied tartness that even now I could not explain. "I was far younger then, and had seen a bit less of the world."

"What of the world have you seen now?" His tone was so jocular that it unaccountedly offended me. Certainly he expected this country mouse to have ventured not much farther than the parson's pantry. Yet I knew myself to be no match for the exotic adventures that had occupied his life.

I folded my hands upon my lap, as they become restless when idle. Naturally Lucifer, who had been sitting docilely enough upon the elbowboard at the window, proceeded to loft into my lap. Mr. Stanhope awaited my answer.

"I have worked as a drapery clerk at Whiteley's and as a typewriter-girl in the Temple. I have been privileged, if you can call it that, to see several freshly murdered corpses and to have solved a cryptic cartograph that led to buried archeological treasure. I have been to Bohemia and have met a king, although I did not much like him. I have also met a princess-to-be, and came to like her despite myself. I have never liked Sarah Bernhardt or Oscar Wilde, however much they may claim to cherish me; nor do I have anything but the most profound distaste for snakes, satin slippers, French cuisine and the dreadful Casanova. Lucifer is not among my favorites, either, though I would never neglect him."

Poor Mr. Stanhope struggled more upright among his feather pillows, which were as overblown and airy as French pastries. "The King of Bohemia? A princess? Bernhardt and Wilde? Casanova and Lucifer? I fear my fever has not waned, after all."

I smiled at his agitation, a sign of recovering strength, and stroked the black cat, who at least felt amiable if he did not behave so. "This is Lucifer. He is Persian and Parisian. A gift from Irene upon my arrival here last year. Most unwanted, I might add."

"Afghan," Mr. Stanhope said in a clear, bitter voice. "The breed is Afghan. Persian is a misnomer."

"He is misbegotten, I'll give you that," said I. "But you mean to say that such cats originated in the unhappy land where you fought in that battle, My . . . My—?"

"Luckily for you, it is not 'your' anything. The battle was called Maiwand, after an insignificant village on the site." Lucifer, like all cats knowing himself to be under discussion and reveling in it, bounded soundlessly to the bed and stalked over to inspect its resident. "He's a handsome fellow. This sumptuous breed of cat is the only exportable product of that unhappy landscape, though I've spent enough years scraping over it like a scorpion. You must have been referring to domestic pets with all that King of Bohemia and Bernhardt and Wilde business."

"Certainly not! I am not personally fond of those persons but I would never compare them to animals. That would be quite . . . disrespectful. To the animals, no doubt. That would be something—"

"Something that your friend Madame Norton would do."

"Exactly," said I righteously. "Irene can, at times, be shockingly irreverent. But she means nothing by it."

"Of course not." He did not sound at all convinced, but I am used to the people around me contradicting my convictions, having resided for so long with Irene.

"Why did you take such a dislike to Mr. Wilde?" he asked. "I have overheard much of him in the cafés since I came to Paris."

"You habituated the cafés?"

"Only the fringes. But tell me how Wilde offended you."

"For one thing, he is such a man with the ladies, always throwing himself into tortured metaphors in our praise and flinging flowers and quips at our feet. I may know little of the world, but I know that nothing good can come of it. He was quite taken with Irene, I'm mortified to say that she insists he also harbored a fondness for myself."

"And Madame Sarah Bernhardt?"

"Quite an immoral woman, and utterly willful. She let Irene fight a duel disguised as her son, can you imagine it? I tried to stop it, but Sarah, of course, can be quite forceful for such a small woman. And I am not at all certain that her hair is its natural color."

He shook his head. "I fear I still suffer from delirium, Miss Huxleigh. The picture you paint is exceedingly different from what I would expect of our placid governess of Berkeley Square."

"There are times that I find my life since then a delirium, too, Mr. Stanhope. Really and truly, it is for the most part excessively dull, unless Irene becomes involved in one of her tangles."

"She has ambitions of making me into one of these 'tangles,' does she?"

"Possibly, but the tangles come to her, rather than vice versa. I would not underestimate her, Mr. Stanhope. She found a missing girdle of diamonds that belonged to Marie Antoinette. Later, she saved a young Parisian girl from disgrace and freed the demoiselle's poor aunt from a charge of murder. Ignore her flamboyant ways; Irene has done much good, despite herself."

"No doubt due to your good example."

"Well . . ." I smiled modestly. "Certainly I have offered advice on occasion. She, being an opera singer by training, suffers from an impetuous nature and requires the moderation of a cooler head. That is where Godfrey comes in so usefully, although he is so besotted at times with his bride that his normal sensible nature can be corrupted—only in the most minor ways, of course. If it were not for me, who is to say upon what questionable ventures Irene might lure him?"

"Not I!" Lucifer had settled at the invalid's side and had begun grooming his glossy black flank. Mr. Stanhope stroked the cat's flowing ruff. "You are a virtual Scheherazade, Miss Huxleigh, spinning exotic tales. I cannot believe that you are the same diffident, lonely young person I knew."

"You did not know me, Mr. Stanhope. A governess is but one step up from a servant. And I was not lonely! I had my two charges, Charlotte and Allegra—how grown they must be by now. Young ladies . . ." My sigh was echoed by Mr. Stanhope's.

"I cannot tell you how many times I thought about Berkeley Square when I was abroad," he said fiercely. "It came to symbolize the innocence of England in a world vastly more dangerous. Once I found myself captivated by that crueler, older world. Once I thought I could be at home in that landscape of clashing opposites and raw gemstones and crude hopes. Yet I always came back to dreaming of England, particularly of Berkeley Square. Remember a day when I surprised you and the girls and their friends—little wren-haired Mary Forsythe, remember her? You were barely taller and older than they, playing blindman's buff. I joined in for a few moments. Do you recall such a day?"

"I—I may," said I, brushing the black cat hair from my cream wool skirt. I could not quite look at him, so my eye focused on Lucifer, disapprovingly. "That animal is most inconsiderate of his leavings! Perhaps I could spin these wasted quantities of his hair into yarn and put some part of him to good use in my crochet work. Did they spin cat hair in Afghanistan, Mr. Stanhope?"

He was regarding me strangely. Indeed, my face had blossomed with sudden warmth. I was again that speechless girl of two-and-twenty, not a woman of the world who could regard a corpse without blanching and had resisted the overtures of such scandalous persons as Oscar Wilde and Sarah Bernhardt. Now a virtual stranger was unraveling me simply because he had seen me as I was and would not be again, and had not forgotten.

"You do remember?" he pressed so eagerly that I had not the heart to deny him.

"Yes, I do. You were . . . amused by me."

"Not amused. Surprised. You always seemed so grave and stern in company, like a little tin soldier sent out from your father's parsonage in Shropshire. Huxleigh, the prim and proper governess. Then there you were blindfolded, stumbling about the schoolroom like a schoolgirl yourself. How shocked you were to find me suddenly in the game."

"Yes, I was. You played a rather . . . startling trick on me. I had not meant for any of the family to see me in such an undignified state."

"But it was charming! I knew, of course, your circumstances. How your father's death had left you orphaned; how well suited you were to teach my dear nieces. Yet it must have been difficult for one so young and strictly reared to shepherd girls so near to her own age."

"Not difficult at all! The girls were delightful, the situation most pleasant. I often . . . recall those days, that day, myself. We were all so innocent then."

"Yes." His hazel, searching eyes turned inward again, much to my relief. "We were all so innocent then," he parroted in an astringent tone.

The silence grew so long and awkward that I cast desperately about for some safe topic of conversation, for a matter not rooted in the past, but the present.

"But you must tell me about yourself!" I blurted with forced brightness.

Those pale, piercing hazel eyes penetrated me as a knitting needle transfixes a ball of yarn. "Why must I?"

"It is what . . . old acquaintances do: they recall old times by revealing more recent ones. I merely wish to make conversation."

He frowned at me with suspicion. "Why should you wish to make mere conversation now? You had no time for such frivolities years ago."

"Obviously, I have consorted with the frivolous since then."

"Indeed." Amusement crimped his mouth. "I can see that you are vastly changed. As am I. There is no point in conducting a Cook's tour of my alterations; they are visible enough in my appearance and my circumstances."

I leaned forward in my eagerness to convince him. "But you left England a young officer on the brink of a brave military adventure! Your family was well connected, your future promising—er, not to say that it is no longer so, of course. What I mean is . . ."

"What you mean is that Miss Huxleigh desires to know the full extent of my fall from what this world calls position and what some might call 'grace.' You wish to satisfy your curiosity about how I have come to such a low state."

"No! Not I! I wish to know nothing of a sordid nature. Though your . . . er, circumstances, of course, are not sordid. I merely wish to offer the solicitude of one who knew you when, when—"

My blathering discomfort finally stirred him to response. His brown hand, surprisingly warm, clasped mine as he confessed, "My dear Miss Huxleigh! You must forgive a man who has led a hardened life among a foreign people for failing to realize that only Christian concern motivates your questions. Of course I see that it is your duty to learn as much of me as possible, so that you may better minister to my depraved soul. But, I warn you, my confidences may be shocking in the extreme. There are certain episodes involving the harem of the emir of Bereidah and various social practices of the Kafkir tribesmen in regard to manhood rituals—"

"No!" I snatched my hand back though his grip was disconcertingly firm. "I wish to know none of this. It is Irene who has an insatiable appetite for unseemly knowledge, not I."

"Ignorance is bliss," he quoted. I detected an unbecoming slyness in his tone that I chose to ignore.

"Ignorance is peace of mind," I returned.

"But you shock me," he went on.

"I? How could I shock anyone?"

"You underestimate yourself. For one thing, you seem utterly in the control of this American woman."

"That is untrue."

"Yet you spy for her."

"I only inquire into matters that are for your own good. How can you expect anyone to help you unless you reveal yourself?"

"I expect no help," he said in an uncompromising tone that sent chills through my veins. Gone was the merry youth who had stooped to play a schoolgirls' game. The man who spoke now could kill, I think, and he was no longer amused by me. "I did not ask to be taken to this pleasant cottage," he went on, "to be charitably tended and uncharitably interrogated. I suspect you have no personal interest in me at all."

I blushed, this time from an all-too familiar emotion, shame. "I did not wish to pry, but Irene is determined to help you. She insists on aiding anyone caught in the skeins of a puzzle that is beyond their ken. There is no arguing with such an impulse."

"Irene, Irene! You quote her as the vicar cites Scripture on Sunday. Can you not speak for yourself, Miss Huxleigh?"

I straightened. "You misunderstand our relationship. Although I have at times . . . assisted Irene in her good works, shall we say, I have never hesitated to give her the frankest benefit of my advice and opinions on any subject."

"I am sure that she is much the better for that," he murmured. "So you admit, then, that although you seek the secrets of my past on your friend's suggestion, your own curiosity—your own sense of duty, I should say—requires you to ferret out the truth."

"Of course. It is clear that you have led an adventuresome and possibly irregular life. Any decently helpful person would wish to understand the difficulties you have faced so as better to encourage you to . . . to put the past behind you and resume the life you left."

"And you always try to be a decently helpful person?"

"I do hope so."

He reached again for my hand, and indeed he was an invalid of sorts. A charitable woman can hardly withhold comfort from such a person, no matter his state of grace, or lack of it. Yet my heart began to beat most unevenly as his lean brown fingers brushed my palm and his eyes burned into mine with a mélange of amusement and keen insight and an odd flicker of challenge. I was appalled to find that during our conversation I had unthinkingly leaned nearer and nearer the bed, until we seemed to be in conspiratorial closeness, something resembling what the confessional must be for the Papists. The thought crossed my mind that whatever poor Mr. Stanhope might confide in me, I would be the judge of whether it was fitting or proper to pass on to Irene or not . . . and he had leaned toward me, as well, as the moment stretched into a strangely unsettling silence. I scarcely knew what to think, could scarcely think at all, gazing into his hazel eyes . . .

Then Lucifer, finding his luxurious position pinched as Mr. Stanhope shifted upon the bed, leaped down between us. We both started with surprise, and bent simultaneously to prevent the cat from landing askew when a sound like a sharp clap of hands exploded in my ear.

My heart spurted into a racing rhythm not at all pleasant as Mr. Stanhope seized my arms and conveyed me to the floor, falling atop me. The cat screamed like a banshee and writhed between us. Before I could catch my breath to protest this indignity as loudly and more articulately than Lucifer, the door of the chamber sprung open so violently that it clapped back against the wall like thunder. My heart pounded in the charged silence.

Godfrey and Irene stood on the bedchamber threshold, the small revolver so familiar from Irene's early adventures poised in her hand. I lay smothered and speechless in the tight clasp of Mr. Stanhope, unable to stir if my life had depended on it.

"When I asked you to entwine yourself in Mr. Stanhope's affairs, my dear Nell," Irene drawled in odious amusement, "I did not expect you to take my suggestion so literally."

While I sputtered without the breath to defend myself, Godfrey went swiftly to the window and from the side, flung the shutters closed. I cannot recall whether Mr. Stanhope helped me to rise, or I him, but we at least struggled halfway up before Irene raised a hand (not the one bearing the revolver, I am happy to report).

"Pray do not be overambitious of rising in the world just yet, my friends. At least come nearer the door."

And so I was herded like some two-legged sheep to the threshold, where Mr. Stanhope and I were at last permitted to stand upright. I put my hand through Irene's arm for support—Mr. Stanhope had offered himself in that role quite enough for one morning—and kept my eyes averted, not knowing what kind of foreign bedclothes our guest might be wearing—or not.

A whistle from the garden below caused Irene to tighten her grasp on the pistol. Godfrey cocked his head to listen intently beside one window. Then the amiable French of our coachman André shouted up the all-clear from below: "*Paré, Monsieur, Madame—paré.*"

Godfrey released a breath and strode for the bed, where he began flinging the pillows about. Lucifer, on the floor, shook himself in royal outrage and strutted before us as if to demonstrate his valor, pausing only to swagger against each of us in turn and leave a swath of black hair glistening like a decorative horsehair band on our skirts and—I risked a glance—on Mr. Stanhope's quite respectable white linen nightshirt, no doubt borrowed from the coachman or Godfrey.

As Godfrey wreaked ruin on the pillows, feathers drifted over the disrupted bed's pale linen landscape like the winter's last and fleeciest snowflakes. I wondered why they had sprung a leak.

"Nothing here," Godfrey muttered. "So far."

Mr. Stanhope joined him in pillaging the pillows.

"I do not understand," I quavered to Irene.

She patted my hand where it curled around her forearm. "Someone has shot at you, Nell, or at Mr. Stanhope, rather. Or perhaps—" the stimulation of a new thought gave her lovely face a look of radiant delight "—at you both! Most interesting."

I found myself unwilling to cling to such a cold-blooded defender and moved my hand to my heart, which pumped feebly but evenly beneath my basque.

"Here." Mr. Stanhope's hand blended with the walnut finish of the left rear bedpost over which it hovered. "The bullet hit here."

Godfrey went over to look, then whistled softly again, a most vulgar habit he had acquired since meeting Irene. Certainly I had never heard him whistle so when engaged upon the practice of the law in the Inner Temple off Fleet Street.

"Went clear through," Godfrey said. "The power must have been tremendous."

Mr. Stanhope's forefinger filled the path the murderous bullet had ploughed through the wood. "An air rifle," he declared.

"Air rifle?" For once Irene sounded at a loss.

Mr. Stanhope eyed the revolver in her rock-steady hand with passing respect, then answered briskly. "A modern weapon, Madame, and deadly. The bullet is propelled by a burst of compressed air, and in the hands of a master marksman . . . Such weapons are sometimes used for shooting tigers in India."

"We are not tigers," I protested.

Mr. Stanhope regarded me—dare I say?—fondly.

"No, Miss Huxleigh, we are not." His expression darkened. "Though I was once, in Afghanistan, called 'Cobra.' "

Irene lowered her weapon but not the stern regard of her magnificent eyes. "I believe, Mr. Stanhope, it is high time for you to enlighten us all about what you have done since leaving England a decade ago."

Stillness—both of sound and motion—swelled in the small bedchamber as the tension does at the climactic moment in an opera. Then the cat Lucifer bounded across the rough floorboards, his claws skittering. Something clicked against something (I fear the chamberpot). Godfrey bent to retrieve what Lucifer had found for a plaything: a large misshapen blot of lead that even I recognized for a spent bullet of awesome and lethal size.

Chapter Nine

RETIRED, DUE TO DEATH

In the same cheery parlor where we three—Irene, Godfrey and I—had first heard the puzzling story of poor little Louise Montpensier and the odious forced tattoo, Mr. Stanhope unfolded another tale as compelling, one that would draw us from our rural Paris nest and into greater danger than any of us suspected that placid summer day.

He had dressed for the occasion in some clothes of Godfrey's that hung quite as limply on his spare frame as the shapeless foreign robes in which we had found him. Despite his privations, I sensed in this onetime acquaintance the same tenacious survival spirit I had seen in the late Jefferson Hope, the American frontiersman who had tracked wrongdoers for twenty years before seeing them punished only days before his own death from a heart condition.

I recalled Mr. Stanhope's odd comment that he had been called "Cobra" in Afghanistan, and his teasing hints to me that he knew intimately the customs of such a savage place, even those between its men and women. I really did not care to hear his tale for fear it should deprive me of a young girl's one moment of breathless admiration. Such moments were sufficiently rare in my life that I did not care to have one tarnished, not even by the person who had inspired it a decade before.

Irene had ensconced our guest in the tapestry-covered bergère, a kind of French easy chair, with—appropriately—an afghan over his knees. I had made it during Irene's many private singing concerts, when she was often accompanied by the parrot Casanova's razor-edged counterpoint.

Godfrey had filled Mr. Stanhope's lean brown hand with a snifter of the finest French brandy. Irene sat back, veiled in her favorite accessory for hearing bizarre tales, a haze of cigarette smoke. Mr. Stanhope accepted another vile cylinder from Godfrey with a faint smile of pleasure.

"Egyptian." He nodded to Irene. "Excellent taste, Madame, for an American."

"I do have excellent taste, Mr. Stanhope, as you can see by the quality of my associates."

Mr. Stanhope eyed Godfrey and me in turn, then grinned. "Call me 'Stan,' I beg you. I have been too long among strangers, among those who would call my name only to distract me while a dagger tickled my ribs."

"Stan?" I repeated unhappily. It is a common name, more suitable for a plumber than a gentleman or a soldier. I admit that "Emerson" had reverberated in my memory and imagination much more euphoniously through the years.

"An Army nickname," he explained gruffly. "It is short and it is sweet, and it does not remind me of days forever lost."

I dropped my eyes, unable to argue with the depth of emotion evident on his face.

"It began in the Army, the story you will tell us," Irene prodded thoughtfully. She was ever impatient for the meat of the matter.

"Indeed. So do most tales of death and betrayal and bloody incompetence. The details of our country's Afghanistan adventure from eighteen seventy-eight to eighty-one have faded already in the public awareness, and for good cause. The Great Game Russia and Britain played across the barren steppes of Afghanistan was not glorious for England."

"You refer to the eighteen-fifties' rout, the retreat from

Kabul and the slaughter of the civilians," Godfrey put in. "The Afghans do not appear to be governed by the rules of civilized warfare."

Mr. Stanhope gave him a sharp glance. "No nation wages civilized warfare, Mr. Norton, though we emphasize the atrocities done to us rather than those our own side commits."

Irene inhaled impatiently from her slender, dusky cigarette. "Why would someone wish to kill you now, over a war that you admit is already long forgotten?"

"Perhaps because I do not forget."

"Ah." She settled into the armchair with the innocently arch pleasure of Lucifer curling himself up before the fire. "Those who refuse to forget can be troublesome indeed. What memory do you carry that is so valuable—or so inconvenient—to someone? We already know that you seek to save the life of a man you do not know. Why is your own in danger?"

"I still am not convinced that it is." At this assertion, Godfrey elevated the distorted lead ball without comment. Mr. Stanhope nodded wearily. "Hard to argue with a spent bullet, but I think I know the marksman. He would not have missed unless he had meant to."

"But," I put in, "we had bent down to catch the cat just then, do you not remember? Our heads were down."

"According to where it entered the bedpost," Godfrey added, "the bullet would have passed through your head had you remained decently abed instead of chasing cats with Nell."

"Nell?" Our guest stared at me with some confusion.

"A nickname," I explained a trifle smugly. "It, too, is short, far more efficient than 'Penelope,' and Mr. Wilde cannot make endless coy classical allusions on it."

He nodded slowly and savored his brandy. "I forget that you have traveled far, as well. This is better than salty tea," he declared suddenly.

"Whyever should you drink salty tea?" I wondered.

"Sugar is a rare and expensive item in Afghanistan, so precious that they drink their tea with salt. Even salt is so treasured that it is saved for only the tea."

"A most uncivil place for an Englishman!"

"You are right, Miss Huxleigh, which is why, after this second Afghanistan war, we English retreated to the civilities of India. Even the ferociously ambitious Russians appear to have tempered their hopes in regard to the area."

"Then why did you stay on?" Irene demanded.

"I could not return."

"Why not? You were unwounded, and you had a medal. That is more than most men take from wars."

"How did you—?" He attempted to rise but his weakness—or the brandy, or both—forced him to fall back.

"I searched your most intriguing apparel and found it in your shoe."

"That is no way to treat a guest, Madame."

Irene's golden-brown eyes glittered like murky gaslights through the blue fog of her cigarette. "You are not a guest, my dear Stan; you are a puzzle."

He frowned. "I begin to fear I have fallen into the lair of one more lethal even than Tiger."

"Your suspected marksman," Godfrey prompted.

Mr. Stanhope looked at me. "Your friends are formidably quick, Miss Huxleigh."

"They are curious as cats, I admit, but I do nothing to encourage their tendencies. Despite this indefensible interest in the most private affairs of others, they have been of actual assistance to some. Pray do not judge them harshly."

My comment brought a bitter laugh. "The opposite case is more likely," he said. "Very well. I will tell you what you wish to know, though it's an ugly story."

Irene held his gaze. "First, does that medal I found in your shoe belong to you?"

He started up again, fire burning in his pale eyes. "Before God, Madame Norton, you tread where the Tiger himself would hesitate. I would not dishonor myself by bearing another man's medal."

Irene shrugged. "A good part of mankind is more casual in such matters than you, and I imagine a great many of them populate Her Majesty's troops, especially in these degraded days."

He subsided, noticing that each of his aggressive gestures had caused Godfrey to sit forward in his chair with a decidedly tigerish expression. Once again he looked to me for enlightenment. "I trust that Miss Huxleigh does not suspect me of purloining medals."

"Never!" I replied. "I fear that my friends are more influenced by your present appearance than your honorable past, Mr. Stanhope."

He laughed then, softly, at himself, his hand stroking his beard. "I look a bloody wild man, I suppose. I had forgotten . . . Even when I first came to Kabul, and found myself adept at the local languages, my fellow officers looked at me aslant. It is not the done thing, you know, speaking the lingo like a native. Better to shout at them in English; they will not do what we wish in either case. But an ear I had, and few could speak Afghan or the various dialects. So they made me a spy."

"Ah!" Irene exclaimed rapturously, lighting another cigarette with a lucifer snatched from a dainty Limoges box painted with hyacinths. The scent of sulfur starched the air. Irene imbued even the most masculine occupation with an instinctive feminity—unless she wished to pass for a man, and then she doffed her ladylike habits in one fell swoop, like an opera cloak.

Godfrey nodded. By the engaged arch of his raven eyebrows I could see that the milieu of the mystery—a foreign clime, military matters, past treachery—were capturing Godfrey's interest as Irene's earlier, more domestic investigations had failed to do.

I, of course, could not have been more indifferent, save for the subject of our inquiry.

"A spy," Irene repeated in a dreamy, thrilling voice. "Sarah would love it."

Mr. Stanhope shook his head. "Grubby, thankless work, but Army life did not suit me. I liked being off on my own in the crowded native bazaars, eavesdropping among them, dressed like them, bandying a few words, as I realized that I could indeed pass as one of them."

"You must have been invaluable to the command," Godfrey commented.

"Not I. I was too lowly to report directly. I needed Tiger for that."

"Who is this Tiger?" Irene asked. "He sounds intriguing."

"I do not know. That was the point of the names, was it not? He was just Tiger, and I was Cobra."

"Cobra," I breathed. "It sounds so, so—"

"So much more dramatic than it was," he finished. "Serpents are supposed to be silent and swift, and that is what the occupation of spy demanded. My task was almost too easy," he mused. "My mastery of language is instinctive. I can hardly explain it—"

"An ear," Irene put in. "Singers call it perfect pitch. What others need to study, one can reproduce in an instant. I myself am able at languages, but you must be a born master. Do you sing?"

He looked confused, for good reason. "I've joined a chorus or two at camp. I'm reasonably true, but no soloist."

"Irene," I put in, "is an opera singer."

"Retired," she added swiftly.

He nodded. "Due to death."

"Due to *reported death*, which is much the same as the real thing."

"Naturally," I explained, "Irene has this perfect pitch she mentions. So she understands your gift."

"More of a curse," he said wearily. "It has kept me from England for a decade. But you ask about the medal. It was awarded to me for spying. That was before the court-martials came, and the charges in the aftermath of Maiwand. I might have lost it if I had stayed around, but I did not."

"You did not go home to England," Godfrey said, frowning. "Where then did you go?"

"Where no Englishman and no Russian would find me. I went the length and width of Afghanistan. To the brutal mountains of the Hindu Kush that thrust against the ceaselessly blue skies, to the farther mountains north of Kabul, through the eye of the Khyber Pass's twenty-seven miles of legend and death where brigands play gatekeeper, into the far eastern Afghan hills toward China, to the ice-bound lake along the Russian frontier. Into no-white-man's-land."

"You lived among the natives for ten years?" Irene's question was not so much incredulous as admiring. "You passed as they? You vanished, Mr. Stanhope, from the world of Berkeley Square, even deserted the comfortable hill stations of India's English settlements? What a . . . role . . . you must have played, have lived. And in all that time no one disturbed you?"

"No. Even when I visited India again, I buried myself in obscure native villages. Few civilized men ventured into that terrain. I wanted to lose myself, and it was easier than one might think."

"Why?" I asked, appalled at the waste of this fine man in that ungodly wasteland.

"I was sickened of war, of my kind, of myself. We lost at Maiwand, and there was treachery in it. Our troops took their stand in a deep ravine outside the village, but Tiger had failed to report a subsidiary ravine meeting it at a right angle. Through that sheltered slash in the terrain the Ayub Khan poured his formidable artillery. I was able to warn only one man the night before the battle, a friend, Lieutenant Maclaine. He pushed his own battery of artillery forward to cut off the Ayub's secret secondary attack, though Brigadier Burrows ordered him back to the agreed-upon battle lines."

"Where did you spend the battle?" Godfrey asked with interest.

"Unconscious near the village," Mr. Stanhope said bitterly. "I was attacked leaving camp. When I awakened, our forces were in retreat. Some British medical man came to tend my battered head. Even as he bent over me, a bullet knocked him aside. I now wonder if that ball was meant for me, even then. But I was swept up in the panic of retreat, and still half out of my head. The Afghanistan fighters harried our flanks through the mountains to Kandahar, which was the nearest Afghan city where we had troops garrisoned."

"And Maclaine?" Irene asked. "The young lieutenant who defied orders to forestall the treacherous attack. What happened to him?"

Mr. Stanhope regarded her with empty eyes, over his empty brandy snifter. "Captured while foraging for water near the village of Sinjini during the retreat. Held along with five sepoys in the camp of the Ayub Khan."

Irene winced, while Godfrey rose to refill Mr. Stanhope's glass. My old acquaintance stared into that bubble of crystal as if he saw the battle of Maiwand in it.

"You cannot imagine the heat and the dust," he said. "Our troops had recorded temperatures at one hundred and fifteen degrees Fahrenheit in June, when the *bad-i-sad-o-bist-roz,* the hot west winds-of-a-hundred-twenty-days, whip up dust devils all month, and this was almost July. We danced with dust until all was swirling, murky confusion punctuated by the screams of men and horses and camels. We had to abandon some of the field guns, abandon some of our wounded. Luckily, I had been attacked before I had managed to change from uniform back into my spy garb. I would have been a dead man for certain in my native robes amidst that mob of rampaging men.

"We stumbled back to Kandahar, an organized retreat in name only. The public soon knew the outcome: how we settled in to defend the city against siege; General Roberts's famous forced march to Kabul of ten thousand fighting men, eight thousand ponies, mules and donkeys and eight thousand followers, in three weeks, over three hundred miles of desolation at the very apex of the heat. This turning tide washed over the Ayub Khan's forces and resulted in his retreat, although he promised that the five prisoners would not be harmed. In the changing fortunes of war, soon the British were sweeping into Ayub's abandoned camp."

"And your friend, the lieutenant, and those sepoys? Were they there when our troops arrived?" I asked breathlessly.

"They were there," he answered.

"Alive?" Irene inquired sharply.

"Five sepoys were."

"And your friend Maclaine?" Godfrey asked.

"There, as promised." Mr. Stanhope sipped the brandy, then held its forbidding fire in his mouth for long moments before swallowing it in one great gulp. "Except his throat was cut. One long cut that nearly severed the head from the body. The body was still warm when our men got in."

I gasped, but no one looked at me. Mr. Stanhope stared into the yawning amber eye of his brandy snifter. Godfrey regarded his interlaced fingers; sometime during the tale he had sat forward, supporting his arms upon his legs. Irene drew on her cigarette until the ember at the tip glowed hellishly red, then snuffed it in a small crystal tray as if she found it suddenly distasteful.

"Afghan treachery," she said, but she was watching Mr. Stanhope carefully.

"No." He did not even look up. "According to the sepoys, Ayub had left instructions before he retreated that the prisoners were not to be killed. Yet a guard cut Maclaine's throat and wounded one sepoy who tried to stop it. Why would the Khan secretly countermand his orders in regard to only one man?"

"The only Englishman," Godfrey reminded him.

"No. Afghanistan breeds fierce fighters, and fiercer palace intrigues, but they are forthright folk in actual battle. Maclaine was of no danger to the Afghans."

"These five sepoys," Irene finally said. "Explain to me their part in the battle."

I was most relieved that she had asked that, as I had no idea what a sepoy was. As far as I was concerned, it could be some rare breed of lapdog.

"Native Indian troops. Noncommissioned," he said. "Good soldiers."

"They would have no reason to lie," Irene said.

"No."

"Unless—"

"Yes?"

"Unless they killed Lieutenant Maclaine. The guards had fled. There is only their word on it."

"But why?" Godfrey wanted to know.

"Perhaps they were bribed to absolve this Khan, this Ayub, of blame. Perhaps, as Stan's story implies, someone British wished to prevent Lieutenant Maclaine's testimony about his actions on the battlefield, about the unreported subsidiary ravine leading straight to the British line."

"What happened about that?" Godfrey asked, sitting straighter. "Surely there was a military inquiry?"

"There were inquiries, and a court-martial. The generals produced their reports, which varied depending on how long after the battle they were written. Much blame was laid on Mac. Of course he was the only one not there to defend himself."

"And where were you?"

He avoided our eyes. "In the Afghan hills. I did not learn of the charges, which came out a full year after the battle, until years later. By then it did not seem to matter."

"Why?" I asked. "Why did you . . . retreat so far beyond Kandahar? Into the wilderness? For all those years?"

"I was honorably discharged and free to go where I would. Native tales of treasure buried in the remote mountains intrigued me. Also, I was sickened by the method of Mac's death. If he had not acted on my information, he might be living today!"

"So you have refused to return to England and live the life you were born to because Lieutenant Maclaine could not, and you felt responsible for that." Irene spoke as dispassionately as a doctor.

Mr. Stanhope cupped the snifter in both of his bronzed hands and let the silky liquid roil like a brazen sea from side to side. "It is not so simple as that. I had reason to think that my life was wanted, too. So I saved it. By remaining lost in Afghanistan."

"Where you have been totally untroubled by anything, until—"

"Until I returned to Europe," he admitted.

Irene leaned forward, her hands taut upon her chair arms. "Why, Mr. Stanhope? Why have you returned? And why now?"

He sighed heavily. "I have learned a thing or two. I now believe that the physician who tended me in the field at the retreat from Maiwand survived also. I believe that he may be in danger. I will not have yet another man die on my account!"

"But how will you find him?" Exasperation tinged Irene's facile voice. She used it as a goad or a lure, that voice, and even when speaking she could imbue her words with all the emotional command of a coloratura soprano. "Ah. You are not quite as lost as you would have us think. You have a clue. You have—his name!"

He recoiled from her words as from a whip. "What is one name in a world full of so many?"

"A thread, Mr. Stanhope. And from a single thread whole cloth can be woven. Tell me his name."

"It will mean nothing to you! It is common beyond counting. You have no reason to know."

"We can search him out if something should befall you."

"How would you recognize him?"

"How will you, with all that battlefield dust and many years between you two?"

"This is pointless, Madame. I regret I have told you so much as my own name."

"Do you not see? It was your knowing something and

confiding it to so few that may have caused Maclaine's tragedy! Secrets aid conspirators, not truth-tellers."

"But this bloody name would mean nothing to you! None of this means anything to you. You are implacable, Madame. You are damn near Afghan."

"I reserve," Godfrey put in quietly, "the right to shout at my wife to myself."

Mr. Stanhope grew immediately silent, then ebbed back into his chair, exhausted. "Do you ever do it?"

Godfrey smiled. "No."

"I can see why not. She is . . . not to be denied."

"No," Godfrey said.

Mr. Stanhope set his brandy snifter on a side table and threw up his brown hands. "Watson," he said. "The name was Watson." He regarded us with weary triumph. "You see! The information is utterly useless. All you have learned is that curiosity can not only kill the cat, but also can be a cul-de-sac, Madame."

"Good Lord, man," Godfrey commented in awed tones. "Do you know how many thousands of Watsons there are in England? How many hundreds may be physicians?"

Nevertheless, Irene shut her eyes and clapped her hands together as if just offered a rare gem before inclining her head toward poor unknowing Mr. Stanhope.

"Ah, but you need not despair, my dear sir," Irene said, glancing significantly at me. "I may already know a most excellent place to start our search for the mysterious Dr. Watson. And Godfrey," she almost literally purred in closing the subject, "I believe that I will have some of that excellent brandy now."

Chapter Ten

KISSMET

Mr. Stanhope had to be assisted upstairs. The strain of sitting up to tell his tale had weakened a constitution already tested by years of privation and most recently—if Irene was right—an attempted poisoning. And although brandy is reputed to buttress the backbone, in this case it further sapped the system, in my opinion.

At his bedchamber door he thanked Godfrey for his support, wished Irene good night now that her questions had been answered, and requested that I remain a few moments, as he wished to speak with me.

I opened my mouth to decline—morning would do, but Irene rushed to speak for me.

"An excellent idea! You seem pale, sir, after recounting your Afghanistan ordeal. A watchful nurse for a short time would set all our minds at rest."

Her suggestion was sensible, at least, but to call Mr. Stanhope "pale," no matter how worn his condition, was a great stretch of the imagination, if not the sympathy.

So the pair of them helped Mr. Stanhope to bed, where he reclined fully dressed upon the feather quilt with a relieved sigh. Godfrey and Irene took a somewhat hasty leave, it struck me.

The paraffin lamp had been turned very low while the

chamber was unoccupied—Sophie was a tyrant about saving oil. I was expected to read and sew in a level of lamplight barely sufficient for seeing one's hands at arm's length. I went to turn up the light.

"Leave it be," he said.

At my inquiring look, he gestured to the window. "We do not wish to be too visible to the world outside."

"Oh." My hand darted back from the little brass turnkey as if it had been a viper's fangs. "Perhaps it is not safe to remain in this chamber."

"The odds are long that he will try again, but it is best not to tempt chance."

In the dimness of the tapestry bed curtains, his face was unreadable; only the extraordinary pearly glimmer of his teeth and eye whites caught the scant light. I sat on the straight-backed chair that would insure no nodding off and fell into an uneasy silence.

In my father's parsonage, visiting the sick was an obligation of the highest regard. Since a child I had sat for long hours beside many a sickbed; there I had learned patience and a respect for mortality.

Despite the nobility of the role, I found myself uneasy in Mr. Stanhope's presence. Perhaps it was the fact that he was fully dressed, oddly enough, although that should allay any notion of impropriety in my sitting up with a man in his bedchamber. Long custom makes clear that only when a man is laid utterly flat by illness can he be regarded as safe enough not to make improper advances to any nearby female.

Mr. Stanhope did not seem sick enough to erase any suggestion of scandal, at least from my mind.

"He," I said, my voice froggy from the long silence.

"He?"

"Your marksman. You know, or suspect, his identity."

"She did not pursue that."

"She?"

"Your friend. She cared only about the name of my battlefield rescuer."

"That is true, and also odd. But Irene has her instincts, and they will not be denied. Nor can I deny that such apparently wild guesses have served her well. Perhaps it is the artistic temperament."

He laughed. "Perhaps. I have not a jot of it."

"Yet you have led quite a . . . Bohemian life."

"Not at all, Miss Huxleigh. I have led an irregular life. There is a difference. That is even worse than being a Bohemian," he added mockingly. "And you . . . you surprise me. You have led an adventurous life."

"I? Not at all! I am a complete homebody. Although," I was compelled to add in all honesty, "I did once travel from London to Bohemia by train unescorted. It was highly improper of me, but the situation was desperate."

"By train? A woman alone? You see my meaning! That is the civilized equivalent of daring to dwell solitary among the brigands of Afghanistan, my dear Miss Huxleigh."

"Ah, but I have never been called 'Cobra.' "

He sobered at that; at least I no longer glimpsed the pale scimitar of his teeth.

"Although," I was again compelled to add in all frankness, "I once signed a cablegram by the code name 'Casanova.' "

"You! Casanova?" He leaned forward until the light limned his features.

At the time I had thought the ruse rather clever myself. "The parrot," I explained modestly.

"Ah, of course. A sagacious old bird. But you see? Coded cablegrams, unescorted train journeys. You have been quite an adventuress."

"Never! And only because Irene had summoned me to Prague. Even Godfrey—who barely knew her then—advised me against going, but I knew Irene would never call on me for a frivolity. And it was a good thing I went, for she trembled upon the verge of a fearsome scandal. I am happy to say that my mere presence insured that no one could speak against her dealings with the King of Bohemia. Quite a nasty little man, that, though he stood several inches over six feet tall." I shuddered in remembrance of the arrogant monarch.

"A cat may look at a queen," Mr. Stanhope said in amused tones, "but only a Miss Huxleigh may despise a king. You are so British, my dear Nell, and so innocently charming. I had quite forgotten."

I froze. "We had not agreed upon using Christian names, Mr. Stanhope."

"I asked you all below to call me 'Stan.' "

"That is a variation of a surname, not a Christian name. And even"— I took a great mental breath before I uttered it —"Emerson . . . is not a truly 'Christian' name."

"Perhaps I should not confess that my middle name is . . . Quentin, then."

"Quentin?" Alas. That, too, struck me as a highly euphonious, if unconventional, pair of syllables. "Quentin is quite—"

"A variation on the Roman Quintus. Quite pagan," he added, a teasing glint in his cairngorm eyes. "Yet I prefer it to Emerson, and was so called among my family and closest friends before I left for Afghanistan. I prefer it."

"Quentin is not uncomely," I admitted, "but it is decidedly un-Christian."

"So is 'Penelope,' " he shot back with alarming accuracy.

"Well—!" I did not know quite how to defend my poor parents' nonconformist choice of a baptismal name. "True, the name is of classical origin, but my father was highly learned, though a humble Shropshire parson. Penelope was an admirable and virtuous woman, who remained faithful to her roving husband Ulysses despite the clamor of suitors and his twenty-year absence."

"Yes, that does resemble Christian denial," he murmured, sounding alarmingly as Irene does at times.

"At least she was not consorting with some sorceress who enjoyed turning men into pigs!"

"Ulysses was a bounder to leave the lady languishing for so long," he admitted soothingly. "But if I have no true Christian name, and neither do you, is there any impropriety in using them between us?"

"I am certain that there is, but you have talked me out of it in that silver-tongued way that Irene puts to such good use. You are both too much for me."

"I doubt that, Nell. And would it be too much for you to assist me to rise? I wish to see the fabled garden that I am now forbidden to visit because of my usefulness as an apparent target. Sophie said the window overlooks it."

"Is it safe?" I looked uneasily to the window.

"Perhaps not, but it would be a shame to live in total safety. Besides, how can I sleep certain that nobody lurks unless I look?"

"You and Irene are two of a kind," I muttered as he shifted on the bed. I really had serious qualms about serving as his support. What if I could not bear up to the weight? I did not relish another humiliating tangle on the floor, this time without the excuse of an assassin's shot. But the ill often take odd notions, and I was not one to refuse them small comforts.

As he stood and lay an arm along my back and shoulder, my heart sank at the impress of alien weight. I should buckle like an overburdened banister, I feared. But then no more pressure came, and we made an awkward progress to the window, where he leaned a hand on the broad elbowboard and pushed the shutters carefully open.

It was as if a clumsy wooden curtain had been dragged away from the fairyland scene in a play. I confess I had never observed our formal French garden by moonlight, had never thought to enjoy it then. By daylight it displayed a rainbow row of hollyhock and heliotrope, larkspur and snapdragons.

But night's cool silver hand soothed the garden's fevered daytime brow, creating a pale landscape of subtle shape and shimmer and shadow. Utterly beautiful. Its perfume drifted up in a delicate, sheer curtain that was almost tangible.

We stood in silence.

He finally spoke. "When I thought of England in the ice house of an Afghanistan winter, in the sweltering swamp of

India, I pictured such serene, uncrowded beauty. I thought of Berkeley Square, teacups and crumpets, my rosy-cheeked nieces in organdy pinafores. I also thought of you, Nell, and the certainty that however the Empire sizzled abroad under brutally blue skies amid dirt and dust and a dozen vicious not-quite-wars, somewhere London fog danced a saraband on the paving stones and among hidden rosebushes in the back garden, and somewhere Miss Huxleigh was putting her charges through their gentle paces."

"And so I should have been," I burst out in frenzied self-incrimination, "save for the war which drove you from that vision! When your sister's husband, Colonel Turnpenny, was posted to India again, the family went, too, as did many such. I found myself unemployable, with governesses a glut on the market. I was forced to become a drapery clerk, and not very successfully. Had it not been for Irene, no doubt I would have starved on the streets. I am sorry to have disappointed you, but it was quite impossible for me to remain a governess. I was fortunate to become a lowly typewriter-girl, and actually was rather proficient at it, though it is a common enough skill now—"

He had grasped me by the shoulders partway through this speech, still leaning upon me somewhat and also, in an odd way, supporting me. A flutter like a caged bird beat within my breast as he spoke with rapid, even joyous conviction.

"But I am not disappointed! That is the point, Nell. I am astounded. The England I painted, that I painted myself into a far corner of the world to avoid, no longer exists except in the musty trunk of my memories. People have changed, even as I have. Times have, manners have. I have felt an outcast incapable of returning. And you, Nell, have shown me just how foolish I have been."

"Well." I could hardly take exception to serving as a model for seeing the error of one's ways. "That is quite . . . reassuring—" I decided to plunge into the deep waters I had so clearly been invited to enter "—Quentin." I would *never* call him 'Stan,' and that was that.

"You see," he said with a quite irresistible smile, "the old barriers crumble. You are not the governess Huxleigh anymore and I am not—"

I interrupted before he could finish. "—the dashing young uncle."

"Is that what you thought?" he asked.

I blushed in the dark and hoped the molten moonlight did not betray me. "That is what we all thought in the schoolroom. The girls adored you, as girls that age will."

He sighed, and his hands loosened on my shoulders. I swayed a little, surprised to discover that I had been relying upon his grip to stay upright, to find that I had willingly surrendered some of the usual effort of standing on my own two feet.

"You were hardly much older than they. That is why I will not hear talk of your disappointing me," he said, "when I have disappointed so many."

"You have not even given them an opportunity to be disappointed; you have deprived them of yourself. You must let them see you anew and judge for themselves. You have condemned yourself unheard, unseen."

"And you, Nell? How do you judge me?"

"I—I have no right."

"Forget our once-separate classes! You have opinions, that was always clear."

"I cannot say! You are so . . . different, and I have never known you, besides. You have lived a life I cannot even imagine; perhaps some of it would shock me. I would say, judge yourself. Go home! See your sisters, your old friends, your nieces."

"It would raise a hornet's nest—about the war, about wounds long healed. I fear the bad opinion of those I love more than bullets."

"Bad opinion can hurt more," I admitted, "but one thing I can tell you: whatever you have done, you do not have mine."

His hands tightened again on my shoulders, so swiftly it

quite took my breath away. "Bless you," he said in a low, intense tone that induced further threats of self-asphyxiation. "If *you* can say that, is there anyone I cannot face?"

He released one of my shoulders but I remained frozen, gazing up at his bronze face bathed in a sickle of icy moonlight. He seemed utterly familiar and utterly foreign at one and the same instant, and I felt that way myself.

In a daze, I felt his fingers pause at the point of my chin, and he tilted my face up as if to study a sculpture in better light. And then his face filled my vision. I felt a teasing tickle that reminded me of a boar's-bristle brush, his beard . . . and then his lips touched mine as lightly as moonshine. The faint flowery scent burst into full bloom around me as my closed eyes suspended me in a place with no bottom or top and no time.

How that moment—moments? minutes? eternity?—ended I cannot say. I felt myself drowning in a fragrant sea of alien yet not unpleasant sensations, so that my fingers curled into the soft folds of his nightshirt to keep myself from sinking. I was one adrift a maelstrom, embracing the strange, tender wave that sucked the very air from my soul, lost again in a suddenly adult game of blindman's buff. I recall that odd internal flutter in my chest bubbling over into breathless if belated retreat, and then a babble of parting inanities.

I next came to myself outside the bedchamber door, in the passage softly lit by the moonlike globe of the paraffin lamp. Its painted roses glowed as if alive and for a moment I held my trembling fingertips, suddenly cold, over its warmth. By its illumination I stumbled to my bedchamber, but though it was pleasant and familiar, it seemed confining. I wanted to burst outdoors, to run into the garden, but that was impractical and would cause comment, and I most of all wished to be alone, as alone as I had ever been. I rushed back into the passage. No, I must speak to someone—to Irene! I must hurry to Irene and tell her, ask her . . . but I could not rouse Irene and Godfrey at such a time, for such a matter.

I quivered in the hall like a hare frozen in the bright, silent blare of a full moon with no place to run. Then a long-ago refuge crossed my mind. I opened the door to what served as our linen closet. The space was cramped under an angled ceiling; it resembled my notion of a priest's hole from a distant century. I darted in and drew the door shut behind me. In pristine dark and quiet, I embraced a bolster smelling vaguely of camphor, and thought.

Time was irrelevant to my state of suspended confusion. The utter dark suited my mood, and so it remained for a long time, until light suddenly sliced into my surroundings—not the mellow bar of daylight dawning under the door that one would expect, but a vertical slash of lurid lamplight.

I had not thought so far ahead as to dread discovery. Its actuality stirred a mortification more profound than when I had been found raiding the parsonage tea tray at the age of four. I quailed before the questing shadow that bore the lamp, whoever it was.

"Nell!"

Irene's voice. I suppose it could have been worse, but not much.

"Nell, you were not in your bedchamber. You were not in our guest's bedchamber. You were not—"

"Why should I be in Mr. Stanhope's bedchamber?!"

"That is where I left you last," she answered reasonably. "What on earth are you doing here? And why—?"

"Must you shine that miserable light in my face?"

"No." Irene lowered it, then stepped fully into the crowded space. She closed the door behind her, taking care to sweep the lace-flounced train of her nightgown into the closet with her first. My hidey-hole glowed in all its homely clutter, lamplight reflecting from the white linens stacked around us.

Irene herself seemed a shining though girlish ghost, her burnt-honey hair backlit into an auburn aura that curled loosely over her shoulders, her snowy nightdress afoam with a phosphorescence of lace and satin ribbons.

She crouched beside me in a spindrift of silk and shook my wrist cautiously. "Are you quite all right?"

I still blinked in the sudden dazzle. "Did you need me for something?"

"No—"

"Then why bother looking?"

"I merely wanted to ensure that you had gotten safely to bed."

"Then you thought I was in some danger!"

"Well . . . a shot was fired into this house not a day ago."

"Yet you encouraged me to remain in Mr. Stanhope's chamber."

"Another attempt did not seem imminent. Was there trouble?"

"Nothing . . . of that kind."

"Ah." Irene placed the lamp on a vacant shelf and settled against a stack of coverlets, tucking her lacy hem over her bare feet.

"And you have gone roaming without your slippers!" I admonished.

"You have gone roving without your night clothes," she observed, eyeing my fully dressed state.

I suppose I did appear ridiculous, but then the look matched how I felt.

"I wanted to think," I explained in a rush, "but the garden is not safe, and I would not leave the house at night in any case. My room was too . . . familiar, and I did not want to rouse the household by going downstairs and being mistaken for a housebreaker. Besides, Casanova would no doubt squawk, and Godfrey might shoot me."

Irene received my confused recital with commendable sobriety. "Now that you explain your reasoning, I can see that the linen closet is a most ideal place to think. I am only amazed that I have not thought of it before. I have sorely wished a retreat myself from time to time."

"Oh, do not be so understanding! You know that I am in a perfectly inane position. You would never back yourself into such a ridiculous corner!" I clutched my bolster closer.

"My dear Nell, we are three unrelated adults sharing one

household, along with the servants. What is so ridiculous about seeking solitude? Even Lucifer wanders off and cannot be found at times."

"That is true. And Casanova has his cage cover to hide under, I suppose. At least he is quiet then. Usually."

"Indeed. Isolation is a rarity in modern life, yet we all need it. If nothing you wish to share is troubling you, I will leave you to your solitude." She began to struggle upright in her voluminous gown.

"That piece of frivolity is utterly impractical," I noted.

She paused to gaze at me with naked bemusement. "I did not don it in hopes of being practical."

"I can see not. You should have stayed in your bedchamber instead of hunting me down."

"Hunting you down? My dear Nell, I was merely looking— you are always exactly where you are supposed to be. Can you not see that I was mildly alarmed—?"

"No! You were merely curious. There is a difference."

She had reached her knees and was about to retrieve the lamp, but froze to regard me. "You *are* upset. You are annoyed with me."

"Not with you."

"Who then?" She settled down again, a look on her face that would not be satisfied without answers.

"With myself."

"You have annoyed yourself? How original, Nell. Most people confine their annoyance to others."

"You will quickly encourage me to reconsider," I snapped, then clapped my hands over my mouth. "Forgive me, Irene. I am frightfully out of temper. But I do think it was most . . . wicked of you to insist that I remain to talk with Mr. Stanhope."

"Why?"

"The hour was late and the circumstances most improper."

"You know that my notions of late hours and improper circumstances do not concur with yours. So how could I lead you into wickedness where I saw none?"

"You placed . . . an occasion . . . I would not have encountered by myself in my path."

"Which was—?"

"Irene, I have never in my life been alone with a man unless he was a relation, or an employer, or a member of the clergy, and it was absolutely necessary."

"Well, Mr. Stanhope is not an employer, and I doubt he will ever be a member of the clergy. But he did ask us to call him 'Stan.' "

"I have it on good authority—his—that he prefers being addressed by his middle name."

"Which is?"

"Q-Quentin," I whispered like a guilty child.

"Quentin it shall be then," she said, "and could we not consider Quentin a quasi-relation, since he is the uncle of former charges of yours?"

"No, we could not! That was far too long ago, and he has changed much. He tried to say that I have changed, which is utterly untrue. He even tried to say that I was adventurous, can you imagine? He behaved most . . . strangely, Irene. I did not know what to make of him. And then . . . then—"

"Then, Nell? Clearly something of great moment has occurred."

"No, it is nothing! It would be nothing to most women, I know that. I am being a silly goose, but I do not know what to think. I—I do not know what to feel. Except that I have the headache from not knowing anything. Oh, ignorance is not bliss!"

Irene took my hands, which were as cold as ice and knotted around each other, into each of hers. "How true, Nell; ignorance is no virtue, and to feel ignorant is a great indignity. How has this Stanhope man managed to make you feel inferior?" She sounded dreadfully angry. "What has he said? Has he had the arrogance to denigrate your former place in his sister's household? Does he dare hold to your supposed difference in stations despite his fallen circumstances? I am weary beyond words of these European notions of 'place'!

They are cruel and archaic, whether coming from a so-called king or an ex-officer of Her Majesty the Queen! I will not have such a person in my house, no matter the personal danger he faces, not if he dares to offend you!"

Irene's grip on my hands had tightened alarmingly, and she made to rise again.

"Irene, no! He has done no such thing. No offense of that sort was given. Quite the contrary. He has . . . violated the very heart of his heritage. He said that *I* was the embodiment of England, and then he—he kissed me."

"He what?" Irene sank back into her billows of nightdress, her features as slack as a drowning person's.

It was harder to say a second time. "He k-kissed me."

"Oh my." Her mouth closed again.

"You knew that something had shifted in the terms of our acquaintanceship since this sudden reunion. That is why you were always urging me to spend time with him."

"Yes, but I did not expect him to kiss you."

"I am relieved."

"Where?"

"Where?"

"Where did he kiss you?"

I swallowed. "By the window."

"Not where in the room, my darling ninny!"

"Then where . . . where?"

"Where upon your person?"

"Really, Irene. That is too . . . personal an inquiry."

"It makes all the difference."

"Truly? How?"

"In analyzing the event."

"You speak as if we were discussing one of your investigative matters."

"We are." Irene sat back, brisk and clinical. Her change of manner relieved me. Suddenly we were dissecting an interesting deviation of remote behavior. I began to believe I could learn something from my bewildering experience and my even more bewildering reaction to it.

"Quentin has been under great emotional stress." Irene began to enumerate his stresses on her fingers. "He is still ill from fever, and has recently survived an attempted poisoning and a shooting. He has encountered a figure from a past he renounced before it could reject him, at least in his own eyes. He feels he has neglected to right a past wrong that he witnessed, which now may cost a man his life. He has long lived apart from his own kind—and from all the conventions of the society that nourished him—as penance for some perceived failure, of which he will not speak. A most thoroughly romantic figure, Nell," Irene finished with a flourish. "And yet, in the midst of all this peril, he pauses to kiss you. Why?"

"Yes, why me?" I wailed. "I am the most unlikely person for such a man to fasten upon. I have led a sheltered life, despite his misguided admiration for my 'adventures.' He must be mad!"

Irene laughed. "No, *you* are. He does admire you, as do I and Godfrey. You are the fiber that holds our flights of fancy to earth. We rely upon you, Nell. For sense. For correction. For innocence. No doubt Quentin sees that in you also. Perhaps he had thought all that lost to him."

I nodded soberly. "Then you believe that he is sincere."

"Oh, a man may be sincere, my dear Nell, and still be dangerous. Now where did he kiss you?"

"I thought we had decided why he did. Where should not matter."

"It always matters, as does how. A man may kiss one's hand as either a social gesture or a seductive one. He may kiss one's cheek as a greeting or an invitation. He may kiss one's lips as an old friend or as a new lover."

"I see," said I, and I did.

"And?"

"And I see that such information is none of your affair, Irene." This time I struggled upright, not easy to do after hours of crouching on a closet floor. My ankles buckled but I braced myself by grasping a shelf edge. "Your comments have been most enlightening, but I really do not care to discuss the matter further. Good night." I opened the door into the darkened hall, blinking, then smiled over my shoulder at Irene.

She was still sitting on the floor, her head leaning on her hand, her arm propped on her knee. She looked most unsatisfied.

"Are you coming to bed?" I asked airily.

"No," she replied. Her tone was almost acid. "I am staying here. To think."

On that ominous note I closed the door and tripped off to bed with a lighter heart and an unspoken chuckle. I was seldom priviledged to know a secret that Irene was mad to learn.

Chapter Eleven

WHEREFORE ART THOU?

A mere ceiling is seldom praised in song or story as the source of revelation, but when my eyes opened on morning, I knew that my life had changed. At first I only sensed the miracle of daylight filtering through the lace festooning the window and bathing the rough plaster ceiling in sheen and shadow. Then, on that blank parchment, slowly, the memory of my retreat to the linen closet flashed into my mind with the starkness of a daguerreotype—along with the incident that preceded it.

Mortified, I pulled the covers over my head, forming a linen tent. How Irene must be laughing at me! And Mr. Stanhope! Quentin . . . Oh! The early birds' muffled caroling sounded like titters through my makeshift linen closet. What a fool I must seem—to everyone!

At last I crept out of bed and into my clothes. Ordinarily I arose first, save for Sophie. Neither Irene nor Godfrey was sufficiently industrious in the mornings. Indeed, both of my friends practiced the decidedly un-American and un-English inclination to linger abed well past the breakfast hour. Had they not been models of energy later in the day, I would have been forced to ascribe their habits to slothfulness.

This morning I blessed their tardiness. I had no wish to accost anyone in the passage—oh, dear. I recoiled into my bedchamber after cracking the door to the hallway. A step. Had I heard the creak of one of the ancient floorboards? I had no desire to see a single occupant of the household until I should compose myself.

The door inched open at my push. I again peeped out into the murky passage. Someone shoved the door closed. Well! I did not appreciate such games, and would confront whoever played them. I swung the door abruptly open. The passage was empty, not even dust motes dancing in the tunnel of light from the far window overlooking the stable yard.

The door wobbled on its hinges again. I looked down.

"Lucifer!" I hissed in annoyance; the name sounds especially sinister when whispered. The black cat curved around the skirts swaddling my ankles, self-satisfied Shadow Incarnate. I whisked up the surreptitious beast and closed my door, then tiptoed down the hall, pausing at every squeal of the floorboards. The dark and narrow staircase was equally vocal. My heart was pounding as much as . . . as much as it had the previous night. At last I stood on the front-hall paving stones. Lucifer billowed down from my arms and shook himself.

How peaceful it was to be up—alone—at dawn. My breathing eased to match the placid tick of the parlor clock, a rococo French porcelain affair much decorated with roses that ill suited this dwelling so humbly called a country cottage. Congratulating myself upon my discreet avoidance of any awkward encounters, I moved toward the music room and froze at a shrill squeak from my first footfall upon the flagstone. Was even mute stone to turn traitor and betray me?

The squeak repeated, though I had not moved, and declared itself: "Errrack!" drifted from the music room. "Cassie want a crumpet. Cassie want a crumpet. Yo ho ho and a bottle of rum."

I hastened into the chamber, where the parrot cage sat shrouded in chintz. Such nightclothes were supposed to silence the creature.

"Hush," I hissed again, lifting the cover to fix the parrot

with my most imposing look. "You shall get neither crumpet nor rum from me, or anyone, if you do not keep still!"

Feathers ruffled into upstanding rows of green. The bird's jet-black pupil shrank to a pinpoint as it sidled away along the wooden perch, squawking: "Cassie want a strumpet. Cassie want a strumpet."

"Now where did you get that?!" I plucked a leftover grape from the ceramic dish that served as Casanova's dinner tray and quickly silenced the bird.

He lifted a revolting foot to take the grape into his claws, tilting his head as quizzically as Hamlet contemplating the skull of Yorick. Then the fierce scimitar of his yellow-gray beak darted at the grape's ruddy surface.

I backed away, hopeful that Casanova would remain distracted, but an unholy yowl issued from beneath my feet. Lucifer, of course. So much for discreet early rising. So much for gathering my shattered nerves. So much for deciding upon a calm course of meeting the house's inhabitants.

"You are up even earlier than usual, Mademoiselle Huxleigh." Sophie stood in the doorway, and spoke with disapproval.

"So I am. I have decided to improve the parrot's language skills. Such birds are said to learn more easily in the early morning hours."

"Hmph." Sophie gave one of those Gallic shrugs that bundle indifference, skepticism and superiority into one portmanteau gesture serviceable for all occasions. "A pity that men are not parrots. My husband wishes to do all his learning at night—in the bistros."

Thankfully, she vanished before I could muster an answer to this statement. I did not wish to think of men—and the night—this morning. Lucifer had cast himself down on the carpet in a spot that in several hours would be drenched with sunlight. Evidently he preferred the afternoon. Casanova was whistling and crooning to himself as he ravaged the grape. I arranged his cage cover over the back of a rush-seated chair and went to the window. Here the interior shutters opened on the garden, which lay under a glistening net of dew, its colors lush in the returning sunlight.

I did not wish to contemplate gardens, either, so I went to the bookshelves and hunted up and down the spines until the graceful gold letters of Milton's *Paradise Lost* caught my troubled eye. I retreated to an upholstered chair and here I intended to read until the others arose and breakfast was served. If my hunger grew irresistible before then, I could always beg for one of Casanova's grapes.

Perhaps an hour and a half later the venerable boards overhead began creaking in succession. By then I was deep in *Paradise Lost*. Casanova began croaking in time with the protesting architecture. I steadied myself, preparing to look and behave with perfect calm. After reading Milton for ninety minutes I have no difficulty in miming a state of utter ennui.

Hence I was installed at our breakfast table blissfully supervising the brewing of my morning tea when the master and mistress of the house descended.

Irene honored me with her sharpest examination, all under the guise of accommodating her Paris morning gown of sky-blue silk on the rush-seated chair. Godfrey wore a maroon house-jacket over his shirt and tie, along with an air of utter innocence. But then he had been a barrister, and they habitually assume such poses.

Apparently, our guest did not yet feel well enough to join us at table. I breathed a sigh of salvation when I saw Sophie lift a laden tray and clatter into the hall passage.

"Did you have a good night, Nell?" Godfrey inquired in a robust, brotherly tone.

Irene darted him a warning glance. "Do have some sugar in your coffee, darling!" she urged with such unusual domestic solicitude that he was immediately distracted from awkward questions. Godfrey frowned as he stirred the offered sweetener into his bitter brew. I could see the moment when he recalled in whose company and in what room he and Irene had bid me good night. I had never seen Godfrey off balance before, but he gave a passing imitation of it then.

"A . . . fine morning it is," he said next. "Would you care for some coffee, Nell?"

"You know that I never drink that vile foreign liquid."

"No. Of course not." Godfrey returned the modern aluminum pot to its stand. He resumed stirring sugar with more vigor than called for, the spoon scraping the china with predictable shrillness.

"Tea is a foreign beverage," Irene observed, sipping smugly, "and some consider it vile, too. If we wanted to honor our ancestors, no doubt we'd have ale for breakfast."

"Speak for your own ancestors," I responded tartly.

"Speaking of ancestors," she added idly, "do you think, Nell, that the Dr. Watson who tended Mr. Stanhope at the battle of Maiwand could be 'our' Dr. Watson?"

My hands flew to my face. "Oh! I had forgotten in all the, the . . . excitement. I devoutly hope not."

"What Watson is this?" Godfrey asked.

I sighed. "I saw it last night when Irene looked as satisfied as Lucifer with fresh cream on his whiskers. Your wife cannot resist pursuing the unlikely, Godfrey. A Dr. Watson apparently is an associate of *the* man, but he is certainly not 'ours.' I cannot even be sure of ever having seen this person."

"So you swore not many days ago in another case," Irene put in wickedly, "and were proven spectacularly wrong."

"*The* man?" Godfrey sounded confused and a trifle worried.

"Sherlock Holmes," I said grimly.

Irene allowed me to instruct Godfrey on another aspect involving the London detective: that a Dr. Watson was listed in an early-'Eighties *Telegraph* agony column along with the address, 221 B Baker Street. That a mortally ill American murderer, Jefferson Hope, held the reins during Irene's and my first hansom ride together. After Hope collapsed and regaled us with a tale of perfidy and revenge, he gave Irene a simple wedding band that he had lost and recently reclaimed from this Dr. Watson at the Baker Street address, the residence of Sherlock Holmes. To this very address, Irene had followed the detective a year and a half earlier before fleeing England with Godfrey.

Godfrey frowned. "The early 'Eighties? Surely this Dr. Watson established his own household and practice years ago."

Irene leaped to the defense of her notion. "What of the man who accompanied the disguised detective back to Baker Street from Briony Lodge only eighteen months ago?"

"Have you ever seen Dr. Watson?" Godfrey riposted.

"No, but Nell may have!" They looked expectantly at me, Irene hoping for confirmation, Godfrey, like myself, hoping for discouragement.

I shook my head. "A third man accompanied Sherlock Holmes and the King of Bohemia to Briony Lodge when only I remained behind in the guise of an elderly housekeeper, but he could have been anybody. We have never seen more than his title and surname. I agree with Godfrey. To hunt for a Dr. Watson in England is to pursue a myriad of needles through an island haystack; we shall only prick ourselves. To suspect that the same Dr. Watson who tended Quentin nearly a decade ago in Afghanistan is also a henchman of Sherlock Holmes is utter madness!"

Irene's fingers mutely, and mutinously, drummed the linen tablecloth. Before she could argue, Sophie returned, still bearing the breakfast tray.

"Monsieur is not in his room."

"Not in his room?" Irene half rose. "But that is . . . dangerous." Sophie's look of surprise forced her to perform a verbal minuet. "I mean that is dangerous—unwise—for his fragile state of health, of course. He was not to be found in the retiring room?"

"I did not investigate, Madame. I heard no sound above stairs." Sophie set down her tray on the wooden table with an emphatic clank. There are no people like the French for resenting unrewarded effort. "The gentleman is absent. See for yourselves." Sophie's elaborate intonation of "gentleman" made plain her own judgment of our houseguest.

"Impossible." I, too, rose from my seat. "Quentin would never depart without the proprieties."

Godfrey stood last. "Quentin?"

Irene intervened as smoothly as an actress delivering a line. "Apparently the only thing of interest that Nell learned from our guest last night was his preference to be addressed by his middle name. 'A rose by any other name,' et cetera. Now we may not have a guest to address by any appellation whatsoever. We had best see for ourselves."

And so I found myself following my companions upstairs in pursuit of a meeting that I would have given anything to avoid but an hour before.

Sophie had been regrettably correct. The Stanhope bedchamber was empty; so was the bathing room tucked so cozily under the eaves. We returned to his chamber in bewilderment.

"Perhaps he is in the garden—" I went to the window. The casement was ajar; birds peeped contentedly under the eaves. The garden radiated no mysterious, misty aura in broad daylight. It seemed cold and aloof, the usual Gallic grid of walks and flower beds. How I longed for the friendly tangle of an English garden—for a vista that was not foreign!

"No." Irene sounded quite definite, and utterly serious. "He understood the danger of exposing himself."

"Then why would he leave?" I demanded, whirling on her.

"*You* must tell *me*."

"I?"

"You were the last to see him."

I stared at her, then at Godfrey's innocently puzzled face, his silver-gray eyes darkened to charcoal in the chamber's dimness. I spun again to face the garden. Spears of hyacinth bowed in the breeze. Purple, orange and blue shades of heliotrope, lily, and what we English call bachelor's button ran together like flooded watercolors before my eyes. I could not see clearly, and could not say why.

"My dear Nell—" I heard the firm forward step of Godfrey's shoe.

"Godfrey, please! Stay back."

"Let us examine the chamber," Irene put in hastily, and I blessed her for that.

Behind me came the squeak of wardrobe hinges, the rustle of bedclothes. I almost laughed to think of Irene hunting under the bed for her quarry. Yet laughter seemed an alien response when all I could see were the blurred flowers melting into a potpourri of waxen blots.

"Here are my clothes," Godfrey announced from the direction of the wardrobe. "He has taken nothing."

"Only the odd garb he wore when we found him," Irene added. "And here—look!"

I almost turned but did not dare.

"In this dish upon the bureau. His medal."

Godfrey went over to examine it. "He must have forgotten it."

"Forgotten it?" Irene demanded skeptically. "With even the bedclothes straightened? No, our visitor has left this room too tidy to have overlooked anything. His military training has not forsaken him. Perhaps he left the medal as a token."

I could sense her face and voice turning to me.

Their talk, the matter at hand, drifted toward me through layers of muffling curtains. At this window less than twelve hours before I had stood with our departed guest. At this window not twelve hours before—

"Nell." Irene's clear stage voice penetrated my mental miasma. "What do *you* think? What possible reason would Stan have to vanish like this, without a word?"

"I would not presume to say, as I would not presume to still call him 'Stan.' "

"Mr. Stanhope, then," Irene said impatiently. "Something has caused him to bolt. What?"

I whirled on her, goaded beyond the wisdom to resist facing them, and facing the empty room. "Not I!"

Godfrey stepped forward, looking grave and concerned as well as puzzled. I could never resist Godfrey when he insisted on being sincere. I backed away, into the window.

"My dear Nell," Godfrey said, "what is the matter?"

"Mr. Stanhope," Irene interjected before I could answer, "expressed a small tenderness toward her last night."

Godfrey stopped moving. "What kind of small tenderness?"

"Er, in the nature of a kiss."

"Nature of a kiss?"

I could stand this speculation no more. "Godfrey, must you repeat everything Irene says? If I had wanted two parrots I would have acquired another."

"Is what Irene says true? He took a liberty?"

"Yes—and no! It does not matter. It was nothing. Obviously such a trifle would have nothing to do with his disappearance. Perhaps he has been—kidnapped."

"Without a struggle?" Irene's skepticism was gentle but unavoidable. "Leaving his borrowed clothing neatly hung and his bedclothes drawn up? A commendably cooperative kidnapping victim. No, I am sorry, Nell. Stan has left of his own free will, and you are the only person who can possibly tell us why."

"*Must* you call him that?"

"He asked us to," she reminded me. "Why do you object to the nickname so much?"

"It . . . denies his past, his place. It is something rude soldiers would use."

"He was a soldier," Godfrey put in.

"An officer," I corrected, "and a gentleman. I am the only one here who knows that for a certainty."

"You hold him to more than he claims for himself," Irene pointed out. "Is that why he left?"

"It has nothing to do with me!"

"Yet you two spoke last night, and there passed between you more than ordinary chitchat, however vague you are about the particulars. Something you said, that happened, must have persuaded him to leave—quickly, without farewell. I agree with you, Nell, your Mr. Stanhope is a gentleman still. He would never have departed without expressing his gratitude unless he felt compelled. Perhaps to save us—you—from himself," she speculated. "You must tell us what you said."

"*I* said very little! He prattled on, about the garden, about my representing England to him. And then he said that he had always expected me to be minding some charge, to be a governess. And when I explained how I had become a typewriter-girl, he behaved as if this were a kind of achievement and said that I had shown him that his memories of home had been mistaken. That we all had changed, though, of course, *I* had not. . . . He must have been feverish, though the moonlight from the window was as cool as ice water. He did ask if I judged him, which I never do. 'Judge not lest ye be judged.' And the last thing he said, the very last thing was so odd. I told him that he did not have my ill opinion. He said that then there was no one he could not face—but surely I am of no consequence to him! Why would he say such a thing? Why would he *do* such a thing?"

"What thing, Nell?" Godfrey asked.

I paused, tangled in conflicting thoughts and emotions. And then I did the unforgivable. I lied. Baldly. "Why . . . leave without a word. It is most impolite."

"A soldier cannot always be expected to be polite," Irene said with a smile. "And it is obvious that matters deeper than mere death threats trouble Mr. Stanhope."

A sudden wave of guilt engulfed me. "I—I must have behaved badly. I drove him to flee. What I said . . . I do not even remember what I said."

The strain of the long, wakeful night, of sitting up in a linen closet, of explaining what to me was still inexplicable, caught up with me in a gallop. I put a hand to my surprised mouth too late to smother a hiccough, or a sob. I was horrified to find my demeanor melting like wax, and hid my face in my hands before anyone should see it cracking.

A silence held, during which I heard the snap of Godfrey's long stride toward me. Then a hand was patting my shoulder and another stroking my hair and I was held close against his maroon satin shoulder as he murmured, "There, there."

I felt as I had at some long-forgotten childhood crisis, when I'd sought refuge in my father's gentle embrace, and heard those heartbroken sobs echoing and felt the saltwater leaking through the tight barrier of my fingers.

"We will find him, Nell," Godfrey promised in tones that thundered with resolve. "We will find him and demand an explanation, and if it does not satisfy me, I will thrash the bounder within an inch of his life."

"Should he still possess a life," Irene broke in coolly, "after facing assassin's bullets and lethal hatpins. Yes, we will find him. He must at the least explain his shocking lack of manners in the face of hospitality. And he has managed to intrigue me."

"There!" Godfrey bent toward me with a smile. "Woe to the man who intrigues Irene and runs away. She is a merciless hound on the trail and will not stop until she has her answers."

I blinked through my sopping eyelashes at my two friends. How could I tell them that learning anything more of Quentin Stanhope and his astonishing affairs was the last thing on earth that I wished?!

Chapter Twelve

SAVING SARAH'S ASP

We began our search where the man had fallen at our very feet but two days before, in the ponderous shadow of Notre Dame.

Irene visited the surrounding cafés, the greengrocers' stands, the fruit dispensers at their carts, her fluid French cascading with descriptions of the "*monsieur exotique*" and the Turkish trousers and loose jacket he wore. "*Très basané et très brunet,*" she would say, passing her hands over her face to indicate his bronzed aspect and his beard. Godfrey, presumably, was performing the same mimes in his designated territory, the Left Bank.

I was a mute witness, fascinated by Irene's endless energy. Each waiter and street sweeper was pounced upon as if he commanded the source of the Lost Chord. At every repetition, the description expanded, requiring more gestures, more discussion. "*Costume Égyptien,*" she would say. "*Nationalité, Anglais.*"

At this last attribution, I endeavored to look totally indifferent to the inquiry. The French already displayed ample *hauteur* toward the English; I had no wish to encourage their unfounded prejudices by claiming this outré person Irene described as one of my own kind.

At last an individual responded to Irene's badgering with as many nods as a street puppet. "*Oui, oui,*" he squealed like a transported pig, and released a spume of French so rapid that I understood almost none of it.

"Excellent." Irene pulled me away from the vendor's river of information. "He has seen Mr. Stanhope in the vicinity—and more. He often goes to Les Halles, the great Paris market near Montmartre, and has seen our quarry about very early in that quarter. It sounds as if Quentin had rooms there."

"Montmartre? But the district is a refuge of lowlife."

"And high life, remember, Nell—if you count the fashionable Bohemian cafés."

"I count them for naught," I returned. "And Quentin did not strike me as one to frequent cafés."

"No, not in his current guise, though certainly no one in Montmartre would look twice at him. Visitors expect such examples of Bohemian dress to lounge about there. A wise address for a man who wishes to disappear." Her eyes fastened on the distance. "And *there* is a man whom I wished to appear, just when I want him. Godfrey has impeccable instincts for an Englishman."

I turned to see her husband striding across the bridge over the Seine toward us, his polished ebony cane swinging jauntily, its gleam vying with the sheen of his plush beaver top hat.

"Nothing to be learned at the bookstalls," Godfrey said as he drew near. "Evidently our friend Quentin had little time for dallying among the encyclopedias."

"Ah, but he had a definite taste for the Bohemian. Nell and I are directed to Montmartre."

"Speak for yourself," I told Irene. "I want nothing to do with such a depraved place."

"Then Godfrey will accompany me tomorrow, and you need not trouble yourself about how our search for Mr. Stanhope progresses." Irene took her husband's arm and they strolled on.

Moments later, and breathless, I caught them up as Godfrey was whistling for a hansom. "I will go to Montmartre,"

I said. "I fear that were I not present, one or the other of you might do some violence to poor Quentin."

"Very wise," Godfrey confided as he helped me into the conveyance. "One never knows what Irene will do with that discreet little revolver of hers."

Of course the day's entire agenda—from the hunt for traces of Quentin to a full schedule of social outings—was designed to distract me from my "loss." A pity we were in Paris. We were taken first to the Louvre, where I wore myself out crossing large expanses of marble floors and endless staircases to view paintings almost as large as the exhibition halls—I think of David's series on the coronation of Napoleon and Josephine—all bordered in miles of rococo gilt frame. In a short time I felt I had surfeited myself on Swiss chocolates and was glad when our party withdrew to take another cab to a fine restaurant in the Latin Quarter. There, once I had eliminated such items on the menu as tripe, octopus, squid and liver in various innovative forms, I was able to consume a *crème* soup and a small *salade.* Much of the so-called "beauty" of the French language is adding a mere fillip to ordinary English words, which last the French would no doubt spell "fillipe."

To end what had been a perfect day in Paris—that is, fatiguing and over-self-indulgent—we adjourned to the Porte Saint-Martin Theatre to view Irene's friend Sarah Bernhardt in *Lena.* A note that morning from Sarah herself had urged our attendance. I had hopes for this production, for it was based on an English novel, *As in a Looking Glass.* Alas, I would have found a looking glass far more entertaining than what transpired on the stage for several hours.

Although the Divine Sarah is famed for her death scenes, this one was most repugnant. After caressing a dagger, she snatched a nearby bottle of poison, emptied it into a rather showy goblet and consumed it. Then she sat and faced the audience. Such were her powers of concentration that I detected a green tint to her skin. I seized the opera glasses from Irene to confirm it, just in time to see Sarah mime a most unnecessarily convincing convulsion and fall face forward onto the floor. The curtain fell in great wallowing swaths of crimson velvet. I found myself heartily pleased that I had supped so lightly, especially when I noticed whey-faced gentlemen and ladies rushing from the theater for the retiring rooms after the play.

"She should have tried *Hamlet*," Irene observed, replacing her opera glasses in their velvet-lined case.

A mistress of backstage maneuvering, Irene forged a path against the current of the departing crowd, while Godfrey escorted me. The press was not as great as I expected, yet the dressing room was crowded, not only with people but with the miasma of powder and perfume that accompanied the actress as invariably as her diaphanous scarves and marabou boas. Sarah herself was the center of a frenzy of admirers, her extraordinary strawberry-blonde hair exploding from their midst like a firework.

She sizzled through them the moment she spotted our party.

"Irene! My darling child! And my dear Godfrey, how splendid you look. And Miss Uxleigh—"

Irene and Godfrey suffered her kisses upon their cheeks. The actress merely clasped my hands instead, which would have been acceptable, or at least endurable, save that I glanced down to find living green bangles circling each wrist.

I pulled my poor hands free with a genteel shriek.

Sarah regarded her embellished wrists. "Ah, Miss Uxleigh recognizes my darling little Oscar, the so-sweet snake she gave me in Monte Carlo! Do you see, Miss Uxleigh, I have found such a charming companion for the poor dear. A mate. I plan to introduce them as the asp in *Cleopatra* soon. Only one serpent will play the part at once, but the footlights are hot, the death scene much extended, and I writhe about quite intently. Each snake will alternate appearances, lest the rigors of performance overcome it. Are they not a handsome pair?"

Here she thrust her ghastly bracelets under my nose. One raised a narrow scaled head to hiss.

"Most engaging," said I, backing away. "I must not keep you from your public."

"Ah, but my dressing-room guests are always my private public," she answered. She flitted to her dressing table, opened a damask jewelry box and cavalierly stripped the serpents from her wrists into its padded velvet interior.

"They thirst for peace and quiet after their hour in the limelight. I wish I could say the same for myself. Ah, thank you, darling Maurice."

I was intrigued to inspect the person from whom Sarah accepted a flute of champagne. Maurice was her son from her illicit union with a supposed nobleman. I observed an even-featured, polite youth of twenty-some, waiting on his energetic mother like a devoted pageboy.

This paragon of young manhood appeared at my side with a companion flute to his mother's. "You are the so amusing Miss Uxleigh that Mama speaks of most fondly," he said in French. "She has many an endearing anecdote about your adventures in Monte, and is most enamored of your gift of Oscar. Few women appreciate Mama's taste in accessories."

I would have been compelled to correct this young man's lamentable miscomprehension about my opinions of his Mama and her menagerie, save that Irene, waving about one of the champagne flutes that Godfrey had procured for them both, burst forth with an announcement.

"You will never believe it, my dear Sarah. Our Nell has unearthed a most intriguing gentleman."

"Miss Uxleigh? A gentleman? French?"

"Only English, I fear," Irene returned, "but he has lived in Eastern climes."

"Ah. An adventurer. Is he rich? Has he found King Solomon's mines? Or simply a small diamond mine would do."

"We do not know. He has vanished."

"Ah." Sarah smiled knowingly at me. "Gentlemen often do. And ladies are often more grateful for the fact than they admit."

"Irene is misleading you," I said. "This gentleman is merely a member of a London family which I served as governess many years ago."

"It would not make a play," Sarah declared with a small shake of her head.

I was tempted to answer that her current property did not make much of play either.

Sarah whirled to the mirror again before I could phrase my comment in the correct—or at least comprehensible—French, though the language is never more incomprehensible than when it is spoken correctly.

"I am so delighted to see my dear friends again. How did you like the play?" she asked.

"Mere words cannot convey our reaction," Godfrey said with suave diplomacy.

"I, too, am speechless," Irene put in demurely.

"How good to be among honest friends!" Sarah declaimed. "But I am so *glad* of your presence! Irene, I have had the most marvelous news. The Empress of All the Russias, Maria Feodorovna, has expressed a desire to meet you. She has heard from her acquaintance, the Duchess of Richelieu—our friend Alice from our amusing scheme in Monte—of your singing privately for Prince Albert there. Her husband, a great stick-in-the-mire, as you say, frowns upon French and German connections for his aristocracy, and the Empress never consorts with mere artists like myself. Yet I have been assured that she would honor my salon with a visit if *you* would be there. Say that you will, and I will be the happiest woman on earth. All the other actresses in Paris will be jealous, as they should be, no?"

"No," Irene answered promptly. Sarah began to frown, but Irene laughed. "And yes. How can I resist satisfying an empress's curiosity? And I confess that the Empress has stirred mine by requesting my presence. What do you know of her?"

"How should I know anything, my dear Irene? She has held herself above me."

"Sarah, if it has to do with aristocracy, art or money, you know all. Tell me."

The actress preened, dropping her air of innocence as if it were a snake she had been toying with. "A lovely little lady, this empress. Danish by birth. Dagmar by birth name and a sister to the Prince of Wales's enchanting Princess Alexandra. She adores the dressmakers of Paris, in whom she shows excellent taste. She obeys her husband in all minor matters and rules him in most major ones. Someone must! Alexander the Third is six feet six inches tall. Can you imagine a man of such height? And a royal personage as well? That is doubly commanding, no?"

Irene kept notably still, for the czar's physical presence was a twin to that of the King of Bohemia, with whom she had such unpleasant dealings not two years before. I myself wondered if some relationship existed between the two rulers, though the Czar of All the Russias was a far more formidable regent than Wilhelm von Ormstein, King of pretty little Bohemia at the edge of the Austro-Hungarian empire. A common ancestor, perhaps?

"The Czar is a complete autocrat, I understand," Sarah said. "So rigid, these northern European men. No wonder many keep mistresses of artistic temperament—the ballerina, the actress or the opera singer. Something must melt that Nordic ice, no?"

Sarah rattled on, oblivious of Irene's sudden quiet, or of Godfrey's instant attention, as her words cut dangerously close to Irene's past.

"It would be a superb coup for me, the Empress of the Stage, to welcome the Empress of All the Russias to my salon. So you must come and sing a bit, but only a bit. It is my salon, after all. Say you will! And bring the adorable Godfrey, of course. And your Miss Uxleigh of the intriguing but lost gentleman. I must hear more of this fellow. Perhaps I can locate him. There is not a man worth knowing in Paris who does not find his way to my doorstep on the boulevard Péreire."

"That is one place, I venture, where we will never find him," I murmured, "nor anything that will aid our search."

"What do you say, Miss Uxleigh? Speak up!"

"Nell says," Irene interjected tactfully, "that she is feverishly awaiting this next occasion to visit you at home. She had feared that she would never encounter such an opportunity again."

We left soon after on another wave of social insincerities, which are to theater people as air is to the rest of humanity.

Chapter Thirteen

HISSTERIA

Moving from the tawdry glitter of the dressing room to the decadence of Montmartre resembled a plummet from the gargoyle-ridden spires of Notre Dame into the rank river that lapped at its foundations. So Irene and I were hurtled after luncheon the next day as our open carriage bore us up to the infamous environs of Montmartre.

Oh, both the Seine and the Montmartre window glass sparkled in the sunlight of a Paris afternoon. So did the rooftops of the city visible below the *Butte*, the highest part of Montmartre upon which shone the white bulwarks of Sacré Coeur, still under construction. Far away and below us, the rusted steel pin of the audacious tower of Eiffel, also under construction, poked into a ragged pincushion of clouds. It reminded me of some monstrous modern bridge piling bereft of its span.

Godfrey did not accompany us. Irene had suggested that he inquire into certain immigration matters at the embassies. He was at first loath to allow us to venture unescorted into such a notorious section, but Irene insisted it was safe by daylight.

She also had pointed out that since he had detected the King of Bohemia's incognito entrance into England and made possible their flight (not to mention their marriage) in the nick of time, his talents were needed more at the bureaus than in the bistros. I knew from my time as his typewriter-girl in the Inner Temple in London that Godfrey suffered from the barrister's love of obscure and hard-to-ferret-out information. He was one of the few men in the world who would take such a humble quest as an opportunity for a romp through the official records. He often claimed that entire novels by Dickens lay tacit in the entrails of the French bureaucracy, and he relished following these paths of paper to their unexpected endings.

So off he went, and thus Irene and I broached this legendary and shocking "mountain" unescorted. It is seldom the case that the higher one ascends in any landscape, the meaner become the dwellings, the shops and the populace, but such was the perverse way of things in Montmartre. Our carriage climbed the rue de la Chaussée d'Antin and the boulevard de Clichy, and the surrounding view degraded. Unkempt, long-haired men shambled alongside us in the streets. Women of a certain kind lounged in doorways, regarding us with bored, hostile eyes imbedded in lampblacked smudges. Articles of clothing seemed little more than discarded rags woven into some fanciful new application.

Modest two-, four- and six-story buildings offered little architectural detail save askew shutters hanging by one hinge. Although geraniums bloomed in the window boxes, slop stains drooled down stucco walls. The odors of onion soup and ownerless dogs overwhelmed any perfume the cheerful red blossoms could offer. Cries rang off the nearby walls—screaming children, caterwauling hawkers, even carousing habitués of the bistros, lurching about the streets in broad daylight.

The ubiquitous loaves of French bread thrust from the figures of passersby like umbrellas. He who was not carting about his bread—or wine—would bear a wrapped canvas under one arm. Few men wore hats. (I hesitate to describe them as "gentlemen.") Their uncut, unkempt hair perhaps explained the omission.

"Here!" Irene commanded our coachman to a stop with

vocal gusto. She surveyed the daunting surroundings like a general overlooking a particularly well-situated battlefield. "We will walk from here and meet you in this square later."

The driver drew our open landau under the shade of a queenly chestnut tree and dismounted to help us alight. I smiled to guess the impression we made upon Montmartre residents: Irene in her Worth gown, a Nile-green-and-tea-rose striped silk visiting dress with a rosette-edge hem and pointed Vandykes of Irish lace girding bodice and sleeves; I in my Bon Marché blue-and-cream lightweight wool gown with the broad sash of Republican red, also available in Empire green and cream, or rosewood and white. Even Paris department stores emphasized whimsy and extravagance.

Yet I spied some redemption in the surroundings. Above us windmills churned lazily in the breeze and cows grazed on green pastures. In some ways, Montmartre was still the picturesque village it had always been.

Irene eyed this bucolic scene. "A pity we do not have time for a picnic. Come, we must survey the neighborhood."

I was relieved to see that the strolling crowds included shopkeepers' wives and even members of the French aristocracy, whose delicacy of dress and manner contrasted with the boisterous common folk around us. Irene took my arm, whether for her protection or mine I cannot say.

"You see, Nell," she confided, leaning close as if to exchange a girlish confidence, "your Mr. Stanhope would be quite unnoticeable here."

"Indeed." I would not give her the satisfaction of again protesting that "your."

"And this is nothing," Irene went on, "as compared to when the quarter throngs with merrymakers of an evening, and the cafés are alight and the *cancan* dancers perform their gymnastics."

I eyed the tawdry café fronts. "Are these *cancan* dancers truly as scandalous as they say?"

"It depends upon who is doing the saying. However, I say—" Irene leaned inward to confide again "—that women so swathed in petticoats and ruffles as these can hardly manage all that yardage and be scandalous at the same time."

"Still, they show their knickers," I sniffed.

"And dingy ones they are, too, I hear. Odd that a washerwoman is the most famous of these *cancan* dancers."

"A washerwoman! Where do you learn such things, Irene?"

She shrugged in a suspiciously Gallic way and stopped to unfurl her parasol. "One hears things."

"Hmm." With Irene, such eavesdropping was likely to be done in person, if not always in her own guise. "I should be most disappointed to learn that you had been visiting these low cabarets."

"Then I shall try my best not to disappoint you," she promised. Whether she meant that she would avoid such places, or merely avoid telling me that she had visited them, was not clear. Such matters never were with Irene. To me, truth was as obvious as an ax; to Irene, truth was like the wood chips that splintered from the ax blade: it changed, depending on which piece of it you grasped at the moment.

"We must inspect the work of these Montmartre artists," Irene suggested, pointing her parasol ferrule in the direction of a shabby cafe whose exterior walls were papered with ragged posters. Under the cafe's tattered red awnings sat even more tattered men surrounded by sketch pads and canvases.

I liked their looks no more than I did the district's. "Why?"

"Because artists use their eyes. While we examine their wares we can cross-examine them. Surely Quentin's Turkish trousers would have been worthy of note, if nothing else."

I studied the baggy-trousered men shambling over the cobblestones. "I doubt it, among these clowns."

"Still, we must begin somewhere. Humor me, darling Nell. I am trying to be logical."

"I see very little of sense in such rude dabbles. These men must be mad. Nothing looks like anything at all in their paintings," I grumbled as we approached the tables.

That they aspired to be artists of a sort was obvious. Their fingers were stained with oils, pastels, watercolor and charcoal. Many sketched passersby as they sat beside their unappetizing wares, which included tasteless depictions of young women casting their black-stocking-clad legs into the air against frothy clouds of petticoats. Whether these articles of underwear were indeed dingy, or merely ill lit by the murky gaslight of the dance halls, was difficult to tell. In fact, I was extremely dubious that the human form could assume such outré positions.

"Their mastery of anatomy is pathetic," I murmured to Irene as we strolled past a brotherhood of artists all engaged in depicting the same sordid subject matter. "Look! That poor sitting girl's legs go in two different directions—not only an unladylike posture, but also utterly unlikely."

"The position is called 'the splits,' Nell, and it is astounding what feats a devoted dancer may assume. I myself have been required to attempt unlikely—not to mention unladylike—positions during my performing career, though I am far from a dancer. Have you never seen a ballet?"

"My father frowned upon theatrical mummeries."

"You must see one, then," Irene declared, blithely dismissing my late father's wishes. "The Paris ballet is not what it was—the blue ribbon in ballet now goes to St. Petersburg—but some small spark remains. We will attend the ballet at the new Paris Opera House as soon as we retire the mystery of Mr. Stanhope's whereabouts."

"I really would rather not find him, Irene! If he chose to withdraw he must have some reason."

"Of course, but what?"

"That is his affair."

"Not any longer. Now that we know about it, we are obliged to assist him. The benighted man has not lived in civil climes for nearly a decade."

I examined the scene. "If he has been residing here, that certainly is true."

At that moment one of the grubby artists took a large cigar

from his lips, balanced it on the edge of his small round table and eyed Irene.

"Madame seeks a Paris scene to take back to England?" he asked.

She took the small canvas he extended in her gloves—lily-white today—and tilted it so the daylight should catch the blotches of blue, yellow and orange in their blurred glory, apparently a garden.

"I was looking for something colorful, in the way of street scenes," she said. "With figures."

The cigar was plucked up again, and the canvas rudely reclaimed. "See him, then." The cigar jerked toward a fellow smoker among a farther grouping of artists. "I never paint human subjects. They only trivialize the truth."

"I fear that I am always in search of such trivial truths," Irene said. "My companion seeks a dear friend who has been lost to the spell of foreign climes. He is European, but dusky of skin and dresses in the eccentric manner of the East."

"You have come to the proper quarter for the eccentric, Madame." The painter spread his arms, displaying a coarse shirtfront decorated with food and wine. In my opinion, it offered more artistic promise than his miserable paintings. "Here wander poets, painters and scribblers of every sort among shopgirls, bakers and street-sweepers—and sometimes ladies and gentlemen in search of originality. How should one man stand out among so many?"

Irene replied with a most eloquent Gallic shrug and moved on.

"That painter is correct, no matter how personally repugnant," I pointed out. "How can we find one man amid this mob?"

"Our search is not as random as it may appear." Irene's parasol tip indicated the windmill topping the hill ahead of us. "I found a matchbook in our guest's pocket from the Moulin de la Galette, the most famous music hall in Montmartre, and wellspring of the scandalous *cancan.*"

"You did not tell me!"

"Why? It was his affair," she said, repeating my earlier answer with a mischievous smile. "I dared not tell you. No doubt you would have objected to the idol of your youth visiting a common French dance hall in order to eye dirty laundry, no matter how artistically presented."

"A man," said I slowly, "must have his amusements."

Irene stopped abruptly, causing a swarthy urchin to careen into us. "A most tolerant sentiment, Nell!" She whirled to watch the rude child stumble away. "You still have your reticule?"

"Of course. I am no foolish country girl now. I have been wary of such pernicious little street thieves since our fortuitous meeting at the decade's other end." In demonstration I lifted my right forearm, from which dangled the green satin strings of my . . . missing reticule!

Irene was already plunging into the crowd, shouting "*Arrêtez, voleur!*" in a voice that would have awakened Napoleon in Les Invalides. It was not sufficient, however, to halt a cutpurse. Her parasol, raised like a lacy lance, beckoned from a swirl of figures. I scurried to join her, finding Irene at last amid a melee of Frenchmen with the very urchin we sought. The boy tried to eel away, but Irene thrust her parasol between his legs. He tripped, scrabbled under an artist's table and at last collapsed under an avalanche of canvases.

"*Ici, Madame.*" The artist was the very one indicated earlier, a bearded dark-haired man with coarse features that well suited the cigar smoking noxiously in a small porcelain dish beside a bilious green glass of absinthe. He was dressed well enough: wide-brimmed straw hat, spotted tie, vest and even a coat despite the warm day. Nevertheless he cut a slightly sinister figure as he dredged up the lad, and my reticule. "I doubt this rascal needs such a dainty accessory." The vile man winked as he extended the article to Irene.

She promptly passed it to me.

"What to do with this rogue?" the man debated.

"Let him go," Irene said. I was about to make an uplifting comment on the quality of mercy when she added: "We have no time to waste on guttersnipes. We are after bigger quarry."

"So I see," the man replied, staring rather too long and too intently at Irene. "Madame is a formidable hunter. Pause a minute, and I will sketch you."

She was already dusting off her abused parasol and righting her bonnet. "I have been sketched before," she said, turning away.

"But, wait! I must capture this thing I see. You have an impressive face, Madame. It belongs on canvas."

Irene paused, trapped by her vanity. Her vanity had nothing to do with her beauty, which she took for granted and thus forgot. No, the canny painter had snared her attention by ignoring her beauty, instead perceiving her unusual will and intelligence. The result was the same; his charcoal was scratching over the sketchpad even as hesitation gave Irene's features a rare look of distraction.

I bent to restore order among the tumbled canvases. I found what Irene sought, charcoal sketches and portraits whose paints had been watered down to transparent, ghostly slashing lines: an old woman with a face as fine as Spanish lace, an urchin as impudent as our thief, a vulgar blonde dancing girl: these played through my hands like the face cards from an ancient deck as I tidied the mess. He had skill, the man with the face of a comic professor, but all of his subjects seemed to be wearing masks that were melting. I feared that his likeness of Irene would offer the same jaundiced distortions, a far cry from the pretty, facile pen-and-ink portraits of the newspapers.

This artist's eye was utterly democratic, almost perverse: the faces of debauched aristocrats, haughty, top-hatted beggars, worn shopgirls and dissolute *cancan* dancers peered back from his small canvases. Then I uncovered one with a jolt of recognition! Quentin Stanhope, as we had first encountered him near Notre Dame—bearded, bone-deep desperate, sitting in some murky café with a glass of opalescent, poison-green liquor before him, a burnt-out cigar on a chipped plate and a small box of matches between his fingers.

I crouched there, staring at this seeming apparition from the attic of my mind. Ordinarily I was one to announce a discovery to the world; yet I was not often privileged to be the exclusive caretaker of anything, even knowledge.

Now I froze in contemplation. Why should not my fingers let the canvas fall face-forward into the pile I had already examined? Why should not Quentin Stanhope remain buried in his unconventional past? More to the point, why should Irene pursue him until he ran where he did not want to go?

Whether I would have concealed this find from my friend, and whether I would have kept that secret for long, I cannot say. A pair of disembodied gloved hands reached down to gently extract the work from my grasp.

"Now this is a fine piece," Irene said in bartering tones as she straightened again. "Exotic. Do you know the subject? Ah, merely another anonymous face captured in the bistros. Recently? Seen once, and never again? Oh, yes. Around Montmartre. How much?"

"Irene, I—" Perhaps she did not hear me. I had not yet managed to rise.

"Forty francs, Monsieur—!" her artful voice rebuked above me. "Twenty. Thirty if you can tell me where to find the gentleman. Ah, it does not matter. Art is supposed to be elusive, is it not? Twenty-five, then."

The clink of coins reminded me to ensure that my reticule was firmly clasped in my hand. I would have to carry it about like a dead rat until I could return home and repair the broken strings.

"No, no wrapping, Monsieur," Irene insisted. "This piece is too fine to hide. We shall take great care with it, I assure you."

By the time I rose and straightened my skirt folds, Irene was holding the canvas at arm's length, dreamily studying its subject. The artist himself had risen to conduct the transaction, and stood no higher than five feet! I blinked. He resembled a nasty, masquerading boy, with his beard, cigar, hat and—I cannot describe it any other way—the appreciative leer that he fixed upon Irene, and . . . as I rose, myself!

Grinning, he tilted his sketch pad so that only Irene could see it. She lifted one eyebrow. "An original approach, Monsieur; I have never before seen myself portrayed as an advertisement for absinthe. I look as deadly as *La fée verte* herself."

Thus the French characterize this lethal liquor of the bistros, as the Green Fairy, a femme fatale of addictive, toxic beauty. I snatched a glimpse of the sketchpad: Irene's features looking quite wicked. She remained nobly indifferent to the familiar fellow as we strolled away. Little did he suspect that Irene had bought his work for its subject rather than its feeble execution, this cheeky creature who signed his work by the overlong name of Toulouse-Lautrec. I hoped never to see such a signature, or its owner, again.

"A splendid likeness, Nell," Irene rapsodized over Quentin's sordid portrait as we strolled away. "A mere phantom of loose lines but quite an uncanny evocation. This artist will make a name for himself. I knew we should find some trace of Quentin in the district, but to unearth a portrait—*quelle chance*, as our French hosts would say. Now we will certainly find him!" She turned a discerning eye on me. "Do not fret about the urchin; they are as common in Montmartre as fleas. Oh, and I have not given you proper credit for finding Mr. Stanhope again. You show a positive genius for stumbling over him in one form or the other. Certainly we will encounter some genuine clue to his whereabouts before the day is over! Well, what do you say to that? Is it not marvelous?" She tucked the portrait under the arm not occupied with her reticule and parasol. Its addition to her accoutrements made her an instant *habituée* of Montmartre.

Irene's high spirits only increased my vague feeling of dread. Why was I so reluctant to see Quentin again? His flight should have buried forever any illusions I might cherish about his character or his seriousness.

Irene's shrewd gaze waited upon my response. I saw in an instant that her chatter was no more than compensation for my introspection, my odd momentary paralysis. I straightened my shoulders and reached up to do the same for my bonnet. Quentin believed that I had developed an adventuresome nature. Today, in Montmartre, we would discover just how adventuresome I was. I nodded to the crooked, climbing path ahead, and we walked on.

The afternoon grew long, and warm, and interminable, and then hot. I donned my pince-nez to consult my lapel watch. Surely there was a limit to how long respectable women could linger in Montmartre, and twilight was its borderland. At the least Godfrey would fret.

"Irene, we must return to the carriage," I protested as we climbed yet another winding lane to yet another row of shops and lodgings. The aged stucco cracked away from the corners of the buildings, so that they seemed to have a skin disease. In these shadowed streets the scents of garlic and human excrement mingled uneasily. Cats were thin and wary. Hoarse dogs barked.

Irene flourished her painting like a badge. "Here, Madame? This gentleman? Have you seen him, Monsieur? Our poor friend. Yes, much fallen in the world. He may be ill."

Our search met indifference unless Irene evoked cooperation with sou coins. I began to squint toward the roofline; by the sky's paler hue, daylight must be slipping out of sight behind Sacré Coeur. My thin boot-soles burned at the long admonishment of the cobblestones, but Irene on a hunt felt no fatigue.

"When you are searching for a needle in a haystack, Nell, it is utterly necessary to inspect every shaft of straw."

She paused at a surprisingly respectable door and pulled the bell. A pansy-faced maid answered, listened politely, glanced at the painting and nodded cheerfully.

"*Oui.*"

One word, but it proved Irene's stubborn optimism and put a dampness in my palms that gloves of the sturdiest Egyptian cotton could not absorb.

"Above," the little maid added, "the attic." I gazed up past the house's steep peak, six stories above us. The sky had paled to an anemic aquamarine color, a blue so bland that it seemed no more than dissolving watercolor.

Irene handed me the portrait. "You can be trusted to take proper care of this, I think, Nell." We began to climb the common stairs at the girl's innocent invitation. "*Monsieur l'Indien*," she had said. As we left the maid's sight, Irene produced her revolver from her reticule.

"Surely we do not need that, Irene?"

"When one is sure that one does not, the need is greatest." She spoke softly.

"What kind of place is this? The entrance, the maid—it seemed respectable."

"It is. Some of the bourgeoisie find it fashionable to live in Montmartre now, but such folk occupy the lowest level. The longer the climb the poorer the occupant." Irene nodded to a nondescript door on the next landing. "A washerwoman lives here, perhaps, who dances the *cancan*. We must reach the last floor."

The stairs grew steeper. I clutched the portrait to my side, wondering what our quarry would think of our purchase, of our pursuit. I had lost count, but my protesting lower limbs screamed that we must have climbed five flights by now. The street din faded as we rose, the paint thinned on the walls and disrepair became utter neglect.

It was again an ascent into greater deprivation. Irene had paused, obscuring my view. Or shielding me with her body.

"Carefully, Nell," she whispered, nodding to the mean little door before us. There the stairs ended. There we must enter, or leave unsatisfied.

Irene listened. Others may pay attention, but Irene had made listening into an art. Perhaps it was due to her musical training, for she gave the appearance of hearing on several levels at once—hearing not merely the footfalls or voices or the creaking furniture springs that one would expect, but sensing movement, sensing presence as an animal might. Her entire attention was devoted to listening so fiercely that she seemed to see beyond the wretched wooden door. Only when her posture subtly relaxed did I believe that there was nothing to hear.

Still, her glance cautioned me as she tried the latch.

It squealed like a piglet. I nearly dropped the canvas, which would have added to the explosion of sound in our tiny cul-de-sac. The stairs narrowed into plunging grayness below us. We seemed to be balanced atop a soaring tower.

Irene listened again, then pushed the door fully open. The flimsy wood banged to a stop on some piece of furniture behind it. I wanted to push past the uneasy perch of the stairs, but Irene did not move. I sensed her surveying the room in the gathering twilight. We had stayed too late in Montmartre. This was worse than the eerie Old City in Prague!

"I-I—" I began, meaning to intone her name, not express an opinion.

"Shhh!" She edged finally through the door.

I followed, glad to have my feet on a level, even if it was raw wood undressed by so much as a rag rug. A meager row of windows spit blurred squares of ebbing daylight onto the floor. The smell of old, and distinctly odd, food lingered like rank perfume. I sensed other odors, vaguely animal, definitely wrong.

Irene moved silently to where the raked attic ceiling almost met the floor and swung the casements as wide as possible. Light like skimmed milk pooled on the floorboards. I saw two narrow cots against the opposite wall. A chest. A basin on a small table between two casements. A slop pail. I had not yet left the doorway. There I stood, dangling between two alternatives equally loathsome: that rude, unlovely room and the twisted stairway that led to it.

"He is gone, Nell." Irene's normal speaking tone nearly startled me into leaping off the threshold and down the yawning throat of steps.

"You are certain?"

She nodded, the revolver still loosely clasped in one hand.

And then I heard a rasp, like a fingernail being drawn across faille silk. "Oh, Irene . . ."

"No one is here." She sounded almost angry in her disappointment. "Nothing remains. Except for that bundle of discarded rags—" She moved toward it.

I heard again—no, sensed—movement. Subtle, hidden, threatening movement. "Irene—?"

"I know, Nell." Her voice was taut, in a higher register, thin, anxious. "I have heard it from the first moment we entered."

"What . . . is it?"

"I do not know, but I doubt that it is human."

"Ohhh!" If she expected *that* intelligence to reassure me she was mistaken.

"Rats, perhaps," she speculated casually.

I leaned against the filthy doorjamb, my knees suddenly as supportive as water. "Shoot them!"

"Nell." Irene sounded amused, even relieved. "They cannot hurt us. I will just inspect that bundle, and perhaps the trunk, and we can leave."

She walked briskly toward the cots while visions of fleas and even more disgusting vermin hopped in my head. My skin crawled. My hair itched. My hands burned on the edges of the canvas, so tightly did I hold it.

Something moved again, at every step Irene made, an unseen mirror of her motions. Something slow, hidden . . . and intelligent.

She bent over the uncertain darkness on the floor, pulled up a length of cloth, and drew back then against a cot, a recoiling melodrama heroine. The gesture was madly unlike Irene.

"W-w-what?" My teeth chattered now, although it was hot under the eaves and perspiration trickled invisibly down my spine in an unpleasant serpentine tracery.

She was backing away as if she did not hear me. "A dead man," she muttered. "Dressed as a native of India. A terrible death."

Speechless, I clung to the portrait, rejecting time and truth, refusing to believe that a man I had seen only two days before should lie lifeless in this squalid attic.

Irene glanced at me, her pale face pocked with the holes of her eyes and mouth and not beautiful at all, unless a skull is so. "Not . . . him. The beard is white and the face so swollen and dark, my God—stay back! It could be . . . plague."

"Quentin was ill even before the poison," I began, appalled at the specter she had raised: an alien disease, with all of us exposed. One man dead of it, and Quentin gone, unable to be told. Unable to tell us what it might be. Plague. "What can we do?"

"Remain calm." Irene seemed to be advising herself as much as me. I had never known her to be so uncertain. It was like seeing Queen Victoria screaming at a mouse—unlikely and frightening.

"I *am* calm," I said with an emphasis that I am sure fooled no one for a moment, not even the . . . corpse. "But I still sense something here—"

"Rats," Irene repeated. "The man has been dead for some time. Rats will come, especially to a garret like this. He looks so ghastly. Perhaps they have been here already." She edged away, toward the sad puddles of waning daylight, toward the stairs.

A rasp again, across the wooden floor, similar to a heavy damask train dragging, snagging on splinters and still being drawn along. A womanly ghost in a court gown? I stared into the haze that heat and unfamiliarity and twilight made of this place. Then I saw something rising, something . . . probing the air. Something that lifted of its own accord, and lifted long, supple and rasping. Irene was backing directly into it.

I had no voice. I had no voice! My throat, my lips moved. My fingernails thrust through the stretched canvas with a wrenching sound. My foot had stepped forward without my willing it, but still I could not speak.

Irene turned toward my motion, turned away from the

silent shadow at her rear now looming as high as her hand, then her waist.

"There!" I screeched at last, pointing. "Shoot! Shoot!"

She whirled. Her silk skirt brushed, actually brushed the swaying shadow. What poised there was no thicker than her furled parasol, which suddenly thrust out like a rapier to engage something long and lethal. At the same time, the pistol spat red smoke in the dusk. Clap, clap, clap! A sound of admonishing hands. Her parasol hurled something limp into a shaded corner. I would have rushed to her side, but she flung a hand behind her to stop me.

For a long while I heard nothing but Irene panting softly and my blood thundering in my ears until these sounds were slowly snuffed by the spreading darkness. I could still see the pale edges of Irene's gown, a bit of light threading through her hair and edging her profile. Her voice came husky, almost hoarse.

"A lamp sits on the table by the door, Nell. I'm going to throw you a box of lucifers. Stanhope's box," she added ironically. "I want you to light the wick and turn it up. Stay as close to the door as you can, but be quick and quiet about it."

Something hurled toward me; I fought the impulse to dodge. The object hit the canvas I clutched to my bodice and slid down until my hand caught and cupped it against my skirt. I set the portrait against the wall and worried the small cheap paper box open. The wooden lucifer was tiny, fit for a doll's hand. I struck it on the tabletop, breathing easier as warmth and light flared. It flickered out before I could even find the lamp Irene had spied on the way in.

I underwent a second struggle to extract another miniature wand and produce another burning flare. This time I touched it to the wick, but it seared my fingertips and I dropped it. Irene said nothing. I heard nothing. I saw little beyond the hot circle of my struggle. I must not fail. The next lucifer licked at my fingers, but I held on until sparks spawned light. When

I dropped the lucifer, the lamplight remained and grew as I turned up the key.

"Bring it here."

I approached Irene as if fearing to wake an infant—or a fiend. Irene handed me her parasol and took the lamp. She moved forward, putting me in darkness that iced my soul. Something on the floor commanded her attention. I edged nearer to view a dark, mottled, sinuous form coiled like massive loops of nautical cable. She bent down, the revolver at the ready, then straightened suddenly.

"Yes, thoroughly dead." She moved more briskly to the bundle she had identified as a dead man, a possible plague victim.

"Irene—?"

She sighed. "Now I understand. Venom. Snake venom. Quantities of venom, from an indecently large snake."

"Not like . . . Oscar?"

"Not like any serpent even Sarah Bernhardt dares to keep. A cobra, I think, but I will let someone else identify the species. And its presence explains that." She stopped by the table where the lamp had rested. "I noticed it when I entered."

I had not, but my eyes now took in all its sinister implications. Some sort of abandoned chest, I would have said but minutes before. Now I saw that it was a cage, perhaps two feet long, pierced with tiny air holes, a small door eloquently ajar. A scum-slimed saucer sat beside it.

Irene sniffed the contents fastidiously. "What did Oscar drink, before you bestowed him on Sarah?"

I shuddered. "Milk. A small saucer of milk."

"Empty, save for dirty residue. The serpent must have been neglected these last days, been hungry."

"But the dead man?"

"Did not live here. He came here. Perhaps he knew of the snake, perhaps not. The maid spoke of only one occupant."

"But, Irene, Quentin Stanhope *lived* here, according to your investigation. Quentin Stanhope—and cobras, assassins? I cannot credit it. It makes no sense. This cannot be the same man I knew in London, though I barely knew him."

She looked at me, all insouciance fled, and nodded grim agreement as she replaced the revolver in her reticule and drew the strings securely shut. "I know, Nell. I know."

Chapter Fourteen

SLEEPING SNAKES LIE

"**If our** main objective, Irene, is to find Mr. Stanhope—and I am not at all sure that it should be—then why are we rattling across the cobblestones of Paris en route to a soirée *chez* Sarah?" I inquired with what I thought was admirable restraint.

"Because," Irene answered imperiously, "I wish to meet the Empress of All the Russias."

"Truly?" returned I. "From your costume, I had concluded that you were intending to *play* the Empress of All the Russias."

"That she could." Godfrey's smile looked doubly dazzling under the dark portcullis of his mustache. He eyed his wife with an approval that I could not fault, for Irene did indeed look fit to hobnob with an empress, if not to be one herself.

"I have renounced thrones for more interesting pursuits," she said, unfurling her gauze and ostrich-feather fan rather theatrically. Her evening jacket was a transparent affair of black lace and jet that glittered like fairy netting in the soft light from the carriage lamps. "For the time being," she added wickedly. "Besides, I am most curious to know why the Empress of All the Russias acquired such a sudden desire to meet me that she would break long custom and deign to visit Sarah's salon."

"We know why," I put in. "The Czar is fond of opera. No doubt he has heard of your private concert in Monaco—Sherlock Holmes himself warned you then that you had become too public for one supposedly dead—and recommended you to his wife."

Godfrey's smile had grown dubious, perhaps at mention of Sherlock Holmes. "And for this the Czarina violates her customary refusal to mingle with commoners and begs an invitation to one of Sarah Bernhardt's notoriously Bohemian soirées? No, Nell. Irene is right. Something more lies behind this invitation."

"I am always right, except when I am wrong." Irene regarded me closely. "Why are you so reluctant to visit the boulevard Péreire again, Nell? You know that Sarah is especially fond of you, and, more importantly, all the men in Paris eventually turn up at Sarah's," she added with a particularly sly smile.

"I rather doubt that! Even the Divine Sarah's appetite for novelty must have limits. And the woman barely knows me! How can she be so 'fond' of me for so little reason? It is most illogical, even perverse of her."

"Are you saying, Nell," Godfrey said with lawyerly patience and a hint of laughter in his voice, "that to like you one would have to be perverse?"

"I am saying that . . . That Woman persists in paying me more attention than I welcome. And after our adventure in Montmartre today, I am not excessively enthusiastic about encountering any more . . . serpents."

"Not even poor little Oscar?" Irene asked.

"Not even Oscar," I answered. "And I resent that actress treating me as another exhibit in her menagerie."

"Sarah means nothing by it, Nell. She merely finds you fascinating. She can never resist the exotic, even when it is so merely domestic."

"I am *not* fascinating! I am not adventuresome. I am English."

Too late I saw the corner into which I had painted myself

and my entire race. Luckily, my two friends had amused themselves sufficiently at my discomfiture and did not press their advantage.

So Godfrey joined us at last in passing under the engraved *S.B.* over the door. From the murmur and clink emanating from our hostess's salon, other guests had already arrived. A manservant took Irene's lacy jacket and my fitted black silk jacket with the ruffle of black lace under its wide reveres.

"Why, Nell, you look quite empress-worthy yourself tonight." Godfrey turned me like a top by the shoulders. "I could not see by the dim hall light of the cottage how splendidly you were gowned."

I flushed, as I always did when a gentleman noticed my attire, which was a bit excessive this evening: Nile-green China crape sashed with black watered silk. A rosy epaulet of flowers decorated my left shoulder and more roses perched at the top right of my coiffure, a most pleasing and subtle touch, Irene assured me. "Opposing sides, my dear Nell," she had said while torturing my hair into ringlets with her curling iron. "Flowers or jewelry best play off each other when mounted on opposing sides. It is a question of balance."

"So are my slippers," I had complained then, for her own Nile-green shoes and stockings clad my feet. The two-inch heels were more than I was accustomed to, especially if I was to curtsy to an empress.

I still was uncertain that the lily of the valley scent she had sprinkled liberally on me had overcome the lingering singed odor of the curling iron. It did not matter. The Bernhardt rooms sprouted heavy aromas the way they did tropical blooms and exotic wildlife.

The first trophy I glimpsed in the salon ahead was the brown bearskin rug that had nearly devoured me on my first visit. The huge, ferocious head confronted all guests with glassy staring eyes the size of monocles, and bared fangs set in massive jaws a full foot apart. One misstep into the maw of this mighty floor covering, and Irene's silken Nile-green stockings would be reduced to threads.

"It does pose a problem for trains," Irene murmured, having followed the, ah, train of my unspoken thoughts. "Luckily, neither of us is wearing one."

She bearded the bear first, sweeping ahead of the ever-courteous Godfrey and my ever-reluctant self. Into this hothouse of Oriental decadence Irene wore an insouciant gown of Rose Dubarry, the skirt and bodice draped with pink tulle dotted with black velvet and touched at the shoulders, décolletage, waist and bustle with black velvet bows tipped in gold. The Tiffany necklace of diamonds mounted between opposing rows of pearls circled her neck, and affixed to it was the Tiffany pin Godfrey had given her: the diamond-studded clef and key device, signifying her twin interests of music and mystery. This was Irene's commoner coat of arms, signifying an aristocracy of wit and talent that no amount of blue blood could contest.

Her dark hair was banded by a narrow fillet of gold over the forehead. A high panache of pink ostrich tips vibrated above her topknot like an amusing crown. Long flesh-pink gloves of undressed kid gave her arms a scandalously unattired look. She stepped over the snarling bear head in this most dainty of costumes, pink silk slippers with black velvet bows on the toes mincing expertly around the fearsome impediment.

Irene's entrance was not unobserved by the two dozen guests present, although some were no doubt expecting the Empress. Men in formal black-and-white stood interspersed among a glittering flower bed of pastel evening gowns. Heads turned and lifted, cigarettes paused midway to mouths, conversation faded as Irene became the focus of all eyes. In the hush, I found my gaze focusing on a regal blonde woman opposite us. This commanding creature, as statuesque as a Greek goddess, wore a violet taffeta gown so lavishly encrusted with turquoise, copper and silver beadwork that it formed a rich, Oriental carapace. I wondered if she would crackle when she walked.

For a startled moment, I thought we faced the Empress of All the Russias and fought a mad impulse to curtsy. Then the guests' chatter resumed and their ranks closed, removing this savagely attractive figure from view. Her presence had not escaped Godfrey's notice.

"I know," he bent to confide as he followed me into that crowded chamber of crimson walls and caged birds where scent and smoke mingled into a heady fog, "that you will record every exotic detail of this evening in your diary, including Irene's ensemble. Do you ever report my mode of dress?"

"Well . . . not often. It is not so interesting."

"Thank you."

I belatedly eyed him. He looked handsome enough to be a play actor, as usual, the severe black-and-white of evening dress emphasizing his almost-black hair and pale silver eyes. Had he not been my employer, and now my dearest friend's husband, of course, I might once have cherished illusions on his account. But to record the details of his attire—

"I am sorry, Godfrey, but this is a restrained age. Men dress as they should: with little vanity or display, in unchanging style. You will forgive me if I speak plainly. Men are judged more for what they do than for what they wear."

"Yet I had to don a horsehair wig and antiquated robes to practice law," he mused with a glint in his eye. "It seems that when men do really serious things, such as wage war, they must resort to silly attire. And consider that models of uniform dress, like our former military man Stanhope, often adopt the exotic, free-flowing wardrobe of the East. It speaks of male dissatisfaction with dull tailoring. Perhaps you could note that observation in your diary."

"Perhaps," said I, making no promises. My diaries were one area in which I was the final judge and arbiter, a deity unto myself on a modest and private scale.

We had maneuvered around the bear and past a buffet table laden with the usual (and often inedible) excesses of French cuisine and spirits. This cornucopia of the unappetizing was implemented with such barbaric fare as raw oysters and mounds of Russian caviar shining like beady black little serpent eyes.

We next confronted the richly carpeted dais upon which our hostess reclined on her famous divan, in a loose gown of Chinese brocade with a great billowing train of heavy smoke-blue velvet. None of the windows were open, for Sarah's multitude of wild pets might escape, so the atmosphere was warm and soporific.

Madame Sarah herself wielded a massive peach-colored ostrich fan which clashed violently with her masses of red-gold hair. It nearly made me sneeze to look at her, though I did not dare, for fear I should undo my coiffure.

She saw us immediately.

"Irene!" Kisses cheek to cheek, Irene's delicate ostrich headdress almost colliding with a sweep of Sarah's intimidating fan.

"My adorable Godfrey!" A kiss (his) on the hand; a kiss (hers) blown over the trembling horizon of the fan.

"And the amusing Miss Uxleigh!" A nod (mine) and a playful, admonishing finger-wagging (hers). "But where is your vanished gentleman?"

"On canvas," I replied.

She turned immediately to Irene with a shocked expression. "He is one of these brutal pugilists?"

Irene smiled. "Nell means that she has only a painted portrait to remember him by."

The Divan One turned to me with a conspiratory leer. "Sometimes I think that this is the ideal place for men—in oils, preferably burning." She examined my attire with mercurial speed. "But you look ravishing, my dear Miss Uxleigh, in green. Nile green like a queen. You require an asp for the evening. If I can find Oscar you may carry him for the night—"

She began uprooting brocaded pillows, and I am sorry to say that something long and sinuous stirred amid the patterned cloths. I felt a sudden panic.

"Let sleeping snakes lie," Irene urged. "Our poor Nell had a rather upsetting encounter with a reptile today."

"Upsetting? Snakes are the soul of tact. Where is the naughty serpent that has upset my adorable Miss Uxleigh? I shall tie it in a knot until it promises to be good."

"I am afraid that I cannot produce it," Irene admitted. "I was forced to shoot it."

"So sad," Sarah hissed sympathetically. (Lest any suppose me so prejudiced against the actress that I exaggerate, I must stress that the French word for "sad" is *triste*, and Sarah lisped it, thusly: *trisssste*.) The actress made sure that all eyes in the salon were fixed on her before speaking further. "I also was forced to shoot a snake. Otto was eating my sofa cushions. He went quite berserk."

"This snake did not have a name that we know of," Irene said, "other than cobra."

The Divine Sarah sat up amid her cushions. "A *cobra?* You shot a venomous snake? Otto was merely a boa constrictor; like most men, he was not dangerous unless one wished to embrace him. But a cobra—again you amaze me, my enterprising Irene. I salute your marksmanship. A cobra is a much smaller target than a boa." She pointed to a lengthy pair of loudly patterned serpents as thick as top hats that coiled decoratively around an ironwork torchère and a potted tree.

"The room was dark," I added.

Sarah fanned herself in agitation. "And in the dark! Even more astounding."

"Not really," commented a new voice in impeccable French. "I imagine the lady aimed for the hood, which would be fully fanned if the snake were raised to strike. The head is the only place to shoot a snake."

We turned to face a gentleman in evening dress. For all his refined garb and perfect French, I should not have judged him a gentleman in the oldest sense of the word. I have never regarded a pair of blue eyes that seemed colder. Despite his fifty or more years, his features were energetic, with a jaw so powerful I was immediately reminded of the bear at our feet.

His white hair had receded from his brow, but baldness did not make him a figure of fun. Rather, it stripped away all softening influences from those pugnacious features, and seemed an affront rather than an accident of nature. His baldness resembled the tonsured sleekness of a fanatical monk. I am not often aware of men as men, but this one struck me as wielding an innate power over his fellow creatures, as if he were a law unto himself. His effect on the others was as potent. Irene had not changed outwardly, but I saw that she had gathered her most incisive instincts about her like a cloak. She radiated an air of instantly rising to the occasion, like a hunter who, stalking dangerous prey, suddenly finds it before her eyes.

Godfrey was no less wary, although one who did not know him would not see that fact. His expression grew noncommittal, guarded. He, too, was concentrating all his faculties on this stranger.

"My dear Captain Morgan!" Sarah actually rose, her gown coiling around her in folds of taffeta and velvet, and advanced—rustling in a way that set my teeth on edge—down the dais steps to offer her hand.

Captain Morgan bowed over it like a Bohemian princeling, which breed I have observed, in a stiff salute, though the kiss was perfunctorily proper. Certain recent events had made me newly aware of the nuances that may be hidden in a kiss.

"What have you brought me?" the Shameless Sarah purred deep in her throat.

"If Madame wishes me to present it in the presence of her guests . . ." He clapped his hands.

Two turbaned servants, their faces the color of *café au lait*, came bearing a great furry bundle over the prone bearskin on the floor.

"This is . . . magnificent!" Sarah exclaimed when the men knelt to unfurl the bundle at her feet, a mammoth pelt. The three of us edged back to avoid the tide of white fur lapping at our shoe tips. "Extraordinary!"

"No more than the mistress of the world stage deserves," Captain Morgan said grandly.

As the bearskin foamed over his feet I noticed that he wore black boots with his evening dress—polished to obsidian sheen, but boots, not shoes! I was beginning to revise my notions on the unimportance of men's dress. Certainly this man's boots spoke of a disregard for civilized niceties.

The huge white pelt ended in a head larger than that of the brown bear, with even sharper teeth. We all gazed speechlessly at this incredible hide.

"I shot it once," the captain boasted idly. "Through the eye, so the skin should bear no mark. Of course a glass eye now covers the bullet hole."

"How clever of you," Sarah said. "But where—?"

Captain Morgan altered his face in a way that might have suggested a smile to the undiscriminating, revealing teeth as yellow and prominent as his massive prey's more pointed armament. "As you know, I hunt the brown bears in Russia. In the northern reaches of that land, where the glaciers creep south toward the tents of man's farthest-flung outposts, the great polar bear rules, virtually invisible against an endless carpet of ice and snow. They call the place Siberia. I donned the hide of a seal, skin-side out, so I wore the bone color of that icy wasteland to stalk these great white bears."

"You took more than one?" Irene asked quickly.

Captain Morgan bowed his bald head in mock-humble pride. "The Czar permits my Russian hunting expeditions; I am privileged to reward my host." He turned to Madame Sarah. "This is the only polar bear pelt I have brought further than St. Petersburg."

"You will be outrageously rewarded," she promised with a happy pout, "much to the displeasure of my manager, Herr Heine. This is too wonderful to resist. Lay it upon my divan."

The turbaned servants understood French, for they instantly bent to lift the heavy bearskin into place. There it lay in barbaric splendor. Sarah reclined upon it in calculated inches, finally pushing her hands into the thick fur to the wrists.

"To think that I will be honored in the same night with the presence of the Empress of Russia and the emperor of polar bears. You are a peerless hunter, Captain. I quite quiver for your prey."

He laughed, a harsh, humorless sound. "And so you should, Madame."

He withdrew to our side as Sarah's other guests came to examine her prize, then turned to Irene. "I would be interested in your cobra skin—Madame, is it?"

"It is," Godfrey answered in French so blandly that the man whirled as if confronted by an enemy from ambush. He was a good judge of character, that hunter, for I have never known Godfrey to be so dangerous as when he is quiet.

"*Monsieur—?*" the captain began, seeking his identity.

"Godfrey Norton," Godfrey said sharply in English.

The captain's strong jaws snapped shut, as if he had been struck an invisible blow. Then the fierce blue eyes narrowed and focused on me. "And Mrs. Norton—?" he asked in a perfectly proper British voice.

"Mrs. Norton is the lady behind you," Irene said in her impeccable French, "who shot the snake. This is Miss Huxleigh, our friend."

"American!" He turned, unfooled by her perfect French, and his blue eyes drilled into Irene like bullets. "You are merely visiting the Continent, then?"

"I am a bird of passage, Captain," she said airily, "as are we all."

"But your home is in America."

"One of them. Once."

"I am serious about the cobra. I have a large collection of cobra skins."

Irene considered, casting her eyes down to her fan and biting her lip in mock-girlish fashion. "I cannot swear that I shot it precisely through the eye, sir. It might not be suitable for your collection."

"I do not require snakeskins to be whole. I rather enjoy shooting cobras. I like to see the evidence of it."

"It would have killed me," Irene answered. "That is why I shot it. And the Paris police are as interested in the skin as yourself. Perhaps you should inquire there."

"Perhaps." His icy gaze regarded us all. "I did not mean to interrupt your discussion. Pray continue."

With another bow so smart it seemed an insult rather than a courtesy, he left the dais.

Sarah looked up from caressing her new pet to address us. "I must confess—" her large, blue-green eyes drooped into Lucifer-size slits "—that few Englishmen impress me. That one does. He has passion. Unfortunately, the game that obsesses him is not human."

"Who is he?" Godfrey asked.

"Captain Sylvester Morgan, late of Her Majesty's forces in India. He has brought me all these lovely bears. I will not have heads of the big cats mounted about me; those I can import to my salon alive, like Minette." She nodded at the tiger cub clumsily cavorting in one corner of the salon. "But bears—they are too big for domestic pets."

"How did you meet him?" Irene wondered.

"He is not a man to trust to chance. He introduced himself, as an admirer."

"How long ago?"

"Does any truly intelligent woman keep count of such things? As well ask me to number my lovers, dear Irene. It is impossible! One must live life so that it cannot be caged behind mere dates. But for some years I have known him. He comes and goes. I hear that no tiger in India is safe from his marksmanship, but of course he knows better than to confront me with his tigerskins." She absently stroked the bear pelt.

"I imagine," Irene said after a slight pause, "that specific times are equally tiresome to the truly intelligent woman, but can you venture to say when the Empress will arrive?"

"Oh, that, yes! Her equerry was most officious about it. She will arrive at nine and depart within half an hour. You must sing in that interval. I trust that you have selected something brief. The instrument is there."

Her furled fan indicated something huddled in a corner of the room. It could have been a draped tiger cage. It could have been a piano. Irene glided over to it, Godfrey and I following.

She lifted the thread-encrusted throw, which was emblazoned with the actress's ubiquitous motto: "*Quand même*," Despite Everything. "Here, I think, is Oscar, Nell. Sarah is right; you should carry him as an accessory."

Irene lifted the coiling Indian green snake from the dusty key cover with one hand. He responded by winding himself several times around her forearm. Her flesh-colored gloves too artfully mimicked bare skin. I repressed a shudder at the picture the pair presented, reminding me of a foolish Eve in a lethal Eden.

Godfrey peeled Oscar from Irene and draped him over a twittering, thick-leaved plant. In fact, the twittering came from the contents of a birdcage concealed by the foliage.

Irene lifted the key cover and struck a note. "I doubt it is in tune. Music is not Sarah's forte. This will be a poor excuse of a concert."

"It *is* an excuse, Irene," I reminded her, managing not to sound at all sympathetic.

She smiled. "Quite right, Nell. What does Madame Norton's musical reputation matter, if she satisfies her curiosity?"

"There is more to it than that." Godfrey withdrew a pair of dusky cigarettes from his gold case and offered one to Irene.

A moment later a lit lucifer twinkled in our shadowed corner of the salon, and then two scarlet embers burned as bright as animal eyes in the dark. The charred lucifer made a burnt offering for the shallow porcelain dish atop the piano.

"Yes," Irene agreed at length, gazing toward the guests through a contemplative curtain of smoke.

I followed her example, recognizing no one but the noxious bear-killer, and then only by his bald head. The salon had become as mysterious as any Montmartre bistro, so fogged was it with smoke. I am sorry to say that cigarette smoking, even by women, had become the fashion at artistic assemblages such as this. Few objected to the petite cigarette as strenuously as they might to a cigar; certainly the odor was milder. And more than the occasional woman carried a bejeweled cigarette holder in her reticule, as Irene did. It occurred to me to wonder if the Empress of All the Russias would smoke.

"Godfrey," Irene said of a sudden, "you pore over the political columns in the newspapers. What do they say of Russia and its royal family?"

"A large subject for a summary."

"You summarize divinely," she said, smiling. "Pray do it."

"Alexander the Third is said to be an utter autocrat."

Irene nodded. "And his wife?"

"The mother of his six children. Much loved. Her only flaw is a fondness for Paris fashion."

"An utter paragon, then."

"So it seems. But czars' heads rest uneasily on their shoulders. The Romanovs have a history of internal treachery and outside assassination for possession of the throne. Germany is nibbling at the Russian bear's borders. England bristles over Russia's intentions toward India, past and present."

"So France is Russia's most obvious ally."

"For now."

Irene straightened suddenly and extinguished her cigarette in the small dish. "Politics is so dull, Godfrey! But, look, here comes royalty and fashion to rescue the evening. I predict that the reception is about to become far more interesting."

Indeed, a flurry at the doorway resolved itself into an ornately bemedaled Russian officer, who announced: "Her Imperial Majesty, the Czarina Maria Feodorovna, Empress of All the Russias."

"I should think, Godfrey," Irene commented sotto voce, "that, from what you have said, one Russia is enough to lord it over, just as a single cobra is sufficient for target practice."

"Indeed," I said, gathering myself to observe the progress of my first empress.

Imagine my surprise to see a tiny, dark-haired woman as slender as a schoolgirl enter the chamber. Her exquisite gown and jewels, however, commanded a respect her diminutive person could never enforce alone.

She illuminated that smoky, decadent salon like the sun bursting full power upon the sulky shadows of a swamp. Her yellow taffeta gown dripped blonde lace. Canary diamonds circled her neck and wrists and glittered in a tiara against her raven hair. Most glorious of all was the cheerful smile on her face.

Sarah had risen and curtsied deeply to this doll-like figure. After exchanging a few, unheard words, she turned to present Irene, who had appeared behind the actress. Irene sank into her rosy skirts in a profound but less effusive curtsy than Sarah's.

Godfrey was presented next. I had never seen him bow from the waist, but he managed it quite nicely. Then I, oh dear . . . I hardly recall the actual moment, a propensity of mine under great stress. We Shropshire girls had always practiced our curtsies in the unlikely case that we ever "met the Queen." I had never expected to meet an empress, but gave her slightly less than the same curtsy I would our own Queen, and thought that should suffice. After all, Godfrey had described the relations between my country and hers as "uneasy." A bit of coolness seemed appropriate. I most remember her remarkable eyes, darker than Irene's, but bright with amiable pleasure.

Others were presented, as well as the six or seven with the Empress—large, blonde, uniformed men like the King of Bohemia, tall women glittering with jewels and foreign eyes whether blonde or dark. The faces are a blur, save for the tall blonde woman I had noticed earlier; so she *had* been Russian! I asked Godfrey for the time, to which he produced a gold pocket watch and the answer, "nine-fifteen."

I suddenly found Irene at my side. She took my arm while

Godfrey took the opportunity to pay his respects to the barbaric buffet table, much to my surprise. Irene never ate before a performance, and Godfrey knew that I would never consume a crumb from the Divine Sarah's table; some men, however, can eat anything, anywhere. It made me speculate unpleasantly on Quentin's past eating habits.

"Now, Nell," Irene told me, unworried by Godfrey's culinary intemperance. "You must sit at Sarah's rather decrepit piano and play an F-minor chord."

"I? You mentioned no such necessity before!"

"I expected to accompany myself, but had not inspected Sarah's piano before. Utterly unreliable. Do not fret. I anticipated as much and came prepared to sing a cappella, but I must start someplace. One chord. Surely you can manage that."

"F-minor?"

"F-minor."

"I . . . believe that I remember where that is."

"I will show you before we start."

"And then what do I do?"

"Remain seated and try not to draw untoward attention to yourself," she answered dryly.

"F-minor?"

"Yes!"

"I did play a bit of piano as a child."

"I know."

"But I've never *performed* before."

"This is not a 'performance.' Casanova could do as much. With two feet. I only need one hand."

"How long should I hold the chord?"

"Until I start singing."

"Oh." I was being steered to the piano corner and seated on the small stool upholstered in leather—leather well scored by rather large cat claws. "Oh!"

"Never mind, Nell." Irene placed my right hand on the keyboard and guided my fingers to the appropriate keys.

"There. Simply press down, hold and then—gently—release."

How gently? I was going to ask, but Irene had turned to face the salon. I looked beyond her to see that during our intense discussion the Empress and her entourage had been seated in a semicircle around us, to see even Sarah Bernhardt sitting on an ordinary upright chair! I glanced quickly to my fingers. They had not moved. Apparently. Unless a finger had slipped onto an adjoining key when my attention had been distracted and I would strike a disastrously off-key chord . . .

Irene stood but two feet from me, calmly shaking out her skirt folds and clearing her throat. I had meant to tell her: smoking could not be doing her voice any good. I would misstrike the keys, and she would croak, and that would be the end of this little charade *chez* Sarah!

Several gentlemen were standing at the back of the room among the parlor palms, birdcages and hidden snakes, among them a flash of flesh-pink bald head and relentless blue eyes. In their evening dress they resembled a phalanx of penguin-like little tin soldiers. That comparison immediately made me think of the purported reason for this expedition, the abruptly absent Quentin Stanhope. Could he possibly resurface here, now? Would I truly see him again . . . or would he see me making a fool of myself at the keyboard of a neglected piano? Oh, dear . . .

"My most honored guest and her companions, and my dear friends," said Sarah, rising to stand beside her chair. "I present at Her Majesty's request my own friend, Madame Norton, performing a song of her selection. She will be . . . ah, accompanied by her friend, Miss Uxleigh."

I shook my head violently, but Sarah was sitting down with the blithe satisfaction of one who has performed her duty.

The striking blonde woman broke from the knot of the Empress's attendants and came crackling toward us, her glittering bodice clicking violently.

"Her Imperial Highness is ready," she told Irene in French

with a throaty accent. "I myself anticipate your performance. I have heard your talents spoken of most highly."

"I hope you will not be disappointed." Irene answered the odd undercurrent in the other woman's voice. "I am but a modest avocational singer," she added lightly.

"Oh, you do yourself an injustice, Madame," the woman returned, her eyes the color of Russian cherry-amber glittering in tandem with her gown's beadwork. "Begin when you are ready." She clicked and rustled off . . . to join Captain Sylvester Morgan at the back of the salon!

Irene had not followed her departure, instead reaching inward. A moment of concentrated quiet always prefaced a performance. Then she glanced over her shoulder at me and nodded.

My miserable hand pressed down the miserable keys upon which my fingers rested. The chord that rang out was certainly minor, but where one might find a starting note in it I could not imagine.

Then Irene's voice began, deep and mournful as a bell. She poured out pure sound, not song. Melancholy, ponderous sound, mourning made music. I cannot say how long it was before I realized that the sound had become words, and that those words were not German or French, or even Bohemian, but something very near the latter—Russian! When had Irene learned Russian? And when had she mastered this alien piece, which was a far cry from the robust peasant melodies of Dvořák?

While I pondered the strange new music, I kept my fingers tensed upon the keys. I was terrified that taking my hand away, even though the chord had long since faded, might disrupt the song. Yet my hand protested its unnatural position. Just when I decided to ease one finger from the keys at a time, a motion on the piano top caught my eye.

The fringe of the piano scarf that draped the closed top and dangled over the front and sides was wavering. While Irene's voice seemed at times to make the walls vibrate in sympathy, I seriously doubted that silk should follow suit . . . especially since the area that trembled now *migrated* slowly from one side of the piano case to the other.

I remained unmoving, my right hand crippled into its awkward position, my eyes never daring to leave the cloth as its horrid undulations seemed to sink and swell in response to the expression in Irene's voice.

Where was little Oscar? More to the point, where were the larger snakes that Sarah Bernhardt kept: the huge muscular spotted species familiarly called boa constrictors? I had heard of snake charming; was it possible that Irene was a born snake singer? That I would be the first "accompanist" to perform in tandem with a reptile?

I eyed my general vicinity for a discreet means of escape. None; I had no recourse save tumbling over backward on the stool and hoping to arise from the tangle of my gown in time to avoid the snake's following me into disgrace.

Although Irene's voice throbbed with the pathos of a violin while delivering the strange, thick-throated words she sang; although one part of my mind noted that she was giving a magnificent and moving performance, and that her unaccompanied voice had a rich power I had scarcely suspected before; although I had to concede that her musical selection was brilliantly chosen and was delighting her audience, I simply could not sit here mesmerized by the ever-nearing manipulations of a snake, no matter what it was wearing!

I lifted first my forefinger. Then my ring finger and my smallest finger. It only remained for me to remove my thumb from the ivory and I would be free of the piano. Perhaps tiny pushes of my feet could ease the stool backwards, and then I could unobtrusively edge sideways, jump up and run!

Sound exploded around me, and I did exactly that in a flash, save that I could not run. Everyone was standing to applaud Irene, except the Empress, who would have stood had she been sitting where I was, even if she *was* an Empress.

"May I?" came a male voice from much closer to me than it should have been.

I glanced toward the piano to find the odious bear-slayer awaiting my permission for something. I nodded numbly.

He tore back the cloth.

I gasped and covered my mouth to muffle the sound.

A long, dark, furry . . . appendage writhed on the polished wood.

Captain Morgan smiled that mirthless smile of his and lifted the slightly open piano top. From within he extracted a hairy little gnome of a creature.

"A Capuchin monkey," he said. "A good thing that you did not actually play the instrument. The rascal was inside, with only his tail—keeping time to the music, I think—protruding. I trust that he did not disconcert you."

"Not in the least," I managed to croak.

Captain Morgan let the creature run up his arm to his shoulder and loop its extraordinarily long tail around his neck. He looked to Irene, who had been called over to receive the Empress's congratulations.

"She is a politician, this Madame Norton," he mused, oddly, since Irene had earlier professed finding politics dull. "Beautiful women make very dangerous politicians. Tell her that my interest in the cobra remains keen. Tell her that she should surrender it to me."

" 'Surrender'? A most odd phrasing, sir."

"Tell her exactly what I said. Can you do that?"

His condescending question reminded me that in some quarters I was considered an adventuresome woman. I drew myself up. "I will report your words precisely."

He nodded, that awful man, with the monkey cradled around his head, its clawed paws curving over his bald scalp. For a moment, the two seemed a hellish hybrid of man and beast.

"You had better," said he curtly, and left me.

Chapter Fifteen

HOMEWARD BOUND

"I have only one question," Godfrey said on the morning after our command performance on the Boulevard Péreire.

We were gathered after a late breakfast—Irene's and Godfrey's had been taken in bed—in the small front parlor that served as music room. At least Casanova's cage shared the space with a handsome, square grand piano, on whose shawl-strewn top he was forever casting grape stems and seed hulls.

"What is that, my darling?" Irene asked lazily. (Though she usually possessed an almost demonic energy, she all too easily evinced that post-performance sloth so deplorably common to those of a theatrical bent.)

Godfrey put down the Paris papers, which were printed on exceedingly thin tissue, like that which wraps pastries. I often suspect that the word "insubstantial" was invented in Paris.

"What was the name of the piece you sang for the Empress last night?" he queried further.

Irene wrapped herself tighter within her violet taffeta robe with a self-congratulatory rustle. Her feet, clad in purple satin slippers, were crossed upon an ottoman.

"I am so delighted that you asked. It was an aria from the most recent Tchaikovsky opera, *Eugene Onegin*. Melancholy stuff, but then there is so much of Russia, and so few Russian cities of gaiety and style. No wonder that everything composed there sounds like a dirge."

"Melancholy suits you," Godfrey replied, "or, rather, your voice. Not a soul in the salon moved an eyelash while you sang."

Irene sat up to regard me over her balloon-sleeved shoulder. "Our dear Nell, I understand, was a veritable pillar of salt during my rendition: so smitten that she could not even lift a finger to remove it from the keyboard."

"I did strive to prevent any distraction," I replied, rising from my chair to approach Casanova's cage.

The bird waddled over to the brass bars, actually welcoming company, especially when it bore an olive branch of plump Muscat grapes.

"You succeeded admirably," Irene admitted, sipping from the coffee cup that accompanied her from rising until noon on mornings after such late evenings. "What did Captain Morgan say to you? I saw him showing you the clever little monkey."

"Eerie beast!" I could not help shuddering when I recalled the creature clasped in that man's arms like some demonic infant. "And Captain Morgan made no sense, though he insisted that I convey a message to you. I am thinking better of it this morning."

Godfrey and Irene exchanged a glance. "You had better do so," he said.

"But Captain Morgan is an odious fellow! Why should I serve as his messenger? And why should Irene be of interest to him?"

"Exactly, my dear Nell." Irene's eyes shone like the almost-black coffee that filled her cup. "Once again you state the obvious with scintillating originality. And you are quite right that I am utterly insignificant. Still, I would like the captain's message."

"Cut the cackle!" croaked Casanova, thrusting his ruffled head forward for another grape. I had neglected his supply in the heat of the discussion.

He got his grape and Irene got her answer.

"Captain Morgan was most rude," I said. "He insisted that he was still interested in the skin of the cobra that you killed. He said that you would do well to surrender the skin to him."

"That is exactly what he said?"

I sighed. "If you wish me to go upstairs and consult my diary—?"

"I do," she answered. "There is nothing for accuracy like the words when they are first set down."

I forsook Casanova, who kept calling "Cassie want a crumpet" after my departing figure, and thumped up the stairs to my bedchamber.

Irene was still lounging in the upholstered chair, feet up, when I returned, except that a cigarette was decorating her small enameled holder and filling the room with tendrils of smoke. "And?"

I stood before them like a well-drilled schoolgirl and read from my own hand: "The Awful Evening ended with the removal of the monkey from the piano chamber. The dreadful bear-slayer said, 'She is a politician, this Madame Norton. Beautiful women make very dangerous politicians. Tell her that my interest in the cobra remains keen. Tell her that she should surrender it to me.' "

I shut my diary, pursed my lips and waited.

Irene looked at Godfrey, who looked at me.

"That is exactly what he said—his interest in the cobra remains keen?" she asked.

I nodded. "It could not be clearer."

Irene laughed then, a cascading gale that somehow made my taut lips want to twitch. "Oh, Nell, much about this affair could be made a great deal clearer, but I am glad that you are here to take such convoluted matters at face value."

"Captain Morgan was *not* speaking literally?"

"Captain Morgan was warning me. His 'cobra' is *your* 'Cobra.' "

"I have no such thing as a snake!"

"He spoke of a man, not a man-biter. Quentin Stanhope.

Remember? He used the spy name 'Cobra' in Afghanistan."

I looked back to my diary pages, and the neat ink-blue words took on a sudden sinister significance. "Then the 'cobra' in which Captain Morgan remains keenly interested is . . . Quentin. And he wants you to surrender Quentin to him!"

"As if I had Mr. Stanhope to do so," Irene pointed out good-humoredly.

I clasped the open diary to my bodice. "You would betray him?"

"No, but I do wonder what Captain Morgan would attempt to do if he knew Mr. Stanhope's whereabouts. Do not worry, Nell; at the most I would use your Mr. Stanhope as a Judas goat."

"The poor man! No wonder he fled this cottage as one might a trap."

"I think his flight had more to do with Captain Morgan—perhaps the possessor of an air gun, do you think?—and a great deal to do with you."

"Myself? But I am of no significance in this matter."

"At the moment you are a go-between for hunter and prey."

"And what role do *you* play in the game of cat-and-mouse?"

"Ah." Irene inhaled the smoke from her cigarette as if it were food for thought, and expelled a dreadful one. "Call it, rather, a game of cobra-and-mongoose—or tiger. I am convinced that Captain Morgan is the person that Mr. Stanhope knew as 'Tiger' in Afghanistan."

Even Godfrey sat up at that. " 'Tiger'? Are you certain, Irene?"

"I am, but my facts are not. I will have to ask you to do more pottering amongst the official papers."

"There will be no record of the English-Afghanistan War in Paris!" I pointed out triumphantly.

Irene regarded me as if I were auditioning for the role of a madwoman. "Of course not. In London."

"You are sending Godfrey to London?"

"No, I am going with Godfrey to London."

He laughed softly, obviously hearing for the first time this latest intemperate scheme. Unfortunately, Godfrey was a good deal more accommodating than myself.

"Well, Irene, you cannot go to London!" I said.

"It may mean Mr. Stanhope's life," she advised me.

"I am sure that he is well suited to preserving it himself."

"Matters must be investigated there if we are to get to the bottom of this."

"I am not at all convinced that I wish to get to the bottom—or the top—of this. And certainly *you* cannot go to London!"

"Why not?"

"Irene, must I constantly remind you of the obvious? You are presumed dead. You are living in virtual anonymity by your own wish. You are known in London. If you go there, you will betray your existence. You may attract the attention of the King of Bohemia's agents—who may not truly have given you up. And you will certainly risk drawing the notice of Mr. Sherlock Holmes of Baker Street."

"He knows that I am alive."

"But he warned you in Monte Carlo to avoid the kind of matters he delves in. I know what you are up to, do not deny it! You will immediately seek out the Dr. Watson who is associated with Mr. Holmes. In so doing, you will stride right into the serpent's jaws. You will ruin your anonymity!"

"Goodness," said Irene calmly. "Quite a case you have built up. Indeed, it is awkward for me to venture from the Continent. You are quite right, Nell," she added with becoming contriteness. "I would, of course, immediately find this Dr. Watson to learn whether he is Mr. Stanhope's Dr. Watson, although the likelihood is . . . well, unlikely." She sighed and was silent.

I closed my diary and glanced at Godfrey, who was regarding Irene's bowed head with concern, or at least surprise. She sat up abruptly, her entire manner animated for the first time that morning.

"But of course! That is the solution! Once again, Nell, your inescapable logic has shown me the way. *You* must go to London with Godfrey while I remain safe and undetected in Paris. How could I miss such an obvious conclusion?"

"I? And Godfrey? But—"

"*You* are not in danger of detection; nor is Godfrey. Neither of you had a public reputation in London, as I did. Unless you led a double life—? No. Certainly you can both be more discreet than I. And since Nell would worry during my absence in London—"

"I would indeed."

"I will remain at home here in Neuilly and worry about *you!*"

Irene sat back with the happy expression of a child who has successfully protested a bedtime by persuading the governess to stay up with her.

"Why must anyone go to London at all?" I muttered.

"Because, dear Nell, Captain Morgan is a very dangerous man who is not only on the trail of poor Mr. Stanhope, but also of the man whom Mr. Stanhope hopes to protect. And now Captain Morgan is convinced that we are involved in the matter. We must delve deeper into the affair for the sake of our own skins, if nothing else. Is that not true?"

"I do not like your figure of speech."

"Which figure?"

"Skins," I intoned. "I have had enough of bearskins. Nor do I care to encounter snakes in any form, even metaphorical, as in this Captain Morgan's case."

Godfrey laughed. "We must, dear Nell. Irene has requested that the Paris police surgeon inspect the, er . . . form . . . of the deceased cobra as well as its victim. He promised to call tomorrow, and I suspect that he will."

"You agree with this scheme, Godfrey?"

He thought for a moment, while regarding Irene fondly. "I agree that we must take action. Whether we like it or not, our taking in Stanhope has attracted the attention of those with the most noxious motives . . . to Stanhope himself—and to us all."

"Then it is settled!" Irene rose and shook out her taffeta robe until it crackled. "I will remain here and pursue snakes, of various sorts, while you two will visit London and interview medical men named Watson who served in Afghanistan." She sighed and gave me a grave look. "I think, my dear Nell, that you have chosen the better part."

"All the world's a stage," the parrot proclaimed as if cued.

I suspect that he was.

One good thing can be said about preparing for travel: it so occupies the mind that the ordinary shocks and surprises of life seem strangely muffled.

Thus I was like a person moving rapidly through a fog in the two days preceding Godfrey's and my untimely departure. Thoughts of Quentin Stanhope collided in my mind as I dealt with shirtwaists and stockings, corsets and collars.

Though I well knew that this trip—like all of Irene's schemes—was designed to distract me from the case of reason and restraint, I also sensed a hidden purpose. Yet I could not argue with her intent to safeguard Quentin, no matter how rudely he had behaved toward me. I was so triumphant at having persuaded Irene to remain safely behind that I did not contemplate one obvious fact until I was alone with my thoughts and my wearables: by going to London, I would almost certainly encounter Quentin again, should Godfrey and I have any success in our inquiries.

So I often found myself standing with a knot of petticoats clutched to my bosom, my heart pounding. I moved my latest diary from one hidden place to another, and finally burdened my trunk with the volume. If anything should happen to me, if the steamer should sink in the Channel, so too would my tenderest thoughts.

I did not give much thought to Irene or to my traveling companion, Godfrey. For the first time, I faced a matter so pressing that my own affairs, such as they were, took precedence over my lifelong dedication to the welfare of others. I had not the slightest thought to spare for the most commonplace things around me. Even Lucifer had a downcast look as he lounged on my counterpane and watched the contents level of the trunk rise. Casanova serenaded me with such innovative variations as "Cassie want a trumpet" to catch my attention, in vain.

With customary efficiency, Godfrey had dashed out to book our passage from Calais. We faced a short train journey followed by a hopefully calm crossing and another short train journey at the other end. I confess that the notion of seeing London again, of breathing British air, quite excited me. Certainly it was only that which caused my heart to give little, breathless skips now and then.

"He is here!" Irene announced the next day, pausing breathlessly on the threshold to my bedchamber.

Only one type of personage (excluding Godfrey) could cause that sudden exuberance, the pink on her cheeks and the fire in her eye: an emissary from the realm of crime and chaos beyond the ken of most gentlefolk.

I set down my small pile of handkerchiefs and went below, where our parlor housed a representative of the Paris Prefecture of Police.

Godfrey paused in the pouring of a sherry—these Paris police are ever ready to mix business with pleasure—and nodded to me as I entered after Irene.

"Our dear friend, Miss Huxleigh. Dr. Sauveur."

I nodded at a hedgehog of a man with a quantity of unruly brown hair erupting around bright brown eyes and an unfortunate, though imposing, nose.

"Dr. Sauveur is associated with the Paris police," Irene explained unnecessarily. I can make some deductions quite unassisted. "He has examined both the unhappy Indian man who perished in Montmartre and the cobra I killed."

"How fortunate," I murmured as I sat.

"Most unfortunate," the doctor contradicted me. "This incident is a complete puzzle." He flipped up his coattails and sat, cradling his glass in both hands with a familiarity all too common to the French when it comes to alcoholic beverages. "I am more baffled than when I first heard of the case."

"Perhaps," Godfrey suggested after he had brought me a glass of Vichy water, "you could begin by telling us the condition of the man."

"Dead." The doctor laughed. "And by cobra venom, though there were no fang marks upon the body. Most puzzling."

At this Irene nearly leaped out of her chair. "No bite marks? But the snake I shot—"

"Was venomous, Madame. You did well to dispatch it. Yet it was not the means of the Indian gentleman's death."

"Do you mean to say, Dr. Sauveur," Godfrey demanded, "that my wife and Miss Huxleigh found a man dead of snakebite alone in a room with a poisonous snake—and the snake was innocent?"

Dr. Sauveur shrugged and sipped sherry. "That is what Inspector Dubuque asked. But facts are facts. There were no fang marks on the dead man."

"Were there any other marks upon him?" Irene inquired.

The doctor looked up with a moue of distaste. "I understand, Madame, that in your . . . past you were a theatrical performer and were thus accustomed to arming yourself as you went to and fro at night. Or so Inspector Dubuque tells me that you told him."

Irene smiled mysteriously at his disapproving tone. Once she would have told him sternly that she had been a prima donna, not some obscure supernumerary one corset-cover removed from scandal. Now she dared not advertise her past respectability without betraying her past identity.

"My wife," Godfrey put in for her, "is American. It is not uncommon that respectable women there carry weapons for self-defense."

"Ah, America. Always the Wild West Show, no? So the Inspector told me that he was told. Still . . . for a woman to go armed in Paris is as unusual as for a man to die of snakebite without a mark upon his skin."

"Unusual," I put in despite my uncertain French pronunciation, "but fortunate in this case. The creature was preparing to strike Irene."

"It was frightened, Mademoiselle," the doctor began.

"So was I!"

"Miss Huxleigh is not terribly sympathetic to snakes," Irene said, "and I do not blame her. What have you learned, then, of the man and the snake, beyond the intriguing fact that they had nothing to do with one another despite a common Indian origin and their admittedly . . . close association in death?"

"From what the inspector tells me, the Indian is unlikely to be identified. Such men are nameless, usually of the servant or sailor class. They come and go as their masters and ships do; few know or note their progress. The cobra is as common, at least in its native land. An Asian cobra is only one and a half meters long—some five feet in your measurement in England, or America, Madame 'Sharpshooter'—" the last word was delivered in English with a pronounced French emphasis "—no very great length as cobras go. It is not as if it was a king cobra. Now those reach—you would say?—eighteen feet."

I must have made a whimper of distaste, for all regarded me attentively.

"A most royally attenuated serpent," I admitted. "Madame Sarah would adore it."

Dr. Sauveur shook his grizzled head at me with some sympathy. "What eccentrics, these performers, eh?" He smiled unctuously at Godfrey, who regarded him with the cold, cobralike stare that a good barrister can produce in court.

The physician swallowed the last of his sherry in one greedy gulp and rose. "There is little more to say. I was asked to report and have done so. The man is dead by cobra venom. The cobra was not the source and it is also dead, by pistol shot."

"Have you no speculations?" Irene asked incredulously.

The doctor's lip curled. "No, Madame. I am not paid to

speculate, only to examine. However, a colleague of Inspector Dubuque's, Inspector Le Villard, suggests that only one man may be able to unravel such a conundrum, a Mr. Sherlock Holmes of London. He is an English amateur who has written monographs on various matters. Le Villard is translating them to our language. Perhaps you have heard of this man?"

"No," said Godfrey quickly, as quickly as Irene said "Yes."

It was left for me to tread the thin line between truth and self-interest. "Perhaps," I said airily. "Theatrical people can be so eccentric."

Dr. Sauveur frowned, as if unsure how to take my meaning. Indeed, I was uncertain of that myself. Then he picked up his top hat and bowed sketchily before leaving the room. Sophie waited in the hall to let him out.

"Well!" Irene's ambiguous eyes sparkled with the pure honey of speculation. "I am minded to reconsider and journey with you. Perhaps this Mr. Sherlock Holmes we 'perhaps' have heard of should be consulted in the case! Quite a pretty puzzle."

Godfrey frowned and lit one of his cigarettes, dropping the lucifer into a crystal dish. "What do you think, Irene? Victim and weapon in the same room, but not related."

She tented her long fingers and rested her chin upon them, a pose that would have been piquant had she not been thinking so hard.

"Could there," I suggested tentatively, "have been another snake?"

"Another snake!" Godfrey nodded approvingly at me.

"That is the heart of the problem," Irene said. "Where did the snake come from, and were there two? We have assumed that the snake was an occupant of the chamber, because its cage was there. But was the Indian also an unacknowledged lodger? We cannot know for sure until we find Mr. Stanhope and ask him."

"Until *we* find Mr. Stanhope," I corrected. "Godfrey and I. You are remaining here in Paris."

"Ah! So I am. And a pretty puzzle remains here in Paris with me: the two snakes, the mysterious dead Indian who may or may not be acquainted with Mr. Stanhope, and the sinister Captain Morgan." Irene rubbed her hands together in anticipation.

"Godfrey!" I demanded. "Do you think we should leave her?"

"We have no choice," he retorted cheerfully. "I hazard that the London end of the matter will be fully as nettlesome. But the questions Irene raises are fascinating. Did the Indian bring the lethal snake—or snakes—to Stanhope's garret intending to kill him? Did one bite his trainer and escape—you said there were several open casements? Did Irene shoot an innocent bystander?" Godfrey laughed and rubbed his hands in imitation of his wife.

"Or . . ." Irene sat up with a demonic expression. "Was the Indian a manservant, even a friend of Mr. Stanhope's? Was the snake his, and did someone, not knowing of either the Indian's or the snake's existence, import his own snake to kill Mr. Stanhope? Only the lethal snake escaped, after ridding itself of its venom. But no matter how many snakes we import to the scene, we are missing something. The man was killed by snake venom . . . administered somehow. Not necessarily by a reptile. Did the same venom coat the needle that pierced Mr. Stanhope, I wonder, only in that instance, in an insufficient amount? Inspector Le Villard was right. This case requires some sophistication in chemistry. I will have to persuade the inspector to let me see whether the English detective's works include any methods of transmitting venoms. Perhaps the good inspector could use a proofreader for his translations?"

"Irene, even you would not dare!"

"Why not, Nell? One can always learn from a rival."

"You and Sherlock Holmes are not rivals."

"We are certainly not allies."

"I hope not," Godfrey put in significantly.

Irene eyed him. "Surely, Godfrey, you have not resided

near Paris long enough to contract the French national disease?''

"And what is that?'' he asked.

"A rivalry of your own.''

He was quiet for a moment. One of Irene's eyebrows arched in surprise. He said slowly, "I agree with Nell. You are like a moth playing with the fire. I understand that for you it is an amusing game, but it makes me uneasy at times. There is the matter of the King of Bohemia as well—''

"That, too?'' She, also, had become unnaturally quiet.

"Only in that he is not likely to have forgotten you so quickly. He is an autocratic, unpredictable man, and a spoiled ruler. It is best not to tempt him into something rash. The more you plunge yourself into sensational matters, my dear Irene, the more likely you are to attract unwelcome attention, even exposure.''

"Oh, pooh, Godfrey! You are sounding like Nell. Shortly Casanova will be carping at me, urging caution. The King is in Prague and Sherlock Holmes is in London. I will be in Paris, will I not?'' she added almost coquettishly. "What harm can come of that? Better you should worry about the safety of Quentin Stanhope and his long-ago friend, Dr. Watson. Better you both should fret about the explanation our former houseguest owes to us all, and especially to Nell.''

Once more all eyes fastened on me, as Irene skillfully turned an inquiry into her own situation into an unwanted and intimate examination of mine.

Chapter Sixteen

INNOCENT UNRELATED ERRANDS

England lay ahead, visible on the heaving silver breast of the sea. How was it that the land that I approached with so much fond eagerness should strike me as ominous when I saw the chalk cliffs of Dover rising like a ghostly barrier from the crashing sea?

Godfrey stood beside me at the rail, his feelings perhaps as mixed as mine. Neither of us was used to traveling without Irene, and we were both forlorn, yet relieved that we need not worry about her.

"I have not forgotten," Godfrey remarked.

"Forgotten what?"

"My promise to you."

"Oh, please, Godfrey, it is not necessary to speak of it."

"Yes, it is. You must not think that either Irene or I take you for granted. You are our friend, and we cannot allow this man to take advantage of you—"

"No such thing happened!"

"Or allow him to renew a friendship and then leave so callously, without explanation. Gentlemen do not do such things."

"I do not think he had any choice. If the man who died in his rooms was a friend or acquaintance, perhaps he feared that same fate for myself—for you and Irene, who had only tried to help him. An honorable man would have no choice but to flee."

Godfrey nodded slowly. "I hope for your sake that he is honorable still, Nell. If he is not—"

"Then we shall know, shall we not? And I suppose that knowing is better than . . . not knowing."

He suddenly smiled down at me. "So serious, Nell, for a lady under a Paris bonnet. You have changed, you know. Stanhope was right about that. And now you espouse the motto that drives Irene, and sometimes myself and most of the human race."

"What is that?" I asked, unaware of any recent profundity that had dropped from my lips.

" 'Knowing is better than not knowing.' I trust we shall soon know more about this tangle than we did."

"What if 'Dr. Watson' is *the* Dr. Watson?"

Godfrey's gray gaze suddenly twinkled like the water around us. "Then we will have a most interesting puzzle piece to deliver to Irene. Perhaps we will even surprise her and solve the puzzle altogether on this end."

"Oh, do you think so, Godfrey?! That would be . . . amusing, would it not? That would be adventuresome."

"Yes, my dear Nell, it would. Even my incomparable Irene can benefit from an outwitting now and again."

I would have never believed that London could strike me as terra incognita, yet it looked like an utterly unfamiliar charcoal sketch through which we rode by some magical means of progress—though a four-wheeler has seldom been mistaken for an altered pumpkin. The soot-blackened buildings seemed limned by some absent artistic hand rather than by reality. Viewed in the high noon of summer rather than through the romantic misty lens of gaslights and fog, the streets appeared cramped, commercial and tawdry compared to the broad, tree-strewn boulevards of Paris. The constant clatter of omnibuses and carriages, the calls of street mongers through the narrow lanes, quickly gave me the headache.

Godfrey directed the driver to Brown's Hotel.

"That sounds a rather common establishment," I commented.

Godfrey merely smiled. I had long ago learned to interpret that response: he knew something which I did not.

As our vehicle drove past Green Park to Dover Street, I realized that we had crossed into Mayfair, which made me lilt my eyebrows as Irene often did. "Is this not an excessively extravagant address?"

"We have an extravagant amount of money from the sale of the Zone of Diamonds," he replied.

I could not argue with fact, however much I might wish to. Brown's Hotel appeared as respectable as the Duke of Kent's country house, not that I have ever been a guest at such an establishment, but a governess does hear things, and I had forgotten nothing that I had heard during those days. And, of course, even then I kept my diaries, though they were not so interesting as they had become since my involvement with Irene, and now Godfrey.

For me the greatest obstacle to Irene's scheme of sending Godfrey and myself a-hunting medical Watsons in London was not the formidable consulting detective sure to be lurking there. No, the most dreaded barrier now rose up before me in a wall of coffered mahogany: the embarrassment of registering at a hotel.

Although some benighted young women nowadays, who consider themselves thoroughly modern, think nothing of remaining unchaperoned with a man for whole hours at a time, the true gentlewoman cannot permit the slightest miscomprehension of her position vis-à-vis any male person at any time. Dear as Godfrey was to me as both employer and friend, I could not bear to have a hotel clerk reach any wrongful conclusions about our relationship.

Godfrey broached the main desk. "I have made reservations for a pair of suites," said he, very commandingly, I thought.

"And the name, sir?" inquired the man on duty. The wall

behind him resembled a gigantic pigeonholed desk bristling with messages, mail and unclaimed keys.

"Feverall Marshwine," said Godfrey without batting an eyelash. "Of Paris."

"Feverall Marshwine of Paris," repeated the clerk without a pause. "Here it is, sir. And a two-room suite for Miss Lucy Maison-Nouveau."

"My cousin," Godfrey said with a courteous nod at me. The desk clerk inclined his head politely. He eyed the trunks a man had deposited in the lobby and rang for a manservant.

Shortly after we and our baggage were escorted by a modern lift to our rooms high above Old Bond Street. They were adjacent, but no one could accuse us of cohabiting without a lewd imagination.

It was not until Godfrey had paid our baggage toter an unholy amount of coinage for the herculean task of conveying our baggage up six flights in a lift that I was able to doff my bonnet and gloves and speak my mind.

We stood in the sitting room of my suite, where my trunk had been deposited until a maid could unpack it.

"This is splendid accommodation, Godfrey," I admitted, "but it is shockingly extravagant for us to occupy two rooms each. I could do quite nicely with one."

"Surely, Nell, you do not wish to be perceived as entertaining gentlemen in your bedchamber? And I will find it necessary to visit you, or vice versa, so we can compare notes on the day's investigations."

"Yes," I agreed, "but you are my 'cousin.' And what do you mean by 'gentlemen' plural? Surely my rooms are not to become an interrogation center for cabmen and snake charmers?"

He smiled. "How quick you are. I was thinking, of course, of Stanhope. Well, Nell, if—when—we locate him, it is possible that we will need to offer him the discretion of a private talk. So you see, our parlors are needed as interview rooms, so to speak, as well as for our own consultations."

"A long way around to justify extra expense," I said. "And

where did you come by those ridiculous pseudonyms? Irene, no doubt?"

He bowed. "Irene had nothing to do with it. I am in charge of this expedition."

"Feverall Marshwine?!"

"It leaped into my mind at the cable office. Have you never wanted to pretend to be someone else?"

"No, I have not. I know what I myself have been up to, but some other identity may be another case entirely. And how did you come by 'Lucy Maison-Nouveau'? Do not tell me it was another inspiration of the cable office."

"But it was! Based upon your sterling example, as always. I recalled the cable from Belgium you signed with the code name Casanova."

"Oh. I see. Maison-Nouveau is French for the same thing. In English it would be Newhouse. Perhaps the better choice, Godfrey. No one will ever mistake me for a Frenchwoman. And the 'Lucy'?"

Like many a delinquent charge from my governess days, Godfrey guiltily eyed his boot tips, polished to as glossy a black as Lucifer's fur after an hour's licking.

"*Luci*fer! Godfrey, how could you?" I managed to avoid laughing.

"A hasty and desperate invention, Nell," he said contritely, "and 'Lucille' is a French name. Forgive me, but I thought it better for us to travel incognito."

His apology was approximately as sincere as Irene's respect for the literal truth. At least no one in London who had known me would suspect that I was masquerading as a French female who had no objections to engaging a suite adjacent to that of an unrelated man, which, I admit, was decidedly "French" behavior.

"Now that we are here, what is our plan?" I asked.

"First, to eliminate the obvious."

"You mean this 'Dr. Watson' who Irene is convinced shares rooms with Sherlock Holmes?"

"Irene saw *two* men entering 221 B Baker Street late at night after the rather underhanded charade in St. John's Wood."

"I agree with you on the underhandedness of Mr. Sherlock Holmes, Godfrey. I cannot comprehend how Irene can profess such admiration for a man who would stoop to impersonating a clergyman while attempting to trick a helpless woman out of the sole artifact that defends her from another man's unwanted attentions, and a king's at that!"

"I agree with you," he said, "except for the 'helpless.' In fact, I consider it highly charitable of you, Nell, to campaign for the life of a man who very likely pitched the plumber's rocket into our drawing-room windows at Briony Lodge. It was a shabby if all too effective ploy to trick Irene into revealing the hidden chamber in which lay the photograph of her and the King of Bohemia."

"You think that Dr. Watson did such a despicable thing? He is a medical man."

"You are a former governess, but I believe that you have essayed a deceptive mission or two for Irene's sake."

"That is quite different! Nothing I have ever done could possibly be construed as malicious mischief."

"Oh? What of your masquerade as Irene's housekeeper, gloating over Mr. Holmes and King Willie when they found their trap sprung and their quarry gone?"

"Perhaps that was the tiniest bit mischievous, but it was hardly malicious, Godfrey. No, you will have to find a better apologist for Dr. Watson's failing than myself. Irene's freedom and happiness were at stake then. Sherlock Holmes had nothing to gain but a mere fee. His only interest was financial."

"Odd that he has not pursued the Zone of Diamonds now that he knows Irene is alive. . . ."

"Nothing odd, only ignorance. He knows nothing of the Zone!"

"He knows it existed, for Tiffany himself said he hired Sherlock Holmes as well as Irene to look into its whereabouts. And from your own account of the trio's visit to

Briony Lodge, it is obvious to me that Mr. Holmes had hoped to find a far more glamorous prize than a photograph, or even Irene herself."

"Obvious? To you? I wrote the account to which you refer, and it was more than obvious to me that no such undercurrent existed."

"Ah!" Godfrey spread his hands in surrender. "Useless to argue with the author of the document in question. Perhaps I am seeing undercurrents on dry land. So you are convinced now that Sherlock Holmes's Dr. Watson—should he prove also to be Quentin Stanhope's Dr. Watson—is a heartless trickster and a lying lackey not worth the effort of saving?"

"If we doled out our acts of charity according to who is worthy, we might have no objects left for our concern," I said stoutly. "And if Quentin thinks it worth risking his life for this man who saved him in Afghanistan, I can only do my best to aid in this enterprise. Besides, I am convinced that the Dr. Watson from Afghanistan in eighteen-eighty has never set foot in Baker Street except for innocent, unrelated errands! He may not even be in London, or England."

"Then the only thing to do is to test your—I hesitate to call such a rousing opinion a mere theory—assertion, shall we say?"

" 'Assertion' is a fine, forthright word that does not shilly-shally. So shall we sally forth?"

"First we have two separate duties to perform."

I grew instantly serious, as the word "duty" invariably encourages me to do.

Godfrey smiled in a way that was eerily reminiscent of Irene. "I must repair to my suite and make some alterations of a personal nature. Irene, I believe, equipped you for slight disguise?"

I produced a length of heavy black veiling, diligently spotted with velour, from the upper shelf of my trunk. "Not efficient for seeing, but most appropriate for mourning—or for not being seen."

"Excellent. And I believe now would be a good time for

you to take the hotel stationery in hand and pen a note to the family of your former employer. Mrs. Turnpenny, was it not?"

"The Turnpennys left Berkeley Square for India. I have no notion where they might reside today."

"I refer to Mrs. Turnpenny's family—the Stanhopes."

"The Stanhopes of Grosvenor Square—Quentin's parents? You expect me to address them at this late date? I have never met them!"

"But you have encountered their son recently, which may be of some interest to them if he has not already returned to England and made himself known. Merely send them a note identifying your earlier connection with the family and expressing your desire to visit them on a matter concerning their son, et cetera. You composed such communications for me innumerable times at the Temple, dear Nell. What makes you pale at the idea now?"

"They are . . . well-placed people. I cannot intrude . . . they would not see me."

"You underestimate yourself, as usual," he said with a smile. "Simply write the note, and we will leave it at the hotel desk for a messenger to deliver. And do not look so appalled! Not even Mr. Sherlock Holmes can investigate a mystery without rushing in where he is not wanted; consider his surprise descent on Briony Lodge."

"Yes, that was cheeky. Very well, I will write the Stanhopes, but I cannot guarantee any response."

"Who can in this hurly-burly world, Nell?" Godfrey said cheerfully, bowing out of my sitting room.

I spent the next half hour penning the wretched note. Several versions lay crumpled in my wastepaper basket, a pitiable waste of Brown Hotel's stationery, which was exceptionally fine cream parchment-paper. Finished at last, I struggled to affix Irene's disguising veiling to my bonnet, a process that involved several short hatpins and even more prickings of my poor fingers. Thus far I was not impressed with the business of being a private inquiry agent.

When Godfrey rapped upon my door, I opened it in not very good temper. The sight that greeted me did little to amend my mood.

"Godfrey?! What on earth have you done to yourself?"

He stepped in past me and ducked to regard himself in the small oval mirror near the door. "I have removed my mustache. Does it alter my appearance?"

"Indeed it does! And I am not sure for the better."

"I thought that you disliked facial hair upon men."

"Yes . . . but I had become accustomed to yours, and it was just a mustache, after all. Oh, what will Irene say?" I was suddenly reminded of the more intimate effects of mustaches, and blushed furiously.

"We will find out when we return to Paris. In the meantime, I congratulate myself upon the idea. At least I have changed my countenance enough to deceive Sherlock Holmes if we encounter him, for I doubt he ever much noted my appearance," Godfrey added dryly.

"You expect to encounter *the* man? Really, Godfrey, I have no desire to come that close to him again. He quite terrifies me."

"The person I expect to encounter is Dr. Watson, of whom I have never seen hide nor hair, and of whose existence and exact relationship to Holmes even you cannot be certain. Perhaps he is a figment of Irene's imagination, or a blind that Holmes uses for his advertising convenience in the agony columns, hm?"

"A third man accompanied Mr. Holmes and the King to Briony Lodge. It could have been—"

" 'Could have beens' are not evidence. We must venture to Baker Street to test our theory, and we must be prepared to elude the master detective. There, now that you have donned your bonnet and I have doffed my mustache, we look quite unlike ourselves, do we not?"

Godfrey bent so that his face and mine were both visible in the mirror.

"I look like Her Majesty in mourning," I murmured unhappily from behind my layers of veiling, "and you look like"—now that Godfrey was clean-shaven the resemblance suddenly struck me—"a rather handsome Sherlock Holmes."

Godfrey recoiled as if snake-bitten, finding the comparison too close for comfort. Yet both men were more than six feet tall, dark-haired and the same age. If both wore top hats, it would take an artist no great skill to sharpen Godfrey's nose, thicken his brows and produce a creditable simulacrum of the famed detective. I could not help smiling to myself at his discomfort. He took much harmless amusement in nudging me beyond the bounds of my strict upbringing, but the shoe distinctly pinched the other foot when I pointed out that he and his rival for Irene's professional interest bore more than a passing similarity in form.

I gave Godfrey my note, addressed to the Stanhopes of Grosvenor Square, then offered my brightest smile. "Shall we sally forth, as I said before?"

Godfrey drew my hand through his arm and we left, stopping at his rooms to gather hat, stick and gloves. The man at the desk assured us that the note would be delivered by the afternoon. I watched it vanish from my care with regret. So much can be set in motion by an innocent note. Perhaps Quentin did not wish his family to know of his return. Or perhaps he did not wish them to know of us. But at least with Irene absent, Godfrey and I were proceeding in a logical manner, rather than rushing into the unknown on pure instinct and panache.

Thus it was with some surprise that I heard Godfrey direct our cabman to "Madame Tussaud's Wax Museum on the Marylebone Road."

"Godfrey, why are we going to that awful place?"

"It is not far from Baker Street, and until recent years occupied a Baker Street address," he replied.

"That would apply to a great many other less loathsome establishments, I would suppose."

"But none draw as many sightseers. A visit to this attraction will allow us to survey the neighborhood before we concentrate on our quarry at 221 B. I suspect even the Great Mr. Holmes first reconnoitered the Serpentine Mews when he was spying upon Irene."

"Why, Godfrey, I believe that you *do not* like him at all either!"

"Why should I? He attempted to wrest from Irene her one means of protection against the King; he was willing to confront her with the King again, despite all her efforts to prevent contact. In addition, despite your opinion, I suspect that he knew of the Zone of Diamonds and hoped to capture that, as well. I cannot think of a single good turn the man has done us, save for keeping his peace about Irene's and my survival after our supposed deaths. Even there he may have some self-serving motive. He is, after all, available for hire. Irene offers her . . . diagnostic services for nothing."

"You *are* indeed a bit jealous, as you said in Monte Carlo!"

"A serious charge, and nothing to smile about, Nell, I assure you." Godfrey idly rapped his cane tip on the hansom's wooden floor. "Say rather that I am uneasy. We do not really know where this Holmes sits when it comes to secret knowledge and profit."

"That is why I am relieved that Irene remained abroad," I put in. "I feared she could not resist the opportunity to engage a foe of such caliber again. She does relish challenge," I admitted, "to an alarming degree. Now there is a woman that Mr. Stanhope could honestly call adventuresome, although he has not seen her in action."

"Hopefully, he has left France and will not. And hopefully the sinister Captain Morgan has left France also. I did not fancy leaving Irene behind with that man circulating. Please do not attribute my concern there to jealousy also, Nell. A husband may worry, that is all."

"That is most becoming, Godfrey. I can imagine no greater good fortune than that someone would worry about me one day."

"There are other emotional apexes than worry, my dear Nell."

"Such as—?"

Godfrey looked about to say something, then shook his head. "Some things one must discover for oneself. Look at the lines! We have arrived at the temple of La Tussaud."

How amazing that so many people should queue up to see some dressmaker's dummies, I thought as Godfrey helped me out of the cab and paused to pay our driver. Once we were ushered into the dim-lit building, my tune changed. Perhaps it was the cleverly manipulated lamplight and settings, but many of the waxen figures seemed eerily real, especially those in the horrific tableaux displayed in "The Chamber of Horrors."

Godfrey and I emerged into the daylight blinking, and London came into clean, bright clarity for the first time since my return.

"How wonderful to view a street crowded with carriages and horses, and omnibuses topped with signs and people, and peddlers and pedestrians," I said. "I had no idea that so many dreadful historical events required memorializing in wax. Those guillotine scenes—"

Godfrey nodded. "That is the real reason I wanted to view this exhibit. Lives are at stake in this matter we meddle in. Who can say what really happened in Afghanistan so many years ago? Yet I believe Stanhope when he says that Maclaine was brutally killed and as brutally libeled after his death, that Stanhope's own life has never been the same, and that at least one other, innocent life stands in danger today from the repercussions of whatever conspiracy unwound then."

"When you put it that way, I feel quite foolish for presuming to play a part in this drama."

"You are foolish." Godfrey looked as serious as I had ever seen him. "So is Irene, and so am I. Danger comes to a boil in the world around us. Your chance acquaintance with Quentin Stanhope—not to mention your unexpected reunion—has immersed us in the nastiest cauldron we have stirred up yet. Remember that in the days to come. Our guard must be up constantly. Nothing is more dangerous than old secrets that span many borders."

"You think our world is as ugly as the one depicted in the wax museum's Chamber of Horrors?"

He nodded. "Sometimes, Nell, it is. For the most part it presents a fairer face, but we must not allow that benign visage to lull us."

"What now, then?"

"Now that we are suitably impressed with the seriousness of our task," said he, hailing a cab with his lifted cane, "on to Baker Street and the trail of the mysterious Dr. Watson."

Chapter Seventeen

WATSON'S FEVERED FRIEND

"**What is** it, John, dear?"

"A matter for Holmes, I am afraid."

"Afraid? When something turns up that could benefit from Mr. Holmes's talents you are more often intrigued than regretful."

I handed the letter across the toast rack. My wife accepted it with her usual grace, preventing the lace-trimmed sleeve of her combing gown from trailing in the clotted cream, while never taking her eyes from the letter in her hand.

"Oh, how sad!" she exclaimed after reading it.

Holmes's evaluation would be far more forthcoming about the nature of the paper and penmanship, but Mary's sympathetic response echoed my own immediate reaction. Well I remembered the writer from our school days: Percy Phelps, known rather more familiarly as "Tadpole." A bright if somewhat fragile boy, he had gone on to a glittering Cambridge career, followed by a Foreign Office appointment, while I was still wallowing in enteric fever in India.

"Brain fever for nine weeks!" Mary shook her head. "The poor man." A woman's compassion is a wondrous thing. There is no man, even one hardened by life and its disappointments, who will not stir some woman to pity when he is truly down and out.

"I can well sympathize myself," I added, grimly recalling my own months of fever and forgetfulness nearly nine years before.

"What disaster can he refer to in his letter?" Mary wondered, her large blue eyes all concern.

"That is for Phelps to say, or, rather, for Holmes to discern."

"Yes, you must present the matter to Mr. Holmes at once! No one can dissect the unthinkable as he can."

"You are certain that you will not mind my running off for the day, Mary? Phelps gives his address as Briarbrae, Woking, and Woking is far from the city smokestacks."

"Nonsense! The poor man has asked you for help. I have never known you to refuse it. Besides, a jaunt to the country will be good for you."

Blessed the man who is joined to a compassionate woman! I kissed Mary good-bye and within twenty minutes was bound for Baker Street. If Mary's company was a balm, Holmes's was sure to be an astringent. Of that I was soon reminded when I arrived to find my friend hunched over one of his chemical experiments.

"Ah, Watson, the married man!" he greeted me without surprise. He went on to warn me that should the chemical solution turn the litmus paper red, it would cost a man's life. I watched the paper suffuse into a telltale maroon the moment Holmes thrust it into a test tube.

Holmes spent the next moments scrawling telegrams for the pageboy. "A very commonplace little murder," he commented before settling into his favorite velvet-lined armchair and giving me his utter attention, his gray eyes keen with anticipation.

I produced my mysterious letter with a tinge of hesitancy. Phelps's dilemma seemed mild in comparison with murder, no matter how commonplace. Indeed, Holmes found nothing of interest in the missive besides the fact that it had been written for my friend by a woman—a woman of extraordinary character, Holmes claimed airily without further explanation.

Yet this poor, vague spoor was enough for the hound always lurking within him. Despite declarations to the contrary, he harbored a drop or two of the milk of human kindness; in minutes we were off for Waterloo and within an hour walking toward the large house and lavish grounds at Woking where my former schoolmate lived.

We found my friend Phelps, looking pale despite the summer sunlight pouring in from the garden window, with his fiancée, Annie Harrison, a handsome, tiny woman with a madonna's eyes and a diva's glossy black hair.

Phelps's tale was sobering. He had been asked by his uncle, the Foreign Minister, to transcribe the original of a secret treaty between England and Italy, whose contents "the French or the Russians would pay an immense sum to learn."

Percy had retired to his office and stayed late in order to accomplish the task in privacy. When he went to inquire after a cup of coffee he had ordered from the commissionaire's lodge he found the old soldier asleep at his post.

At that moment, a bell rang from the very room poor Phelps had left unattended.

He dashed back to the chamber, seeing no one in the hall or its intersecting passage while coming or going. Yet Phelps found the original treaty gone. Only his copy of eleven of the twenty-six articles remained.

Although in the nigh ten weeks since the tragedy not a whisper indicated that the treaty had reached the wrong hands, be they French or Russian, this fact was small comfort to my friend. He had collapsed completely at the discovery of the theft, and only now had emerged weak and anxious from lost weeks of delirium, spent in the ground-floor bed-sitting room at Briarbrae, from which his sudden illness had evicted Miss Harrison's brother Joseph. Miss Harrison had come to Briarbrae to meet her fiance's parents, with her brother as escort, when the tragedy occurred. Despite a sickroom bedecked with dainty bouquets from the tending hand of Miss

Harrison in every corner, despite her brother Joseph's cheery optimism, I could see that the only thing that heartened Percy's spirits was the intervention of my friend Holmes.

Yet Holmes offered no false hopes during the interview with Percy and Miss Harrison, pronouncing the case very grim indeed. We returned to London. A call on Inspector Forbes at Scotland Yard produced no obvious direction to the mystery. At least Percy's eminent uncle, Lord Holdhurst, the Foreign Minister, at Downing Street confirmed that France or Russia should have acted by now had either nation obtained the treaty.

Imagine Holmes's chagrin, after we traveled again to Woking the next day, to learn that Phelps had surprised an intruder at his window the previous night. Truly, the mystery had deepened. Holmes responded by ordering the recovering Percy to come to town with us. Holmes's actions took a further odd turn at the train station in Woking, when he left Phelps and me to proceed to London while he remained behind on errands of a peculiarly vague nature.

I had rarely been so annoyed with Holmes during our acquaintance. I would be forced to spend the entire day with Percy, a fine enough fellow but one in a strained and nervous condition.

"If your Mr. Holmes remains at Woking to trap last night's burglar, his efforts are vain," Phelps confided as we rattled along toward London.

"Why do you think so?"

"Because *I* am no longer at Briarbrae. Oh, you may eye me askance, Watson; you never were a decent mummer even at school, but I am not still off my head. I tell you that no common burglar broke in with that long knife last night. And if I am the target of this mania, now that I have left Briarbrae there will be no further incidents."

"Holmes does not usually act against the grain of the situation."

"He underestimates the political depth of this conspiracy."

"Perhaps so," I said mildly, "but why are you the focus of

such a grandiose scheme? Who would have cause to destroy you?"

"I do not know," Phelps said despondently, lapsing into a silence all the more unnerving because his hands and feet were never still.

By late afternoon we returned to Baker Street, where I sent a message to Mary that I would be staying the night with a sick friend. As a doctor's wife, she was accustomed to my extended absences. We shared one of Mrs. Hudson's substantial dinners—roast beef—then settled in for a worrisome evening. I attempted to distract my charge from matters that upset him.

"I must say, Phelps, we have come again to a common path by unfortunate events, but I have faced more dire circumstances than this and come through."

"You, Watson?" His hand patted nervously at his face in the pallid gas light. "How could anything be more dreadful than this pall over my life and reputation? Nine weeks of my life unremembered; my career in limbo, awaiting only an awful disclosure to complete my ruin; my fiancée, the sweetest woman who ever stood by a man, facing only shame and revilement for her loyalty—"

"You are not dead yet, man! And Holmes is helping you. I would that I had acquired such assistance at Maiwand."

"Maiwand?" Phelps looked totally mystified and bit at his lips. I could as well have spoken of Katmandu.

"Yes, the battle of Maiwand in Afghanistan in 'Eighty. I joined as an assistant surgeon with the Northumberland Fusiliers, but when I arrived in India the Afghan war had broken out, so I was assigned to the Sixty-sixth Berkshires at Kandahar under Brigadier General Burrows. At Maiwand I took a jezail bullet in the shoulder. . . .

"You were wounded, Watson?"

"I seldom speak of it, but I was very nearly killed, Phelps, and suffered enteric fever for weeks afterward, during the entire month-long siege of Kandahar, before Roberts's troops came marching to our rescue. Then we turned and drove the

Ayub Khan's men back into the Afghanistan mountains. So, you see, I know more of brain fever than even my medical degree would attest."

"You, too, forgot everything while you were ill?"

"My dear fellow, you must keep this to yourself, but I never even remembered taking a second bullet in my leg, yet that is the inexplicable scar that reminds me of itself every rainy day, though it has been less bothersome of late."

"I was never military material, Watson," Percy said with a wan smile. "It is hard to imagine you in such a shabby fray. One does not hear much about the Afghanistan adventure these days. I had forgotten all about it."

"So have most people. I do not fancy many military reputations were polished in that rough arena. Of course, I was just doing my duty and seeing something of the world, a lad in my twenties. And there is much to see in that quarter of the globe, exotic bits, Phelps: snake charmers and belly dancers and some astounding mating rituals—"

Phelps suddenly clasped a hand to his mouth. "What do you suppose Holmes is doing all day at Woking?"

"Walking," I suggested shortly.

"I am sure that he underestimates the influences at work here." He rose to pace the chamber anxiously, his fingers twitching. "It could be foreign spies; the interests of strong nations are at stake."

"Holmes is aware of such influences. He has often represented the reigning houses of Europe in matters of such sensitivity that they are far too dangerous to speak of even now."

"Perhaps he has served the interests of the French and the Russians in those matters," Phelps said darkly.

"He serves his own country first and foremost," I admonished gently. The man's melancholy grew wearing. At that moment I could have done with a dose of Mary Watson's patient kindness. "When Holmes can assist a foreign personage without harming England, he does—there was the scandal involving the King of Bohemia, for instance, and the astonishingly beautiful I—"

"Bohemia is a pretend-dukedom sewn onto the selvage of Austro-Hungary!" Phelps interrupted petulantly. "This stolen treaty could irritate a Russian emperor and the ruling body of all France!"

"Holmes has been of service to individuals as highly placed as those," I replied a trifle stuffily, "though I can say nothing of the specifics. You underestimate him, and myself, Phelps. I am not merely a dull and domestic London physician. I have aided the world's first consulting detective, and am a veteran of one of the most grueling conflicts of the past decades."

"It is true, it is true!" Phelps cried pathetically, pressing his trembling hands over his pale face. "Pray excuse me. I am distraught. Of course your friend Holmes is my only hope! Of course you are an absolutely splendid fellow to come to my aid! But, Watson, I am sorry, I have been through too much of late. At the moment, I simply am not up to hearing your war stories."

"Oh. I see." Certainly I had heard enough of his difficulties all the day.

"I cannot concentrate on anything trivial when I am bedeviled by larger issues. Where has the treaty gone? Who removed it in such a devastating manner? And what is your Mr. Holmes doing in Woking?"

Trivial! "I am only trying to distract you. I have told you before that you must remove your mind from this current puzzle. Such fruitless speculation will only excite your nerves—and mine. You must retire and manage a good night's sleep, dear fellow. I beg you to rest and think no more about it. In the morning we will know more."

I finally persuaded him to lie down in the spare bedroom, though he was still visibly fretting. I myself did not find Morpheus easily that night. My attempts to show Phelps that others had survived circumstances as difficult as his had only revived my few memories of Maiwand and the fever.

I found it hard to lie upon my left shoulder and seemed to sniff Afghanistan's dust-laden air in the high summer of July. It was the same month, nine years later. Phelps had suffered from brain fever for nine weeks. A woman bears a baby for nine months before it is delivered fully formed. For a moment, I glimpsed fragments of Maiwand I had not recalled before: wounded faces beseeching me for aid; a sudden dull shattering sensation in my shoulder; a bone-rattling ride over a packhorse led by the loyal Murray; delirious days and nights on my back in some makeshift dispensary, during which I imagined poisonous serpents writhing around me and my comrades on the adjoining cots.

I knew that I had made the unpleasant overland trek to Sinjini where the new railway began after the siege of Kandahar was lifted at the end of August, but I remembered nothing of it. My memories of the difficult train journey from Sinjini to Peshawar in India were fuller, and unappetizing, especially in regard to the scanty sanitary arrangements. I certainly recalled my relapse into fever once I reached Peshawar, where the bitter taste of quinine baptized all my liquid intake.

For the first time since I had received Phelps's letter I began to regret my involvement in the case. For the first time since my association with Holmes I was moved to wonder if a middle-aged doctor belonged at home with his wife, rather than nursing querulous acquaintances in questionable circumstances and reviving old campaign days long gone and forgotten.

Chapter Eighteen

THE THIRD MAN

In a great, humming metropolis of four million persons it is possible to live for many years without traversing every street. I approached Baker Street for the first time with a sense of visiting an alien locale, and yet, the sensation of finally seeing what I had always known. Godfrey's companionship in the hansom cab was little comfort.

Our sturdy horse's hooves clattered on the pavement, a sound magnified by dozens of drumming hooves. Around us, the very air dispensed the mingled odors of horse and hazy summer heat. The interior of the hansom cab, the shopfronts and signs passing beyond the windows, the sounds and the smells were all as familiar as tea. Yet . . . yet.

Baker Street.

Those words were inextricably associated with the key event of my life, my chance meeting with Irene Adler outside Wilson's Tea Room in 1881. Never mind that I was homeless, hungry, unemployed, desolate. Perhaps that merely sharpened my senses, for every detail of the following twenty-four hours is engraved upon my brain: Irene, in all her intimidating, energetic splendor, which I soon discovered to be gallantly counterfeit, for she was as impoverished as I, had seemed like some glamorous machine, an urban Titania descending upon a lost child in the forest of the great city.

I had followed her, benumbed, into a world of ghastly figures (consider the tragic Jefferson Hope, doomed murderer and avenger, who had driven our first shared, extravagant cab) and treachery hidden in homely symbols (consider the unholy wedding ring that was the sole souvenir of that episode).

Thus I had come in a sinister London twilight to the modest but eccentric rooms Irene rented in Saffron Hill, the Italian district, where arias and sausages scented the everyday air. I remember Irene's purloined pastries toasting on the fireplace fender that evening, and her faded, crackling Oriental robe; a bottle of wine prized open with a button hook.

My confusion, my concern, my disorientation at the unaccustomed wine. My relief at being in hands as certain as hers, however Bohemian. And later, the newspaper column announcing the death of Jefferson Hope. And Baker Street, 221 B Baker Street, where dwelt the amateur detective, Mr. Sherlock Holmes, was where Jefferson Hope had sent a crony to collect the unholy wedding ring from a certain Dr. Watson only days before his death. . . .

So, Baker Street. From the first mention of that locale my life had changed, and so had Irene's, and ultimately, Godfrey's. We were all three hopelessly entwined with that plain address, and *the* man who lived there. Now I was, at last, to see it.

Godfrey was watching out the hansom window with an intensity so like Irene's on a quest that I smiled. He seemed consumed by an unadmitted curiosity about the man who had piqued Irene's competitive instincts.

Baker Street itself was commonplace—a series of functional four-story Georgian facades, some performing as shops on the street level, other as entries for offices or lodgings. Wrought iron fenced the fronts, bracketing doorways and guarding windows and below-street trade entrances.

"There!" Godfrey said, a trifle tensely. His cane urgently rapped the ceiling to signal the driver to stop. "I want to approach on foot."

We disembarked upon a well-maintained pavement, and I

gratefully took Godfrey's arm. For some reason I needed moral support. We ambled along in a current of hurried passersby. Brass numerals and a letter flashed into my mind like daggers. Two. Two. One. B.

"There it is," Godfrey said unnecessarily in a low tone.

We strolled past a perfectly ordinary entryway: two stone steps, a graceful break in the wrought-iron railing, a fanlight over the door greeted us.

In only a moment, we had walked past it.

"Well," I said, sounding breathless.

"An ordinary address," said he.

"I could not agree with you more. What do we do next?"

For the first time in my experience, Godfrey seemed uncertain. He examined the street both ahead and behind us, then nodded at a shop across the way.

"There is an ABC tearoom, Nell. We can quite properly stop for refreshment there, and keep watch on the address we are concerned with."

"Oh, tea should be quite proper," I answered, "but can we ensure a proper view?"

"We will," said he, guiding me across the street with nary a brush with a hansom or a misstep into the unfortunate residue of an equine engine.

And so we settled in for the afternoon. Godfrey had requested, nay demanded, a window table. Men do have their uses. Ensconced in it we had a fine view of bustles, canes, horse hindquarters and, when the intervening traffic permitted, the entrance to 221 B Baker Street.

From all that we could survey in the first hour, no one came or went from that benighted address. Finally Godfrey expressed a pressing need to visit the tailors of Regent Street, so I occupied the window seat alone for another two hours, dutifully noting any who came and went from number 221 B.

A resident left just after Godfrey did, a white-haired old lady in a violet cape somewhat out of fashion, with a straw bonnet tied firmly under her ample chin. Remembering that *the* man had once deceived us in the guise of an elderly clergyman, I placed a faint question mark next to the description. Irene had warned me to overlook nothing with an adversary of Sherlock Holmes's caliber.

A rough-looking boy in a tweed cap several sizes too large came along twenty minutes later. He rang the bell, to no avail, leading me to speculate that the old lady was a housekeeper off on her day's errands. The lad jigged his feet, turned his cap this way and that, and generally fidgeted until it was obvious he would get no response. At that he drew away from the doorway, looked cautiously in all directions, then jerked on the bill of his cap and leaned back to hurl something from his pocket up at the first-floor bow window.

I could not hear the impact, but saw a fistful of small stones rain down from the glass. "The ruffian!" I muttered, looking about for a constable. But no such person appeared, and the rude boy was off, tossing his cap in the air and whistling quite boldly.

I noted the incident and his description, in case a constable should arrive on the scene later.

"Well, miss, and you've a right lot of work to do there." The serving girl nodded at my notations as she brought a fresh pot of tea.

I shifted the papers discreetly out of view. "Merely catching up on some entries in my diary."

The girl's blue eyes widened to match the Delft saucer under my cup. "Lor', miss, an' you must lead an excitin' life, with so much writin' to do about it!"

"I manage," was my curt reply. I kept her gaze until she bobbed a slovenly curtsy and went about her business.

Shortly after that an elegant equipage drew up to disgorge a heavily veiled lady attired all in summer white. She poised upon the stoop of 221 B like a bride; one small gloved hand reached out three times to ring the bell. The door was as indifferent to this intriguing figure as to the others. She retreated to her carriage and was barely out of sight when the old lady waddled back into view, bearing a number of brown paper parcels tied with string.

This, too, I noted down, along with my guesses as to the contents of the parcels. Lemon curd for tea tarts, I decided, and perhaps some crochet string. That is where I wished to be: at home having tea and doing my crochet work, even with Casanova and Lucifer at hand.

I began to keep a worried eye out for Godfrey. We had not been in London for more than a year. I was not anxious to lose him. Just then a hansom cab drew up across the thoroughfare, obscuring the entry. I sipped my Earl Grey in great impatience, but the hansom crouched before the door like a great shiny black beetle too lazy to move.

At length the driver bent down for his pay and the cab crept off, revealing two men by the door. Both wore soft country hats, but one appeared rather pale and weak. The second was a sturdy man with a mustache. The old lady, sans bonnet, cape and parcels, opened the door and they vanished within. And that was that. Surveillance work, I concluded, could be quite boring.

I ate an inordinate amount of tea cakes, then removed my pince-nez and settled in for a good bout of worrying.

"Well, Nell!" Godfrey arrived at half-past four in a flurry of top hat and cane, looking flushed. "The traffic seems to have increased since my departure. What have you observed?"

"A good deal of nothing," said I, turning my notebook around.

He frowned at the entries. "None of these visitors looks like Mr. Holmes. So you have not seen him?"

"Not in his own guise, certainly. But he is a 'consulting' detective; perhaps he seldom leaves his domicile."

"He got about well enough in St. John's Wood," Godfrey said ruefully. "So no one was admitted until the two men. . . . Your notes express suspicion of the old lady and the young boy."

"Either could be a disguise, since both are the sort of persons often overlooked, as no one expects much from either."

Godfrey laughed as he drank the tea the serving girl had rushed to him upon his arrival. Men, even of the most superior sort, are invariably oblivious to how thoroughly they are catered to.

"You sound like Irene," he noted.

"That is where all resemblance ends," said I. "Despite drinking four pots of Earl Grey and consuming as many tea cakes as Irene once kidnapped from Wilson's in lieu of lunch, the static nature of my vigil has not altered. Irene would never have stood for such a tame train of events."

"Then—" he obligingly gulped down the rest of his tea and rose to draw back my chair "—we must accelerate matters."

As Godfrey paused to pay the bill the serving girl brushed past, leaned toward me conspiratorially. "Now I see why your diary takes so much writing," she whispered in a forward but mystifying way, casting her eyes toward Godfrey.

I blushed, not quite sure why, but I had been well reared and knew when I ought to. Soon we were on Baker Street again, facing the enigmatic facade of 221 B.

"I had expected a famous detective's door to be a modicum more busy," Godfrey admitted. "If you tire of surveillance, there is only one course left to us. We must inquire within."

"Ring the bell?" I asked incredulously.

"It would seem so, Nell," he conceded sadly. "I realize that Irene would never resort to so simple a stratagem, but I am, after all, a barrister, and used to taking the direct route."

I was not so sure. Never had the door to 221 B been so forbidding. Never had I felt more obvious. Nevertheless, we marched up to the establishment. Godfrey rang the bell with a fine, determined flourish.

The plump, white-haired woman answered. "Yes, sir?"

Godfrey presented this simple soul with a dazzling smile. "We seek the residence of Dr. Watson."

"You would have been successful, sir, only months ago, but since his marriage, Dr. Watson keeps his own establishment in Paddington. Is it Mr. Holmes you would wish to see instead?"

"No," said I firmly, before Godfrey could say the opposite. "It is a medical matter."

"Paddington, you say," Godfrey added politely, at which prompting the woman disgorged the doctor's new address.

We withdrew with murmured thanks.

"Well," said Godfrey ten paces down Baker Street. "I had not anticipated that the doctor would be on his own."

"All the better for us. We can inquire forthrightly into his past without fear of *the* man interfering."

"Still . . ."

"Godfrey! You are fully as fascinated by *the* man as Irene is. You should be grateful that we can conduct our inquiry without having to tread near Mr. Holmes again."

"You really think that she is so fascinated by him, Nell?"

I sighed. "A figure of speech, Godfrey. You know that Irene is devoted to you. It borders upon the sickening on occasion."

"Really?"

He sounded most interested, but exploring such topics now would not advance our inquiry. It was too late to call on Dr. Watson in Paddington, so Godfrey quickly hailed a hansom and was amenable, if silent, on the journey back to Brown's Hotel, where we received another surprise of the day.

Our routine inquiry at the desk produced a communication on pale-blue parchment paper addressed to me in a hasty hand. The return address was Grosvenor Square.

"Excellent!" Godfrey chortled in the lift, eyeing the communication.

I attempted to calm myself in the face of my most immediate concern: being in the interior of an overdecorated moving closet.

Godfrey had been correct about one thing. We required a discreet place to repair and compare notes—or at least peruse notes. My sitting room proved to be ideal.

"Well?"

"Please be patient, Godfrey. I must remove this rather smothering bonnet and veil, and my gloves first."

He was so impatient that he seized my hatpin as soon as I had released it and began stabbing at the envelope.

"There is an opener here," said I, taking the now-mangled correspondence to the small writing desk. Godfrey had never shown a subtle hand with the correspondence in chambers. I neatly slit the seam and pulled out a folded paper.

"Very fine quality," I noted, as Irene might.

Godfrey sighed. "What does it say?"

"It is from Mrs. Waterston. Quentin Stanhope's married sister, as Mrs. Turnpenny was."

"What does she say?"

"Only that . . . my goodness!"

"Nell!"

I sat down. "She recalls me as her sister's governess—is that not nice?"

"Wonderful! Sublime! What does she—?"

"She wants us to call as soon as possible. This evening if possible."

"Marvelous!"

"She says that her aged mother is most interested in news of her long-lost, dear son Quentin . . . Oh, Godfrey—"

"What?"

"She does not know of his . . . condition. We cannot disabuse poor old Mrs. Stanhope of her illusions."

"We will not. We will relieve his relations of the information we require and give them next to nothing in return."

"Is that fair?"

"No, but it is useful."

"You sound like Irene!"

"Thank you."

I sank unhappily onto the Louis XIV chair before the escritoire.

"We are here to serve the greater good, Nell. That may require . . . compromise."

"I am not used to compromise."

That gave him pause. "Neither was Quentin Stanhope. Until Afghanistan."

"Oh!"

Godfrey came and leaned over me in a most emphatic manner, his hands braced on the chair arms. "Nell, we are thrust into matters of great moment. Nicety has no place in our calculations. We must steel ourselves to serve the truth, and hope that it will hurt no one for whom we care."

"I do not even know these women."

"No, but you know their lost loved one. Irene would never have let you come if she had suspected that you would succumb to such qualms of conscience."

"*Let* me come! Irene cannot come because she is known here!"

"Would that stop her? She thought that the trip would do you good."

"Do me good? Why?"

Godfrey withdrew, suddenly subdued. "You are the springboard of the current puzzle. Irene thought you deserved the opportunity to investigate your own mystery."

"I see."

"Do you?"

"You need not glower like the Queen's Counsel, Godfrey. I understand that I am broaching my past, and Irene's past as well, in this affair. Very well; I will call upon Mrs. Waterston and endeavor to learn what we must know in order to best serve her true interests, even if we cannot confide fully in her."

"Brava, Nell." He smiled like a man relieved of a burden not his.

Godfrey glanced at my veiled bonnet lying like a wounded pheasant on the pier table. "And I think you can dispense with that bonnet. The idea is for you to be recognizable in Grosvenor Square."

Chapter Nineteen

A NOSY NIECE

Godfrey again perused my list of Baker Street visitors in the cab en route to Grosvenor Square, shaking his head. "Not promising, Nell. Obviously Holmes is either gone or keeping to his rooms. None of the visitors is a candidate for the doctor, except this stocky chap who arrived with the pale-looking man. The old lady is likely the housekeeper, or landlady, as you surmise. When our interview on Grosvenor Square is done, we shall have to take steps."

"What do you mean?"

"I mean that we will have to inquire after Dr. Watson ourselves," he said.

"I as well? Mr. Holmes could be lurking about, and I have been seen by him."

"But in circumstances in which he would be likely to overlook you."

"I thought he was a formidable detective. How should he overlook me?" I asked.

"Irene has said that he has a weakness for women."

"Indeed! That is the first that I have heard of such a failing."

Godfrey smiled. "Not in the common way that the phrase is meant. She claims that he is uninterested in women to a fault, so that he is forever underestimating their importance and wit. That gives women a kind of invisibility."

"He appeared perfectly capable of noticing Irene, and found her on the crowded terrace of the Hôtel de Paris in Monte Carlo."

His smile faded. "Ah, but that was Irene. Irene is always noticeable unless she is taking especial care not to be. Here is number forty-four."

Anyone who has lived in London is well aware that Grosvenor numbers among the city's most lordly squares. Our cab drew up before an imposing stone fence. A piece of antique statuary peeked from beyond the manicured greenery of high summer.

"In truth, Godfrey," I said, my eyes surveying the blank expanse of windows lining the great house, "I dare not confront this family again. I am but a mere mote in their memories . . ."

"Fortunately their son and brother is not," he said in firm tones, stepping down from the cab to help me out before he paid the driver. "And we are expected."

I sighed. "I suppose it is my duty."

"Of course it is." He drew my hand through the crook of his elbow. "Yet it would be more amusing to regard this as an adventure."

His use of that particular, overadvertized word reminded me of Quentin. How could I tell a man who had faced the unthinkable in India and Afghanistan that I was reduced to a quailing girl by his own family? Not that I was ever likely to see Quentin Stanhope again. Still, passing up that long, formal walk into that long, formal house was for me a return to a once-pleasant past that now seemed beyond reach. I was nothing to these people except a link between our common history and their lost member.

The butler who answered the door was impeccably noncommittal. I felt like a pair of galoshes that had been inadvertently left on the steps. Godfrey's hat, stick and gloves were swiftly stripped from him; at least women could retain the accessory armor of hat and gloves indoors.

We were shown into a front receiving room full of strangers.

"Please, come right in!" cried a pretty young woman in a buttercup-yellow mousseline tea-gown, rising to draw us in as we paused politely on the threshold. "Why, Miss Huxleigh, you have grown so smart!"

Her words astounded me, but her identity amazed me even more.

"And you have simply grown! Miss Allegra?" I asked rather than exclaimed. "Miss Turnpenny now, rather."

"No, I am Allegra still," said this ingratiating creature, taking my hands and laughing. "But what has happened to Miss Huxleigh's mouse-gray skirts and cream cotton shirtwaists?"

"I have . . . changed," I said, "and so have you."

"And are you still Miss Huxleigh?" inquired the impertinent young person, eyeing Godfrey with an interest unbecoming to a well-brought-up girl.

"Indeed," I said hastily. "That has not changed. May I introduce Mr. Godfrey Norton, a barrister who practices in Paris? He, too, is aware of the news I have come to convey." At least here we could use our true identities.

"Then you must meet the others."

The young woman spun to introduce the array of middle-aged ladies seated behind her: her aunt, Mrs. Waterston; her mother, Mrs. Codwell Turnpenny, who had grayed greatly since Berkeley Square; her other aunt, Mrs. Compton. These three women were Quentin Stanhope's older sisters, I realized with a jolt. Looking into their genteel, concerned faces, I wondered what on earth I should tell them about the fate of their baby brother.

We were seated and plied with tea and crumpets of a vastly superior variety. Godfrey accepted the female doting they bestowed with calm good grace, refusing all offers of cucumber sandwiches until the social flutter had died a natural death.

"It is wonderful to see you, Miss Huxleigh," Mrs. Turnpenny finally ventured over her cup of tea. "You do not look a day older." I could not truthfully say the same of her, so remained attentively silent. "Now, please, you must tell us what you know of Quentin."

"Perhaps," Godfrey intervened, capturing their instant attention by being both handsome and a man of affairs, "you should tell us what you know first."

Their eyes, all pale watercolor shades of blue and gray, gently consulted each other. I imagined a family portrait—perhaps by the Florence-born American, Singer Sargent, who in his London studio attired his female subjects in such a swooning shimmer of pale paint—with the sisters portrayed as the fading Three Graces. I then pictured the brother and beloved uncle we had first seen in Paris—bearded, bronzed, berobed, ill—thrust into their midst. No. Quentin Stanhope as he now was made a more proper subject for one of those Bohemian bistro painters of Paris—a Mucha or a Chéret.

Mrs. Turnpenny spoke. "I am a widow. Yes, my dear," she explained with a glance at me, "Colonel Turnpenny died in Afghanistan. Not at Maiwand, but ironically in the victorious battle that followed it."

"I am so sorry," I murmured.

"Our elderly mother is a widow also," Mrs. Turnpenny added. "She is upstairs in her rooms. We did not wish to upset her unnecessarily. We knew Quentin had been wounded at Maiwand, and that he had been reported missing or dead. Later, the Army insisted that he was alive, and indeed, we finally received a letter in a shaky hand that was certainly his. So we waited for him to recuperate and come home."

"He never did!" Allegra interjected this in the aggrieved tone of a disappointed child. "Uncle Quentin never came back. The others had given him up, and certainly it was better for Grandmama to think him dead if we had no word or sign of him, but I have never understood why he left us. Do you know something more, Miss Huxleigh, please? Can you tell us something more?"

"Allegra!" the young woman's mother rebuked softly, turning to us. "She remembers him with a child's freshness. You must forgive her enthusiasm. I would be most grateful for any information you could offer us. We had hoped when the other gentleman called—"

"Other gentleman?" Godfrey asked.

Mrs. Turnpenny paused at the urgency in his tone. "Yes, a war veteran, like Quentin. A former member of his company."

"When did this gentleman call?" Godfrey wanted to know.

Again the three older women silently consulted one another, both to bolster their common recollection and to protest Godfrey's intrusive curiosity.

"In May," Mrs. Waterston declared in a no-nonsense voice. "It was my wolfhound Peytor's birthday."

"May," Godfrey repeated without further comment, in the irritating way of barristers everywhere.

"*Do* you know anything of Quentin, Miss Huxleigh?" Allegra beseeched me.

Suddenly my qualms tumbled like a wall of stone turned to sand before their heartfelt concern.

"We know that he is relatively well, and alive," I said briskly. "We encountered him in Paris last week. He has lived in the East for many years."

"He was well?" Mrs. Turnpenny demanded. "Why did he not contact us? Why has he not come home, then?"

"He was not well," Godfrey put in quite rashly. "We think he had been poisoned."

Shock sighed through the room, and their pale powdered faces grew more ashen.

I said quickly, "Quentin had reasons for staying abroad. There may have been danger to those he came too near. He is quite all right now, save for a troubling touch of fever now and then."

"Quentin?" Mrs. Turnpenny repeated with a polite frown.

Godfrey regarded me with a deeply interested expression, like any barrister curious to see how a witness would extricate herself from an unpardonable blunder.

I flushed as scarlet as the velvet footstool at Mrs. Turnpenny's aristocratic feet.

"Oh, Mama, don't be a stick!" young Allegra urged with flashing blue eyes. "Miss Huxleigh has known me since the schoolroom, and Uncle Quentin was a favorite visitor there."

"It was Nell who roused Mr. Stanhope's memories of home," Godfrey added in my defense at last. "He recognized her in Paris."

"Nell?" Mrs. Turnpenny murmured again, this time faintly, as if confused beyond the point of fretting about it.

"That is how my wife and I call Miss Huxleigh," Godfrey explained.

Mrs. Turnpenny nodded, reassured that Godfrey had a wife. If only she had met Irene! "And Paris is where Quentin was . . . poisoned?"

"We think so," I said, "or rather Irene does." A silence. "Godfrey's wife. Irene. She has remained behind in Paris. It was not serious, the poisoning, only Qu—Mr. Stanhope feared for our own safety and vanished. We thought he might have come here, but of course if he fears that whoever he approaches is endangered—"

"Quite a tale, from what sense I can make of it," the formidable Mrs. Waterston noted. "Yet it might explain the gentleman caller in May if Quentin has been seen in Europe."

"Indeed," said Godfrey. "So while we can offer no particulars about your loved one at present, we can tell you that he was well not many days ago, and that his long absence has apparently been forced by circumstance, not inclination. But take care to whom you speak of him."

"He has always kept you in his mind and heart," I added. "You must not think that he has not. I hope that one day he can tell you so himself."

"As do we," Mrs. Turnpenny said feelingly. "And what

has brought you from Paris to London, so that you could deliver this news?"

"Shopping," said Godfrey promptly and somewhat truthfully, given his afternoon activities. "The French are quite inferior at men's tailoring, but excel in women's styles. As you can see, Miss Huxleigh has become a formidable fashion plate since her sojourn in Paris."

The older ladies blinked politely at his mock-serious tone, but Miss Allegra laughed until her eyes watered. "Oh, you remind me of Uncle Quentin, Mr. Norton. He was such an unreformed tease! What fun we had when I was young."

"That is usually the case, miss," I reminded her primly.

"In some ways you have not changed at all, Miss Huxleigh," she answered, "and I am glad."

I smiled at the dear child, who reminded me of her uncle, though she found me less changed than he did.

The rest of the tea was spent in polite chitchat, which Godfrey handled with masterful blandness. As we rose to leave, Godfrey inquired casually, "By the way, what did the gentleman who asked after Mr. Stanhope look like?"

The ladies exchanged another blank glance.

"Quite unremarkable looking," Mrs. Turnpenny said, consulting her sisters. "Middle-aged, respectable." Mrs. Compton nodded soberly.

"I was not at the house at the time," Mrs. Waterston declared, and that was that.

"I will see them out, Mama," the charming Allegra offered, frothing to my side in her jonquil gown to lay a hand on my arm like a favorite niece.

As we walked into the tiled entry hall, Allegra spoke in a voice lowered to an excited whisper. "Not so tall as Mr. Norton," she said, slipping her arm through his so we three were conspiratorially linked. "Bald as a cue ball. Fierce lapis-lazuli eyes, cold as stone. A most sinister individual. Mama has absolutely no powers of observation," she added sadly.

She delivered us to the cruising butler, who circled us like a shark, so eager was he to rid the house of its unconventional visitors.

"Do find dear Quentin," she finished, shaking our arms in light admonishment. "He is quite my favorite uncle."

"I am afraid," said I, "that you take after him a great deal."

"Thank you, Miss Huxleigh," she said with a last, roguish smile and a curtsy, before melting down the hall.

Out in the square we paused, staring across the vast garden to the line of stately houses beyond.

"Quite helpless and unforthcoming, the ladies of the house," Godfrey mused as he smoothed his French kid gloves over his knuckles, "but your former charge is a charmer. She reminds me of Irene."

"I did not have a very long time with her in the schoolroom," I admitted. "She does take a great deal upon herself."

"Someone must, in that household." He sighed. "So Captain Morgan was already hunting for Stanhope in May. Why?"

"Of course! *That* is who the inquiring gentleman was!"

"The real question is what the devil—sorry, Nell—was Stanhope involved in, and why has it turned so urgent now?"

"Oh," I said without thinking, "I wish Irene were here. She would know what to do."

Godfrey smiled fondly. "We can cable her, if you like, in the morning, to tell her what we have learned."

"Oh, yes! But Godfrey—"

"Yes?"

"We must use a code name, in case that odious man Morgan has henchmen in Paris."

"We already have one," he pronounced as we strolled toward New Bond Street, where we could more readily hail a cab.

"What is that?"

"Lucy Maison-Nouveau."

"Oh."

Chapter Twenty

SHE SNOOPS TO CONQUER

At last a Watson in the flesh!

Godfrey and I had decided that we would have more luck finding a physician free later in the day, so we stood before the doctor's door in Paddington at four o'clock the next afternoon, I in a froth of excitement at finally meeting the figure who might serve as the key to Quentin Stanhope's dilemmas. We confronted a semidetached brick residence that sat close to the street but was domestic enough in appearance to promise a garden in the back. A brass lozenge attached to the brick wall read, JOHN H. WATSON, M.D. Was he the same Dr. Watson who had aided Quentin Stanhope on the blazing battlefields of Afghanistan?

The door opened. Instead of a gentleman who had consorted with *the* man of Baker Street, a lady stood in the doorway, regarding us with an air of pleasant but unsurprised inquiry.

"We are here to see Dr. Watson," Godfrey said. "This is Miss Huxleigh and I am . . . er, Feverall Marshwine."

"I am Mrs. Watson. The house girl has the day off. Have you an appointment, Mr. Marshwine?"

"No," he admitted, "but we will wait."

"You will wait in either case, for the doctor has been called out suddenly," she answered with a slight smile. Then she stepped back to allow us in. Mrs. Watson was a dainty, self-possessed woman, whose vivid cornflower-blue eyes eclipsed any plainness in her refined face.

We followed her down the passage, which was dim, as such hallways usually are, into a back parlor that had been furnished as an office with a large mahogany desk and several leather upholstered chairs. An open door to the room beyond showed a cabinet filled with medical preparations.

"Can you say when you expect him, Mrs. Watson?" Godfrey asked.

"Hardly. Like most physicians', my husband's days are filled with long, empty hours broken by sudden flurries of patients or the emergency call."

"No doubt such enforced idleness encourages a taste for other pursuits," I commented.

"Why, yes." The lady glanced rather fondly toward the desk, where some papers lay piled near a crystal inkstand and a Gray's *Anatomy*. "As a matter of fact, my dear husband has a literary bent. Unfortunately, I cannot guarantee his prompt return. He has left the town."

I glanced doubtfully at my lapel, about to consult my watch, when Godfrey spoke.

"Thank you, Mrs. Watson. We will wait nevertheless."

She nodded and left us, closing the passage door behind her.

"Why did you use that ridiculous name?" I demanded.

"Marshwine?" Godfrey seemed genuinely hurt. "I thought that Dr. Watson might recognize my own name. Remember, Sherlock Holmes implied that he knew of Irene's marriage to me when they all descended on Briony Lodge to trap Irene."

"Then . . . why use my real name?" I demanded with some agitation.

"Because, dear Nell, I believe it is always better to tell the truth than to lie, and surely neither Holmes nor Watson can know your name."

"At any rate," I declared, "the doctor may be gone for hours—for the day."

"I sincerely hope so," Godfrey replied, going to the passage door and listening intently. "We could not have arranged a better opportunity to learn a thing or two about Dr. Watson." He had paused before a photograph of a gaunt, medal-decorated man framed on the wall. "General Gordon of India. An Afghanistan connection already. I wonder what others may be hidden in drawers."

"Godfrey! You would use this occasion to spy?"

"Yes, and so will you. Have a look at the desk, will you, Nell? You have a sublime instinct for paperwork."

Godfrey darted into the neighboring chamber, leaving me no time to object. I gingerly approached the doctor's large mahogany desk decorated with Chippendale fretwork, still unsure that I would actually stoop to the act required.

A small red Turkish carpet, perhaps two by five feet and somewhat worn, ran from the chair between the desk's flanking pedestals of drawers, ending at the pair of side chairs for guests. Obviously intended to protect the chamber's overall Axminster carpeting, the Turkish rug reminded me of a royal runner, which the desk straddled like a throne to be approached at my own risk. It made the desk look as tempting of exploration as a covered candy dish set upon a brightly colored doily.

My gloved fingers trailed along the desk's exposed wooden top, then paused at the piled papers. A casement window behind the chair wafted the drone of bees from the honeysuckle bush flowering beyond it. If I wished to investigate, I would have to remove my gloves. Proper paper shuffling requires agile fingers. I tugged the tight cotton off my right hand and soon was riffling through the pile.

As quickly I discovered that this was not the usual stack of unconnected documents, but rather a continuous narrative. I could not believe my eyes, even as they read the opening sentence: "To Sherlock Holmes, she is always *the* woman."

I sank onto the huge chair behind the desk, though its upholstery was lumpy and its legs were mounted on little wheels that gave me an uneasy seat, like a nervous mare. The shocking words leaped into stark emphasis before my eyes, all the more horrible for being penned in a neat, quite legible hand.

> *In his eyes she eclipses and predominates the whole of her sex. It was not that he felt any emotion akin to love for Irene Adler. All emotions, and that one particularly, were abhorrent to his cold, precise, but admirably balanced mind.*

More than ever was I convinced that *the* man was a monster who, as his biographer admitted, "never spoke of the softer passions, save with a gibe and a sneer . . . who loathed every form of society with his whole Bohemian soul," and who, buried among his books in his Baker Street lodgings, alternated "from week to week between cocaine and ambition. . . ."

My feet had pushed forward on the rug as I read. Beneath my boot soles, the material had rolled into a hard hummock as adamant as a doorstop, which made a useful footrest as I read the awful words before me.

"And yet there was but one woman to him, and that woman was the late Irene Adler, of dubious and questionable memory."

She? Dubious and questionable? My gasp was echoed by the breeze sighing through the casement and buffeting the flowered curtains, as my hands—one gloved and one ungloved—made outraged fists.

The narrator, surely the selfsame doctor in whose rooms Godfrey and I now pried to our joint shame and my sole and swiftly receding regret, recounted how his recent marriage had created "complete happiness, and the home-centered interests . . . sufficient to absorb all my attention." To this I could not take exception.

Then, one March night a year ago, this same upright doctor wrote, he was returning from a journey to a patient when his path led him through Baker Street. The events could have been set down in a modern *Faust* or perhaps in *Dr. Jekyll and*

Mr. Hyde, as the ordinary physician finds himself drawn again into the web of his evil genius: He finds himself passing That Doorway, which first recalls the circumstances of his wooing the woman now responsible for his bliss. But unhappy chance also reminds him of "the dark incidents" of the case during which the blissful couple had met. Soon the doctor is "seized" by "a keen desire" to see *the* man again and discover how he is using his "extraordinary powers."

And there, within, he did indeed find *the* man "at work again. He had arisen out of his drug-created dreams, and was hot upon the scent of some new problem."

A noise behind me made me start so guiltily that my foot kicked the rumpled rug with a dull thump. Something about the hummock was oddly . . . pliant. Godfrey was emerging from the inner room, frowning.

"Nothing in the consulting room but the usual remedies and supplies. Have you made any progress with those papers, Nell?"

"No!" I shouted, collapsing them back into a single pile like a flimsy deck of cards. "Ouch!"

"What is it?" Concern brought Godfrey even closer, when I wished to prevent him from seeing the outrageous papers beneath my hands.

"Nothing, Godfrey, nothing," I said, rising awkwardly. I always have been a most unconvincing prevaricator. "Only . . . my foot has struck some untoward object under the desk."

"Oh?" At least Godfrey was peering now at the carpeting and need never read: "And yet there was but one woman to him . . ."

I turned the papers upside down and weighted them with the Gray's *Anatomy*. "It is nothing, really, Godfrey, merely some household appliance that I stubbed my toes on."

"Why were you sitting at the desk, Nell?" He had bent to inspect the area beneath it.

"I was . . . feeling faint."

"But the casement is open. Surely there was sufficient fresh air."

"I, ah, am not used to criminal activities."

"Hardly criminal, Nell." Godfrey's voice was muffled now as he burrowed under the desk. "Yes, there's something here—and heavy. Stand by the other side of the desk and I'll push it through. That will be easier."

I took my position as requested. The papers were safe beneath their bookish disguise. "You really ought not to disorder the office, Godfrey. Dr. Watson might notice."

"This is extremely odd," he said in an annoyed voice, ignoring my advice. "There!" He grunted, and something long and heavy rolled out from under Dr. Watson's desk and onto my boot toes.

"Well?" Godfrey, somewhat flushed in the face, popped his head above the desktop.

I looked down.

I would have screamed, save that I did not have the breath for it. I stiffened as if turned to stone by a Medusa.

"Nell?" Godfrey rose and came around the desk. "Nell—?"

I could not find words, or the breath to speak them.

He looked down.

Then he bent, cautiously pinched the rug into a pair of folds and gingerly eased the five-foot-long cobra from my feet.

"I believe that it is dead, Nell."

"Believe?" I began to breathe again.

"Hope and pray, rather. It has not moved except by my exertions."

"How reassuring."

"It cannot be long dead," he mused, "for the body is still amazingly flexible."

"Godfrey! Please keep such revelations to yourself."

"It could be the twin to the one Irene shot in Montmartre."

"Good. We can call it the one my feet pummeled to death in Paddington."

"I mean that it seems more than coincidence to find two dead Asian cobras of similar type in Paris and London."

"Of course it is more than coincidence. It is appalling!"

He knelt over the long form on the rug. "The head seems almost jointed. I believe the neck is broken."

"Can a serpent be said to possess a neck?"

"Certainly. A serpent is all neck."

"I see. Godfrey?"

"Yes, Nell?"

"I appear to have dropped a glove under the desk. Could you—?"

"I am not anxious to explore and find another cobra."

"Please."

He sighed, returned to the desk's other side, and vanished beneath it.

Moments later he surfaced, waving a white glove of surrender. "No nest," he reported cheerfully.

I regarded the mottled corpse. It all too precisely matched Dr. Sauveur's description of the Asian cobra Irene had shot in Montmartre: perhaps five feet long but thick as a table leg, a speckled pattern of scales tapering to a tail end as delicate as little Oscar's entire body. A depraved mind might find beauty in its lethal, whiplike pliancy.

"Perhaps Dr. Watson was going to have it stuffed, *à la* Sarah Bernhardt," I suggested.

"I think not. I believe that someone intended to have Dr. Watson stuffed full of cobra venom."

"But who?"

"Come, Nell! Obviously the person that Stanhope wished to warn Watson against. Our outing is a success: we have found the very Watson we wanted."

"I am most relieved," I said faintly. "I doubt I could invade doctors' consulting rooms on false pretenses indefinitely." A thought came to me. "Godfrey, if cobra venom is so deadly, why are we coming upon dead cobras instead of dead victims?"

"Put like a prosecutor, Nell," he congratulated me, bending to take hold of the carpet, which I was all too happy to vacate.

A few vigorous shakes of the rug and the cobra was once more concealed beneath the desk. "There, tidy again."

"You are not going to simply leave it there?"

"It is not my desk, and certainly not my business."

"But what shall we do, then?"

Godfrey grinned and smoothed his hair. "Wait for Dr. Watson, as we intended, and ask him some questions about Afghanistan."

Chapter Twenty-One

DOCTOR'S DILEMMA

After forty uneasy minutes, during which I watched Godfrey snooping about the premises when I was not eyeing the carpet beneath the desk for signs of movement—after all, some snakes hibernated, I understood, and there was no guarantee that this one should not rise from the dead—the door opened.

I do not know what kind of man I expected. A rather weak one, perhaps, to be so easily led from domestic and professional rectitude by an individual as apparently erratic as this Sherlock Holmes. Certainly I had wondered whether Watson had in fact visited Briony Lodge in company with the vaunted detective and the foiled King. I remembered the detective's companion as an ordinary, quite overlookable sort of person. I had not anticipated the solid citizen who now stood before me, a man not yet forty who was built like a boxer and possessed of a certain symmetry of feature as well as an unassuming mustache that made me miss Godfrey's adornment.

"Mr. Marshwine?" the gentleman inquired. "Miss . . . er, Buxleigh?"

"Indeed," said Godfrey as he rose, thereby avoiding an outright lie.

I myself was pleased to be mistaken for the fictional Miss Buxleigh, given our violations of hospitality in our host's absence. This Dr. Watson certainly did not look like a writer, nor like a person who could be led willy-nilly by an extravagant but strong personality. He had the demeanor of a physician—and a former military man.

"What may I do for you?" the doctor inquired as he started for his desk. My eyes flew to the rug.

"Actually," Godfrey began easily, "we are not here to consult you on a medical matter."

"Oh?" The doctor sat, and yawned. "You must forgive me. I have been attending a nervously exhausted individual." I heard his feet stretch out beneath the desk as he leaned back in the chair, which creaked.

The rug before the front of the desk wrinkled in response. I bit my lip.

"We are here on a personal matter," Godfrey went on. He was being alarmingly frank for a person who only minutes before had been searching the premises.

"And that is—?" Dr. Watson's tone had become a bit gruff. Now I recognized him! He was the hatted man who had helped the pale one into 221 B Baker Street yesterday.

"We are searching for a man missing since Maiwand."

"Missing since Maiwand! My dear sir, odd that you should mention Maiwand; I had occasion to think of it for the first time in years only recently. How did you decide to approach me on this matter?"

Godfrey, like any perspicacious barrister, leaned forward persuasively in his chair even as he lowered his voice.

"You see, Dr. Watson, we have met one who remembers you ministering to the very man we seek during the battle of Maiwand. In your memories of that time we might discern some clue by which we could trace poor Blodgett."

"Blodgett?"

"Ah, Jasper Blodgett, Miss . . . er, Buxleigh's fiancé, gone missing these nine years."

Dr. Watson looked from one to the other of us. "Blodgett? Buxleigh? Nine years?"

"Exactly. A tragic tale in its simple way. A man called up

to war. A woman waiting at home. The confusion of a battle waged on alien soil. Men wounded, men killed, men gone off their heads and simply . . . lost. Miss Buxleigh has waited faithfully for almost a decade, Doctor, and now has received reports from India indicating that poor Blodgett is yet alive, if not wholly himself."

"This Blodgett has been seen?"

"Indeed. And if we could find some kernel of incident in your memories of the wounded you tended, that might help us find poor Blodgett."

The doctor's face grew distressed. "My dear sir, my dear Miss Buxleigh, my own memories are uncertain. I was wounded myself at Maiwand."

"Oh!" I exclaimed in my disappointment that our long-sought connection was so useless. Dr. Watson took my interjection for sympathy and went on more warmly.

"Jezail bullet in the shoulder," he confided to Godfrey in a bluff man-to-man way that I was not supposed to overhear, though I did. "If it had not been for my orderly Murray slinging me belly-down over a horse and leading me from harm's way, I would not be here." He flung one of his limbs beneath the desk. "Took another in the leg and never knew it, I was so fever-ridden. Most embarrassing for a physician to suffer a phantom wound. I doubt I can help you."

The wounded leg, once mentioned, thrashed again beneath the desk, like a child fidgeting when it hears its name called. I saw a mottled semicircle of snake protruding from under the bottom lip of the mahogany desk.

"Still, Dr. Watson," I put in, "what you may have witnessed before your wounding could help us."

The doctor nodded. "Many men escaped injury that day, but on my knees amid the battle dust it seemed that every man around me was half done-for. Well, Miss Buxleigh, I confess that I admire a woman eager after many years to reunite with the man who has commanded her love and loyalty. Jasper Blodgett is a lucky man."

"Thank you, Doctor," I said modestly, wringing the cords

of my reticule and looking significantly at Godfrey rather than at the slow but steady resurrection of the cobra. Time for Godfrey to play the barrister and begin questioning.

"Perhaps you remember Maclaine—?" he began dutifully.

"Poor devil! He was taken prisoner during the retreat, but I never knew him. Died, of course, at savage hands."

"If he had not died, do you think he would have been blameless?"

A sharp glance from eyes used to making diagnoses appraised us. "That is politics, sir. I fear that war brings out the worst as well as the best in men, as do political skirmishes. I heard talk that Maclaine, being dead, made a good target on which to pin hindsight, though I have no opinion either way on the affair. I was a lowly medical officer in a battle that was no more than a rout for our forces. There is a tale with a different twist to it for every man who was at Maiwand."

"Our man," said Godfrey, "was wounded early in the afternoon, early in the retreat. He had a head wound."

"How do you know if you have not found him?"

The doctor's piercing eyes did not meet mine, for I was looking modestly down—at the carpet. Godfrey answered this challenge, as well he should, since the entire fairy tale was of his spinning.

"Those who have seen him in Peshawar saw the scar."

Dr. Watson nodded. "I remember a man with a blow to the head—odd, for we had not come to hand-to-hand combat. Of course, in the scramble to retreat one of our own might have given him a knock. It was not a pretty sight, miss, almost three thousand men trying to elude bullets and blood in blinding dust and artillery fire. I do not wonder that your Jasper lost his wits afterwards—and the head blow could have done it. The fellow I remember had a desperate air, raved that he needed to see the command. He did not want to retreat, or save his skin, so much as to see someone in authority, if anyone was then. Clawed at my uniform as if he were drowning, would not let me leave. Yes, the head blow could explain much, even the fact that he has not been seen in civilized climes since—"

"Hazel!" I said. "Were his eyes hazel?"

"Eyes, Miss Buxleigh? A field surgeon does not notice such things. Pallor, perhaps, and what is broken or battered."

"J-Jasper had very compelling hazel eyes," I insisted. "If you remember him as being agitated, you must have noticed. He must have looked directly at you, imploring you—"

The doctor leaned back in his creaking chair, his bootheels thumping the floor, his chin resting on his chest. "If I had a bit of something to induce a trance, I might recall," he said with a wry expression I understood more than he suspected. "My mind has fixed on Afghanistan more than usual lately. Perhaps it is this leg acting up." He banged his foot on the floor for emphasis, and his boot shifted the rug as it landed.

More of the cobra coiled into full view at my and Godfrey's feet. Despite the provocation, we both managed to present Dr. Watson with rapt faces.

The physician suddenly clapped his hand to the desktop. "By St. Harry, you are right, miss! Peculiarly light hazel they were, like murky lakes in all that evil ocher dust. I remember thinking that it was a pity another brave young fellow was going to carry Afghanistan in his kit bag for the rest of his life, and that is when—" Dr. Watson's own eyes blinked, as if again in the heat and dust of the battlefield "—that is when something ripped into my left shoulder as cold as ice in that devil's oven. I have never recalled it before, the actual moment of my being wounded."

"What happened to—to Jasper?" I put in before the doctor's memories should fade again.

He shook his head in a daze. "I next remember Murray. 'Can you hang onto the mane for a minute, sir?' he was saying. I was swaying by the side of a horse—a stringy packhorse—and then Murray slung me over and I thankfully remember nothing until I awoke in the makeshift hospital in Kandahar. It was four weeks of fever and short rations until Roberts came to relieve us."

"And that is all you remember of poor Jasper?"

Dr. Watson nodded soberly. "That is more than I remembered yesterday. But, yes, how he clung to me, as if I were more than a mere lifeline! They will do that, you know, in the field, but this man was desperate beyond fear for his life. He would not release my arms, and as I moved to leave, his hands clung even to my medical bag. Then that icy furrow ploughed through my being, quickly followed by the heat of fever. Jezail bullets are manufactured crudely and often bear disease as well as death." Dr. Watson sighed. "Sometimes forgetfulness is a blessing."

We both nodded somberly, there being little else to say. Godfrey rose. "I thank you, Doctor, for your time and recollection. Your story explains at least why Jasper may have lost his head and failed to return to England and Miss Buxleigh."

I rose also, and the doctor saw us to the door. "Certainly," he said, with a gallant glance at myself, "he would never have neglected to return to as charming a lady as Miss Buxleigh of his own will."

I was unable to savor or shrug off this gallantry; my eyes flicked back into the room. From the door, the dead cobra looked like a wrinkle in the rug. I wondered if the Watsons' maid had good, steady nerves like myself. . . .

We started down the passage to the outer door.

"I hope that I have been of help," said the doctor.

"You have indeed," Godfrey said heartily. "I'm sure that Miss Buxleigh's mind is more at rest for our interview."

Godfrey had ever been an optimist.

"I fear," the doctor added, "that my attention has been somewhat distracted by a matter of some moment apart from my practice. If you have gleaned anything useful from me, you are welcome to it."

Godfrey donned his top hat and smiled as he took my arm in a solicitous way. "You have been an invaluable help, sir, and will never know how deeply I and Miss Buxleigh appreciate your assistance. It has been most enlightening in every respect. Thank you again. Good day, Dr. Watson."

"Good day, Miss Buxleigh, Mr. Marshwine."

On such cordial commonplaces we parted company.

Paddington unfolded before us in all its everyday homeliness. I had almost expected to exit into a dusty, throbbing battlefield full of wounded men and dead snakes.

"Godfrey!" I demanded as soon as we had walked a decent distance from the Watson abode. "What of the cobra? We have left it simply lying there, halfway revealed, without warning anyone."

"It is not our cobra," he said with something of Irene's offhanded manner.

"But what shall they do when they find it?"

He smiled as he spied a hansom to take us back to the heart of the town. "It should make a fine puzzle for Dr. Watson's friend, Mr. Holmes."

"The doctor will say that we were there, that we were inquiring about Afghanistan."

"All the better. I would like to see Sherlock Holmes try to track down Mr. Marshwine and Miss Buxleigh."

I settled into the cab in some unease, glancing out the window on the fine day. I clutched Godfrey's arm.

"Look! That street boy. I saw him before—yesterday in Baker Street—the one with the cap that is too large!"

Godfrey leaned to peer out. "Only a lad trying to make a few pence running errands. I would not fret about him, Nell."

"Baker Street is a far way from Paddington for a lad afoot."

"Perhaps he was hired to escort some elderly person home by hansom cab."

"He is signaling another cab—an urchin like that! How can he pay?"

Our vehicle jerked into motion, wresting away my view of the boy.

"Likely his patron gave him the fare back, though I admit that a cab is rather royal for his sort."

"He could be a minion of Sherlock Holmes, set to follow us."

"My dear Miss Buxleigh," Godfrey said, drawing the curtain on the passing scene of the street outside, "did I ever tell you that you are possessed of a most ungoverned imagination?"

Chapter Twenty-Two

DIVINELY INSPIRED

A cable from Irene awaited us at the hotel: "*Mes amis,* you get on splendidly. I am having abominable luck finding the captain of my heart in Paris. I await your next developments breathlessly." She had signed it with an unmistakable code name, "Sarah."

"How odd. She says nothing personal," I noted to Godfrey. "No word of missing us. You."

"It is only a cablegram, Nell. Brevity is the soul of clarity." Godfrey was pacing my small sitting room, his hands locked behind his back, his long legs scissoring across the thick Turkish carpet. "What Irene has chosen to say is significant. If she can find no trace of Captain Morgan in Paris, with all her resources of intelligence and connection, then he is no longer there. I doubt it is coincidence that cobras have emigrated from Paris of late as well."

"Snakes stick together," I sniffed. "So you suspect Captain Morgan of perpetrating the bad business in Montmartre?"

"Suspect? I am certain of it, and so is Irene."

"Yet you left her behind to his supposed mercies."

"Actually, Nell, I believe that you and I have drawn him here. In that our jaunt is an unqualified success."

"Indeed, if I wish to spend my life entering rooms into

which serpents have preceded me, I have been uncannily successful!"

"Morgan, mysterious as he is, must be the key to Stanhope's difficulties. Obviously, he is also trying to murder Dr. Watson."

"And yet we have not warned the poor man!" I remonstrated. "We have left him defenseless."

"Hardly." Godfrey stopped pacing to eye me with a twinkle. "The dead snake cannot fail to alarm him. He will immediately acquaint his friend with the mystery. So Dr. Watson will have as guardian the formidable Sherlock Holmes."

I remained silent, aching to add "Formidably given to strange drugs," but I dared not. If I did, I would be obliged to confess to my forbidden reading. Nor did I want to mention my knowledge of the intense impression Irene had evidently made on this man who sneered at women and softer emotions, but reverenced hypodermic needles.

"But we must not rest on Mr. Holmes's laurels," Godfrey said. "Tomorrow we will begin hunting the hunter. I will make inquiries at the gentlemen's clubs devoted to sporting pursuits. You can try the hotels."

"You wish me to inquire after a male resident at a series of hotels? That is most improper, Godfrey."

"Would you rather visit such institutions as The Royal Rhinoceros Regiment? Besides, many clubs forbid women the premises."

"And what sensible woman would wish to visit those masculine enclaves? No doubt they are filled with decorative weapons, rank odors, hollow elephant feet, stuffed snakes and such."

"Yes," he said, laughing, "just like Madame Sarah's Paris salon. What woman could possibly relish such an environment?"

"I am glad that Irene is not here, for she would surely grasp any pretext to storm the gentlemen's clubs in false whiskers. I have it! We will make our rounds together. Admittedly we will lose time, but we will have the advantage of two viewpoints to compare. That is the solution."

"Not so soon!" said he, taking my new determination for instant action. "We must devise a plan of attack. The hotel will have a recent map of London, as well as some suggestions of where a former military man might stay. I suggest that we repair to the dining room. Brown's *table d'hôte* was famous even in my Temple days."

I smiled tentatively. "I have never dined alone in public with a male escort, but I am sure the experience will be bracing."

And so it was. After a tasty dinner in the quite respectable hotel dining room—whitebait and brown bread, followed by summer pudding, all so delectably English, so fresh, so garlic-free!—we retired to my sitting room again to plan the next day's campaign.

"There is just one thing that troubles me, Godfrey."

"Only one?" He seemed pleasantly surprised.

"If Quentin intended to warn Dr. Watson, why has he not done so?"

"We cannot be sure that he has not."

"Dr. Watson seemed a bit weary, but not at all wary. There is a great difference, Godfrey. He was quite willing to sit down and speak of Afghanistan with two virtual strangers. No, I am certain that he knows nothing of this matter. He will be as mystified by the dead cobra in his study as I would be to find an expired toad in my glove box."

An unwilling smile tweaked the corners of Godfrey's lips, much more visible now that he had shaved off the mustache. "When you put it that way, I must confess that the circumstances are comical despite their seriousness."

"Yes, the world finds much that is serious laughable. That is its main trouble."

"You must admit the melodramatic nature of finding these dead serpents, and realizing that whatever sinister purpose they may have had is moot."

"The motive, whatever it was, is not moot," I pointed out.

"Oh, I do wish Irene were here! She has a genius for taking some totally unforeseen course that nevertheless cuts to the heart of the matter. And what will we do about finding Quentin?"

Godfrey sat on a small tapestry-covered chair with a woebegone expression. "That is the purpose of our visit, true, and yet our only routes to the mysterious Mr. Stanhope are indirect. Well—" he rose with a sigh, his hands clapping his trouser legs "—our tasks are set for the morrow. Perhaps we will encounter some piece of luck."

Luck, I was tempted to answer, was not something Irene relied upon in the slightest. After Godfrey had bid me good night, I reread her cablegram. The blithe good humor underlying it ill became an Irene forced to keep a safe distance from anything. Yet Godfrey was almost supernaturally calm in the face of our frustrating search, and remarkably resigned to the absence of his wife. . . .

Of course I smelled what is known in certain, cruder circles as a rat, and it was not Captain Morgan, no matter how well qualified for the role. This would not be the first time that my two friends had conspired to keep me ignorant for my own good. They might even be acting from some misguided impulse to "spare" me the ugly truth about Emerson Quentin Stanhope. I neither welcomed nor wanted such protection. From now on I would keep a weather eye out for well-intentioned subterfuge.

The next morning we set out from Brown's Hotel in fine weather. Flowers bloomed in window boxes above the shopfronts and the ubiquitous pubs. A pure blue sky dipped down between the five-story rooftops of the great city's buildings.

Gentlemen's clubs, I soon discovered, are like vermin: they lurk everywhere, but are seldom seen. Discreet doorways marked only by severe brass plates that would mean nothing to the uninitiated lead to such eccentric environs as "The Oryxians," "The Fox and Hounds Club," and "The Norfolk Jacketeers."

Godfrey was quite right that I would not be admitted, although I was permitted to teeter on the stoop while he inquired within. My presence was helpful, however. I donned a perpetually doleful look so that Godfrey could point out "poor Miss Huxleigh, who has lost her only brother. Yes, quite genuinely lost. In Injah." Would the hearer know a certain Captain Morgan who had served in that quarter, a renowned heavy-game hunter, particularly of tigers—?

His hearers always denied knowledge of renowned tigers or their hunters, although almost every club kept a mounted tiger head about the place. They were most adamant on their ignorance of "Captain Morgan."

As we made our rounds, I became ever more annoyed at having to stand on the stoop like a domestic servant. However, I was not too lost in indignation to fail to notice the ebb and flow of people around us. Mother London's thronging four millions never allow a citizen to feel lonely.

Godfrey, recognizing my irritation, paused at a flower vendor's near Covent Garden to comfort me with a posy.

"Please, no, I do not require such an extravagance," I protested.

The flower girl, a young person with an extremely freckled face liberally powdered by soot, grimaced at me for discouraging a sale. She need not have worried.

"Nonsense." Godfrey presented me with a knot of pansies and fragrant verbena that was all the more charming in contrast to its grimy vendor.

I had bent my face to sniff the posy, when I spied a familiar face in the crowd.

"Godfrey!"

"Yes, Nell?"

"It is that ruffian again!"

"Which ruffian?"

A good question, for the area teemed with ragged folk of all sorts.

I lowered my voice, speaking as I sniffed the posy in the best Irene-approved method of surreptitious communication.

"That boy that I saw outside 221 B Baker Street," I mumbled into the petals, "and then in Paddington near Dr. Watson's. I am convinced that he is following us."

"That may be, Nell," Godfrey said without alarm. "Then let us give him something to do and go along to the next club."

So we did. It was a fine day, and despite my concern over the ragamuffin I savored the sights of Covent Garden. The vicinity attracted people from the opposite poles of London life; though it literally shone as the theatrical district each night, by day it merely twinkled in the sunshine, genial and friendly.

Here the unlovely strains of pure Cockney echoed off the stone buildings, sounding like a convention of Casanovas. Here, too, strolled retired military men wearing old-fashioned muttonchop whiskers, their backs ramrod straight, their shoes mirror-polished. Fashionable ladies in flower-strewn summer bonnets of Neapolitan straw and summer wraps of the lightest lace, silk and wool ambled among them.

Children too wove through the passing parade, young girls in pleated skirts and wide-brimmed shade hats and very young boys in long curls and short skirted frocks, looking like miniature courtiers from another and more gilded age.

These small ladies and gentlemen capered like kittens beneath the benign summer sunlight. I realized that my visit to Grosvenor Square, as well as my warm encounter with the ingratiating Allegra, had led me to attach only the rosiest memories to my governess days. I reminded myself of tantrums and falsehoods and stubborn silences. No burst of nostalgia should lead me to seek such employment again.

"Your pardon," snapped a dowager in mourning dress as she collided with me, the words courteous but the tone outraged.

I flushed, aware that I had been moonstruck. "I am so very sorry." I reached out a hand to steady her. She glared at me from under wild iron-gray brows before crabbing forward again without acknowledging my apology. On she went, navigating these crowded streets like a sable ship with her sails broken-backed, clothed from neck to toe in braided camel's hair, mantled in a crape-banded black and bonneted in gauze and beads. Though stooped as if by a terrible, invisible weight bundled to her shoulders, her person suggested no fragility.

"I must have been sleepwalking, Godfrey, to have collided with that poor creature."

"She seems none the worse for wear," he said to comfort me. Indeed the old dame was scuttering away at a brisk pace. "In truth, the fault was hers. She careened into you. No doubt her sight is failing."

I sighed. "Certainly my foresight is. I seem to be walking in a fog. Perhaps I have been away from London too long."

"Perhaps your distraction began in Paris," he said.

"What do you mean?"

"Only that you have confronted your past. That is always a shock to the equilibrium."

"That is the whole trouble, Godfrey! I have no past, only a history, like a public edifice. Sarah Bernhardt once said that a woman without a past is like a poodle without a pedigree: alive, but who is interested enough to notice?"

"And for how long have you heeded what Sarah Bernhardt says?"

"Never! But I remember. Even Irene seems to have a past."

"Irene 'seems' a great deal of things."

"Have you never wondered, Godfrey, about her life before you two met?"

He shrugged. "She lived with you for several years."

"But before that? She did not burst upon London fully formed at the age of three and twenty. And she will say nothing of her American days."

"Assuredly that makes them more interesting. Irene is never one to neglect sowing subtle seeds of interest."

"As long as no one around her reaps the result! Perhaps that is what Sarah means by 'a past': the assurance that at some time one has been interesting. I have never been 'interesting'; I have been in Shropshire."

"Shropshire is, I am sure, most interesting."

"But you have no desire to go there."

"Not in the immediate future, no."

"Never."

"It is not likely," he admitted at last.

"I even come from a dull place. Irene would never allow herself to come from a dull place."

"Nell, I am certain that New Jersey is a dull place, or else Irene would not be so close-mouthed about it. Has it ever occurred to you that an unmentioned 'past' may simply be unmentionably dull?"

"No, Godfrey, it has not."

"Well, it may. Besides, the present is all that matters, and here is the next sporting club on our agenda, The Frontier Fusiliers."

Another black-painted door with a brass knocker inset discreetly into a row of redbrick Georgian facades confronted us. Godfrey rang the bell, then introduced us and our business. This time the porter suffered me to enter the hall, where I waited on cold marble, not wishing to sit upon the red-velvet upholstered chair formed from animal horns, and glimpsing a warm red-damask room beyond where deer antlers bristled on the walls.

Godfrey soon returned, his face transparently disappointed.

"This club had a directory of the memberships of all the others; no Sylvester Morgan, Captain or not, honors their rolls. The senior member present suggested that Morgan may have been expelled from one of the other clubs years ago."

"Expelled?"

"Hunters' clubs on occasion resemble their game for behavior. The odd member of the pack 'goes rogue' from time to time. He said this Morgan sounded like 'a bad 'un' who may have had less than honorable dealings with both the hunters' fraternity and the public, if he dealt in rare pelts."

"A perceptive gentleman. So what is our next course?"

"Retreat, I suppose." Godfrey escorted me down the few stairs to the street.

"You are remarkably calm in the face of defeat," I commented.

"I am remarkably calm at all times," he retorted with a smile that I found winning. I found the absence of his mustache disconcerting. Much as I deplore facial hair on men, I confess that I had grown used to it in mild amounts. Or at least I had made an exception to my prejudice with Godfrey.

We walked in silence. Irene made her investigative efforts look like larks, but without her we made a plodding pair.

"Something bracing is called for," Godfrey announced suddenly, steering me with a featherweight pressure on my elbow toward an ABC tea shop. He was also guiding me away from a convention of beggars sprawled upon the walkway.

I hesitated. Under normal conditions, I am not swayed by public beggary, no matter how pathetic. Much of it is polished into a vehicle for the greed of the beseecher rather than the generosity of the giver.

Yet only weeks before in Paris one such unappetizing person had proved to be not only truly needful but an acquaintance. Impulsively, I cannot say why, I dug in my reticule for a few pence.

As I was about to drop them into the grimy hand extended, something flashed past with the utmost speed. My reticule was snatched from my hands, the proffered coins clinking to the pavement. The beggar was too stunned to even scramble for the coppers, although his younger fellows hurled themselves atop the bounty.

Godfrey was bounding after the cutpurse, coattails flying, and I hurried after. I had my suspicions. I had nursed them all along, and now I was certain. No one would make off with my reticule twice in the same week, and only one person would remember a similar incident of many years ago. . . .

I shortly came even with Godfrey, who had paused to search the crowd from his not unrespectable height.

"I fear the scamp has escaped, Nell," he told me.

"No," I told him, "I fear that you have *let* 'the scamp' escape."

"Why, what do you mean?"

"Only that I am tired of this charade! I am not the oblivious fool you take me for! Cablegrams from Paris indeed! Such 'foreign' communications may be arranged from London. It has all been a farce: our search for the mythical Captain Morgan; Irene remaining in France. She is here in London, do not bother to deny it, and hot on a more rewarding trail. Do you think that I have failed to notice the suspicious persons along our route? I have seen that miserable boy three times, and I warrant that you were unable to catch him only because you did not want to!"

"Nell, come into the tearoom and sit down until you collect yourself—"

"No!" I shook off his gentlemanly hand. "I will not be made a public fool, and if Irene does not produce herself soon, I cannot say what I will do!"

"Excuse me," came a deep voice.

Godfrey's eyebrows lifted at the new arrival behind me.

I turned. An old soldier stood there, snowy muttonchops frothing at his jaws, thick spectacles with a dark tint shading his weak old eyes. Apparently there was nothing wrong with his weak old legs, or his weak old arms, for he had the very lad in question by the scruff of his tatterdemalion jacket.

"I caught this one running as if the Queen's Guard were behind him. Since street lads seldom dress with such nicety, he plainly was the reason for the furor down the street. Might this be yours, miss?"

The old man extended my reticule, which I took with relief.

"Anything gone?" Godfrey inquired.

"Not a thing," I replied triumphantly, eyeing the writhing youth. He was a strapping lad. Such street urchins looked depressingly similar, but no matter how he hunched and wriggled, it was obvious he had attained the size of a grown woman.

"Really," I said, regarding the lad unpityingly. "You could

not resist the grand gesture, could you? Was it not enough that you cast yourself in my path at every opportunity? Did you expect me to remain completely duped?"

"Nell—" Godfrey said urgently at my rear. I turned on him with great pleasure.

"And you, you . . . henchman! Oh, I have been very thick, but that is past now."

"Nell, in all good conscience—"

"Godfrey, do not try to dissuade me. I am certain that it will be most mortifying, but she needs to be taught a lesson. Sir, will you keep a good hold on that lad? Thank you."

I took a handkerchief from my retrieved reticule and reached out to scrub at the filth smudging the boy's features. Immediately a lighter cast of skin shone through.

"You see?" I spared Godfrey a triumphant glance. He had a most odd expression. I turned back to my victim, who was cursing in a Cockney screech that was so unintelligible it fortunately spared my sensibilities.

"Irene, it's no use," I advised the captive. "You cannot fool me, though of course you had to rub my nose in your deception. Now I am rubbing your nose and it looks far better so. And as for this ridiculous cap—" I reached for the item of apparel in question "—anyone could see it was a clumsy disguise, too large only because it hid a great, feminine quantity of hair—"

At this I lofted the offending headgear. By now my demonstration had drawn a crowd of onlookers: the beggar family, more used to entertaining than being entertained; several nicely dressed children; even the old lady in mourning, with whom we had apparently caught up again.

"You see," I said to my mesmerized audience. "The game is up. This is not a lad," I announced. "This is a grown woman who likes to play silly games!" I looked back at the miscreant.

The sunlight shone down on a dull tangle of cropped black hair, not the shimmering lengths of cinnamon-brown I had expected to unveil. The captive's squirmings and epithets increased.

Well, I had heard of theatrical wigs before. I grasped the unappealing head of hair and jerked.

"Owwwwwww!" The creature howled as if to wake any dead within earshot and every living soul all the way to Gretna Green.

"I cannot hold him much longer," the old soldier gritted between a set of wooden teeth. "Do you want to call a bobby or continue on your own?"

"Nell," said Godfrey in soft rebuke that only I could hear, "this is not Irene."

My hand tugged again, to no avail. My gloved fingers uncurled, suddenly aware of the thick, oily texture of the hair they grasped. Even a theatrical wig did not have to be so disgustingly . . . dirty.

Every onlooking eye was nailed to me with lively interest.

"I—I thought . . ."

As my own grip collapsed, so the old gentleman's loosened. The lad wrenched free with a blazingly indignant face, now striped from the cleansing offices of my handkerchief. The young thief whirled to leave, then spun back to glare at me before snatching his . . . truly filthy . . . cap from my nerveless fingers.

"Mad as a moonbeam," he spat at me with perfect clarity before dashing away through a crowd that did nothing to prevent him.

I looked around. "He did steal my reticule."

"Quite so." The old gentleman dusted off his palms as if that would remove his contact with so much uncleanliness.

Gradually, but not soon enough, the onlookers ebbed, going about their business. I stood in the street drawing my reticule strings tight and loose in turn.

"Nell—" Godfrey began, more gently than I should have had the circumstances been reversed.

"Do not say it! I was wrong, but I was right as well. Irene

is in London," I said, raising my eyes defiantly to his at last.

He did not deny it. "Would you care for some tea now?"

Godfrey and I did not discuss the matter further, not even at dinner that night. I recognized that by avoiding the topic he avoided having to deliver any falsehoods. Of course Irene was lurking about London.

At least my reticule had been returned.

Alone in my room, I examined it to see if it required mending or cleaning. As I had told Godfrey, my coin purse was still there, along with the handkerchief, which would require laundering, and a vial of smelling salts, an item that no woman should ever be without. I sniffed it delicately in case any lingering miasma remained from my strenuous afternoon.

The reticule's lining appeared unbesmirched, I noted with relief, for the lad's filthy fingers had not escaped my notice. What had escaped my notice until that moment was a cylinder of pale paper that lay upright against the cream silk lining.

I withdrew it gingerly.

Scratched in faint pencil were the words: "*You must come to the Natural History Museum vertebrate rooms at 11* A.M. *tomorrow (the 8th). Urgent!*" One letter signed the note: "Q."

My heart began pounding. How had this message gotten into my reticule? When? By whom had it been delivered? I rose, intending to fetch Godfrey. Then I paused.

I would not make an idiot of myself again in anyone's presence, least of all his. No proof existed that the message was from Quentin Stanhope, but who else should it be from? And as for the method of delivery, that I must puzzle out for myself.

I took the note to my dainty Louis XIV desk. Brown's Hotel was liberally equipped with gaslight, but the desk bore as well an oil lamp, which I lit. I held the tiny piece of rolled paper down by the edges of a crystal stamp box and an ink bottle.

The words had been hastily written, but I was no judge of Quentin's handwriting in any case. I desperately wished I was, having seen Irene dissect the character of correspondents with a glance and a blithe pronouncement.

The penmanship was legible; a pencil—none too sharp—had been used, which bespoke a hasty scrawl made on the street without premeditation; and the words were impossible for me to ignore.

When and how had this missive come into my possession? Certainly not at the hotel; I had filled the reticule myself before leaving. The most obvious choice of messenger was the unfortunate thief. Had he actually been adding to the contents of my reticule rather than subtracting from them?

Perhaps that was why he had "let" himself be caught. I had glimpsed this unwholesome figure several times. Obviously he had been commissioned to watch us. Of course, he could simply be a thief who had decided that my reticule was tasty prey and who had followed us for that reason only. But if the young thief had not thrust this note into my bag, who else could have?

I rose to fetch the reticule, a common kind of faille sack with a wide mouth pulled shut by pursing the strings interwoven into the folds. I drew the cords, noticing that while the reticule was throttled shut, so to speak, the moment that I released the cords they loosened slightly. Sufficient room remained among the puckered pleats to thrust a slender pipe of paper into the depths of the bag.

So. Anyone could have done it. The dowager in mourning who had bumped into me . . . the old soldier who had captured the young thief . . . the flower girl who had handed me the posy, for that matter . . . the ragamuffin . . . even Godfrey.

One of these figures—or even another, unnoticed person—could have been Quentin in disguise. Or Irene in disguise. Or even—never underestimate *the* man—Sherlock Holmes in disguise. Or none of them could be anybody at all.

I leaned my head on my hands and shut my eyes. On the blackness before me floated the figures of the day, as if inviting me to choose one. But my choice that afternoon had been horribly wrong. I would not make that mistake again! And I would attend that rendezvous on the morrow. Of course I dared not tell Godfrey. Besides suspecting that he and Irene had left me out of their game, I could not risk letting him see Quentin again. Godfrey's last promise had been to thrash an explanation for his disappearance from Quentin. I had no intention of allowing such an occurrence.

No, I must somehow elude Godfrey without his suspecting anything. But how? And then I sat up straight, divinely inspired.

I would tell Godfrey that I wished to go to church!

Chapter Twenty-Three

'ONEST CITIZENS

''**Church?**'' **Godfrey** said in startled tones, as if I had proposed visiting a Whitechapel opium den.

"Yes. Church," I reiterated at breakfast. "I have had no opportunity to attend Anglican services since joining you and Irene in France nearly a year ago."

"I have not been in a church since Irene and I were married," he mused.

"Neither has she."

"I suppose," he began with little enthusiasm, mangling his kipper, "I can accompany you."

"You can indeed, and that would be commendable, save that this expedition of mine is a private pilgrimage. I make it once a year upon the anniversary of my dear father's death."

"Oh." Godfrey looked as taken aback as I had ever seen him. Referring to a death in the family is a proven method of ensuring other people's rapid loss of interest in one's personal affairs.

He frowned. "I never noticed such an annual outing during the years that I employed you at the Temple."

I rather oversalted my kidney pie while composing my next venture into falsehood. "Ah . . . such visitations are more spiritually salubrious if not boasted about, Godfrey."

"No doubt, no doubt," he agreed. "You are the parson's daughter and should know."

"Indeed."

"What church do you honor with your pilgrimage?"

Now I trod upon very delicate ground. My difficulty was the fact that Brown's Hotel was located close to the theatrical district called by the silly name of Piccadilly. Unfortunately, but not unexpectedly, no reputable church was within suitable distance. I would have to name one near my true destination.

"Holy Trinity," I said firmly, hoping Godfrey would inquire no further.

He was not a barrister for nothing. "Holy Trinity?" He spoke with some astonishment. "Why on earth would you wish to go there?"

"Why on earth not?"

"I read about it in yesterday's *Telegraph*. It will be a splendid homage to the Arts and Crafts Movement when completed, with its Burne-Jones and Morris stained glass windows, but it cannot be the goal of your pilgrimage. It is still unfinished, Nell."

"Where is this so-called 'Holy Trinity'?"

"Sloane Square," he replied, watching me carefully.

"Heavens, no! That Holy Trinity is quite the wrong one, Godfrey. Goodness. *My* Holy Trinity is in Knightsbridge, near the Victoria and Albert Museum, an excellent, restrained example of the Gothic style."

He buttered his muffin. "You are certain that I cannot persuade you to allow me to escort you?"

"I prefer going alone, so that I may think about things."

"Things," he echoed in his newly annoying way, so like Casanova.

"Things," I repeated firmly. At least that part was utterly true.

I insisted on taking an omnibus to Kensington, as I had not done for many months. Godfrey argued in favor of a hansom cab, but I resisted. As my association with Irene and her early "cases" had shown me, a cab journey is easier to track than the crowded comings and goings aboard a public omnibus.

My late father, I told Godfrey, would not have approved such extravagance as a hansom cab, even on his own behalf. Since it is virtually impossible to argue with the dead, Godfrey relented, and soon I was on my separate, if not merry, way.

As I jolted out the Brompton Road toward Kensington among an anonymous mob of fellow travelers, all of us advertising "Dr. Morton's Amazing Foot Powder," I brooded on the extremes to which my attempt to help Quentin Stanhope had driven me. I had never willfully deceived anyone to whom I owed so much. Yet I had known Quentin before I had ever met Godfrey, if one may call such a brief acquaintance as ours "knowing." The poor man had quite literally stumbled across me after all these years and had seemed to take some comfort in that. I had no choice but to see him.

I felt obliged to stop at Holy Trinity and offer a prayer for my father, who had died in mid-February rather than July. Still, my visit to Holy Trinity did me good, and steeled my resolve. I set out for the museum.

This entire quarter of London just south of the velvet-green summer quilt of Kensington Park bristled with new constructions. In the near distance I could spy the awesome spires and domes of the Queen's monuments to domestic bliss and connubial bereavement: the Gothic spires of the Prince Albert Memorial bristling beyond the redbrick bulk of Albert Hall, a modern glass-and-iron domed concert arena.

The Museum of Natural History and Modern Curiosities dated only to the early 'Seventies, and faced the strong sunlight as yet unstained by London's smoke-misted autumns and wet, sooty winters. With its twin spires and central nave, the terra-cotta and slate-blue exterior offered a most reassuring, contemplative and churchlike appearance, though it was a bit Byzantine for my taste.

Within, the religious similarity ended. In the vast entry area loomed some monster of the primordial swamps in all its bony glory. Yet, like a church, the Museum of Natural History and Modern Curiosities was ever mindful of death. As I wandered its many exhibit rooms, for I had arrived well in advance of the appointed time, I felt I toured a mausoleum rather than a museum. All of the exhibits, whether insect, reptile, bird or mammal, were dead, whether shown in the bare bones or in the furred and feathered simulacra of life.

Bright glass eyes stared at me without wavering. Creatures posed as patiently as if for a photograph, only these subjects would never move again, and I was the moving camera that recorded their bizarre forms. I almost wished that I could huddle under a black cloth and peer at them in secret. This public display of so much death, of so many creatures killed that so few of us could gawk at them in echoing marble splendor, seemed truly primitive.

I passed the bloated reptiles coiling in their great wooden cases, stopping before a cobra raised up as I had seen one do in life only recently, its famous "spectacle"-marked hood wide as an eighteenth-century lady's calabash. The maw was open so the fangs glimmered bone-white under the electric lights. This serpent looked as regal as any Queen of the Nile; for a moment I saw it not as a thing of loathing or the Form of the Fall, but rather as a bejeweled and magnificent creation wrested from its true setting, the natural world. And then I shuddered, for it was a serpent after all, and deadly.

Yet the true predator was not the venomous serpent, but the one who sought to put the snake's natural weapons to unnatural, human ends, unthinkable crimes in garrets and consulting rooms.

As I looked about, the vastness of the museum oppressed me. I felt as if I had been immured in some gigantic sarcophagus. What a site Quentin had selected for our clandestine meeting!

With relief I entered the vertebrate area, devoutly hoping that fur would mask all the macabre zoology exhibits. Instead, I was again unnerved. Exotic creatures were fastened high on the walls or imprisoned in glassed-in wooden cabinets oddly reminiscent of Mr. Tiffany's well-secured jewelry cases at 79 rue Richelieu. A faint odor of stale fur and formaldehyde reminded me of the Paris Morgue.

Weaving past the room's mounted occupants, I concentrated with some relief on the moving, human exhibit, the visitors. How should I recognize Quentin? Certainly he would not be attired in the fantastic foreign garb that he had worn in Paris. In that City of Lights the lunatic is a patron saint. In London, only mild eccentricity is tolerated.

As I passed a pair of towering ostriches (such glamourous plumes upon a bonnet; such gawky and unpleasing creatures), I heard a rustle like a great bird's quills. I turned to see a familiar figure bearing down on me—an old woman in mourning dress!

She brushed past impatiently to approach a stuffed ostrich. Even her stooped posture could not disguise her once-great height. She lifted a lorgnette on its black silk cord and bobbed her head upon its scrawny neck to scrutinize the exhibit. Her gestures were so like a chicken's in a hen yard that I could not repress a smile, despite my lively suspicions.

Could this be Quentin Stanhope? Certainly that hump-shouldered carriage could disguise a man's height. I had seen enough of Irene's wonder-working with crape hair and veiled bonnets to know that the unruly gray eyebrows could be false and that a black veil could soften a man's harsher features into those of an elderly woman. As women age their feminine features harshen into those of old men, as if all our differences are designed to melt away by life's end.

The dowager turned from the ostrich, keeping her lorgnette raised while she favored me with the same openly bobbing inspection. Then she nodded, once and briskly, and rustled on.

I did not know what to think. Had she recognized me from the street? Or was this inspection a signal to accost her? What if I were wrong and mere coincidence had brought her here?

"Mere coincidence, Nell?" I could almost hear Irene's amused tones. "I do not know if there is such a thing as the

God defined by the self-declared men of God, but I do know that there is no such thing as 'mere coincidence.' "

I looked around. Figures passed, vaguely seen among the stuffed animal life—or death—surrounding me. An overwhelming sense of observation oppressed me. Perhaps it was engendered by the myriad of glass eyes, shining as if every creature came equipped with spectacles.

I drew out my pince-nez, presumably to better inspect the exhibits, but in fact because my naked face felt so vulnerable. I wished for one of Irene's lavish veils. No wonder she affected them; they allowed her to see without being fully seen—not only an advantage for an actress, but a necessity for the inquiry agent.

And here was I, armed with nothing but my determination and a note that—oh! For the first time the dreadful thought struck: a note that might not even be from Quentin Stanhope, that might be a ruse to lure me here for purposes . . . purposes . . . purposes unguessed at but not good!

I looked about with the intent of making my exit—and spied the old soldier who had collared the thieving boy of yesterday. He was leaning down, whisker to whisker with a gigantic, sprawling male seal!

I hastened around the rear of a most impressive giraffe, and tried to hide behind one of its tall but extremely slender spotted legs. Another unwelcome discovery greeted me. Yes, my eyes were not deceiving me; there, not twenty feet away, was the boy who had stolen my purse, strolling among the monkeys with his hands in his pockets and an innocent expression on his still-filthy face!

I fixedly contemplated the giraffe's tail high above my head: a most ridiculous appendage considering the owner's great height, terminating in a broomlike brush of whisker-stiff hairs. The spots before my eyes were as nothing compared to the mad pattern of notions colliding in my brain.

The boy could not be Quentin, but he might be bearing another message for me. Or . . . I looked about. A number of children gamboled through the rooms, as the animals were a drawing card for the younger set. I would have taken my charges here myself, had I been a governess longer. Most instructive and suitable entertainment, given the number of families in attendance.

But lone, purse-snatching street urchins . . .

I had half convinced myself that certainly all of the previous day's population of Covent Garden had now convened to the Museum of Natural History and Modern Curiosities. The retired soldier was looking in my direction. As our eyes intersected, he nodded and bowed slightly, and why should he not? He had assisted in the recovery of my reticule but a day before.

Coincidences bred like monkeys around me, and so did my own speculations. It seemed as if I were center stage at the Grand Guignol, the leading actress in a gruesome play. Was it Irene's fine Machiavellian hand airily pulling a set of invisible strings high in the building's vaulted ceilings? An air of intense expectation hung above the macabre blending of man and beast executing a clandestine pavane in the scene below.

Then from behind an aardvark hobbled the strangest creature yet: a hunchbacked old scholar buttoned into a rusty black coat despite the warm day, a yellowed beard trailing down his concave chest, his eyes vigilant and owlish behind a pair of yellow-tinted spectacles. He might have been the twisted twin of the stooped dowager . . .

I could not resist glancing at her; she had interrupted her close inspection of a mole peering out from a mossy log to glare at the newest arrival.

Suddenly inspired, I realized that both figures could have been men in disguise; men, moreover, who were gifted, or cursed, with telltale eyes—men like Quentin Stanhope, with his clear hazel gaze that a veneer of foreign sun only emphasized, or Captain Sylvester Morgan, whose compelling cold azure stare was that of the professional hunter!

Could hunter and prey have both found their way here? Which could I trust, if both approached me? And what part did the retired soldier play?

I watched them circle in the exhibition room: the young urchin, the old soldier, the elderly scholar, the stooped dowager. It was not lost on me that three of my four suspicious fellow citizens were apparently old. "Age is the best disguise," Irene had remarked long ago. "It is so commonplace, yet so unspokenly dreaded, that we seldom look it in the eye, much less examine its traces in ourselves."

So. Which of these enfeebled browsers was Irene, then? And why was that idle boy present, if he was not Irene? No matter how I counted up my suspicions, I had one candidate for disguise too many. Quentin; Irene; Captain Morgan.

To give myself time to think, I extracted my pince-nez from my reticule and exchanged soulful gazes with a two-toed sloth that depended most artistically from an artificial tree within a glassed-in case. In its faint reflection I could follow the actions of the principal parties.

The scholar had pressed himself to an opposite case as if to obtain the same once-removed view of us all that I had of them. The dowager was rummaging in her reticule. The boy was surreptitiously removing the prettiest of the small rocks arrayed around the corpulent seal. The soldier was honoring the giraffe with a long inspection, and seemed, viewed through the gaudy bars of the beast's legs, confined in a cage. One must be Quentin, one Irene and one Captain Sylvester Morgan.

But who was the fourth? Who?

When the logical answer occurred to me, I plucked a linen handkerchief from my reticule—no easy task, as I had taken to wrapping the cords twice around my wrist since the attempted theft—and buried my face in it.

The fourth in our game of hide and seek must be: Sherlock Holmes! Now I must conceal my identity. No doubt Dr. Watson had alerted him to the cobra in swift enough time for the detective to discover where our cab had taken us and follow me from the hotel this morning.

My face muffled in white linen embroidered with love knots, I sneezed delicately from time to time and shuffled along to the next cabinet, which featured an array of goggle-eyed lizards.

Someone bumped into me from behind.

I whirled, one hand clutching my reticule, one clasped to my mouth and nose.

The retired soldier stood there, ramrod straight, his features florid against the snowy frame of his muttonchops and mustache, his eyes in the shadow of a jaunty straw boater a very familiar hazel.

I felt the hand with the handkerchief sinking into a sea of surprise and confusion. My mouth opened to say the only possible thing, which was "Quentin . . ."

"Kweh . . . kweh . . . kweh," I began, only catching myself in time at a sudden warning cramp in the very pith of my being. I must not betray his true identity! "Kweh-choooo!" I declared, muffling my face again.

A long, dark tube like the barrel of a rifle thrust through the fraudulent foliage of the thick, junglelike display in which a half-dozen jeering monkey faces perched.

Another figure crashed into us. I reeled as the retired soldier moved to catch me. Something sped past my bonnet ribbons. At the same instant, the glass case behind me exploded and a shower of pebbles pelted my back. I recognized the phenomena as issuing from a firearm, but the other museum visitors screeched and milled madly, unsure of what transpired. Amid all this mayhem, someone was again pulling on my poor reticule cords.

"No!" I shouted. "Stop, thief!"

The old soldier collared the lad again. I had an overwhelming sense of what the French (they have their few uses) call *déjà vu.* Over the soldier's shoulder the wizened scholar stared at us and then darted away. The dowager rustled after him at a startlingly efficient pace. A stranger was striding toward us, a black-suited figure with a vertical line of small suns blazing down his coat front and a helmet upon his head. He swelled until he blocked out all the rest.

" 'Ere now," said he in a great authoritarian grumble, putting a firm hand on the soldier's narrow elbow. "We will all come along quietly. This 'ere's a public institution, you know. No disturbances in a public institution."

"Let him go!" I screeched, thinking of Quentin, if he *was* Quentin.

Unfortunately, two "hims" were in custody. The supposed Quentin, startled, immediately liberated the boy, who thanked him by tightening his grip on my reticule, which he had never released, and turning to run.

Unfortunately, I had bound it to my wrist all too well. I lurched forward, my feet slipping on shards of shattered glass. I found myself falling toward the sparkling, diamond-strewn floor.

I was arrested in my plummet by a strong arm around my waist, even as the bobby leaped to snag the wretched urchin with the law's long arm.

"Thank you." I adjusted my bonnet as the old soldier righted me. "And there is your thief," I told the bobby while I unwound my snarled reticule and glared at the captive boy.

"You'll all 'ave to come along to the magistrate," the bobby returned in the bored tones of a policeman used to all sorts. "We'll need testimony. And someone's got to pay for that spoiled glass. Was it a slingshot done it, lad?"

His captive squirmed and hunched and muttered unintelligibly.

The soldier was eyeing the blasted cabinet with a sober expression, then caught my glance. Quentin he was! I knew it now. He must not, of course, be forced to name himself to any official. His current identity would no doubt melt like a vanilla ice under the hot regard of the law.

"Come then," the bobby urged, his thick black mustache, most ill trimmed, vibrating with emphasis. " 'Onest citizens must do their dooty, or wot kind o' an example is set for lads like this?"

I would have resisted strongly, save that the sullen lad looked up suddenly from under the brim of his tweed cap and said, "Oh, give it up, Nell; you'll ruin everything if you cause a fuss now."

I would have recognized the unadulterated, bell-like tones of Irene Adler anywhere, even in the Museum of Natural History and Modern Curiosities, and even when she was sounding utterly annoyed with me.

Chapter Twenty-Four

FORAGING AT FORTNUM'S

The bobby rushed all three of us into a four-wheeler outside the museum. I was unsure by whom to be the more amazed—Quentin Stanhope in the guise of a retired soldier, or Irene Adler as the boy in the disreputable cap.

"Irene, is that you?" I demanded the moment I was seated within the dim interior.

"Of course." She flung herself into the vehicle after Quentin and me, then immediately strained halfway out the open window again. "If I had not been so efficiently restrained, I could have followed Tiger—but it is too late now. We must lose no time in being off! Oh, where is Godfrey?"

"I have no idea, Irene, but I do believe that this bewhiskered old gentleman is Quentin."

Irene flung herself into the seat opposite to regard him. The inspection was intensely mutual.

"It had better be Quentin Stanhope," Irene noted at last, "else we have the honor to share a four-wheeler with Sherlock Holmes, which would suit none of us at the moment, I think."

"Who is this impertinent boy?" the perhaps-Quentin demanded, turning to me. "And why do you keep calling him 'Irene'?"

The streetside coach door opened at that awkward instant,

and in bounded the bobby. "Chelsea, and be quick about it," he shouted over his uniformed shoulder to the driver as he sat.

"Chelsea?" I demanded in shock.

"We must mislead pursuers," Irene answered as, ahead, the reins snapped over the horses's hindquarters.

The carriage gave a fearful lurch, and we began to rattle over the cobblestones at a smart pace. The motion jolted the Disreputable Cap askew on the Disreputable Boy's head . . . and down fell the rich lengths of gilt-tinged brown curls I had envisioned revealing the previous day.

"It is Mrs. Norton!" exclaimed the old soldier beside me, thus sealing his identity.

"Only yesterday you were simply a miserable street lad!" I complained bitterly.

Irene smiled through her filthy ragamuffin's face. "Yesterday I was a Covent Garden flower girl," she corrected me. "Since you so thoughtfully demonstrated that the young thief was utterly authentic in front of so many crucial witnesses, it made the perfect, foolproof guise today. Thank you, dear heart."

"I suppose I am the fool against which it was proof," I said.

"Oh, no. I rather hoped it would be Captain Morgan and Mr. Holmes. We shall soon see." She pressed against the window and peered out. "No hansom in apparent pursuit, but smugness is premature." She rapped the roof of the carriage and shouted, "On to Brixton after you reach Chelsea, and drive like the wind incarnate. There's a half-sovereign in it."

She sat back and beamed at the bobby, who had remained a dark, silent presence in our midst. "I hope you do not mind my borrowing a page from your book, my dear."

At this Quentin turned his dignified head to glare at the bobby. I studied the policeman's eyes under the helmet brim, the slightly aquiline nose that bridged helmet and mustache, the chin strap that slashed across his cheek to the tip of the chin, much altering the features. . . .

"Godfrey?" I attempted.

He doffed his official headgear with a bow. "For God and country and Sir Robert Peel."

"Well." I sat back feeling very put upon. "It appears that I am the only person in honest guise among you. Would any of you care to explain?"

"It is Mr. Stanhope who has the real explaining to do," Irene said a trifle sternly, "and much of his explanation is owed to you, Nell. But Godfrey and I will unburden our deceptive souls first, because it is such fun to reveal the moves of a game once the object has been won."

"And what is the object of your game, Mrs. Norton?" Quentin inquired stiffly.

"You," Irene replied with an urchinlike grin. Her expression and tone sobered as she continued. "The ensuring of your bodily safety, as well as that of the distinguished Dr. Watson. Also the uncovering of the plot that enmeshes you both in death and deception, so that your futures can be secure. And the disarming of the villainous and implacable nature behind this scheme that has unwound for nearly ten years. And lastly, my object is the well-being and peace of mind of my dear companion, Miss Penelope Huxleigh, who has come to expect from a gentleman a private explanation rather than a hasty departure by night."

I would have thought it impossible for the old soldier's florid complexion to flush further, but it did.

"Miss Huxleigh's safety and that of yourself and your husband were my sole concerns in Paris," he said. "Hence my abrupt departure. You have no idea of the dangerous waters into which you plunge, Madame."

"Do you?" Irene asked with a wicked gleam in her eye. "And I think a liquid analogy does not become a matter which began in arid Afghanistan."

"Yes, this did begin with attempted murder years ago in Afghanistan. Now more of the same erupts in Paris and London. The situation is far too volatile for new and uninformed players in the game, as you call it."

"Oh, fiddlesticks, Quentin. The Great Game between England and Russia has been waged on the steppes of Afghanistan for decades. While you play the noble spy and tell half-truths and melt into the shadows, the real villain is getting away with murder. What do you know of the Indian gentleman who died of cobra venom in your Montmartre lodgings?"

"Dalip is dead?" Quentin performed the impossible again and paled beneath his greasepaint choler. "By cobra bite?"

Godfrey bestirred himself at the sight of a fine point slithering free. "Cobra *venom.* A cobra was on the premises, but was not the source of poison. Irene shot it."

"Good God." Quentin turned to her in wonder.

"Only after Nell had alertly pointed it out to me," Irene admitted modestly.

Quentin turned to me in even greater disbelief.

"The room was quite dim," I explained. "I only saw a . . . swaying silhouette, but Irene had her revolver and so—"

Quentin abandoned his upright military posture and let himself thud back against the tufted leather cushions with a stunned sigh. "Poor Dalip. A sepoy soldier at Maiwand, and my sole friend in the years after. I begin to feel my supposed age. Do you mean to say that you two ladies were alone in my Montmartre quarters with a cobra and a dying man?"

"He was dead by the time we arrived, Quentin," I assured him. "It was perfectly proper."

"What was most improper," Irene said, retrieving something glittering from her urchin's garb, "was leaving this token behind in Neuilly. You cannot outrun your past, Quentin."

He hesitated before taking the small golden object Irene extended. "Medals make a tawdry memorial for the costs of Maiwand."

"Medals are not made to memorialize the dead, my dear man," Irene told him, "but to remind the living of just those costs. If you choose to give it away, I hope you would do it for better reason than that it weighs heavily on your memory."

His closing fingers eclipsed the small glimmer. "Perhaps you are right. Mementos must be tended gladly, not outrun. I will keep it—for now—as a remembrance of my last peaceful days, in Neuilly."

"What is the plan now?" Godfrey asked in the lengthening silence.

Irene rubbed her grimy face with her hands, a sign more of mental fatigue than a desire for cleanliness. "We must return to Brown's and change hotels. Obviously, Nell was followed to and from it. Nell, since you alone are yourself, you must handle the transfer. Once we have found new headquarters we can restore ourselves to normal, and then compare notes."

Godfrey groaned. "Must we change hotels? That is much to ask poor Nell to stage-manage alone."

"Indeed," I seconded him.

"Unless you care to find a sleeping cobra as a foot-warmer, I suggest that we do so immediately."

No one objected after considering this argument, and the confused driver was instructed to make his way to Piccadilly. How I arranged for payment and the packing and transfer of Godfrey's and my things to the waiting carriage does not make for absorbing reading even in a diary. Let me state merely that I managed it.

"Now, where is Irene staying?" I asked when our luggage was finally piled atop the four-wheeler and I had joined the other three within it.

A silence. "Well?"

Godfrey answered. "Irene was staying with me, Nell."

"With you? From the very beginning? Then that is why you insisted that I required a sitting-room suite, and why our conferences were always held in my room! My sitting room, that is," I added with a quick glance at Quentin. "It was utter deception from the first."

"I am afraid so," Irene said with no compunction. "And great fun it was. Hovering about unbeknownst to you was most amusing." Her expression grew misty-eyed. "There is no place like London for surreptitious following. These grim gray buildings and narrow streets and byways, the gaslit evenings when fog becomes one's uninvited accessory. The broad boulevards, sprawling public buildings and all the electricity of Paris cannot hold a candle to it!"

Godfrey cleared his throat, a favorite courtroom signal of his for attention. Irene reluctantly shook herself out of her reverie, sending more locks of hair cascading over the shoulders of her ragged jacket.

"I digress," she admitted. "Well, Mr. Stanhope, shall we repair to your lodgings for the time being?"

"My—?" He glanced at me askance. "They are not suitable for ladies."

"Wonderful! Where else would such a desperate character as yourself go to ground? I do so long to see them!"

"Truly, I cannot allow it," the poor man said. "A fellow who has lived in the squalor of India or in the wilds of Afghanistan may camp out in a metropolitan sinkhole, but ladies . . . see here, Norton, can you not talk her out of it?"

"Not a bit," Godfrey answered. "Besides, I am curious myself."

"But Miss Huxleigh—" Quentin finished with a plea in my direction.

"—lived in Saffron Hill with me in the early 'eighties," Irene pointed out. "We are both adapted to the Bohemian life."

"Saffron Hill was merely a foreign section, not beyond the pale," he argued. "I am mortified enough as it is that you saw the garret I occupied in Paris."

Irene clasped her hands as if about to deliver a most heart-wrenching aria. "It was superb, my dear Quentin. Quite perfect for a setting in *La Bohème*. You underestimate the attractions of the tawdry. The romanticism. The adventure."

"You *are* speaking of that unspeakable garret in Montmartre?"

"Indeed. Where else could a civilized woman go to shoot a cobra?"

"The salon of Sarah Bernhardt," I interjected in acid tones.

Quentin laughed. "She has got you there. Even I have heard of La Bernhardt's menagerie."

Irene refused to be ruffled. "If I am to shoot a cobra, which I really do not wish to do unless it is a matter of self-defense, I certainly would not want to do it in a drawing room. No. A garret in Montmartre provides the proper artistic ambience. When you know me better, Quentin, you will understand that the proper artistic ambience is always a major consideration with me. Now, tell this most impatient driver where to take us. I do hope it will be interesting."

First, however, Quentin and I were ejected at nearby Fortnum & Mason's in Piccadilly near Duke Street, under orders to return with enough comestibles for an impromptu luncheon at our destination. Godfrey showered me with pound notes before we descended from the carriage, and soon we were wandering the impressive aisles in canyons of piled tinned goods from the world over.

"Mrs. Norton is right," Quentin murmured to me once we were inside the famous emporium. "I owe you an explanation, and an apology. But I must ask why we have been delegated to feed our party."

"We are the least likely to attract undue attention, as we are the most respectable-looking of the quartet. I know Irene's methods. An urchin and a bobby would hardly be shopping partners at Fortnum and Mason."

"And you and I?"

I glanced at his most successful disguise. "A retired colonel, widowed, on an outing with his . . . spinster daughter."

"Not a retired colonel, widowed, on an outing with his second wife?"

I could have sworn that there was a teasing gleam in the pale eyes under the bushy white eyebrows.

"Mine is the more likely assumption. Besides, I have never been anyone's first wife, so I should not know how to enact a second one. Oh, really, I do not know what to buy." I gazed at a depressing display of tins with French labeling. "Irene loved this goose-liver mess in Paris, but I cannot abide it. Do choose what you want to eat. I have quite lost my appetite."

"Are you ill?"

"No! Merely . . . feeling a fool."

He laughed and smoothed his full, white and totally false mustache. "How do you think I feel? My clever plan to approach you without attracting notice apparently drew a full house. Now I am compelled to draw you all further into my sordid life—"

"Oh, you must not think of it that way! Irene is right, you know, in her maddening way. Interesting people often lead . . . irregular lives. I suppose I notice that because I am not interesting."

"My dear Penelope, I cannot tell you how interesting you are to me. Norton has his hands full with Mrs. Norton, I see."

"I do not believe that he would have it any other way, Quentin." We had begun walking down the aisles, Quentin taking my arm, or rather leaning upon it in what I chose to consider quite a fatherly way as befitted his semblance. "I suppose we do not want any tinned peas? No."

"Your friend Mrs. Norton does not strike me as one highly enamored of tinned peas."

"You must call her 'Irene,' as I do, and she has asked you to."

"I prefer calling her Mrs. Norton," he said.

"Then you must take the state of matrimony very seriously." I was suddenly aware of what a personal intrusion this comment was.

"Not necessarily," he returned easily, "but calling such an exotic woman as your friend by the utterly commonplace name of 'Mrs. Norton' amuses me."

The warmth in his eyes unnerved me, and I fell back on my best governess behavior. "I am afraid that you are amused by very trivial matters."

"All amusement is trivial, Penelope. That is why there is so little of it in learned books."

"Does 'Miss Huxleigh' amuse you?" I made my next, bold offer rather breathlessly. "Otherwise, you may call me 'Nell.' "

"And will you call me 'Stan'?" he asked so gently that I was quite undone and spoke more sharply than I meant, spoke in the most contrary tone to what I felt.

"I think not."

"You see, commonplace names do not suit us; we are too ordinary to begin with. We shall have to go a long way before we do anything so dignified that it would be droll to call us by nicknames. But I would be delighted to call you 'Nell.' "

His logic had become convoluted, or else I was too distracted to follow it. I would have thought that he was mocking me, were it not that a man whose life is in danger, it seems evident, will not stoop to frivolity . . . or flirting. Of course he meant nothing by it, but our chitchat did not settle the matter of what we should eat. I told him so.

"Why then," said he, "we must outfit ourselves." With that he steered me to the picnic hampers—great, wicker contrivances large enough to house a dozen cobras—and told the gentleman in morning coat who attended us that he wished a good supply laid within of game pies, lobster, prawns, smoked salmon, Parma ham, sandwiches, Stilton cheese and (unfortunately) *pâté de foie gras*, as well as champagne and a trifle for dessert.

"We must celebrate our reunion," he said with a grin at the clerk and a wink at me. Old age apparently entitles a gentleman to all manner of liberties.

Godfrey's pound notes vanished as if swallowed by anacondas, but the hamper was soon full and fitted out as well with napery, cutlery, pottery, china and crystal. Two men carried it out behind us to the waiting carriage, and if we had desired discretion, it was a vain wish.

"Oh, I am famished!" Irene exclaimed as the booty was set on the floor amongst us, for there was no room atop.

"I am afraid that my lodgings will be less appetizing," Quentin said, "but I have given the driver the address."

"You have not been followed there so far?" Irene asked. "You are sure?"

"I am alive," he answered wryly. "No, I have been doing the following these latter days, and busy work it is, too."

"You must tell us more." The backs of Irene's graceful fingers tapped Godfrey's breast pocket, a familiar gesture to me, but new to Quentin. He watched Godfrey produce a cigarette case with lucifers stored in the side, then offer Irene an Egyptian cigarette and a lit match.

She soon had swathed herself in an airy scarf of smoke.

"You smoke away from home, Madame?" Quentin, I noticed, always fell back on the French form of address when amazed by Irene. No "Mrs. Norton" then.

"And you do not?"

"Only the occasional cigar."

"I smoke only the occasional cigarette. It helps me to think."

"I would not believe that you require any assistance in that area," Quentin responded.

Godfrey laughed. "There, Irene. You will have to give up all your beloved props, since peerless logic alone makes you fascinating to Quentin here."

"Ne-vair," Irene answered in a perfect imitation of the Bernhardt manner. "Where are we going for our picnic?" she asked Quentin.

"Houndsditch," he said.

"Fascinating," was all Irene said, crossing her arms and lounging in her seat like the rude boy she enacted.

I bestirred myself. "You have said nothing of your own activities."

Her half-shut eyes lifted to me. "No," she said, and let them fall shut again.

I turned to Godfrey, but he was also lost in his own thoughts, looking most uncomfortable in his bobby uniform. Quentin, too, wore an abstracted, exhausted expression. I could not understand how three such energetic people had tired so easily, when I was as fresh as a . . . a nosegay.

The driver required a generous fare when he deposited us at a doorway that resembled something from the more depressing and lengthy fictions of Dickens.

"It is reasonably clean," Quentin said as he stood and looked up at the four dilapidated stories looming above us.

"You are, I presume," Irene said, "on the topmost floor?"

When Quentin nodded, she asked, "Can your landlady be trusted?"

"To a degree."

"Then I propose we leave our baggage in her care on the ground floor. We shall have to find new quarters this evening. In the meantime, we will take the hamper and ourselves upstairs to plot and picnic."

Chapter Twenty-Five

A MESSY PICNIC

The "we" who took the hamper was Godfrey and Quentin, once they had transported our baggage into the dim front parlor of one Mrs. Bracken. This spare, gray-haired, gray-apron-clad figure made me long for the rosy cheeks and flyaway white hair of the landlady who presided over 221 B Baker Street.

The stairs were cramped and dim; I was unhappily reminded of the Montmartre stairway and the creature that met us at the top.

But the one large room, though roughly finished, was dusty rather than dirty. Sunlight slanted through a half-moon window and the chamber had the indolent, secret charm of a lumber room remembered from childhood games of hide-and-seek.

"Excellent!" Irene declared. She whisked the coverlet from the large old bed and spread it on the floorboards as on a close-cropped lawn.

Godfrey was unearthing the treasures of the hamper with the air of a blissful epicure. "By Jove, lobster! And ham."

"Parma ham," I corrected him.

"By Juvenal, then. Roman ham. And an inordinately assertive bottle of champagne." He eyed Quentin with approval, even though his money had underwritten this bounty.

"Cleanliness before gluttony," Irene declared. "We must doff our disguises. Where are your theatrical supplies?"

Quentin pointed to a small table surmounted by a basin and a mirror near the little window. She retrieved a damp square of linen from the tabletop, drew a wooden chair into a shaft of sunlight, and stood behind it, a barber welcoming a customer.

"Come, sit, Quentin. I must be utterly certain of the identity of those with whom I dine. A most creditable job of disguise," she noted as he took the seat. "Had your posture not betrayed you, I should never have recognized you."

"But I took great care to mimic a lifetime of military bearing!"

"Exactly. I knew you had been a military man. Your imitation was too excellent. A retired soldier no longer has to take such pains, and that shows the merest bit—a fine point only an actor would notice. Hmm. The false facial hair and florid greasepaint well served to hide your sunburned skin. . . . You know, I often have used this red paint for lip and cheek rouge, but mixed with white it makes a splendid base for a splenetic gentleman—it also covered your difficulty."

Irene had whisked the crape hair and paint away. Godfrey and I stared at the denuded face of Quentin Stanhope, which looked as if he wore a tawny half-mask over the eyes and nose.

He grimaced at our expressions. "I shaved off the beard thinking to disguise myself, but forgot that the pale skin beneath it had seen no sunlight in many a year. And there was no time to grow another beard."

Irene fetched two small jars from the table, the contents of which she blended in her palm. Then her fingers passed quickly over Quentin's upper face. When they came away, the top half had lightened to match the lower portion.

"Goodness, Irene!" I could not help exclaiming, though I'd seen her perform such tricks with her own appearance. "He looks as if he had never left Grosvenor Square."

She smiled. "Not fine enough to fool a mortal enemy, but sufficient among friends. Next I shall 'shave' Godfrey and then wash myself. Nell we can leave alone; as usual she has done nothing to alter her natural appearance, not even so much as apply a bit of color on the tip of a rabbit's foot."

"I should hope not." I colored quite naturally at this attention drawn to my appearance—or lack of one.

Godfrey had happily removed his overbearing bobby's helmet the instant we were secure in Quentin's lodgings. Calling him to the chair, Irene quickly softened the adhesive holding on his dreadful, bristly false mustache, which was the color of a bleached muskrat.

"You too have a wan upper lip, my love," she said when the mustache fell away like a dead rat-tail, rubbing a forefinger over her palm and then passing it under Godfrey's nose. As if by magic his skin color was of a piece all of a sudden.

Irene finished her transformations by rinsing the artistic arrangement of "dirt" from her delicate features. She turned, still clad like an urchin, but angel-faced.

"There. We are a better-looking crew, except for Nell, who was always lovely." Irene collapsed on the coverlet like the street arab she had impostured. "We can discuss our situation while we eat."

Quentin turned to me, gallantly extending his arm. "May I assist you to the floor?"

"You already did that most effectively in Neuilly," Irene pointed out archly.

I blushed like a schoolgirl while Quentin took my hand in his to steady me until I was safely seated on the floor.

"What is 'our situation'?" I asked Irene, bending my knees into a "side-saddle" position to sit more comfortably. "And why on earth did you suggest that Quentin might be Sherlock Holmes in disguise?"

"Because Mr. Holmes was there, or else I have seriously misjudged his interests and his intelligence!"

"Who is this Holmes?" Quentin asked as Godfrey opened the food containers while Irene and I passed out utensils, plates and goblets.

"Ah!" Irene clasped her now-clean hands in mock rapture.

"Do you hear that, Nell? An innocent who is mine to educate. Sherlock Holmes, dear Quentin, is the foremost consulting detective in Europe—"

"England," Godfrey interrupted sternly.

Irene flashed him a melting look. "Thank you, my dear. What is not debatable is that Mr. Holmes is the greatest master of disguise in—"

"England," Godfrey put in again, opening the champagne with a pop that made me jump.

"In England," Irene repeated docilely. "And by the most delicious of coincidences, he is the dear friend, nay, the former chambermate of the same Dr. Watson who aided you in Afghanistan."

Quentin frowned even as he accepted a large slice of cold game pie from Irene. "You mean that you have found my Watson and that he has a protector?"

"I mean that we have found your Watson and that now he has a barrier against both the assassin and ourselves. So far as I could determine during my own investigations, Mr. Holmes has been engaged on a matter of extreme delicacy. It involves an unfortunate young man who was well placed in the Foreign Office until a violent illness overtook him more than two months ago. I followed Mr. Holmes and Dr. Watson to Woking the day before yesterday and the matter appears to be settled, although after Dr. Watson returned home to Paddington yesterday, Mr. Holmes paid a visit to an extremely discreet and odd establishment called the Diogenes Club. My instincts tell me that the case is not as settled as Sherlock Holmes wishes his old friend to think."

"And this Holmes fellow was at the museum today?"

"Mmm." With great relish Irene was doing something disgusting involving the *pâté de foie gras* and soda crackers. "That means that he was following one of the principals in the case. He was either Queen Victoria's grandmother or the Quasimodo-like scholar."

"And you cannot be sure which one you libel with your suspicion?" Quentin asked.

"I libel neither of them. The other was decidedly the man who has been pursuing you so lethally, and who tried to murder Dr. Watson through the intervention of an Asian cobra."

"Good God!" Quentin would have started up, except that Godfrey had filled his hand with a brimming flute of champagne, which he quickly downed as if it were pale ale. "*He* was there? You cannot know what you say, Madame."

"Indeed I can. I have met the gentleman."

"What gentleman?"

"The man you fear more than death itself, whom you call 'Tiger.' The man who once called you 'Cobra,' and who reminds you of that fact by using cobras as assassins. Did you ever know his true name?"

Godfrey refilled Quentin's glass, but he sat regarding Irene as if she had suddenly turned into the many-armed goddess Kali.

"You are a sorceress." Quentin watched Irene sip her champagne with a regal air, cross-legged on the coverlet. "No," he answered at last. "I doubt that anyone knows his genuine name. He used many identities, for he was a spy, as I was. How then have you 'met' him?"

"We were introduced at the Paris salon of a friend. Does the name Captain Sylvester Morgan mean anything to you?"

"He could call himself Peter Piper and it would mean nothing to me. How can you be sure we allude to the same person?"

"Because this man is a killer—oh, I speak not in any moral sense. I refer only to his nature. It is as brutally and honestly devouring as that of a shark. I am convinced that he is as adept at that specialty as Mr. Holmes is at problem-solving, as Dr. Watson is at healing, or as I am at singing. Or Nell at blushing, for that matter."

"Irene!" I objected.

"I am hurt," Godfrey put in, perhaps to distract her from teasing me so unmercifully. "You have left out my specialty."

Irene was not contrite. "I am ever aware that Nell records

our doings in her diary; I do not wish to force her into censorship," she said primly, "but you are certainly most agile at the law, too."

Quentin paid not the slightest mind to this banter, but was staring into the single shaft of sunlight as if the dust motes that drifted lazily through it were golden. "How are you so sure that you have met my nemesis?" he asked Irene again.

"For one thing, our meeting with this Captain Morgan occurred after your stay with us at Neuilly. For another, it was arranged by the Empress of Russia, who broke custom to ensure that I would meet her—and especially him, I think. For the last and most damning reason, it was after I slew the snake in your Montmartre garret. This Captain Morgan showed a most persistent interest in my reptilian victim. He wanted the skin. He said that he collects cobras and wanted mine."

Quentin shuddered suddenly. "He wants my skin. He said as much nine years ago, before any of this transpired, that the man who crossed him was . . . tiger bait."

"Not yet," Godfrey noted.

"I presume," said I in a small voice, "that threat applies to women as well."

"Nonsense," Irene said. "Women and doctors are only *cobra* bait, from the evidence so far. And some cobras are very nice indeed." Mortified, I blushed. Again. "One of them saved Dr. Watson's life."

I glanced wildly at Quentin, who was looking startled.

"We have a mystery," Irene announced with suppressed amusement. "Perhaps you can solve this one small matter, Quentin, being an old India hand. Your friend Dalip died of cobra venom, but the cobra that confronted me in that garret was not the snake who bit him. And now Godfrey tells me that the dead snake he found in Dr. Watson's consulting room had not been shot or stabbed, but appeared to have had its neck broken. I believe that you had been keeping watch on Dr. Watson's establishment, that you found the cobra in the consulting room, or saw it introduced there—and disarmed it, shall we say?—before it could harm the good doctor."

"You credit me with too much. I cannot crush snakes with my bare hands," Quentin said evasively.

"But you did have an accomplice, one who has traveled with you since Paris, and before. One brought with you from India, who escaped that fatal Montmartre garret along with you."

"Irene! He has admitted to the company of the dead Indian, but no other. Are you accusing Quentin of lying?"

"Not yet, Nell. He has not yet answered me."

Quentin's hazel eyes narrowed, which only increased his distinguished appearance, in my opinion. "It is impossible to conceal anything from Mrs. Norton. How did you guess—?"

"I never guess, my dear man! I merely put myself in your place, quite literally. I asked myself who and what I might take with me from India for protection from a madman who would use any means to harm me. How, I wondered, would a 'Cobra' protect himself against one of similar cunning and subtlety? Of course the empty milk dish was a clue, though I was misled by the fact that Nell's little green snake, Oscar, drank milk. On reflection I realized that Oscar was an aberration and only warm-blooded animals drink milk, so the resident of the vacant cage was unlikely to be reptilian."

Quentin made a resigned gesture, then rose and approached the dilapidated trunk at the foot of the bed. He threw off a torn scarf and opened it, bending to withdraw something—a boa of sorts, a dark fur-piece perhaps two feet long . . . that wriggled!

"Poor little beast." Quentin stroked the object he held. "The trunk admits air enough to keep her alive, but it is not home. I had to leave her cage behind in Montmartre. She had killed the first cobra, but I never dreamed that a second was still loose to slay Dalip when he came in after I'd left. Out the window and over the rooftops we fled together with a sack of my belongings and money. I did not want my absence to cause a stir, so I took the cobra's corpse with me."

Irene's eyebrows raised. "And—?"

Quentin looked sheepish. "I . . . deposited it in a handy drainpipe. This one"—he stroked the dense, coarse fur—"rode inside my tunic front, which she likes to do. I've had her for many years."

He placed his pet on the floor, a long, low, weasel-like creature with clever clawed paws. It pattered swiftly to our picnic, thrusting its ratlike snout among the remains of the game pie.

"Oh, the darling!" Irene laughed and applauded. "I've never seen one. Does she bite?"

"Only to eat," Quentin replied wickedly.

"How would she kill a cobra?" Godfrey asked.

"With speed, daring and skill. She darts in and out at a great rate, teasing the snake until its guard is down. Then a quick twist and a pounce, and she is behind it, the snake's head caught in her tenacious teeth. A proper shake, and the cobra's skull is cracked, with one bite."

"Ah!" Irene sat back and nodded. "Rather like a rat terrier. I thought so. You see, Nell and Godfrey, that explains the deceased cobra in Dr. Watson's consulting room. One must set a thief to catch a thief. In this case it took a Cobra to forestall a cobra's killing: a human Cobra and his pet mongoose."

"Is that what this is?" I inquired carefully. I dared not move, as the creature was nuzzling my lace-edged sleeve.

"Her name," Quentin said, "is Messalina. I call her 'Messy' for short."

"That is undoubtedly true," I noted, watching the animal overturn a tin of Irene's beloved *pâté* and lick it clean. "And Irene guessed its existence from an empty milk dish?"

"And from the empty cage, which we first assumed had been used to contain the snake," she said, handing Godfrey a fresh tin of *pâté* to open. "But if the cobra had been imported to the premises in order to kill someone, why leave the evidence of the cage behind? Therefore, the cage must have belonged to another—and now missing—animal. Besides, I could not envision Quentin traveling with a cobra, a rather large and infamous snake to conceal, whereas a mongoose might be mistaken for a weasel or a monkey, and accepted as a pet in the poorer quarters he haunted. Still, having the creature forced him to seek even tawdrier lodgings than his finances or inclinations required."

"She is a remarkable creature," Quentin said fondly, offering Messalina a bit of boned chicken. "To see her dance with a cobra is to watch an ultimate exercise of beauty and terror. I often feel pity for the cobra."

"A misplaced emotion," Irene declared, waving about a *pâté*-smeared cracker, "in a world where cobras abound and mongooses are far too rare. Now that you have finally introduced your accomplice, you must tell me everything you know or guess about this Tiger. Hold nothing back. You do realize that the mysteries of the Montmartre garret reveal him to be a formidable opponent who will stop at nothing?"

"How so?" Quentin asked.

"Surely you have reconstructed the sequence of events that produced the dead cobra you found, and later left your friend Dalip dead of venom not administered by a snake, as well as a second cobra hidden to attack Nell and me when we arrived after you and Messy had fled."

Quentin was most sober, almost stunned. "No, Madame, I have not."

"Ah." Irene wriggled happily into a more comfortable and therefore less ladylike position on the coverlet. "Allow me. Tiger, seeking your death and unaware of your association with poor Dalip and the mongoose, entered your garret while you were out and left two cobras to ensure your demise. Before he could release them, he was surprised by the return of Dalip, overpowered him, and resorted to a more sinister method of administering venom: via human snake."

"Tiger is poisonous?" I exclaimed, for I would put nothing past this abhorrent man.

"Not quite literally, but almost. Twice he has used an air rifle to attack Quentin: once in Neuilly and now again in the

Museum of Natural History and Modern Curiosities. A famed heavy-game hunter would have a mastery of weapons, would even invent his own. I posit that Tiger has applied the spring-loaded mechanism of the air rifle to a smaller and more subtle form, one that can be silently and discreetly used at close quarters—"

"By Jove!" said Godfrey, sitting up. "Quentin's poisoning near Notre Dame—a spring-loaded syringe of sorts!"

Irene nodded sagely. "And the same weapon was used on Dalip, to preserve two full measures of cobra venom for Quentin. Of course Tiger could not know of Messalina."

Quentin nodded. "I kept her cage in the trunk, but I found it open when I returned. When I saw the dead cobra, I knew she had escaped in her frenzy to confront the creature; she is clever. But I never saw Dalip dead. . . ."

"My dear Quentin, Nell and I barely noticed him in that dusky garret. I assume the second cobra could have been dormant for some reason, and hidden."

"Or hiding," Quentin added. "It had seen its fellow killed by a mongoose and would not wish to repeat the ritual."

"This Tiger must be the very devil," I finally put in, "to so cold-bloodedly kill poor Mr. Dalip!"

Irene for once agreed with my estimation of someone's character, and looked severely at Quentin. "That is why you must be absolutely frank with me now, my friend. Tiger has already marked me and mine for his loathsome interest. I cannot afford to tangle with the likes of Sherlock Holmes while only possessed of a smattering of the truth."

"What I know is only half-truths and suspicions," Quentin said.

"They were enough to have stirred you out of Afghanistan," Godfrey pointed out. "We are all endangered now. And the first explanation you owe is to Nell."

"Not at all!" I objected in confusion. I would never aspire to claim that Quentin Stanhope "owed" me any attention whatsoever, nor could I bear to have him think that I so presumed.

"Godfrey is right," he said with a level look at me. "I fell upon your hospitality, upon your friendship, like a starving wolf, and then absconded at the first opportunity. You must understand my state of mind. I was ill when I met you, and half poisoned, if Mrs. Norton's theory is credible. Further—" he regarded me with a troubled gaze "—I had encountered unexpected forces from my past. It was as if I was awakening from a dream that had lasted for almost a decade.

"First my life was attempted in Afghanistan, after years of safe obscurity. Suspicious that the attempt stemmed from the sad events of the past, I attempted to trace this Dr. Watson through the military and medical records, and found that another had been there before me, and had abstracted those very documents." Quentin glanced sharply at Irene. "You are not the only person to become addicted to a mystery. I became uneasy in my soul to think that this Watson's life might be sacrificed because I was moldering in obscurity in Kandahar. I came west, but apparently did not come unnoted. That is why I left Neuilly, Penelope; my self-exile, once voluntary, was fast becoming necessary, enforced by a lethal threat that could destroy all that I knew and loved should I attempt to see England again. The shot from the garden was a reminder that there is no rest for an outcast."

"But why?" Irene was adamant. "You admit that the events that cause these attacks today are almost a decade old. What does this Captain Morgan stand to lose that he would resort to such desperate ploys—and to attempt to slay by the means of a cobra an associate of the foremost detective in—" she caught Godfrey's implacable eye "—er, England?"

"If Morgan is the man I knew as Tiger, he has been abroad. He may know nothing of your Sherlock Holmes."

"I am sure that by now the reverse is not true. Pity the man or woman who attracts the concentrated attention of Sherlock Holmes. Holmes will not rest until he knows everything, once he is convinced that serious matters are involved. Morgan's bizarre attempt on Dr. Watson's life, as well as your equally exotic counter to it, have truly stirred a sleeping cobra."

"He is an enemy of yours, this man?"

"Call him rather a competitor," Godfrey suggested. "Still, Irene treads a fine line. To the European public she is dead. Her presence in London compromises her privacy, and perhaps her safety."

"You have not said why Mrs. Norton must conceal herself."

"Nor have you said why someone would wish to kill Dr. Watson and yourself," Irene pounced.

Quentin had the grace to look abashed.

"I have crossed swords with a king," Irene said. "Oh, not literally, but in a matter of will. He is not a very important king as kings go, but in his little corner of the world his will is law, and he is not used to having it scoffed. He is not likely to forget it. Sherlock Holmes was his agent in England, where our . . . duel ended. Neither the king nor Mr. Holmes got what he expected—or wanted. Therefore, it behooves me to avoid drawing the attention of either, that is all."

Quentin stroked the mongoose, which had settled near him, its glossy sides panting with the excesses of freedom, which included devouring all the remaining smoked salmon, the last bits of lobster, and the Parma ham, as well as the first tin of *pâté*. "Turnabout is fair play. I tell you my suspicions only because you have encountered risks on my behalf. It was to spare you all that I left Neuilly so rudely. Since you have not allowed me the privilege of disappearing, I agree that you are too involved to remain ignorant. Yet I am not sure where the significance may be found in my tale."

I shifted my position for what promised to be a long recital. My knees and ankles were aching and one foot had gone completely numb. However Bohemian it may be to lounge on garret floors drinking champagne and gobbling lobster in the company of a mongoose, it is exceedingly hard on the lower extremities.

Quentin Stanhope rubbed the back of his neck with his

hand, but his hazel eyes seemed fixed on a distant place and time despite whatever discomfort he felt in the present. Irene leaned forward to offer me a half glass of champagne. I took it, hoping it might have a medicinal effect on my sorely tried joints. I did not want to miss a word of Quentin's testimony.

Godfrey leaned forward in his turn to offer Quentin a cigarette from his case, and of course then Irene must have one, and there must be an intricate ceremony of lucifer lighting and cigarette lighting and lucifer snuffing and cigarette inhaling, and I must end up smothering in clouds of smoke like an explorer in a camp of Wild West Indians. . . .

"Please," I suggested, coughing discreetly, "may we get on with it? I am eager to hear Quentin's story."

"Spoken like a true adventurer," he said with a smile. And then he sighed. "You have heard me confess that I had a facility for native languages and that this skill drew me deeper into the landscape than my superiors approved. Yet they were eager to employ me as a spy, and I confess that I preferred that work, despised as it was, to my ordinary camp duties."

"You must harbor a streak of the actor in you," Irene said, "and acting under the threat of discovery and death must add an excitement that even the most adoring audience cannot provide."

He nodded. "I took a perverse pride in going among the natives, be they Indian or Afghan, as one of them. This man Tiger was a British officer in India who also had a taste for dangerous assignments. He would don native dress, as I did, but his aim was to slip through their lines, not to mingle with them. He ranged Afghanistan from the barbaric Russian cities on the northern border to the eastern skirts of China and south to the cool hill country of India. He had a wicked reputation as a hunter of dangerous game. He was older than I and my senior as a spy. The command trusted him implicitly."

"You did not." Irene blew a soft plume of smoke into our midst.

"No."

"Why were spies needed?" I asked. "Surely the Afghanistan troops were not so sophisticated."

"Afghanistan is the greatest sinkhole of skulduggery on the globe. It has been considered a 'land' for barely a century, being little more than a loose alliance of squabbling tribes and lawless brigands. Its ruling families are fraught with brother slaying brother, father betraying son, and vice versa," Quentin added. "Oriental politics are intricate and utterly vicious. The loser may sacrifice not only his life, but first his eyes, his ears, nose, hands, feet, even—most brutal torture of all—his beard, which is holy to Allah."

"Even," Irene added, "more delicate appendages, I imagine."

"*I* cannot imagine. What appendages?" I put in.

"We are speaking of savagery beyond imagining, Nell," Godfrey said quickly. "I believe that we have a sufficient picture of the scale."

"I do not! They would cut off his ears and his nose, put out his eyes, cut off his hands and feet . . . what else is there to truncate but his beard?"

"His . . . pride," Irene put in. "We were speaking metaphorically, Nell."

"Oh." I still did not see, but did not wish to interrupt the tale for a fine point.

"We did not need to spy only on the Afghans," Quentin went on.

"The Russians," Godfrey suggested. "They have spent several decades dancing all over that region trying to get their bearclaws into India."

"Yes, exactly. And while the Russians are not quite as savage as the Afghans, they are far more consistent, being a bit less casual about killing off their leaders. So any mischief against our troops was as liable to be plotted with a Russian accent as a Pushto or an Uzbek one."

"Do you speak Russian?" Irene asked suddenly.

"A smattering, but my specialty was the difficult dialects of Afghanistan. As engagement became more inevitable, I was expected to go amongst the enemy and report his numbers and weapons."

"Which you did at Maiwand."

"Yes." Quentin crushed his cigarette in a well-licked *pâté* tin. "Except that the command did not take my report of the Ayub Khan's intimidating number of artillery pieces seriously. We were British, you know, and bound to beat the turbans off these savages who so outnumbered us." He laughed bitterly. "And then I became suspicious of Tiger, who had not been where he had claimed to be, as I knew from my own native contacts."

"Where *had* he been?" Irene wondered with raised eyebrows.

"Tashkent, near the Russian border."

"Just before Maiwand?" Godfrey asked.

Quentin nodded soberly. "I did not like it either, especially since a formidable Russian spy known as 'Sable' was also in Tashkent, and Tiger was the senior spy on the battleground. Then, the day before the battle, Tiger laid a pretty obvious tidbit on my plate, expecting me to run howling back to the command with it."

"Maclaine's supposed betrayal."

Quentin nodded again. "Mac was a friend of mine, unbeknownst to Tiger. Suspicious, I searched Tiger's kit bag and found an odd bit of paper, not really a map but similar to one, with some backwards Russian alphabet markings on it. I took it, meaning to slip it back into his kit later if it proved innocuous.

"Then I went on an errand before returning to camp to confront Mac, who acted as innocent as a Paschal Lamb, as I expected. That was the night of twenty-six July. I had already scouted the immediate area and discovered a secondary, unreported ravine near the one our troops would defend, one at right angles to it. I slipped out of camp to explore further, but when I was digging up my native clothes I was knocked unconscious."

"Oh!" I winced in sympathy.

"A wicked blow," Quentin recalled, lifting his hand to the old wound, "meant to kill. I next awoke to find the ground thrumming beneath me, the sky veiled by yellow dust, and gunpowder perfuming the evil air. Men and horses screamed in tandem. Smoky figures milled in the murk. I viewed a scene from a Renaissance hell. I was frightfully dizzy, and could hardly focus my eyes, but managed to stagger up and head for what English voices I heard. To make a sad story short, I found myself in the ignoble retreat from Maiwand to Kandahar some sixty miles south. We left good guns behind, and horses and camels. And men. I staggered along unnoticed until I finally collapsed. Luckily, I'd gotten far enough from the front lines that some plucky medical officer sprinted to my side through the dust. The Sixty-sixth Berkshires had valiantly stood their ground so that the rest of us could retreat, and this surgeon must have been attached to them.

" 'Water,' I croaked, and he had a canteen of warm spit that helped some. 'Thank you, Doctor—' I knew enough to say.

" 'Dr. Watson,' said he, as if we were meeting in Pall Mall. 'Take it easy, lad, I'll find your wound.'

"Well, I'd bled all down my back, so he naturally thought I'd been shot and spent some time turning me over and finding me whole where I should not have been. The fighting was not hand-to-hand, and my head wound puzzled him when he found it. He seemed more a stickler for the how and why of my wound rather than just the tending of it. I was not coherent then, but I knew the battle had been a disaster. I did not expect to live to tell the true tale of it, so I worked the paper I'd taken from Tiger into the doctor's kit bag. My fingers found a nice little tear in the bottom, the answer to a spy's prayer, though one gets clever in moments of desperation, even when off one's head. I was about to drift into sleep or death or whatever would come when a piece of thunder exploded in my ear and the doctor's fingers slip and he falls down in a faint beside me. Now it is my turn to probe for a wound, and I see that a jezail bullet has sliced into his shoulder. His uniform is slowly soaking as red as my bloody back.

Right shoulder it is, but the heart seems safe. So I use the bandages in his bag to poke over the wound when some young fellow stops beside us.

" 'Tis Dr. Watson!' says he, 'can you help me wi' him, soldier? I have a horse.'

"So it is patient tending doctor, and we two get him belly-down over the poor beast's back. The orderly snatches up the bag and straps it to the saddle, leading horse and doctor off.

"I realize that I must look fairly hale from the front at least, and start walking again for the rear, knowing my paper will stand a better chance of getting to Kandahar and being found than if it was with me. That orderly was a goer, and a horse is better than gold in an out-and-out rout. I truly expected to die," Quentin said, and was quiet.

"Why didn't you?" Irene asked shrewdly.

"Irene!" I remonstrated, shocked that she would speak so.

She ignored me. "The most important part of the story is yet to come, Nell." She leaned forward, the better to fix Quentin with her magnetic eyes. She reminded me of a queen cobra at the moment, bewitching a victim. "Why didn't you die as Tiger intended?"

He stared at her, equally shocked, then he laughed. "Perhaps because I almost wanted to, and Maiwand was not an occasion when I got what I wanted."

Irene, startled, settled back on her coverlet for further interrogations. Like a mongoose, she relished a foe—even a friendly one in a duel of words—capable of surprising her. And like a mongoose, she intended to ensure that she surprised him last.

If Godfrey Norton had one facility that proved invaluable on innumerable occasions, it was his ability to arrange things. Such talents are seldom hailed as they deserve.

Leaving our oddly companionable picnic under the dusty gables, Godfrey vanished into the great maelstrom of London life. He returned two hours later with a fresh carriage and assorted outer garments for our more oddly attired members, namely Irene in her street urchin's rags. In the interim he had also obtained rooms for our party of four. Quentin, Irene and Godfrey said, must reside with them for safety's sake until the threat to his well-being was resolved.

We were whisked to a private hotel in the Strand with as much discreet ceremony as if we had been Cinderellas in search of coronation balls rather than errant cobras and double-dealing spies.

In the company of Irene and Godfrey I often found myself being snatched from the most humble, even disreputable of circumstances to the most glorified. Certainly I never learned more of the world than when I accompanied them, and if I did not always like the nature of my lessons, I could not quarrel with their necessity.

At the new hotel once again I was provided with a sitting room. Irene and Godfrey took a two-bedroom suite that would accommodate Quentin and his trunk as well. I, for one, was relieved that the clever but lethal mongoose remained on the other side of my door.

We met again that evening, all properly attired, in Irene and Godfrey's sitting room. This was a grandiose salon with gilt cornices crowning scarlet brocade draperies and an inordinate number of small tufted settees upholstered in shades of lavender. I finally brought myself to sit upon one of these dollhouse sofas. Quentin joined me, looking utterly urbane in one of Godfrey's city suits, which fit him surprisingly well.

"You have transformed yourself completely," I said in some surprise. "You could walk up to the door of number forty-four Grosvenor Square and enter without a challenge."

He frowned at the familiar address. "You have visited in Grosvenor Square?"

"We had to learn," Irene put in quickly, "whether you had informed your relations of your return."

His face grew remote. "I have made a point of keeping them clear of my miserable affairs for almost a decade. If you have betrayed my existence, my condition—"

"We have not," Irene said in firm tones. "Or rather, I

should say, Nell and Godfrey have not, for they were my emissaries to Grosvenor Square. However, they did learn a useful piece of information."

"Which is?" Quentin was not mollified, and I could not blame him.

"Which is that a certain commanding blue-eyed gentleman called upon them two months ago, seeking news of yourself."

"Two months ago!" Quentin had risen abruptly. "That is before I was attacked, before I even left India. Why did Tiger wait to renew his persecution of me until this time?"

"Because," Irene said thoughtfully, "something of his is at stake at this particular moment. Some . . . scheme which that paper you took from him years ago could harm."

"But that scrap likely does not exist anymore. Tiger is pursuing a phantom. The piece of paper must have been lost in Afghanistan or at Peshawar years ago."

Godfrey nodded. "Dr. Watson lay delirious with fever for many weeks, even months. He does not even recall how a second wound to his leg occurred. Certainly his medical bag was taken from him during this illness, or more likely was destroyed during the month-long siege of Kandahar."

"Still, it may survive," Irene said. "We have little else to pursue. In fact, unless we wish to wait for Captain Morgan to find us and subject us to more reptilian chambermates, we shall have to resort to desperate measures at once."

"How desperate?" I asked dubiously.

She sighed and shifted upon the overupholstered love seat she occupied alone, like Sarah Bernhardt reclining on her polar-bear-pelt-strewn divan.

"Some of us," Irene answered, "will have to return to Paddington and search Dr. Watson's residence."

"Some?" I pursued with foreboding.

"I have not decided who will execute this delicate task," Irene said airily.

"I will go," Quentin said manfully. "I can identify the bag."

"No," Irene answered, "you will not."

"And why not?" I asked indignantly on his behalf. Irene

was entirely too high-handed with virtual strangers. Godfrey and I were used to serving as milady's equerries, but Quentin had never enlisted in her army.

Her warm golden-brown eyes, all innocent inevitability, regarded me. "Because anyone who ventures near Dr. Watson risks seeing Sherlock Holmes, or worse, being seen by him. And that would be ruinous, since in the near future Quentin Stanhope will be in Baker Street consulting with Mr. Sherlock Holmes on precisely the problem that faces us."

Chapter Twenty-Six

A BRACE OF BURGLARS

"**The matter** involves Afghanistan, I presume," my friend Sherlock Holmes pronounced as he viewed the dead cobra beneath my desk. "You have not moved it?"

"Not a bit. I know your methods."

"Hmm. Someone has, and rather rudely." Holmes wriggled farther under my desk, lost in that utter concentration that any sort of mystery evoked in him. "There also has been someone sitting at your desk, Watson."

"Someone sitting at my desk?"

"A woman with a small foot attired in a boot, not new, with the heel worn evenly. Most unusual, one might even say irregular. A preternaturally well-balanced lady. A Turkish rug is better than fresh-mown grass for absorbing slight imprints. I see that your leg has been bothering you again, for the shoe that leaves the lighter impression has been most active . . . Were it not for the interesting marks behind the head, I'd say that you yourself had kicked the snake to death. A pity that you did not apprise me of this situation sooner."

This was unjust. "It was not discovered until the girl came to clean this morning, and after all, you were not in until evening yesterday."

Holmes emerged carefully from under my desk, his thin cheeks flushed from his efforts and the compelling oddity of the mottled souvenir. "I had some tidying up to do in the naval-treaty affair. How is Mrs. Watson taking this intriguing discovery?"

"She, of course, had a thrilling introduction to the world of mystery and crime in 'The Sign of the Four,' and—"

" 'The Sign of the Four,' Watson? That is an abstruse figure of speech."

I found myself at a loss, for Holmes had no notion about the extent of my literary recreations of his cases, even to the liberty of titles. "That is to say, the matter of the Agra treasure, in which her late father was involved. Mary, I can report, is absolutely unruffled, although she has no wish to inspect my late . . . visitor."

"Hah!" barked Holmes in an outburst that passed for laughter. "Quite wise on the lady's part. This fine fellow has grown a tad fragrant and had best be removed soon. Now I must inspect the windows."

He went to the casement, magnifying glass in a white-knuckled grip, his sharp features bent to the lens with the intensity of a hound's nose to the spoor.

"Keeping a ground-floor office has its drawbacks. You have had a brace of burglars in the last two days, Watson, although I doubt either of them were London cracksmen in search of remnants of the Agra treasure. Yet each bore something with him—a middling-size box. See where the wood has been rubbed raw? When a man swings one leg and then the next over a windowsill, anything that he is carrying is likely to scrape the frame."

"But what is the point of bringing a poisonous snake into my office, Holmes?"

"The point is all too obvious. The motive is less so." Holmes dropped to his knees before the window and undulated across the Turkey carpet to my desk. "Our number-one man is powerful. Stealthy strides taken far apart. Boots of foreign manufacture—I should say German. Cologne. I see the impress of a most assertive nail in the right front sole. This was our cobra importer. See the line in the carpet where the container rested while our snake charmer prodded it under the desk? The man had no fear of his lethal partner, that is certain."

"I see a small line in the carpet, Holmes, that is all. It could be the tracery of a design element."

"Nonsense, Watson. It is the right front impression of a box two feet in length and, from the depth of the impression, roughly eighteen inches in height. The corner is marked because that is where the man leaned his not inconsiderable weight as he rose again once he had loosed the snake."

"How could he be sure that it would stay hidden beneath my desk?"

"That is elementary." Holmes rose to stalk to the window again. "He simply had to feed it beforehand. Snakes are torpid after eating, but if roused from slumber will strike at the interruption."

"That is what Mary claims that I do following Sunday dinner," I remarked.

"You make light of your uninvited guest, Watson, but its purpose was anything but to amuse," Holmes said sharply. "And what is this in the flower bed outside the window? Traces of a lighter man, one still showing the effects of a recent illness. Note the uncertain footprints. This chap did not advance beyond the window frame. Ah—here is where he set down his casket."

"These men sound more like the suitors in *The Merchant of Venice* than housebreakers, Holmes."

"Their business was deadly serious, Watson. This second fellow does not set toe to carpet, so he suspects the nature of his vile precursor into the room. I refer to the serpent rather than to the human reptile who brought it. And examine the sill, where the new man's fingernails have scored the wood . . . he was well aware of the cobra lying in wait. He must have watched for a while, then left—why?"

"I am sure that I cannot guess, Holmes."

"No, I doubt that you can."

Holmes returned to my desk and began to pull the carpet

from beneath it until the snake's long mottled form lay exposed. He then pored over the corpse, the magnifying glass to his eye.

"You can see where the scales are rubbed against the grain; the tender mercies of your unheeding foot. Do you remember doing this?"

"I remember the carpet being rumpled, that is all."

"Fortunate for you that the reptile was already dead. The bite of an Asian cobra is deadly within minutes."

"Do you mean to say that the first man deposited a dead cobra on my premises?"

"Absolutely not. The creature was alive, and ready to take lethal exception to your habit of rug-kicking, when the first man left it."

"Then the second man killed it."

"From the window, Watson? I have heard of snake charmers, but I doubt even they can induce death at a distance. Think how the annals of crime would swell were such a dread skill added to the murderer's arsenal."

"Then the second man left me to my fate."

"I think not. He managed to disarm the snake somehow. Hmm. Those are tooth marks behind the head."

"Human teeth?" I asked in horror.

Holmes rose from his inspection, his thin lips pursed. "No." He walked to the back of my desk and gazed down at the surface and the empty chair before it. "Nothing was taken?"

"Er, no."

"You sound uncertain."

"Some . . . papers were disturbed."

"What papers?"

"Simply . . . notes I had jotted to myself."

"On your cases?"

"On . . . cases in which I was involved, yes."

"Watson, you are hiding something from me. Out with it, dear fellow. This matter is too serious to allow for anything but total candor."

"I merely noticed that some papers I had lying atop my desk were disturbed, but that was after I had returned to find the couple waiting in my rooms."

"They could have riffled the papers at least, or killed the cobra, though I think that highly unlikely. Who did they say they were?"

"The man introduced himself as a solicitor, Feverall Marshwine. The woman was a Miss Buxleigh, who sought news of her missing suitor, who was lost at the battle of Maiwand."

"Ahhh." Holmes cast himself into my chair. "I knew it involved perfidy abroad."

"Maiwand was a terrible battle, but I doubt that there was much perfidy in it."

"The perfidy is evidencing itself here. Consider the cobra." Holmes pointed eloquently with his magnifying glass to the front of the desk. "And these visitors are most suspicious."

"They seemed quite credible."

"Feverall Marshwine? My dear Watson, that is a childishly obvious pseudonym."

"Why do you say so?"

Holmes smiled thinly. "You often chide me for my patchwork education, but even I know that Feverall Marshwine was a notorious eighteenth-century highwayman."

"I have never heard of him!"

"We each have our areas of expertise. Mine is crime. Rely upon it, Watson. So what did these fictional personages Marshwine and Buxleigh want?"

"Tales of my experiences at the battle of Maiwand."

"Did you oblige?"

"As much as I could. My memory of the disaster is clouded."

"Much like poor Phelps's memory of more recent events. Odd. His dilemma involved a treaty between nations; your puzzle seems to revolve around an old war between nations."

"There can hardly be a relationship, Holmes."

"The more unlikely the possibility of connection, the more

likely the probability. Did this pair of visitors say why they specifically required your recollections of Maiwand?"

"Only that I may have tended the lady's lost fiancé there."

"Nine years is a long time to mourn."

"That is just it. The fellow went off his head and vanished. One Jasper Blodgett."

Holmes raised a dubious eyebrow. "Blodgett. That name is ridiculous enough to be true. Perhaps your callers were innocent, though I am by no means convinced. Certainly the snake was not."

"But nothing came of it, Holmes."

"That does not mean that something cannot come of it. Quite the contrary. Do you have any paper—? Ah, here is some, under the Gray's *Anatomy.*"

"Here is fresh paper." I leapt for the drawer and seized my poor scribblings from the desktop. I put several clean sheets of writing paper before Holmes, while he shook my pen until it drizzled ink.

"Excellent, Watson. That is what is so utterly valuable about you, old fellow. You are prepared for anything. Now pray do not worry about that cobra. I fancy that there is more dangerous human game about, and I vouchsafe I will catch it."

Chapter Twenty-Seven

DR. WATSON'S BAG

On the morrow we had our marching orders.

Godfrey and Quentin set off first thing, bound for the Military Archives to seek records of the military careers of John H. Watson, M.D., Emerson Quentin Stanhope and one Sylvester Morgan.

"What of . . . Grosvenor Square?" Quentin asked before he left.

Irene turned from adjusting her bonnet in the mirror. "I suggest that you not venture there yet, Quentin, unless you wish the residents to come under the closer scrutiny of Tiger."

Quentin nodded, added a plush beaver top hat and cane to his attire, courtesy of Godfrey's well-stocked trunk, and left with a last quizzical look at me. I was swathed once again in the feature-blurring veiling that I had found the simplest and most effective disguise for someone of my theatrical ignorance.

"Do I look suitably demure?" Irene asked me. She did not often request the loan of my clothes. I was astounded to see her in them; the effect was much like confronting a distorted image of myself.

"You will never look demure," I told her.

"Tsk, Nell, I am an actress. I can look like anything I wish."

"Here," said I, going over to assist her. "For one thing, you have tied the bonnet ribbons too successfully. There. Uneven tails and a loop turned inside-out looks much more ordinary. And your handbag straps are not twisted . . . that's better. I do presume you wish to resemble a parson's daughter with no deep abiding concern for the frivolities of fashion?"

"You do presume, Nell," she chided me. "You are not nearly so dowdy as you imply."

"Nearly?" said I.

Irene had swept away from the mirror. "Well?" she demanded.

She had donned my spring gown of Empire-green serge, with cream border stripes that edged her high neck, the mid-forearm-length sleeves, the bodice reveres and the pleated flounce on the hem. All in all a neat and quiet toilette that did nothing for her coloring. The skirt was a trifle too short, revealing two-tone brown spectator shoes tied with dull orange tassels.

"Irene, the shoes are dreadful with that gown!"

She grinned. "I thought so too. And now, for the *pièce de résistance*." She whipped something from her thoroughly utilitarian leather handbag, which I had not seen since it had transported the photograph the King of Bohemia sought to Godfrey's Temple chambers more than a year before. On her nose perched my pince-nez, now accompanied by a brown cord that was affixed to her bodice with a brooch bearing a cheap, foil-backed glass stone the color of tobacco spit.

The indignity done to my spectacles was as nothing compared to the transformation that now occurred. Somehow Irene's posture altered: her shoulders rounded, her bosom sank, her toes pointed ever so slightly inward. A more gawky, unfortunate creature I had not spied since first catching sight of myself next to a full-blown Irene in Wilson's Tea Room windows eight years before.

"How shall I see?" I wailed, that being the only issue I dared address.

"It will not be necessary. Besides, a squint will add a 'character' touch to your portrayal." Irene eyed me critically over the gold-wire frames of my purloined pince-nez. "You will have to be the Lady Bountiful of our pair, while I play the shortsighted church mouse. But you must take care not to put on too grand airs, or the whole effect will be ruined."

"*I*? Put on airs? Irene, what can you be thinking of?"

She paused near the door to snatch up my umbrella, which was plain and black. "Ours is the more delicate mission, Nell. It may even be the more dangerous."

"What could be more dangerous than consulting Sherlock Holmes?" I thought of poor Quentin soon to be sent to beguile the foremost detective in . . . England in the service of some master plan Irene would not disclose.

She lifted the umbrella like a standard and swept open the door into the hotel's dim-lit hall. "Broaching the second-most dangerous woman in London: Mrs. John H. Watson."

"Who is the first, pray?" I inquired.

Irene simpered modestly over the pince-nez. "Myself."

We took the Metropolitan Railway to Paddington. A carriage, Irene said, would attract attention, and we were humble seekers after pence for the poor, unable to afford such grand transportation.

I cannot say I much cared for the ultramodern urban railway. Most of the line ran underground in great steam-choked tunnels, which magnified the racket of the carriage wheels over the tracks to ear-jarring proportions.

What a noisy, dirty method of transport! Yet many respectably attired women milled among the crowds thronging to board these metal monsters.

"Really, Nell," Irene urged cheerfully as an unattractive area of the city sped past during one of our infrequent aboveground transits, "you needn't look so sour until we arrive in Paddington. It is true we are on an ostensible mission of good works, but we do not have to look like it quite yet."

"Nothing good has ever come of a rail journey in my life," I retorted.

She paused to consider. "That is true. First to and from Bohemia under great duress. Then to Monaco, in the company of the Lascar and Jerseyman—" She did not, I am glad to say, mention the incident of the yet-unnamed Oscar and the gasolier. "But the return trip from France was without incident!" she reported triumphantly.

"You did not share my unfortunate encounter with the traveling corset salesman."

Irene looked instantly chastened. "No, that is true. I did not." And she said no more in praise of trains.

Once above ground in Paddington, Irene pulled a small sketch from her large handbag and squinted at it through her—that is, my—pince-nez. "Can you read this, Nell dear? I am not used to spectacles. Godfrey has drawn directions to the Watson residence."

I sighed and took the paper, bringing it to eyelash distance. "It is only a short walk," I determined. "But what is this phrase in French here in the corner? I do not recognize those words. . . ."

"Nothing!" Irene snatched the map back. "Godfrey has a habit of leaving unanticipated messages. I will, er, interpret it later."

Luckily, I had seen the map long enough to commit its simple directions to memory. We set out, attracting little attention. Apparently Irene's transformation was dazzlingly successful.

"I still do not see," I fussed as we neared the Watson domicile, "why you think that the medical bag Dr. Watson carried in Afghanistan is still in his possession, or how you expect to wrest it from him without revealing yourself."

"I do not plan to wrest it from Dr. Watson, but from Mrs. Watson. There is nothing so reliable as a wife's innate instinct to dispose of any articles of her husband's that she believes he has kept for no good purpose for far too long."

"Dr. Watson keeps his office on the premises. He will not permit you past him."

"I will not have to 'pass' him. Now, where is this establishment that is so attractive to cobras?"

I told her that we were about to turn into the proper street; Dr. Watson's house was only three doors around this corner, on the opposite side. She pulled us both to a halt before a chemist's window. While we stared at bunion remedies she doffed the pince-nez and surveyed the quiet thoroughfare.

"I need an idle boy, Nell. Do you see one?"

"Usually the London streets teem with them."

"This is bucolic Paddington, with fewer enterprising urchins."

"Will an idle girl do?" I asked.

Irene turned to regard a young miss attired in a navy-blue sailor dress sitting atop the steps leading to a dressmaker's establishment across the street.

"Even better!" Irene smiled and waved the child over.

The little girl gave one cautious over-the-shoulder glance, then decided that her mother would be occupied for some time and that we, despite our painstaking dowdiness, looked much more interesting. Over to us she skipped, poor lamb.

"Oh, my dear," Irene began, bending down and declaiming in a voice that would wring pity from an oyster. "My uncle is so very ill. I have just stopped at the chemist for a remedy, but he desperately needs a doctor."

The child started to look in the desired direction. "There is Dr. Watson—"

"Wonderful! Now." Irene was scribbling frantically on a scrap of paper, using her handbag for a writing desk. "You must give him this note. It will tell him where to find my uncle . . . Frost. Jonathan Frost. He must hurry! Uncle is having a terrible chill. White as a sheet. And for your trouble—" Irene produced a five-pence piece.

"No, miss," the child trilled. "I'm not allowed to take pay for a good deed."

Off she trotted, all officious, Irene's note clutched in her hand. Irene grasped my arm and bustled me into the chemist's, which smelled of wintergreen and mothballs.

Through the murky window glass facing Dr. Watson's domicile we watched the plain and simple pantomime: child reaching up to ring the bell. Maid answering. Child vanishing within. Child reappearing, sans note. A few moments later, the door opening to disgorge Dr. Watson.

"Hastily, Nell," Irene hissed. "We must both get a good look at the bag. If we have sent him off with the one we want, a different scheme will be necessary." She thrust my appropriated pince-nez at me. I was able to position it in time to see the doctor's bag swinging beside him as he trotted past us toward the underground station.

"Brass!" I gasped.

"What?"

"I saw the glimmer of bright brass fittings. Surely a new bag."

Irene nodded. "I thought so, too. Then we wait until our little miss leaves."

This looked to take some doing. The child had returned to her step across the way. I scouted the chemist's and found some French pastilles—the only thing of French manufacture for which I had developed a taste—but Irene hailed me to the window again.

"Gone inside to watch Mama's fitting at last, thank God."

We scuttled around the corner like thieves, Irene donning my pince-nez again despite my warnings. There are none so blind as those that will not see. Soon we were poised before the door that Godfrey and I had broached but three days before.

I rang the bell. When the maid's broad pale face appeared behind an opening door I recalled that this poor unsuspecting soul must have been the one to "discover" the dead cobra. For a moment I was tongue-tied with shame.

Into the breach leaped the golden tongue of my shameless companion. "Is the master or mistress of the house in? We are seeking donations to St.-Aldwyn-the-Bald's-on-the-Moor. A most worthy cause."

The maid's lips folded in undecided reluctance.

"What is it, Prudence?" came a kindly voice. "The doctor is out on a case," the speaker continued, drawing the door wider to see us and thus revealing herself to be Mrs. Watson.

"That ith quite all righth," I found myself saying, "you would do nithely." Irene had decided that pretending to a catarrh would allow me to press a handkerchief to my lower face, and the concurrent lisp would serve to disguise my voice. All I need do was breathe through my mouth, as I had on one key occasion in France. . . .

"Do?" The poor lady looked utterly puzzled.

Irene made a great business of glancing at the brass plate proclaiming the resident's name and business. "Mrs. Watson, is it? We would most appreciate speaking with you in your husband's absence. We are parishioners of St.-Aldwyn-the-Bald's-on-the-Moor, a church in nearby Notting Hill, which has suffered from a fire."

"Oh, dear." Mrs. Watson frowned at the notion of the mythical fire. "I have not heard of your congregation . . . or your conflagration—"

"Of course not," Irene said sadly. "The fire has grievously reduced our numbers and resources. That is why we must go door-to-door seeking what charity we can."

"I suppose I could—" the good woman began. "But, how rude I am. Come in, ladies."

Thus we entered the Watson house, I for a second occasion. We were led into a charming little parlor, with a lace-covered table in the street-facing window. A stereopticon upon it caught a stray beam of sunlight.

"Now," Mrs. Watson said, once we were seated. She was a tiny, fine-boned woman; it would be unforgivable to lie to her transparent blue eyes. I cringed on both our behalves. "I can spare a few coins—"

"Oh, no!" Irene raised a forbidding hand. "Please. We do not seek money."

"Then how can I help you?"

"If you have some unused item about, something that

could prove useful to our congregation . . . old books, for instance, that you would rid yourself of anyway."

"Books? I do not think John would care to donate those. Nor would I . . . I could never part with my Mrs. Gaskells, or the Waverlys, or Miss Austen . . ."

"Since your husband is a doctor," Irene said briskly to stop what promised to be a complete catalogue, "perhaps you could spare some older medical books, even a medical bag he no longer uses."

Mrs. Watson shook her head. "There is nothing of that sort that I could give away in his absence. You must admit that a husband's possessions are sacred."

"I am sure of it," Irene said.

Mrs. Watson looked politely to me.

"I would nod know." I sniffled sadly into my lacy bit of Irish linen. "I am not married."

"Oh," she said sympathetically. "And you?" she asked Irene.

"Oh, yes. That is why I asked if there were something lying about that you could spare. My own husband is so determined to cling to every old pair of hunting boots or souvenir of his youth, things he would not possibly use in a hundred years! But there it is. Men must have their clutter."

Mrs. Watson smiled. "The doctor is remarkably neat about his possessions. It comes from his sharing lodgings with a bachelor friend in the days before we married. Excellent training."

Irene joined her in a wifely laugh at the expense of the absent spouses. "Your good fortune is our misfortune," she said lightly, rising and blinking pitifully behind my pince-nez. "We must look elsewhere. A cast-off medical bag would be just the thing for parish sick calls, but if you are wed to a wonder of organization we will have to seek elsewhere."

"Wait!" Mrs. Watson cried as we neared the doorway to the passage. "There is some musty old thing at the bottom of the wardrobe. I believe John had it with him in Afghanistan. He has had no earthly use for it since . . . would not even miss it after all this time, I am sure. I will fetch it. If it is in any proper condition—"

"Oh, bless you, Mrs. Watson," Irene murmured fervently (and most sincerely), clasping her gloved hands. "You are an angel of mercy."

The poor woman flew up the stairs, returning shortly with a battered brown leather satchel.

"It is not new looking," she said, turning it over in her hands. "It survived a war, after all. If you think that it would serve—?"

"It will serve magnificently." Irene clutched the flattened old bag to her bosom. "You have no idea how delighted we are to see this. How . . . useful it will be. I vouchsafe to say that you and your husband will walk safer these next few days because of this good deed. Heaven has a way of helping those who help others."

Mrs. Watson's faced showed sudden anxiety. "How odd that you should say that. I have been worried, actually. We had an . . . incident at the house recently. But I'm delighted to help St.-Ethelwed-the-Bold's-on-the-Mire. Are you certain that a monetary donation—?"

"No, no," I said firmly. "To take mere money is begging."

"To take cash is to take trash," Irene paraphrased *Othello* shamelessly, and somewhat disjointedly, on our exit, "but he—or she—who offers hard goods will always have a sterling reputation."

We stood again on the stoop. Mrs. Watson, shadowed in her doorway, still looked puzzled, and even slightly worried. Perhaps the recent incident with the cobra troubled her.

"There is a sign in the Bible," Irene said, abruptly employing a serious tone. "To find a dead snake upon one's doorstep signifies that a powerful protector is watching over you and yours."

"Truly?" Shock paled Mrs. Watson's complexion even more. "How odd you should say that." A sudden smile made that poignant face radiant. "Certainly my husband does have such a benefactor—the most mentally powerful man in London."

"Doubtless the Good Book had other, unseen allies in mind, Mrs. Watson," Irene said, "but an honest soul can never have enough angels on its side."

Chapter Twenty-Eight

SHERLOCK HOLMES'S LAST CASE

Irene spent the next evening brooding.

This she managed with the panache of Sarah Bernhardt on the stage. First she attired herself after dinner in a close-fitting crimson velvet gown of the princess cut. A heliotrope taffeta caftan over her shoulders swept to a wide train in the back and was edged in snowy ermine along the front floor-length reveres.

This garb was ideal for pacing, which she proceeded to do, the hotel's rococo decoration fading to a dull backdrop indeed for her formidable foreground presence. Mind you, I do not claim that this performance was planned; merely that Irene's nature required the properly dramatic setting before her mind could explore its most creative and instinctive territories.

Naturally, she smoked during this exercise, but fitfully, letting the cigarette in its gold-entwined mother-of-pearl holder smolder unheeded in a dish, until a pale length of ash crowned it like an eighteenth-century French lady's powdered wig.

Or she would suddenly seize the holder and her pace would quicken, even as her eyebrows plunged together in a concentrated frown. She would sip swiftly from the delicate holder until her cigarette end burned a constant ember-red. And always wreaths of smoke drifted around her like the fine-net veiling they call "illusion."

She finally stopped, turning at the same time, so her heliotrope train crackled before swirling to rest in a graceful spiral around her lower limbs.

"No doubt you all have wondered what I did today."

We waited attentively, the gentlemen nursing after-dinner cigars whose odor reminded me of burnt burlap. I suffered much in their rank company, but confined myself to embroidering a handkerchief. The one with which I had attempted to clean the actual urchin's face not four days earlier had been sullied beyond redemption.

"Dare we suppose that you have done as Quentin and I, and visited the London shops?" Godfrey said.

I glanced at Quentin, dashing in evening dress like Godfrey, as all good hotel dining rooms required. I had not inquired into the funds for Quentin's outfitting, suspecting one of my friends' quiet but spectacular acts of charity, from which I also had benefited in the past.

Irene sighed. "Not yet, I fear. I wish I had done something as interesting as that; I do not often have the opportunity to shop in London. No, my activities were far more commonplace. I was in Woking."

"Woking again? Whatever for?" I burst out. "That is an excessively idyllic locale for one with your proclivities for mayhem."

Irene smiled at me. "Mayhem is not snobbish about address; it may reside as well behind the moss-grown facade of the manse as the Whitechapel pub. Perhaps you have heard of the Poisoning Parson of Tunbridge Wells."

"No, I have not. I think that you have made that up."

"I? Make something up? Heaven forbid, Nell."

"It often does, but you never listen."

"Do go on, Irene," Quentin said. "I am most anxious to learn what you found so fascinating in Woking, though any place that you would honor with your presence would perforce become irresistible."

Irene laughed heartily. "Clothes do make the man! Put a desperate exile into white tie and tails and he spouts drawing-room hyperbole."

Quentin bit at his infant mustache and smiled shyly. He seemed a stranger in civilized clothes. I found that I actually missed his air of wild incongruity.

Irene laid her cigarette holder in a tray, from which supple ribbons of smoke wafted up like visible incense. She crossed her arms and eyed us with that suppressed excitement that betokens revelations.

"I went to Woking because that is where resides the young gentleman upon whose behalf Sherlock Holmes's most recent efforts have been made. Briarbrae is a most impressive house with extensive grounds, and in it dwell Mr. Percy Phelps and his fiancée, Miss Annie Harrison. Mr. Phelps has been ill and under a great strain, but I had a most pleasant tea with Miss Harrison."

"I do not know how you do it," Godfrey said. "How you persuade strangers to give you not only tea but confidences."

"That is because you were trained as a barrister, Godfrey, and expect people to resist telling you things. I, on the other hand, tell them everything about me. They are so overcome that they reciprocate in kind."

"It is more than that," I put in. "You make it seem that only by telling you everything will they have any possible chance of doing the right thing. It is a pity that women cannot take holy orders; you would make a most effective clergyman."

"It is all a matter of convincing others of an Unreality," Godfrey added. "Clergymen and actors are not so different."

"Be that as it may," Irene said, bringing our attention upon herself once again; indeed, in her flowing, royal-hued gown she did resemble a pagan priestess. "That simple tea in Woking answered an entire menu of questions."

"The first one is why are you concerned about Sherlock Holmes's last case?" Godfrey put in.

She smiled at him in sweet patience, faultlessly acted. "Because it is linked to the matter that Quentin presented to us."

"I?" the man cited objected. "Surely not."

"Surely so," she replied, absently stroking the soft ermine of one revere. "I first sniffed the matter when I followed Mr. Holmes to the Diogenes Club—an extremely intriguing establishment! The membership is gentlemen only, but of course that was no barrier to me."

I sighed pointedly. Quentin, who had seen Irene only as a street boy, not in the full and impressive range of her talents as a male impersonator, looked puzzled.

"I entered the premises," Irene explained, "as a waiter in hopes of a position. I regret to say that I failed to achieve one. It must have been my Italian accent." She shrugged soulfully. "However, I did learn two or three interesting points about the place. The Diogenes Club is one of the oddest, if not the oldest, in London. Members retreat there for utter isolation and silence, not fellowship. Among them is a certain Mycroft Holmes. According to my hasty but thorough reading of the visitor's ledger, this Mycroft Holmes is indeed sought after by the most highly placed men in London, including his relation—a brother, I'd think—Sherlock."

"So after penetrating the Diogenes Club, you next go gadding off to Woking?" I asked.

"Yes. How nicely put. I gadded off to Woking. But first I made a few other trifling inquiries. At the Foreign Office, for instance, I had a long chat with the commissionaire's wife, a rather surly woman. However, once I professed myself a friend of 'poor Percy'—remember, he worked there—she kindly revealed that he had been under suspicion over a 'missing paper.' She also indicated that 'even a decent God-fearin' woman' was suspect in the case, namely herself. She was not treated gently by Scotland Yard, I gather, when she was subjected to a search, always a mistake with the humbler classes. They take offense and are exactly the type to fume and fuss about the matter to all comers."

"That paper sounds like a sensitive document." Godfrey thoughtfully knocked the ash from his cigar into a low dish.

She answered his comment with a question. "How sensitive would you consider a secret naval treaty between England and Italy?"

Quentin looked puzzled. "I have long been ignorant of current foreign affairs, thanks to my sojourn in Afghanistan."

Godfrey pondered the question. "The only interested parties would be those who would lose by the alliance. Perhaps . . . France," he suggested. "Both Italy and France have Mediterranean ports."

"Bravo!" Irene said. "That is exactly it."

"And how did you know this?" I asked her.

She donned a modest expression. "Rumors of this event reached the press last spring. I looked up back copies of the *Telegram* and the *Times*."

"Anyone could do that!" said I indignantly.

"Of course. But would anyone? And would anyone know what to make of this fact as regards our end of the tangle?"

" 'Our' end?" I repeated.

"Ah, you do miss Casanova, Nell, but I do not require an echo at the moment. There is another nation, as well, that would squirm at news of any such English alliance abroad, and that is her ancient enemy in another quarter of the world."

"By Jove—that I do know!" Quentin was sitting up, his precious cigar abandoned in the dish beside him. "Russia! Russia has no European ports. She would be most uneasy with such a treaty, especially since Czar Alexander spurns European connections, except for those few French ones he tolerates for his Empress's sake."

Irene's smile grew radiant. "There speaks the soul of a spy. There stands the link to the two puzzles: the Afghanistan Events of 'Eighty and the recent hushed scandal of the missing English-Italian naval treaty. I propose that solving one muddle will resolve the other."

"It is preposterous," Quentin said, sadly. "Ingenious . . . Ireneous, even, but erroneous," he added with a flash of humor I had not yet seen in him. "If you can posit a connection between the disaster at Maiwand, Maclaine's death, my and Dr. Watson's recent brushes with death and this obscure treaty, my hat—nay, my head—is off to you, Madame Mystery-solver."

Irene positively glittered at the challenge. "You think it is impossible? Then listen to what Miss Harrison told me at tea."

"Irene, how did you persuade the young woman to tell you anything at all about such a secret matter?"

"I told her the truth," Irene answered.

"Shocking," Godfrey muttered. "You must have been desperate."

"We did not have much time together," she said tersely. "I had already learned that her fiancé, Mr. Phelps, had spent several weeks abed with brain fever and that recently, to gather from the behavior of Lord Holdhurst, his uncle, and others in the Foreign Office, all pressure had lifted from him. A significant figure present in this matter was Sherlock Holmes, I might add. So when I called upon Miss Harrison I told her of my concern for a noble-spirited Englishman who was a virtual exile from his homeland because of a false disgrace in war. I also told her that I had heard rumors of her recent trouble and that a Mr. Sherlock Holmes was said to have assisted in the matter. Did she think Mr. Holmes could do anything for me?"

"Who did you tell her you were?" I asked suspiciously.

"You," she answered promptly. "The poor wronged gentleman's fiancée."

"Irene!" I could not look at Quentin—an agonizing surge of pleasure made my cheeks burn at Irene's blithe endorsement of our mock engagement as an actuality to be appropriated for her own purposes—though I was well aware that he looked at me. "And what did you learn as a result of this outrage?"

"Much." Irene rubbed her palms together in the approved Del Sartian acting method for conveying intense satisfaction.

She resembled a glamorous Lady Macbeth immediately after the Gruesome Deed.

"You see," she went on, "a woman will confide almost anything to another woman if it involves a matter of the heart. And the treaty has been safely returned—yes, thanks to Mr. Sherlock Holmes. Her Percy is now blameless. She could not praise Mr. Holmes more highly. The only trace of sadness was when she confessed that her brother, Joseph, who had recently lost heavily in the stock market and knew that the Russians or the French would pay heavily to see the document, was the culprit who had taken the treaty, it was thought impulsively."

" 'It was thought,' " Godfrey repeated.

"Yes, Casanova?"

"*You* do not think it was a spur-of-the-moment theft?"

"No, I most certainly do not, and there is where Mr. Sherlock Holmes has made a fatal mistake. By the way, Joseph was punished for his act by an awful irony. He hid the treaty in his bedroom at Briarbrae—but that was the very room where Percy Phelps was confined when he collapsed at once of brain fever and where he stayed for almost two months. And there the treaty sat, unreachable to either man.

"According to Miss Harrison, Mr. Holmes lured Joseph into attempting to recover the document, then took it by force when Joseph attacked him and fled. Mr. Holmes presented it to Percy over breakfast in Baker Street, after first pretending that the document was unrecoverable. Poor Percy fainted, but luckily Dr. Watson was present to revive him. I told you years ago, Nell—" she glanced my way "—that a detective like Mr. Holmes would find association with a physician handy. Suffice it to say that this 'surprise' has redeemed Phelps and the Foreign Office. Joseph fled, and no one is minded to apprehend him now that the treaty is recovered. In a matter of weeks the alliance will be public knowledge, anyway."

"So the treaty matter is closed," Quentin said. "That has

nothing to do with cobras appearing in my Montmartre garret or Dr. Watson's Paddington consulting room."

"One would think not," Irene said demurely.

"One would," I parroted. "What would Irene think?"

"Ah, Nell, you do anticipate my methods. First there is this puzzling paper we have retrieved from Dr. Watson's Afghanistan bag. I wonder if he will ever miss it?" She shrugged. "Quentin, you have had time to study it, as you did not nine years ago."

He lifted it from the marble-topped side table with a shake of his head. "I have played with it until my eyes ache. It is written in Cyrillic Russian, and combines elements of a map and a communication. Frankly, I believe it is a fragment and I cannot make head or tail of it. Certainly it was not worth my pains to preserve it," he added ruefully.

"It is worth great pains to someone. If it is not for the contents, could it be for the mere fact of its existence?"

Quentin dubiously regarded the heavy, soft paper that wilted in his grasp like a leaf of yellowed cabbage. "Only one person might wish to destroy this, and I know you suspect him of the evildoings. Tiger."

"Tiger." She articulated the word with relish. "Whom we suspect to be Captain Sylvester Morgan, whom in turn we now know to be one Colonel Sebastian Moran, late of Her Majesty's Indian Army. Thank you, Godfrey, for your investigations among the military records."

He bowed his head slightly and smiled.

I could not help commenting. "This fabled Tiger certainly showed little imagination when it came to false identities."

"This man secretly wishes credit even for his misdeeds," Irene answered. "And the long, lashing tail of his arrogance will be the thing that will trip him up. Quentin, does the word 'Tiger' appear anywhere on that paper?"

"Why, yes. The salutation. That is why we had code names."

"Then if that paper came into hands that could trace the

identity of Tiger then and now, it would link him to the Russians?"

"I suppose so," he answered doubtfully. "Certainly there were rumors that he had been seen in their territories, which is why I suspected him of betraying us at Maiwand. But I cannot prove any of it! No one cares at this late date. The villains have been designated for the history books. The issue is moot."

"Perhaps not to Tiger," she replied. "Perhaps not to Tiger's current activities. Consider that he may protect not the past, but the present and the future. Perhaps he cannot afford the slightest trace of suspicion about him. To prevent it, he would stoop to murder."

"That would mean," Quentin said slowly, lifting his abandoned cigar to his lips, "that he had *monitored* me in Afghanistan and India; that he only sought my life when my existence endangered his current activities and I began my return to Europe, and to England."

Irene nodded soberly. "Perhaps he did not observe you in person. He was in London in May inquiring about you from your family. He was a spy. He must have had henchmen. Or henchwomen."

"So it was Tiger—Moran—or his minions who looked up Dr. Watson's name in the military files in India, and purloined the documents of his service!"

"Yes. Do you see what that means?"

"It means that . . . that I was safe only so long as I remained abroad; that my journey has brought these attacks on myself, perhaps even on Dr. Watson."

"My dear Quentin, you are too swift to blame yourself in everything," Irene rebuked him. "Do you see what it means for the battle at Maiwand? How it colors every incident, from Maclaine's killing to Dr. Watson's wounding even as he tended you?"

"My God—" Quentin's voice was hardly audible. "Even then . . . even then."

"What does he mean?" I asked Irene, whose attention was utterly bent on Quentin's bowed head. "Godfrey?"

Irene swiftly turned to me. "If Tiger/Moran was spying for the Russians in Afghanistan, he not only misled thousands of men into a battle they could only lose, he is responsible for Lieutenant Maclaine's posthumous slandering."

"And *he* hit me over the head after I'd talked to Mac, meaning to kill me!" Quentin exclaimed. "Except—"

"Except that you not only survived," Irene interjected, "but Tiger later discovered you had taken a paper that was extremely dangerous to him. He suspected you the moment he found the paper missing, of course. He could not risk letting anyone survive to reveal his role in neglecting to report the secondary ravine. Obviously you had told Maclaine about it, or your friend Mac would not have dashed beyond the ordered lines to fire upon the Afghanistan forces."

Quentin's head shook dully. He seemed as dazed as when we had found him—or he had found me—in Paris. "Then Tiger saw that I had survived the retreat. You believe that the bullet that wounded Dr. Watson in the shoulder was meant for me?!"

She nodded slowly, watching him. "Most likely. You mentioned dust and confusion. I suspect that Tiger was not among the confused at that time. I doubt he knew you had put the paper in Watson's medical bag, but now that events have come to a head in London, he knew that he could not take the risk that you had told Watson anything. Some happening here in London in the past year made him see ghosts of the conscience from the past and move to make them ghosts indeed; first you in India and en route to London; then hapless Dr. Watson in Paddington."

"What about Maclaine's death?"

Irene reversed direction and paced toward the draperies, resting her chin on her tented fingers. She seemed to change the subject. "Were not the Russians and the British both aching to claim Afghanistan? Would they not attempt to do so by subterfuge if force couldn't prevail?"

"Of course. The game has gone on for decades. We British had 'our' candidate for Khan who would favor our interests; the Russians had theirs. Spies were everywhere, and the Afghans, being long used to treachery in their own ruling families, played both ends against the middle. Who can blame them?"

"In this case, I think the Ayub Khan behaved honorably. He did leave orders for his six British prisoners—Lieutenant Maclaine and the five sepoys—to survive. Instead, Tiger intervened. Dressed as an Afghan and disguised by his desert robes—he hardly needed your command of their language for this work—he swirled into the prisoners' midst even as the rescuing troops were riding in, and slit Maclaine's throat."

Irene stopped and turned, her hands dropping to her sides. "Maclaine's death was murder, Quentin. Cold-blooded murder in the guise of a casualty of war. With one ferocious stroke Colonel Sebastian Moran virtually beheaded the one credible witness to your suspicions. Maclaine could never testify to the unreported second ravine, testimony that would lead to more damaging investigations."

"Maclaine murdered. I had not considered that." Quentin looked up with eyes whose luster had been dulled by shock. "A fiendish use of a fiendish weapon: war itself. Then why did I survive so long?"

"What did you do after the battle?" Irene asked with a terse smile.

He frowned. "I . . . arrived at Kandahar in one piece, which was a significant achievement. They needed a scout to try for headquarters in India, so I volunteered. My suspicions about Tiger were only that, and no one but Maclaine could confirm them. I knew Mac had been taken prisoner—there were witnesses—but his death would not come for another month. They gave me a horse, and I made my way to the new railway at Sinjini and then on to Peshawar in India, where I collapsed."

"Hence the medal," Irene interrupted him, "not for the collapse but for the deeds before it."

Her words scarcely touched him. "I had recovered by the time of the relief of Kandahar at the end of August and was gone long before the wounded from Maiwand were transported to Peshawar."

"So you and Dr. Watson never crossed paths again?" Godfrey asked.

"No. News of Maclaine's dreadful death came to Peshawar before the wounded, of course. I thought only that a witness to the treachery was dead by an ironic stroke, not by . . . murder. Yet, spying was still needed, and the waste of lives at Maiwand had sickened me. I went out, as commanded, into the godforsaken wasteland, which was still sweeter to me than the waste we had made of ourselves and our enemies at Maiwand. Out of sight, out of mind. Everyone seemed to forget about me. Eventually, I was honorably discharged." Quentin laughed bitterly. "What a phrase for an honorless place and time! I took my bit of brass and lived where I wished, among those I liked."

"And your life was never threatened?"

He eyed Irene with a sudden glint. "Many, many times, but not by anyone European, and most often by nothing human. Why did Tiger spare me then?"

"He had better things to do, and he found you no threat as long as you remained in the wilds. He probably supposed that you would never return to civilization as he knew it."

Quentin nodded. "I would have struck some as a broken man. Life was simpler with those complicated people of the steppes. Goat cheese and salty tea and hospitality with a vengeance, if they were not trying to kill you for your boots or a bit of brass." He shook his head.

Godfrey—at last—extinguished his cigar, rather thoughtfully. "What events here have compelled Moran to reach back into the past?"

Irene strode to the marble-topped table to pick up her cigarette holder and fit it with an Egyptian cigarette. Quentin leaped up to light a lucifer for her, a useless gallantry that made Godfrey smile like a complacent cat. A woman who had shot a cobra needed no help striking a match.

As soon as Irene had drawn a veil of smoke around her, she spoke again. "Recall my most extraordinary invitation *chez* Sarah."

"There was nothing at all extraordinary about it," I said promptly. "You are invited to that address all too frequently, in my opinion."

"Perhaps." Irene shrugged. "Yet never at the behest of the Empress of All the Russias. Why? Surely not because she wished to meet an obscure English barrister's wife who was known to sing a little."

"I hope," Godfrey put in, "that you mean that the wife is obscure, not the barrister."

"Of course I do," Irene said with a bow. "You are gaining quite a reputation in Paris."

"Irene," I interrupted, my eyes on Quentin's distracted visage, "we did not come all this way to sharpen fine points between ourselves. Can you not simply come out with it?"

"But it is so much more amusing to edge up to the obvious, rather than pouncing outright upon it!"

"I see nothing so obvious that it merits pouncing upon," I returned.

"My command performance before the Empress was an excuse. She no more wished to meet or hear me than she wished to sail a balloon over Lombardy! Obviously her influence was used so that 'Captain Morgan' could inspect us. He knew that we had sheltered Quentin Stanhope; he wanted to know why, and he wanted to gauge our mettle. Like any good hunter, he studied the lay of the land and the disposition of his prey."

"Why should so dreadful a man have influence over an Empress?" I demanded.

Quentin came to life. "If you mean, Irene, that Tiger is still spying for St. Petersburg, and I am now certain that he is, it would be no great thing for the Russian embassy to convey his wishes to the traveling monarch. Royal figures often smooth the path for clandestine subterfuge. They are told nothing of the true reason for such requests, only that they are necessary to the state, and think nothing more of them."

Irene nodded. "Then, I ask, why has this Moran now made his headquarters in London? He has indeed, for once Godfrey found out his real name he immediately returned to The Frontier Fusiliers and discovered the hunting club to which Moran belongs, the Anglo-Indian. His membership dates to more than a year ago."

"He has business here." Quentin leaped up to join Irene in pacing. "Why had I not thought of it? He is English by birth. He could do the Russians inestimable service—he could do England irreparable harm—in London. With his hunting credentials and his military title, no one would suspect him. He is the perfect Russian agent because he is not Russian!"

"Honestly, Irene," I put in, "you have asked an excessive number of questions but you have been remarkably stingy with answers. I believe you do not know precisely why this Colonel Moran is here."

"But I do," she retorted. "He has been the key agent in the case which Sherlock Holmes thinks that he has just solved: the stolen naval treaty. Moran may even be a double agent representing Russia and France; both nations yearn to glimpse that interesting document. More likely, I think that he represents only himself, planning to award the treaty to the highest bidder."

"But Joseph Harrison took it!" I objected. "You said his own sister admitted that."

"Joseph Harrison took it, and for the reason that she gave: he was in debt because of bad investments. Yet Joseph Harrison never had the sophistication to deal with the embassies of foreign nations. He was recruited for the task by Colonel Moran, who may even have arranged for his investment disaster. Moran has used agents before: remember the striking but nameless blonde woman at Sarah's soirée? Was she not possibly among the strollers near Notre Dame when Quentin was injected with poison? I never forget a stunning ensemble."

I nodded vigorously with sudden, shocked recall, aching to go and consult my diaries on the matter, but Irene returned to the immediate question.

"Yes, Joseph was ideally positioned to take the treaty, and did. As for Joseph's eluding the infallible Sherlock Holmes, I am not convinced that Mr. Holmes failed to prevent Joseph's escape as much as permitted it."

"Why?" I asked.

"For one thing, the awkwardness. Poor Percy Phelps might be cleared of losing the treaty once he returned it with Mr. Holmes's help, but having his own brother-in-law-to-be arrested for the theft would hardly enhance Phelps's reputation or his personal life."

"You think that Sherlock Holmes let Joseph go out of the goodness of his heart? That is hardly likely, Irene."

She smiled, started to say something, then smiled again. "Even the foremost consulting detective in—" she glanced at Godfrey "—England . . . may have a trickle of mercy in his veins. And I am not certain that Mr. Holmes has actually ended his investigation."

"Yet," said Godfrey, still sitting comfortably as Irene and Quentin paced and I fumed, "Moran has been balked. The treaty is safe. I doubt even he would try to steal it again."

Irene sighed. "Nothing is so ferocious as a wounded tiger. He may blame the old Afghanistan business for his failure here, seeing its survivors as a continuing threat to his future enterprises in London. Surely he must know by now that Dr. Watson, whose life he has threatened on two widely different occasions at two opposite ends of the globe, is a close and valued associate of the one person most dangerous to his future freedom."

"The one person who resides in London most dangerous to his future freedom," Godfrey corrected.

"No," she added, pacing again in opposite rhythm to Quentin so that as he came, she went. "Quentin still is not safe, nor is Dr. Watson. Nor are we three, for that matter."

She paused before Godfrey and extended both her hands, which he took.

"Forgive me, dear and glorious barrister, but there is only one person in London who can pull the teeth of this Tiger; who can expose him to the secret community of diplomacy and subterfuge; who can reveal his perfidy then and now. And to him we must go. Set a thief to catch a thief. Moran is not only a Tiger, but as treacherously toxic as a cobra. And to stop a cobra, we need a clever mongoose domesticated to our defense. We need Mr. Sherlock Holmes."

Chapter Twenty-Nine

HOLMESWARD BOUND

"Nell!" Irene sounded utterly exasperated, like a nanny at odds with an obstreperous child. "You are being completely unreasonable!"

We were in my hotel bedchamber the following morning, each tugging at opposite ends of the same paisley silk shawl.

"I am not being unreasonable! Even you must admit that I am impeccably reasonable. You cannot go. I will go."

"It is too dangerous."

"Dangerous! Irene, if Sherlock Holmes recognizes you, the entire scheme will be ruined and who knows what measures against you he may take? Besides, Dr. Watson may be present, and he has already seen me."

Irene drew breath but let go of the shawl not one whit. "When I have finished dressing in character, you and I will look like twins. Besides, I am sure that Dr. Watson did not engrave your features upon his memory during the brief visit you and Godfrey paid to Paddington."

"You always tell me not to underestimate Mr. Holmes, but you underestimate Dr. Watson. Merely because he associates with *the* man does not mean that he is equally as indifferent to women."

She tugged on the shawl, but I held fast. "Quentin's riveting story will mesmerize them both, Holmes and Watson," Irene insisted. "Do you think two such Englishmen, already addicted to domestic malfeasance to an alarming degree, will be able to resist an international stew reeking of blood and thunder and battle and infamy—not to mention venomous serpents? The woman's role in this scheme merely reveals the unity of the two incidents. Now stop being such a ninny and do give me that shawl!"

"No! It is mine. If you wish to impersonate me impersonating someone else, you will have to find your own costume!"

"Nell—!" Irene sighed gustily and released the remarkably tenacious material so abruptly that I tumbled back onto the bed. "This is ludicrous."

"I only wish to protect you from yourself. You are far too tempted to flit near this awful man on Baker Street. Godfrey does not like it, either."

That gave even Irene a moment's pause. "Godfrey does not—? What are you saying, Nell?"

I was sorry I had brought it up. "He thinks you overly fascinated by this fellow."

"Godfrey is jealous?"

"Perhaps. A little."

She collapsed beside me, as only Irene could, in her most gracefully unladylike manner. "Well then, it is decided. I *must* go!" she said in Sarah Bernhardt tones. "As the French say, nothing is bettair for the average 'usband than a little jealousy, no?"

I could not help smiling. "Godfrey is not the average husband. Truly, Irene, you should not risk going near that man. He warned you in Monte Carlo to stay out of his affairs."

"I should not breathe then, in this London smog," she erupted, ready to explode temperament as Mount Etna spews hot lava. Then she eyed me narrowly. "Nell, are you certain that your true objection is not to the fact that I wish to go to Baker Street, but to the role I will be playing?"

"What do you mean?" I edged myself and the shawl out of her easy reach.

"You know what I mean! I will be posing as Quentin's fiancée. *You* are jealous!"

"I am not! I am not," I repeated in a lower, more restrained tone. "I merely point out what is logical: I have already approached the doctor in the guise of someone's fiancée, that of Jasper Blodgett, late of Godfrey's imagination. Dreadful name."

"Blodgett, you mean," Irene said, nodding.

"No, Jasper."

"Blodgett will be harder to make credible," she muttered, "but I expect Quentin to carry it off. A successful spy is an actor first and foremost. What poetic justice to leave both you and Godfrey behind on this venture—Godfrey especially, for creating Jasper Blodgett. Besides, you are both jealous and there is something of the Feydeau farce in all this."

"I am not jealous! But if you persist in this madness, you may not have a stitch of my wardrobe for it." I clasped the shawl to my bosom.

Irene lunged forward and shook the fringe. "Oh, keep it, Nell. Wear it in good health, Miss Buxleigh. At least we were fortunate that Mrs. Watson misheard your surname. You shall go with Quentin, and mind you that you do not miss a detail of the conversation. I expect you to report every word and every nuance."

"Oh, thank you, Irene!" I leaped up, still embracing my shawl.

Irene stood as well.

"Where are you going?" I asked.

"To my chamber, to cross-examine Godfrey on certain behavior unbecoming a barrister, such as jealousy."

"You cannot," I wailed.

"Whyever not?"

"You have to help me choose what to wear."

"But you are going as yourself."

"But I am pretending to be someone else."

"Nell, that is still the same thing."

I regarded her with silent rebuke until she clapped her

hands to her sides. "Very well. What to wear: your 'surprise dress'—the housedress that closes into a plain, side-buttoning coat for street wear. A fiancée of Jasper Blodgett would be practical to a fault, I think. Boots, of course, no dainty slippers for her. Pale kid gloves and a most subdued bonnet, perhaps the ecru straw with the ghastly spotted ribbon."

I paled. "I never knew you thought the spotted ribbon ghastly."

"I am usually diplomatic, despite those who think me brazen," she said pointedly.

I had begun assembling the items in question as she spoke and draped them over the bed, except for the boots. "You don't think that this ensemble will be too . . . dowdy?"

"For the fiancée of Jasper Blodgett? Any woman engaged to a man whose Christian name is Jasper cannot be too dowdy."

I dared not mention that the first man to engage my romantic interest was a Jaspar, but I determined to remove and destroy the spotted ribbon as soon as my mission to Baker Street ended.

"Besides . . ." Irene bent over the severe, black silk surprise dress that was trimmed only by a five-inch hem of ruching. When she flipped open the front, the pale old-rose lining embroidered in black bloomed like a flash of color on a blackbird's wing. She leaned conspiratorially near to whisper, "When your task is done, you can return to the hotel, swiftly fold back the gown's reveres to reveal its sumptuous undergown, and 'surprise' Mr. Jasper Blodgett at dinner."

She left the room before I could answer that I had no such ambition, a typical example of how aggravating Irene could be on occasion.

Early that morning, we had sent a note to Baker Street requesting an interview with Mr. Holmes. Irene had composed it with an eye to making it impossibly irresistible.

"Mr. Holmes would detect any discrepancy between the penwomanship and the purported fiancée," she insisted, so I copied it in my own hand:

Dear Mr. Holmes,

Your help is desperately required in a most mystifying matter upon which may hang the fortunes of several nations, as well as our own lives.

The problem involves my poor fiancé, Jasper Blodgett, missing in India these nine years and now miraculously returned to me with his life in grave danger. We have no notion what to make of these awful events.

We have made what inquiries we can on the matter ourselves, and now find our lives in danger in a most repellent manner, which I cannot even commit to paper without a shudder.

Please do us the honor of hearing our tale. We should be forever grateful for any assistance you may be able to render us.

Yours very truly,

Irene paused in dictating this breathless missive. "What name shall we give you, Nell?"

"Mrs. Watson has already renamed me 'Buxleigh.' Surely that is disguise enough?"

"I mean for a first name. It is best not to offer such a quick man as Mr. Holmes too many genuine clues. Have you never longed for another Christian name?"

I shook my head.

"Never yearned to be called 'Chloe,' say, or 'Aurelia'?"

"Never."

"Not even 'Melisande' or 'Cressida' or—"

"Irene, please! Penelope is classical enough for my tastes. If I must choose a pseudonym, I have always been partial to 'May.' "

" 'May'! That is all? 'May'?" My plain choice appeared to plunge Irene into a minor melancholy. "The entire world unrolls before you and you are content with 'May'?"

"Yes," I answered. "I am, after all, from Shropshire." And

I had already signed the missive "May Buxleigh," so that was that.

Within three hours, a note penned in a brash but legible hand was returned to us by our messenger. This was a street youth who had been instructed to wait for Holmes's reply, but to indicate another hotel as his destination, if pressed.

"*You intrigue me,*" it read. "*Three o'clock today. S.H.*"

"A man of few words," Irene observed, smiling tightly, then tying the paisley shawl over my plain-Jane coat-dress.

Quentin and I set out by hansom cab taken from a neighboring hotel at two-thirty.

Returning to Baker Street filled me with anxiety, despite my having seen it previously. Irene had draped my bonnet with the spotted veiling, but other than making me dizzy, it likely had little effect on muting my appearance, should Mr. Holmes choose to remember that he had met me twice before: in my servile role at Briony Lodge and as myself in Godfrey's Temple chambers. Quentin looked most proper but ordinary in a suit he and Godfrey had bought earlier in the day at a department store, quite nice broadcloth but not personally tailored. It perfectly fit his part of returned prodigal son.

We said little in the hansom, both aware of the roles we must soon assume before a man reputed to see through criminal subterfuge.

"That is the key," Irene had prompted us before we left. "You are there to speak the truth, after all. You must only omit certain inconvenient facts."

"Such as you and me," Godfrey added wryly.

So Quentin and I rehearsed the truth in our minds as we left the cab poised before 221 B Baker Street.

This time Quentin, not Godfrey, pulled the bell. My tongue suddenly cleaved to the roof of my mouth. Why had I fought Irene for this dreadful privilege? I remembered *the* man's piercing iron-gray gaze, fixed on me for a few, unnerving minutes when I had undertaken the role of housekeeper at Briony Lodge. This interview could last an entire hour. Or more.

"Yes?" The cheery white-haired woman opened the door with a welcoming smile. "Mr. Holmes said he was expecting visitors. Go right up."

So I climbed another momentous flight of stairs, this one with only a figurative cobra awaiting us at the top.

"Come in, come in!" A cordial, though slightly high voice greeted us as we entered the room above. "Miss Buxleigh, Mr., er . . . Blodgett."

I recognized the Holmesian manner. He was tall, thin and quick in motion and speech. We were shown to a sofa while our host cast himself with a kind of caged energy into a basket chair that should be cool seating indeed at midsummer.

"Now," said he, "you must tell the tale that your—that Miss Buxleigh's—uncommonly intriguing letter began. I have requested a colleague of mine who is peculiarly suited to throw some light upon the matter to join us later. For now, however, I must hear the facts." He laid an elbow upon the chair arm and leaned his head upon his hand, a position of rapt attention belied by the sleepy droop of his eyelids.

I immediately recalled Dr. Watson's reference to cocaine use. Had Mr. Holmes been indulging this outré habit before our arrival?

"Begin," he suggested with the brisk command of a maestro to an orchestra, "at the beginning, if you please, Mr. Blodgett."

Quentin and I exchanged an uneasy glance.

"We cannot, Mr. Holmes," I said, "however much we may wish to oblige you. The fact is that a mere three days ago I was in search of—" I glanced at Quentin in a melting manner that Irene would have applauded "—dear Jasper. That we have found each other after so long is a wonder; that our reunion has been shadowed by the most bizarre incidents and danger is a cruel twist of fate."

"Tell me, then, of this most amazing recent reunion. How did it occur?"

I glanced again at Quentin, not having thought to invent this supposed occurrence. He plunged into the dangerous waters of this topic like a trout into a pool.

"On Angel Street," he said promptly. "Quite the most amazing coincidence. I had returned to England only after a long and not totally willing sojourn in India and Afghanistan, sir."

"You are, of course, a veteran of the battle of Maiwand," Mr. Holmes interjected with a kind of weary smile.

"Why—yes! Indeed. That is extraordinary, Mr. Holmes. I can see why your reputation shines so brightly."

Mr. Holmes leaned forward with the speed of a hawk diving on a dove. "How *did* you learn of me, then?"

"Why—" Quentin glanced at me to gain time for his fabricating faculties to grind into gear.

I was inspired. "From my solicitor, Mr. Marshwine."

"I have not heard of him," Holmes said in a way that struck me as deliberately challenging.

"That was not necessary," I replied tartly, "since he had heard of you. He has connections in France—a Monsieur Le Villon of the Paris police, I believe, speaks highly of your amazing deductive abilities." In a bit of inspired deception, I slightly changed the surname, so my story should not be too neat.

"Monsieur Le Villard," Mr. Holmes corrected me.

I bridled a bit, then feigned confusion. "I beg your pardon?"

"Is the French connection you speak of Monsieur Le Villard, not Le Villon?"

"Yes, you are right! These French names are so similar."

Mr. Holmes nodded and leaned back in the basket chair, his eyes on the gasolier. "Continue."

Quentin accepted his invitation. "As I said, I was strolling down Angel Street when I spied Miss Buxleigh in the window of a . . . I suppose it was a draper's shop. I was so startled that I paid little attention to the surroundings. You see, my fiancée and I have been separated for nine years. Imagine meeting one another purely by chance!"

"Yes, it is unlikely to the point of incredulity," Mr. Holmes noted dryly. "Why had you not returned from that rough quarter of the world for so long, Mr. Blodgett?"

Quentin and I kept our innocent visages bland.

"Severe fever following the battle of Maiwand," Quentin answered. "I lost my senses and ultimately my memory. It was only in March when I was set upon by thieves in the bazaar at Peshawar and hit upon the head that I woke up whole again."

"I have heard of such miraculous returns to the senses," Mr. Holmes said. "It appears your path of late has been salted with happy mishaps."

"Indeed." Then Quentin drew a long face and took my hand. I was wearing kid gloves, naturally, but still could not quell a thrill of excitement utterly unrelated to the terrors of our impersonation. "Poor May has had restored to her a fiancé who is dogged by some malign god. An attempt was made on my life when I embarked from Bombay. Another occurred in Belgium; the latest and most exotic transpired in my hotel room on Oxford Street."

"What was this latest assault?" Mr. Holmes inquired.

I gave a mock shudder, quite without guile.

"An . . . object was left in my room while I was out. A poisonous snake."

"An Asian cobra, in fact," Mr. Holmes interjected.

"Exactly!" Quentin regarded me with innocent joy. "Utterly amazing. You see, my dear, this is just the man to aid us."

"How did you," the detective inquired next, "live to tell the tale?"

Here Quentin looked modestly down. "I have lived in India for nearly a third of my life, sir, and have picked up some exotic habits, perhaps. One of my acquisitions is a devoted pet. I go nowhere without it."

Holmes leaped out of the chair. "Of course! A mongoose."

Quentin regarded me with another wondrous look. "Is not this wonderful, my dear! Mr. Holmes is quick to the point of prescience. Surely he can help us. As you evidently know, Mr. Holmes, there is nothing a mongoose likes better than a dance-to-the-death with a cobra. My Messalina was out of her cage in a wink—clever with her feet, she is. All I found when I returned was a dead cobra . . . sorry, my dear . . . and a bit of damage to the draperies. Messalina can be quite a climber on occasion."

Mr. Holmes drew a pocket watch and studied it in silence while its gold chain swung hypnotically. From the links swung a small yellow sun—a gold sovereign set into a bezel; an odd souvenir. I was pleased to have spotted a detail about Sherlock Holmes that I could legitimately report to Irene, as ordered. (Certainly I could never tell Irene the dreadful words Dr. Watson had penned about *the* man's obsession with her!)

Mr. Holmes lifted his head intently like an animal. "Ah, I hear my associate's step upon the stair. How convenient that your tale has reached a point where it should prove most interesting to him."

He rose and opened the door to a man who was no surprise to me; the same Dr. Watson among whose writings I had shamelessly read and from under whose desk I had quite unintentionally kicked a dead snake.

I experienced some nervousness during the introductions, while Miss Buxleigh professed great amazement that Mr. Holmes knew Dr. Watson, but the doctor merely nodded politely at me and Quentin. All of Dr. Watson's attention was on his friend.

"I am happy to see, Miss Buxleigh," he said bluffly, "that you have managed to retrieve your missing fiancé, uh, Blodgett, is it?" He turned to the much taller, thinner man beside him. "Holmes, what has this to do with the Paddington mystery? Your note promised revelations."

"And we shall have them, Watson," Mr. Holmes said with great good humor, gesturing his friend to a velvet-lined armchair that must have been hot for the day. "Pray continue, Mr. Blodgett."

"Not much more to say. I discreetly disposed of the snake—"

"Therein lies a tale," Mr. Holmes commented sotto voce.

"—but I fear that an old tangle I have remembered from the war underlies this perfidy."

"War?" Dr. Watson asked. "Perfidy?"

"Mr. Blodgett will explain directly." Mr. Holmes fixed his disconcerting attention on Quentin.

That was Quentin's cue to unravel the true tale within the false construct of our fiction as he told the detective and his companion what he had revealed to Godfrey, Irene and myself.

Quentin spoke thrillingly of his spy-work in Afghanistan and of his suspicions toward another British espionage agent called Tiger when the man libeled his friend, Lieutenant Maclaine. He dramatically described the blow to the head after his talk with Maclaine, and his awakening the next day in the midst of a harrowing British retreat.

Dr. Watson listened intently at first, then began to fidget subtly, tapping his fingers on the velvet pile of his armchair, shifting to find a more comfortable position for his leg.

"Yes," Dr. Watson interrupted when Quentin paused for breath, "Miss Buxleigh thought I might have treated you. I remember encountering only one case of a blow to the head at Maiwand. I received a wound from a jezail bullet to my shoulder shortly after. The man I treated could have been you, but I cannot swear to it, Blodgett. I am sorry."

Quentin sat forward on the sofa. "I am not, Dr. Watson, for I am sure of it! I was indeed he whom you tended moments before being shot in the shoulder yourself. Heavens, man, how amazing that we should meet again nearly a decade after Maiwand. Remember the dust?"

Dr. Watson laughed shortly. "Dust and Ghazi fanatics by the yard—who could forget? And the infernal heat. But I confess, Blodgett, that I did not even recall the exact instant of my wounding until Miss Buxleigh brought it back by inquiring after you a few days ago."

"How did you find Dr. Watson?" Sherlock Holmes inquired suddenly.

Quentin was ready for him. "The last name. He mentioned it at Maiwand, one of the first things I remembered once my memory was resurrected from the past." Quentin turned to the doctor with genuine emotion. "You will never know how relieved I am to see you again, Doctor! I feel in some way that my mislaid past has been redeemed."

"I have recaptured some lost memories myself," the doctor admitted.

"These mysteries unravel at a fearsome pace without my aid," Mr. Holmes noted wryly. "You two gentlemen would seem to have more in common than a battlefield meeting and bad memories. You both have been recent recipients of Asian cobras."

"Blodgett, too?" Dr. Watson demanded. "What is going on, Holmes? Is London infected by some sort of imported-serpent ring?"

"For that answer we will have to apply to Mr. Jasper Blodgett. He can begin by explaining how he managed to find you in time to set his trained mongoose on the cobra in your consulting room."

"No!" Dr. Watson appeared sincerely shocked. "A mongoose. Why, I never thought of that, Holmes."

"It is fortunate that I did, then, although I had not yet tracked the owner of the mongoose. Remember the nail marks on your windowsill? Obviously an animal's. Well, Mr. Blodgett?"

"Utter simplicity, Mr. Holmes. Having finally remembered Watson's name, I had determined to find any physicians named Watson in England, for by last month I had realized that Tiger was tracking me. In fact, when I attempted to look up Dr. Watson in the records at Peshawar, I discovered that a previous party had recently found—and removed—them. That is when I knew your life to be in danger, Doctor, and why I came to London. That you were the proper Dr. Watson came clear shortly after I found your residence and set watch upon it, planning to introduce myself to you if I thought you a likely candidate. That very night I saw a housebreaker import a box into your study. I may not be a detective—" here Quentin nodded at Mr. Holmes with some pride in his voice "—but I know the average cracksman doesn't convey goods, beyond a few tools, into a house he's planning to rob. I looked in from the windowsill after he had gone—a good clean job he made of it, too—and soon heard the rasp of a creature that chills the blood of any man who has spent time in India, the cobra."

"You happened to have the mongoose with you, no doubt," Holmes suggested with a trace of disdain.

"After the cobra I found in my hotel bedchamber, I went nowhere without it," Quentin said with such feeling that it took me a moment to realize that this was a complete untruth.

In the ensuing silence, Quentin and Mr. Holmes regarded each other with narrowed eyes. Quentin radiated conviction. I was quite perversely proud of him, even though he was lying through his teeth. Mr. Holmes exuded another attitude, one I could not quite name. Perhaps it was skepticism.

"Go on," the detective urged my supposed fiancé.

Quentin only said, "So I nipped onto the sill, set the cage down, and let Messalina loose to do her work—"

"Oh, Jasper," I found myself simpering like any genuine fiancée (and for a brief second, in a strange way, felt that I was), "weren't you frightened that your adorable little pet would succumb to the awful snake, especially in the dark?"

"There, there, May," he said, startling me, for I had forgotten my recent rechristening. "I had not a thing to worry about. No mongoose can choose when to confront a cobra, and Messalina has never lost yet. Cobras can be a sluggish, slow-swaying sort of snake as well as deadly."

"Yes, Miss Buxleigh," *the* man said in obviously insincere consolation, "we humans may learn quite a lesson from the interaction of mongoose and cobra. Its results are applicable to London affairs daily."

I had the dreadful sense that the detective was playing with us all, including his friend, as a mongoose may taunt the slower-moving snake. In this he reminded me of Irene at her most sphinxlike. I shuddered slightly at the insight. Mr. Holmes seemed as cold-blooded as his friend had described him in the pages I had read in Paddington. "*. . . his cold, precise but admirably balanced mind.*" Now I suddenly saw that Irene shared some of that same clinical distance.

"Messy nipped back to her cage when the job was done," Quentin said, describing, I am sure, exactly what had occurred. "I shut her up and slipped away, knowing Dr. Watson's maid might have a bit of noxious tidying up to do on the morrow, but the doctor's life was safe."

"Indeed." This time Dr. Watson shuddered. "The serpent was discovered under my desk, quite dead, but well positioned to bite me in the leg."

"So Mr. Blodgett's imported mongoose averted a tragedy and a second leg wound, Watson," drawled the detective in an odiously knowing manner.

"There is no first leg wound, Holmes!" Dr. Watson insisted with some irritation. "I merely get a bit stiff in the joints as a lingering symptom of enteric fever. This London weather is dank to one who has broiled in the kiln of Afghanistan and India."

"Utterly true," Quentin put in fervently.

Mr. Holmes turned to him with an air of having toyed enough with too-tame prey. "So is there an explanation for this villainy, Mr. Blodgett, or is that what I am being consulted to detect?"

Quentin paused as if perplexed. "There you have me, Mr. Holmes. I have my suspicions, and we have the two dead cobras to show that something is up."

"Not to mention the irregularities at the battle of Maiwand," I prompted.

Quentin nodded soberly. "They are more than mere irregularities, my dear. If my suspicions are correct that the spy I knew as Tiger was secretly working for the Russians, it could mean that our troops lost that day only by treachery. Many more lives hang on that than poor Maclaine's."

"What are you saying, Blodgett?" Dr. Watson asked. "That an Englishman betrayed his own kind? Maiwand saw much carnage. I witnessed that before I myself was wounded. The Sixty-sixth Berkshires standing to cover the retreat took dreadful losses. I would be most angry to learn that all of this waste could have been avoided."

"If I am right, Dr. Watson," Quentin returned, "your own wounding could have been avoided. I now believe that the bullet that shattered your shoulder was intended for me. Tiger knew that I was suspicious. I am certain that he struck me on the head the night before battle, intending to kill me and have me taken for a casualty. During the retreat, he saw me still alive under your care, and used the dust and confusion as a cover to try again to kill me. That is why I have come all this way after all this time: to warn you and preserve you. To my mind, you saved my life that day by taking a bullet meant for me."

Nothing could belie the sincerity of Quentin's words, the concern that had driven his return to an England that was not only personally dangerous, but dreaded. The two veterans sat silent, affected by the emotion of his voice as much as by what he had said.

"My dear fellow," Mr. Holmes told Quentin with more warmth than he had yet used, "there is no doubt in my mind that you saved Watson's life by introducing your animal ally into his consulting room, and for that I am most grateful. On that score rest easy. That does not mean that the puzzle is solved, or the wrongdoers brought to justice. Do you have any proof that this Tiger is the traitorous spy that you claim he is?"

"Only this, Mr. Holmes." Quentin reached into the breast pocket of his department-store suit and withdrew the paper

Irene and I had prized from Dr. Watson's Afghanistan bag only a day before.

I quite loathed to see Quentin hand it over to the detective, who bounded up and swooped it away to the light of the bow window. Irene had insisted that a copy of this nine-year-old document would not deceive the eminent detective, that Quentin had to surrender this precious paper, his only proof of Tiger's betrayal, if indeed the cryptic scrawls could prove that. Still, I hated seeing Quentin surrender another piece of the past in which he had submerged so much of his life.

"Now we have something to grasp," Mr. Holmes exclaimed. "Watson, my glass!"

He hunched over the document as if to consume it with his eyes. When his associate brought a magnifying glass, Mr. Holmes swept it across as well as up and down both sides.

"Hah! St. Petersburg deckle with a rag content that is no less than forty percent—and cut so that the watermark is conveniently missing." His thin fingers rubbed the paper as appreciatively as Irene's sensitive fingertips judged the weight of Chinese silk.

"This paper is so fine, so sturdy, it has virtually aged like cloth. First it was kept in arid circumstances—some of the fibers are desiccated."

"That is not so mystifying," Quentin said, "I obtained it in the Afghanistan steppes in the horrid heat of July."

Mr. Holmes barely glanced his way. "Since then, I mean . . . most odd. I would judge it to be on the brink of rotting, having spent most of its span in a cool, damp climate. Where has this been kept all these years, Mr. Blodgett?"

I kept my glance from straying accusingly to Dr. Watson, who had allowed this invaluable document to languish in a London wardrobe, all unknowingly, of course, but ignorance is no excuse.

"Ah," Quentin was saying as he flailed for an explanation that would not betray our latter-day acquisition of the paper. "With me. In India. I lived in the cooler hill country most of the time," he lied with such conviction that I listened admiringly. "During the rainy season the climate there can indeed be hideously humid."

"Hmm." Mr. Holmes did not sound convinced. "Certainly little care has been taken with it."

"I had forgotten much that occurred before the blow upon my head," Quentin said. "It is a piece of luck that I kept it at all."

"Yes," Holmes mused, "luck and coincidence have a great deal to do with this case. As to the characters upon the paper, a language expert could translate them better, but they are written in Cyrillic Russian and list geographical locations. I recognize the Russian word for tiger." The detective smiled briefly. "I have been invited to contribute to a matter or two in Russia, including the Trepoff murder in 'Eighty-eight. You may have heard of it. These Russians are a most . . . er, assertive people."

Mr. Holmes suddenly lowered the magnifying glass and strode to the sofa. "I am afraid that I cannot help you. This scrap contains nothing incriminating. There remains only your word that you took it from the belongings of this 'Tiger,' whose actual name you do not even know."

I cannot convey the idly dismissive tone that the detective used, as if all of his interest in the matter had vanished.

"Mr. Holmes!" I said sharply. "For a famous detective you have omitted to ask the obvious. We *do* know the name of Tiger, for my solicitor has discovered his military records. We even know the name of his London club. Since he is the individual responsible for throwing live cobras into everyone's path—it is not his fault that they die before they can do damage, thus far—I should think that a person deeply interested in crime in our metropolis could show a little less ennui and a bit more . . . energy."

Dr. Watson spoke hastily. "You must overlook the lady's distress, Holmes. She is remarkably devoted to Mr. Blodgett, as you can see."

At this the detective leaned forward to sear me with his

disconcerting gaze. I bit my lip, unsure whether I should suddenly confess all under that merciless inspection.

"Yes, Watson, a woman's loyalty is commendable, if often misdirected, as may be her anger." He turned to Quentin. "Do you have any notion why this Tiger would wait nine years to stalk you and Dr. Watson?"

"He thought me harmless," Quentin answered promptly. "My memory was gone, and I was marooned in India and Afghanistan. Yet he still might fear that I had raved about the paper, about his treachery, to the good doctor. It was only as I ventured from the East that these attempts on my life began."

Mr. Holmes softly rapped the paper against his open palm. "The entire affair reeks of the operetta stage. Were Watson not involved I would not waste my time on it, but I will look into your terrifying Tiger, though I suspect that London has tamed him. What is his name?"

"Colonel Sebastian Moran. His club is the Anglo-Indian."

"To your knowledge, Mr. Blodgett, you have not seen him since you arrived in London?"

We shook our heads in unison.

"Watson, does my *Index* list the gentleman?"

The doctor once again rose to do the great man's bidding, picking a massive volume off the bookshelf above the desk, which was cluttered with much domestic effluvia, such as pipes, vials and other oddities, no doubt including whatever appliances are necessary to the consumption of cocaine.

"There is indeed a reference, Holmes! Colonel Sebastian Moran, here between 'Morais, Sabato, born 1823 in Leghorn, Italy, expert on Italian straw fabrication; emigrated to the United States in 1851' and the Countess of Morcar."

"We need no specifics on Her Ladyship," Mr. Holmes said. "What are the particulars on Colonel Moran?"

" 'Moran, Sebastian, born 1840. Unemployed. Formerly First Bangalore Pioneers. Educated at Eton and Oxford. Heavy-game hunter in India. Served in Jowaki Campaign, Afghan Campaign at Charasiab, Sherpur and Kabul. Clubs:

The Anglo-Indian, the Tankerville, The Bagatelle Card Club.' "

Mr. Holmes fixed Quentin with a stern eye. "No mention of Maiwand, then?"

"Tiger was a spy," Quentin returned. "He did not always say where he was, and neither did the military reports."

"Hmm. Anything more, Watson?"

"He is the author of two monographs: *Heavy Game of the Western Himalayas* published in 'Eighty-one, and *Three Months in the Jungle*, in 'Eighty-four."

"To a hunter used to such prey, one would think a domestic Paddington doctor would be something of a comedown," Mr. Holmes said with a sudden twinkle in his formidable gaze. "Any threat, however unlikely, to my associate is one I take very seriously," he added, his eyes again cold and speculative as they fastened on us. "I will look into the affairs of this Moran. Call on me tomorrow at four o'clock."

"That is wonderful—" I began.

"Four o'clock tomorrow?" Quentin echoed. "Surely that is not time enough to unravel such a mystery."

"It is time enough for me," Mr. Holmes said sharply. "I have, in fact, one or two notions about the case that may bear rapid fruit." He turned his back on us to rummage among the objects atop the rather crowded mantel. I saw him lift a Persian slipper, the most decorative of the objects to my view, and prod the toe.

Quentin and I had risen in a daze, recognizing our sudden dismissal. Then, to my horror, my wandering eyes found a familiar object among the odious and untidy assortment—the cabinet photograph of Irene in evening dress! It stood near a mass of papers skewered to the wooden manteltop by a large knife.

I may have whimpered during my sudden intake of breath. For whatever reason, Dr. Watson rushed anxiously to my side. "Now do not worry," the good physician counseled me. "Holmes can be brisk about his work once he sets his mind upon it, but he has rarely failed to help those in far more desperate circumstances than yours."

"Oh, I do hope so, Dr. Watson," I said in perfect honesty. It was time for Quentin to lead a free life without Tiger's ominous shadow at hand, and certainly Mr. Holmes should do something to earn the trophy he flaunted from the Briony Lodge Affair. Irene had intended it as a consolation prize for the king; instead this detective, this . . . commoner . . . had claimed it. I had seen the claiming at the time, yet I had not known then of Sherlock Holmes's cold and cocaine-consuming nature, nor of his apparent obsession with my dearest friend. How fortunate that I had insisted she not come in my stead! No good could come of these two individuals' further association.

"Be cautious yourself," Quentin advised the doctor during their parting handshake, as I nodded vigorously. "My tale may sound extravagant, but it is true. You have seen the proof of it on your consulting-room rug."

"If there is any way to pull the fangs of this human pit-viper whom you suspect of being responsible for the deaths of so many good men at Maiwand, you may be sure that Sherlock Holmes, however reluctant, is the man for the job."

"Thank you for your assurances," I told the doctor in farewell, wondering if he would ever discover that his Afghanistan bag was missing, poor man.

"Good day, Miss Buxleigh, Mr. Blodgett. Many happinesses to you both," he added warmly.

I blushed like a bride at his remark, however well intended, yet it pleased me enormously in an odd way.

Quentin took my arm in a most proprietary manner, all in his role of Jasper Blodgett, of course.

"We will see what the morrow brings," he said vaguely.

"Thank you," I added to our good-hearted physician. I longed to tell him that he would find far more satisfaction keeping to his own hearth than in accompanying his unconventional friend on wild adventures of a criminal sort. Nothing good could come of such an association; certainly his pathetic scribblings would never amount to more than kindling, from what I had glimpsed of them.

But discretion sealed my lips. Instead of endowing Dr. Watson with my honesty, I simply mumbled a cowardly "Good day" and left.

"Oh, it is too delicious! Better than a Punch and Judy show. Are you saying that by four o'clock tomorrow the unenthusiastic Mr. Holmes expects to have done with Colonel Sebastian Moran? That is a contest I should like to witness. You must tell me everything!"

Irene stopped pacing in the salon of her suite and flounced down onto an embroidered ottoman, sitting raptly as a child, staring at Quentin and myself.

We told her what we could, but none of our efforts satisfied her hunger.

"What sort of 'odd things' were 'lying about' and where, Nell? Do you realize how maddeningly vague such a description is? You should memorize an environment as an actor commits a stage setting to the senses. No detail is unimportant. A man with so little patience for triviality as Sherlock Holmes would tolerate nothing unessential about him."

"I did notice a gold coin upon his watch chain," I put in hesitantly.

"Excellent!" Irene's exuberantly clasped hands showed thanks for any small crumb of intelligence that escaped me. "A gold coin. Not a terribly original watch-charm, but still . . . an observation."

"What kind of gold coin?" Godfrey put in with a frown.

"A sovereign."

Now Irene frowned. "A sovereign? But that is the—" She suddenly stopped speaking.

"Is what—?" Godfrey asked.

"Is the oddest thing," she finished with a light laugh. "Who would expect Sherlock Holmes to adorn himself with such a commonplace token?" And she sank into silence even as I stuttered my way through a few more vague and uninteresting details, such as the Persian slipper and the basket chair.

"The most important fact," Quentin said, "is that this Holmes is willing to pursue the matter despite himself. I sensed that he has other objectives than the obvious."

"Ah!" Irene revived again, like a puppet whose strings have been pulled. "He always has his own objectives, I fancy. Such a man never fails to be working on a master puzzle. Why else do you two babes-in-the-woods think I sent you to him?"

"Out of perversity," I answered a bit crossly.

I was not pleased to be found wanting for not having made a mental inventory of the clutter at 221 B Baker Street. Naturally I said nothing of the prominent place accorded to Irene's photograph. It would encourage an elevated opinion of herself, and Godfrey would fret to hear it.

Irene shrugged blithely. "I really must see this fountainhead of crime-solving for myself. I am determined to go as Miss Buxleigh tomorrow."

"Irene! You cannot."

"I most certainly can. You wore a concealing veil, Nell, and I will, too. My acting and camouflaging techniques are sufficient to overcome any discrepancy in our height or hair color. Oh, I am longing to see this den of detection for myself. Who knows when we may be in England again?"

"Irene, I have sacrificed myself and committed several untruths to masquerade as a fictional person's fiancée. It shall not be for naught. I absolutely will not hear of you interjecting yourself into a plan that is working well only so that you may satisfy your abominable curiosity."

"I agree," Godfrey said suddenly. "No matter how well you do it, Irene, you risk the greater venture. Besides, to substitute yourself for Nell treads far too close to exposure. It is one thing to hide behind the unlikely facade of a street urchin or a grande dame; aping Nell would allow for very little disguise and too much risk."

"Thank you, Constable," she grumbled in return, for Godfrey was right. The more out-of-character the guise, the more likelihood of deception. It was the very fact of my never expecting to see Godfrey in the role of a bobby that allowed him to sweep us all into a carriage without Quentin's or my recognizing him, though he wore virtually no disguise other than the helmet and a false mustache.

"I do not suppose I could wear a false mustache as Nell," Irene admitted glumly. "Oh, well. Another time."

We dined that night at Simpson's in the Strand, a restaurant famed for its rare roast beef, which Quentin savored with the intensity of an exile. That entire evening was a pleasant, almost tranquil time. Our foursome chatted like old friends, as Quentin and I recalled new details of our outing to Baker Street that amused our companions. I truly felt that Quentin and I had been fellow adventurers in a sense, even as I considered with a pang that the necessity should soon be over and our paths would part.

The evening ended with the usual smoking session in the Norton sitting room—I was thankful that my draperies were not subjected to such a cloud of ill-smelling smoke. But how could I deny my friends their small vices, especially in the face of looming triumph?

"Sherlock Holmes is the key," Irene said expansively, lounging rather casually on the sofa in her pale peach-colored *mousseline de soie* gown. "The problem that has enmeshed Quentin also echoes in far-off corridors of power. I am convinced that Mr. Holmes can disarm Colonel Moran for us, or I never would have sent you to him."

"A pity," Quentin noted, "that we will have to wait until tomorrow to know anything."

"Yes, it is." Irene offered a sympathetic smile. "How you must long to see your family again."

"Actually . . . I rather dread it. I do not know how they will accept me after my foreign sojourn."

"With open arms!" she insisted. "I propose that after your second interview with Mr. Holmes, and if his results assure you that your life is not in such danger that your family must be avoided, you and Nell pay a visit to Grosvenor Square."

"Oh, Irene, I could not intrude at such a time!" I objected.

"Whyever not? You were associated with the family years ago. They have met you again recently. Your presence will cushion any awkwardness. You are the perfect go-between in this instance."

"That is true," Quentin said with pathetic eagerness. "Will you go with me, Nell? After all, had I not found you in Paris, I would not be contemplating a return to my family."

"I do not see the necessity—"

"This would not be necessity, Nell," Irene told me. "It would be nicety."

"Of course I cannot object to nicety . . ."

"Then it is decided," Irene said, with an air of having settled a vital matter.

She was the most definite of persons, and never more so than immediately after her will had been thwarted.

Chapter Thirty

A LUKEWARM SOLUTION

A message from Holmes summoned me from Paddington to Baker Street at noon the day following his interview with Jasper Blodgett and his fiancée. Our maid Prudence had refused to cross my carpet since the incident with the cobra, so I was forced to take the note at the consulting-room door, then went to the window to read it.

"Watson," it read. "Come at once. All is solved."

In this case, I had a more than casual interest in Holmes's effort to stop a man determined to kill me as well as Jasper Blodgett. No patients had appeared all morning, so I had been writing my memoir titled "The Adventure of the Devious Diva." As much as Holmes might pooh-pooh my literary ambitions and my taste for "sensation," as he called it, I was loath to leave my desk, being in the midst of a stirring account of *the* woman's trickery at Briony Lodge.

Once I had informed my wife of my destination and taken a brisk walk to Paddington Station, my enthusiasm for real life as opposed to fiction had revived. I was, after all, fairly twitching to know what Holmes had learned of the bounder who had introduced a venomous serpent into my home.

I found the windows of 221 B open and Holmes sitting in the basket chair, his feet upon an ottoman and the familiar pipe perfuming the balmy air.

"Ah, Watson, as prompt as the tax collector, as usual. Sit down. Mrs. Hudson left some lemon curd tartlets from elevenses."

"Oh, excellent, Holmes. I thought, though, that I was to return at four o'clock."

Holmes set his black clay pipe in an empty gravy tureen. "No. I am afraid that you have seen the last of Mr. Jasper Blodgett and his most definite fiancée, Miss Buxleigh."

"Surely they have not been attacked again—and successfully?"

Holmes's smile was weary. "Of course not, my dear fellow. They are as safe as houses, or as safe as anyone can be in modern-day London, and so are you."

"Then you've performed the miracle of permanently cutting the Tiger's claws?"

"Not I, Watson. My brother Mycroft."

As I frowned in puzzlement, he rose and went to lean against the mantel, his eyes idly resting on the photograph of the very woman whose actions occupied the current exercises of my pen.

"The matter is far more complicated—and dangerous—than assassin cobras and spoiled spy-work long ago at Maiwand. It involves the most eminent figures in the governments of three nations, Watson. Colonel Moran has influence with two of them, so it was a tricky bit of work, but he will trouble you and Mr. Blodgett no longer. He now has worse worries that render his past concerns moot."

"What wonderful news, Holmes! Mary is the most understanding of women, but the matter of my reptilian visitor was most unsettling."

"I do not doubt it. That is why I am informing you as quickly as possible of how things stand. Certain facts in the matter must not be made public, not even to the pair who commissioned me to investigate. Too much would be risked. This Colonel Moran is a vicious piece of work, Watson. His reptilian emissaries are creatures of great integrity compared to their keeper."

"You have seen this man?"

"More than that. I was very nearly required to horsewhip him from the Anglo-Indian Club."

"Indeed!"

"You see, Watson, I was not entirely unaware of his existence even before the unfortunate Blodgett called. Yet matters were of such delicacy that I was forced to appear more ignorant than I was." Holmes's dark eyebrows clashed above his aquiline nose. "A most unpleasant necessity, Watson; I trust I shall not be compelled to do so again."

"But what more evil has this man Moran done beyond our suspicions of skulduggery at Maiwand, wounding me and harassing poor Blodgett?"

Holmes sighed. "I must ask you to keep this in strictest secrecy, old fellow. You cannot even begin to dream of so much as committing it to paper."

I nodded and assumed a sober expression as proof of my worthiness.

"Pray do not look so gloomy! The worst is over, and the odd thing is that this new case is linked to the old one."

"Old one? Which old one?"

"The matter I have just dealt with involving your old school friend Percy Phelps."

"But that was solved, Holmes. I sat here in Baker Street not a week ago as you passed Percy his missing papers under cover of Mrs. Hudson's breakfast dishes. I will never forget his expression as he lifted the cover and found the cylinder of paper in place of the likely kippers."

"I will never forget his faint," Holmes added with a smile. "The poor chap was exhausted by his ordeal, or the surprise solution to his dilemma would not have had such a severe effect on him. At least a doctor was present to tend him."

"I have never seen a more grateful man."

"Or a luckier one, Watson. His precious paper was safe.

You know, of course, that the culprit, Joseph Harrison, escaped after surrendering the treaty to me, and taking something of a beating at my hands."

"Yes," said I. "You felt that both the young couple and Percy's uncle the Cabinet Minister would prefer discretion over justice in this matter."

"And so it is with the case of Jasper Blodgett." Holmes suddenly rose and went to the open bow window to gaze down on Baker Street in all its hustle. "Have you ever noticed how crime follows a certain natural law, Watson? Where a flower will put forth petals that mirror one another, so too the unhappy works of the criminal mind often produce a parallel symmetry?"

"No, Holmes, I cannot say that I have."

"Consider the engaged couples in the two cases: both faithful and devoted women; both men whose reputation and future have been sullied by events beyond their control. Granted that Blodgett's unhappy circumstances began nine years ago, but otherwise these two men's situations are not that different.

"Now, Watson, consider the fact that the same evil influence has governed both men's lives: Colonel Sebastian Moran, late of India and Her Majesty's forces, and now all too thoroughly of London."

"Then Blodgett was right!"

"Oh, Blodgett was right enough, but he can never know how much so. Had it struck you that the naval-treaty affair had a rather lukewarm ending, Watson?"

I pondered his question. "I must say that if I had any desire to turn it to fiction, I would find the ending rather inconclusive and unsatisfactory. Happy enough for poor Percy, of course."

"And that is how we must leave poor Blodgett as well, Watson: reunited with his fiancée, safe but in the dark. You see, however in debt Joseph Harrison was, and however well placed to seize the document from his future brother-in-law in the Foreign Office, and however vicious his temperament, he is not the sort of mastermind who could begin to handle the delicate business of hawking this stolen treaty to either France or Russia, or most likely to the higher bidder of the two. Joseph was the thief, but he was a mere hireling."

"Then this Colonel Moran—?"

"Watson, once again you leap on the train of my logic with your usual promptitude. Colonel Moran commissioned Joseph to take the treaty and planned to force France and Russia to pay a pretty penny to see it. He has had a Russian connection since his Afghanistan days, from Blodgett's rather damning testimony. I don't doubt that his nefarious career has taken him to France. In fact, I have sent cables to both Inspector Dubuque and Le Villard on the matter."

"How fortunate, then, that Blodgett found me. Without him, you would never have been able to link the two cases."

"Yes." Holmes went to the mantle to delve in the Persian slipper that contained his shag tobacco, but paused to lift the photograph of Irene Adler. "How . . . amazingly fortunate." He abruptly set the frame down and returned to burrowing for more tobacco.

"How have you disarmed this renowned game hunter, Holmes? He does not strike me as one easy to discourage."

"He is not," Holmes said grimly. "First I spoke to Mycroft, who had already been making inquiries among his diplomatic sources. There is no man in London better placed than Mycroft to stir the subtle threads of international relations. Mycroft has discredited Moran with his supporters in both camps by revealing his double-dealing nature. Every nation needs spies but none need counterspies. I predict that the colonel will be much occupied with finding work, now that his important supporters in foreign capitals have melted from him like snow leopards in winter. He has no reason to kill to protect his past since it is no longer worth protecting, nor is his present. Besides, he now has sworn to kill me instead, and that should serve to divert him from lesser prey."

"Good God, Holmes! Is he serious?"

"Absolutely. I had a most unpleasant interview with him at the Anglo-Indian. It seems that my call interrupted a crucial card game. A powerful and intelligent man, Watson, gone over totally to evildoing. All life to him is a game, a tiger hunt, and he is the supreme predator. I fancy I can teach him a thing or two about that game. Certainly he knows that if he lays a hand upon a hair of your head he will have more to answer for than even he would care to."

"Did you really horsewhip him out of his club, Holmes?"

My friend's often melancholy face took on a rare radiance of joy. "The club walls were accoutred with every exotic weapon known to man and many of the exotic animal victims of those weapons. In fact, an Argentinean bullwhip was at hand—actually at shoulder level. Moran tried to surprise me with a revolver."

Holmes flexed his knuckles, which still bore the marks of Joseph's knife attack of a few days before. "See how crime blossoms in parallels, Watson? Moran's hand bears a slash much like mine, only from a bullwhip, not a knife. There is a certain justice, do you not think, in a man who has used snakes to do his dirty work being disarmed with the long, leathery length of a bullwhip?"

"Perhaps . . ." said I, even then envisioning a parallel literary construction: two tales told in matching tracks like a train's that met and entwined into complementary denouements. . . .

"But you must not write a word of this, Watson. I know your habits. Even though your scribblings are unlikely to ever see the light of public print, it would be too dangerous to commit them to paper. See how an old piece of paper, miraculously preserved, helped undo Moran? You must say nothing of this to anyone."

"Someday perhaps, Holmes, it will all come out." *The Puzzle of the Naval Treaty,* my mind formulated. And *The Adventure of the Catatonic Cobras.*

"Someday, Watson, but not while you and I yet live."

"Let us hope that day is long after the demise of the unpleasant Colonel Moran."

"Let us hope, Watson," he answered as he relit his pipe with a series of cheek-hollowing puffs. "And let us ensure that it is so."

Chapter Thirty-One

A MOTHER NOSE

The day following our first interview with Sherlock Holmes brimmed with errands. Immediately after breakfast, we again repaired to the Norton sitting room, where Irene declared herself bound for Liberty's of Regent Street and a fitting for the flowing gowns in the oriental mode for which the establishment was famed.

"I will go, too," I suggested.

"Nell, you know you loathe the fashion for aesthetic dress," Irene said quickly. "I plan to order a gift for Sarah as well as a few things for myself."

Godfrey rolled his eyes at this announcement; Irene's "a few things" invariably filled trunks.

"I might reconsider," I said, glancing at Quentin. It occurred to me that a gown *à la* Saracen might find favor in his Eastward-oriented eyes.

Irene was stuffing a formidable roll of pound notes into her reticule. "Nonsense," said she even more abruptly. "We are not suited as shopping partners. You always reject my suggestions and I yours. Besides, we shall all be returning to France soon and I wish to accomplish a great deal in one swoop. I should return before your appointment with Mr. Holmes."

With that she swept out, the empty carpetbag she carried certain proof that she intended to collect items for immediate consumption as well as ordering gowns to be sent along later.

At her exit, Quentin, too, bestirred himself. He had seemed distracted this morning. I fear the afternoon's meeting with Mr. Holmes and the proposed reunion with his family were occasions for anxiety as well of hope. He also had errands to accomplish, he announced, among them a pressing need to "find fresh food for Messalina." I did not offer to accompany him, nor did I inquire into the specifics of this process, being hopeful that it involved the butcher's rather than the domestic pet vendor's. He left soon after Irene.

Godfrey smiled over the *Times* at me. "Time will hang heavy today, Nell. Perhaps we should arrange an outing of our own."

"I have nowhere I wish to go."

"Not even 'church'?" he jibed me wickedly.

"Godfrey, you know that fiction was necessary to deceive you. Quentin's life was at risk."

"Not among that crowd at the British Museum."

"It was a charade, was it not?"

"Still . . ." Godfrey lowered the paper as if beset by an unpleasant thought. "If Colonel Moran was among those odd folk milling around that exhibition room—and he must have been, given the air gun fired into the exhibit case—he is fully as duplicitous as the incomparable Irene, or even Mr. Sherlock Holmes, or—lately—Miss Penelope Huxleigh."

"Godfrey, you do me an injustice to place me in such professionally duplicitous company," I answered with a mock pout, for I knew that he enjoyed teasing me. "But you are truly worried?"

He nodded, running a forefinger over his bare upper lip, no doubt missing his mustache. "I fear that Irene underestimates the rapacious nature of Moran. Such men do not lose easily, and never give up if once they develop a grudge. I only hope that we do not become the object of it. She also overestimates the esteemed investigator of Baker Street."

"Then you think that Quentin's difficulties may not be solved?"

He sighed and folded the newspaper. "I will not know what I think until the events of this afternoon, but meanwhile I have thought of the perfect diversion for you and me to make the hours fly until you can return here and depart for Baker Street again."

"Oh, really, Godfrey? What is this treat?"

"The zoo," he said, with an expression of immense self-satisfaction. "You and I are going to the Regent's Park zoo."

I could hardly tell him that my distaste for dead animals, as displayed in the Museum of Natural History and Modern Curiosities, was only exceeded by my abhorrence for live animals, especially eccentric ones.

We returned at three o'clock, my vision spotted from gazing upon so many beasts of conflicting patterned hides. Sarah Bernhardt would have been ecstatic.

The Norton suite was not unoccupied, but Irene had not yet returned. Instead, a strangely subdued Quentin greeted us. With him was a lady of such age and frailty that she barely seemed able to sit upright despite the ebony cane around whose golden top her blue-veined hands were curled.

"Godfrey. Nell." Quentin paused as if to gather his thoughts. "I should like to present my mother, Mrs. Fotheringay Stanhope."

Godfrey and I nodded dazedly at this fragile figure in rich shades of half-mourning: heliotrope, lavender and gray. The white-haired head inclined in greeting.

Quentin spoke on quickly, as if embarrassed or unusually nervous. "I must apologize for surprising you in this way, but I had given some thought to Irene's advice of yesterday that it was high time I overcame my shame and approached my family. I decided to visit Grosvenor Square, in suitable disguise to protect the family. Only Mama was at home, but when I gave the name 'Quentin,' she saw me at once. Her health has been fragile and she has mostly kept to her rooms upstairs, but when she heard my story, and that you and I, Nell, were to hear the end of it today in Baker Street, she insisted on accompanying me there to personally thank Mr. Holmes for safeguarding my return to England and to her."

We stood in shocked silence, Godfrey and myself, as Quentin must have done only hours before in the upper rooms of number forty-four Grosvenor Square.

For how could anyone deny the request of this lovely little old lady whose hazel eyes—so like her son's—had faded to the color of old gold?

"I—I am most pleased to meet you, Mrs. Stanhope," I said, falling into a sort of schoolgirl curtsy. I glanced quickly at Quentin. "I imagine it will not be necessary for me to accompany you to Grosvenor Square from Baker Street now."

"Quite the contrary, Nell!" he replied as if cut to the quick. "Mama must be taken home, and I cannot think of revealing myself to my dear sisters without having at my side the woman who first convinced me to return."

"You said that Irene—"

"Irene suggested that I no longer put off the time of the reunion, but you were the one who made me see that such a thing was possible when we first spoke at Neuilly. I hope I have not angered you."

"No. I seldom anger."

"And only in defense of her friends," Godfrey put in. He went to the old lady and bowed. "Good afternoon, Mrs. Stanhope. It is a pleasure to meet you." The grande dame carefully lifted one slightly trembling hand from the head of her cane, which Godfrey saluted with a very Continental kiss. Then he turned to me. "You will wish to refresh yourself before leaving for Baker Street, Nell. As soon as you are ready, I will see you all down to a carriage."

"Yes," I said pointedly before I left. "The zoo was hot and crowded. And . . . pungent." I was not angry but I was a bit annoyed.

One could not blame Quentin for an impulse to visit a mother who thought him long lost, I told myself as I retreated to my rooms to don my Miss Buxleigh garb. Still, I was bitterly disappointed, and could not say why. Perhaps I saw that once Quentin had been reclaimed by his family, his regard for me would pale. I was, after all, only a means, not an end.

The journey to Baker Street required a four-wheeler rather than a hansom cab, and was quieter than the trip Quentin and I had made the previous day. The lavender ostrich plumes on Mrs. Stanhope's hat nodded dolefully at me as we jolted along. She and Quentin occupied the opposite seat. Already the "fiancée" was being usurped by the mother, even in our fictional relationship. I no longer looked forward to my return to the Stanhopes, although I wore the "surprise" dress Irene had suggested I wear yesterday, so I could smarten my ensemble in the carriage with a few discreet adjustments on the way to Grosvenor Square.

Again the elderly woman admitted us to 221 B Baker Street. Again we climbed the stairs. Again Mr. Holmes invited us in and assigned us seats. This time Quentin and his mother occupied the sofa. I took the velvet armchair claimed yesterday by Dr. Watson, who was absent today.

"Delighted to meet you, Mrs. . . . er, Blodgett," the detective said. "I believe I have excellent news for your son." (Despite her advanced age, Mrs. Stanhope had understood the need to muddy her son's identity and readily accommodated the charade.)

She nodded graciously, if a bit vacantly, and withdrew a lorgnette from her ruched violet satin reticule. She gravely unfolded it, then brought the device to her eyes and honored Mr. Holmes with the kind of up-and-down inspection only the very elderly—or the very young—are permitted in polite society.

"Thank you . . . Mr. Holmes, is it?" Her voice, which I had not yet heard, was one of those that ages like apricots: dry, fruity and shriveled. Her tones wavered in the midst of words, producing an unfortunate tremolo. Quite frankly, it would grate on anyone with any ear for music. Mr. Holmes's features became pained of a sudden, and he took a sharp intake of breath.

"Holmes it is, Madam, as Blodgett is your name."

This statement, and that unlovely, fraudulent name, he left hanging in the air. I was quite unsure what this imperious lady would say in answer. She was perfectly capable of forgetting our pose and telling the truth.

"Fine, upstanding English names, both," she finally asserted in her voice so like an ill-sawed violin. "I am relieved to hear that you have released my long-lost Jasper from impending danger. How was it done, young man?"

Mr. Holmes turned to Quentin and myself with an apologetic look and a conspiratorial smile. "I am sorry to say that the particulars must remain veiled. Certainly you realize that the matter of Maiwand involved persons who are now highly placed in the government. Yet I can assure you that some of these same public and private figures are also in a position to see that this Colonel Moran troubles you no more."

Quentin frowned. "Then poor Maclaine's reputation must remain compromised?"

"I fear so." Mr. Holmes strode to the mantle from where he could fix us all with his compelling gaze. "Past injustices must on occasion not only go unpunished but celebrated in monuments. Such is the history of war since the Trojans. Maiwand was a minor battle in a far quadrant of the globe in which our nation no longer invests any real interest. I vouchsafe to say that Russia's ambitions there are also fading and by the new century will be nonexistent. Colonel Moran only resurrected the past because his current activities were endangered by those who might know of it."

"You still do not say how it was done, sir," Mrs. "Blodgett's" commanding quaver piped up like a creaky old organ. "I was given to understand that you are some latter-day wonder-worker. A Daniel come to judgment."

"Even a Daniel may not necessarily name his lions," Mr. Holmes returned. He turned to include us in his remarks. "Suffice it to say that I have taken the teeth and claws from the man. No one he was accustomed to dealing with in his spywork will associate with him. There is no reason for him to protect his past when his future ground has been cut out from under him."

"Will not such a beast be dangerous, rather like a wounded tiger?" Quentin's mother asked.

Holmes smiled condescendingly, although his tone remained ever courteous. "A terrifyingly apt expression, Madam. No. Colonel Moran will be too busy hunting for his own survival to harass others in theirs."

"Humph." The old lady leaned slowly forward, putting all her weight on those two frail hands folded over her cane top. Then she pushed herself slowly upright, inch by inch. We all stood, feeling we should assist her, yet fearing to topple her with the very offer of our aid.

Straightening gingerly, she began to hobble about the room, the lorgnette at her face, as she inspected the furnishings.

"That basket chair needs a bit of reweaving, Mr. Holmes," she said. "I hope that my son has recompensed you sufficiently for your services that you can afford a bit of repair to your belongings."

"Not yet," Quentin put in hastily, "but I will before we depart."

"Speaking of which, we should—" I began, watching Mrs. Stanhope scuttle along the opposite wall toward the cluttered desk.

She stopped suddenly and pointed with her cane to an object in a dark corner of the chamber. "Ah, a fiddle. Play, do you?"

"It is a Stradivarius, Madam," was all Mr. Holmes said, in an icily polite tone.

She bent over it, viewing the instrument through her lorgnette. "Needs oiling, young man." Then she was skittering along the well-worn red carpet to pause before the sofa Quentin and I occupied. Her neck craned to study, not us, but the wall above us.

"Most patriotic, sir," she trilled approvingly and traveled

on around the chamber to a cluttered corner where hand-labeled bottles and vials glimmered in the low lamplight.

I turned to inspect the dusky damask-pattern wallpaper behind us: what I had taken for some unevenness in the pattern now stood revealed as bullet holes in the graceful script of *V.R.*, complete with a small crown above them.

Mrs. Stanhope had paused before the hearth. Her cane tapped the head of a brown bear that lay prostrate before the fender. "You are more partial to bears than tigers, it appears, Mr. Holmes. A pity this Colonel Moran who has caused my dear boy such grief cannot be trapped and turned into an object of use, if not beauty."

She eyed the jackknife stuck into the middle of the wooden mantel to pin down a fan of papers and cocked her head in a most uncouth manner to try to read some of the text thereon. I glanced at Quentin, feeling wretched for his mother's appalling behavior. And he was worried that his family would find his life abroad irregular and spurn *him!* So much for a house on Grosvenor Square, apparently no guarantee of gentility.

"Now," Mrs. Stanhope croaked in a tone all too reminiscent of Casanova, "there is a lively-looking lass. A mother could not ask better than that for her son to marry. Your sister, sir, no doubt? Perhaps you will introduce my boy when he gets his feet on the ground."

I gasped, for the old woman had stopped before the photograph of Irene. The very idea of proposing Irene for Quentin as a fiancée in my presence was too appalling to entertain for even one moment. Did this dreadful old busybody have no limits?

Mr. Holmes's expression hinted that he, too, had been goaded beyond his endurance. He went to the mantel and lifted the frame from the elderly woman's rapt gaze. "A lady of my acquaintance," he said coldly, "a rather private person." He paused. "Of my 'late' acquaintance," he added finally.

Mr. Holmes had also discovered how admirably mention of death deters impertinent inquiries. Mrs. Stanhope recoiled at this implied rebuke, but a moment later lifted a hand from her cane to jab a crooked finger at Mr. Holmes's midsection.

"Now that is a lovely charm, sir. No doubt a memento from a grateful client, eh? Jasper, son, you must find Mr. Holmes something suitable, too. A sovereign would hardly do, as he has one already. Why, sir," she jibed him slyly, "if you are as successful in the detection business as they claim and receive a small token from every satisfied client, you will hardly be able to walk, your watch chain will be so laden with booty."

He drew his jacket over the chain with great dignity, like a man closing a curtain, or perhaps veiling a wound unsuitable for public viewing.

"Please be seated, Mrs. Blodgett. I fear you will trip upon a wrinkle in the rug; though your eyes seem remarkably sharp, you are somewhat unsteady on your feet."

With that he took her elbow and guided her back to the central table and into a chair beside it, bending his remarkably penetrating, almost fierce, gaze upon her.

"Now," said he, "our business is concluded. Ah, thank you, Mr. Blodgett, an entirely satisfactory commission."

"I hope," Quentin said, "that pound notes will not inconvenience you, Mr. Holmes. Being newly arrived in the country, I have not yet had time to establish credit."

"Not at all, not at all. I have accepted gold coin as happily," he added, with a sharp look to the elderly lady.

Mrs. Stanhope looked a bit taken aback and began her pained rising once again, the cane wobbling between her clasped hands until every eye was fixed upon her in the same breathless way one watches rope dancers at a circus.

Her trembling hand paused on Mr. Holmes's forearm. "Sir," she said, "I hope you will accept a mother's full measure of joy at witnessing the restoration of her son's safety and freedom."

"Indeed I will, Madam," he said swiftly, guiding her once again with such courteous skill toward the door that for a moment he almost seemed a courtier escorting a great lady to a moment of mutually lamented farewell.

Quentin and I followed, mortified; at least I was. And then it was over—the charade. We stood on the threshold. I could glimpse beyond Mr. Holmes a room that had become, after two visits, familiar in an odd way. What bizarre experiments unfolded under the bright glow of those gaslights high on the walls! What high- and low-born clients passed over this very threshold, bearing problems of every description like gifts to the strange man who lived there!

I saw the chamber for an instant as an exotic private railroad car hurtling through time with its cargo of crime and punishment. I felt I would never be able to return to Baker Street with quite the innocence with which I had first viewed it, just as I would never be able to return to Saffron Hill or Shropshire. And then I realized that *I* was the train, and that my life was the tracks that were hurtling me away from my past into an uncertain, an ever-mysterious future. I began to understand Irene's fascination with the curious and the criminal; these things were the velocity that made the journey fast and frightening and . . . interesting.

Mr. Sherlock Holmes rode such a track as well. I could tell by studying his quick, nervous and yet admirably controlled features that he would never forsake it, and never could forsake it.

"Thank you," I found myself saying quite sincerely, not as Miss Buxleigh or even as Miss Huxleigh but as my Real Self. He was Irene's last resort. He had served to complete the rescue of Quentin Stanhope from his past, and—unfortunately, I feared—from my future.

Quentin helped his mother down the stairs and to the street while I slowly followed, wrapped in uncustomary emotions. I was once again the odd one out, but had anything other been destined for me?

Baker Street was dim. A fleecy black sheep of cloud had rolled over the town like an endless, billowing coverlet of smoke. The air had grown still, just as time seemed to have stopped.

Quentin drew out a whistle and blew twice. A four-wheeler veered across the thoroughfare at a reckless pace to fetch us. Even the horse sensed the storm sulfur in the air; its hooves churned the pavement and its eyes rolled nervously despite the driver's hard hands on the lines.

After Quentin seated his mother, he took my arm to assist me within, where it was even darker than the drab day. None of the gaslights had been lit yet, but they ought to have been.

We clicked away from the curb, Mrs. Stanhope covering her face with a fall of lace handkerchief. Her entire fragile frame quivered at the mercy of a coughing spell.

"Your mother must have overdone," I said, trying to sound properly sympathetic.

"I fear so," he answered, bending nearer the old woman to inspect her. "It should pass in a moment."

I stared politely, for Mrs. Stanhope was shaking now as with an ague and was burying her face in the folds of handkerchief in paroxysms of breathlessness.

"Quentin, perhaps we should stop—"

"We will," the old lady croaked, "just as soon as I remove my nose."

Chapter Thirty-Two

THE DREADFUL TIFFANY SQUID

"**Irene, this** is your most appalling mischief yet! It was unspeakable—and most unwise."

"You are quite right as usual, Nell," she admitted cheerily, peeling away theatrical putty wrinkles like some giddy reanimated corpse on Judgment Day. In fact, this was the first thing I could picture Irene doing on Judgment Day. "I will be out of your way in a twinkle, once I have restored some semblance of myself."

She reached under her crackling taffeta petticoats to draw out the carpetbag, into which went the literal pieces of her face as well as a snow-white flock of various "rats" and hairpieces. Only a bit of white remained at her hairline, and that she was vigorously shaking out, until the powder clogged the carriage like smoke.

"How did you manage to turn your eyes yellow?"

Irene flourished a small vial. "The opposite of belladonna, which enlarges the pupil and makes the eyes appear darker. This handy potion reduces the pupil for the opposite effect. Of course, it makes it a bit troubling to see. Mrs. Stanhope's bumbles through the chamber were not fakery." Still, she glanced at me sharply enough. "You need not fear, Nell. I will not intrude on your pilgrimage to Grosvenor Square. *Two* Mrs. Stanhopes might cause confusion, and Quentin's triumphant return is excitement enough."

"Quentin." I turned to him, shaken from the strange reverie that leaving Baker Street had caused. "You must have known about this ruse even before we left the Strand."

"Guilty," said he with no more contriteness than a boy who had eaten all the teatime scones. He smiled at my rising indignation. "My dear Nell, after all Irene has done to insure my safety, even my sanity, during this troubled time, I could hardly deny her an opportunity to play my mother."

"And I was mad to get inside Baker Street!" Irene pled her own case even as she resumed her own face with quick, skilled movements. "What a glorious hodgepodge in which to find such a supremely logical man living! It is quite endearing."

" 'Endearing' is not a word I would apply to Sherlock Holmes or his environment," I retorted.

"No, I am sure that you would not," Irene said, leaning over to jerk at my hem.

I recoiled, both from startlement and from a sense that she had wronged me. I would not accept additional liberties from her at the moment.

"Now, Nell, I am only hitching up the side on your overskirt. We both have transformations to accomplish in this miserable little carriage and not long to do them. You do not wish to look . . . dowdy at Quentin's homecoming, do you?"

The word "dowdy" instantly drove all other considerations from my mind. Irene began unbuttoning the diagonal closing of my bodice as if I were a recalcitrant child who had to be guided through even the most elementary process.

"Irene!" was all I could say in objection to the notion of being undressed with a gentleman present.

"Hush!" she ordered. "I am merely folding back the reveres. Old rose," she told Quentin. "Quite the thing on Grosvenor Square, I assure you."

He laughed, a carefree sound I had not heard from him in a very long time, not since Berkeley Square days. "Do not apply to me for approval. I am ten years behind the times."

"Then you will have to take my word on it." Irene fluffed the folds of rose chiffon at my bodice. "As will Nell. There.

And see what I brought!" She plucked something from her carpetbag and then her fingers lunged at my throat. "Oh, do be still, Nell! I'm not trying to garrote you, merely affix this brooch."

"Oh!" My fingers went to my collar. "It's not the dreadful Tiffany squid, is it?" My fingertips traced a cool, irregular shape.

"Nell, you wound me." She shook her hair into a lavishly ungoverned mane, then twisted it up with a few flicks of her wrists and transfixed it with long pins she had grasped in her teeth. No doubt she would argue that her cigarette smoking was the ideal preparation for dressing her hair in a moving carriage. "Lish-en," she articulated fairly well through her diminishing mouthful of tortoiseshell quills as her fingers swiftly drove them one by one into place. "You must not tell Godfrey about this. He will be cross."

"I cannot abet a woman who intends to deceive her husband!"

"Goodness, Nell, most of the wives in Mayfair and Belgravia make a religion of it. I am merely following Fashion. Besides, you know how obsessed he can be on the subject of Sherlock Holmes."

"Godfrey? *Godfrey* is obsessed?"

"It was my plan," she said. "I had a right to see it accomplished, though Mr. Holmes was annoyingly coy about the exact means. Never mind, I can guess it, and if we are lucky there may be some cryptic reference in the newspapers. Now—" she opened the carpetbag, drew out a bonnet and donned it "—I am ready to leave you to your next interview. For some reason I do not have the same curiosity about the goings-on in Grosvenor Square as I do about the doings in Baker Street."

Irene leaned to the window. "Quentin, signal the coachman to stop at the next corner. I will take an omnibus back to the hotel."

I could only shake my head, my nerveless fingers still massaging the brooch at my throat.

The carriage jerked to a slower pace as soon as Quentin rapped on the ceiling. He leaned across to release the door when the vehicle stopped, and Irene darted out with the zest of a street urchin. I leaned after her.

"Wait! Irene . . ." She was grinning back at me, and then she blew me a kiss. "Irene—this brooch. Tell me that it is not the ruby star given you by the King of Bohemia—?"

"It should look very well in Grosvenor Square," she caroled back, even as she hurried away.

"But rubies . . . and old rose don't go together—"

"Rubies go with everything, like blood," came her fading answer as the carriage jerked us past all sight of her.

I shuddered as my fingers fell away from the gemstones.

"Are you cold?" Quentin inquired with a certain solicitude that would have been warming had I really been chilled.

"No. Merely outmaneuvered."

He laughed again. "Pray do not be angry with her. She must have her masquerades or she does not feel quite alive."

"Is that what spying was like?"

"I suppose so. The times of greatest danger are also those of the greatest exhilaration."

"You will miss it," I said.

He shrugged, but his eyes had a faraway look. "I will have to find something other to do, that is all. I am not sure what."

"What did you do when you were abroad after the war for so long?"

"I traveled among strange peoples, learned odd languages and odder customs." His eyes fell to the jewel at my throat. "Rumors abounded of a lost ruby mine in far northeast Afghanistan among a blue-eyed, yellow-haired people. I convinced myself that I was looking for it, that this intriguing treasure was why I stayed."

"Was it?"

He shrugged. "It was a convenient reason to stay. Going home has become frightening. There is too much to explain."

"Then do not do it all at once," I advised.

He nodded and fell silent until the carriage stopped again.

By now dusk had crept like smoky ground fog over the square, between the great houses, and curled like a sleeping black panther around the statuary in the square's central gardens.

Quentin helped me down from the carriage. The wheels rattled away behind us, drowning out the patter of my heart as we approached the ranks of windows glowing with the evening's first-lit lamps.

"Perhaps we should have warned them," I suggested.

"No." He took my arm, and I had the oddest sense that this gesture was for his support, not mine.

The black-painted double door bowed away from us at Quentin's knock, revealing the austere butler. I paused, wondering if he would recognize Quentin, but apparently he had not been in service until after Quentin's departure.

"Whom shall I announce?" this personage asked in disapproving tones, his eyes pausing respectfully on my borrowed brooch.

"Quentin Stanhope of Afghanistan and Miss Penelope Huxleigh of Paris," Quentin said, a twinge of humor in his voice.

I found my fingers curling into his coat sleeve. His hand briefly covered mine. Even through kid leather I could feel its warmth. We followed the butler across the marble-floored hall as vast as a ballroom, past a dining room where linen lay like melting snow and candles gleamed like stars. Our footsteps reverberated with the same soft patter the rain makes in autumn on fallen leaves.

We were announced at the open double doors of a drawing room, in which the family had gathered before dinner. After passing through the spreading dusk outside and the inner shadows of the hall, we crossed that threshold into a room that exploded with blinding light.

The family sat as frozen as in the Sargent portrait I had imagined, dressed for dinner, the men in regulation black and white, the women a blurred watercolor swirl of gowns and skin tones and startled blue-gray eyes.

"Uncle Quentin!" cried one vague pastel pool. Then Allegra Turnpenny was tripping across the Aubusson carpet and over the marble floors like a child on Christmas Eve. She flew at him, throwing her arms around his neck while he repeated, "Allegra? Allegra—is it you, really?"

And those calm, composed Stanhope women deserted their places in the portrait and came flowing over in clouds of silk and satin, followed at a more sedate pace by the puzzled men in evening dress.

Introductions were made, of myself, of course, of the two married sisters' husbands. Even Quentin required a formal greeting from each member of his family, as if to place them once again in his current landscape.

I watched Quentin sink into his family as one might ease onto a down-upholstered sofa, talking with first one, then another, pausing to embrace a sister who only now had overcome the strangeness of this reunion. The men, the brothers-in-law, kept circling back to him with hand pumpings and astounded looks.

Then came a pilgrimage to the upstairs domain of his elderly mother. If I had any tendency to smile after the travesty of Irene's impersonation, old Mrs. Stanhope's condition crushed it in an instant. She was a frail, silent lady in a wheeled chair attended by a capped nurse. Her memory was a gray hummock of ashes from which no phoenix would arise. While she smiled her tremulous pathetically polite pleasure at the hubbub, she clearly had no recall of her son whatsoever, and virtually none of the older siblings who cooed around him.

Sobered, we went downstairs again, the family keeping up a gay repartee as if to drown out the old woman's utter silence of voice and mind.

Dinner, needless to say, was delayed. By the time we all migrated into the long dining chamber, the butler's expression had hardened into an icily polite, harried fury.

At table Allegra quite literally took me in hand and plied

me with questions, all the while admiring her favorite uncle from afar.

"He doesn't look a bit different. Not really," she added. "Not even older."

"That is because as a child you considered every adult as ancient as Egypt."

Her giggle implied guilt, but she denied my charge with newly adult dignity. "That is not true; I have never considered you at all Egyptian, Miss Huxleigh. Or may I call you 'Nell,' as Quentin does?" she added mischievously.

"It remains to be seen whether we two will associate enough in future that such issues will require settling."

"You are not leaving London?"

"My home is in France now, near Paris."

"Near Paris, how divine!" Allegra's eyes sparkled like star sapphires, soft and fugitive with youthful illusion. "Oh, the couturiers, the courtiers, the utterly romantic French gentlemen—!"

"I see that you have not seen much of Paris."

"Oh, but I may come and visit you! Do say I may! I have never known anyone who lived in Paris."

"Near Paris," I corrected, "and you must ask Mr. and Mrs. Norton, at whose cottage I reside."

"A cottage. How picturesque. What else have you there?"

"A rather fiendish black cat named Lucifer. He is of the breed called Persian, but Quentin informs me that the animals are actually Afghan in origin. We also are endowed with a parrot I inherited from one of Godfrey's—Mr. Norton's—clients, a nasty gaudy prattlewit named, er, Casanova."

"It all sounds such fun," Allegra said wistfully with the optimism of the very young. "Not dull and stuffy and dark like London. And I think your friend Godfrey must be as charming and handsome as real Frenchmen."

I omitted pointing out that her experience of Frenchmen vied only with her experience of Paris. "Godfrey is also married."

"Oh, yes, you said so." She was young enough to sound disappointed.

"His wife is my friend Irene, who used to be my chambermate in Saffron Hill years ago."

"Saffron Hill? You really lived there? How Bohemian."

"Yes, Irene and I are devout Bohemians," I said. "We always seem to be poking around the more colorful quarters of great cities."

"You know, Miss Buxleigh," Allegra said as she leaned back in her chair to accept a bowl of exceedingly thin soup in which floated several unidentifiable objects sliced unbearably fine, "I am sure that Uncle Quentin's war stories will be quite interesting, as well as his life in the East, but I am also convinced that your adventures since we last saw you in Berkeley Square are much more enthralling."

"Such delusions apparently run in the family," I muttered as the serving man presented me with my own pallid pool of soup. The lusty bouillabaisse of Provence began to look edible in comparison. "I doubt that your uncle will speak of his war days. His work was secret and he has suffered much since then."

"Secret?" She looked down the glittering tabletop to Quentin, who was speaking with her mother. "He is always so amusing and I adored him, but I can't imagine Uncle Quentin doing anything actually important, can you?"

So much for the adoration of nieces. It required biting my tongue, which fortunately rendered sampling the soup impossible, but I refrained from telling her in detail just how exciting and vital a life her uncle had led of late.

The tall-case hall clock had rung half-past ten before we took our leave of Grosvenor Square. After dinner the gentlemen had slipped away to the study for cognac and cigars. I did not much miss the miasma of smoke such masculine pursuits engendered, but found my time in the drawing room with the ladies almost as stifling. Save for Allegra, they had little to say to a governess turned acquaintance of the family Lost Sheep. I had even less to say to them. The London scandals and sensations that struck them as cataclysmic seemed trivial matters indeed compared to the international plots and attempted assassinations of the past few days. As I listened, I realized that Quentin had been right. However low-born and obscure, I led a more adventuresome life than most women.

Once again Allegra escorted me and a gentleman out, but on this occasion she hung upon her uncle and myself a trifle desperately.

"Please do come again to call, Miss Huxleigh," she begged, "or at least invite me to Paris. And Uncle Quentin, say that I shall be seeing more of you. I have missed you dreadfully!"

He sighed and gently untangled her arm from his. "It seems like yesterday, dear Allegra. I was the youngest of my family. Miss Huxleigh can tell you how deeply I was impressed by you and your schoolroom friends when I was . . . mislaid in Afghanistan. It was for you I fought, the new and vibrant generation. I am delighted to see what a charming and lively young lady you have become. Whatever you do, never surrender your spirit."

She clung to his arm as if afraid of losing him to another decade-long exile. He patted her hand and kissed her cheek and finally extricated himself.

Mrs. Turnpenny had offered the Stanhope family carriage for our return to the hotel in the Strand, but Quentin had expressed a polite wish to stroll into the square before seeking a hansom.

"I hope you do not mind, Nell," he commented after we had traversed the walkway to the square.

I had indeed been anticipating a ride in the family's undoubtedly first-rate carriage after a lifetime spent on public transportation, but I said only, "It has been a busy day."

"Busy indeed," he answered. "My head is spinning."

"No doubt that is the cognac."

He laughed and led me down one of the diagonal walks crisscrossing the square's central garden. It was quite dark, yet the gaslights circling the square, if such a contradiction is possible, glowed like multiple moons in the misty distance.

"Ah, smell that cool, London summer air, Nell. It was growing close inside."

"Was it?"

He paused to take my gloved hand. "I wonder if you know what you have escaped, what you would have been like after ten years more in a household like that."

There seemed no answer to such a question, to such a mood. Certainly I recognized that this reunion had been a crucial one for Quentin and that his emotions must be at a high pitch. Yet I had been privileged to witness him encompassed by his own kind, and to see how separate I stood from that kind, as did my friends, Irene and Godfrey, however gloriously they improvised their lives.

Chapter Thirty-Three

FALLEN ANGELS

"**Will we** find a hansom?" I asked timidly after we had been walking for some few minutes. While I applauded Quentin's optimism, I was certain that no cabs could be had at this late hour.

He laughed again. "Hansoms hover about the squares looking for fares. They like such fares even better when they are tipsy, for the tips will match the condition of the riders."

"We are not tipsy."

"No." He sounded sorry.

Yet once we had crossed the square we heard the crisp clop of a single horse's hooves. They seemed to be pacing us.

"It could be a resident carriage," I suggested.

"Resident carriages invariably sport at least two steeds. That is a hansom."

"You are right."

Yet there was something ominous about that invisible equipage gaining on us in the cool mist of a midsummer evening, about the tick-tock rhythm of the unseen horse's hooves. It seemed ordinary life was bearing down upon us both after a sojourn in fairyland. It seemed the past was grinding closer on its steady orbit toward the future. It seemed a time had ended, and with it an understanding between ourselves that was unsaid and would ever be so.

"You see!" Quentin announced as the vehicle came into view. "A cab. Soon we will be regaling Irene with the details of our outing."

"You believe that she will wait up for us?"

"Can you doubt it?" Quentin nodded to the cabman at the back of the shiny black vehicle that loomed from the darkness, its twin lamps shining like beast eyes at midnight.

"The Strand," he called up to the driver, who in his top hat and muffler seemed a Christmas pantomime figure rather than a humble London cabbie.

Quentin helped me inside, his hand resting for a moment on my waist. How intimate a hansom cab is at night! One sits side by side with another, bound for a common destination. The way was unexpectedly deserted, so alone we seemed to be journeying. I reflected that Irene and Godfrey and I would leave Quentin behind, as he and I should leave this vehicle behind once our goal was reached. Quentin had come home at last.

"You do not have any family," he said of a sudden.

"No." I was surprised. I had not thought of it that way, but it was true. "Father was a widower who died more than a decade ago. I had no siblings, no known cousins. Except for—"

"Irene and Godfrey. They do not have much family either."

"No, you are right. Godfrey's mother died long ago, and he is estranged from his brothers. He despised his late father, rightfully so. As for Irene, who knows?"

"It is apt that Irene sprang unaccoutred, like Athena, the goddess of wisdom, from her father Zeus's forehead. She invents herself and does not require antecedents."

"I am sure," I said, "that Irene would have given any father a gruesome headache. She has done sufficiently well with me, and I am not even related. You are fortunate to have found your kin again."

"Am I? Forgive me, but I feel crowded among them. I have lived among . . . clans, tribes, in which there were more individuals and more individual freedom. They all expect something of me."

"I thought you would . . . rejoin them, live with them. What else does one do with a family?"

"Fight them, escape them." Amusement salted his voice. "Explain to them."

"If civilization wears upon you, you are welcome to visit us in Neuilly again. And bring Allegra as well. She seems in need of a change. I am certain that Irene can provide something provocative in that area."

"I do not doubt it!" He was silent, the dreary beat of the horse's hooves marking time to his discontent, to the exhausted evening.

"Is something wrong?" I asked finally. I am ever blunt.

"Only that I expected my returning home to answer questions instead of pose them."

"Do you mean that you will not . . . rejoin your family, and resume your place in society?"

"What is that 'place'?" he asked, his voice bitter. "What is 'society'? I do not 'fit' any longer. I do not recognize my own, and they do not recognize me."

"You must allow some time."

"Perhaps I will return to France."

My heart leaped up, as if a poor dray horse had leaped ahead when its only lot was to plod.

"France?"

"And then—"

He said no more, for the horse suddenly did hasten under the quick flick of a whip. Our hansom was spinning faster along the dark thoroughfare. Quentin was leaning against his window, his face brushed with the yellow rays of the sidelight and his hair riffled by the increased wind. We lurched to our left.

"We must have been traveling South Audley Street," Quentin murmured. "Why would we go left, then? Ah, I remember now. We must make a jog and go down Hamilton

Place before we arrive at Hyde Park corner and proceed east up Piccadilly."

"Oh, then that is the park." It unfolded rapidly on my side of the street, a blot of darkness lit by such distant gaslights that they winked like tiny stars.

"We are at Stanhope Gate," Quentin pointed out with amusement, his features catching the glimmer of a passing gaslight.

A whip snapped in the darkness and our cab veered abruptly right.

"Quentin!" I exclaimed as the sudden turn tossed me against his side.

Moments later we were rattling under that so aptly named keystone into Hyde Park itself, into the deep velvet darkness.

He had caught me firmly and did not let go, and well it was, for the poor horse had been whipped to a frightful pace. Its hooves tattooed a rapid clickety-click like a railroad car as we shot straight ahead at the heart of darkness, the wind raking into our faces.

My heart played a staccato tune, not helped at all by Quentin's unflagging grip upon my person; totally necessary, of course, given the wild progress of our vehicle.

Suddenly we veered right again, the cruel snap of the whip answered by the hooves' frantic speed. I was struck with a flare of fury at our driver for abusing the poor beast so. Quentin's gloved hand tightened on my shoulder.

"He is taking us along the Serpentine!" he said. "This is not the way to the Strand, but its opposite."

Our speed had pressed me against Quentin, and his window was now my window. I saw the water, glimmering like buoyant diamonds in the vague light. We lurched left again. I was slammed against my own side of the hansom, Quentin pressing me close to the tufted upholstery.

"This is mad," said he, rising in his seat to rap frantically on the ceiling. "Stop it, man! Stop this race at once! You are going in the wrong direction."

The water on our left flickered like dying embers as we

careened past, then winked out. For a moment we rode in total darkness, silent and bewildered. Then the hansom tilted violently left again. Quentin and I were again tossed like dice in a box against my side of the hansom.

I glimpsed an ironic address in the fleeting light of a corner gaslight: Stanhope Terrace.

"Bayswater Road," Quentin gasped, straining to see. "We are bound west from London. What deviltry is this—?"

Gaslights sped by, precious smudges of light in an onrushing blackness. The hansom's sidelights illuminated only our own worried faces washed in a harsh yellow glare resembling a Paris painter's impression of a bistro.

I had no doubt been bruised by the jostling, but felt nothing but a sense of wild, untrammeled danger. Quentin was wrenching the mechanism that opened our half-door.

"It is damned difficult—or stuck somehow," he said.

His language did not shock me, only the bouncing of the well-tried springs, the pounding of the runaway horse.

"The driver must be mad," he said again.

"Or stricken," said I, thinking of Jefferson Hope.

"Dead," Quentin speculated with a grim look at me. "Stay here," he ordered.

Where did he think I would go?

He leaned back in his seat and kicked both feet at the half-door. It remained shut.

"I'm going atop," he shouted, turning to face me, then sitting on the half-door while gripping the top of the hansom, thus riding backwards in the streaming wind.

I nodded then, assurance being all I could offer, and clung to the seat with one hand.

Slowly, Quentin vanished above as if being devoured by a rather dilatory dragon. It was awful to watch: first his head and shoulders rising out of sight, then his trunk and finally his legs.

I cast an anxious glance out the window. Our speed made observation nearly impossible, but I saw warm tavern lights wink by and the occasional wagon. We rattled through terra incognita now. My poor mind could not even conjure what lay beyond this outskirt of London besides utter dark and empty wilderness.

We climbed a hill. We passed under another, more ancient gateway than the one named Stanhope near the corner of Hyde Park. We were far from such civilized venues now, hurtling into nothingness.

Thumps above indicated Quentin's presence. Still our horse's wild race continued. I was tossed from window to window and saw nothing I recognized, saw nothing, in fact.

Ahead unwound a tunnel of darkness, and then within it, an arrow of tiny lights, gaslights beaming through heavy mist under a boiling charcoal sky lit by a suddenly revealed full moon. I saw towers. Soaring, churchlike towers. And flying buttresses. A bit Romanish for my taste, but any port in a storm of this proportion.

The thumping aloft doubled, and redoubled. I could hear reins slapping, and the horse screamed like a woman. Then the hansom veered and jolted over some obstacle, creaked, swayed, stopped. . . .

I swayed with it, clutching at anything and finding only the fastened half-door, which never gave.

Rudely tossed and turned, beaten and bruised, I finally sat still in my seat. My bonnet had fallen onto one ear. I could hear the horse gasping like a giant bellows.

For I moment I did not move; then I struggled upright. There was no other course but to climb over the half-door as Quentin had done. I did so, my skirts catching on the impediment. I tugged and they would not loosen, so I tugged again until I heard the rip of cloth. Then I clambered over until I was snagged again, and further ripped my dressmaking.

At last I desisted. I was hopelessly snagged, but at least I could see ahead. Then I regretted even that. My place of sanctuary, my "church," was no refuge. The twin towers that drew me repeated into the distance, mere architectural decoration on the supports of a bridge. The flying buttresses were the bridge's spans, upheld by wrought-iron bars.

Gaslights lit the way across, reflecting on the night-damp paving stones. On either side a body of water, so broad that it must be the Thames, shimmered like Irene's most lavishly bejeweled black velvet evening gown, reflecting the sad, drowned face of the moon.

Quentin stood beside the stalled vehicle, his top hat fallen away. The driver had dismounted, too: a bulky silhouette blocking the river's glitter, he still wore his battered top hat. The long pointed line of his whip seemed to pierce the churning gray clouds.

Quentin glanced back to assure himself of my survival. Then he spoke to the driver. "You are quite, quite mad."

A voice spoke that I thrilled to recognize. "No, only damned inconvenient to those who thwart me."

"You are a long way from the jungles of India, Tiger," Quentin said in a tight, careful voice.

"And you are far from the forbidding steppes of Afghanistan, Cobra," Colonel Sebastian Moran answered with a guttural laugh quite awful to hear. "They are hunting old Tiger because of you. You took that damned paper nigh ten years ago, and now they have hung me with it. I told you then and I tell you again that it is not profitable to meddle with a tiger."

"Let the lady go."

"You let her go, if you survive to do so."

They spoke of me, but I was miles removed from their calculations. I was a distant pawn upon a board that had broadened to encompass two continents and ten years. I could do nothing but watch.

"What will revenge gain you?" Quentin asked, moving carefully away from the hansom.

"Satisfaction," Tiger articulated so precisely that he hissed like a great cat, or a snake.

"Small meat for one used to triumph."

"It was that meddling detective! Did the fool think that I would not see his hand in this—and yours?"

"And mine," Quentin agreed calmly, "no thanks to your efforts."

"I sent a snake to catch a snake. Pity it didn't work."

"Your emissary killed on one occasion, but not me."

"A greater pity."

"Will you shoot me?" Quentin asked coolly.

"I would not waste a bullet on such poor game," Tiger snarled.

Those words acted as a signal, for then Quentin knew that a pistol was not pointed at him. He leaped—one shadow pouncing on another. Tiger and Cobra, snake and mongoose, Moran and Stanhope. These words were symbols of the elemental battle unfolding; even I knew that, even as I knew I was powerless to prevent or alter one bit of it. Oh, for Irene's wicked little revolver! Oh, for Irene, or Godfrey!

Tiger's long agile whip lofted against the boiling sky like black lightning. It cracked and then struck Quentin. I recoiled, but he did not. He advanced on Tiger, shadow stalking shadow until the spitting whip was too close to snarl, a scuffle, and then it rose . . . in Quentin's hand.

He advanced like a madman himself, cracking the whip until the poor stalled horse trembled in its traces, wielding the lash with a demonic energy that drove the figure of Tiger back against one looming gatepost of the bridge.

Tiger leaped onto the stone dais some four feet up and crouched at the foot of a leafy stone scroll as high as a man. The whip danced in the air beside him until he scrambled up the carved scrolls to the next level.

"This is the way to train a cat," Quentin announced, himself a shadow that leaped lithely atop the first level.

And so they progressed, ever upward on that strange man-made mountain. Perhaps the gatepost was not so very high. It seemed Mount Everest to me, and both men like quarreling fallen angels contending against a murky, ill-lit sky.

The gatepost ended in a three-pronged bloom of ironwork across the way, etched against the cauldron of the sky. I watched them labor upward in their common enterprise of individual destruction.

My heart had long since left my body for my throat. I was

aware of nothing but the contention so near and yet so far. Around them the thin sinuous line of the whip wove like a script. Quentin wielded it, for emphasis rather than defense. It was as if he would drive Tiger back to Afghanistan, back to the past to undo the waste of Maiwand, undo the deaths of countless men. He seemed to me at that moment an avenging angel, a Michael to a Lucifer. One must fall, I knew that. Yet, for all my worry, it was a thrilling scene.

And then one figure leaped suddenly down a notch on the face of the gatepost. The whip lashed out one final time—upon the tried horse's haunches—as Quentin cast it away.

"Go!" Quentin shouted.

Whether he addressed me or the horse did not matter. The poor beast sprung forward as if released from the gates of hell.

"Go, dearest Nell!" I heard these extraordinary words end as if choked off. Still standing at the half-door like a charioteer, I looked back to see the figure of Tiger leap down on Quentin's silhouette. They struggled just beneath the gatepost's crest. For a moment both men teetered under the impact of their clash and then . . . and then they fell. Against the ghastly, moonlit clouds above the silver river, their silhouettes hung larger than life, the fleeting moments of their plunge stretched into a dreadful, false eternity.

I saw them both: together yet separate, falling . . . oh, falling. By some divine blessing, in those horrific seconds the lovely lines of Lucifer's fall from Milton's *Paradise Lost* flared into my brain like a burning brand even as I watched:

> *From morn to noon he fell, from noon to dewy eve,*
> *A summer's day; and with the setting sun*
> *Dropp'd from the zenith like a falling star.*

I had memorized those lines at my father's school table, as well as the sad plaint from Isaiah: "How art thou fallen from heaven, o Lucifer, son of the morning?"

Two men fell, my becalmed heart accompanying only one. Then I recalled that "Lucifer" meant light, despite the name's dark associations, and thought it bitter irony that one man's light must die in order to snuff out another's darkness.

At the last, I briefly saw them diminished, as birds or bats against the lowering clouds at the horizon. Then they plunged together into the glittering moonlit maw of the Thames and the black waters below.

My driverless hansom cab bolted on, its impetus pushing me back into the seat. I do not believe that I screamed; the situation was beyond such trivial measures. The hansom rattled across the empty bridge, spans and bars and proud towers flashing past me. . . . I heard nothing and saw very little.

I returned to the hotel in the Strand at two the following morning. A kindly fruit vendor bound for Covent Garden had come upon my vehicle and taken charge of both the winded horse and myself. Godfrey was in the lobby waiting. I managed to stammer out some version of the events before he whisked me to the Norton suite and plied me with brandy. They both had been mad with worry at our long absence and Irene, he said, was out interrogating cab drivers. I never asked in what guise she undertook this assignment. I barely remember her coming in, though someone bundled me into bed, for that is where I awoke the next day.

When we three met again in the morning, I related the circumstances more coherently. My friends instantly realized that any action was useless, that both men had plunged together into the swift current, and perished.

That afternoon we traced the route in a four-wheeler until we came to what proved to be the Hammersmith Bridge. By day the impressive architecture seemed puny. I seemed to observe it from a distant point, like the invisible moon. A drive along the river revealed nothing but gray water. Irene and Godfrey were indefatigable for the next few days, but their inquiries uncovered nothing. New Scotland Yard reclaimed no bodies from the Thames that day or in the next five. The visit we three made later to Grosvenor Square drains through my mind like muddy tea to this day. I remember that

Allegra wore black and did not ask to visit Paris. I seemed to have contracted the amnesia that follows brain fever.

We prepared to return to Paris. Irene packed. I do not know what she did with Quentin's new clothing.

Shortly before we left, Godfrey came out of the bedchamber that had been Quentin's.

"I have been seeing to it," he told me, "but I don't know what to do with it now."

"I beg your pardon?"

"The mongoose."

"Oh." I had forgotten about it.

"Should I . . . dispose of it here?"

"How exactly do you propose to . . . dispose of it?"

"Perhaps there are rare-pet dealers."

"It is a bit late to think of that," I reminded him.

"We could take it on the boat-train to Calais."

"Would they allow it?"

"Would they dare *not* allow it if Irene insisted?"

"Messalina is as untidy as Casanova and as predatory as Lucifer."

"Undoubtedly."

"Most inconvenient."

"I cannot argue with you."

"We will take it."

And so we went.

On the Channel passage, I was standing by the rail watching the white cliffs of Dover pale to vague clouds on the horizon, when someone came to stand beside me.

It was Irene, the wind blowing her veiling back. Her face was as sober as I have ever seen it.

"We have miscalculated dreadfully, Nell," she said. We had not spoken privately since the morning after the awful night on the Hammersmith Bridge Road.

"How have we miscalculated?"

"Not you and I. He and I."

"He?"

"Sherlock Holmes and I."

"I did not know that you were in partnership."

"We were, unknowingly, and we both failed horribly. Neither of us guessed that Colonel Sebastian Moran would be so ferocious when cornered. Neither of us anticipated that he would strike out at the one who first foiled him in Afghanistan. We were . . . too prideful. We each pictured ourselves contending with the Tiger. We did not see that his oldest enemy was most likely to be his target once we had frustrated him."

"Is Mr. Holmes as remorseful as you?"

She smiled wanly. "He is unaware of this tragic outcome. He did not even know Quentin's true name."

"Quentin is dead," I said, as I had not before.

"It seems so."

"And Tiger as well."

"Likely."

I looked at her directly for the first time in days. "Do you truly believe it so?"

She paused, then brushed the veiling back from her face as if it were hair. "I will not if you do not."

I lifted my chin to the sea breeze. It was salty and raw and I did not care for it. "Then I have not decided yet."

Chapter Thirty-Four

THE CARDBOARD BOX

One thing can be said for French skies: they are more frequently blue than English ones.

Unfortunately, an abundant animal life wishes to share in this natural bounty, so the garden at Neuilly that August hummed with cricket song while birds darted down for seeds among the beds of fading roses.

I had persuaded André to move Casanova's cage outside for the afternoon, and sat in the shade of a plane tree, where I could keep an eye on both the bird and the mongoose. Lucifer was no difficulty; since I was doing some stitchery, he was at my feet alternately unraveling a ball of crochet string and snagging my petticoats.

Messalina had adapted well to country life. At least she waxed fat and sleek and had proved a tireless guardian of the garden, retreating to her cage near the kitchen door only now and again.

A mongoose, I had decided, fell between a cat and a parrot as a pet: Messy was far cleverer than Lucifer, less lazy, yet even more independent than Casanova. If she mourned her master, I was not expert enough in mongoose manners to detect any sign.

That August was quiet to the point of stagnation. Most Parisians fled the city during the last blast of summer heat.

The country hummed and chirped in tuneless monotony, and nothing disturbed the sunlight or the breeze or the endless days and long, light-bathed evenings in which the setting sun seemed reluctant to depart.

"And, Nell, what are you doing today?" Godfrey asked as he strolled up the flagstones toward me.

"What I did yesterday: fancy work."

"That seems fancier than usual."

I glanced at my project. "It is a pillow cover for Messy, composed of a new stitch—French knots. Being French, they are needlessly intricate and time-consuming, but the result is bright and flamboyant."

"So I see. I am sure that the mongoose will appreciate it."

I let my handiwork rest in my lap. "Truly, Godfrey, we cannot know whether a mongoose even appreciates a mouse for lunch. I am merely occupying time."

He sat beside me on the stone bench. "I never told you what Irene and I discovered during the days before we left London." I regarded him with a blank gaze. He added, "After the . . . bridge incident."

"Was there anything to do beyond comb the riverbanks?"

Godfrey laced his hands and kept his eyes on them. He seemed ill at ease, as everyone had seemed with me since what Godfrey called 'the incident' at Hammersmith Bridge—everyone except the animals, who were as obnoxious as usual and quite a relief.

"I—I kept an eye on Moran's club, in case he had survived and should return, secretly or otherwise."

"Did you really? I had no idea, Godfrey."

He looked rather sheepish. "Irene insisted on it. She will never give up."

"I know." My sigh drifted into the lazy air. "She is too hopeful for her own good."

"At any rate," he said with forced enthusiasm, "Moran never came back, so I finally represented myself as an interested barrister and gained admittance to the chamber he kept there. I also learned of a fearsome dustup at the club the day before Moran left, never to return. It seems a tall, thin gentlemen came to see Moran on some private matter and nearly bullwhipped the colonel from the premises. You can guess, of course, who the high-tempered visitor was," Godfrey added archly.

"No, Godfrey, I cannot." He regarded me with disbelief. "I have not much had my mind on past events. It seems . . . better."

"Well, that gentleman certainly was Sherlock Holmes himself. I had no idea he was such a Tartar."

"I am not surprised," I said, thinking of the glimpses that Dr. Watson's clumsy scribblings had offered of Mr. Sherlock Holmes's temperament and habits. A cold and precise personality was exactly the sort to explode with self-indulgent emotion, especially if he had been drugging himself with cocaine.

Godfrey sat back, then began again. "Perhaps you would be more fascinated by what I found in Moran's abandoned chamber, which even Mr. Holmes has not likely penetrated."

"Perhaps." I finished a knot and broke it from the skein with my teeth, a technique that disconcerted Godfrey, but I am a practical woman, and I had not invited spectators to my homely pastimes.

"Dr. Watson's service and medical records," Godfrey said with a pride that reminded me of Lucifer presenting me with a dead field mouse.

I paused. "Then Quentin was correct in guessing that Tiger had taken them in India."

"Yes, but the contents were most . . . puzzling. The papers record all that we know—Watson's wounding at Maiwand and the fever that followed, his orderly Murray rescuing him, his stay in Kandahar, his transportation by pack train to the railway at Sinjini and hence to Peshawar—"

"Godfrey, at the moment I am not up to a geographical tour of Indian frontier settlements." I still could not bring myself to more than glance at my sole remembrance of Quentin: the disreputable Montmartre portrait Irene had bought.

"I am sorry, Nell," he said so meekly that I immediately regretted my petulance. "Yet I found an astounding fact among the papers: an account of a cobra that had gotten into a patient's cot at Peshawar. The snake was found before it could strike, but an overzealous guard drew his sword to kill the creature—and accidentally stabbed the patient in the leg."

I did pause in my French knotting at that juncture. "Dr. Watson? Wounded again?"

Godfrey nodded. "Is that not odd? He was still incoherent with fever at the time, and likely did not even recall it, but I should say that our old friend Tiger was having another lethal go at the much-tried doctor. It certainly proves that Colonel Moran had resorted to cobras before."

"Imagine being stabbed in the leg by a clumsy defender!" I shuddered despite the warm day. "At least we have managed to protect Dr. Watson."

"Assuredly," he told me quickly.

"So Quentin achieved what he wished," I mused, setting down my work and staring into the distant poplars shivering silver in the breeze.

"Yes, he did. He saved another man's life—perhaps many more—by ridding the world of a predator like Moran."

I regarded Godfrey. "No doubt that thought is supposed to be comforting, but I do not find it so."

"My dear Nell," Godfrey began, reaching for my hand at a moment that was edging perilously close to treacle. . . .

The wooden kitchen door banged shut, a sound that turned us both like vigilant watchdogs. Only Irene was impetuous enough to leave the cottage in such a loudly advertised manner.

She came quickly toward us, walking on the flagstones only when their artfully meandering path crossed her direct one. "Look at what has come! The post."

I understood her excitement. As exiles from our own land and strangers in France, we seldom received mail, except the overscented invitations of that Bernhardt woman. Irene in the presence of an unopened missive was like a child handed a surprise present: curious, excited and greedy all at once.

"Look." She sat between us, her buoyant mood altering our more somber one by mere proximity. "From Grosvenor Square for you, Nell! If it is from that delightful child Allegra, tell her, yes, of course, she must visit. It would do us all good."

"You mean me," I said, struggling to slit the heavy parchment paper with my only implement at hand, a crochet hook. Naturally Irene had not thought to bring a letter opener with her.

"I mean us all," she iterated. "Nell, we too are devastated by the loss of . . . of one who meant a great deal to us all. Well, is it from Allegra? Does she want to come?"

"No." My eyes could hardly read the script, despite my pince-nez. I removed the spectacles the better to see through a glaze of sudden tears. "It is from Mrs. Turnpenny. Mrs. Stanhope has died."

Silence held for a few moments, while Casanova juggled consonants and vowels in his cage, mingling phrases and producing a model for Mr. Carroll's jabberwocky.

Irene's hand closed around mine. "I am so dreadfully sorry, Nell. I had hoped for better news." She patted my hand as her voice reached a more cheerful, albeit forced, tone. "But see, this package is for you as well. You must open it."

I held it on my lap as if it contained a cobra. "There is no law that I must."

"If you will not, I will!" She reached for it.

"It is addressed to me."

"Then open it!"

"I do not recognize the hand," I said, "and even without my spectacles, I can tell that the paper and string employed are quite coarse and common, even cheap."

Irene sighed dramatically. "Heavens to Hecuba! You are not Sherlock Holmes, Nell. It is a simple package. You will not know what it contains, or who sent it, until you open it.

Perhaps it is a present from Allegra. She seemed quite taken with you."

I finally found my curved little embroidery scissors. Irene watched stormily while I methodically cut the string and carefully unfolded the brown paper wrapping back from what appeared to be . . . "a cardboard box," I said in disappointment. I had spent enough time in Irene's vicinity to know that nothing very valuable ever came in a hard-paper box.

Even the ever-optimistic Irene drew back. Godfrey was frowning behind her, wearing a look that said that Cruel Circumstance must not deal me another blow or he would know the reason why. . . . Dear Godfrey and Irene, they were so helpless in the face of real adversity.

Then I opened the box. A trinket shone there, a small gold brooch.

"Nell." Irene's voice sounded very strange. "I believe that you had better don your pince-nez to examine this very . . . rare . . . gift."

I put my fingers to the hollows impressed on the bridge of my nose; one notices the price of modern aids only when one ceases using them. Then I snapped the spectacles onto my face again and lifted up the box and its contents.

I would have dropped it had Irene's hands not been fanned beneath mine, ready for just such an event.

"Irene! Godfrey! It is Quentin's medal."

"Yessss," Irene hissed under her breath, her glowing eyes resting on it with a nameless emotion. "Is there a message?"

I turned over the medal, and moved the cotton fabric upon which it rested. "Nothing. Who has sent it?"

Irene was already scrambling for the wrapping paper, which had slipped off my lap in the excitement. "How provident that you were so agonizingly cautious about opening the parcel, Nell. Ah! As I feared. It has been posted from Marseilles."

"What is wrong with being posted from Marseilles?" Godfrey inquired.

"Only that it is a port city," she retorted. "The person who sent this could be on his way . . . anywhere."

"The person?" I asked.

"Oh, Nell, do you not see? It must have been Quentin!"

I stared again at the humble package in my lap, at the bright bit of brass, as he had named it, and shook my head. "There must be another explanation. You found no trace of him in London. Perhaps this was recovered at his lodgings and—"

"And the landlady immediately knew to mail it to you at Neuilly. Besides, I believe that he kept it upon his person after I returned it to him. There was no medal among his effects. Nell, do not be such a dedicated dolt! Of course Quentin sent it. Who else knew where we lived?"

"Irene," Godfrey began in a warning tone, putting his hands on her shoulders.

"Of course it is Quentin," she repeated to me, her beautiful face even lovelier, abrim with the hope she meant to give me. "There is no other answer."

"Irene," Godfrey said, turning her to face him. "There is another."

She stared at him for a confused moment, she who so delighted in outthinking everyone, who was so adept at it unless concern for another clouded her judgement. "Who else would care to send Nell—us—a message that he still lived?" she demanded.

I looked gratefully at Godfrey for sparing me unfounded hope. "Colonel Sebastian Moran might, Irene," I said. "He might wish to tell us that *he* still lived and that Quentin did not."

Irene twisted back to face me. "Oh, no . . . Nell. No." She sighed as Godfrey released her, and cruel inescapable reason returned. "Yes, Colonel Moran, if he survived, could have. He could have wrested the medal from Quentin's . . . form. He did know we lived at Neuilly since he shot at Quentin here, but he is not the kind of man to tease his game in such a way. His message would come on a bullet, or the fang of a serpent."

"Perhaps it already did—" I nodded to Messy's lean brown form; the mongoose was pattering along the flagstones making for her cage "—and was stopped."

Godfrey spoke suddenly. "I congratulate you, Nell, on your gruesome turn of mind. You outdo Irene. But in this case I think Mrs. Norton is right, however overhasty she may have been. Moran would go for Holmes, not us. We are incidental to his downfall, at least as far as he knows."

"Perhaps," I said.

Irene lifted the box. "Quentin left the medal here before, only I returned it. I thought then that he sought to elude his past, and the glory due him. I was wrong. Quentin left the medal for you even then. Now he has survived this duel with Moran and sends the medal to announce his triumph, and to acknowledge yours."

"Which is?" I demanded incredulously.

"You are an admirably adventuresome woman, Miss Huxleigh." Irene pinned the token to my shirtwaist below my left shoulder. "If not for you, Quentin Stanhope would have never gone home and Dr. Watson would be dead."

"Then why has he not come himself?" I had not meant the words to blunder out in such a childishly distraught way.

Godfrey lent the matter its final fillip. "Perhaps Colonel Moran survived the contest, too. Perhaps Quentin dares not show himself, not with a man of Moran's mettle on his trail."

"Then he is an exile again, after all that has happened! Why must everyone I know be presumed dead? Except that . . . that miserable Sherlock Holmes?!"

Irene's expression grew bittersweet. "But Quentin is alive, my dear! Surely that is better than the alternative."

"And we shall never know for certain what transpired?" I asked.

They were silent. Finally Irene spoke. "At least you know that he is alive."

I remembered what I had said to Godfrey on our way to England. I caught his concerned gray eyes and smiled ever so wanly. "I have concluded before that knowing is better than not knowing."

Irene leaned back against Godfrey's shoulder, her half-shut eyes sharpening in sudden speculation. "And even better is knowing of ways to find out. . . . Another tantalizing question arises: Do you think that in future Mr. Sherlock Holmes should be on the watch for cobras?"

A BRIEF AFTERWORD

The foregoing selections from the Penelope Huxleigh diaries and newfound Watsonian fragments in my possession shed welcome new light on two areas dear to minutiae hunters in the so-called Holmes canon: Dr. Watson's vacillating wound and the hitherto unknown history of the man Holmes would later call "the second most dangerous man in London," Colonel Sebastian Moran.

Sherlockians have long debated the whys and wherefores of Watson's injuries at Maiwand. The author of these tales (i.e., John H. Watson himself) first mentions a shoulder wound and later refers to a leg wound, with no explanation of how the second occurred, if it actually did.

We can now see plainly in these additional Watsonian fragments and the new Huxleigh material that the good doctor was wounded unawares in the second instance, and was naturally sensitive to admitting to his loss of memory in Afghanistan, especially in the presence of his prescient detective friend. No wonder his accounts are inconsistent; he never made peace with this situation, or fully understood that both wounds were attempts on his life, made not in the heat of battle but through the cold-blooded designs of a murderous spy.

As for the revelations of the history of Watson's attacker,

the spy "Tiger" who is revealed to be Colonel Sebastian Moran, anyone acquainted with the Sherlockian canon must heave a sigh of comprehension. Diplomatic considerations compelled Watson to delay recounting what he called *The Adventure of the Naval Treaty*; the same reasons forced him to suppress all mention of the first encounter between Holmes and Moran, that was to bear such bitter, better-known fruits in latter escapades of Holmes that Watson was free to relate. These newly narrated events clearly show how Moran lost his credibility as a spy, thanks to the efforts of Sherlock Holmes and Irene Adler acting in unknowing (on Holmes's part) concert. His livelihood cut out from under him, Moran was forced to enlist his nefarious but formidable talents in the service of Sherlock Holmes's archenemy, Professor James Moriarty. Of that association came only grave ill, with which every dedicated reader of the Watsonian canon will be familiar.

As for the Nortons and their chronicler, further probes of the Huxleigh diaries will indicate whether the events in this narrative had equally severe repercussions on their lives.

Fiona Witherspoon, Ph.D., F.I.A.*
November 25, 1991

*Friends of Irene Adler